UTILITY THEORY: A BOOK OF READINGS

Utility Theory:
A Book of Readings

ALFRED N. PAGE

ASSOCIATE PROFESSOR OF BUSINESS ECONOMICS AND QUANTITATIVE METHODS
UNIVERSITY OF WASHINGTON

JOHN WILEY & SONS, INC.

NEW YORK   LONDON   SYDNEY

PREFACE

Economics, of course, deals with the allocation of scarce resources in a world filled with risk. The evolvement of a set of generally accepted optimal allocation rules to be used across time by individuals and collections of individuals is a heady and fascinating task.

Vital to any such set of rules is the concept of utility—one of the oldest concepts, yet in its present stage of development, one of the most useful modern concepts in economics.

This volume is the first collection of articles and excerpts from books that relate primarily to utility. It concentrates on the historical development of the concept, ranging from Bentham's doctrine of pleasure and pain and Edgeworth's development of the indifference curve to the impressive contributions of Arrow and von Neumann and Morgenstern. The book also provides the first English translation of portions of Pareto's *Manual D'Economie Politique*, including the important discussion and appendix pertaining to Pareto optimality.

The articles communicate for themselves without introductory comment. I sincerely thank all of the authors and publishers who allowed this book to come into existence. Finally, I acknowledge tacit encouragement from Noble Crichton, a utility-maximizing canine.

Alfred N. Page

University of Washington
January, 1968

v

CONTENTS

vii

UTILITY THEORY: A BOOK OF READINGS

PART I
Utility and Utilitarianism

AN INTRODUCTION TO THE PRINCIPLES OF MORALS AND LEGISLATION

Jeremy Bentham

CHAPTER I. OF THE PRINCIPLE OF UTILITY

I. *Mankind governed by pain and pleasure.* Nature has placed mankind under the governance of two sovereign masters, *pain* and *pleasure*. It is for them alone to point out what we ought to do, as well as to determine what we shall do. On the one hand the standard of right and wrong, on the other the chain of causes and effects, are fastened to their throne. They govern us in all we do, in all we say, in all we think: every effort we can make to throw off our subjection, will serve but to demonstrate and confirm it. In words a man may pretend to abjure their empire: but in reality he will remain subject to it all the while. The *principle of utility*[1] recognizes this subjection, and assumes it for the foundation of that system, the object of which is to rear the fabric of felicity by the hands of reason and of law. Systems which attempt to question it, deal in sounds instead of sense, in caprice instead of reason, in darkness instead of light.

But enough of metaphor and declamation: it is not by such means that moral science is to be improved.

II. *Principle of utility, what.* The principle of utility is the foundation of the present work: it will be proper therefore at the outset to give an explicit and determinate account of what is meant by it. By the principle[2] of utility is meant that principle which approves or disapproves of every action whatsoever, according to the tendency which it appears to have to augment or diminish the happiness of the party whose interest is in question: or what is the same thing in other words, to promote or to oppose that happiness. I say of every action whatsoever; and therefore not only of every action of a private individual, but of every measure of government.

III. *Utility, what.* By utility is meant that property in any object, whereby it tends to produce benefit, advantage, pleasure, good, or happi-

Source: Chapters I–IV, 1823.

ness (all this in the present case comes to the same thing) or (what comes again to the same thing) to prevent the happening of mischief, pain, evil, or unhappiness to the party whose interest is considered: if that party be the community in general, then the happiness of the community: if a particular individual, then the happiness of that individual.

IV. *Interest of the community, what.* The interest of the community is one of the most general expressions that can occur in the phraseology of morals: no wonder that the meaning of it is often lost. When it has a meaning, it is this. The community is a fictitious *body,* composed of the individual persons who are considered as constituting as it were its *members.* The interest of the community then is, what?—the sum of the interests of the several members who compose it.

V. It is in vain to talk of the interest of the community, without understanding what is the interest of the individual.[3] A thing is said to promote the interest, or to be *for* the interest, of an individual, when it tends to add to the sum total of his pleasures: or, what comes to the same thing, to diminish the sum total of his pains.

VI. *An action conformable to the principle of utility, what.* An action then may be said to be conformable to the principle of utility, or, for shortness sake, to utility (meaning with respect to the community at large), when the tendency it has to augment the happiness of the community is greater than any it has to diminish it.

VII. *A measure of government conformable to the principle of utility, what.* A measure of government (which is but a particular kind of action, performed by a particular person or persons) may be said to be conformable to or dictated by the principle of utility, when in like manner the tendency which it has to augment the happiness of the community is greater than any which it has to diminish it.

VIII. *Laws or dictates of utility, what.* When an action, or in particular a measure of government, is supposed by a man to be conformable to the principle of utility, it may be convenient, for the purposes of discourse, to imagine a kind of law or dictate, called a law or dictate of utility: and to speak of the action in question, as being conformable to such law or dictate.

IX. *A partizan of the principle of utility, who.* A man may be said to be a partizan of the principle of utility, when the approbation or disapprobation he annexes to any action, or to any measure, is determined by and proportioned to the tendency which he conceives it to have to augment or to diminish the happiness of the community: or in other words, to its conformity or unconformity to the laws or dictates of utility.

X. *Ought, ought not, right and wrong, &c. how to be understood.* Of an action that is conformable to the principle of utility one may always say either that it is one that ought to be done, or at least that it is not one that ought not to be done. One may say also, that it is right it should be done; at least that it is not wrong it should be done: that it is a right action; at least that it is not a wrong action. When thus interpreted, the words *ought,* and *right* and *wrong,* and others of that stamp, have a meaning: when otherwise, they have none.

XI. *To prove the rectitude of this principle is at once unnecessary and impossible.* Has the rectitude of this principle been ever formally contested? It should seem that it had, by those who have not known what they have been meaning. Is it susceptible of any direct proof? It should seem not: for that which is used to prove every thing else, cannot itself be proved: a chain of proofs must have their commencement somewhere. To give such proof is as impossible as it is needless.

XII. *It has seldom, however, as yet been consistently pursued.* Not that there is or ever has been that human creature breathing, however stupid or perverse, who has not on many, perhaps on most occasions of his life, deferred to it. By the natural constitution of the human frame, on most occasions of their lives men in general embrace this principle, without thinking of it: if not for the ordering of their own actions, yet for the trying of their own actions, as well as of those of other men. There have been, at the same time, not many, perhaps, even of the most intelligent, who have been disposed to embrace it purely and without reserve. There are even few who have not taken some occasion or other to quarrel with it, either on account of their not understanding always how to apply it, or on account of some prejudice or other which they were afraid to examine into, or could not bear to part with. For such is the stuff that man is made of: in principle and in practice, in a right track and in a wrong one, the rarest of all human qualities is consistency.

XIII. *It can never be consistently combated.* When a man attempts to combat the principle of utility, it is with reasons drawn, without his being aware of it, from that very principle itself.[4] His arguments, if they prove any thing, prove not that the principle is *wrong,* but that, according to the applications he supposes to be made of it, it is *misapplied.* Is it possible for a man to move the earth? Yes; but he must first find out another earth to stand upon.

XIV. *Course to be taken for surmounting prejudices that may have been entertained against it.* To disprove the propriety of it by arguments is impossible; but, from the causes that have been mentioned, or from some confused or partial view of it, a man may happen to be disposed not to relish it. Where this is the case, if he thinks the settling of his opinions on such a subject worth the trouble, let him take the following steps, and at length, perhaps, he may come to reconcile himself to it.

1. Let him settle with himself, whether he would wish to discard this principle altogether; if so, let him consider what it is that all his reasonings (in matters of politics especially) can amount to?

2. If he would, let him settle with himself, whether he would judge an act without any principle, or whether there is any other he would judge and act by?

3. If there be, let him examine and satisfy himself whether the principle he thinks he has found is really any separate intelligible principle; or whether it be not a mere principle in words, a kind of phrase, which at bottom expresses neither more nor less than the mere averment of his own unfounded sentiments; that is, what in another person he might be apt to call caprice?

4. If he is inclined to think that his own approbation or disapprobation, annexed to the idea of an act, without any regard to its consequences, is a sufficient foundation for him to judge and act upon, let him ask himself whether his sentiment is to be a standard of right and wrong, with respect to every other man, or whether every man's sentiment has the same privilege of being a standard to itself?

5. In the first case, let him ask himself whether his principle is not despotical, and hostile to all the rest of human race?

6. In the second case, whether it is not anarchical, and whether at this rate there are not as many different standards of right and wrong as there are men? and whether even to the same man, the same thing, which is right today, may not (without the least change in its nature) be wrong tomorrow? and whether the same thing is not right and wrong in the same place at the same time? and in either case, whether all argument is not at an end? and whether, when two men have said, "I like this," and "I don't like it," they can (upon such a principle) have any thing more to say?

7. If he should have said to himself, No: for that the sentiment which he proposes as a standard must be grounded on reflection, let him say on what particulars the reflection is to turn? if on particulars having relation to the utility of act, then let him say whether this is not deserting his own principle, and borrowing assistance from that very one in opposition to which he sets it up: or if not on those particulars, on what other particulars?

8. If he should be for compounding the matter, and adopting his own principle in part, and the principle of utility in part, let him say how far he will adopt it?

9. When he has settled with himself where he will stop, then let him ask himself how he justifies to himself the adopting it so far? and why he will not adopt it any farther?

10. Admitting any other principle than the principle of utility to be a right principle, a principle that it is right for a man to pursue; admitting (what is not true) that the word *right* can have a meaning without reference to utility, let him say whether there is any such thing as a *motive* that a man can have to pursue the dictates of it: if there is, let him say what that motive is, and how it is to be distinguished from those which enforce the dictates of utility: if not, then lastly let him say what it is this other principle can be good for?

CHAPTER II. OF PRINCIPLES ADVERSE TO THAT OF UTILITY

I. *All other principles than that of utility must be wrong.* If the principle of utility be a right principle to be governed by, and that in all cases, it follows from what has been just observed, that whatever principle differs from it in any case must necessarily be a wrong one. To prove any other principle, therefore, to be a wrong one, there needs no more than just to show it to be what it is, a principle of which the dictates are in some point or other different from those of the principle of utility: to state it is to confute it.

II. *Ways in which a principle may be wrong.* A principle may be different from that of utility in two ways: 1. By being constantly opposed to it: this is the case with a principle which may be termed the principle of asceticism.[5] 2. By being sometimes opposed to it, and sometimes not, as it may happen: this is the case with another, which may be termed the principle of *sympathy* and *antipathy*.

III. *Principle of asceticism, what.* By the principle of asceticism I mean that principle, which, like the principle of utility, approves or disapproves of any action, according to the tendency which it appears to have to augment or diminish the happiness of the party whose interest is in question; but in an inverse manner: approving of actions in as far as they tend to diminish his happiness; disapproving of them in as far as they tend to augment it.

IV. *A partizan of the principle of asceticism, who.* It is evident that any one who reprobates any the least particle of pleasure, as such, from whatever source derived, is *pro tanto* a partizan of the principle of asceticism. It is only upon that principle, and not from the principle of utility, that the most abominable pleasure which the vilest of malefactors ever reaped from his crime would be to be reprobated, if it stood alone. The case is, that it never does stand alone; but is necessarily followed by such a quantity of pain (or, what comes to the same thing, such a chance for a certain quantity of pain) that the pleasure in comparison of it, is as nothing: and this is the true and sole, but perfectly sufficient, reason for making it a ground for punishment.

V. *This principle has had in some a philosophical, in others a religious origin.* There are two classes of men of very different complexions, by whom the principle of asceticism appears to have been embraced; the one a set of moralists, the other a set of religionists. Different accordingly have been the motives which appear to have recommended it to the notice of these different parties. Hope, that is the prospect of pleasure, seems to have animated the former: hope, the ailment of philosophic pride: the hope of honour and reputation at the hands of men. Fear, that is the prospect of pain, the latter: fear, the offspring of superstitious fancy: the fear of future punishment at the hands of a splenetic and revengeful Deity. I say in this case fear: for of the invisible future, fear is more powerful than hope. These circumstances characterize the two different parties among the partizans of the principle of asceticism; the parties and their motives different, the principle the same.

VI. *It has been carried farther by the religious party than by the philosophical.* The religious party, however, appear to have carried it farther than the philosophical: they have acted more consistently and less wisely. The philosophical party have scarcely gone farther than to reprobate pleasure: the religious party have frequently gone so far as to make it a matter of merit and of duty to court pain. The philosophical party have hardly gone farther than the making pain a matter of indifference. It is no evil, they have said: they have not said, it is a good. They have not so much as reprobated all pleasure in the lump. They have discarded only what they have called the gross; that is, such as are organical, or of which the origin is easily traced up to such as are organical: they have even cherished and magnified the refined. Yet this, however, not under the name of pleasure: to cleanse itself from the sordes of its impure original, it was necessary it should change its name: the honourable, the glorious, the reputable, the becoming, the *honestum*, the *decorum*, it was to be called: in short, any thing but pleasure.

VII. *The philosophical branch of it has had most influence among persons of education, the religious among the vulgar.* From these two sources have flowed the doctrines from which the sentiments of the bulk of mankind have all along received a tincture of this principle; some from the philosophical, some from the religious, some from both. Men of education more frequently from the philosophical, as more suited to the elevation of their sentiments: the vulgar more frequently from the superstitious, as more suited to the narrowness of their intellect, undilated by knowledge: and to the abjectness of their condition, continually open to the attacks of fear. The tinctures, however, derived from the two sources, would naturally intermingle, insomuch that a man would not always know by which of them he was most influenced: and they would often serve to corroborate and enliven one another. It was this conformity that made a kind of alliance between parties of a complexion otherwise so dissimilar: and disposed them to unite upon various occasions against the common enemy, the partizan of the principle of utility, whom they joined in branding with the odious name of Epicurean.

VIII. *The principle of asceticism has never been steadily applied by either party to the Business of Government.* The principle of asceticism, however, with whatever warmth it may have been embraced by its partizans as a rule of private conduct, seems not to have been carried to any considerable length, when applied to the business of government. In a few instances it has been carried a little way by the philosophical party: witness the Spartan regimen. Though then, perhaps, it may be considered as having been a measure of security: and an application, though a precipitate and perverse application, of the principle of utility. Scarcely in any instances, to any considerable length, by the religious: for the various monastic orders, and the societies of the Quakers, Dumplers, Moravians, and other religionists, have been free societies, whose regimen no man has been astricted to without the intervention of his own consent. Whatever merit a man may have thought there would be in making himself miserable, no such notion seems ever to have occurred to any of them, that it may be a merit, much less a duty, to make others miserable: although it should seem, that if a certain quantity of misery were a thing so desirable, it would not matter much whether it were brought by each man upon himself, or by one man upon another. It is true, that from the same source from whence, among the religionists, the attachment to the principle of asceticism took its rise, flowed other doctrines and practices, from which misery in abundance was produced in one man by the instrumentality of another; witness the holy wars, and the persecutions for religion. But the passion for producing misery in these cases proceeded upon some special ground: the exercise of it was confined to persons of particular descriptions: they were tormented, not as men, but as heretics and infidels. To have inflicted the same miseries on their fellow-believers and fellow-sectaries, would have been as blameable in the eyes even of these religionists, as in those of a partizan of the principle of utility. For a man to give himself a certain number of stripes was indeed meritorious: but to give the same number of stripes to another man, not consenting, would have been a sin. We read of saints, who for the good of their souls, and the mortification of their bodies, have voluntarily yielded themselves a prey to vermin: but though many persons of this class have wielded the reins of empire, we read of none who have set themselves to work, and made laws on purpose, with a view of stocking the body politic with the breed of highwaymen, housebreakers, or incendiaries. If at any time they have suffered the nation to be preyed upon by swarms of idle pensioners, or useless placemen, it has rather been from negligence and imbecility, than from any settled plan for oppressing and plundering of the people. If at any time they have sapped the sources of national wealth, by cramping commerce, and driving the inhabitants into emigration, it has been with other views, and in pursuit of other ends. If they have declaimed against the pursuit of pleasure, and the use of wealth, they have commonly stopped at declamation: they have not, like Lycurgus, made express ordinances for the purpose of banishing the precious metals. If they have established idleness by a law, it has been not because idleness, the mother of vice and misery, is itself a virtue, but because idleness (say they) is the road to holiness. If under the notion of fasting, they have joined in the plan of confining their subjects to a diet, thought by some to be of the most nourishing and prolific nature, it has been not for the sake of making them tributaries to the nations by whom that diet was to be supplied, but for the sake of manifesting their own power, and exercising the obedience of the people. If they have established, or suffered to be established, punishments for the breach of celibacy, they have done no more than comply with the petitions of those deluded rigorists, who, dupes to the ambitious and deep-laid policy of their rulers, first laid themselves under that idle obligation by a vow.

IX. *The principle of asceticism, in its origin, was but that of utility misapplied.* The principle of asceticism seems originally to have been the reverie of certain hasty speculators, who having perceived, or fancied, that certain pleasures, when reaped in certain circumstances, have, at the long run, been attended with pains more than equivalent to them, took occasion to quarrel with every thing that offered itself under the name of pleasure. Having then got thus far, and having forgot the point which they set out from, they pushed on, and went so much further as to think it meritorious to fall in love with pain. Even this, we see, is at bottom but the principle of utility misapplied.

X. *It can never be consistently pursued.* The principle of utility is capable of being consistently pursued; and it is but tautology to say, that the more consistently it is pursued, the better it must ever be for humankind. The principle of asceticism never was, nor ever can be, consistently pursued by any living creature. Let but one tenth part of the inhabitants of this earth pursue it consistently, and in a day's time they will have turned it into a hell.

XI. *The principle of sympathy and antipathy, what.* Among principles adverse[6] to that of utility, that which at this day seems to have most influence in matters of government, is what may be called the principle of sympathy and antipathy. By the principle of sympathy and antipathy, I mean that principle which approves or disapproves of certain actions, not on account of their tending to augment the happiness, not yet on account of their tending to diminish the happiness of the party whose interest is in question, but merely because a man finds himself disposed to approve or disapprove of them: holding up that approbation or disapprobation as a sufficient reason for itself, and disclaiming the necessity of looking out for any extrinsic ground. Thus far in the general department of morals: and in the particular department of politics, measuring out the quantum (as well as determining the ground) of punishment, by the degree of the disapprobation.

XII. *This is rather the negation of all principle, than any thing positive.* It is manifest, that this is rather a principle in name than in reality: it is not a positive principle of itself, so much as a term employed to signify the negation of all principle. What one expects to find in a principle is something that points out some external consideration, as a means of warranting and guiding the internal sentiments of approbation and disapprobation: this expectation is but ill fulfilled by a proposition, which does neither more nor less than hold up each of those sentiments as a ground and standard for itself.

XIII. *Sentiments of a partizan of the principle of antipathy.* In looking over the catalogue of human actions (says a partizan of this principle) in order to determine which of them are to be marked with the seal of disapprobation, you need but to take counsel of your own feelings: whatever you find in yourself a propensity to condemn, is wrong for that very reason. For the same reason it is also meet for punishment: in what proportion it is adverse to utility, or whether it be adverse to utility at all, is a matter that makes no difference. In that same *proportion* also is it meet for punishment: if you hate much, punish much: if you hate little, punish little: punish as you hate. If you hate not at all, punish not at all: the fine feelings of the soul are not to be overborne and tyrannized by the harsh and rugged dictates of political utility.

XIV. *The systems that have been formed concerning the standard of right and wrong, are all reducible to this principle.* The various systems that have been formed concerning the standard of right and wrong, may all be reduced to the principle of sympathy and antipathy. One account may serve for all of them. They consist all of them in so many contrivances for avoiding the obligation of appealing to any external standard, and for prevailing upon the reader to accept of the author's sentiment or opinion as a reason for itself. The phrases different, but the principle the same.[7]

XV. *This principle will frequently coincide with that of utility.* It is manifest, that the dictates of this principle will frequently coincide with those of utility, though perhaps without intending any such thing. Probably more frequently than not: and hence it is that the business of penal justice is carried on upon that tolerable sort of footing upon which we see it carried on in common at this day. For what more natural or more general ground of hatred to a practice can there be, than the mischievousness of such practice? What all men are exposed to suffer by, all men will be disposed to hate. It is far yet, however, from being a constant ground: for when a man suffers, it is not always that he knows what it is he suffers by. A man may suffer grievously, for instance, by a new tax, without being able to trace up the cause of his sufferings to the injustice of some neighbour, who has eluded the payment of an old one.

XVI. *This principle is most apt to err on the side of severity.* The principle of sympathy and antipathy is most apt to err on the side of severity. It is for applying punishment in many cases which deserve none: in many cases which deserve some, it is for applying more than they deserve. There is no incident imaginable, be it ever so trivial, and so remote from mischief, from which this principle may not extract a ground of punishment. Any difference in taste: any difference in opinion: upon one subject as well as upon another. No disagreement so trifling which perseverance and altercation will not render serious. Each becomes in the other's eyes an enemy, and, if laws permit, a criminal.[8] This is one of the circumstances by which the human race is distinguished (not much indeed to its advantage) from the brute creation.

XVII. *But errs, in some instances, on the side of lenity.* It is not, however, by any means unexampled for this principle to err on the side of lenity. A near and perceptible mischief moves antipathy. A remote and imperceptible mischief, though not less real, has no effect. Instances in proof of this will occur in numbers in the course of the work.[9] It would be breaking in upon the order of it to give them here.

XVIII. *The theological principle, what—not a separate principle.* It may be wondered, perhaps, that in all this while no mention has been made of the *theological* principle; meaning that principle which professes to recur for the standard of right and wrong to the will of God. But the case is, this is not in fact a distinct principle. It is never anything more or less than one or other of the three before-mentioned principles presenting itself under another shape. The *will* of God here meant cannot be his revealed will, as contained in the sacred writings: for that is a system which nobody ever thinks of recurring to at this time of day, for

the details of political administration: and even before it can be applied
to the details of private conduct, it is universally allowed, by the most
eminent divines of all persuasions, to stand in need of pretty ample interpretations; else to what use are the works of those divines? And for
the guidance of these interpretations, it is also allowed, that some other
standard must be assumed. The will then which is meant on this occasion, is that which may be called the *presumptive* will: that is to say,
that which is presumed to be his will on account of the conformity of its
dictates to those of some other principle. What then may be this other
principle? it must be one or other of the three mentioned above: for there
cannot, as we have seen, be any more. It is plain, therefore, that, setting
revelation out of the question, no light can ever be thrown upon the
standard of right and wrong, by any thing that can be said upon the
question, what is God's will. We may be perfectly sure, indeed, that
whatever is right is conformable to the will of God: but so far is that
from answering the purpose of showing us what is right, that it is necessary to know first whether a thing is right, in order to know from thence
whether it be conformable to the will of God.[10]

XIX. *Antipathy, let the actions it dictates be ever so right, is never of
itself a right ground of action.* There are two things which are very apt
to be confounded, but which it imports us carefully to distinguish: the
motive or cause, which, by operating on the mind of an individual, is
productive of any act: and the ground or reason which warrants a legislator, or other by-stander, in regarding that act with an eye of approbation. When the act happens, in the particular instance in question, to be
productive of effects which we approve of, much more if we happen to
observe that the same motive may frequently be productive, in other
instances, of the like effects, we are apt to transfer our approbation to
the motive itself, and to assume, as the just ground for the approbation
we bestow on the act, the circumstance of its originating from that motive. It is in this way that the sentiment of antipathy has often been
considered as a just ground of action. Antipathy, for instance, in such or
such a case, is the cause of an action which is attended with good effects:
but this does not make it a right ground of action in that case, any more
than in any other. Still farther. Not only the effects are good, but the
agent sees beforehand that they will be so. This may make the action indeed a perfectly right action: but it does not make antipathy a right
ground of action. For the same sentiment of antipathy, if implicitly deferred to, may be, and very frequently is, productive of the very worst
effects. Antipathy, therefore, can never be a right ground of action. No
more, therefore, can resentment, which, as will be seen more particularly
hereafter, is but a modification of antipathy. The only right ground of

action, that can possibly subsist, is, after all, the consideration of utility, which, if it is a right principle of action, and of approbation, in any one case, is so in every other. Other principles in abundance, that is, other motives, may be the reasons why such and such an act *has* been done: that is, the reasons or causes of its being done: but it is this alone that can be the reason why it might or ought to have been done. Antipathy or resentment requires always to be regulated, to prevent its doing mischief: to be regulated by what? always by the principle of utility. The principle of utility neither requires nor admits of any other regulator than itself.

CHAPTER III. OF THE FOUR SANCTIONS OR SOURCES OF PAIN AND PLEASURE

I. *Connexion of this chapter with preceding.* It has been shown that the happiness of the individuals, of whom a community is composed, that is their pleasures and their security, is end and the sole end which the legislator ought to have in view: the sole standard, in conformity to which each individual ought, as far as depends upon the legislator, to be *made* to fashion his behaviour. But whether it be this or any thing else that is to be *done*, there is nothing by which a man can ultimately be *made* to do it, but either pain or pleasure. Having taken a general view of these two grand objects (*viz.* pleasure, and what comes to the same thing, immunity from pain) in the character of *final* causes; it will be necessary to take a view of pleasure and pain itself, in the character of efficient causes or means.

II. *Four sanctions or sources of pleasure and pain.* There are four distinguishable sources from which pleasure and pain are in use to flow: considered separately, they may be termed the *physical*, the *political*, the *moral*, and the *religious:* and inasmuch as the pleasures and pains belonging to each of them are capable of giving a binding force to any law or rule of conduct, they may all of them be termed *sanctions.*[11]

III. *The physical sanction.* If it be in the present life, and from the ordinary course of nature, not purposely modified by the interposition of the will of any human being, nor by any extraordinary interposition of any superior invisible being, that the pleasure or the pain takes place or is expected, it may be said to issue from or to belong to the *physical sanction.*

IV. *The political.* If at the hands of a *particular* person or set of persons in the community, who under names correspondent to that of *judge,* are chosen for the particular purpose of dispensing it, according to the will of the sovereign or supreme ruling power in the state, it may be said to issue from the *political sanction.*

V. *The moral or popular.* If at the hands of such *chance* persons in the community, as the party in question may happen in the course of his life to have concerns with, according to each man's spontaneous disposition, and not according to any settled or concerted rule, it may be said to issue from the *moral* or *popular saction.*[12]

VI. *The religious.* If from the immediate hand of a superior invisible being, either in the present life, or in a future, it may be said to issue from the *religious sanction.*

VII. *The pleasures and pains which belong to the religious saction, may regard either the present life or a future.* Pleasures or pains which may be expected to issue from the *physical, political,* or *moral* sanctions, must all of them be expected to be experienced, if ever, in the *present* life: those which may be expected to issue from the *religious* sanction, may be expected to be experienced either in the *present* life or in a *future.*

VIII. *Those which regard the present life, from which soever source they flow, differ only in the circumstances of their production.* Those which can be experienced in the present life, can of course be no others than such as human nature in the course of the present life is susceptible of: and from each of these sources may flow all the pleasures or pains of which, in the course of the present life, human nature is susceptible. With regard to these then (with which alone we have in this place any concern) those of them which belong to any one of those sanctions, differ not ultimately in kind from those which belong to any one of the other three: the only difference there is among them lies in the circumstances that accompany their production. A suffering which befalls a man in the natural and spontaneous course of things, shall be styled, for instance, a *calamity;* in which case, if it be supposed to befall him through any imprudence of his, it may be styled a punishment issuing from the physical sanction. Now this same suffering, if inflicted by the law, will be what is commonly called a *punishment;* if incurred for want of any friendly assistance, which the misconduct, or supposed misconduct, of the sufferer has occasioned to be withholden, a punishment issuing from the *moral* sanction; if through the immediate interposition of a particular providence, a punishment issuing from the religious sanction.

IX. *Example.* A man's goods, or his person, are consumed by fire. If this happened to him by what is called an accident, it was a calamity: if by reason of his own imprudence (for instance, from his neglecting to put his candle out) it may be styled a punishment of the physical sanction: if it happened to him by the sentence of the political magistrate, a punishment belonging to the political sanction; that is, what is commonly called a punishment: if for want of any assistance which his *neighbour* withheld from him out of some dislike to his *moral* character, a punishment of the *moral* sanction: if by an immediate act of *God's* displeasure, manifested on account of some *sin* committed by him, or through any distraction of mind, occasioned by the dread of such displeasure, a punishment of the *religious* sanction.[13]

X. *Those which regard a future life are not specifically known.* As to such of the pleasures and pains belonging to the religious sanction, as regard a future life, of what kind these may be we cannot know. These lie not open to our observation. During the present life they are matter only of expectation: and, whether that expectation be derived from natural or revealed religion, the particular kind of pleasure or pain, if it be different from all those which lie open to our observation, is what we can have no idea of. The best ideas we can obtain of such pains and pleasures are altogether unliquidated in point of quality. In what other respects our ideas of them *may* be liquidated will be considered in another place.[14]

XI. *The physical sanction included in each of the other three.* Of these four sanctions the physical is altogether, we may observe, the groundwork of the political and the moral: so is it also of the religious, in as far as the latter bears relation to the present life. It is included in each of those other three. This may operate in any case (that is, any of the pains or pleasures belonging to it may operate) independently of *them:* none of *them* can operate but by means of this. In a word, the powers of nature may operate of themselves; but neither the magistrate, nor men at large, *can* operate, nor is God in the case in question *supposed* to operate, but through the powers of nature.

XII. *Use of this chapter.* For these four objects, which in their nature have so much in common, it seemed of use to find a common name. It seemed of use, in the first place, for the convenience of giving a name to certain pleasures and pains, for which a name equally characteristic could hardly otherwise have been found: in the second place, for the sake of holding up the efficacy of certain moral forces, the influence of which is apt not to be sufficiently attended to. Does the political sanction exert an influence over the conduct of mankind? The moral, the religious sanctions do so too. In every inch of his career are the operations of the political magistrate liable to be aided or impeded by these two foreign powers: who, one or other of them, or both, are sure to be either his rivals or his allies. Does it happen to him to leave them out in his calculations? he will be sure almost to find himself mistaken in the result. Of all this we shall find abundant proofs in the sequel of this work. It behoves him, therefore, to have them continually before his eyes; and that under such a name as exhibits the relation they bear to his own purposes and designs.

CHAPTER IV. VALUE OF A LOT OF PLEASURE OR PAIN, HOW TO BE MEASURED

I. *Use of this chapter.* Pleasures then, and the avoidance of pains, are the *ends* which the legislator has in view: it behoves him therefore to understand their *value.* Pleasures and pains are the *instruments* he has to work with: it behoves him therefore to understand their force, which is again, in other words, their value.

II. *Circumstances to be taken into the account in estimating the value of a pleasure or pain considered with reference to a single person, and by itself.* To a person considered by *himself,* the value of a pleasure or pain considered by *itself,* will be greater or less, according to the four following circumstances:[15]

1. Its *intensity.*
2. Its *duration.*
3. Its *certainty* or *uncertainty.*
4. *Its propinquity* or *remoteness.*

III. —*considered as connected with other pleasures or pains.* These are the circumstances which are to be considered in estimating a pleasure or a pain considered each of them by itself. But when the value of any pleasure or pain is considered for the purpose of estimating the tendency of any *act* by which it is produced, there are two other circumstances to be taken into the account; these are,

5. Its *fecundity,* or the chance it has of being followed by sensations of the *same* kind: that is, pleasures, if it be a pleasure: pains, if it be a pain.
6. Its *purity,* or the chance it has of *not* being followed by sensations of the *opposite* kind: that is, pains, if it be a pleasure: pleasures, if it be a pain.

These two last, however, are in strictness scarcely to be deemed properties of the pleasure or the pain itself; they are not, therefore, in strictness to be taken into the account of the value of that pleasure or that pain. They are in strictness to be deemed properties only of the act, or other event, by which such pleasure or pain has been produced; and accordingly are only to be taken into the account of the tendency of such act or such event.

IV. —*considered with reference to a number of persons.* To a *number* of persons, with reference to each of whom the value of a pleasure or a pain is considered, it will be greater or less, according to seven circumstances: to wit, the six preceding ones; *viz.*

1. Its *intensity.*
2. Its *duration.*
3. Its *certainty* or *uncertainty.*
4. Its *propinquity* or *remoteness.*
5. Its *fecundity.*
6. Its *purity.*

And one other; to wit:

7. Its *extent;* that is, the number of persons to whom it *extends;* or (in other words) who are affected by it.

V. *Process for estimating the tendency of any act or event.* To take an exact account then of the general tendency of any act, by which the interests of a community are affected, proceed as follows. Begin with any one person of those whose interests seem most immediately to be affected by it: and take an account.

1. Of the value of each distinguishable *pleasure* which appears to be produced by it in the *first* instance.

2. Of the value of each *pain* which appears to be produced by it in the *first* instance.

3. Of the value of each pleasure which appears to be produced by it *after* the first. This constitutes the *fecundity* of the first *pleasure* and the *impurity* of the first *pain.*

4. Of the value of each *pain* which appears to be produced by it after the first. This constitutes the *fecundity* of the first *pain,* and the *impurity* of the first pleasure.

5. Sum up all the values of all the *pleasures* on the one side, and those of all the pains on the other. The balance, if it be on the side of pleasure, will give the *good* tendency of the act upon the whole, with respect to the interests of that *individual* person; if on the side of pain, the *bad* tendency of it upon the whole.

6. Take an account of the *number* of persons whose interests appear to be concerned; and repeat the above process with respect to each. *Sum up* the numbers expressive of the degrees of *good* tendency, which the act has, with respect to each individual, in regard to whom the tendency of

it is *good* upon the whole: do this again with respect to each individual, in regard to whom the tendency of it is *good* upon the whole: do this again with respect to each individual, in regard to whom the tendency of it is *bad* upon the whole. Take the *balance;* which, if on the side of *pleasure,* will give the general *good tendency* of the act, with respect to the total number or community of individuals concerned; if on the side of pain, the general *evil tendency* with respect to the same community.

VI. *Use of the foregoing process.* It is not to be expected that this process should be strictly pursued previously to every moral judgment, or to every legislative or judicial operation. It may, however, be always kept in view; and as near as the process actually pursued on these occasions approaches to it, so near will such process approach to the character of an exact one.

VII. *The same process applicable to good and evil, profit and mischief, and all other modifications of pleasure and pain.* The same process is alike applicable to pleasure and pain, in whatever shape they appear: and by whatever denomination they are distinguished: to pleasure, whether it be called *good* (which is properly the cause or instrument of pleasure) or *profit* (which is distant pleasure, or the cause or instrument of distant pleasure,) or *convenience,* or *advantage, benefit, emolument, happiness,* and so forth: to pain, whether it be called *evil,* (which corresponds to *good*) or *mischief,* or *inconvenience,* or *disadvantage,* or *loss,* or *unhappiness,* and so forth.

VIII. *Conformity of men's practice to this theory.* Nor is this a novel and unwarranted, any more than it is a useless theory. In all this there is nothing but what the practice of mankind, wheresoever they have a clear view of their own interest, is perfectly conformable to. An article of property, an estate in land, for instance, is valuable, on what account? On account of the pleasures of all kinds which it enables a man to produce, and what comes to the same thing the pains of all kinds which it enables him to avert. But the value of such an article of property is universally understood to rise or fall according to the length or shortness of the time which a man has in it: the certainty or uncertainty of its coming into possession: and the nearness or remoteness of the time at which, if at all, it is to come into possession. As to the *intensity* of the pleasures which a man may derive from it, this is never thought of, because it depends upon the use which each particular person may come to make of it; which cannot be estimated till the particular pleasures he may come to derive from it, or the particular pains he may come to exclude by means of it, are brought to view. For the same reason, neither does he think of the *fecundity* or *purity* of those pleasures.

Thus much for pleasure and pain, happiness and unhappiness, in *general*. We come now to consider the several particular kinds of pain and pleasure.

NOTES

CHAPTER I

[1] Note by the Author, July 1822:

To this denomination has of late been added, or substituted, the *greatest happiness* or *greatest felicity* principle: this for shortness, instead of saying at length *that principle* which states the greatest happiness of all those whose interest is in question, as being the right and proper, and only right and proper and universally desirable, end of human action: of human action in every situation, and in particular in that of a functionary or set of functionaries exercising the powers of Government. The word *utility* does not so clearly point to the ideas of *pleasure* and *pain* as the words *happiness* and *felicity* do: nor does it lead us to the consideration of the *number,* of the interests affected; to the *number,* as being the circumstance, which contributes, in the largest proportion, to the formation of the standard here in question; the *standard* of *right* and *wrong,* by which alone the propriety of human conduct, in every situation, can with propriety be tried. This want of a sufficiently manifest connexion between the ideas of *happiness* and *pleasure* on the one hand, and the idea of *utility* on the other, I have every now and then found operating, and with but too much efficiency, as a bar to the acceptance, that might otherwise have been given, to this principle.

[2] *A principle, what.* The word principle is derived from the Latin *principium:* which seems to be compounded of the two words *primus,* first, or chief, and *cipium,* a termination which seems to be derived from *capio,* to take, as in *manicipium, municipium;* to which are analogous, *auceps, forceps,* and others. It is a term of very vague and very extensive signification: it is applied to any thing which is conceived to serve as a foundation or beginning to any series of operations: in some cases, of physical operations; but of mental operations in the present case.

The principle here in question may be taken for an act of the mind; a sentiment; a sentiment of approbation; a sentiment which, when applied to an action, approves of its utility, as that quality of it by which the measure of approbation or disapprobation bestowed upon it ought to be governed.

[3] Interest is one of those words, which not having any superior *genus,* cannot in the ordinary way be defined.

[4] "The principle of utility (I have heard it said) is a dangerous principle: it is dangerous on certain occasions to consult it." This is as much as to say, what? that it is not consonant to utility, to consult utility: in short, that it is *not* consulting it, to consult it.

Addition by the Author, July 1822:

Not long after the publication of the *Fragment on Government,* anno 1776, in which, in the character of an all-comprehensive and all-commanding principle, the principle of *utility* was brought to view, one person by whom observation to the above effect was made was *Alexander Wedderburn,* at that time Attorney or Solicitor General, afterwards successively Chief Justice of the Common Pleas, and Chancellor of England, under the successive titles of Lord Loughborough and Earl of Rosslyn. It was made—not indeed in my hearing, but in the hearing of a person by whom it was almost immediately communicated to me. So far from being self-contradictory, it was a shrewd and perfectly true one. By that distinguished functionary, the state of the Government was thoroughly understood: by the obscure individual, at that time not so much as supposed to be so: his disquisitions had not been as yet applied, with any thing like a comprehensive view, to the field of Constitutional Law, nor therefore to those features of the English Government, by which the greatest happiness of the ruling *one* with or without that of a favoured few, are now so plainly seen to be the only ends to which the course of it has at any time been directed. The *principle of utility* was an appellative, at that time employed—employed by me, as it had been by others, to designate that which, in a more perspicuous and instructive manner, may, as above, be designated by the name of the *greatest happiness principle*. "This principle (said Wedderburn) is a dangerous one." Saying so, he said that which, to a certain extent, is strictly true: a principle, which lays down, as the only *right* and justifiable end of Government, the greatest happiness of the greatest number—how can it be denied to be a dangerous one? dangerous it unquestionably is, to every government which has for its *actual* end or object, the greatest happiness of a certain *one,* with or without the addition of some comparatively small number of others, whom it is matter of pleasure or accommodation to him to admit, each of them, to a share in the concern, on the footing of so many junior partners. *Dangerous* it therefore really was, to the interest—the sinister interest—of all those functionaries, himself included, whose interest it was, to maximize delay, vexation, and expense, in judicial and other modes of procedure, for the sake of the profit, extractible out of the expense. In a Government which had for its end in view the greatest happiness of the greatest number, Alexander Wedderburn might have been Attorney General and then Chancellor: but he would not have been Attorney General with £ 15,000 a year, nor Chancellor, with a peerage with a veto upon all justice, with £ 25,000 a year, and with 500 sinecures at his disposal, under the name of Ecclesiastical Benefices, besides *et caeteras.*

CHAPTER II

[5] *Asceticism, origin of the word. Principles of the Monks.* Ascetic is a term that has been sometimes applied to Monks. It comes from a Greek word which signifies *exercise.* The practices by which Monks sought to distinguish themselves from other men were called their Exercises. These exercises consisted in so many contrivances they had for tormenting themselves. By this they thought to ingratiate themselves with the Deity. For the Deity, said they, is a Being of infinite benevolence: now a Being of the most ordinary benevolence is pleased to see others make themselves as happy as they can: therefore to make ourselves as unhappy as we can is the way to please the Deity. If any body asked them, what motive they could find for doing all this? Oh! said they, you are not to imagine that we are punishing ourselves for nothing: we know very well what we are about. You are to know, that for every grain of pain it costs us now, we are to have a hundred grains of pleasure by and by. The case is, that God loves to see us torment ourselves at present: indeed he has as good as told us so. But this is done only to try us, in order just to see how we should behave: which it is plain he could not know, without making the experiment. Now then, from the satisfaction it gives him to see us make ourselves as unhappy as we can make ourselves in this present life, we have a sure

proof of the satisfaction it will give him to see us as happy as he can make us in a life to come.

⁶ The following Note was first printed in January 1789:

It ought rather to have been styled, more extensively, the principle of *caprice.* Where it applies to the choice of actions to be marked out for injunction or prohibition for reward or punishment (to stand, in a word, as subjects for *obligations* to be imposed), it may indeed with propriety be termed, as in the text, the principle of *sympathy* and *antipathy.* But this appellative does not so well apply to it, when occupied in the choice of the *events* which are to serve as sources of *title* with respect to *rights:* where the actions prohibited and allowed the obligations and rights, being already fixed, the only question is, under what circumstances a man is to be invested with the one or subjected to the other? from what incidents occasion is to be taken to invest a man, or to refuse to invest him, with the one, or to subject him to the other? In this latter case it may more appositely be characterized by the name of the *phantastic principle.* Sympathy and antipathy are affections of the *sensible* faculty. But the choice of *titles* with respect to *rights,* especially with respect to proprietary rights, upon grounds unconnected with utility, has been in many instances the work, not of the affections but of the imagination.

When, in justification of an article of English Common Law, calling uncles to succeed in certain cases in preference to fathers, Lord Coke, produced a sort of ponderosity he had discovered in rights, disqualifying them from ascending in a straight line, it was not that he *loved* uncles particularly, or *hated* fathers, but because the analogy, such as it was, was what his imagination presented him with, instead of a reason, and because, to a judgment unobservant of the standard of utility, or unacquainted with the art of consulting it, where affection is out of the way, imagination is the only guide.

When I know not what ingenious grammarian invented the proposition *Delegatus non potest delegare,* to serve as a rule of law, it was not surely that he had any antipathy to delegates of the second order, or that it was any pleasure to him to think of the ruin which, for want of a manager at home, may befall the affairs of a traveller, whom an unforeseen accident has deprived of the object of his choice: it was, that the incongruity, of giving the same law to objects so contrasted as *active* and *passive* are, was not to be surmounted, and that *-atus* chimes, as well as it contrasts, with *-are.*

When that inexorable maxim (of which the dominion is no more to be defined, than the date of its birth, or the name of its father, is to be found), was imported from England for the government of Bengal, and the whole fabric of judicature was crushed by the thunders of *ex post facto* justice, it was not surely that the prospect of a blameless magistracy perishing in prison afforded any enjoyment to the unoffended authors of their misery; but that the music of the maxim, absorbing the whole imagination, had drowned the cries of humanity along with the dictates of common sense.† *Fiat Justitia, ruat coelum,* says another maxim, as full of extravagance as it is of harmony: Go heaven to wreck—so justice be but done: and what is the ruin kingdoms, in comparison of the wreck of heaven?

So again, when the Prussian chancellor, inspired with the wisdom of I know not what Roman sage, proclaimed in good Latin, for the edification of German ears, *Servitus servitutis non datur* [*Cod. Fred.,* tom. ii, par. 2, liv. 2, tit. x, § 6, p. 308.], it was not that he had conceived any aversion to the lifeholder who, during the continuance of his term, should wish to gratify a neighbour with a right of way or water, or to the neighbour who should wish to accept of the indulgence; but that, to a jurisprudential ear, *-tus -tutis* sound little less melodious than *-atus -are*. Whether the melody of the maxim was the real reason of the rule, is not left open to dispute: for it is ushered in by the conjunction *quia,* reason's appointed harbinger: *quia servitus servitutis non datur.*

Neither would equal melody have been produced, nor indeed could similar melody have been called for, in either of these instances, by the opposite provision: it is only when they are opposed to general rules, and not when by their conformity they are absorbed in them, that more specific ones can obtain a separate existence. *Delegatus potest delegare,* and *Servitus servitutis datur,* provisions already included under the general adoption of contracts, would have been as unnecessary to the apprehension and the memory, as, in comparison of their energetic negatives, they are insipid to the ear.

Were the inquiry diligently made, it would be found that the goddess of harmony has exercised more influence, however latent, over the dispensations of Themis, than her most diligent historiographers, or even her most passionate panegyrists, seem to have been aware of. Every one knows, how, by the ministry of Orpheus, it was she who first collected the sons of men beneath the shadow of the sceptre: yet, in the midst of continual experience, men seem yet to learn, with what successful diligence she has laboured to guide it in its course. Every one knows, that measured numbers were the language of the infancy of law: none seem to have observed, with what imperious sway they have governed her maturer age. In English jurisprudence in particular, the connexion betwixt law and music, however less perceived than in Spartan legislation, is not perhaps less real nor less close. The music of the Office, though not of the same kind, is not less musical in its kind, than the music of the Theatre; that which hardens the heart, than that which softens it: sostenutos as long, cadences as sonorous; and those governed by rules, though not yet promulgated, not less determinate. Search indictments, pleadings, proceedings in chancery, conveyances: whatever trespasses you may find against truth or common sense, you will find none against the laws of harmony. The English Liturgy, justly as this quality has been extolled in that sacred office, possesses not a greater measure of it, than is commonly to be found in an English Act of Parliament. Dignity, simplicity, brevity, precision, intelligibility, possibility of being retained or so much as apprehended, every thing yields to Harmony. Volumes might be filled, shelves loaded, with the sacrifices that are made to this insatiate power. Expletives, her ministers in Grecian poetry are not less busy, though in different shape and bulk, in English legislation: in the former, they are monosyllables [men, toi, ge, nun, &c.]: in the latter, they are whole lines. [And be it further enacted by the authority aforesaid, that—Provided always, and it is hereby further enacted and declared that—&c. &c.]

To return to the *principle of sympathy and antipathy:* a term preferred at first, on account of its impartiality, to the *principle of caprice.* The choice of an appellative, in the above respects too narrow, was owing to my not having, at that time, extended my views over the civil branch of law, any otherwise than as I had found it inseparably involved in the penal. But when we come to the former branch, we shall see the *phantastic* principle making at least as great a figure there, as the principle of *sympathy and antipathy* in the latter.

In the days of Lord Coke, the light of utility can scarcely be said to have as yet shone upon the face of Common Law. If a faint ray of it, under the name of the *argumentum ab inconvenienti,* is to be found in a list of about twenty topics exhibited by that great lawyer as the co-ordinate leaders of that all-perfect system, the admission, so circumstanced, is as sure a proof of neglect, as, to the statues of Brutus and Cassius, exclusion was a cause of notice. It stands, neither in the front, nor in the rear, nor in any post of honour; but huddled in towards the middle, without the smallest mark of preference. [Coke, Littleton, 11. a.] Nor is this Latin *inconvenience* by any means the same thing with the English one. It stands distinguished from *mischief:* and because by the vulgar it is taken for something less bad, it is given by the learned as something worse. *The law prefers a mischief to an inconvenience,* says an admired maxim, and the more admired, because as nothing is expressed by it, the more is supposed to be understood.

Not that there is any avowed, much less a constant opposition, between the prescriptions of utility and the operations of the common law: such constancy we have seen to be too much even for ascetic fervor. [*Supra,* par. x] From time to time instinct would unavoidably betray them into the paths of reason: instinct which, however it may be cramped, can never be killed by education. The cobwebs spun out of the materials brought together by "the competition of opposite analogies," can never have ceased being warped by the silent attraction of the rational principle: though it should have been, as the needle is by the magnet, without the privity of conscience.

Additional Note by the Author, July 1822:

Add, and that the bad system, of Mahometan and other native law was to be put down at all events, to make way for the inapplicable and still more mischievous system of English Judge-made law, and, by the hand of his accomplice Hastings, was to be put into the pocket of Impey—Importer of this instrument of subversion, £ 8,000 a-year contrary to law, in addition to the £ 8,000 a-year lavished upon him, with the customary profusion, by the hand of law. See the Account of this transaction in *Mill's British India.*

To this Governor a statue is erecting by a vote of East India Directors and Proprietors: on it should be inscribed—*Let it but put money into our pockets, no tyranny too flagitious to be worshipped by us.*

To this statue of the Arch-malefactor should be added, for a companion, that of the long-robed accomplice: the one lodging the bribe in the hand of the other. The hundred millions of plundered and oppressed Hindoos and Mahometans pay for the one: a Westminster Hall subscription might pay for the other.

What they have done for Ireland with her seven millions of souls, the authorised deniers and perverters of justice have done for Hindostan with her hundred millions. In this there is nothing wonderful. The wonder is—that, under such institutions, men, though in ever such small number, should be found, whom the view of the injustices which, by *English Judge-made law,* they are compelled to commit, and the miseries they are thus compelled to produce, deprive of health and rest. Witness the Letter of an English Hindostan Judge, Sept. 1, 1819, which lies before me. I will not make so cruel a requital for his honesty, as to put his name in print: indeed the House of Commons' Documents already published leave little need of it.

ᵗ*Various phrases that have served as the characteristic marks of so many pretended systems.* It is curious enough to observe the variety of inventions men have hit upon, and the variety of phrases they have brought forward, in order to conceal from the world, and, if possible, from themselves, this very general and therefore very pardonable self-sufficiency.

1. *Moral Sense.* One man says, he has a thing made on purpose to tell him what is right and what is wrong; and that it is called a *moral sense:* and then he goes to

work at his ease, and says, such a thing is right, and such a thing is wrong—why? "Because my moral sense tells me it is."

2. *Common Sense*. Another man comes and alters the phrase: leaving out *moral*, and putting in *common*, in the room of it. He then tells you, that his common sense teaches him what is right and wrong, as surely as the other's moral sense did: meaning by common sense, a sense of some kind or other, which, he says, is possessed by all mankind: the sense of those, whose sense is not the same as the author's, being struck out of the account as not worth taking. This contrivance does better than the other; for a moral sense, being a new thing, a man may feel about him a good while without being able to find it out: but common sense is as old as the creation; and there is no man but would be ashamed to be thought not to have as much of it as his neighbours. It has another great advantage: by appearing to share power, it lessens envy: for when a man gets up upon this ground, in order to anathematize those who differ from him, it is not by a *sic volo sic jubeo*, but by a *velitis jubeatis*.

3. *Understanding*. Another man comes, and says, that as to a moral sense indeed, he cannot find that he has any such thing: that however he has an *understanding*, which will do quite as well. This understanding, he says, is the standard of right and wrong: it tells him so and so. All good and wise men understand as he does: if other men's understandings differ in any point from his, so much the worse for them: it is a sure sign they are either defective or corrupt.

4. *Rule of Right*. Another man says, that there is an eternal and immutable Rule of Right: that that rule of right dictates so and so: and then he begins giving you his sentiments upon any thing that comes uppermost: and these sentiments (you are to take for granted) are so many branches of the eternal rule of right.

5. *Fitness of Things*. Another man, or perhaps the same man (it's no matter) says, that there are certain practices conformable, and other repugnant, to the Fitness of Things; and then he tells you, at his leisure, what practices are conformable and what repugnant: just as he happens to like a practice or dislike it.

6. *Law of Nature*. A great multitude of people are continually talking of the Law of Nature; and then they go on giving you their sentiments about what is right and what is wrong: and these sentiments, you are to understand, are so many chapters and sections of the Law of Nature.

7. *Law of Reason, Right Reason, Natural Justice, Natural Equity, Good Order.* Instead of the phrase, Law of Nature, you have sometimes, Law of Reason, Right Reason, Natural Justice, Natural Equity, Good Order. Any of them will do equally well. This latter is most used in politics. The three last are much more tolerable than the others, because they do not very explicitly claim to be any thing more than phrases: they insist but feebly upon the being looked upon as so many positive standards of themselves, and seem content to be taken, upon occasion, for phrases expressive of the conformity of the thing in question to the proper standard, whatever that may be. On most occasions, however, it will be better to say *utility: utility* is clearer, as referring more explicitly to pain and pleasure.

8. *Truth*. We have one philosopher, who says, there is no harm in any thing in the world but in telling a lie: and that if, for example, you were to murder your own father, this would only be a particular way of saying, he was not your father. Of course, when this philosospher sees any thing that he does not like, he says, it is a particular way of telling a lie. It is saying, that the act ought to be done, or may be done, when *in truth*, it ought not to be done.

9. *Doctrine of Election*. The fairest and openest of them all is that sort of man

who speaks out, and says, I am of the number of the Elect: now God himself takes care to inform the Elect what is right: and that with so good effect, and let them strive ever so, they cannot help not only knowing it but practising it. If therefore a man wants to know what is right and what is wrong, he has nothing to do but to come to me.

Repugnancy to Nature. It is upon the principle of antipathy that such and such acts are often reprobated on the score of their being *unnatural:* the practice of exposing children, established among the Greeks and Romans, was an unnatural practice. Unnatural, when it means any thing, means unfrequent: and there it means something; although nothing to the present purpose. But here it means no such thing: for the frequency of such acts is perhaps the great complaint. It therefore means nothing; nothing, I mean, which there is in the act itself. All it can serve to express is, the disposition of the person who is talking of it: the disposition he is in to be angry at the thoughts of it. Does it merit his anger? Very likely it may: but whether it does or no is a question, which, to be answered rightly, can only be answered upon the principle of utility.

Unnatural, is as good a word as moral sense, or common sense; and would be as good a foundation for a system. Such an act is unnatural; that is, repugnant to nature: for I do not like to practise it: and, consequently, do not practise it. It is therefore repugnant to what ought to be the nature of every body else.

Mischief they produce. The mischief common to all these ways of thinking and arguing (which, in truth, as we have seen, are but one and the same method, couched in different forms of words) is their serving as a cloke, and pretence, and aliment, to despotism: if not a despotism in practice, a despotism however in disposition: which is but too apt, when pretence and power offer, to show itself in practice. The consequence is, that with intentions very commonly of the purest kind, a man becomes a torment either to himself or his fellow-creatures. If he be of the melancholy cast, he sits in silent grief, bewailing their blindness and depravity: if of the irascible, he declaims with fury and virulence against all who differ from him; blowing up the coals of fanaticism, and branding with the charge of corruption and insincerity, every man who does not think, or profess to think, as he does.

If such a man happens to possess the advantages of style, his book may do a considerable deal of mischief before the nothingness of it is understood.

These principles, if such they can be called, it is more frequent to see applied to morals than to politics: but their influence extends itself to both. In politics, as well as morals, a man will be at least equally glad of a pretense for deciding any question in the manner that best pleases him, without the trouble of inquiry. If a man is an infallible judge of what is right and wrong in the actions of private individuals, why not in the measures to be observed by public men in the direction of those actions? accordingly (not to mention other chimeras) I have more than once known the pretended law of nature set up in legislative debates, in opposition to arguments derived from the principle of utility.

Whether utility is actually the sole ground of all the approbation we ever bestow, is a different consideration. "But is it never, then, from any other considerations than those of utility, that we derive our notions of right and wrong?" I do not know: I do not care. Whether a moral sentiment can be originally conceived from any other source than a view of utility, is one question: whether upon examination and reflection it can, in point of fact, be actually persisted in and justified on any other ground, by a person reflecting within himself, is another: whether in point of right it can properly be justified on any other ground, by a person addressing himself to the community, is a third. The two first are questions of speculation: it matters not, comparatively speaking, how they are decided. The last is a question of practice: the decision of it is of as much importance as that of any can be.

"I feel in myself," (say you) "a disposition to approve of such or such an action in a moral view: but this is not owing to any notions I have of its being a useful one to the community. I do not pretend to know whether it be an useful one or not: it may be, for aught I know, a mischievous one." "But is it then," (say I) "a mischievous one? examine; and if you can make yourself sensible that it is so, then, if duty means anything, that is, moral duty, it is your *duty* at least to abstain from it: and more than that, if it is what lies in your power, and can be done without too great a sacrifice, to endeavor to prevent it. It is not your cherishing the notion of it in your bosom, and giving it the name of virtue, that will excuse you."

"I feel in myself," (say you again) "a disposition to detest such or such an action in a moral view; but this is not owing to any notions I have of its being a mischievous one to the community. I do not pretend to know whether it be a mischievous one or not: it may be not a mischievous one: it may be, for aught I know, an useful one." "May it indeed," (say I) "an useful one? but let me tell you then, that unless duty, and right and wrong, be just what you please to make them, if it really be not a mischievous one, and any body has a mind to do it, it is no duty of yours, but, on the contrary, it would be very wrong in you, to take upon you to prevent him: detest it within yourself as much as you please; that may be a very good reason (unless it be also a useful one) for your not doing it yourself: but if you go about, by word or deed, to do any thing to hinder him, or make him suffer for it, it is you, and not he, that have done wrong: it is not your setting yourself to blame his conduct, or branding it with the name of vice, that will make him culpable, or you blameless. Therefore, if you can make yourself content that he shall be of one mind, and you of another, about that matter, and so continue, it is well: but if nothing will serve you, but that you and he must needs be of the same mind, I'll tell you what you have to do: it is for you to get the better of your antipathy, not for him to truckle to it."

[8] King James the First of England had conceived a violent antipathy against Arians: two of whom he burnt [Hume's Hist. vol. 6.]. This gratification he procured himself without much difficulty: the notions of the times were favourable to it. He wrote a furious book against Vorstius, for being what was called an Arminian: for Vorstius was at a distance. He also wrote a furious book, called *A Counterblast to Tobacco,* against the use of that drug, which Sir Walter Raleigh had then lately introduced. Had the notions of the times co-operated with him, he would have burnt the Anabaptist and the smoker of tobacco in the same fire. However he had the satisfaction of putting Raleigh to death afterwards, though for another crime.

Disputes concerning the comparative excellence of French and Italian music have occasioned very serious bickerings at Paris. One of the parties would not have been sorry (says Mr. D'Alembert [Melanges Essai sur la Liberté de la Musique.]) to have brought government into the quarrel. Pretences were sought after and urged. Long before that, a dispute of like nature, and of at least equal warmth, had been kindled at London upon the comparative merits of two composers at London; where riots between the approvers and disapprovers of a new play are, at this day, not unfrequent. The ground of quarrel between the Big-endians and the Little-endians in the fable, was not more frivolous than many an one which has laid empires desolate. In Russia, it is said, there was a time when some thousands of persons lost their lives in a quarrel, in which the government had taken part, about the number of fingers to be used in making the sign of the cross. This was in days of yore: the ministers of Catherine II, are better *instructed* [Instruct. art. 474, 475, 476.] than to take any other part in such disputes, than that of preventing the parties concerned from doing one another a mischief.

⁹ See ch. xvi. [Division], par. 42, 44.

¹⁰ *The principle of theology how reducible to one or another of the other three principles.* The principle of theology refers every thing to God's pleasure. But what is God's pleasure? God does not, he confessedly does not now, either speak or write to us. How then are we to know what is his pleasure? By observing what is our own pleasure, and pronouncing it to be his. Accordingly, what is called the pleasure of God, is and must necessarily be (revelation apart) neither more nor less than the good pleasure of the person, whoever he be, who is pronouncing what he believes, or pretends, to be God's pleasure. How know you it to be God's pleasure that such or such an act should be abstained from? whence come you even to suppose as much? "Because the engaging in it would, I imagine, be prejudicial upon the whole to the happiness of mankind;" says the partizan of the principle of utility. "Because the commission of it is attended with a gross and sensual, or at least with a trifling and transient satisfaction;" says the partizan of the principle of asceticism: "Because I detest the thoughts of it; and I cannot, neither ought I to be called upon to tell why;" says he who proceeds upon the principle of antipathy. In the words of one or other of these must that person necessarily answer (revelation apart) who professes to take for his standard the will of God.

CHAPTER III

¹¹ *Sanctio,* in Latin, was used to signify the *act of binding,* and, by a common grammatical transition, *any thing which serves to bind a man:* to wit, to the observance of such or such a mode of conduct. According to a Latin grammarian [Servius. See Ainsworth's Dict. ad verbum *Sanctio.*], the import of the word is derived by rather a far-fetched process (such as those commonly are, and in a great measure indeed must be, by which intellectual ideas are derived from sensible ones) from the word *sanguis,* blood: because, among the Romans, with a view to inculcate into the people a persuasion that such or such a mode of conduct would be rendered obligatory upon a man by the force of what I call the religious sanction (that is, that he would be made to suffer by the extraordinary interposition of some superior being, if he failed to observe the mode of conduct in question) certain ceremonies were contrived by the priests: in the course of which ceremonies the blood of victims was made use of.

A Sanction then is a source of obligatory powers or *motives:* that is, of *pains* and *pleasures;* which, according as they are connected with such or such modes of conduct, operate, and are indeed the only things which can operate, as *motives.* See Chap. x [Motives].

¹² Better termed *popular,* as more directly indicative of its constituent cause; as likewise of its relation to the more common phrase *public opinion,* in French *opinion publique,* the name there given to that tutelary power, of which of late so much is said, and by which so much is done. The latter appellation is however unhappy and inexpressive; since if *opinion* is material, it is only in virtue of the influence it exercises over action, through the medium of the affections and the will.

[13] A suffering conceived to befall a man by the immediate act of God, as above, is often, for shortness' sake, called a *judgment:* instead of saying, a suffering inflicted on him in consequence of a special judgment formed, and resolution thereupon taken, by the Deity.

[14] See ch. xiii. [Cases unmeet] par. 2. note.

CHAPTER IV

[15] These circumstances have since been denominated *elements* or *dimensions* of *value* in a pleasure or a pain.

Not long after the publication of the first edition, the following memoriter verses were framed, in the view of lodging more effectually, in the memory, these points, on which the whole fabric of morals and legislation may be seen to rest:

> *Intense, long, certain, speedy, fruitful, pure—*
> Such marks in *pleasures* and in *pains* endure.
> Such pleasures seek if *private* be thy end:
> If it be *public,* wide let them *extend.*
> Such *pains* avoid, whichever be thy view:
> If pains *must* come, let them *extend* to few.

BENTHAM'S FELICIFIC CALCULUS

Wesley C. Mitchell

Jeremy Bentham has one service yet to perform for students of the social sciences. He can help them to work free from that misconception of human nature which he helped their predecessors to formulate. This role of emancipator he plays in the following paper.

In the social sciences we are suffering from a curious mental derangement. We have become aware that the orthodox doctrines of economics, politics and law rest upon a tacit assumption that man's behavior is dominated by rational calculation. We have learned further that this is an assumption contrary to fact. But we find it hard to avoid the old mistake, not to speak of using the new knowledge. In our prefaces and introductory chapters some of us repudiate hedonism and profess volitional psychology or behaviorism. Others among us assert that economics at least can have no legitimate relations with psychology in any of its warring forms. In the body of our books, however, we relapse into reasonings about behavior that apply only to creatures essentially reasonable.

Bentham cannot help toward making the social sciences valid accounts of social behavior. But better than any one else he can help us to see the absurdity of the intellectualist fallacy we abjure and practice. For Bentham has no rival as an exponent of the delusions that haunt the backs of our heads, and gain control over our speculations when we are not thinking of psychology. The way to free ourselves from these delusions is to drag them into the light of full consciousness and make them face our other thoughts about behavior. We can perform this psychoanalytic operation upon our own minds best by assembling in orderly sequence the pertinent passages scattered through Bentham's writings.

I

Bentham dealt not only with many branches of jurisprudence—criminal law, evidence, procedure, codification, international law, constitu-

---

Source: Reprinted with permission from the *Political Science Quarterly,* XXXIII: 161–183 (June 1918).

tional law—but also with economics, psychology, penology, pedagogy, ethics, religion, logic and metaphysics. Yet all his books read as one. They work out a single idea in diverse materials. They apply the sacred principle of utility whether the subject matter be colonies or Christianity, usury or the classification of the sciences, the crimes of judges or the reformation of criminals.

But utilitarianism as such is not the differentiating characteristic of Bentham. A line of Englsih philosophers running back at least to Richard Cumberland in 1672 had expounded that doctrine before him. About these predecessors Bentham knew little; but "Utilitarianism had been so distinctly in the air for more than a generation before he published his *Principles of Morals and Legislation* that he could not possibly have failed very substantially to profit by the fact."[1] Indeed, Bentham was conscious of doctrinal indebtedness to Hume, Hartley and Priestley in England, Helvetius in France, and Beccaria in Italy.[2] Among his own contemporaries Utilitarianism prevailed widely outside the circle of professed philosophers. The regnant theologian of the day, William Paley, was as grim an exponent of the sacred principle as Bentham himself.[3] In the English controversy about the French Revolution all parties agreed tacitly or explicitly in accepting utility as the final test of political institutions—Burke as well as Godwin, the respectable Whig Mackintosh as well as the agitator Tom Paine. And when Malthus, a clergyman, answered Godwin on the population issue he showed himself as good a utilitarian as his atheistical opponent.[4] No one has studied currents of

[1] Ernest Albee, *A History of English Utilitarianism*, 1902, p. 167.

[2] For Bentham's numerous references to these writers see the index of *The Works of Jeremy Bentham*, published under the superintendence of his executor, John Bowring, 11 volumes, Edinburgh, 1843.

[3] Compare Paley's famous definition of virtue: "the doing good to mankind, in obedience to the will of God, and for the sake of everlasting happiness." *Principles of Moral and Political Philosophy*, bk. I, ch. vii (21st edition, 1818, vol. i, p. 42). Further see Paley's remarks upon population in bk. vi, ch. xi. "The final view of all rational politics is, to produce the greatest quantity of happiness in a given tract of country . . . the quantity of happiness in a given district, although it is possible it may be increased, the number of inhabitants remaining the same, is chiefly and most naturally affected by alteration of the numbers: . . . consequently, the decay of population is the greatest evil that a state can suffer; and the improvement of it the object which ought, in all countries, to be aimed at in preference to every other political purpose whatsoever." Vol. ii, pp. 345–7.

[4] See particularly bk. iv, ch. iii, of the second and later editions of the *Essay on the Principle of Population*. For example, "I do not see how it is possible for any person, who acknowledges the principle of utility as the great foundation of morals, to escape the conclusion that moral restraint, till we are in a condition to support a family, is the strict line of duty. . . ." 2d. ed., 1803, p. 504.

English thinking in these times so thoroughly as Elie Halévy, and he remarks: "Towards the end of the eighteenth century, it is not only the thinkers, it is all the English who are speaking the language of utility."[5] "It was plain," he adds in another volume, "that the doctrine of utility was becoming the universal philosophy in England, and that the reformers must speak the language of utility if they wished their opinions to be understood—let alone accepted—by the public they were addressing."[6] This view certainly accords with Bentham's own impression as recorded in his commonplace book: "The opinion of the world (I am speaking of the people in this country) is commonly in favour of the principle of utility. . . ."[7]

What did distinguish Bentham from other utilitarians, what made him the leader of a school, what keeps his work instructive to this day, was his effort to introduce exact method into all discussions of utility. He sought to make legislation, economics, ethics into genuine sciences. His contemporaries were content to talk about utility at large; Bentham insisted upon measuring particular utilities—or rather, the net pleasures on which utilities rest.

The ideal of science which men then held was represented by celestial mechanics; its hero was Newton, whose system had been popularized by Voltaire; its living exemplars were the great mathematicians of the French Academy. Bentham hoped to become "the Newton of the Moral World." Among the mass of his papers left to University College Halévy has found this passage:

> The present work as well as any other work of mine that has been or will be published on the subject of legislation or any other branch of moral science is an attempt to extend the experimental method of reasoning from the physical branch to the moral. What Bacon was to the physical world, Helvetius was to the moral. The moral world has therefore had its Bacon, but its Newton is yet to come.[8]

II

Bentham's way of becoming the Newton of the moral world was to develop the "felicific calculus." There are several expositions of this calculus in his *Works;* but the first and most famous version remains the best to quote.[9]

[5] *La Formation du Radicalisme Philosophique,* 1901, vol. i, p. 231.

[6] *Ibid.,* vol. ii, pp. ii, iii.

[7] *Works,* vol. x, p. 141. Written sometime between Bentham's thirty-third and thirty-seventh years.

[8] Halévy, *Radicalisme Philosophique,* vol. i, pp. 289, 290.

[9] "Introduction to the Principles of Morals and Legislation," *Works,* vol. i, pp. 1, 16. The exposition in "Logical Arrangements, or Instruments of Discovery and

Nature has placed mankind under the governance of two sovereign masters, *pain* and *pleasure*. It is for them alone to point out what we ought to do, as well as to determine what we shall do. On the one hand the standard of right and wrong, on the other the chain of causes and effects, are fastened to their throne.

Hence to know what men will do, to tell what they should do, or to value what they have done, one must be able to measure varying "lots" of pleasure or pain. How are such measurements to be made?

To a person considered *by himself*, the value of a pleasure or pain considered *by itself*, will be greater or less, according to the four following circumstances: 1. Its *intensity*. 2. Its *duration*. 3. Its certainty .... 4. Its *propinquity* .... But when the value of any pleasure or pain is considered for the purpose of estimating the tendency of any *act* by which it is produced, there are two other circumstances to be taken into the account; these are, 5. Its *fecundity* .... 6. Its *purity* .... [When a community is considered, it is also necessary to take account of] 7. Its *extent;* that is, the number of persons to whom it *extends* ....

The unit of intensity is the faintest sensation that can be distinguished to be pleasure or pain; the unit of duration is a moment of time. Degrees of intensity and duration are to be counted in whole numbers, as multiples of these units. Certainty and propinquity are reckoned as fractions whose limit is immediate actual sensation; from this limit the fractions fall away. In applying the calculus, one begins with the first distinguishable pleasure or pain which appears to be produced by an act, multiplies the number of its intensity units by the number of duration units, and then multiplies this product by the two fractions expressing certainty and proximity. To bring in fecundity one computes by the preceding method the value of each pleasure or each pain which appears to be produced after the first one; the resulting values are to be added to the value previously obtained. To bring in purity one computes the values of all pains that attend a given series of pleasures, or of pleasures that attend a given series of pains; these values are to be subtracted from the preceding sums. That is, pleasure is a positive, pain a negative quantity. Since the unit of extent is an individual, one completes the computation

---

Invention employed by Jeremy Bentham," *Works,* vol. iii, pp. 286, 287 is a convenient summary. Another brief statement is given in "A Table of the Springs of Action," *Works,* vol. i, p. 206. The value of the calculus is best stated in the curious "Codification Proposal," *Works,* vol. iv, pp. 540-2. A more discursive version appears in ch. iv, of *Deontology,* vol. i (not included in the *Works*). As will appear below, several of the most important points are best explained in passages which remained unpublished until Halévy's day—see the notes and appendices of his first and third volume.

by multiplying the net resultant pain or pleasure ascertained as above by the number of individuals affected. Usually however this last step is more complicated: not all the people affected are affected in the same way. In that case one does not multiply by the number of individuals, but makes a separate computation for each individual and then strikes the algebraic sum of the resultants.[10]

III

If these technical directions for measuring "lots" of pleasure and pain be taken seriously, the felicific calculus is a complicated affair at best. In addition it is beset by subtler and graver difficulties, some that Bentham saw clearly, others that he barely glimpsed. Unfortunately the disciples who pieced his manuscripts together into books did not think fit to publish his sharpest bits of insight into the haze, so that later writers had to rediscover much that their master had descried. The type of social science on which Bentham worked might have been completed and superseded much sooner than it was had his difficulties been made known in his own lifetime.

(1) That all comparisons of the feelings of different men are questionable Bentham was perfectly aware. In his *Principles of Morals and Legislation,* indeed, he enlarged upon this topic by discussing thirty-two "circumstances influencing sensibility" to pleasure and pain.[11] Since these thirty-two circumstances exist in an indefinite number of combinations, it would seem that the felicific calculus can scarcely be applied except individual by individual—a serious limitation. So long as he was thinking only of the problem of punishments Bentham accepted this conclusion. The legislator and the judge ought each to have before him a list of the several circumstances by which sensibility may be influenced: the legislator ought to consider those circumstances which apply uniformly to whole classes, for example, insanity, sex, rank, climate and religious profession; the judge ought to consider the circumstances which apply in varying degrees to each individual, for example, health, strength, habitual occupation, pecuniary circumstances, etc.[12]

[10] "Principles of Morals and Legislation," *Works,* vol. i, p. 16, and extracts from Bentham's mss. published by Halévy in *Radicalisme Philosophique,* vol. i, p. 398 *et seq.*

[11] Ch. vi. The list includes health, strength, firmness of mind, habitual occupations, pecuniary circumstances, sex, age, rank, education, climate, lineage, government, religious profession, etc.

[12] *Works,* vol. i, pp. 31, 32. Compare the discussion of this theme in Bentham's essay "Of the Influence of Time and Place in Matters of Legislation," *Works,* vol. i, pp. 172, 173, 180, 181.

But as Bentham's problems widened he concluded that his calculus must apply to men at large, if it was to yield scientific generalizations, although he still thought that this application rested upon an assumption contrary to fact. One manuscript found by Halévy runs:

> 'Tis in vain to talk of adding quantities which after the addition will continue distinct as they were before, one man's happiness will never be another man's happiness: a gain to one man is no gain to another: you might as well pretend to add 20 apples to 20 pears . . . . This addibility of the happiness of different subjects, however when considered rigorously it may appear fictitious, is a postulatum without the allowance of which all political reasoning is at a stand: nor is it more fictitious than that of the equality of chances to reality, on which that whole branch of the Mathematics which is called the doctrine of chances is established.[13]

(2) Of course, this postulate of the "addibility" of the happiness of different men tacitly assumes that numerical values can be set on the feelings of each individual. But is that really true? Indeed, can any individual put a definite figure upon his own pleasures and pains, let alone compare them with the pleasures and pains of other men? The more Bentham dwelt upon this aspect of his calculus, the more difficulties he developed and the more assumptions he found necessary to his type of social science.

One fundamental doubt he sometimes overlooked, and sometimes admitted. Intensity is the first "element" in which feelings differ. Can any man count the intensity units in any one of his pleasures or pains, as he counts the duration units? Bentham usually assumes that he can, without telling how.

> . . . the degree of intensity possessed by that pleasure which is the faintest of any that can be distinguished to be pleasure, may be represented by unity. Such a degree of intensity is in every day's experience: according as any pleasures are perceived to be more and more intense, they may be represented by higher and higher numbers. . . .[14]

In his *Codification Proposal*, however, Bentham frankly grants that intensity is not "susceptible of measurement."[15]

(3) With a closely-related problem, Bentham wrestled frequently: can a man make quantitative comparisons among his qualitatively unlike pleasures or pains?

[13] Halévy, *Radicalisme Philosophique*, vol. iii, p. 481.
[14] *Ibid.*, vol. i, p. 398.
[15] *Works*, vol. iv, p. 542.

The difficulty here was aggravated by one of Bentham's favorite ideas. He held that most of our feelings are complexes made up of simple elements. One of the tasks which he essayed was to enumerate exhaustively the "simple" pleasures and the "simple" pains, which like the elements in chemistry cannot be decomposed themselves, but which can combine with each other in the most diverse ways. In his *Principles of Morals and Legislation* he listed fourteen simple pleasures (counting the alleged pleasures of the senses as one) and twelve simple pains.[16] In his *Table of the Springs of Action* he, or his editor, James Mill, modified the lists somewhat, but kept the general idea that in the last analysis our pleasures and pains are compounded of qualitatively unlike elements.[17] Now, if that be literally true, how can one apply the felicific calculus even in the case of a single individual? Some common denominator seems needed for the two dozen or more elements; but if there exists a common denominator, are not the elements themselves homogeneous?

When he wrote his *Principles of Morals and Legislation* Bentham did not discuss, perhaps did not think of these questions. Despite all the trouble he took to describe "the several sorts of pains and pleasures," he referred to pain and pleasure as "names of homogeneous real entities."[18] Throughout the book he assumed tacitly not only that different pains and different pleasures, but also that pains and pleasures are commensurable. Yet the one passage most to the present purpose shows that his method of comparing quantities was strictly limited. He says:

> The only certain and universal means of making two lots of punishment perfectly commensurable, is by making the lesser an ingredient in the composition of the greater. This may be done in either of two ways. 1. By adding to the lesser punishment another quantity of punishment of the same kind. 2. By adding to it another quantity of a different kind.[19]

Indeed in this whole treatise Bentham relies upon classification, and not upon calculation.[20] He splits everything he discusses—pleasures, pains, motives, dispositions, offenses, "cases unmeet for punishment" etc.—into kinds, limits his quantitative comparisons to relations of greater and less, and makes even these comparisons chiefly among phenomena belonging to the same kind. He does indeed bid the authorities do things which imply bolder comparisons, as when he rules that "the value of the

---

[16] *Works,* vol. i, pp. 17–21.
[17] *Ibid.,* pp. 195–219.
[18] *Ibid.,* p. 22, footnote.
[19] *Works,* vol. i, p. 92.
[20] Compare Halévy, vol. i, pp. 47, 48.

punishment must not be less in any case than . . . the profit of the offence;"[21] but he does not make such comparisons himself.

And yet Bentham did find a way of reducing qualitatively unlike pleasures and pains to a common denominator, and so of putting figures on felicity. There are traces of this method in his published works,[22] but much the best exposition remained in manuscript until Halévy's day. The following passages have peculiar interest as anticipations of Edgeworth's use of "indifference" and more definitely of Marshall's "money measures."

> If of two pleasures a man, knowing what they are, would as lief enjoy the one as the other, they must be reputed equal . . . . If of two pains a man had as lief escape the one as the other, such two pains must be reputed equal. If of two sensations, a pain and a pleasure, a man had as lief enjoy the pleasure and suffer the pain, as not enjoy the first and not suffer the latter, such pleasure and pain must be reputed *equal*, or, as we may say in this case, *equivalent*.
>
> If then between two pleasures the one produced by the possession of money, the other not, a man had as lief enjoy the one as the other, such pleasures are to be reputed equal. But the pleasure produced by the possession of money, is *as* the quantity of money that produces it: money is therefore the measure of this pleasure. But the other pleasure is equal to this; the other pleasure therefore is as the money that produces this; therefore money is also the measure of that other pleasure. It is the same between pain and pain; as also between pain and pleasure.
>
> . . . If then, speaking of the respective quantities of various pains and pleasures and agreeing in the same propositions concerning them, we would annex the same ideas to those propositions, that is, if we would understand one another, we must make use of some common measure. The only common measure the nature of things affords is money. . . .
>
> I beg a truce here of our man of sentiment and feeling while from necessity, and it is only from necessity, I speak and prompt mankind to speak a mercenary language. . . . Money is the instrument for measuring the quantity of pain or pleasure. Those who are not satisfied with the accuracy of this instrument must find out some other that shall be more accurate, or bid adieu to Politics and Morals.[23]

(4) That Bentham did not follow up this promising lead was due to a further difficulty. Every time he began thinking about money measures of feeling he was checked by the diminishing utility of wealth. The

---

[21] *Works*, vol. i, p. 87.

[22] For example, "Codification Proposal," *Works*, vol. iv, pp. 540–2; *Deontology*, vol. i, pp. 76, 131, 192.

[23] Halévy, vol. i, pp. 410, 412, 414.

"quantity of happiness produced by a particle of wealth (each particle being of the same magnitude) will be less and less at every particle; the second will produce less than the first, the third than the second, and so on."[24] ". . . for by high doses of the exciting matter applied to the organ, its sensibility is in a manner worn out."[25] Consider the monarch with a million a year and the laborer with twenty pounds:

> The quantity of pleasure in the breast of the monarch will naturally be greater than the quantity in the breast of the labourer: . . . But . . . by how many times greater? Fifty thousand times? This is assuredly more than any man would take upon himself to say. A thousand times, then? a hundred? ten times? five times? twice? which of all these shall be the number? . . . For the monarch's, taking all purposes together, *five times* the labourer's seems a very large, not to say an excessive allowance: even *twice*, a liberal one.[26]

Quite apart from differences in the sensibility of different men to pleasure, then, equal sums of money can by no means be supposed to represent equal quantities of feeling.

Once, at least, Bentham thought he had found a solution of this difficulty. In the manuscript last quoted he argues:

> . . . money being the current instrument of pleasure, it is plain by uncontrovertible experience that the quantity of actual pleasure follows in every instance in some proportion or other the quantity of money. As to the law of that proportion nothing can be more indeterminate. . . . For all this it is true enough for practice with respect to such proportions as ordinarily occur (var.: small quantities), that *ceteris paribus* the proportion between pleasure and pleasure is the same as that between sum and sum. So much is strictly true that the ratios between the two pairs of quantities are nearer to that of equality than to any other ratio that can be assigned. Men will therefore stand a better chance of being right by supposing them equal than by supposing them to be any otherwise than equal. . . .

Speaking then in general, we may therefore truly say, that in small quantities the pleasures produced by two sums are *as* the sums producing them.[27]

This passage lies on the frontier of Bentham's realm of thought. It shows that the idea of dealing with small increments of feeling occurred to him, as a method of avoiding the embarrassment caused by diminishing utility and still using money as a common denominator. But all this

---

[24] "Pannomial Fragments," *Works,* vol. iii, p. 229.
[25] "Constitutional Code," *Works,* vol. ix, p. 15.
[26] "Codification Proposal," *Works,* vol. iv, p. 541.
[27] Halévy, vol. i, pp. 406, 408, 410.

was rather dim; the idea did not develop vigorously in his mind. He missed, indeed, two notions that his disciples were to exploit later on: Bernoulli's suggestion that, after bare subsistence is provided, a man's pleasure increases by equal amounts with each equal successive percentage added to his income; and the plan of concentrating attention upon the increments of pleasure or pain at the margin.

The net resultant of all these reflections upon the felicific calculus collected from Bentham's books and papers might be put thus: (1) The intensity of feelings cannot be measured at all; (2) even in the case of a single subject, qualitatively unlike feelings cannot be compared except indirectly through their pecuniary equivalents; (3) the assumption that equal sums of money represent equal sums of pleasure is unsafe except in the case of small quantities; (4) all attempts to compare the feelings of different men involve an assumption contrary to fact. That is a critic's version of admissions wrung from Bentham's text; a disciple's version of his master's triumphs might run: (1) The felicific calculus attains a tolerable degree of precision since all the dimensions of feeling save one can be measured;[28] (2) the calculus can handle the most dissimilar feelings by expressing them in terms of their monetary equivalents; (3) in the cases which are important by virtue of their frequency, the pleasures produced by two sums of money are as the sums producing them; (4) taken by and large for scientific purposes men are comparable in feeling as in other respects. . . . Heat these two versions in the fire of controversy and one has the substantial content of much polemic since Bentham's day.

IV

The quintessence of Bentham's social science is the double role played by the felicific calculus. On the one hand this calculus shows how the legislator, judge and moralist ought to proceed in valuing conduct; on the other hand it shows how all men do proceed in guiding conduct. That is, Bentham blends utilitarian ethics with a definite theory of functional psychology. The ethical system has been more discussed, but the psychological notions are more important to students of the social sciences.

1. Human nature is hedonistic. It is for pain and pleasure alone "to determine what we shall do . . . . They govern us in all we do, in all we think. . . ." These words from the first paragraph of *Principles of Morals and Legislation* put simply the leading idea. "Nothing"—Bentham remarks in *A Table of the Springs of Action*, "nothing but the expectation of the eventual enjoyment of pleasure in some shape, or of exemp-

---

[28] This is substantially Bentham's own language. "Codification Proposal," *Works*, vol. iv, p. 542.

tion from pain in some shape, can operate in the character of a *motive. . . .*"[29]

The psychological processes by which pleasure incites to action are more fully described in later passages. "Every operation of the mind, and thence every operation of the body," says the *Essay on Logic*, "is the result of an exercise of the will, or volitional faculty."[30] The relations between will and intellect are explained by the *Table of the Springs of Action:*

> To the *will* it is that the idea of a pleasure or an exemption [from pain] applies itself in the *first* instance; in *that* stage its effect, if not conclusive, is *velleity:* by velleity, reference is made to the *understanding, viz.* 1. For striking a *balance* between the *value* of this *good,* and that of the *pain* or *loss,* if any, which present themselves as eventually about to stand associated with it: 2. Then, if the balance appear to be in its favour for the choice of *means:* thereupon, if *action* be the result, *velleity* is perfected into *volition,* of which the correspondent *action* is the immediate consequence. For the process that has place, this description may serve alike in *all* cases: *time* occupied by it may be of any length; from a minute fraction of a *second,* as in ordinary cases, to any number of years.[31]

2. Human nature is rational. There is nothing in the felicific calculus "but what the practice of mankind, wheresoever they have a clear view of their own interest, is perfectly conformable to." This passage from Chapter IV of the *Principles*[32] is supported in Chapter XVI by an answer to the objection that "passion does not calculate." But, says Bentham:

> When matters of such importance as pain and pleasure are at stake, and these in the highest degree (the only matters, in short, that can be of importance) who is there that does not calculate? Men calculate, some with less exactness, indeed, some with more: but all men calculate. I would not say, that even a madman does not calculate. Passion calculates, more or less, in every man: in different men, according to the warmth or coolness of their dispositions: according to the firmness or irritability of their minds: according to the nature of the motives by which they are acted upon. Happily, of all passions, that is the most given to calculation, from the excesses of which, by reason of its strength, constancy, and universality, society has most to apprehend: I mean that which corresponds to the motive of pecuniary interest. . . .[33]

---

[29] *Works,* vol. i, p. 215.

[30] *Ibid.,* vol. viii, p. 279.

[31] *Ibid.,* vol. i, p. 209.

[32] *Ibid.,* vol. i, p. 17.

[33] *Works,* vol. i, pp. 90, 91. Compare the similar passage in *Principles of Penal Law,* vol. i, p. 402.

3. Human nature is essentially passive. Men do not have propensities to act, but are pushed and pulled about by the pleasure-pain forces of their environments.

> . . . on every occasion, *conduct*—the *course* taken by a man's conduct—is at the absolute command of—is the never failing result of —the *motives*—and thence, in so far as the corresponding interests are perceived and understood, of the corresponding *interests*—to the action of which, his mind—his will—has, on that same occasion, stood exposed.[34]

Of course, this view of human nature as a passive element in the situation greatly simplifies the task of social science. Whenever one can make out what it is to men's interest to do, one can deduce what they will do. The only uncertainty arises from the actor's imperfect comprehension of his interest, of which more in a moment.

Human nature is also passive in the sense that men are averse to work. In his *Table of the Springs of Action*, Bentham includes both pleasures and pains of the palate, of sex, of wealth, of amity, of reputation, and so on through eleven heads until he comes to labor—under that head he recognizes nothing but pains. If any pleasure in activity is to be found in this table we must read it into the pleasures of power or of curiosity.[35] Enlarging upon this point, Bentham says *"Aversion*—not *desire*—is the emotion—the only emotion—which *labour,* taken by itself, is qualified to produce: of any such emotion as *love* or *desire, ease,* which is the *negative* or *absence* of labour—*ease,* not *labour*—is the object."[36]

4. Since men ought to follow the course which will secure them the greatest balance of pleasure, and since they do follow that course so far as they understand their own interests, the only defects in human nature must be defects of understanding.

> *Indigenous* intellectual weakness—*adoptive* intellectual weakness— or, in one word, *prejudice*—*sinister interest* (understand self-conscious sinister interest)—lastly, *interest-begotten* (though not self-

---

[34] "A Table of the Springs of Action," *Works,* vol. i, p. 218.

[35] This omission of pleasure in labor is clearly no oversight; indeed it must represent a deliberate change of opinion; for in his *Introduction to the Principles of Morals and Legislation* Bentham had included "The pleasures of skill, as exercised upon particular objects. . . ." *Works,* vol. i, p. 18.

[36] *Works,* vol. i, p. 214. In "Chrestomathia" Bentham discusses the "pain of ennui." "Ennui is the state of uneasiness, felt by him whose mind unoccupied, but without reproach, is on the look out for pleasure . . . and beholds at the time no source which promises to afford it . . . the pain of ennui soon succeeds to the pleasure of repose." *Works,* vol. viii, p. 8.

conscious) *prejudice*—by one or other of these denominations, may be designated (it is believed) the cause of whatever is on any occasion amiss, in the opinions or conduct of mankind.[37]

There is no such thing as a bad motive—or a disinterested action—but men may blunder.

Similarly, whatever lack of uniformity in human nature we find must be due to differences in men's intellectual machinery for calculating pleasures and pains. Such is the sole reason for the gulf that separates civilized men from savages. In "the variety and extent of the ideas with which they have been impressed . . . may be seen the only cause of whatsoever difference there is between the mind of a well educated youth under the existing systems of education, and the mind of the Esquimaux, or the New Zealand savage at the same age."[38] Men do vary in sensibility, as we have seen; but the thirty-two "circumstances influencing sensibility"[39] act by associating the motor ideas of pleasure and pain with the ideas of different objects or actions. So Bentham asserts, "Legislators who, having freed themselves from the shackles of authority, have learnt to soar above the mists of prejudice, know as well how to make laws for one country as for another." They must master the peculiar local circumstances affecting sensibility—that is all.[40] In the *Codification Proposal addressed by Jeremy Bentham to all Nations professing Liberal Opinions* he even argues that a foreigner is in a better position to draft a general code of laws than a native.[41]

The understanding, it will be noted, is conceived as a matter of associations among ideas. As hedonism explains the functioning of mind, so the "association principle" explains the structure of mind. Bentham derived this principle from Hartley, and left its working-out to James Mill.[42]

5. Since whatever is amiss in the opinions or conduct of mankind is due to "intellectual weakness, indigenous or adoptive," education must be the one great agency of reform. And since the understanding is made up of associations among ideas, the forming and strengthening of proper associations must be the great aim of education.

In the possibility of establishing almost any desired associations in a

---

[37] "Springs of Action," *Works,* vol. i, p. 217.

[38] "Chrestomathia," *Works,* vol. viii, p. 11.

[39] "Introduction to the Principles of Morals and Legislation," *Works,* vol. i, p. 22.

[40] "Influence of Time and Place in Matters of Legislation," *Works,* vol. i, pp. 180, 181.

[41] *Works,* vol. iv, pp. 561–3.

[42] *Works,* vol. x, p. 561; Mill's *Analysis of the Phenomena of the Human Mind* appeared in 1829, three years before Bentham's death.

child's mind, and even in the possibility of dissolving old and forming new associations in an adult mind Bentham had considerable faith. "As respects pleasures, the mind of man possesses a happy flexibility. One source of amusement being cut off, it endeavours to open up another, and always succeeds: a new habit is easily formed. . . ."[43] Hence Bentham's interest in the educational experiments of the day, hence the time he spent in planning a "chrestomathic school . . . for the use of the middling and higher ranks in life," hence his financial support of Robert Owen's scheme of industrial education at New Lanark, hence his claims for the Panopticon Penitentiary as "a mill for grinding rogues honest, and idle men industrious."[44]

In a larger sense, Bentham conceived all his work on law as part of an educational program. "The influence of government," says one of Dumont's treatises, "touches almost everything, or rather includes everything, except temperament, race, and climate. . . . The manner of directing education, of arranging employments, rewards, and punishments determines the physical and moral qualities of a people."[45] A sharper point and a graver meaning were given to this task by Bentham's slow discovery that men do not all spontaneously desire "the greatest happiness of the greatest number."[46] Thereafter the "self-preference principle"

---

[43] "Principles of Penal Law," *Works,* vol. i, p. 436.

[44] See "Chrestomathia," *Works,* vol. viii, and the following passages in Bowring's life of Bentham—*Works,* vol. x, pp. 476, 477, 226.

Bentham once suggested—not more than half in jest—that "metaphysics" might be made an experimental science by applying his "inspection-house principle" to the training of children. That plan would enable the instructor to determine what sensible objects, conversation, books should have part in forming the child's mind. Then, "The geneology of each observable idea might be traced through all its degrees with the utmost nicety: the parent stocks being all known and numbered." "Panopticon," *Works,* vol. iv, p. 65.

Mr. C. E. Ayers has just propounded a modern version of this suggestion. Epistemology, he argues, is becoming a science, "whence the mental content of every man's mind, what are the limitations that are imposed upon that content by its sources? The solution of this problem lies along the path of the investigation of the social sources of all mental content and of the limitations which are imposed upon the human mind by the fact that it is always the product of some particular environment and so must always receive an environmental bias. This investigation is the business of social psychology." *Journal of Philosophy, Psychology and Scientific Methods,* January 17, 1918; vol. xv, p. 43.

[45] Quoted by Halévy, vol. i, pp. 139.

[46] In his earlier period Bentham had tacitly assumed that the authorities would spontaneously adopt any plan that promised to increase social happiness. It took him sixty years to learn that the authorities were seeking their own happiness, not that of the nation. See his own account of how his eyes were opened, *Works,* vol. x, pp. 79, 80 and vol. i, pp. 240–259.

was a regular component of human nature as Bentham saw it, and the great task of statecraft was to contrive cunning devices by which necessarily selfish individuals must serve the pleasure of others to get pleasure for themselves. While Adam Smith and his disciples assumed that a natural identity of interests bound men together in economic affairs, Bentham thought it necessary to establish an artificial identity of interests in law and politics.[47] The ruler himself was to be kept in tutelage his whole life long.

But robust as was Bentham's faith in the potency of schools and government to improve man's character and lot, it was modest in comparison with the expectations cherished by certain among his masters and his contemporaries. Helvetius and Priestley, Condorcet, William Godwin and Robert Owen believed in the "perfectability" of man. Bentham put his views in opposition to Priestley's:

> Perfect happiness belongs to the imaginary regions of philosophy, and must be classed with the universal elixir and the philosopher's stone. In the age of greatest perfection, fire will burn, tempests will rage, man will be subject to infirmity, to accidents, and to death. It may be possible to diminish the influence of, but not to destroy, the sad and mischievous passions. The unequal gifts of nature and of fortune will always create jealousies: there will always be opposition of interests; and, consequently, rivalries and hatred. Pleasures will be purchased by pains; enjoyments by privations. Painful labour, daily subjection, a condition nearly allied to indigence, will always be the lot of numbers. Among the higher as well as the lower classes, there will be desires which cannot be satisfied; inclinations which must be subdued: reciprocal security can only be established by the forcible renunciation by each one, of every thing which might wound the legitimate rights of others.[48]

V

Social science nowadays aims to give an intelligible account of social processes, to promote the understanding of social facts. While we may value such "science" mainly for its practical serviceability, we profess to distinguish sharply between our explanations of what is and our schemes of what ought to be.

In Bentham's world, on the contrary, the felicific calculus yields a social science that is both an account of what is and an account of what ought to be. For on the one hand "the chain of causes and effects" and on the other hand "the standard of right and wrong" are fastened to

---

[47] The contrast between these two views of the relations between society and the individual is one of the chief points developed fully by Halévy in the course of his three volumes. See particularly his first and last chapters.

[48] "Of the Influence of Time and Place on Matters of Legislation," *Works*, vol. i, pp. 193, 194.

the throne of our two sovereign masters—whose books the felicific calculus keeps.[49] Indeed, of the two aspects of the science the more reliable, and therefore the more scientific, is the account of what ought to be. The account of what is holds only in so far as men understand their own interests—that is, associate the ideas of pleasure and pain with the ideas of the proper objects and acts. Really to account for what is, on Bentham's basis, one would have either to observe with elaborate care what men do, or to work out their defects of understanding and deduce the consequences for conduct. Needless to say Bentham spent little time on such procedures.

Bentham plumed himself, indeed, upon assigning priority to normative science—in strict accordance with his philosophy. He writes:

> When I came out with the principle of utility, it was in the *Fragment*, I took it from Hume's *Essays*, Hume was in all his glory, the phrase was consequently familiar to every body. The difference between Hume and me is this: the use he made of it, was—to account for that which *is*, I to show what *ought to be*.[50]

Practical conclusions regarding what ought to be done, then, were the chief product of Bentham's science. That, indeed, was what made Bentham the leader of the Utilitarians or philosophical radicals, who were first and foremost reformers. But it must be admitted that Bentham's attitude upon the crucial problem of reform was not derived strictly from his science. The felicific calculus turned out to be a singularly versatile instrument. Men could make it prove what they liked by choosing certain assumptions concerning the relative importance of various imponderable factors, or concerning the relative sensitiveness to pleasure of different classes of people. Some assumptions have to be made on these heads before the argument can proceed far, and the assumptions which seem natural to the utility theorist are those which yield the conclusions in which he happens to believe on other than scientific grounds. "All history proves" anything that a writer has at heart. The felicific calculus is equally obliging.

[49] "Principles of Morals and Legislation," *Works,* vol. i, p. 1.

[50] From a manuscript found by Halévy, *Radicalisme Philosophique,* vol. i, p. 282. Compare the "History of the Greatest-happiness Principle" given in *Deontology,* vol. i, pp. 293–4.

Like many a modern, Bentham held that the value of science consists in its subserviency to art—though he admits that in so far as science pleases it is an end in itself. ("Chrestomathia," *Works,* vol. viii, p. 27; "Manual of Political Economy," *Works,* vol. iii, p. 33.) That is as true of his science of what ought to be as of his science of what is. The peculiarity of his position from the modern viewpoint is in conceiving his account of what ought to be as itself a science—not in taking a pragmatic view of science.

Now Bentham and his school believed firmly in the institution of private property. They might have proved that property, despite its resulting inequalities of wealth, is necessary to produce the greatest amount of happiness if they had been willing to assume that the propertied classes are more sensitive to pleasure than the poor. For, if some men are better pleasure machines than others, then to maximize happiness more wealth—the most important raw material of pleasure—should be fed to the better machines than to the poorer ones. Such is the course Professor Edgeworth was to take many years later.[51] Bentham did not like that course: to make social science possible he felt obliged to assume that men are substantially alike in their capacity for turning commodities into pleasure. But he had another shift, just as effective, just as little needing proof to those who agreed with him, and just as unconvincing to a doubter.

Every code of laws that is to promote the greatest happiness, he argues, must do so by promoting "the four most comprehensive particular and subordinate *ends, viz. subsistence, abundance, security,* and *equality.*"[52] "Equality is not itself, as security, subsistence, and abundance are, an immediate instrument of felicity."[53] It gets its claim upon us from the diminishing utility of wealth—other things being the same, a given quantity of wealth will produce more pleasure if distributed unequally. But other things are not the same. Unless people had security in the possession of their wealth, they would not produce it, and so there would be nothing to distribute—equally or otherwise. Thus from the viewpoint of maximum happiness security is more important than equality. And granted security in enjoying the fruits of labor a certain inequality results. The conclusion is "that, so far as is consistent with security, the nearer to equality the distribution is, which the law makes of the matter of property among the members of the community, the greater is the happiness of the greatest number."[54]

> Equality . . . finds . . . in security and subsistence, rivals and antagonists, of which the claims are of a superior order, and to which, on pain of universal destruction, in which itself will be involved, it must be obliged to yield. In a word, it is not equality itself, but only a tendency towards equality, after all the others are provided for, that, on the part of the ruling and other members of the community, is the proper object of endeavour.[55]

[51] See his *Mathematical Psychics,* 1881, especially pp. 77–82.
[52] "Codification Proposal," *Works,* vol. iv, p. 561.
[53] "Constitutional Code," *Works,* vol. ix, p. 14.
[54] *Ibid.,* p. 18.
[55] "Logical Arrangements," *Works,* vol. iii, p. 294. For still other expositions than the three cited above, see *Pannomial Fragments,* vol. iii, pp. 228–230; *Leading Principles of a Constitutional Code for Any State,* vol. ii, pp. 271–272.

VI

We have seen that Bentham relied upon the felicific calculus to make himself the Newton of the moral world—the felicific calculus which was to treat the forces pain and pleasure as Newton's laws treated gravitation. But he did not really frame a quantitative science of the Newtonian type. His calculus, indeed, bore little resemblance to the mathematical conceptions by which in his own day chemistry and crystallography were being placed upon a secure foundation. No man could apply Bentham's calculus in sober earnest, because no man could tell how many intensity units were included in any one of his pleasures—to go no further. And indeed Bentham did not use the calculus as an instrument of calculation; he used it as a basis of classification. It pointed out to him what elements should be considered in a given situation, and among these elements *seriatim* he was often able to make comparisons in terms of greater and less—comparisons that few men would challenge, though Bentham might not be able to prove them against a skeptic. So his science as he elaborated it turned out to be much more like the systematic botany than like the celestial mechanics of his day. Bentham himself was a classifier rather than a calculator; he came nearer being the Linnaeus than the Newton of the moral world.[56]

Far as he fell short of his dream, Bentham's line of attack upon social problems represented a marked advance upon the type of discussion common in his day—or in ours. Though he could not literally work out the value of any "lot" of pain or pleasure, he had a systematic plan for canvassing the probable effects of rival institutions upon the happiness of populations. By pinning debates conducted in "vague generalities" down to fairly definite issues he was often able to find a convincing solution for practical problems. The defects of the rival method if not the merits of his own stand sharply outlined in what Bentham says about the dispute between England and her American colonies:

> I . . . placed the question . . . on the ground of the greatest happiness of the greatest number, meaning always in both countries taken together. With me it was a matter of calculation: pains and pleasures, the elements of it. . . . No party had any stomach for calculation: none, perhaps, would have known very well how to go about it, if they had. The battle was fought by assertion. *Right* was the weapon employed on both sides. "We have a *right* to be as we

---

[56] Compare Bentham's own reference to Linnaeus in *Deontology,* vol. i, p. 202; his discussion of his own "natural method" of classification by bi-partition—including the reference to botany in a footnote in *Principles of Morals and Legislation, Works,* vol. i, p. 139; and certain other references to the merits of classification in botany, *Works,* vol. vi, p. 442; vol. viii, pp. 121–6 and pp. 254, 255.

now choose to be," said people on the American side. "We have a right to continue to make you what we choose you should be," said rulers on the English side. "We have a right to legislate over them, but we have no *right* to tax them," said Lord Camden, by way of settling the matter. . . .[57]

What he claimed for his results in his *Codification Proposal* may well be granted:

> How far short soever this degree of precision may be, of the conceivable point of perfection . . . at any rate, in every rational and candid eye, unspeakable will be the advantage it will have, over every form of argumentation, in which every idea is afloat, no degree of precision being ever attained, because none is ever so much as aimed at.[58]

Probably every reader of this article will share the impression that Bentham's conception of human behavior is artificial to an extreme degree. That impression is not due, I think, to any trick in my exposition. Nor is it due to any quirk in Bentham's mind. He can hardly be charged with doing violence to the commonsense notions of his day, unless it be violence to develop and accept their full consequences. The real reason why we find the conception artificial is that we have another stock of ideas about behavior with which Bentham's ideas are incompatible. Our business is to be consistent as he was, and to use the set of ideas in which we believe as fully as he used the set in which he believed. Then if our ideas prove wrong, as is not unlikely, we may at least give later comers the same kind of help that Bentham now gives us.

[57] *Historical Preface to the Second Edition of A Fragment on Government, Works,* vol. i, p. 248.
[58] *Works,* vol. iv, p. 542.

IS "UTILITY" THE MOST SUITABLE TERM FOR THE CONCEPT IT IS USED TO DENOTE?

Irving Fisher

In all sciences, and particularly in one like economics, which appeals to the general public and which uses concepts and terms already at least partially familiar, it is a matter of some practical importance to select a suitable terminology.

The concept called "final degree of utility" by Jevons, "effective utility," "specific utility," and "marginal efficiency" by J. B. Clark, "marginal utility," and "marginal desirability" by Marshall, Side and others, "Grenznutzen" by the Austrians, "Werth der letzten Atome" by Gossen, "rareté" by Walras, and "ophélimité" by Pareto, seems still in need of really satisfactory terms by which to express it.

Marshall improved greatly upon Jevons' phrase when he substituted the term "marginal" for "final degree of," and this improvement has been very generally recognized and accepted.

But, as yet, no generally accepted substitute for "utility" has been found. The term is a heritage of Bentham and his utilitarian philosophy. It is misleading to every beginner in economics and to the great untutored and naïve public who find it hard to call an overcoat no more truly useful than a necklace, or a grindstone than a roulette wheel. Economists cannot with impunity override the popular distinction between useful and ornamental, much less that between useful and useless, without confusing and repelling the man in the street.

In the last few years a new source of confusion has arisen for the use, in a special sense, of the phrase "public utilities." This phrase must itself be used by economists who now find themselves discussing the marginal utility of a public utility!—and distinguishing between the marginal utility "in the economic sense" representing the esteem of the political ring or other powers that be for that public utility (which marginal utility imparts economic value to said public utility), and

---

Source: Reprinted with permission from the *American Economic Review,* VIII: 335–337 (June 1918).

utility "in the popular sense" representing the real social serviceableness of that public utility!

Genuine utility for social service must, as Pareto says, be more and more studied by economists as they fulfill their task of working out plans for economic and social betterments. He therefore suggested that we should not abandon the term utility but reserve it to express the genuine article and employ in its place in price analysis the term "ophelimity"— as it has been anglicised—to express the value-making quality.

It is true that coined words have the great advantage of breaking away from the misleading associations which cling to terms already in popular use. But the difficulty has been with "ophelimity" as with most coined words, that, just because it has *no* associations to introduce it, it would not and could not dispossess the old term.

The term "desirability" comes very near the required mark and I have used it in most of my books; but, unfortunately, like utility it carries with it to some extent an ethical connotation. Usage seems to imply that a desirable object is one which *ought* to be desired, rather than one which simply has the potentiality of being desired. We are forced to call the most undesirable articles and services, such as whiskey and prostitution, economically "desirable" in price analysis.

It has occurred to me that the term really needed may be built on the good old economic term "want." Long before the days of "marginal utility" economists spoke of "human wants." Wants include wants for purposes of ornamentation as well as for purposes of real utility; wants for what is trivial or useless as well as for what is important, useful, and desirable; wants for evil as well as for good purposes. So far as the influence on price is concerned the essential fact is that an object is actually wanted, or rather that it is capable of being actually wanted under stated circumstances. Whether it ought to be wanted, or whether it is wanted for a proper purpose is immaterial. It must merely have the capacity for being wanted, it must be wantable, it must have wantability. Ordinarily the short term "want" will suffice. We can speak of a marginal want for whiskey, and if we prefer a phrase in which "of" replaced the "for" we can speak of the marginal "wantability" of whiskey. The two terms "want" and "wantability" might well be used alternatively, affording welcome variety in expression.

The more technical term of the two, "wantability," is only half coined. It is sufficiently coined to serve notice on the reader that he must learn, not assume, its meaning; while the association of ideas it carries, leads the mind along the right path without paradox, contradiction, or confusion. It is readily recognized when seen and easily recalled when wanted. In short, it bears its meaning on its face. As hinted above, it could be piloted into use by speaking of the "marginal want for" as an alternative to "the marginal wantability of."

Another advantage is that these terms afford the means for coining an expression, to me at least much needed, for a *unit* of "wantability." Such a unit might be called a "wantab." In this case we have a free field for a coined word and no term in use to dispute possession. If, as I anticipate, the science of measuring human wants is to be developed in the future a convenient term for this unit will be needed.

No equally suitable term for a unit of "desirability" or "utility" or "ophelimity" seems available; although in my doctor's thesis of 1891 on "mathematical investigations in the theory of value and prices" I made an attempt. The appearance last year of a French translation of this little essay has renewed my interest in a better terminology and, together with the opportunity to secure the necessary data which the war seems to promise, has led me to hope for the statistical measurement of marginal "wantability."

Before attempting to launch any new terms for this concept, I should be glad to receive expressions of approval or disapproval from other economists.

PART II

An Overview of the Development of Utility Theory

THE DEVELOPMENT OF
UTILITY THEORY

George J. Stigler

*But I have planted the tree of utility. I have planted it
deep, and spread it wide.*—Bentham

The history of economic thought can be studied with many purposes.
One may trace the effects of contemporary economic and social conditions on economic theory or—rather more bravely—the effects of economic theories on economic and social developments. One may study the
history to find the original discoverers of theories, spurred on by the
dream of new Cantillons; or one may compare the economics of the great
economists with that of the rank and file, as a contribution to the structure and process of intellectual change. Or one may, and most often does,
simply set forth the major steps in the development of a branch of economic theory, hoping that it can be justified by its contribution to the
understanding of modern economics. This history of utility theory is
offered primarily with this last purpose, although in the final section I
review the history to answer the question, "Why do economists change
their theories?"

The scope of this study is limited in several respects. First, it covers
primarily the period from Smith to Slutsky, that is, from 1776 to 1915.
Second, the study is limited to certain important topics and to the treatment of these topics by economists of the first rank. The application of
utility theory to welfare economics is the most important topic omitted.
An estimate of the part played by utility theory in forming economists'
views of desirable social policy is too large a task, in the complexity of
issues and volume of literature involved, to be treated incidentally. The
omission is justified by the fact that most economists of the period used
utility theory primarily to explain economic behavior (particularly de-

Source: Reprinted with permission from the *Journal of Political Economy,* LVIII:
307–327, 373–396 (August and October 1950).

mand behavior) and only secondarily (when at all) to amend or justify economic policy.[1]

I. THE CLASSICAL BACKGROUND

ADAM SMITH

Drawing upon a long line of predecessors, Smith gave to his immediate successors, and they uncritically accepted, the distinction between value in use and value in exchange:

> The word VALUE, it is to be observed, has two different meanings, and sometimes expresses the utility of some particular object, and sometimes the power of purchasing other goods which the possession of that object conveys. The one may be called "value in use"; the other, "value in exchange." The things which have the greatest value in use have frequently little or no value in exchange; and on the contrary, those which have the greatest value in exchange have frequently little or no value in use. Nothing is more useful than water: but it will purchase scarce any thing; scarce any thing can be had in exchange for it. A diamond, on the contrary, has scarce any value in use; but a very great quantity of other goods may frequently be had in exchange for it.[2]

The fame of this passage rivals its ambiguity.

The paradox—that value in exchange may exceed or fall short of value in use—was, strictly speaking, a meaningless statement, for Smith had no basis (i.e., no concept of marginal utility of income or marginal price of utility) on which he could compare such heterogeneous quantities. On any reasonable interpretation, moreover, Smith's statement that value in use could be less than value in exchange was clearly a moral judgment, not shared by the possessors of diamonds. To avoid the incomparability of money and utility, one may interpret Smith to mean that the ratio of values of two commodities is not equal to the ratio of their total utilities.[3]

---

[1] I have also omitted consideration of the criticisms raised by the anti-theoretical writers, who played no constructive part in the development of the theory. For a discussion of some of their views, see J. Viner, "The Utility Theory and Its Critics," *Journal of Political Economy,* XXXIII (1925), pp. 369–87.

I wish to acknowledge the helpful suggestions of Arthur F. Burns, Milton Friedman, and Paul A. Samuelson.

[2] *The Wealth of Nations* (New York: Modern Library, 1937), p. 28.

[3] Or, alternatively, that the ratio of the prices of two commodities is not equal to the ratio of their total utilities; but this also requires an illegitimate selection of units: The price of what quantity of diamonds is to be compared with the price of one gallon of water? Smith makes such illegitimate statements; for example, "The whole quantity of a cheap commodity brought to market, is commonly not only greater, but of greater value, than the whole quantity of a dear one. The whole

On such a reading, Smith's statement deserves neither criticism nor quotation.

This passage is not Smith's title to recognition in our history of utility. His role is different: it is to show that demand functions, as a set of empirical relationships, were already an established part of economic analysis. The negatively sloping demand curve was already axiomatic; for example, "A competition will immediately begin among [the buyers when an abnormally small supply is available], and the market price will rise more or less above the natural price."[4] The effect of income on consumption was not ignored:

> The proportion of the expence of house-rent to the whole expence of living, is different in the different degrees of fortune. It is perhaps highest in the highest degree, and it diminishes gradually through the inferior degrees, so as in general to be lowest in the lowest degree. The necessaries of life occasion the great expence of the poor. They find it difficult to get food, and the greater part of their little revenue is spent in getting it. The luxuries and vanities of life occasion the principal expense of the rich; and a magnificent house embellishes and sets off to the best advantage all the other luxuries and vanities which they possess. A tax upon house-rents, therefore, would in general fall heaviest upon the rich; and in this sort of inequality there would not, perhaps, be any thing very unreasonable.[5]

This type of demand analysis was continued and improved by Smith's successors, but his example should suffice to remind us that a history of utility is not a history of demand theory.

BENTHAM

Jeremy Bentham brought the principle of utility (to be understood much more broadly than is customary in economics) to the forefront of

---

quantity of bread annually brought to market, is not only greater, but of greater value than the whole quantity of butcher's-meat; the whole quantity of butcher's-meat, than the whole quantity of poultry; and the whole quantity of poultry, than the whole quantity of wild fowl. There are so many more purchases for the cheap than for the dear commodity, that, not only a greater quantity of it, but a greater value, can commonly be disposed of" (*ibid.*, p. 212; see also p. 838).

Nevertheless, this statement can be reformulated into a meaningful and interesting hypothesis: Order commodities by the income class of consumers, using the proportion of families in the income class that purchase the commodity as the basis for choosing the income class. Then does aggregate value of output fall as income class rises?

[4] *Ibid.*, p. 56. Substitution is illustrated by the effects of a royal death on the prices of black and colored cloth (*ibid.*, p. 59).

[5] *Ibid.*, pp. 793–94. This is of course the opposite of modern budgetary findings, but near-contemporary budget studies seem to me indirectly to support Smith.

discussion in England at the beginning of the nineteenth century. In his Introduction to the *Principles of Morals and Legislation* (1789) he suggested the measurement of quantities of pleasure and pain (primarily for the purpose of constructing a more rational system of civil and criminal law). Four dimensions of pleasure and pain were distinguished for the individual: (1) intensity, (2) duration, (3) certainty, and (4) propinquity.[6]

The first two dimensions are clearly relevant to the measurement of a pleasure, but the latter two are better treated as two of the factors which influence an individual's response to a particular pleasure or pain.[7] Bentham did not give explicit directions for calculating a given pleasure and indeed devoted a long chapter (vi) to "Circumstances Influencing Sensibility," which listed no less than thirty-two circumstances (such as age, sex, education, and firmness of mind) that must be taken into account in carrying out such a calculation.

The theory was much elaborated with respect to economic applications in *Traités de legislation* (1802), a lucid synthesis of many manuscripts made by his disciple, Étienne Dumont.[8] Bentham was particularly concerned with the problem of equality of income, and this raised the question of comparisons of the utilities of persons who might differ in thirty-two circumstances:

> It is to be observed in general, that in speaking of the effect of a portion of wealth upon happiness, abstraction is always to be made of the particular sensibility of individuals, and of the exterior circumstances in which they may be placed. Differences of character are inscrutable; and such is the diversity of circumstances, that they are never the same for two individuals. Unless we begin by dropping these two considerations, it will be impossible to announce any general proposition. But though each of these propositions may prove false or inexact in a given individual case, that will furnish no argument against their speculative truth and practical utility. It is enough for the justification of these propositions—1st, If they ap-

[6] *Op. cit.*, chap. iv. In addition, two further "dimensions" were added for the appraisal of the total satisfaction of an "act": the consumption of a loaf of bread might be the pleasure to which the first four dimensions refer; the theft of the loaf might be the act. These additional dimensions were fecundity and purity; respectively, the chance of one pleasure leading to another and the chance of a pleasure not being followed by a pain.

[7] As Bentham indicated elsewhere (see *Works of Jeremy Bentham* [Edinburgh: Tait, 1843], I, 206; III, 214).

[8] The reliability of the presentation of Bentham's views has been attested by Élie Halévy, *La Formation du radicalisme philosophique* (Paris: Germer Baillière, 1901), Vol. I, Appendix I. Here the Hildreth translation of the *Traités* is used (London: Trübner, 1871).

proach nearer the truth than any others which can be substituted for them; 2nd, If with less inconvenience than any others they can be made the basis of legislation.[9]

Thus, he achieved interpersonal comparisons, not by calculation, but by assumption, justified by the desirability (somehow determined) of its corollaries. This resort to a question-begging assumption was a fundamental failure of his project to provide a scientific basis for social policy: the scientific basis was being justified by the policies to which it led. In one of his manuscripts he argued that this assumption was merely an abbreviation and that the conclusions he deduced could be reached (more laboriously) without it,[10] which is not in general true.

Having surmounted this obstacle no better than subsequent economists, Bentham proceeded to establish a set of propositions on the utility of income:[11]

1st. Each portion of wealth has a corresponding portion of happiness.
2nd. Of two individuals with unequal fortunes, he who has the most wealth has the most happiness.
3rd. The excess in happiness of the richer will not be so great as the excess of his wealth.[12]

[9] *Theory of Legislation,* p. 103.

[10] "Tis in vain to talk of adding quantities which after the addition will continue distinct as they were before, one man's happiness will never be another man's happiness; a gain to one man is no gain to another: you might as well pretend to add 20 apples to 20 pears, which after you had done that could not be 40 of any one thing but 20 of each just as there was before. This addibility of the happiness of different subjects, however, when considered rigorously it may appear fictitious, is a postulatum without the allowance of which all political reasoning is at a stand: nor is it more fictitious than that of the equality of chances to reality, on which that whole branch of the Mathematics which is called the doctrine of chances is established. The fictitious form of speech (expression) in both cases, which, fictitious as it is, can give birth to no false consequences or conclusions, is adopted from a necessity which induces the like expedient in so many other instances, merely for the sake of abbreviation: as it would be endless to repeat in every passage where it was used, what it was it wanted to be rigorously true" (Halévy, *op. cit.,* III, 481).

[11] *Theory of Legislation,* pp. 103 ff.; all statement italicized by Bentham.

[12] The use of marginal analysis was even more explicit in his *Pannomial Fragments:*

"But the quantity of happiness will not go on increasing in anything near the same proportion as the quantity of wealth: ten thousand times the quantity of wealth will not bring with it ten thousand times the quantity of happiness. It will even be matter of doubt whether ten thousand times the wealth will in general bring with it twice the happiness.

". . . the quantity of happiness produced by a particle of wealth (each particle being of the same magnitude) will be less and less at every particle" (*Works,* III, 229; see also IV, 541).

Each of these propositions was elaborated, and the utility calculus was used to defend equality ("The nearer the actual proportion approaches to equality, the greater will be the total mass of happiness"), although equality was finally rejected in favor of security of property. As corollaries, gambling was utility-decreasing and insurance utility-increasing.[13]

In a manuscript written about 1782, Bentham attempted to set forth more clearly the precise measurement of utility.[14] We are given a definition of the unit of intensity:

> The degree of intensity possessed by that pleasure which is the faintest of any that can be distinguished to be a pleasure, may be represented by unity. Such a degree of intensity is in every day's experience: according as any pleasures are perceived to be more and more intense, they may be represented by higher and higher numbers: but there is no fixing upon any particular degree of intensity as being the highest of which a pleasure is susceptible.[15]

(This suggested measure will be discussed in connection with the Weber-Fechner literature.) Then, shifting ground, Bentham argues that, although utility does not increase as fast as income, for small changes the two move proportionately,[16] so we may measure pleasures through the prices they command:

> If then between two pleasures the one produced by the possession of money, the other not, a man has as lief enjoy the one as the other, such pleasures are to be reputed equal. But the pleasure produced by the possession of money, is *as* the quantity of money that produces it: money is therefore the measure of this pleasure. But the other pleasure is equal to this; the other pleasure therefore is as the money that produces this: therefore money is also the measure of that other pleasure.[17]

Unfortunately, this procedure is illegitimate; we cannot use an equality (or, more strictly, a constancy of the marginal utility of money) that holds for small changes to measure total utilities.[18] These suggestions are important chiefly in revealing Bentham's awareness of the crucial problems in his calculus and his ingenuity in attempting to solve them.[19]

---

[13] *Theory of Legislation*, pp. 106–7.

[14] Lengthy extracts are given by Halévy, *op. cit.*, Vol. I, Appendix II.

[15] *Ibid.*, p. 398.

[16] *Ibid.*, p. 408.

[17] *Ibid.*, p. 410.

[18] Bentham appears to have recognized this difficulty when, in a passage following a discussion of diminishing marginal utility, he wrote: "[Intensity] is not susceptible of precise expression: it *not* being susceptible of measurement." (*Codification Proposal* [1822], in *Works*, IV, 542).

[19] For more general discussions of Bentham see W. C. Mitchell, "Bentham's

Bentham had indeed planted the tree of utility. No reader could over-look the concept of utility as a numerical magnitude; and the implica-tions for economic analysis were not obscure. But they were overlooked.

THE RICARDIANS

The economists of Bentham's time did not follow the approach he had opened. One may conjecture that this failure is due to the fact that Ricardo, who gave the economics of this period much of its slant and direction, was not a Benthamite. It is true that he was the friend of Bentham and the close friend of James Mill, Bentham's leading disciple. Yet there is no evidence that he was a devout utilitarian and much evi-dence that he was unphilosophical—essentially a pragmatic reformer.[20]

It is clear, in any event, that Ricardo did not apply the utility calculus to economics. He began his *Principles* with the quotation of Smith's distinction between value in use and value in exchange and ended the volume with the statement: "Value in use cannot be measured by any known standard; it is differently estimated by different persons"[21] I should be content to notice that he left the theory of utility as highly developed as he found it—as much cannot be said for the theory of value—were it not for a remarkable interpretation of Marshall's:

> Again, in a profound, though very incomplete discussion of the dif-ference between "Value and Riches" he seems to be feeling his way towards the distinction between marginal and total utility. For by Riches he means total utility, and he seems to be always on the point of stating that value corresponds to the increment of riches which results from that part of the commodity which it is only just worth the while of purchasers to buy; and that when the supply runs short, whether temporarily in consequence of a passing acci-dent, or permanently in consequence of an increase in cost of pro-duction, there is a rise in that marginal increment of riches which is measured by value, at the same time that there is a diminution in the aggregate riches, the total utility, derived from the commodity. Throughout the whole discussion he is trying to say, though (being ignorant of the terse language of the differential calculus) he did not get hold of the right words in which to say it neatly, that marginal utility is raised and total utility is lessened by any check to supply.[22]

Felicific Calculus," in *The Backward Art of Spending Money* (New York: McGraw-Hill Book Co., 1937); and J. Viner, "Bentham and J. S. Mill," *American Economic Review*, XXXIX (1949), 360–82.

[20] See Bonar's Preface to *Letters of Ricardo to Malthus* (Oxford: Clarendon, 1887).

[21] *Principles of Political Economy and Taxation* (Gonner, ed.; London: Bell, 1932), p. 420.

[22] *Principles of Economics* (8th ed.; London: Macmillan, 1920), p. 814.

In the chapter (xx) referred to, Ricardo defines riches as "necessaries, conveniences, and amusements," and value, as usual, is measured by the amount of labor necessary to produce a commodity. The chapter is essentially an exercise in the paradoxes of this definition of value; for example, if the productivity of labor doubles, riches double, but value changes only if the number of laborers changes. We may properly identify "necessaries, conveniences, and amusements" with total utility; but what of marginal utility? Ricardo says that, if a person receives two sacks of corn where formerly he received one, "he gets, indeed double the quantity of riches—double the quantity of utility—double the quantity of what Adam Smith calls value in use."[23] Hence he did not believe that marginal utility diminishes as quantity increases. He continued:

> When I give 2,000 times more cloth for a pound of gold than I give for a pound of iron, does it prove that I attach 2,000 times more utility to gold than I do to iron? certainly not; it proves only as admitted by M. Say, that the cost of production of gold is 2,000 times greater than the cost of production of iron . . . if utility were the measure of value, it is probable I should give more for the iron.[24]

The writer of this passage cannot be said to have been close to the notion of marginal utility. I cannot find a single sentence that gives support to Marshall's interpretation, and I think that it should be added to the list of examples of his peculiar documentation and interpretation of predecessors.

Ricardo's influence was such that James Mill, the logical person to apply Bentham's system to economics, was content to present a rigid simplification of Ricardo's *Principles;*[25] and his son—whose formative work in economics, we must remember, came chiefly in the 1820s—did little more with utility.[26] Only the French utilitarian, J. B. Say, attempted to give utility a substantial place in economic theory, and he was prevented from doing so effectively by his inability to arrive at a notion of marginal analysis. In order to support the thesis that prices are proportional to utilities, he was driven to invent the metaphysical distinction between natural and social wealth:

> One pays 2,000 times as much for a pound of gold as for a pound of iron. Here is how, on my theory, this phenomenon is explained. I assume with you that a pound of iron has the same utility as a

[23] *Principles*, p. 265.

[24] *Ibid.*, pp. 267–68.

[25] In his *Elements of Political Economy* (3d ed., 1827).

[26] *Principles of Political Economy* (Ashley, ed.; New York: Longmans, Green, 1929), pp. 442–44, 804.

pound of gold, although it is worth only one-two-thousandth as much. I say that there are in the iron 1,999 degrees of utility that nature has given us without charge, and I degree that we create by work, at an expense that we will assume only if a consumer is willing to reimburse us; hence the pound of iron has 2,000 degrees of utility (on your assumption), which however can be obtained only on exacting terms, that is to say, . . . by expenses of 2,000. The 1,999 degrees of utility for which we do not pay when we consume iron are part of our natural wealth. . . . The single degree which must be paid for is part of our social wealth.[27]

II. THE UNSUCCESSFUL DISCOVERERS

The principle that equal increments of utility-producing means (such as income or bread) yield diminishing increments of utility is a commonplace. The first statement in print of a commonplace is adventitious; it is of no importance in the development of economics, and it confers no intellectual stature on its author. The statement acquires interest only when it is logically developed or explicitly applied to economic problems, and it acquires importance only when a considerable number of economists are persuaded to incorporate it into their analyses. Interest and importance are of course matters of degree.

Some economists gave clear statements of the principle of diminishing marginal utility but did not apply it to economic problems; they include Lloyd (1833), Senior (1836), Jennings (1855), and Hearn (1864) [28] Others applied utility theory to economic events without explicitly developing the principle of diminishing marginal utility: A. Walras (1831) and Longfield (1834), for example.[29] At least two economists—in addi-

---

[27] Letter to Ricardo, July 19, 1821, in *Mélanges et correspondence* (Paris: Chamerot, 1833), pp. 116–17, 287–89; cf. also *Treatise on Political Economy* (Boston: Wells & Lilly, 1824), Book II, chap. i, and *Cours complet d'économie politique* (Paris: Guillaumin, 1840), I, 65–66, 71–72.

[28] W. F. Lloyd, "The Notion of Value," reprinted in *Economic History, Economic Journal Supplement*, May, 1927, pp. 170–83; N. W. Senior, *Political Economy* (New York: Farrar & Rinehart, 1939), pp. 11–12; R. Jennings, *Natural Elements of Political Economy* (London: Longman, Brown, Green & Longman, 1855), pp. 98–99, 119, 233 n.; W. E. Hearn, *Plutology* (London: Macmillan, 1864), p. 17. Lloyd, the third occupant of the Drummond chair in political economy at Oxford, gave much the most elaborate statement of the principle. Instead of applying it to contemporary economic problems, however, he emphasized the fact that the marginal utility is not the same thing as exchange value and applied the theory to Robinson Crusoe to show this.

[29] A. Walras, *De la nature de la richesse et de l'origine de la valeur* (Paris: Alcan, 1938), esp. chap. xi; M. Longfield, *Lectures on Political Economy* ("London School Reprints" [London, 1931]), pp. 27–28, 45–46, 111 ff.

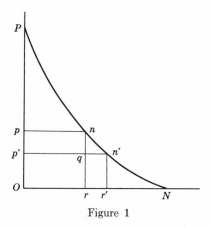

Figure 1

tion to Bentham—elaborated the principle or applied it to economic problems but failed to persuade other economists of its usefulness.[30] Their theories will be summarized briefly.

DUPIT (1844)

Jules Dupuit, a distinguished engineer, was led to the marginal utility theory by his attempt to construct a theory of prices that maximize utility.[31] He distinguished total and marginal utility with great clarity and discovered "une espèce de bénéfice" that we now call *consumers' surplus*. It was defined as the excess of total utility over marginal utility times the number of units of the commodity, but it was actually taken to be the area under the demand curve minus the expenditures on the commodity (i.e., Marshall's measure without his restrictions).[32]

Armed with this concept, he investigated the optimum toll on a bridge. His analysis was as follows. Let NP be the demand (and marginal utility) curve, Op the price (Fig. 1). Then $OrnP$ is the absolute utility

[30] Daniel Bernoulli's much earlier discover will be treated later.

[31] His chief essays (published in 1844 and 1849) are reprinted in *De l'utilité et de sa mesure* (Torino: La Fiforma Sociale, 1934).

[32] Dupuit's instruction for measuring utility reveals the tacit identification of utility and demand curves: "Assume that all the like commodities whose general utility one wishes to determine are subjected to a tax which is increased by small steps. At each increase, a certain quantity of the commodity will no longer be purchased. The utility of this quantity in terms of money will be the quantity multiplied by the tax. By increasing the tax until all purchases cease, and adding the partial products, one will obtain the total utility of the commodity" (*ibid.*, p. 50; also p. 180).

consumers obtain from the use of the bridge, and pnP is the relative utility. If the toll is reduced by pp', there is a net gain of consumer utility of qnn' (equal to the area under the demand curve between r and r' minus the expenditure $rr'n'q$).

Dupuit's general conclusion is: "The utility of a means of communication, and in general of any product, is at a maximum when the toll or the price is zero."[33] This is little more than a tautology, and Dupuit did not draw the further and illegitimate conclusion that the optimum toll rate is zero:

> It will not be our conclusion [that tolls should be small or zero], when we treat of tariffs; but we hope to have demonstrated that [tariff rates] must be studied, combined on rational principles to produce simultaneously the greatest possible utility and a revenue which will repay the expense of maintenance and the interest on the capital investment.[34]

We see that he was not afraid of interpersonal comparisons of utility, and in fact he argued that the effects of price changes on the distribution of income must be ignored because they were merely transfers.[35]

Dupuit could not reach a complete theory of optimum prices because he did not devise a coherent theory of cost.[36] One is impressed by the narrowness of his vision; the explicit formulation of the concept of consumer surplus is elegant, but there is no intuition of the difficulties in the concept, nor is there an attempt to construct the larger theoretical framework necessary to solve his problem.

[33] *Ibid.*, p. 161. I have transposed the axes of Dupuit's diagram.

[34] *Ibid.*, p. 51. Elsewhere he says that the ideal toll would be one proportional to the consumers' total utility, but this is impracticable because of *"l'improbité universelle"* (*ibid.*, p. 141); and the effects of alternative methods of financing public works (e.g., the incidence of taxes) must be studied before a practical recommendation can be made (*ibid.*, p. 161). Multiple price systems were also considered (*ibid.*, pp. 64–65, 140 ff.).

[35] *Ibid.*, p. 52.

[36] This is illustrated by the following quotation, in which price fluctuations are treated as exercises of arbitrary power:

> "In order that there be an increase or decrease in utility, it is necessary that there be a decrease or increase in [a commodity's] cost of production—there being no change in its quality. When there are only variations in market price [*prix vénal*], the consumer gains what the producer loses, or conversely. Thus, when an article costing 20 francs to produce is sold for 50 francs, as a result of a monopoly or concession, the producer deprives every buyer of 30 francs of utility. If some circumstance forces him to lower his price by 10 francs, his income diminishes by 10 francs per unit and that of each buyer increases by 10 francs. There is a cancellation; no utility is produced."

(*Ibid.*, pp. 52–53.)

GOSSEN (1854)

Heinrich Gossen is one of the most tragic figures in the history of economics. He was a profound, original, and untrained thinker who hid his thoughts behind painfully complex arithmetical and algebraic exercises.[37] He displayed every trait of the crank,[38] excepting only one: history has so far believed that he was right. Only a few distinctive features of his work will be commented upon.

First, Gossen's discussion of the laws of satisfaction is concerned only with individual acts of consumption, such as the eating of slices of bread.[39] Correspondingly, in his early diagrams marginal utility is a function of time (duration of the act of consumption), and only after a considerable elaboration of this approach does he take quantity of a (perishable) commodity as proportional to duration of consumption.[40] Yet he does not attempt to work out a theory of the temporal pattern of consumption, and this portion of his theory seems misdirected.

Second, he presents a theory of the marginal disutility of labor that is completely symmetrical with that of the marginal utility of consumer goods. Gossen's curve of the marginal disutility of income is essentially identical with that which Jevons made famous: the early hours of work yield utility, but, as the duration of labor increases, the marginal utility diminishes to zero and then to negative values.[41] He defines the condition of maximum utility as that in which the marginal utility of a unit of product is numerically equal to the marginal disutility of the labor necessary to produce a unit of the product.[42]

Third, Gossen was the first writer to formulate explicitly what I shall call the fundamental principle of marginal utility theory:

> A person maximizes his utility when he distributes his available money among the various goods so that he obtains the same amount

[37] Only a person who has labored through the volume can savor the magnificent understatement of Edgeworth: "He may seem somewhat deficient in the quality of mathematical elegance" ("Gossen," *Palgrave's Dictionary of Political Economy* [London: Macmillan, 1923], II, 232).

[38] His *Entwicklung der Gesetze des menschlichen Verkehrs* (3d ed.; Berlin: Prager, 1927), which is not encumbered with chapters, begins with the famous sentences: "On the following pages I submit to public judgment the result of 20 years of meditation. What a Copernicus succeeded in explaining of the relationships of worlds in space, that I believe I have performed for the explanation of the relationships of men on earth."

[39] For a good summary see M. Pantaleoni, *Pure Economics* (London: Macmillan, 1898), pp. 28 ff.

[40] *Entwicklung*, p. 29; his treatment of durable goods is not sound (see pp. 25, 29–30).

[41] *Ibid.*, p. 36.

[42] *Ibid.*, p. 45.

of satisfaction from the last unit of money (*Geldatom*) spent upon each commodity.[43]

We may translate this statement into semisymbolic form:

$$\frac{MU_1}{p_1} = \frac{MU_2}{p_2} = \frac{MU_3}{p_3} = \cdots ,$$

where MU_i represents the marginal utility of the ith commodity and p_i its price. (We shall adhere to the notation: x_i is the quantity of commodity X_i, p_i is its price, MU_i is its marginal utility, and R is money income.) This equation marked a long step forward in the development of the relationship between utility and demand curves.

Finally, Gossen's views on the measurability of utility are vague but tantalizing:

> We can conceive of the magnitudes of various pleasures only by comparing them with one another, as, indeed, we must also do in measuring other objects. We can measure the magnitudes of various areas only by taking a particular area as the unit of measurement, or the weights of different bodies only by taking a particular weight as the unit, and hence an indefiniteness remains in the measurement of a pleasure. It is a matter of indifference which pleasure we choose as the unit. Perhaps the consequences will be most convenient if we choose the pleasure from the commodity which we use as money.[44]

He did not notice that there might be no unit of utility comparable with that of area or weight; and it is probably going too far to read into this passage the later position that it is sufficient to deal with the ratios of marginal utilities.

III. THE BEGINNINGS OF THE MODERN THEORY

The utility theory finally began to win a place in generally accepted economics in the 1870s, under the triple auspices of Jevons, Menger, and Walras. Independently these economists arrived at positions similar in the main and sometimes in detail.[45] I shall compare their treatments of

[43] *Ibid.,* pp. 93–94.
[44] *Ibid.,* p. 123.
[45] Marshall was a contemporary discoverer of the theory but did not publish it until later (*Memorials of Alfred Marshall* [London: Macmillan, 1925], p. 22). J. B. Clark was a somewhat later discoverer and never developed the theory to a level comparable with the best contemporary European analysis. He became preoccupied with a neglected problem to which he could not find a useful solution: how to apply marginal analysis to variations in the quality of goods (see *The Philosophy of Wealth* [New York: Macmillan, 1931], chaps. xiv–xvi).

certain basic problems of the theory, and henceforth our organization will be by subject.

A. CRITICISM OF RECEIVED DOCTRINE

Each of these founders of utility theory criticized the Ricardian theory of value, but for each this was an incidental and minor point; they deemed the positive merits of the utility theory a sufficient basis for acceptance. Thus, only after completing the presentation of his utility theory did Jevons point out the deficiencies in Ricardo's labor value theory. These deficiencies were three: (1) Ricardo required a special theory for commodities with fixed supplies, such as rare statues. This proved that labor cost is not essential to value. (2) Large labor costs will not confer high value on a commodity if the future demand is erroneosly forecast; "in commerce bygones are for ever bygones."[46] (3) Labor is heterogeneous, and the various types of labor can be compared only through the values of their products.[47] On the other hand, the cost of production theory of value fits in nicely as a special case of the utility theory, for it explains the relative quantities of commodities that will be supplied.[48]

Menger and Walras took fundamentally the same position. The former also gave the first two criticisms listed above and, in addition, made a parallel criticism to the Ricardian rent theory: if the value of land did not depend upon labor cost, this demonstrated a serious lack of generality in the classical theory of value.[49] Walras repeated the criticism that the classical theory lacked generality, emphasized the reciprocal effects of prices of products and of productive services on one another, and denied the existence of the class of commodities whose supplies could be infinitely increased, on the overly literal ground that no productive resource was available in infinite quantity.[50]

The task of elaborating and expounding the theory, and of exaggerating its merits and understating the usefulness of the classical theory— the inevitable accompaniments of intellectual innovations—fell largely to disciples, in particular Wieser and Böhm-Bawerk. These men did not improve on the substance of the theory—in fact, it deteriorated in their hands—so we shall pass them by.[51]

[46] *Theory of Political Economy* (4th ed.; London: Macmillan, 1911), p. 164.

[47] *Ibid.*, p. 166.

[48] *Ibid.*, p. 165.

[49] *Grundsatze der Volkswirtschafslehre* (Vienna: Braumüller, 1871), pp. 69, 120–21, 144–45.

[50] *Eléments d'économie politique pure* (1926 ed.; Paris: Pichon & Durand-Auzias), Leçon 38. The first edition (Lausanne: Carbay, 1874) does not differ materially in substance on the subjects discussed here.

[51] Wieser's paradox of value (that marginal utility times quantity may decrease

B. THE EXISTENCE AND MEASURABILITY OF UTILITY

Without exception, the founders accepted the existence of utility as a fact of common experience, congruent with the most casual introspection. Jevons was most explicit:

> The science of Economics, however, is in some degree peculiar, owing to the fact . . . that its ultimate laws are known to us immediately by intuition, or, at any rate, they are furnished to us ready made by other mental or physical sciences.
> . . . The theory here given may be described as *the mechanics of utility and self-interest*. Oversights may have been committed in tracing out its details, but in its main features this theory must be the true one. Its method is as sure and demonstrative as that of kinematics or statics, nay, almost as self-evident as are the elements of Euclid. . . .[52]

I am inclined to interpret the silence of Menger and Walras on the existence of utility as indicative of an equally complete acceptance.

Menger glossed over the problem of measurability of utility. He represented marginal utilities by numbers and employed an equality of marginal utilities in various uses as the criterion of the optimum allocation of a good.[53] His word for utility—*Bedeutung*—was surely intentionally neutral, but probably it was chosen for its non-ethical flavor.[54] Walras was equally vague; he simply assumed the existence of a unit of measure of intensity of utility and thereafter spoke of utility as an absolute magnitude.[55]

Jevons' attack on the problem of measurability was characteristically frank and confused. He denied that utility was measurable:

> There is no unit of labour, or suffering, or enjoyment. I have granted that we can hardly form the conception of a unit of pleasure or pain, so that the numerical expression of quantities of feeling seems to be out of question.[56]

---

when quantity increases) led to deep confusion (see *Natural Value* [New York: Stechert, 1930], Books I and II). Böhm-Bawerk's greatest polemic is *Grundzüge der Theorie des wirtschaftlichen Güterwerts* ("London School Reprints" [London, 1932])

[52] *Op. cit.*, pp. 18 and 21.

[53] *Op. cit.*, p. 98 n.

[54] On one occasion he states that his numbers represent only relative utilities and that numbers such as 80 and 40 indicate only that the former (marginal) utility is twice as large as the latter (*ibid.*, p. 163 n.).

[55] *Éléments*, pp. 74, 102, 153.

[56] *Op. cit.*, pp. 7 and 12.

Yet he seemed also to argue that one cannot be sure that utility is not measurable but only that it could not presently be measured.[57] He was somewhat more skeptical of the measurability of utility in the first (1871) than in the second (1879) edition; for example, in the second edition he deleted the following passage:

> I confess that it seems to me difficult even to imagine how such estimations [of utility] and summations can be made with any approach to accuracy. Greatly though I admire the clear and precise notions of Bentham, I know not where his numerical data are to be found.[58]

With gallant inconsistency, he proceeded to devise a way to measure utility. It employed the familiar measuring rod of money:

> It is from the quantitative effects of the feelings that we must estimate their comparative amounts.
> I never attempt to estimate the whole pleasure gained by purchasing a commodity; the theory merely expressed that, when a man has purchased enough, he would derive equal pleasure from the possession of a small quantity more as he would from the money price of it.[59]

This position is elaborated ingeniously: We can construct a demand curve by observation (or possibly experiment), and then we can pass to the marginal utility curve by means of the equation,

$$MU_r p_i = MU_i,$$

where MU_r is the marginal utility of income.[60]

> For the first approximation we may assume that the general utility of a person's income is not affected by the changes of price of the commodity.
> .   .   .
> The method of determining the function of utility explained above will hardly apply, however, to the main elements of expenditure. The price of bread, for instance, cannot be properly brought under the equation in question, because, when the price of bread rises much, the resources of poor persons are strained, money becomes scarcer with them, and [MU_r], the [marginal] utility of money, rises.[61]

This procedure is so similar to Marshall's that we may defer comment until we discuss the latter's more elaborate version.

[57] *Ibid.*, pp. 7–9.
[58] *Theory of Political Economy* (1st ed.; London: Macmillan, 1871), p. 12.
[59] *Theory* (4th ed.), pp. 11 and 13.
[60] *Ibid.*, pp. 146 ff. (Our notation.)
[61] *Ibid.*, pp. 147 and 148.

Unlike Walras and Menger, Jevons considered the question of the interpersonal comparison of utilities. He expressly argued that this was impossible[62] but made several such comparisons, as we shall notice later. Menger avoided the subject and did not engage in such comparisons; and Walras made only incidental interpersonal comparisons.[63]

C. UTILITY MAXIMIZATION AND THE DEMAND CURVE

Menger simply ignored the relationship between utility and demand. He was content to set some demand prices (he worked always with discontinuous schedules) which somehow represented marginal utilities[64] and proceeded to an elementary discussion of pricing under bilateral monopoly (the indeterminacy of which was recognized), duopoly (the complications of which were not recognized—a competitive solution was given), and competition (in which the absence of a theory of production had predictable effects).[65]

Jevons' attempt to construct a bridge between utility and demand was seriously hampered, I suspect, by his inability to translate any but simple thoughts into mathematics. His fundamental equation for the maximization of utiilty in exchanges was presented as a *fait accompli:*

$$\frac{MU_1}{MU_2} = \frac{p_1}{p_2}.$$

This equation was satisfactory for an individual confronted by fixed prices, but how to apply it to competitive markets?

Jevons devised two concepts to reach the market analysis: the trading body and the law of indifference. A trading body was the large group of buyers or sellers of a commodity in a competitive market.[66] The law of indifference was that there be only one price in a market.[67]

---

[62] *Ibid.,* p. 14.

[63] See *Études d'économie politique appliquée* (Lausanne: Rouge, 1890), pp. 295 ff.; *Études d'économie social* (Lausanne: Rouge, 1896), pp. 209 ff.

[64] "The value that a good has for an economizing individual is equal to the significance of that want-satisfaction" (*op. cit.,* p. 120; also chap. v).

[65] *Ibid.,* pp. 177 ff., 208–9.

[66] The requirement of competition was indirect: one characteristic of a perfect market was that "there must be no conspiracies for absorbing and holding supplies to produce unnatural ratios of exchange" (*Theory* [4th ed.], p. 86). It is evident that the trading body could not properly be used to explain prices, because its composition depended upon prices.

[67] Jevons (*ibid.,* p. 95) stated the law of indifference as

$$\frac{dx_2}{dx_1} = \frac{x_2}{x_1}.$$

This notation is ambiguous (see Marshall, *Memorials,* p. 98; F. Y. Edgeworth, *Mathematical Psychics* [London: Paul, 1881], pp. 110 ff.).

He proceeded in the following peculiar manner. Let the equation of exchange be applied to each trading body; for each group of competitive individuals the equation will determine the relationship between the quantity offered and the quantity demanded.[68] Hence we have two equations to determine the two unknowns: the quantities of x_1 and x_2 exchanged. Quite aside from the ambiguous concept of a trading body, this procedure was illicit on his own view that utilities of different individuals are not comparable.[69]

Walras succeeded in establishing the correct relationship between utility and demand. He first derived the equations of maximum satisfaction for an individual: if there are m commodities, and a unit of commodity x_1 is the *numéraire* in terms of which the prices of other commodities are expressed (so $p_1 = 1$), we have $(m - 1)$ equations.[70]

$$MU_1 = \frac{MU_2}{p_2} = \frac{MU_3}{p_3} = \cdots$$

Finally, the budget equation states the equality of values of the initially stocks of commodities (x_i^0) and the stocks held after exchange:

$$x_1 + x_2 p_2 + x_3 p_3 + \cdots = x_1^0 + x_2^0 p_2 + x_3^0 p_3 + \cdots .$$

We thus have m equations to determine m quantities of the commodities demanded or supplied by the individual. We may solve the equations for the quantities demanded or supplied as functions of the prices:

$$x_2 = x_2(p_2, p_3, \ldots)$$
$$x_3 = x_3(p_2, p_3, \ldots)$$
$$\cdots \cdots \cdots \cdots$$
$$x_1 = (x_1^0 + x_2^0 p_2 + x_3^0 p_3 + \cdots) - (x_2 p_2 + x_3 p_3 + \cdots).$$

The $x_1, x_2, x_3, \ldots$, are the quantities held (demanded), and $(x_1^0 - x_1)$, $(x_2^0 - x_2)$, $(x_3^0 - x_3)$, $\ldots$, the quantities supplied.[71]

[68] Jevons seems to have introduced the trading bodies to get quickly to market prices, not because of an intuition that bilateral monopoly was indeterminate; at least he overlooked the difficulties in duopoly (*Theory* [4th ed.], p. 117).

[69] "The reader will find, again, that there is never, in any single instance, an attempt made to compare the amount of feeling on one mind with that in another" (*ibid.*, p. 14).

[70] *Éléments*, Lecon 8. Let total utility $= f(x_1) + g(x_2) + h(x_3) + \cdots$. In one of these utility functions, substitute the budget limitation,

$$x_1 + x_2 p_2 + x_3 p_3 + \cdots = x_1^0 + x_2^0 p_2 + x_3^0 p_3 + \cdots ,$$

where $x_1^0, x_2^0, x_3, \ldots$, are the initial stocks. Then maximize total utility to obtain the equations in the text.

[71] This summary differs in notation and detail, but not in substance, from Walras'

To determine the market prices, we simply add the demands of all n individuals in the market for each commodity

$$X_2 = \sum^n x_2 = \sum^n x_2(p_2, p_3, \ldots)$$

$$X_3 = \sum^n x_3 = \sum^n x_3(p_2, p_3, \ldots)$$

$$\cdot \ \cdot \ \cdot \ \cdot \ \cdot \ \cdot \ \cdot \ \cdot \ \cdot \ \cdot \ \cdot \quad \cdot \ \cdot \ \cdot \ \cdot \ \cdot$$

and equate the quantities demanded to the quantities available (X_i):

$$X_2^0 = X_2:$$

$$X_3^0 = X_3,$$

$$\cdot \ \cdot \ \cdot \ \cdot \ \cdot \ \cdot$$

There are $(m-1)$ such equations with which to determine the $(m-1)$ prices of x_2, x_3, $\ldots$, in terms of x_1. It may appear that we have forgotten the budget equation, but it is not an independent relationship because it can be deduced from the other equations. If we multiply the last set of equations by the respective prices of the commodities and add, we obtain

$$p_2(X_2^0 - X_2) + p_3(X_3^0 - X_3) + \cdots = 0.$$

But if we add the individual budget equations we obtain

$$\sum^n x_1 - X_1^0 = p_2(X_2^0 - X_2) + p_3(X_3^0 - X_3) + \cdots = 0.$$

Hence if the quantity demanded equals the quantity available in $(m-1)$ markets, the equality must also hold in the mth market. This is equivalent to saying that if we know the amounts of $(m-1)$ commodities that have been exchanged for each other and an mth commodity, and the rates of exchange, we necessarily know the amount of the mth commodity exchanged.

The (Walrasian) demand function is thus the relationship between the quantity of a commodity and all prices, when the individual's (or individuals') money income and tastes (utility functions) are held constant. We shall adhere to this meaning of the demand function or "curve" (the two-dimensional illustration of course requiring that all prices except that of the commodity are held constant), and the relationship between quantity and money income (all prices and tastes being held constant) will be designated as the income curve.

---

exposition (*ibid.*, pp. 123 ff.). The chief difference of detail is that Walras writes the utility as $f(x_i^0 + x_i)$, where I write it as $f(x_i)$, so his x_i can be negative.

D. THE APPLICATIONS OF THE THEORY

Jevons gave only one application of his utility theory: a demonstration that both parties to an exchange gain satisfaction. The demonstration, as he gave it, was inconsistent with his denial of the possibility of comparing utilities of individuals, for it rested on the marginal utility curves of nations.[72]

Menger was even less specific but surely vastly more persuasive in his applications of the theory: he made it the basis of economic theory. The theory was given many everyday illustrations (mostly hypothetical, to be sure): it explained exchange, the wages of textile workers during the Civil War cotton shortage, the shifts of goods between free and economic, etc. More important, the theory of production became simply an instance of the theory of marginal utility: productive services were distinguished from consumption services only in being goods of higher order. Menger's version had no predictive value, nor did he conjecture any new economic relationships. Indeed at least two of the founders of marginal utility theory—Jevons was the exception—knew much less about economic life than a dozen predecessors such as Smith and Babbage. Yet the theory served to systematize a variety of known facts of everyday observation and seemed to confer an air of generality and structural elegance upon price theory.

Walras also did a good deal of this reorientation of economic theory in terms of utility, whereby the value of productive services was determined by the values of products. But he also attempted a specific and natural application of the theory to demand-curve analysis.

This application was the derivation of the law that price reduction will increase the quantity demanded; price increases will decrease the quantity demanded.[73] Walras treated this as intuitively obvious, but it was a strict implication of his theory. Consider the equations of maximum satisfaction:

$$\frac{MU_1}{p_1} = \frac{MU_2}{p_2} = \frac{MU_3}{p_3} = \cdots$$

Assume p_2 falls by δp_2, and assume that the individual is deprived of his nominal increase in real income, $x_2 \delta p_2$. At the new price, $p_2 - \delta p_2$, the individual obtains a larger marginal utility per dollar from X_2 than from other commodities, hence he will substitute X_2 for other commodi-

[72] *Theory* (4th ed.), pp. 142 ff. In the Preface to the second edition he proposed broader applications much closer to those of Menger and Walras but never worked out this position.

[73] *Éléments*, pp. 131, 133.

ties. Restore now the increment of income $x_2 \delta p_2$, and it will be used to purchase more of every commodity, including x_2. The individual necessarily buys more X_2 at a lower price, and therefore all individuals buy more of X_2 at a lower price: the demand curve for each product must have a negative slope.[74]

A second application of utility theory was made in the theorem on the distribution of stocks: a redistribution of initial stocks of goods among the individuals in a market, such that each individual's holdings have the same market value before and after the redistribution, will not affect prices.[75] It is the amount of income, not its composition in terms of goods, that influences consumer behavior. The most interesting point with respect to this obvious theorem is that Walras stopped here on the threshold of the analysis of the effects of income upon consumption. One may conjecture that his penchant for analyzing what are essentially barter problems in his theory of exchange played a large role in this failure to analyze income effects.[76]

The theory of utility also led Walras to his theory of multiple equilibria.[77] This theory deals with the exchange of one commodity for another in a competitive market, when both commodities have utility to the individual.[78] The possessors of X_1 have a fixed stock—how much will they offer at various prices of X_1 (in terms of X_2)? When p_1 is zero (no X_2 is given in exchange for a unit of X_1), they will naturally supply no X_1; the supply curve begins at (or above) the origin. At higher p_1, they will offer more X_1 to obtain more X_2, but beyond a certain price, L, further increases in the price of X_1 will lead them to reduce the quantity of X_1 offered because they become relatively sated with X_2. Walras illustrates this with Figure 2, where D is the demand curve and S the supply curve. A' and A'' are points of stable equilibrium, because at

[74] The validity of this argument depends on the assumption that the marginal utility of a commodity is a (diminishing) function only of the quantity of that commodity (see Sec. IV).

[75] *Ibid.*, pp. 145–49.

[76] Perhaps mention should also be made of the applications of utility theory to labor. Jevons' theory of disutility was labored and at times confused (see my *Production and Distribution Theories* [New York: Macmillan, 1941], chap. ii). Walras' treatment was more elegant—he introduced the marginal utility of leisure in complete symmetry to the theory of consumption—but not much more instructive (*Éléments*, p. 209). Menger denied that labor was usually painful (*op. cit.*, p. 149 n.).

[77] Marshall's theory of multiple equilibria is independent of utility analysis; it refers only to the long run, whereas Walras' theory is strictly short run. See Marshall, *Pure Theory of Domestic Values* ("London School Reprints" [London, 1930]).

[78] *Éléments*, pp. 68–70; Wicksell restates the theory, *Lectures on Political Economy* (London: Macmillan, 1934), I, 55 ff.

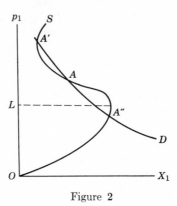

Figure 2

higher prices the quantity supplied exceeds the quantity demanded and at lower prices the quantity demanded exceeds the quantity supplied. Point A, however, is an unstable equilibrium because at higher prices the quantity demanded exceeds the quantity supplied so the price rises even more, and conversely at lower prices. We shall not follow the history of multiple equilibria, in which economists have usually taken an apprehensive pride.

In the area of welfare economics, Walras' most important application was the theorem on maximum satisfaction:

> Production in a market governed by free competition is an operation by which the [productive] services may be combined in products of appropriate kind and quantity to give the greatest possible satisfaction of needs within the limits of the double condition that each service and each product have only one price in the market, at which supply and demand are equal, and that the prices of the products are equal to their costs of production.[79]

This theorem, which is not true unless qualified in several respects, gave rise to an extensive literature which lies outside our scope.[80]

[79] *Éléments*, p. 231; Jevons also stated the theorem (*Theory* [4th ed.], p. 141).

[80] Among the important writings during our period are: A. Marshall, *Principles of Economics* (1st ed.; London: Macmillan, 1890), Book V, chap. vii; V. Pareto, "Il Massimo di utilità dato dalla libera concorrenza," *Giornale degli economisti*, Series 2, No. 9 (July, 1894), pp. 48–66; E. Barone, "The Ministry of Production in the Collectivist State," reprinted in F. A. Hayek, *Collectivist Economic Planning* (London: Routledge, 1938); K. Wicksell, *Lectures on Political Economy* (London: Macmillan, 1934), I, 72 ff.; L. Bortkewich, "Die Grenznutzentheorie als Grundlage einer ultra-liberalen Wirtschaftspolitik," *Jahrbuch für Gesetzgebung, Verwaltung und Volkswirtschaft*, XXII (1898), 1177–1216; and A. C. Pigou, *Wealth and Welfare* (London: Macmillan, 1912).

IV. THE FORM OF THE UTILITY FUNCTION

The three founders of the utility theory treated the utility of a commodity as a function only of the quantity of the commodity. If x_1, x_2, x_3, . . . , are the commodities, the individual's total utility was written (explicitly by Jevons and Walras, implicitly by Menger), as

$$f(x_1) + g(x_2) + h(x_3) + \cdot \cdot \cdot \cdot$$

They further assumed that each commodity yielded diminishing marginal utility. This form of utility function has the implication that the demand curve for each commodity has a negative slope, as I have already remarked. It has also the implication that an increase in income will lead to increased purchases of every commodity. This is easily shown with the fundamental equations,

$$MU_r = \frac{MU_1}{p_1} = \frac{MU_2}{p_2} = \frac{MU_3}{p_3} = \cdot \cdot \cdot \cdot$$

If income increases, the marginal utility of every commodity (and of income) must decrease, but the marginal utility of a commodity can be reduced only by increasing its quantity. This implication was not noticed.

Edgeworth destroyed this pleasant simplicity and specificity when he wrote the total utility function as $\varphi(x_1, x_2, x_3, \ldots)$. He appears to have made this change partly because it was mathematically more general, partly because it was congruent with introspection.[81] The change had important implications for the measurability of utility that I shall discuss in Section V.

With the additive utility function, diminishing marginal utility was a sufficient condition for convexity of the indifference curves;[82] with the generalized utility function, diminishing marginal utility was neither necessary nor sufficient for convex indifference curves.[83]

[81] *Mathematical Psychics*, pp. 20, 34, 104, 108.

[82] Diminishing marginal utility for each commodity was not necessary, however; the indifference curves could be convex to the origin if every commodity except one yielded diminishing marginal utility, and the marginal utility of this exception commodity did not increase too rapidly. This exceptional case was first analyzed by Slutsky (see Sec. VII).

[83] In the two-commodity case

$$\frac{dx_2}{dx_1} = - \frac{\varphi_1}{\varphi_2}$$

Nevertheless, Edgeworth unnecessarily continued to assume diminishing marginal utility, but he also postulated the convexity of the indifference curves.[84]

Even with convexity, the generalized utility function no longer has the corollary that all income curves have positive slopes (or, therefore, that all demand curves have negative slopes). After a price reduction, δp_2, we may again segregate the effect of a change in relative prices by temporarily reducing the individual's income by $x_2 \delta p_2$. When we restore this increment of real income, we cannot be sure that each commodity will be consumed in larger quantity. Suppose an increase in X_1 reduces the marginal utility of X_2. Then when a portion of the increment of real income $x_2 \delta p_2$ is spent on X_1, MU_2 may diminish so much that the amount of X_2 must be reduced below its original quantity to fulfill the maximum satisfaction conditions.[85]

---

is the slope of an indifference curve, and the condition for convexity is

$$\frac{d^2 x_2}{dx_1^2} = - \frac{\varphi_2^2 \varphi_{11} - 2\varphi_1 \varphi_2 \varphi_{12} + \varphi_1^2 \varphi_{22}}{\varphi_2^3} > 0,$$

where the subscripts to φ denote partial differentiation with respect to the indicated variables. It is clear that diminishing marginal utility (φ_{11} and φ_{22} negative) is not necessary for convexity, since φ_{12} can be positive and large, and it is not sufficient, since φ_{12} can be negative and large. In the additive case ($\varphi_{12} = 0$), at most one marginal utility can be increasing, as was pointed out in the previous footnote.

[84] *Mathematical Psychics*, p. 36. He wrote the utility function as $\varphi(x_1 - x_2)$, in my notation, for reasons which will be pointed out below. He postulated that $\varphi_{12} < 0$, where $-X_2$ is work done by the person and X_1 is remuneration received. This is equivalent to assuming that an increase in remuneration increases the marginal utility of leisure, and would be represented by $\varphi_{12} > 0$ if we write the function as $\varphi(x_1, x_2)$, as is now customary. With diminishing marginal utility this condition leads to convexity (see previous note).

[85] The conditions for maximum satisfaction are

$$\frac{\varphi_1}{\varphi_2} = \frac{p_1}{p_2},$$

$$x_1 p_1 + x_2 p_2 = R.$$

Differentiate these equations with respect to R (holding prices constant) and solve to obtain

$$\frac{\partial x_2}{\partial R} = \frac{p_2 \varphi_{11} - p_1 \varphi_{12}}{p_2^2 \varphi_{11} - 2p_1 p_2 \varphi_{12} + p_1^2 \varphi_{22}}.$$

The denominator of the right side is negative if the indifference curves are convex to the origin. The numerator, however, can be positive with $\varphi_{12} < 0$, so the whole expression may be negative (X_2 may be "inferior"). With the additive function, $\varphi_{12} = 0$ (and of course they assumed $\varphi_{ii} < 0$), so the expression must be positive (X_2 [and X_1] must be "normal"). Similarly, differentiate the equations with respect to p_2 holding p_1 and R constant) and solve to obtain

The only further generalization of the utility function (aside from questions of measurability) was the inclusion of the quantities consumed by other people in the utility function of the individual. Thus one's pleasure from diamonds is reduced if many other people have them (or if none do!), and one's pleasure from a given income is reduced if others' incomes rise. This line of thought is very old,[86] but it was first introduced explicitly into utility analysis in 1892. Fisher casually suggested it:

> Again we could treat [utility] as a function of the quantities of each commodity produced or consumed by *all persons* in the market. This becomes important when we consider a man in relation to the members of his family or consider articles of fashion as diamonds, also when we account for that (never thoroughly studied) interdependence, the division of labor.[87]

Henry Cunynghame made the same suggestion more emphatically in the same year:

> Almost the whole value of strawberries in March, to those who like this tasteless mode of ostenation, is the fact that others cannot get them. As my landlady once remarked, "Surely, sir, you would not like anything so common and cheap as a fresh herring?" The demand for diamonds, rubies, and saphires is another example of this.[88]

Pigou took up this argument, used it to show that consumer surpluses of various individuals cannot be added, but decided that these interrelationships of individuals' utilities were stable (and hence did not vitiate the consumer surplus apparatus) when the price changes were small.[89]

$$\frac{\partial x_2}{\partial p_2} = \frac{p_1\varphi_1 + x_2 p_1 \varphi_{12} - x_2 p_2 \varphi_{11}}{p_2{}^2 \varphi_{11} - 2p_1 p_2 \varphi_{12} + p_1{}^2 \varphi_{22}}$$

Again the denominator is negative, and the numerator may be negative if φ_{12} is negative, so the whole expression may be positive. With the additive utility function and diminishing marginal utility, the expression must be negative.

[86] E.g., A. Smith, *Theory of Moral Sentiments* (Boston: Wells & Lilly, 1817), Part III, chap. iii; Part IV, chap. i; N. F. Canard, *Principes d'economie politique* (Paris: Buisson, 1801), chap. v; Senior, *op. cit.,* p. 12.

[87] *Mathematical Investigations in the Theory of Value and Prices* (New Haven: Yale University Press, 1937—reprints of 1892 ed.), p. 102. Edgeworth (*ibid.,* Preface).

[88] "Some Improvements in Simple Geometrical Methods of Treating Exchange Value, Monopoly, and Rent," *Economic Journal,* II (1892), 37.

[89] "Some Remarks on Utility," *Economic Journal,* XIII (1903), 60 ff. He wrote the utility function of the individual as

$$U = \phi[x, y, z, w, K(ab)],$$

where x, y, z and w were quantities consumed by the individual, a_i was the quantity of x possessed by some other individual i, whose social distance was b_i, and K was a symbol "akin to, though not identical with, the ordinary Σ" (*ibid.,* p. 61).

It was only proper that Marshall's leading pupil should postulate the constancy of the marginal utility of prestige.

Pigou's article elicited the first statistical investigation designed to test a utility theory (and apparently the only such investigation during the period). Edgeworth, a Fellow of All Souls, collected statistics from "a certain Oxford College" to determine "whether the size of the party has any influence upon the depth of the potations"—that is, upon the per capita consumption of wine. The data were presented in relative form lest they "should excite the envy of some and the contempt of others"; the conclusion was that the effect of the size of party was inappreciable.[90]

A few subsequent attempts have been made to revive this extension of the utility function to include the effect on one person's utility of other people's consumption, but the main tradition has ignored the extension. This neglect seems to have stemmed partly from the obstacles it would put in the way of drawing specific inferences from utility analysis.

There remain three subordinate topics that may conveniently be discussed here. They are (a) the graphical exposition of the theory of the generalized utility function; (b) the attitude of contemporary economists toward Edgeworth's generalization; and (c) the Bernoulli hypothesis on the shape of the utility function.

A. INDIFFERENCE CURVES

With the introduction of the interrelationship of utilities of commodities, it was no longer possible to portray total utility graphically in two dimensions. Edgeworth devised indifference curves, or contour lines, to permit of a graphical analysis of utility in this case. In itself this was merely an expositional advance, but its merits summarization because of its great popularity in modern times and because it later invited attention to questions relating to the measurability of utility.

We restrict ourselves to the case of two commodities, as Edgeworth and almost everyone since has done in graphical analysis.[91] We define the indifference curve as the combinations of X_1 and X_2 yielding equal satisfaction, i.e., $\varphi(x_1, x_2)$ = constant. Edgeworth chose an asymmetrical graphical illustration of these curves that had a definite advantage for his purpose of analyzing bilateral monopoly. He let the abscissa represent the quantity of X_1 obtained by the individual, and the ordinate represent the quantity of X_2 given up.

It is evident that such indifference curves have a positive slope (if both commodities are desirable), for the individual will require more X_1

---

[90] *Papers Relating to Political Economy* (London: Macmillan, 1925), II, 323–24 n.

[91] The three commodity indifference surfaces are of course the limit of literal graphical exposition, and even they have been deemed unappetizingly complex.

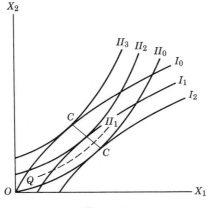

Figure 3

to offset (in utility) the loss of more X_2. In fact, the slope of the indifference curve with respect to the X_1 axis will be

$$\frac{dx_2}{dx_1} = \frac{MU_1}{MU_2}.^{92}$$

In addition, Edgeworth postulated that the indifference curves are concave to the X_1 axis.

Edgeworth's pioneer demonstration of the indeterminacy of bilateral monopoly will illustrate the advantage of this formulation.[93] A trader possessing X_2 but no X_1 would be at the origin; his indifference curves are those labeled I in Figure 3. The second trader, who possesses X_1 but no X_2, will have the corresponding indifference curves (II), for he will be giving up X_1 and acquiring X_2 in exchange. The points where the two sets of indifference curves are tangent form a curve, CC, which Edgeworth christened the contract curve. The ends of the contract curve are determined by the condition that no trader be worse off after trading than before, i.e., by the indifference curves, I_0 and II_0. The final contract between the traders must take place on this contract curve, because if it occurred elsewhere, it would be to the gain of one party, and not to the loss of the other, to move the curve. Thus point Q was not a tenable point of final contract because individual II can move from II_1 to the higher indifference curve II_2, while I remains on the same indifference

[92] For dx_1MU_1 will be the gain of utility from an increment dx_1, and dx_2MU_2 will be the loss of utility from a decrement dx_2, and these must be equal if the movement is along an indifference curve.

[93] *Mathematical Psychics,* pp. 20 ff.

curve, I_1. Any point on the contract curve is a position of possible equilibrium, and the precise position reached will be governed by "higgling dodges and designing obstinacy, and other incalculable and often disreputable accidents."[94]

Although this mode of exposition is convenient in the analysis of trade in two commodities between two individuals, it has no special advantage in the competitive case, and asymmetrical axes are awkward in algebraic analysis. Fisher introduced the new conventional graphical statement, in which the amounts held (or obtained) of the commodities appear on all axes.[95]

B. CONTEMPORARY PRACTICE

Despite the intuitive appeal of Edgeworth's generalized utility function, economists adhered to the additive utility function with considerable tenacity. In the nonmathematical writings, such as those of Böhm-Bawerk, Wieser, and J. B. Clark, the additive function was used almost exclusively. Barone defended it as an approximation.[96] Wicksell used it exclusively in his *Über Wert* (1894), although conceding the greater realism of the generalized function,[97] and found some place for it in his later *Lectures*.[98] Wicksteed used only the additive function in his *Alphabet* (1888)[99] and also in the elementary exposition of the theory in his *Common Sense* (1910) but not in the "advanced" statement.[100] Finally, Marshall and Pareto were so influential as to require more extended discussion.

Marshall also started with the Jevons-Walras assumption, to which he had properly arrived independently. This assumption was not explicit in the first edition of the *Principles* (1890), but one can cite evidence of its presence.

First, in his mathematical characterization of the utility function Marshall ignores any interdependence of utilities.[101] Second, he asserts the law of negatively sloping demand curves in all generality: "There is

---

[94] *Ibid.*, p. 46.

[95] *Op. cit.*, Part II.

[96] *Le Opere economiche* (Bologna: Zanichelli, 1936), I, esp. pp. 22–23.

[97] *Über Wert, Kapital and Rente* (Jena: Fischer, 1894), esp. p. 43.

[98] *Lectures on Political Economy*, I, 46–47, 55 ff.; however, the generalized function is preferred (*ibid.*, pp. 41–42, 48–49, 79 ff.).

[99] *Alphabet of Economic Science* (London: Macmillan, 1888).

[100] *Common Sense of Political Economy* (London: Routledge, 1934), Vol. I, chap. ii; Vol. II, chap. ii; the generalized function is used in Vol. II, chap. iii, esp. p. 479.

[101] *Principles of Economics* (London: Macmillan, 1890), Mathematical Notes II, III, VII, [I, II, VI]. References in brackets will be used for corresponding passages in the eighth edition.

then one law and only one law which is common to all demand schedules, viz. that the greater the amount to be sold the smaller will be the price at which it will find purchasers."[102] This is a corollary of diminishing marginal utility only if the utility function is additive. Third, he was prepared to measure the utility of all commodities as the sum of the individual utilities: "We may regard the aggregate of the money measures of the total utility of wealth as a fair measure of that part of happiness which is dependent on wealth."[103]

In the second edition (1891) the assumption became reasonably explicit:

> Prof. Edgeworth's plan of representing U and V as general functions of x and y has great attractions to the mathematician; but it seems less adapted to express the everyday facts of economic life than that of regarding, as Jevons did, the marginal utilities of apples as functions of x simply.[104]

The facts both of everyday life and of contemporary theory soon led Marshall to make serious qualifications of his theory but never to qualify this statement.

Even in the first edition Marshall had inconsistently recognized the existence of "rival" products, which were defined as products able to satisfy the same desires.[105] Fisher's discussion of competing and completing goods seems to have been the stimulus to Marshall to give more weight to interrelationships of utilities in the third edition of the *Principles* (1895).[106] Once persuaded, Marshall modified his theory on two points. The first was that he slightly modified his assertion of the universality of negatively sloping demand curves and in fact introduced the Giffen paradox as an exception.[107] The second alteration was in his treatment of consumers' surplus: "When the total utilities of two commodities which contribute to the same purpose are calculated on this plan, we

[102] *Ibid.*, pp. 159–60 [99].

[103] *Ibid.*, pp. 179–80, also Mathematical Note VII. His Mathematical Note III [II] also implies an additive function if his p, "the price which [a person] is just willing to pay for an amount [x] of the commodity . . ." is interpreted as our $x_1 p_1$ and the price to the person is treated as constant. See Sec. VII.

[104] *Loc. cit.*, p. 756 [845]. See also the deduction of diminishing marginal utility from negatively sloping demand curves (*ibid.*, p. 159 [101 n.]).

[105] See Sec. VI.

[106] Reference is there made to Fisher's "brilliant" book, precisely on this point (*Principles* [3d ed.; London: Macmillan, 1895], p. 460 n. [390 n.]). For Fisher's discussion see Sec. VI below.

[107] *Loc. cit.*, p. 208 [132]. See my "Notes on the History of the Giffen Paradox," *Journal of Political Economy*, LV (1947), 152–56.

cannot say that the total utility of the two together is equal to the sum of the total utilities of each separately."[108] No imporant changes were made thereafter.

These alterations were only patchwork repairs; Marshall did not reword his theory of utility. He retained to the last a theory constructed on the assumption of an additive utility function.

Pareto also conceded the validity of the Edgeworth generalization but continued to use chiefly the additive function in his early work.[109] Indeed, he offered the remarkable argument:

> One sees now that instead of being able to use the indicated properties of the final degree of utility to demonstrate what laws demand and supply must obey, it is necessary to follow the opposite path, and use the knowledge of such laws one may obtain from experience to derive the properties of the final degree of utility. One cannot rigorously demonstrate the law of demand, but rather, from the directly observable fact that demand diminishes with the increase of price we deduce the consequence that the final degrees of utility may each be considered—as far as this phenomenon is concerned—as approximately dependent only on the quantity of the commodity to which it is related.[110]

In the *Manuel*, however, he showed that the additive utility function leads to conclusions which are contradicted by experience,[111] but defended it as an approximation which was permissible for large categories of expenditure and for small changes in the quantities of substitutes or complements.[112] There is no reason to believe that this is true.

C. THE BERNOULLI HYPOTHESIS

The precise shape of the utility function received little attention in the main tradition of utility theory. Occasionally it was stated that the marginal utility of a necessity falls rapidly as its quantity increases and the like; and there were some mystical references to the infinite utility of subsistence. These were *ad hoc* remarks, however, and were not explicitly

---

[108] He added the less than candid footnote: "Some ambiguous phrases in earlier editions appear to have suggested to some readers the opposite opinion" (*loc. cit.*, p. 207 and n. [131 and n.]).

[109] Considerazioni sui principii fondamentali dell'economia politica pura," *Giornale degli economisti*, Series 2, Vol. V (August, 1892); *Cours d'économie politique* (Lausanne: Rouge, 1897), II, 332 ff.

[110] "Considerazioni sui principii fondamentali . . . ," *op. cit.*, VII (1893), 307.

[111] Below, Sec. VII.

[112] *Manuel d'économie politique* (2d ed.; Paris: Giard, 1927), pp. 253 ff., 274.

developed parts of the formal theory. Only one hypothesis about the marginal utility function ever achieved prominence: it was the Bernoulli hypothesis, which ultimately merged with the Weber-Fechner law, and to this literature we now turn.

In 1713 Nicholas Bernoulli proposed to a French mathematician, Montmort, five problems in probability theory,[113] one of which was equivalent to the following:

> Peter tosses a coin in the air repeatedly until it falls heads up. If this occurs on the first throw, he pays Paul $1.00; if this occurs first on the second throw, he pays $2.00; on the third throw, $4.00; on the fourth throw, $8.00; and on the nth throw, 2.00^{n-1}. What is the maximum amount Paul should pay for this game?

Montmort replied, perhaps too easily, "les deux derniers de vos cinq. Problemes n'ont aucune difficulte,"[114] for this was to become known as the St. Petersburg paradox.

Twenty-five years later Daniel Bernoulli introduced the paradox to fame.[115] Its paradoxical nature is easily explained: The probability of a head on the first throw is $\frac{1}{2}$, so the expected winning from the first throw is $\frac{1}{2}$ times $1.00, or $0.50. The probability of a first head on the second throw is $\frac{1}{4}$ ($\frac{1}{2}$ of tails on the first throw times $\frac{1}{2}$ of heads on the second), so the expected winning is $\frac{1}{4}$ times $2.00, or $0.50. The probability of a first head on the nth throw is $(\frac{1}{2})^n$, so the expected winnings are $(\frac{1}{2})^n$ times 2.00^{n-1}, or $0.50. Since these probabilities are exclusive, we add them to obtain the expected winnings from the game, which are $0.50 times the infinite possible number of throws. Thus the expected winnings of Paul are infinity—an excessive price for Paul to pay for the game, as even the mathematicians saw.

Bernoulli's solution was to take into account the diminishing marginal utility of money. In the later words of Laplace, he distinguished the mathematical from the moral expectation of a chance event upon which a sum of money depended: the moral expectation was defined as the sum of the products of the various advantages accruing from various sums of money times their respective probabilities.[116] To Bernoulli, "it appears in the highest degree probable" that each equal increment of

---

[113] P. R. de Montmort, *Essay d'analyse sur les jeux de hazard* (2d ed.; Paris: Quillau, 1713), p. 402.

[114] *Ibid.*, p. 407.

[115] In *Specimen theoriae novae de mensura sortis;* references are to the German translation, *Versuch einer neuen Theorie der Wertbestimmung von Glücksfällen* (Leipzig: Duncker & Jumblot, 1896).

[116] *Ibid.*, p. 27.

gain yields an advantage which is inversely proportional to the individual's wealth,[117] i.e.,

$$dU = k\frac{dx}{x},$$

where dU is the increment of utility resulting from an increment dx of wealth and k is a constant. It follows that total utility is a logarithmic function of wealth,

$$U = k \log \frac{x}{c},$$

where c is the amount of wealth necessary for existence.[118]

Bernoulli applied this formula to gambling, obtaining the now traditional result that mathematically fair bets are disadvantageous to both parties because the utility of the sum that may be gained is less than the utility of the sum that may be lost.[119] By a converse application, he calculated the maximum amount one should pay for insurance of specified risks.[120] Finally, he solved the paradox: a person with $1,000 should pay $6; etc.[121]

---

[117] *Ibid.*, pp. 27–28. Marshall properly remarked on the difficulties raised by the use of wealth instead of income (*Principles* [8th ed.], p. 842).

[118] On integrating the differential expression we obtain

$$U = k \log x + \text{constant},$$

and the constant is determined by the condition that, when wealth is at the subsistence level c, $U = 0$.

[119] *Op. cit.*, pp. 39–40.

[120] *Ibid.*, pp. 42–44.

[121] The moral expectation of the individual with initial wealth a is

$$U = \frac{1}{2} k \log \frac{a+1}{c} + 1k \log \frac{a+2}{c} + \frac{1}{8} k \log \frac{a+4}{c} + \cdots$$

$$= k \log \left(\frac{a+1}{c}\right)^{\frac{1}{2}} \left(\frac{a+2}{c}\right)^{\frac{1}{4}} \left(\frac{a+4}{c}\right)^{\frac{1}{8}} \cdots$$

$$= k \log \frac{v}{c},$$

where v is the sum of money whose utility equals the moral expectation. Hence

$$v = (a+1)^{\frac{1}{2}}(a+2)^{\frac{1}{4}}(a+4)^{\frac{1}{8}} \cdots$$

and $(v - a)$ is the sum of money whose utility equals the expected gain of utility from playing the game.

We should notice one further point in this beautiful memoir:

> If [the initial wealth] appears to be infinitely large relative to the greatest possible gain, the arc [of the total utility curve from initial wealth to initial wealth plus the gain] may be considered an infinitely short straight line, and in this case the usual rule [for calculating mathematical expectations] is again applicable. This case is closely approximated in all games in which relatively small sums are at stake.[122]

Thus Bernoulli suggested the assumption of a constant marginal utility of wealth for small variations of wealth.

We cannot follow the immense literature of the paradox in mathematics, but a few views may be noticed.[123] Some mathematicians—the foremost was Laplace[124]—accepted Bernoulli's solution. Some, like Poisson, solved the problem by taking into account Peter's inability to pay if he had a sufficiently long run of tails, so Paul should pay an amount for the game determined by Peter's fortune.[125] Perhaps the most amusing solution was one by Buffon, which was based on the "lemma" that all probabilities smaller than .0001 are equal to zero (because this was the probability of dying during the day for a man of fifty-six, which was commonly treated as negligible).[126] Cournot, here as in demand theory, refused to look at utility and resorted to the market evaluation of the game.[127]

Perhaps the most surprising characteristic of this literature to the economist is the mathematicians' chief requisite of a solution: that a finite value be found for the value of the game. This is the only merit one can attach to the "limited-fortune" solution of Poisson and others, and even its spurious plausibility depends upon the particular formula-

---

[122] *Op. cit.*, p. 33.

[123] For the eighteenth century see I. Todhunter, *A History of the Mathematical Theory of Probability* (London: Macmillan, 1865).

[124] *Théorie analytique des probabilities* (3d ed.; Paris: Gauthier-Villars, 1886), p. xix–xx, chap. x.

[125] S. D. Poisson, *Recherches sur la probabilité des jugements* (Paris: Bachelier, 1837), pp. 74–76. Thus if $F = 2^k$ is Peter's fortune, Paul's expected winnings are

$$\frac{1}{2} \cdot 1 + \frac{1}{4} \cdot 2 + \cdots + \frac{1}{2^k} \cdot 2^{k-1} + 2^k \left(\frac{1}{2^{k+1}} + \frac{1}{2^{k+2}} + \cdots \right) = \frac{k}{2} + 1.$$

[126] Todhunter, *op. cit.* At the present time the critical probability is .00005.

[127] *Exposition de la théorie des chances* (Paris: L. Hachette, 1843), pp. 108–9, 334. He reformulated the problem: the state (chosen to avoid Poisson's solution) issues tickets: No. 1 pays $1.00 if the first throw is heads; No. 2 pays $2.00 if the first heads comes on the second throw; etc. He argued that no one would buy the high-numbered tickets.

tion of the problem.[128] Bernoulli was right in seeking the explanation in utility (or, alternatively, as Cournot did, in market appraisals), and he was wrong only in making a special assumption with respect to the shape of the utility curve for which there was no evidence and which he submitted to no tests.[129]

In 1860 this line of thought was joined by the independent series of researches that culminated in the Weber-Fechner law. E. H. Weber had proposed the hypothesis: the just noticeable increment to any stimulus is proportional to the stimulus $(R - Reiz)$, or

$$\frac{dR}{R} = k.$$

Fechner made this constant of just noticeable differences the unit of sensation (S), to obtain

$$dS = C \frac{dR}{R},$$

or, integrating, $S = C \log R/R_0$, where R_0 is the threshold of sensation. Fechner performed a vast number of experiments on weight, temperature, tonal, and other types of discriminations which the formula fitted fairly well, and in the process he devised several methods of measurement (such as the constant method, in which Weber's k is determined by the proportion of [e.g.] "greater" to total responses in weight comparisons).[130] This was construed—by Fechner also—as proof of Bernoulli's hypothesis, with stimulus identified with income, sensation with pleasure.[131]

---

[128] J. Bertrand was surely right in this respect: "If one plays with centimes instead of francs, with grains of sand instead of centimes, with molecules of hydrogen instead of grains of sand, the fear of insolvency may be reduced without limit" (*Calcul des probabilités* [Paris: Gauthier-Villars, 1889], p. 64). Alternatively, one may alter the game, increasing the probability of longer runs and decreasing the rewards correspondingly.

[129] The arbitrariness is illustrated by the fact that the Genevese mathematician, Cramer, had suggested that the utility of income be taken as proportional to the square root of income, in a letter to Nicholas Bernoulli, from which Daniel Bernoulli quotes an extract (*op. cit.*, pp. 55 ff.). It should be noted that, unless the utility of income has an upper bound, it is possible to devise some variant of the St. Petersburg paradox which will have an infinite moral expectation.

[130] *Elemente der Psychophysik* (reprint; 2 vols.; Leipzig: Breitkopf & Härtel, 1889). See also E. G. Boring, *A History of Experimental Psychology* (New York: Appleton-Century, 1929), chap. xiii.

[131] *Psychophysik*, I, 236 ff.

We need not follow the detailed evolution of psychologists' treatment of the Fechner law. For decades it was a lively topic of discussion,[132] but for a generation or more it has been declining in importance. Many exceptions have been found to Fechner's formula.[133] The concept of sensation has been severely restricted in meaning, and the form of response of a subject was found to affect his sensitivity.[134] At present Fechner's *Elemente* is important chiefly for the basic methods of measurement he invented and improved.

Many economists in this later period noticed the Bernoulli or Weber-Fechner "laws." The majority simply referred to the hypothesis, favorably or otherwise, and made no real use of the theory. In this group we may list Edgeworth,[135] Pareto,[136] and Wicksell,[137] as well as many lesser figures.[138]

Marshall took the Bernoulli hypothesis much more seriously than did any other leading economist. In 1890 he was prepared to apply it directly to whole income classes:

> If however it should appear that the class affected [by a particular event] in the one case is on the average, say, ten times as rich as in the other, then we shall probably not be far wrong in supposing that the increment of happiness measured by a given sum of money in

[132] For a summary see E. B. Titchener, *Experimental Psychology* (New York: Macmillan, 1905), II, xiii–clxx.

[133] J. P. Guilford, *Psychometric Methods* (New York: McGraw-Hill Book Co., 1936), chaps. iv and v.

[134] H. M. Johnson, "Did Fechner Measure 'Introspectional' Sensations?" *Psychological Review*, XXXVI (1929), 257–84. Johnson reports a subject whose sensitivity was 18 per cent greater when distinguishing weights by voice than when distinguishing them by pushing the heavier weight toward the experimenter. It would be interesting to know the effect on sensitivity of pushing money.

[135] *Mathematical Psychics*, pp. 7, 62; *Papers*, I, 210; II, 107 ff. Edgeworth flirted with the theory at first but later rejected it as arbitrary and accepted the equally arbitrary view that the marginal utility of income falls faster than the Bernoulli hypothesis suggests.

[136] "Considerazioni . . . ," *Giornale degli economisti*, Series 2, VI (1893), 1–8. Pareto also deemed it arbitrary and pointed out that strictly it pertained to consumption, not to possessions.

[137] "Zur Verteidigung der Grenznutzenlehre," *Zeitschrift für die gesamte Staatswissenschaft*, LVI (1900), 580. Wicksell thought the Weber-Fechner work might eventually permit interpersonal comparisons of utility.

[138] E.g., O. Effertz, *Les Antagonismes économiques* (Paris: Giard & Biere, 1906), pp. 3032; he encountered the theory first at a beer party where a professor of physiology made a "humorous and detailed application to the consumption of beer" (F. A. Lange, *Die Arbeiterfrage* [5th ed.; Winterthur: Ziegler, 1894], pp. 113 ff., 143 ff.; F. A. Fetter, *Economic Principles* [New York: Century, 1915], pp. 40–41).

the one case is, so far at least as its direct results go, about one-tenth as great as in the other.[139]

Whatever the reason, this use of the hypothesis disappeared in the second edition, but lesser evidences of Marshall's affection for the Bernoulli theory persisted.[140]

A group of writers on tax justice, mostly Dutch, made considerable use of the theory in discussions of the ideal rate of income-tax progression.[141] The enthusiasm for the Bernoulli hypothesis diminished when it was discovered that it led to proportional taxation under the equal sacrifice doctrine (each taxpayer to sacrifice an equal amount of utility).[142] Although the doctrine of proportional sacrifice (each taxpayer to sacrifice an equal proportion of his utility) leads to progressive taxation with the Bernoulli utility function,[143] the minimum sacrifice doctrine (which insured progression if the marginal utility of income diminished) soon triumphed.

---

[139] *Principles* (1st ed., 1890), pp. 152–53; also p. 180.

[140] *Principles* (8th ed., 1920), pp. 135, 717, 842–43.

[141] For references and summaries see E. Sax, "Die Progressivsteuer," *Zeitschrift fur Volkswirtschaft, Sozialpolitik und Verwaltung*, I (1892), 43 ff.

[142] If $U = k \log R$, a tax of T involves a sacrifice of

$$k \log \frac{R}{R - T}.$$

On the equal sacrifice doctrine,

$$k \log \frac{R}{R - T} = \text{constant} = c,$$

$$\frac{R}{R - T} = e^{c/k},$$

so

$$\frac{T}{R} = e^{-c/k}(e^{c/k} - 1) = \text{constant}.$$

[143] Using the notation of the previous footnote, the doctrine requires that

$$\frac{k \log \dfrac{R}{R - T}}{k \log R} = \text{constant} = m$$

or

$$\frac{R}{R - T} = R^m,$$

whence

$$\frac{T}{R} = 1 - R^{-m}.$$

Two Italian writers used the logarithmic law in quantitative work: Gini, in the analysis of demand;[144] del Vecchio, in the analysis of budgetary data.[145] These studies belong in the history of demand theory, however; and we shall not discuss them here.

Max Weber's famous essay on the Weber-Fechner law is commonly, and perhaps properly, interpreted as a final demonstration that economists can ignore this law. Weber had three main points. First, the law does not hold in all cases ("Tiffany-Vasen, Klosettpapier, Schlackwurst, Klassiker-Ausgaben, Prostituierten . . ."). Second, the law refers to psychical reactions to external stimuli, whereas economics deals with observable behavior in response to subjective needs. Third, economics can get along with the empirical fact that man has limited means to satisfy competing ends and can allocate these means rationally to maximize the fulfillment of the ends.[146] This pungently written essay is hardly conclusive, however, on whether economists should adopt the law. This turns on whether it yields fruitful hypotheses concerning economic behavior. Since it does not,[147] it should not be used.

V. THE MEASURABILITY OF UTILITY

The first careful examination of the measurability of the utility function and its relevance to demand theory was made by Fisher.[148] He

---

[144] "Prezzi e consumi," *Giornale degli economisti,* Series 3, XL (1910), 99–114, 235–49.

[145] "Relazioni fra entrata e consumo," *Giornale degli economisti,* Series 3, XLIV (1912), 111–42, 228–54, 389–439.

[146] "Die Grenznutzlehre und das 'psychophysisches Grundgesetz,'" (1908) reprinted in *Gesammelte Aufsätze zur Wissenschaftslehre* (Tübingen: Mohr, 1922). The fundamental argument is in the third paragraph (pp. 361–68).

[147] As applied to commodities, it puts unrealistic limitations on the income elasticities; as applied to income, it implies that there will be no gambling.

[148] Walras had already pointed out that only the ratios of the marginal utilities enter into demand analysis:
"What are v_a, v_b, v_c, . . . [the exchange values]? They are absolutely nothing but the indeterminate and arbitrary terms which have meaning only in their proportionate relationship to one another. . . . Thus value in exchange is essentially relative, being always based upon marginal utility, which alone is absolute" (*Éléments,* pp. 139–40). He dropped the discussion at this point.
[G. B. Antonelli, an Italian engineer, anticipated some of the most important work in his *Sulla teoria matematica della economia politica* (Pisa, 1886), which has been reprinted in the *Giornale degli economisti e annali di economia,* X (N.S., 1951), 233–63, with expository articles by G. Demaria and G. Ricci. In this remarkable memoir, Antonelli investigates the possibility that, if an individual is ob-

TABLE 1

Increment of Milk

Symbol	Quantity (Cubic Inches)	Utility of Increment of Milk	Total Utility of Milk
Δm_1	3	1	1
Δm_2	4	1	2
Δm_3	5	1	3
Δm_4	6	1	4
Δm_5	7	1	5

solved the measurability problem quite satisfactorily for the case in which the marginal utilities of the various quantities are independent of one another.[149] His procedure was as follows:

Select arbitrarily a quantity of any commodity, say, 100 loaves of bread. Let the marginal utility of this quantity of commodity be the unit of utility (or util). Grant the ability of the individual to order the utilities of specified amounts of two goods, i.e., to indicate a preference (if one exists) or indifference between the two quantities. Then it is possible to construct the utility schedule of (say) milk. Start with no milk, and find the increment of milk (Δm_1) equivalent to the hundredth loaf of bread, i.e., the minimum amount of milk the individual would accept in exchange for the hundredth loaf of bread. Find a second increment (Δm_2), given the possession of Δm_1, equivalent to the hundredth loaf, etc. We obtain thus a schedule (or function) such as that given in Table 1. This function gives the amounts of milk necessary to obtain equal increments of utility; by interpolation we determine the amounts of utility obtained from equal increments of milk (Table 2).

---

served to consume various combinations at various prices, there exists a (utility) function which is maximized for these quantities. He demonstrates that such a function can always be found by integration when there are only two commodities and states the (integrability) conditions under which the function exists when there are three or more commodities. The sufficient conditions for a maximum are stated but not exploited to derive conditions on the demand functions. The complete lack of contemporary notice or effect is the only excuse for the brevity of these remarks. —Note added, 1964.]

[149] *Op. cit.*, pp. 11 ff.

TABLE 2

Milk (Cubic Inches)	Total Utility of Milk	Marginal Utility of Milk*
3	1.0000	—
6	1.7667	0.7667
9	2.4333	0.6667
12	3.0000	0.5667
15	3.4667	0.4667

* Per 3 cubic inches.

This initial choice of a unit is arbitrary, but this is not objectionable:

> Any unit in mathematics is valuable only as a divisor for a second quantity and constant only in the sense that the quotient is constant, that is independent of a third quantity. If we should awaken tomorrow with every line in the universe doubled, we should never detect the change, if indeed such can be called a change, nor would it disturb our sciences or formulae.[150]

Suppose now that the marginal utility of milk depends not only upon the quantity of milk but also upon the quantities of bread and beer—more generally, suppose the generalized utility function of Edgeworth holds. We could proceed as before in finding the quantities of milk, Δm_1, Δm_2, . . . , whose utilities equaled that of the hundredth loaf of bread. Let us now shift to the marginal utility of (say) 60 bottles of beer as our unit and proceed in identical fashion to find $\Delta m_1'$, $\Delta m_2'$, . . . , and thus measure the utility of milk in terms of beer. We shall find the new increments of milk, $\Delta m_1'$, $\Delta m_2'$, . . . , are not proportional to the old,[151] because the marginal utilities of beer and of bread will vary differently as the quantity of milk increases. Hence the total utility curve of milk will take on an entirely new shape, and not merely differ by a proportionality factor, when we change the commodity in terms of which it is measured. Thus we can no longer use this procedure to measure utility.[152]

Fisher concludes his brilliant dissertation with the argument that the total utility function cannot in general be deduced from the indifference curves and that, for purposes of explaining consumers' reactions to prices and income changes, there is no occasion to introduce total utility:

---

[150] *Ibid.,* p. 18.
[151] That is, $\Delta m_1 : \Delta m_2 : \Delta m_3 :$ . . . will not equal $\Delta m_1' : \Delta m_2' : \Delta m_3' :$ . . . .
[152] Fisher, *op. cit.,* p. 67.

Thus if we seek only the causation of the *objective facts of prices and commodity distribution* four attributes of utility as a quantity are entirely unessential, (1) that one man's utility can be compared to another's, (2) that for the same individual the marginal utilities at one consumption-combination can be compared with those at another, or at one time with another, (3) even if they could, total utility and gain might not be integrable, (4) even if they were, there would be no need of determining the constants of integration.[153]

Fisher's statement of the difficulty of constructing total utility functions from differential equations of the indifference curves was extremely concise,[154] and we shall elaborate it in connection with Pareto. We may note in passing that thirty-five years later Fisher qualified much of this argument. He was now willing to assume independence of utilities (at least for broad categories such as food and housing) and comparability of utilities of different persons—in order, apparently, to achieve concrete results applicable to income taxation.[155]

Pareto was the great proponent of doubts on the existence of unique utility functions and of the relevance of such functions to economic behavior. Apparently independently of Fisher, Pareto noticed the problem of the existence of a utility function as early as 1892.[156] Soon thereafter most of his basic mathematical theory was developed.[157] The import of

---

[153] *Ibid.*, p. 89.

[154] *Ibid.*, pp. 74–75, 88–89.

[155] See "A Statistical Method of Measuring 'Marginal Utility' and Testing the Justice of a Progressive Income Tax," in *Economic Essays Contributed in Honor of John Bates Clark* (New York: Macmillan, 1927), pp. 157 ff.

[156] "Considerazioni . . . ," *Giornale degli economisti*, Series 2, IV (1892), 415. He refers casually to the fact that when the differential equation of the indifference curve is of the form

$$Q(x, y)dx + R(x, y)dy,$$

"it may happen that $P[R]$ and Q are not partial derivatives of the same function and then the function will not exist." This was not quite correct: in the two-commodity case there always exists an integrating factor.

[157] "Considerazioni . . . ," *Giornale degli economisti*, Series 2, VII (1893). He introduces the index functions (p. 297), recognizes that it is always possible to integrate the differential equations when the marginal utilities are independent, and presents the integrability condition for the three-commodity case (p. 300). Let the differential equation of the indifference surface be

$$dx_1 + Rdx_2 + Sdx_3 = 0.$$

Then Pareto gives the integrability condition:

$$\frac{\partial R}{\partial x_3} = \frac{\partial S}{\partial x_2}.$$

the theory was realized only slowly, however: in the *Cours* (1896 and 1897) he was still willing to accept the interpersonal comparison of utilities for welfare purposes.[158] In the *Manuel* (1909), however, measurable utility had fallen into the background—of his theory, if not of his exposition. For Pareto, two questions on measurability were at issue.

The first, and to Pareto the major, problem is this: We can deduce the slopes of indifference curves at (in principle) all possible combinations of goods from the budgetary data, because the slopes of the price lines equal the ratios of the marginal utilities (slopes of indifference curves). Thus we obtain empirically the differential equation of the indifference curves. Can we integrate it to obtain the equation of the indifference curves?

Before we look at the mathematics, we may present the problem verbally. Will the choices that an individual makes between combinations of goods differing by infinitesimal amounts be consistent with the choice he makes between combinations differing by finite amounts? For example, the individual starts with the combination $100X_1$, $100X_2$, $100X_3$. By infinitesimal steps we obtain an infinite number of combinations, each equivalent to the preceding, reaching ultimately the combination $90X_1$, $85X_2$, $120X_3$. Will the individual consider this last combination equivalent to the first? The intuitive answer usually is: Yes, he is consistent in his preferences. The mathematical answer is equivalent: If the preference system displays a proper continuity, the equation is integrable. If we postulate indifference surfaces, there is no problem: then by hypothesis the infinitesimal comparisons are consistent with discrete comparisons. Economists have usually been willing to admit that the individual can well display this type of consistency. Pareto at times did likewise.[159]

He should have given,

$$\frac{\partial R}{\partial x_3} - \frac{\partial S}{\partial x_2} = S \frac{\partial R}{\partial x_1} - R \frac{\partial S}{\partial x_1}.$$

He also corrected the statement in the last footnote: "If there are only two economic goods, equation (52) is always integrable" (p. 299 n.). Subsequently he forgot this again (*Manuale di economia politica* [Milan: Piccola Biblioteca Scientifica, 1919—first published in 1906], pp. 499 ff.). He was gently reminded of it by V. Volterra, "L'Economia matematica," *Giornale degli economisti*, Series 2, XXXII (1906), 296–301.

[158] *Cours d'economie politique* (Lausanne: Rouge, 1897), II, 47–48. The comparisons were limited to types or classes of people to avoid personal idiosyncrasies. The measurability problem was referred to only incidentally (*ibid.*, I, 10 n.).

[159] *Manuel*, pp. 169 n., 264.

Mathematically, the issue is: Does the line integral of

$$f(x_1, x_2, x_3, \ldots) \, dx_1 + g(x_1, x_2, x_3, \ldots) \, dx_2$$
$$+ h(x_1, x_2, x_3, \ldots) \, dx_3 + \ldots = 0$$

exist independently of the path between the beginning and end points? Pareto's first two answers are Fisher's: (1) Yes, if f is a function only of x_1, g only of x_2. . . .[160] (2) Yes, if there exists an integrating factor, that is, if the integrability conditions are fulfilled.[161] He adds: (3) If the integrability conditions are not fulfilled, the integral depends on the order of integration, and if this is known the equation can be integrated.[162]

Pareto displayed a peculiar literalness of mind when he tried to translate this third case into economic terms. He identified the order of integration with the order of consumption of the goods.[163] This was absurd for precisely the same reason that dinner-table demonstrations of diminishing marginal utility are objectionable; they do not bear on the problems economics is interested in. Acts of consumption are of little concern; the purpose of the theory of consumption is to explain the pattern of consumption, not its episodes. Economics is usually interested only in the time rates of purchase and consumption of goods, and it is not interested in whether the soup precedes the nuts, or whether the consumer drinks three cups of coffee at breakfast or one after each meal, or pours them down the sink. The correct translation of the integrability problem was in terms of the consistency of consumer preferences, not of the temporal sequence of consumption.[164] Pareto indicated elsewhere that economics is interested in repetitive patterns of behavior, and we may view this discussion as a minor aberration.[165]

Given the indifference curves, we come to the second issue: Can we deduce a unique total utility surface? In general, "No." There are in general an infinite number of total utility surfaces whose contours constitute these indifference curves. If we construct one utility surface, we can get another by squaring the amounts of utility, another by taking

---

[160] *Ibid.*, pp. 545–46, 555; "Économie mathématique," *Encyclopédie des sciences mathématiques* (Paris: Gauthier-Villars, 1911), I, iv, 614.

[161] *Manuel*, pp. 545 ff.; "Économie mathématique," *op. cit.*, pp. 598 ff. The equations are

$$f\left(\frac{\partial h}{\partial x_2} - \frac{\partial g}{\partial x_3}\right) + g\left(\frac{\partial f}{\partial x_3} - \frac{\partial h}{\partial x_1}\right) + h\left(\frac{\partial g}{\partial x_1} - \frac{\partial f}{\partial x_2}\right) = 0,$$

and similarly for all triplets of goods.

[162] *Manuel*, pp. 553 ff.

[163] *Ibid.*, pp. 251, 270, 539 ff.

[164] Pareto might equally well have debated how one consumer can consume all goods at once, since the equality of marginal utilities divided by prices is a set of simultaneous equations.

[165] *Manuel*, p. 262.

the logarithm of utility, etc. So far as observable behavior is concerned, one utility surface will do as well as another. We shall return to this, Pareto's basic answer.

He gave also an introspective reply. We can construct a unique total utility function if the consumer can tell us the magnitude of the utility gained by moving from one indifference curve (I_1) to a second (I_2) relative to the utility gained by a move from I_2 to I_3. If he can tell us that the move from I_1 to I_2 gains (say) three times as much utility as the move from I_2 to I_3, then utility is "measurable." That is, if we have one utility surface, we may no longer submit it to transformations such as squaring the amount of utility—then we should have increased the utility of the move from I_1 to I_2 to *nine* times the utility of the move from I_2 to I_3. We can still take the utility function (U) and write it as $(aU + b)$, but this merely says that the origin and unit of measurement are arbitrary for utility just as they are for length and other measurements.[166] But Pareto believed the consumer could not rank utility differences.

He did not adhere to these views with consistency. The *Manuel* is strewn with passages that are meaningful only if utility is measurable. Two examples will suffice: First, Pareto's definitions of complementary and competing goods were dependent on the measurability of utility.[167] Second, the marginal utility of income was discussed at length.[168]

Yet much of the foregoing discussion is a digression from the viewpoint of Pareto's mature theory of utility. This digression reflects the heavy hand of the past, and it is justified (rather weakly) chiefly on expository grounds.[169] Fundamentally, Pareto argued that the differential equation of the indifference surface is given by observation and that this is all that is necessary to derive the demand functions:

> The entire theory . . . rests only on a fact of experience, that is to say, on the determination of the quantities of goods which constitute combinations which are equivalent for the individual. The theory of economic science thus acquires the rigor of rational mechanics; it deduces its results from experience, without the intervention of any metaphysical entity.
> [Edgeworth] assumes the existence of utility (ophelimity) and from it he deduces the indifference curves; I instead consider as empirically given the curves of indifference, and I deduce from them all that is necessary for the theory of equilibrium, without having recourse to ophelimity.[170]

[166] *Ibid.*, pp. 264–65.
[167] See below, Sec. VI.
[168] *Manuel*, pp. 579 ff.
[169] *Ibid.*, p. 160.
[170] *Ibid.*, pp. 160, 169 n.; see also pp. 539–44.

Observations on demand consistent with any utility function ϕ will also be consistent with an arbitrary utility index-function $F(\phi)$ so long as the order of preference among the combinations is preserved $[F'(\phi) > 0]$.[171]

Two mathematicians consolidated this position, that all notions of measurable utility could be eliminated from economics. W. E. Johnson demonstrated that the variation of quantity purchased with price and income was independent of the measurability of utility:

> This impossibility of measurement does not affect any economic problem. Neither does economics need to know the marginal (rate of) utility of a commodity. What is needed is a representation of the ratio of one marginal utility to another. In fact, this ratio is precisely represented by the *slope* of any point of the utility curve [indifference curve].[172]

Johnson thereafter dealt only with ratios of marginal utilities.

Two years later E. E. Slutsky published his magnificent essay on the equilibrium of the consumer.[173] To put economics on a firm basis, "we

[171] *Ibid.*, p. 542.

[172] "The Pure Theory of Utility Curves," *Economic Journal*, XXIII (1913), 490. Of course the first sentence is too strong. See M. Friedman and L. J. Savage, "The Utility Analysis of Choices Involving Risk," *Journal of Political Economy*, LVI (1948), 279–304.

[173] "Sulla teoria del bilancio del consumatore," *Giornale degli economisti*, Series 3, LI (1915), 1–26.

E. E. Slutsky was born in 1880 in Novom, Yiaroslavskoi Gubernii, and died in Moscow on March 10, 1948. As a student of mathematics at the University of Kiev in 1901, "because of his participation in an illegal meeting he was drafted as a soldier, and only a large wave of protests by students in the big cities of the country forced the government to return him to the University in the same year. At the beginning of the next year, 1902, E. E. was dismissed from the University without the right to study in any institution of higher education. Only after 1905 was he able to return to the University of Kiev, but this time he entered the law school. "This choice was dictated by E. E.'s desire to prepare himself for scientific work in the field of mathematical economics, an interest which he had developed from a thorough study of works of Ricardo, Marx, and Lenin. He finished at the law school in 1911, and received a gold medal for his final paper. However, because of his reputation for being 'unreliable' he was not asked to continue his academic career at the University." Thereafter he worked intensively in probability and mathematical statistics, teaching at the Institute of Commerce at Kiev from 1912 to 1926, when he went to Moscow "to work in a number of scientific research institutions of the capital."

This information is from N. Smirnov's obituary notice, *Izvestiya Akademiia Nauk SSSR* ("Mathematical Series"), XII (1948), 417–20, a translation of which was kindly made for me by Dr. Avram Kisselgoff.

must make it completely independent of psychological assumptions and philosophical hypothesis."[174] His utility function was accordingly an objective scale of preferences. Slutsky did not deny the interrelations of "economic" utility and "psychological" utility but sought to deduce empirical tests of any psychological hypotheses. If introspection suggests that the marginal utilities of commodities are independent, we can test the hypothesis by the equation it implies.[175] Slutsky assumes that the increment of utility obtained by moving from one combination to another is independent of the path of movement and offers an empirical test of its validity.[176] Conversely, he shows that a full knowledge of demand and expenditure functions is not sufficient in general to determine whether marginal utility diminishes.[177] The beauty and power of the essay are unique.

With Slutsky's development, introspection no longer plays a significant role in utility theory. There is postulated a function which the consumer seeks to maximize, and the function is given the characteristics necessary to permit a maximum. This is perhaps subjective in origin: the notion of maximizing behavior was probably derived from introspection, although it need not be. Slutsky posits such a function merely because it contains implications that observation can contradict, and hence yields hypotheses on observable behavior. We shall return later to the question whether this is an efficient method of obtaining hypotheses.

We have been marching with the vanguard; we retrace our steps now and examine the views of the other leading economists of the period on measurability.

A. CONTEMPORARY PRACTICE

None of the other leading economists of this period rejected the measurability of utility; we may cite Wicksteed,[178] Wicksell,[179] Barone,[180] Edgeworth,[181] and Pigou.[182] It is true that by the end of the period the leading economists were realizing that measurability of utility was not

---

[174] *Op. cit.*, p. 1.

[175] *Ibid.*, p. 25.

[176] *Ibid.*, pp. 3, 15–16. That is, the integrability condition is fulfilled.

[177] *Ibid.*, pp. 19–23.

[178] *Common Sense of Political Economy*, I, 148 ff.; II, 470, 473, 661.

[179] *Lectures*, I, 29 ff., 221; he apparently did not fully understand the Pareto analysis (see his review of the *Manuel, Zeitschrift für Volkswirtschaft, Sozialpolitik, und Verwaltung*, XXII [1913], 136 ff.).

[180] *Principi di economia politica* (Rome: Bertero, 1908), pp. 12–13, 22–24.

[181] *Papers*, II, 473 n., 475.

[182] *Wealth and Welfare* (London: Macmillan, 1912), *passim*.

essential to the derivation of demand curves, but they were loath to abandon the assumption. In part this reluctance was based on the desire to employ utility theory in welfare analysis; in part it was psychological theorizing. Yet with the passage of time, caution increased, as Marshall's evolution will illustrate.

Marshall was at first unqualified in his acceptance of the measurability of utility:

> Thus then the desirability or utility of a thing to a person is commonly measured by the money price that he will pay for it. If at any time he is willing to pay a shilling, but no more, to obtain one gratification; and sixpence, but no more, to obtain another; then the utility of the first to him is measured by a shilling, that of the second by sixpence; and the utility of the first is exactly double that of the second.
>
> The only measurement with which science can directly deal is that afforded by what a person is willing to sacrifice (whether money, or some other commodity, or his own labour) in order to obtain the aggregate of pleasures anticipated from the possession of the thing itself.[183]

Moreover, he fully accepted the intergroup comparisons of utility:

> Nevertheless, if we take averages sufficiently broad to cause the personal peculiarities of individuals to counterbalance one another, the money which people of equal incomes will give to obtain a pleasure or avoid a pain is an *extremely accurate* measure of the pleasure or the pain.[184]

Indeed, as we have already noticed, he believed that one can even compare the utilities of groups with different incomes, by using Bernoulli's hypothesis.

We need not trace in detail the growth of Marshall's caution and reticence in this area. He became unwilling to attribute precision to interpersonal comparisons.[185] The discussion of consumer surplus becomes increasingly defensive. Probably because of the growing criticism of hedonism, many terminological changes are made: "benefit" for "pleasure"; "satisfaction" for "utility"; etc. Bentham's dimensions of pleasure were approved at first;[186] they lose their sponsor and place in

---

[183] *Principles* (1st ed.), pp. 151, 154 n.

[184] *Ibid.*, p. 152. (My italics.) See also *ibid.*, p. 179.

[185] The Bernoulli hypothesis is no longer applied to social classes. The "extremely accurate" comparison of groups with equal incomes becomes "there is not in general any very great difference between the amounts of the happiness in the two cases [two events with equal money measures]" (*Principles* [8th ed.], p. 131).

[186] *Principles* (1st ed.), p. 153.

the text.[187] The distinction between desires and realized satisfactions becomes prominent.[188] Yet Marshall seems never to have been seriously skeptical of the measurability of utility, and the changes in his exposition were not accompanied by any change in the fundamentals of his theory.

VI. COMPLEMENTARITY

Jevons had noticed the case of "equivalent" (substitute) commodities and implicitly defined them by the constancy of the ratio of their marginal utilities.[189] In this he was inconsistent, for he treated the marginal utility of X_1 as dependent only on the quantity of X_1 in his general theory, whereas if X_1 and X_2 are "equivalent," the marginal utility of X_1 depends also on the quantity of X_2. One cannot define the usual relationships among the utilities of commodities with an additive utility function, so the utility theory of complementarity had to wait for Edgeworth's generalization of the utility function. In fact, it had to wait a little longer, for Edgeworth glossed over this problem in the *Mathematical Psychics*.

The first formal definition of the relationship between utilities of commodities was given by the remarkable Viennese bankers, Auspitz and Lieben:

The mixed differential quotient,

$$\frac{\partial^2 \phi}{\partial x_a \partial x_b},$$

indicates what influence (if any) an algebraic increase in x_b—a larger purchase or a smaller sale of B—has on the utility of the last unit of A purchased or not sold. If we consider the simplest case, in which only A and B are consumed,

$$\frac{\partial^2 \phi}{\partial x_a \partial x_b} \gtrless 0,$$

according as B complements the satisfaction derived from A, has no influence on it, or competes with A.[190]

Fisher repeated this definition and illustrated certain limiting cases by indifference curves. He defined two commodities to be perfect substitutes if the ratio of the marginal utilities of the amounts "actually consumed"

---

[187] *Principles* (8th ed.), p. 122 n.

[188] *Ibid.*, p. 92.

[189] *Theory of Political Economy*, p. 134.

[190] *Untersuchuchungen uber die Theorie des Preises* (Leipzig: Duncker & Humblot, 1889), p. 482; see also pp. 154 ff., 170 ff.

TABLE 3

		Total Utility Quantity of X_1		Marginal Utility of X_1
		1	2	
Quantity of X_2	1.......	3.0	5.4	2.4
	2.......	5.4	9.0	3.6

was absolutely constant; they were perfect complements if the quantities consumed were in a constant ratio.[191] Edgeworth gave the same criterion in 1897.[192]

Let us illustrate the use of this criterion with a numerical example. We may construct a table of total utilities as a function of the quantities of X_1 and X_2 and from it calculate the marginal utilities of X_1 (Table 3). Our example has been so chosen that the marginal utility of a given quantity of X_1 increases when the quantity of X_2 increases, hence X_1 and X_2 are complements.

Now let us construct a new table, in which total utility is equal to the logarithm of the total utility in Table 3. This is the kind of transformation we may make if utility is not measurable; it does not preserve the relative differences between utilities, but it preserves their order. We now find (Table 4) that by the same criterion, X_1 and X_2 are substitutes. We have shown that the criterion is ambiguous if utility is not uniquely measurable.[193]

Perhaps Fisher was so casual on this point because he saw the dependence of the definition on the measurability of utility, and Edgeworth was unconcerned because he believed utility was measurable. But

[191] *Mathematical Investigation*, pp. 65–66, 69, 70–71. The definitions of these limiting cases are independent of the existence of a unique utility function.

[192] He was so punctilious in acknowledging predecessors that his tone suggests independence of discovery. See "The Pure Theory of Monopoly," reprinted in *Papers*, I, 117 n. His criterion differed in one detail—ϕ was the utility function in terms of money and hence involved the marginal utility of money (the complicating effects of which were not discussed). This was not inadvertent; he desired symmetry with the definition of complementarity of products in production (*ibid.*, I, 127; II, 123). The Auspitz and Lieben definition was given later (*ibid.*, II, 464).

[193] Equivalently, let φ be a utility function, $F[\varphi]$ a transformation of it such that $F' > 0$. Then

$$U = F[\varphi(x_1, x_2)],$$
$$U_1 = F'\varphi_1,$$
$$U_{12} = F'\varphi_{12} + F''\varphi_1\varphi_2,$$

so F'' must be zero—the transformation must be linear—if the sense of the definition is to be preserved.

TABLE 4

		Total Utility Quantity of X_1		Marginal Utility of X_1
		1	2	
Quantity of X_2	1......	0.4771	0.7324	0.2553
	2......	0.7324	0.9542	0.2218

Pareto was inconsistent; he made extensive use of this definition at the same time that he was rejecting the measurability of utility.[194]

Marshall displayed greater inconsistency than Pareto, for he implicitly followed the Auspitz-Lieben definition even though he employed an additive utility function which did not permit of complementarity. Thus he speaks of "rival commodities, that is, of commodities which can be used as substitutes for it."[195] In the third edition this definition in terms of utility becomes reasonably explicit.[196] I suspect that Marshall was led into the inconsistency by his preoccupation with the role of rival and competing goods in production. That Pareto and Marshall adhered to the criterion is weighty testimony for its intuitive appeal.

W. E. Johnson supplied a definition of complementarity in terms of utility that was independent of the measurability of utility.[197] His criterion turned on the behavior of the slope of the indifference curve when one quantity was increased. That is to say, X_1 and X_2 are complements if the more of X_1 the individual possesses, the larger the increment of X_1 he will give up to obtain a unit of X_2.[198] For the fairly broad

[194] *Manuel*, chap. iv, pp. 576 ff.

[195] *Principles* (1st ed.), p. 160; see also pp. 438 and 178 n., with its accompanying Mathematical Note VI referring to "several commodities which will satisfy the same imperative want. . . ."

[196] "The loss that people would suffer from being deprived both of tea and coffee would be greater than the sum of their losses from being deprived of either alone: and therefore the total utility of tea and coffee is greater than the sum of the total utility of tea calculated on the supposition the people have recourse to coffee, and that of coffee calculated on a like supposition as to tea" (*loc. cit.*, p. 207 n. [131–32 n.]).

[197] *Op. cit.*, p. 495. See also Henry Schultz, *The Theory and Measurement of Demand* (Chicago: University of Chicago Press, 1938), pp. 608–14.

[198] The commodities are complements if both of the following inequalities hold:

$$\frac{\partial\left(\dfrac{\varphi_1}{\varphi_2}\right)}{\partial x_1} < 0, \qquad \frac{\partial\left(-\dfrac{\varphi_1}{\varphi_2}\right)}{\partial x_2} < 0.$$

They are substitutes if one of the inequalities is reversed; the stability condition (convex indifference curves) inhibits the reversal of both inequalities.

classes of commodities usually dealt with in budget studies, all commodities are probably complements on the Johnson definition. Slutsky
offered no definition of complementarity.[199]

It is difficult to see the purpose in Johnson's definition of complements,
or, for that matter, in more recent versions such as that of Hicks and
Allen. They cannot be applied introspectively to classify commodities
(as the Auspitz-Lieben definition could be), so they offer no avenue to
the utilization of introspection. Hence no assumption concerning their
magnitude or frequency is introduced into the utility function—except
for the condition that their frequency and magnitude be consistent with
the assumption of stability.[200] As a result, such criteria can be applied
concretely only if one has full knowledge of the demand functions. If
one has this knowledge, they offer no important advantage over simple
criteria such as the cross-elasticity of demand; if one does not have
this knowledge, the simple criteria are still often applicable. The chief
reason for presenting criteria in terms of utility, I suspect, is that, when
familiar names are given to unknown possibilities, an illusion of definiteness of results is frequently conferred.

VII. THE DERIVATION OF DEMAND FUNCTIONS

Walras' derivation of the demand curves from utility functions was
complete and correct for the generalized utility function of Edgeworth
as well as for the additive utility function. But Walras passed from
utility to demand intuitively and failed to demonstrate that any limitations on demand curves followed from the assumption of diminishing
marginal utility.

Pareto was the first to make this logical extension of utility theory.
Working with the simple additive utility function, he showed in 1892
that diminishing marginal utility rigorously implies that the demand
curves have negative slopes.[201] A year later he partially solved the prob-

---

[199] His compensated variation of price is intimately related to the later definition
of Hicks and Allen.

[200] Thus, in the two-commodity case, both commodities cannot be substitutes on
Johnson's definition; however, neither need be.

[201] "Considerazioni . . . ," *Giornale degli economisti,* Series 2, V (1892), 119 ff. His
demonstration is equivalent to ours (above, Sec. IIII). He also suggested the analysis
of the problem of the simultaneous variation of all prices—which can be made
equivalent to an income variation—but did not solve the problem explicitly (*ibid.,*
p. 125). As we have noticed (Sec. IV), under the less stringent assumption of a
convex utility function, one commodity can have a positively sloping demand curve.

lem when the marginal utilities of the commodities are interdependent.[202] He could no longer deduce any meaningful limitation on the slope of the demand curve, and dropped the analysis. In the *Cours* he went further and argued that the demand curve for wheat may have a positive slope.[203]

A corresponding derivation of the effect of a change in income on the consumption of a commodity was presented in the *Manuel*, but Pareto gave no explicit mathematical proof and the analysis has generally been overlooked:

> If we assume that the ophelimity of a commodity depends only on the quantity of that commodity that the individual consumes or has at his disposal, the theoretical conclusion is that, for such commodities, consumption increases when income increases; or, at the limit, that the consumption is constant when income exceeds a certain level. Consequently, if a peasant subsists only on corn, and if he becomes rich, he will eat more corn, or at least as much as when he was poor. He who has only one pair of sabots a year because they are too expensive, may when he becomes rich use a hundred pairs, but he will always use one pair. All this is in manifest contradiction to the facts: our hypothesis must therefore be rejected . . . .[204]

Despite this admirable test of the hypothesis of independent utilities, Pareto continued to find some use for the additive utility function.

Pareto also made a number of minor applications of utility theory to demand analysis. He showed that the demand and supply curves cannot be linear when there are three or more commodities and that the demand curve of a commodity cannot have constant elasticity when there are three or more commodities. Both demonstrations rested on the independence of the marginal utilities of the commodities.[205] We shall notice later his analysis of the constancy of the marginal utility of money.

Fisher had shown graphically in 1892 that if the utility function is not additive, an increase in income may lead to decreased consumption of a commodity.[206] The compatibility of negatively sloping income curves with convex indifference curves was first shown mathematically by W. E. Johnson.[207] Johnson also demonstrated that a rise in price may lead to an increase in the quantity of the commodity purchased.[208] Moreover,

---

[202] "Considerazioni . . . ," *Giornale degli economisti,* Series 2, VII (1893), 304–6. This is equivalent to our illustration (Sec. IV).

[203] *Cours, II,* 338. The discussion was hypothetical, employing the same argument that Marshall used for the Giffen case.

[204] *Manuel,* pp. 273–74.

[205] "Économie mathématique," *Encyclopedie,* I, iv, 616 ff.

[206] *Mathematical Investigations,* pp. 73–74.

[207] *Op. cit.,* p. 505.

[208] *Ibid.,* p. 504.

Johnson was first to carry through the explicit analysis of utility with the use only of the ratios of marginal utilities. His exposition was concise and peculiar, however, and was slow to receive attention.[209]

The complete and explicit analysis of the general case was given in lucid form by Slutsky.[210] We may illustrate his general logic with a numerical example. Let the individual consumer buy

100 units of X_1 at $1.00, a cost of $100,

60 units of X_2 at $0.75, a cost of $45,

exactly equaling his income of $145. Let now the price of X_1 rise to $1.10. Then the apparent deficiency of income, in Slutsky's language, is 100 times $0.10 = $10, for this is the amount that must be added to the individual's income to permit him to purchase the former quantities. If, simultaneously with the rise in the price of X_1, we give the individual $10, Slutsky calls it a compensated variation of price. Although the individual experiencing a compensated rise in the price of X_1 can still buy the same quantities, he will always substitute X_2 for X_1, because X_2 is now relatively cheaper: Slutsky demonstrated that this is a consequence of the convexity of the indifference curves.[211] The individual will move to perhaps

86.36 units of X_1 at $1.10, a cost of $95,

80.00 units of X_2 at $0.75, a cost of $60.

The changes in quantities

$$86.36 - 100 = -13.64 \text{ units of } X_1,$$

$$80.00 - 60 = -20.00 \text{ units of } X_2,$$

[209] A good discussion was given by Edgeworth, *Papers,* II, 451 ff.

[210] It is summarized by Schultz, *op. cit.,* chapts. i, xix; R. G. D. Allen, "Professor Slutsky's Theory of Consumers' Choice," *Review of Economic Studies,* February, 1936. Slutsky takes the equation,

$$d^2\varphi = \varphi_{11}dx_1{}^2 + \varphi_{22}dx_2{}^2 + \ldots + 2\varphi_{12}dx_1dx_2 + \ldots$$

and by a linear transformation puts it in the canonical form,

$$d^2\varphi = A_1da^2 + A_2db^2 + A_3dc^2 + \ldots.$$

He carries through two analyses, one for all $A_i < 0$, called the normal case, and a second for one $A_i > 0$, called the abnormal case. If two or more A_i are positive, $d^2\varphi$ will not be negative along the budget constraint (*op. cit.,* pp. 4–5).

[211] More precisely, he demonstrated that it is a consequence of the stability of the maximum the consumer has achieved (Slutsky, *op. cit.,* p. 14, Eq. 52).

were called the residual variabilities. If now we withdraw the $10 of income used to compensate for the variation in price, the individual may move to, say,

80 units of X_1 at $1.10, a cost of $88,

76 units of X_2 at $0.75, a cost of $57.

In our example the individual reduces the quantities of both goods when income falls; Slutsky calls such goods relatively indispensable. Had X_1 been relatively dispensable, the decline in income of $10 would have led to a rise in the quantity purchased, conceivably sufficient to offset the residual variation. We have thus the laws of demand:

1. The demand for a relatively indispensable good is necessarily normal, that is to say, it diminishes when its price increases and rises when the price diminishes.
2. The demand for a relatively dispensable good may in certain cases be abnormal, that is to say, it increases with the increase of price and diminishes with its decrease.[212]

In addition, he deduced integrability equations connecting the effects of the price of X_1 on X_2 and the price of X_2 on X_1:

$$\frac{\partial x_1}{\partial p_2} + x_2 \frac{\partial x_1}{\partial R} = \frac{\partial x_2}{\partial p_1} + x_1 \frac{\partial x_2}{\partial R}.^{213}$$

And so we have fulfilled the historian's wish: the best has come last.

MARSHALL

Marshall constructed a demand curve superior to Walras' for empirical use but related it to utility by an exposition less than masterly. This demand curve was of the form

$$x_i = f(p_i, R, I),$$

where I is an index number of all prices. Marshall assumed, of course, that tastes are fixed.[214] The constancy of the "purchasing power of money" (the reciprocal of our I) is an assumption governing the entire

[212] Ibid., p. 14.
[213] Ibid., p. 15.
[214] Principles (1st ed.), p. 155 [94]: "If we take a man as he is, without allowing time for any change in his character. . . ."

Principles, and it is specifically reaffirmed in the discussion of demand.[215] The role of money income is clearly recognized.[216]

I interpret I in Marshall's equation as an index number representing the average price of all commodities excluding X_i. Then his demand curve differs from the Walrasian demand curve in that he holds constant the average of other prices rather than each individual price. Changes in I may be measured by an index number embracing all commodities (including X_i), as in effect Marshall proposes, but only at the cost of inconsistency: when all prices except p_i are constant, I will vary with p_i. Unless the expenditure on X_i is large relative to income, and unless its price varies greatly, however, the quantitative error will be small.[217] We could eliminate this inconsistency (and certain ambiguities too) in Marshall's treatment by interpreting I as the average of all prices, so real income is held constant along the demand curve.[218] But then we should encounter new inconsistencies.[219]

Marshall insists that the prices of rival goods be held constant.[220] This proviso is troublesome to reconcile with his utility theory but not to explain. The reconciliation is troublesome because rival goods are defined in terms of utility and cannot exist with an additive utility function.[221] (We can of course eliminate this difficulty by generalizing the utility function or shifting to a definition of rival products in terms of demand cross-elasticities.) The purpose of the proviso is obvious, however; when p_i rises, consumers will shift to close rivals, and their prices will tend to rise even if the price level is stable, so the effect of changes only in p_i on purchases of X_i will be obscured.[222]

[215] "Throughout the earlier stages of our work it will be best . . . to assume that there is no change in the general purchasing power of money" (*ibid.*, p. 9 [62]).

[216] In addition to a reference discussed below (*ibid.*, p. 155 [95]), we may cite Book III, chap. iii [iv], with its discussion of rich and poor buyers and the "disturbing cause." "Next come the changes in the general prosperity and in the total purchasing power at the disposal of the community at large" (*ibid.*, p. 170 [109]).

[217] It is sufficient, Marshall says, to "ascertain with tolerable accuracy the broader changes in the purchasing power of money" (*ibid.*, p. 170 [109]); elsewhere he proposes to do this with an index number of wholesale prices (*Memorials*, pp. 207–10).

[218] See M. Friedman, "The Marshallian Demand Curve," *Journal of Political Economy*, LVII (1949), 463–95.

[219] Examples are the Giffen paradox and the statement that, in cases of multiple equilibria, consumers prefer to buy the quantity at the largest intersection of the supply and demand curves (*Principles* [1st ed.], p. 451 n. [472 n.]).

[220] "One condition which it is especially important to watch is the price of rival commodities . . ." (*ibid.*, p. 160 [100]). Complements' prices were added in the second edition (*loc. cit.*, p. 158 [100 n.]).

[221] See Sec. VII.

[222] Marshall also assumes in effect that the anticipated future price equals the present price (Principles [1st ed.], p. 161).

This Marshallian demand curve can be derived by the conventional Walrasian technique simply by grouping together all commodities except the one under consideration and identifying their price with the price level.[223] But then what is the role of that famous assumption, the constancy of the marginal utility of money (income)? The answer is that this additional assumption is quite indispensable to his textual instruction on how "to translate this Law of Diminishing Utility into terms of price."[224] Marshall moves directly and immediately from marginal utility to demand price by the (implicit) equation,

$$MU_i = \text{constant} \times p_i,$$

and adds, "so far we have taken no account of changes in the marginal utility to [the buyer] of money, or general purchasing power."[225] The assumption of constancy of the marginal utility of money is essential to his exposition of the relationship between utility and demand curves, and essential also to the substance of the apparatus of consumers' surplus. But it is not essential to the Marshallian demand curve if expositional simplicity is sacrificed.

Precisely what does Marshall mean by the constancy of the marginal utility of income? He tells us (in Book V!):

> There is a latent assumption which is in accordance with the actual conditions of most markets; but which ought to be distinctly recognized in order to prevent its creeping into those cases in which it is not justifiable. We tacitly assumed that the sum which purchasers were willing to pay, and which sellers were willing to take for the seven hundredth bushel would not be affected by the question whether the earlier bargains had been made at a high or a low rate. We allowed for the diminution in the marginal utility of corn to the buyers as the amount bought increased. But we did not allow for any appreciable change in the marginal utility of money; we assumed that it would be practically the same whether the early payments had been at a high or a low rate.
>
> The assumption is justifiable with regard to most of the market dealings with which we are practically concerned. When a person

---

[223] No explicit derivation was given along these lines, but one can be read into Mathematical Note III [II].

[224] The phrase, but not the thought, dates from the second edition (*loc. cit.*, p. 151 [94]).

[225] *Principles* (1st ed.), p. 155 [95]. In the first edition this was the only explicit statement of the assumption in the book on demand; but see also Mathematical Note VI with its cross-reference to pp. 392–93 [334–35]. After the quoted sentence, Marshall discusses the effect of income on the marginal utility of money but is eloquently silent on the effect of price changes.

buys anything for his own consumption, he generally spends on it a small part of his total resources; while when he buys it for the purposes of trade, he looks to re-selling it, and therefore his potential resources are not diminished. In either case the marginal utility of money to him is not appreciably changed. But though this is the case as a rule, there are exceptions to the rule.[226]

It seems beyond doubt that Marshall treated the marginal utility of money as approximately, and not rigorously, constant, and fairly clear that it is constant with respect to variations in the price of a commodity whose total cost is not too large a part of the budget.

The large volume of writing on Marshall's assumption adds an ironical overtone to our phrase "expositional simplicity." Some of the studies have been concerned with the implications of strict constancy.[227] Pareto and Barone gave such interpretations in our period.[228] The approximate constancy of the marginal utility of income has also been discussed.[229] Pareto skirted such an interpretation;[230] it can be elaborated to show that approximate constancy has no implications beyond those already implicit in the additive utility function.[231] The asumption looms large in economic literature but marks a fruitless digression from the viewpoint of the progress of utility theory.

[226] *Ibid.*, pp. 392–93 (334–350); see also (p. 132).

[227] See M. Friedman, "Professor Pigou's Method for Measuring Elasticities of Demand from Budgetary Data," *Quarterly Journal of Economics*, L (1935), 151–63; P. A. Samuelson, "Constancy of the Marginal Utility of Income," in Oscar Lange *et al.* (eds.), *Studies in Mathematical Economics and Econometrics* (Chicago: University of Chicago Press, 1942), pp. 75–91.

[228] In 1892 Pareto argued that the assumption implied that each demand curve has unitary elasticity; "Considerazioni . . . ," *Giornale degli economisti*, Series 2, IV (1892), 493. In 1894 Barone made a more elaborate analysis and reached a similar conclusion: *Le Opere*, I, 48. A few months later he offered a second interpretation: when p_i varies, money income varies by an amount equal to the change in expenditure on X_i (*ibid.*, pp. 59 ff.).

[229] N. Georgescu-Roegen, "Marginal Utility of Money and Elasticities of Demand," *Quarterly Journal of Economics*, L (1936), 533–39.

[230] *Manuel*, pp. 582 ff.; "Économie mathématique," *op. cit.*, p. 631.

[231] Let X_1 be the commodity, X_2 all other commodities. I interpret Marshall to mean that the rate of change of the marginal utility of X_2 is small relative to the rate of change of the marginal utility of X_1, or—introducing prices to eliminate the units in which commodities are measured—that

$$\frac{\varphi_{22}p_1{}^2}{\varphi_{11}p_2{}^2}$$

is approximately zero.

A. THE ABANDONMENT OF UTILITY

Demand functions, as we have already noticed, had been treated as empirical data in the classical economics and in the work of economists such as Cournot.[232] Gustav Cassel was the first of the modern theorists to return to this approach. His theory was developed in 1899 and never changed thereafter in essentials.[233] He attacked the utility theory along two lines.

His first and constructive thesis was that one can employ demand functions directly, without a utility substructure:

> The individual has a value scale in terms of money, with which he can not only classify his needs but also express numerically their intensities. . . . If I adopt the fiction that the needs of individuals A and B are of the same intensity, if both value a given need at one mark, then I have extracted from the psychological assumptions everything that is relevant to the economic side of the matter.[234] The subjective element which we seek to isolate is the relationship between valuation and external factors [income and prices]. In order to discover this relationship, we must allow the external factors to vary; then the value of the individual attributes to the good in question will also vary. This value is therefore a function of the external factors, and in this functional relationship we have the complete and pure expression of the subjective element, that is, of the nature of the individual so far as it affects the formation of prices.[235]

But Cassel made no studies of the properties of the demand functions.

No doubt it was psychologically inevitable that Cassel had also a second thesis: that the utility theory was full of error. This theory, he charged, required a unit of utility that no one could define;[236] it required unrealistic divisibility of commodities and continuity of utility functions;[237] it required, or at least always led to, meaningless inter-

---

[232] A. A. Cournot, *Mathematical Principles of the Theory of Wealth* (New York: Macmillan, 1929), esp. chap. iv.

[233] "Grundriss einer elementaren Preislehre," *Zeitschrift für die gesamte Staatswissenschaft*, LV (1899), 395 ff.; cf. *The Theory of Social Economy* (New York: Harcourt, Brace, 1932), esp. pp. 80 ff., where the tone is much more gentle and conciliatory.

[234] "Grundriss . . . ," pp. 398–99.

[235] *Ibid.*, p. 436.

[236] *Ibid.*, pp. 398 ff.

[237] "The fact is, that every person who is even moderately well off buys the greater part of the articles he uses for much less than the value they have for him" (*ibid.*, p. 417).

personal comparisons of utility;[238] the assumption of constancy of the marginal utility of money is meaningless or objectionable;[239] etc.

Wicksell quickly replied for the utility theorists and with sufficient vigor to estrange Cassel for life.[240] He properly pointed out the weaknesses in Cassel's criticisms of the marginal utility or interpersonal comparisons except for welfare analyses; that Cassel's discontinuity objections were unrealistic and in any event did not affect the substance of the theory; etc. Wicksell also properly pointed out the considerable use of utility language in Cassel's positive theory and his implicit use of utility to reach welfare conclusions. And, finally, Wicksell criticized Cassel for his rough treatment of predecessors on the rare occasion when he recognized them at all—a charge that was exaggerated but not unfounded.[241]

But Wicksell did not meet the substantive claim of Cassel that it was possible to start directly with demand functions and that the utility theory added no information on the nature of these functions. He seemed content at this point merely to argue that the utility theory incorporated reliable psychological information into economics.[242]

Barone employed the same empirical approach to demand in his famous article on collectivist planning:

There is no need to have recourse to the concepts of *utility*, of the *final degree of utility*, and the like; and neither is it necessary to have recourse to Pareto's concept of the *Indifference Curve*. . . .

. . . the *tastes* of the various individuals. On these last we will make no presupposition, no preliminary inquiry, limiting ourselves simply to assuming the fact that at every given series of prices of products and productive services, every single individual portions out the income from his services between consumption and saving in a certain manner (into the motives of which we will not inquire) by which, at a given series of prices, the individual makes certain demands and certain offers. These quantities demanded and offered vary when the series of prices vary.

Thus we disengage ourselves from every metaphysical or subtle

---

[238] *Ibid.*, p. 402.

[239] *Ibid.*, pp. 428–29.

[240] "Zur Verteidigung der Grenznutzenlehre," *Zeitschrift für die gesamte Staatswissenschaft*, LVI (1900), 577–91; amplified in some respects in "Professor Cassel's System of Economics," reprinted in *Lectures*, I, 219 ff. Cassel replied in an appendix to "Die Preduktionskostentheorie Ricardos," *Zeitschrift für die gesamte Staatswissenschaft*, LVII (1901), 93–100.

[241] Cassel was not the equal of Pareto in this respect (see especially the latter's "Économie mathématique").

[242] "Zur Verteidigung . . . ," p. 580.

conception of utility and of the functions of indifference, and rely solely on the authenticity of a fact.[243]

Yet Barone is not an important figure in the movement to abandon utility. He employed this approach only in the one article,[244] and there perhaps chiefly to bring out the analogies between competitive and collectivist economies. What is more important, he did not discuss the crucial problem: Can one say more about the demand functions if they are derived from utility functions?

One final theorist of the period consistently ignored utility in his work on demand—Henry L. Moore. It was Moore's program to join economic theory with the then recent developments of statistical theory to quantify the important economic functions. In this lifelong task he has found no assistance in utility theory and paused only briefly to criticize it:

> In the closing quarter of the last century great hopes were entertained by economists with regard to the capacity of economics to be made an "exact science." According to the view of the foremost theorists, the development of the doctrines of utility and value had laid the foundation of scientific economics in exact concepts, and it would soon be possible to erect upon the new foundation a firm structure of interrelated parts which, in definiteness and cogency, would be suggestive of the severe beauty of the mathematico-physical sciences. But this expectation has not been realized. . . .
> The explanation is to be found in the prejudiced point of view from which economists regarded the possibilities of the science and in the radically wrong method which they pursued. . . . Economics was to be a "calculus of pleasure and pain," "a mechanics of utility," a "social mechanics," a *"physique social."* . . . They seemed to identify the method of physical sciences with experimentation, and since, as they held, scientific experimentation is impossible in social life, a special method had to be devised. The invention was a disguised form of the classical *caeteris paribus*, the method of the static state.[245]

This is not the place to quarrel with certain aspects of Moore's methodological views, nor is it the place to discuss the deficiencies in his statistical work on demand, nor is it the place to give him his due as a major figure in the history of demand theory. It is a suitable place, however, to conclude our history of the theory of utility.

[243] "The Ministry of Production in the Collective State" (1908), translated in F. A. Hayek, *Collectivist Economic Planning* (London: Routledge, 1938), pp. 246, 247.

[244] Conventional utility analysis is used in his *Principi di economia politica,* Part I.

[245] *Economic Cycles: Their Law and Cause* (New York: Macmillan, 1914), pp. 84–86.

VIII. A THEORY OF ECONOMIC THEORIES

We have before us a fairly complete account of the major developments in one branch of economic analysis. I wish now to review this
history with a view to isolating the characteristics of successful (and
hence of unsuccessful) theories, where success is measured in terms of
acceptance by leading economists. (It would require a different history
to answer the interesting question: To what extent, and with what time
interval, do the rank and file of economists follow the leaders?) The
bases on which economists choose between theories may be summarized
under the three headings of generality, manageability, and congruence
with reality.

A. THE CRITERION OF GENERALITY

The successful theory was always more general than the theory it
supplanted. The marginal utility theory was more general than the
classical theory of value (with its special cases of producible and non-
producible goods); the generalized utility function was more general
than the additive utility function; the non-measurable utility function
was more general than the measurable utility function. On the other
hand, the Bernoulli hypothesis was rejected as arbitrary (i.e., par-
ticularizing). There was no important instance in which a more specific theory supplanted a more general theory, unless it was Marshall's
assumption of the constant marginal utility of money, and this assumption had little vogue outside Cambridge circles.

What does generality mean here? Occasionally it is simply an application of Occam's razor, of using a weaker assumption that is sufficient
to reach the conclusion in which one is interested. The nonmeasurable
utility function was the leading instance of this kind of generality,
although I shall argue below that perhaps logical elegance was not the
major reason for abandoning measurability. Very seldom has Occam's
razor beautified the face of economic theory.

More often, generality meant the encompassing of a wider range of
phenomena. The marginal utility theory enabled economists to analyze
the values of non-producible goods and the short-run values of producible goods. The generalized utility function allowed the analysis of
interrelationships of the marginal utilities of commodities, which previously had been outside the domain of utility theory.

Yet we must note that generality is often only verbal, or at least ambiguous. The Walrasian theory was more general than the Ricardian theory in that the former applied to both producible and non-producible goods, but it was less general in that it took the supply of labor as given. Cassel's empirical demand curves seemed more general in that they were valid even if every element of utility theory was banished;[246] but the utility theorist Wicksell could reply that the utility theory was more general because it permitted welfare judgments. Unless one theory encompasses all the variables of the others, their order of generality will vary with the question in hand.

Generality, whether formal-logical or substantive, is a loose criterion by which to choose among theories. It is always easy and usually sterile to introduce a new variable into a system, which then becomes more general. Yet a more general theory is obviously preferable to a more specific theory if other things are equal, because it permits of a wider range of prediction. We turn now to the other things.

B. THE CRITERION OF MANAGEABILITY

The second criterion employed in choosing between theories has been manageability. Economists long delayed in accepting the generalized utility function because of the complications in its mathematical analysis, although no one (except Marshall) questioned its realism. They refused to include in the individual's utility function the consumption of other individuals, although this extension was clearly unimportant only in the social life of Oxford. The non-integrable differential equation of the indifference curves was similarly unpopular. In these cases manageability was the prime consideration: economists tacitly agreed that it is better to have a poor, useful theory than a rich, useless one.

Of course, this is true, although the choice is not really this simple as a rule. Manageability should mean the ability to bring the theory to bear on specific economic problems, not ease of manipulation. The economist has no right to expect of the universe he explores that its laws are discoverable by the indolent and the unlearned. The faithful adherence for so long to the additive utility function strikes one as showing at least a lack of enterprise. I think it showed also a lack of imagination: no economic problem has only one avenue of approach; and the non- and semi-mathematical utility theorists could have pur-

---

[246] Actually he put sufficient conditions on his demand functions to make them logically equivalent to those derived from indifference curves (see H. Wold, "A Synthesis of Pure Demand Analysis," *Skandinavisk Aktuarietidskrift,* XXVII [1944], 77 ff.).

sued inquiries suggested by theories beyond their powers of mathematical manipulation.[247] The investigator in his science is not wholly dissimilar to the child in his nursery, and every parent has marveled at how often unreasoning obstinacy has solved a problem.

C. THE CRITERION OF CONGRUENCE WITH REALITY

The criteria of generality and manageability are formal; the empirical element entered through the criterion of congruence with reality. It was required of a new theory that it systematize and "explain" a portion of the empirical knowledge of the times. It must perform tasks such as accounting for the fact that often goods sold for less than their costs of production (which the marginal utility theory did) or for liking bread more when there was butter on it (which the generalized utility function did).

The reality with which theories were required to agree was one of casual observation and general knowledge. It was composed of the facts and beliefs that the men of a time mostly share and partly dispute and of the observations of men who earned and spent incomes and watched others do so. Of course the type and amount of such information varied widely among economists. Some, like Marshall, had a deep knowledge of their economies; others, like Edgeworth and Pareto, were more worldly scholars; still others, like Walras and the young Fisher, kept the world at a distance.

This casual knowledge was loose and relatively timeless with respect to utility theory; these economists knew little more about utility and not a great deal more about demand than their ancestors. In this respect utility theory is not wholly representative of economic theory; in population theory, for example, casual knowledge changed radically with the times and exercised a decisive influence on the comparative acceptabilities of various population theories. The one changing element in the general knowledge was the growing skepticism of hedonism in academic circles. Economists were surely (if improperly) more susceptible to the proposal to abandon the measurability of utility when the psychologists chided them:

> Important as is the influence of pleasures and pains upon our movements, they are far from being our only stimuli. . . . Who

---

[247] E.g., the generalized utility function suggested studies of the interrelations of prices in demand; the effect of other people's consumption on one's utility suggested the use of relative income status rather than absolute income in demand analysis; etc.

smiles for the pleasure of smiling, or frowns for the pleasure of the frown? Who blushes to avoid the discomfort of not blushing?[248]

The sieve of casual knowledge was broad in its gauge. It could reject the notion (of Cassel) that consumers do not equate marginal utilities divided by prices because they do not know the prices, or the notion (of the abstemious Fisher) that the marginal utility of liquor increases with quantity. But it could not reject even the imaginary Giffen paradox. Casual knowledge is better calculated to detect new error than to enlarge old truth.

This third criterion of congruence with reality should have been sharpened—sharpened into the insistence that theories be examined for their implications for observable behavior, and these specific implications compared with observable behavior. The implication of the diminishing marginal utility of money, that people will not gamble, should have been used to test this assumption, not to reproach the individuals whose behavior the theory sought to describe.

Not only were such specific implications not sought and tested, but there was a tendency, when there appeared to be the threat of an empirical test, to reformulate the theory to make the test ineffective. Thus, when it was suggested that there might be increasing marginal utility from good music, as one acquired a taste for it, this was interpreted as a change in the utility function.[249] Yet if in the time periods relevant to economic analysis this phenomenon is important, it is a significant problem—the defenders had no right to rush to the dinner table. When it was suggested that the marginal utility of the last yard of carpet necessary to cover a floor was greater than that of fewer yards, the theory was modified to make the covering of the entire floor the unit of utility analysis.[250] They did not anxiously seek the challenge of the facts.

In this respect Pareto was the great and honorable exception. Despite

---

[248] William James, *Psychology* (New York: Holt, 1893), p. 445. William McDougall was more emphatic and pointed (as well as absurd and illogical): "Political economy suffered hardly less from the crude nature of the psychological assumptions from which it professed to deduce the explanations of its facts and its prescriptions for economic legislation. It would be a libel, not altogether devoid of truth, to say that the classical political economy was a tissue of false conclusions drawn from false psychological assumptions. And certainly the recent progress in economic science has largely consisted in, or resulted from, the recognition of the need for a less inadequate psychology" (*An Introduction to Social Psychology* [3d ed.; London: Methuen, 1910], pp. 10–11).

[249] Marshall, *Principles* (8th ed.), p. 94; Wicksteed, *Common Sense,* I, 85.

[250] Marshall, *Principles* (8th ed.), p. 94; Wicksteed, *Common Sense,* I, 83; Pareto, *Manuel,* p. 266.

much backsliding and digression, he displayed a constant and powerful instinct to derive the refutable empirical implications of economic hypotheses. He was the first person to derive the implications of the additive utility function, but Pareto—and he alone of the economists—constantly pressed in this direction.

But exception he was. The ruling attitude was much more that which Wieser formulated:

> Any layman in economics knows the whole substance of the theory of value from his own experience, and is a layman only in so far as he does not grasp the matter theoretically—i.e., independently, and for and by itself—but only practically—that is to say, in some given situation, and in connection with its working out in that situation. If this be true, how else shall be better proved our scientific statements than by appealing to the recollection which every one must have of his own economic actions and behavior?[251]

That this criterion was inadequate was demonstrated by the slowness with which utility theory progressed. The additive utility function was popularized in the 1870s; it was 1909 before the implication of positively sloping income curves was derived. The generalized utility function was proposed in 1881; it was 1915 before its implications were derived. The chief of these implications is that, if consumers do not buy less of a commodity when their incomes rise, they will surely buy less when the price of the commodity rises. This was the chief product—so far as hypotheses on economic behavior go—of the long labors of a very large number of able economists. These very able economists, and their predecessors, however, had known all along that demand curves have negative slopes, quite independently of their utility theorizing.

Had specific tests been made of the implication of theories, the unfruitfulness of the ruling utility theory as a source of hypotheses in demand would soon have become apparent. Had these economists sought to establish true economic theories of economic behavior—that is, to isolate uniformities of economic events that permitted prediction of the effects of given conditions—they would not long have been content with the knowledge that demand curves have negative slopes. They would have desired knowledge on the relative elasticities of demand of rich and poor, the effects of occupation and urbanization on demand, the role of income changes, the difference between short- and long-run reactions to price changes, and a whole host of problems which we are just beginning to study. They would have given us an economic theory which was richer and more precise.

These remarks shall have been completely misunderstood if they are

[251] *Op. cit.*, p. 5.

read as a complaint against our predecessors' accomplishments. It would be purposeless as well as ungracious to deprecate their work. They improved economics substantially, and, until we are sure we have done as much, we should find gratitude more fitting than complaint. But we should be able to profit not only from their contributions to economics but also from their experiences in making these contributions. That such able economists were delayed and distracted by the lack of a criterion of refutable implications of theories should be a finding as useful to us as any of the fine theoretical advances they made.

PART III

Utility and the Classical Theory of Demand

THE UTILITY CONCEPT IN VALUE THEORY AND ITS CRITICS

Jacob Viner

The utility theory of value is primarily an attempt to explain price-determination in psychological terms. Some traces of the recognition of the existence of psychological determinants of price can be found throughout the history of value theory. But for our immediate purpose, it will suffice to begin with the English classical school. The classical economists borrowed from the language of common sense the term "utility," and gave to it the technical meaning of the capacity of a good to satisfy desire. They claimed that the existence of utility was pre-essential to the existence of exchange value. It was in costs of production, however, that they found the ultimate[1] determinants of exchange values, and they used ambiguously both psychological (labor pain, abstinence) and objective (money expenditures, hours of labor) concepts of cost. Under the influence of Jevons, Walras, and the Austrians, writing in the seventies and eighties, but with predecessors ignored by their contemporaries,[2] the emphasis was shifted to demand, and demand was derived from the utility of the classical school, but with the latter concept now elaborated into a psychological law of diminishing utility and with special emphasis on marginal utility, or the utility of terminal units in the order of acquisition or consumption, as the ultimate determinant of exchange value. Jevons and the Austrians, however, failed to distinguish clearly between utility schedules and individual demand schedules, and by expressing utility schedules in monetary terms, they practically identified them with demand schedules, with the consequence that they reasoned from equivalence of price-offers by different persons to equivalence of utility for these persons. In this respect, their predeces-

---

[1] Ultimate, that is, in so far as concerned the scope of their analysis.
[2] Notably, W. F. Lloyd in England, 1834; Dupuit in France, 1843; Gossen in Germany, 1854.

Source: Reprinted with permission from the *Journal of Political Economy,* XXXIII:369–387 (August 1925).

sors, Lloyd[3] and Gossen,[4] but not Dupuit,[5] were more acute in their analysis. This error was, however, soon discovered and corrected, especially by the mathematical economists of the utility school.[6] Recognition of and allowance for the difference between the psychological utility schedule and the objective individual schedule of price-offers is now to be found in the writings of all the competent contemporary exponents of the utility theory.[7] Jevons, Walras, and the Austrians either explicitly rejected or ignored the claims of disutility or "pain costs" as an independent determinant of price and explained money costs as a derivative of demand, leaving marginal utility as the sole ultimate determinant. But with few exceptions,[8] the present-day exponents of the utility theory accept disutility as a co-ordinate factor with utility in the determination of price.[9] Under the leadership of Marshall, there later became evident a tendency to shift emphasis from marginal utilities to utility schedules as a whole as factors in the determination of price.

The utility theory, upon the completion of these stages in its development, appeared to have attained its final form, and it has undergone

[3] W. F. Lloyd, *A Lecture on the Notion of Value* (London, 1834), p. 28.

[4] H. H. Gossen, *Entwickelung der Gesetze des menschlichen Werkehrs* (reprint of 1889), pp. 82, 83.

[5] *Vide* Léon Walras, *Éléments d'Économie Politique Pure* (4th ed., Lausanne, 1900), pp. 446, 447.

[6] Cf., for example, Alfred and Mary Paley Marshall, *Economics of Industry* (2d ed.; London, 1881), pp. 69–70 (the first edition was not available for examination); P. H. Wicksteed, *Alphabet of Economic Science* (London, 1888), pp. 68 ff. Walras apparently had been in possession of the correct doctrine in 1873, when he published his first work (see the Preface to his *Éléments d'Économie Politique Pure*, 2d ed., Lausanne, 1889).

[7] Cf., however, B. M. Anderson, *Social Value* (Boston, 1911), chap. v and *passim*, who attributes to the Austrian school and its followers a constant confusion between demand curves and utility curves. In his anxiety to make an impressive list of the utility theorists who have gone astray in this manner, he even includes Marshall and Davenport, who have been particularly expert in avoiding the error. Some glaring and notorious examples of the error have, however, escaped him.

[8] For England, Wicksteed, and for the United States, Alvin Johnson (and Fetter?) appear to be the sole important surviving upholders of the original Austrian position.

[9] Bohm-Bawerk himself, in reply to critics of his doctrine, disclaimed that he had ever rejected disutility as an independent determinant of price, but explained that he had merely ignored it as not being in controversy at the time. He conceded that it was a theoretically co-ordinate factor with utility, though practically of minor importance, in determining price ("The Ultimate Standard of Value," *Annals of the American Academy* [Sept., 1894], pp. 23 ff.; "One Word More on the Ultimate Standard of Value," *Economic Journal* [Dec., 1894], pp. 720, 721). His concessions were inadequate, however, to satisfy his critics, and are hard to reconcile with many passages in his earlier writings.

no modification of importance in the last thirty years or so. In its developed form it is to be found sympathetically treated and playing a prominent role in the exposition of value theory in most of the current authoritative treatises on economic theory by American, English, Austrian, and Italian writers.[10]

In the scientific periodicals, however, in contrast with the standard treatises, sympathetic expositions of the utility theory of value have become somewhat rare. In their stead are found an unintermittent series of slashing criticisms of the utility economics. Its psychology, it is alleged, is obsolete; its logic faulty; its analysis and conclusions tainted with class bias; its service to economic enlightenment nil. The critics vie with one another in finding terms sufficiently vigorous to express to the full their dissatisfaction with it. To cite some characteristic examples: "The hocus-pocus of marginal utility does not explain price";[11] the utility theory is enmeshed in a vicious maze of circular reasoning,[12] "serious injury has been wrought in economic theory by the pernicious concept of utility dragged into economics by Jevons and the Austrians," which "adds nothing to that of value and should be abandoned";[13] "Marginal-utility economics . . . has not contributed and it cannot contribute to the elucidation of any practical problem."[14] The critics are not in doubt as to the damaging effect of their criticisms. As one of them says:[15] "The descriptive powers of some newcomers in the theoretical field have been brought to bear on accepted doctrine with devastating consequences. The results might almost be called an expose."

On some points the critics could be set off against one another, some crediting to the utility economics, as its only contributions, what others attack as its chief errors. But on one point the critics are in unison, in

[10] In France and Germany the developed utility theory has many exponents, but has never attained the position of the dominant value theory.

[11] R. G. Tugwell, "Human Nature in Economic Theory," *Journal of Political Economy* (June, 1922), p. 330.

[12] B. M. Anderson, *Social Value, passim;* O. F. Boucke, "A Unique Situation in Economic Theory," *American Economic Review* (Dec., 1922), p. 603.

[13] F. H. Knight, "Normal Price in Value and Distribution," *Quarterly Journal of Economics* (Nov., 1917), pp. 67 and 70 n. Knight has subsequently recanted somewhat, however. Cf. *ibid.* (Nov., 1921), p. 146.

[14] E. H. Downey, "The Futility of Marginal Utility," *Journal of Political Economy* (April, 1910), p. 268.

[15] Tugwell, *op. cit.*, p. 319. A critic of an older generation can be cited whose "descriptive powers"—more explicitly, his command of the vocabulary of derogation—surpassed even that of these "newcomers," and who was even more outspoken in his expression of contempt for the intellectual caliber of the utility economics. Cf. H. M. Hyndman, *The Economics of Socialism* (London, 1896), chap. vii, "The Final Futility of Final Utility."

the refrain if not always in the pitch, and that is that the utility theory rests on an unsound psychology. The heart of the utility economics is the law of diminishing utility, which maintains that any person acquiring or consuming successive units of a good without important intermission of time will derive from each successive unit less "utility," or "pleasure," or "gratification," or "satisfaction," or "benefit," or "ophelimity," or "capacity to satisfy desire, than he derived from the preceding one.[16] To use this law in the explanation of the mode of determination of particular exchange values or prices, it is necessary to establish a causal sequence between it and price. The utility theorist commonly does this in elliptical fashion and by resort to the assumption or argument, generally implicit, that the intensity of desire for objects is governed by and is quantitatively a more or less accurate reflection of the utility or satisfaction-yielding power of the objects. It is this leap from utility to desire that involves the psychological reasoning which the critics allege to be hedonistic and rationalistic. The causal sequence, fully expressed, is, according to the utility theorists, from (1) a potential or future schedule of diminishing utility of successive units of a good to (2) a more or less accurate and conscious anticipation of this utility schedule, to (3) a corresponding desire schedule, to (4) a comparison, unit by unit, with the desire for what must be given in exchange for this good if it is to be obtained, which gives (5) an individual demand schedule in terms of the price-good, which compounded with the demand schedules of other persons gives (6) the market demand schedule, which is a determinant of (7) price.

The critics deny the reality of this alleged sequence. The hedonism and rationalism which it implies, they assert, are either wholly absent from human behavior or are not dominant characteristics of it. They point out that men commonly seek, not utilities nor pleasure, but objects and that they do not commonly engage in deliberative and careful comparisons and calculations of the units of pleasure which successive units of the same good, or units of different goods, or units at different stages of removal from the present, will yield to them. They ridicule the notion that man's desires are held in leash and spring into action only after completion of fine actuarial comparisons of the hedonic potentialities of different commodities.

Modern psychology is clearly on the side of the critics. Men do not ordinarily have pleasure, or even pleasures, as the realized object of their desires. Human behavior, in general, and presumably, therefore,

---

[16] Utility theorists have used all of the terms listed above, and few of them have consistently used one term only. For our present purposes, we may take them as substantially synonymous.

also in the market place, is not under the constant and detailed guidance of careful and accurate hedonic calculations, but is the product of an unstable and unrational complex of reflex actions, impulses, instincts, habits, customs, fashions, and mob hysteria. In the light of modern psychology, "Let reason be your guide" is apparently a counsel of unapproachable perfection.[17] The utility economics, as ordinarily formulated, is bad psychology. But what of it? How vital is its dependence upon its erroneous psychology? How extensive would be the changes required in its mode of analysis and its conclusions of all of its psychological elements which were in conflict with the current fashions in psychological doctrine were either brought into accordance with it or ruthlessly excised? The critics, of course, have said that the utility economics stands or falls with its psychology, but have they made their case?

THE UTILITY CONCEPT IN PRICE-ECONOMICS

Many of the utility theorists in the main confined their value theory within the limits of price-economics; that is, they made it their chief, if not their sole, concern to explain the mechanism of price-determination, without appraising that mechanism from an economic welfare on other ethical or quasi-ethical standpoint. They probed into the psychological background of objective market demand because they desired more light on the character and the origin of demand and not because they were interested in the consumer's psychology per se. This can, at least, be inferred from the fact that the earliest systematic exponents of the developed utility theory, notably Gossen, Jevons, Walras, Bohm-Bawerk, and Wicksteed, used the law of diminishing utility and the concept of marginal utility only or mainly as a means of introducing and finding a causal background of negatively sloping demand schedules and market-price equilibria,[18] and to explain why, in the terms of the

[17] Though utility economists have pointed out that too fine and constant calculation as to the comparative desirability of alternatives would itself be ill advised from a rational point of view because of the mental wear-and-tear which would result. Cf. Wicksteed, *Alphabet of Economic Science*, p. 129; H. J. Davenport, *Economics of Enterprise*, p. 101 n.

[18] In this connection, confirmation is offered by Pareto's development of a theory of price-determination, on the basis of Edgeworth's "indifference curves" or series of equilibria of individual preference as between combinations of different commodities, which carries the analysis of the mechanism of price-determination behind pecuniary demand schedules without using or reaching utility schedules (Vilfredo Pareto, *Manuel d'Economie Politique* [Paris, 1909], pp. 168 ff.).

current conventional graphics, the market demand schedule always (or as a rule) "slopes downward and to the right." In so far as concerns the main stream of doctrinal development, the clear notion of demand schedules appears to have been the contribution of the utility theorists and to have been suggested by the prior concept of diminishing utility schedules.[19] As has already been pointed out, some of the earlier utility theorists did not distinguish clearly between utility curves and pecuniary demand schedules.

I can find no evidence in the writings of the early utility theorists to support the thesis of many of the critics that they found their utility doctrines ready to hand in the contemporary psychology and that they used these psychological doctrines as major premises from which to derive a priori their price-theories. Their writings do not show any special acquaintance with the psychological speculations current at the time. The references in the earlier literature to psychological sources are very few in number, and not otherwise important. The critics have at times taken for granted that the economists derived their law of diminishing utility from the Weber-Fechner law of the psychologists and have assumed that if they demonstrated, as could readily be done, that psychologists as a rule apply the law to the sensations only, and not to feelings, they had removed from under the utility theory of value the foundation upon which it rested.[20] I can find little evidence that the early utility theorists had ever heard of this law.[21] The resemblance between the Weber-Fechner law and the law of diminishing utility, such as it is, seems to be due to similar but independent processes of observation or to coincidence, but not to direct derivation of the latter from the former. The law of diminishing utility, whether sound or not,

[19] Cournot, of course, had given clear mathematical expression to the schedule concept of demand without relating it to utility, but the early utility theorists were not acquainted with his work.

[20] For a recent example, see A. J. Snow, "Psychology in Economic Theory," *Journal of Political Economy* (Aug., 1924), pp. 493 ff., who refers to Dickinson's appeal to the Weber-Fechner law as if it were a typical example.

[21] The only citation to the Weber-Fechner law that I have encountered in the early literature of the utility theory is by F. Y. Edgeworth in his *Mathematical Psychics* (London, 1881), p. 62. His reference to the law, however, is only by way of analogy, and he plainly recognizes that acceptance to the Weber-Fechner law does not necessarily lead to acceptance of the law of diminishing utility. The only recent instances I can find of economists in the utility tradition who appeal to this law for support of their value doctrines are F. A. Fetter (Economic Principles [1915], p. 42), G. P. Watkins (*Welfare as an Economic Quantity* [1915], p. 26), and Z. C. Dickinson (*Economic Motives* [1922], pp. 233, 234).

has been developed by the economists as a product of their own observation and has not been borrowed from psychology.[22]

Wherever the utility economists may have obtained their psychology, however, it cannot be gainsaid that it is faulty. But for the price-economist who wishes merely to make a first contact between objective price and human psychology, much of the theorizing with respect to utilities, and certainly all the hedonistic and rationalistic elements herein, are irrelevant to his purpose. If there be substituted for the law of diminishing utility a law of diminishing desire—or if utility be defined and used to signify desire—if all references to gratification, satisfaction, benefit, pleasure, pleasantness, pain, irksomeness, and unpleasantness be eliminated, there will remain sufficient to supply an immediate psychological background for the concept of the negatively inclined pecuniary demand schedule, and therefore for the explanation of the mode of determination of market price. Diminishing desire need be referred to only to explain diminishing price-offers as quantity available increases.[23] The variations between the demand schedules for a commodity of different persons can be explained as due either to differences in the intensity of their respective desires or to differences in the intensity of their aversions to surrendering the price-commodity or to both. It is not necessary, moreover, for any purpose proper to price-economics, to insist upon either the comparability of desire as between different persons or the general prevalence of deliberate and reasoned calculation on the part of individuals of the relative intensity of their desires for different units of the same or different goods, or to impute to the desires of any person, even hypothetically, any quantitative relationship inter se beyond that which can be expressed through the primary function of numbers of indicating order. All that the price-economist need assume with respect to an individual's desires is that they vary in intensity and that the desire for a further unit of a good diminishes with the increase in the number of units already acquired.

[22] I do not intend to deny that the utility theorists inherited the hedonic element in their theory, the postulate that utility and desire were quantitative correlatives, from the psychologists.

[23] Cf. Z. C. Dickinson, "The Relations of Recent Psychological Developments to Economic Theory," *Quarterly Journal of Economics* (May, 1919), p. 384: "The law of diminishing utility, a purely psychological postulate, giving greater precision to the tendency of exchange value of a commodity to decrease as the supply of the commodity is increased, has rendered very great service in economic analysis." This particular service can be as fully rendered, and with the advantage of freedom from disputations psychological matter, if there be substituted a law of diminishing desire for the law of diminishing utility.

This avenue of escape from the pitfalls of rationalistic hedonism has long been clear to many utility economists. Gide, as long ago as 1883, suggested "desirability"[24] and Wicksteed, in 1888, proposed "desiredness"[25] as a substitute for utility. These terms are perhaps objectionable because they unnecessarily objectify desire, but they are otherwise in the spirit of the argument presented here. The critics, it is true, have expressed impatience with such attempts as the foregoing, which they have characterized as unsuccessful endeavors to cover up the unsound psychological presuppositions of their theories by minor and deceptive changes in terminology. In so far as price-economics is concerned however, the critics have relied on vigorous assertions to demonstrate that a recasting of the utility theory in the manner indicated will not suffice to render it free from hedonistic taint without lessening its serviceability as an explanation of the mechanism of price-determination.

I have assumed, of course, that there is a law of diminishing desire. Certain apparent exceptions to the law can be cited, but it is not difficult to explain them in terms consistent with it. The collector, for instance, who seeks a complete set of coins, or stamps, or first editions, would ordinarily desire the last unit necessary to complete his set as intensely as, if not more intensely than, the first unit. The matcher of pearls may well have a mounting desire for successive pearls which match with those already acquired, until he has enough for a complete chain. The intensity of desire for the second glove of a pair may well be more intense than for the first in the absence of the second. In all of these instances, however, a complete set is the proper unit to take to observe the operation of the law, and the law may be expected to manifest itself as between successive sets. The perfect miser's attitude toward gold coins is probably not in accordance with a law of diminishing desire, but the miser presents a psychopathic rather than a normal case. He is a collector whose initial set is never complete.

According to the utility theory, as presented above, the market demand curve derives its negative slope from the downward inclinations of the desire curves of the individuals in the market. If instances should be found, therefore, where market demand curves for particular goods were positive in their inclination, it might seem to imply that many if not all of the purchasers of such goods had positive desire curves for

---

[24] Cf. *Cours d' Economie Politique* (4th ed.; Paris, 1894), p. 55 n.

[25] *Alphabet of Economic Science*, p. 8. Cf., also, H. J. Davenport, "Proposed Modifications in Austrian Theory and Terminology," *Quarterly Journal of Economics* (May, 1902), p. 361. The position taken in the text as to the irrelevance to the price-economics of the utility theorists of their hedonistic and rationalistic doctrines is essentially that of Davenport in his *Value and Distribution* (1908), pp. 303–10.

them. Cunyngham has suggested as an instance of a class of commodities for which there might be a positive demand curve a particular edition of a hymnbook which is useful in direct proportion as it is widely used.[26] Goods such as metric measuring instruments or interchangeable parts, or say a telephone, whose direct or instrumental serviceability is dependent to a large degree upon their wide use, belong to this class. So also do fashion and style commodities,[27] as distinguished especially from commodities whose virtue lies wholly in their rarity. But this is not a true instance of a positive demand curve in the static sense, and does not at all imply positive desire schedules. A person's desire for successive units of such goods will vary directly with the generality of their use, but inversely, as for other goods, with the number of units he already possesses. The demand of each individual may rise as the use of the good spreads, but at any given moment, given the extent of its use, he will take fewer units at a high than at a low price.[28]

But instances are conceivable of the existence of true, positively inclined demand curves. Commodities which have prestige value derived mainly from their expensiveness may have demands which for part of their range are positive in inclination, as may also commodities whose quality is judged by purchasers mainly from their price. In both these instances, however, the positive inclination of the demand schedule will be due to the fact that at any given price, x, purchasers will desire any nth unit more than they would have desired an nth unit at a lower price, y. It does not follow that the desire curves will also be positive in their inclination, i.e., that at any given price, or irrespective of price, purchasers will desire second and third units more than first units. The failure in these instances of the demand schedule to follow the desire schedules in its inclination is due to the fact that for such commodities the desire schedules are functions of actual price as well as being variables of it.

Another possible instance of a positively inclined demand schedule may be cited. Assume that wheat is the cheapest food in terms of calories, and that a householder needs $2x$ calories in the course of a year. Assume, further, that he has $200.00 annually to spend on food and that when wheat is $1.00 a bushel he can secure the $2x$ calories as fol-

---

[26] Henry Cunyngham, "Exchange Value, Monopoly and Rent," *Economic Journal* (March, 1892), p. 39.

[27] Fashion commodities, of course, may lose their value if their use becomes too widespread.

[28] If extent of use and price are closely related, it will, however, be difficult to separate the influence of price from the influence of extent of use on the amount which buyers will take.

lows: $100.00 for 100 bushels of wheat, giving $1\frac{1}{2}x$ calories, and $100.00 for other less economical foodstuffs, giving $1/2x$ calories. If wheat rises in price above $1.00 per bushel, the necessary amount of calories can be obtained only by increasing the number of bushels of wheat purchased, and decreasing the quantities of other foodstuffs purchased.[29] Here is an instance where quantity purchased will increase as price rises, even though price itself does not contribute to the appeal of the good. But even this case can be explained consistently with the existence of negatively inclined desire curves, if reference is had to J. B. Clark's reasoning that the desire for a commodity is really a composite of desires for the various qualities of the article.[30] In this simplified case, what the consumer desires is calories and variety, and the desire for calories is urgent and provision must be made for its satiation before the desire for variety can be satisfied. But once the $2x$ calories are obtained, there may be no further desire at all for calories, and the remaining funds will be devoted wholly to the securing of variety. Both the desire for calories and the desire for variety, however, will be negative in their inclination.

It should be clear, also, that the utility theory does not posit a direct relationship between consumers' desire curves and the market demand schedules of professional operators in middlemen's markets, though critics of the utility theory have sometimes failed to see this.[31] The removal of middlemen's demand schedules from consumers' desire schedules, both as to time and as to stages in the process from the beginning of production to final consumption, results in certain differences of behavior as between them.[32] A middleman's demand is governed largely by his opinion as to the prospective demand of consumers—or more immediately, as to the prospective trend of price—and all sorts of influences may contribute to the formation of that opinion, some of them intimately connected with the trading process itself. Where buyers are influenced by the behavior of other operators, whether consciously or not, especially in highly speculative markets, price-rises resulting from eager bidding on the part of some operators are likely to induce like eager bidding on the part of others and to result in still further increases

---

[29] Cf. Alfred Marshall, *Principles of Economics* (6th ed.), p. 132.

[30] Cf. *Distribution of Wealth,* pp. 214 ff. It can also be explained by reference to the existence of very steeply inclined curves of utility or desire for money.

[31] Cf., especially, E. H. Downey, "The Futility of Marginal Utility," *Journal of Political Economy* (April, 1910), pp. 265 ff.

[32] Cf. Alfred Marshall, *Principles,* p. 100 n: ". . . . The demand for a commodity on the part of dealers who buy it only with the purpose of selling it again, though governed by the demand of the ultimate consumers in the background, has some peculiarities of its own."

in price.[33] Under such circumstances volume of sales is for a time likely to show a positive, instead of a negative, correlation with price. But such instances neither necessitate any qualification to the universality of the law of diminishing desire, nor do they serve to discredit the proposition that even middlemen's demand schedules are ultimately dependent upon consumers' desire schedules.

It has been objected against the validity of the use of a concept of diminishing desire in value theory that we have no evidence of diminishing desire except as inferred from diminishing price-offers, and that to explain the negative slope of the demand curve by the existence of a law of diminishing desire and in turn to infer the existence of such a law from the negative slope of the demand curve is to indulge in circular reasoning.[34]

But the negative slope of the demand curve is a direct inference from experience, and the law of diminishing desire is a working hypothesis serving to explain the general recurrence of that phenomenon. Until it is demonstrated to be contrary to established fact, or until a better hypothesis is available, the law of diminishing desire can stand on this fact alone. But the evidence from introspection, for whatever it may be worth, and from the observation of human behavior in other fields than the economic market, lends further confirmation to the hypothesis. As Lloyd pointed out over ninety years ago,[35] our situation with respect to desire is closely comparable with the state of our knowledge with respect to heat prior to the discovery of the thermometer. The existence of different degrees of heat was then a hypothesis supported only by the fact that it was the only available explanation of other resultant phenomena and by introspection with respect to sensations. Nevertheless, the lack

---

[33] For an early reference to the tendency in speculative middlemen's markets of price-increases to lead to increased eagerness to buy, see Eugene Schwiedland, "Étude sur les Rapports existant entre les Prix en Gros et en Détail," *Revue d'Économie Politique* (1890), pp. 48 ff.

[34] Cf., for example, O. F. Boucke, "A Unique Situation in Economic Theory," *American Economic Review* (Dec., 1922), p. 603.

[35] *A Lecture on the Notion of Value,* pp. 29–30: "It would indeed be difficult to discover any accurate test by which to measure either the absolute utility of a single object or the exact ratio of the comparative utilities of different objects. Still it does not follow that the notion of utility has no foundation in the nature of things. It does not follow that because a thing is incapable of measurement, therefore, it has no real existence. The existence of heat was no less undeniable before thermometers were invented than at present." For later instances of appeal to heat for a parallel with desire, cf. Wicksteed, *Alphabet of Economic Science,* p. 15; Edgeworth, "Professor J. S. Nicholson on 'Consumers' Rent,'" *Economic Journal* (March, 1894), p. 155.

of means of direct measurement of heat did not put it out of the realm of scientific discussion even for those most exacting of scientists, the physicists. Even with the thermometer, temperature is arbitrarily defined and is measured only indirectly by its effect on the height of a column of mercury. The parallel would continue to be close if the accepted rule that each equal unit of increase of temperature will bring about an equal rise in the mercury column were a hypothesis no more susceptible of proof than the economic theory of the relationship between diminishing desire and diminishing pecuniary demand.

Some of the critics of the utility economics have not confined themselves, however, to attacks on the validity of its psychological presuppositions, but have claimed to demonstrate that even if its psychology were conceded to be valid it was guilty of various logical errors in making its inferences therefrom. The main conclusion in the field of price-economics resulting from the utility analysis is that for each purchaser of a series of commodities the purchase prices measure the relative marginal utilities of these commodities. For the "marginal utility" concept of the utility theorists, marginal desire may likewise be substituted and will serve equally well the only legitimate function of the concept in price-economics, namely, as a logical device for expressing with greater precision the subjective relationships between small, final increments of different goods. Substituting marginal desire for marginal utility, this proposition may be expressed as follows: The market prices of a series of commodities (if purchasable in small units) measure for each purchaser his relative marginal desires for all of the commodities actually purchased by him. As has already been pointed out, some utility theorists have gone beyond this and in their confusion of utility curves and demand schedules, and especially because of the dangerous practice of expressing utility schedules in pecuniary terms, have spoken of price as measuring the marginal utilities of the same goods to different persons and of different goods to society as a whole. Criticism of this error is fully justified, but it should not be directed against the utility school as a whole.[36]

---

[36] The character and the source of the error can be clearly brought out by a quotation from Böhm-Bawerk (*Positive Theory of Capital*, p. 161): "First, since the relations of Wants and Provision among individuals are extremely various, one and the same good may possess an entirely distinct subjective value [= marginal utility] for different persons . . . without which, indeed, it is difficult to see how there could be any exchanging at all."

To the economist who distinguished utility schedules from individual demand schedules, it would be obvious, especially if he refrained from expressing utility schedules in pecuniary terms, that what was necessary to a profitable exchange between two persons was not that to A goods x and y have a higher marginal utility

On the other hand, there is no merit in the argument of those critics who contend that the attempt to demonstrate a causal sequence from utility schedules to price must necessarily fail once it is admitted that price is not a satisfactory measure of utility as between individuals.[37] The price of a particular commodity is determined in part by the market demand for it, and the market demand is a compound of the individual demands. The individual demands are, in turn, resultants of the contract, for each individual, of his desire to acquire that particular commodity with his desire to retain, or to make other use of, what must be surrendered to obtain it. In this way individual desire schedules are an ultimate determinant of market price and have "market significance."

The utility theory of value has also been charged with the vicious circle of explaining exchange value by exchange value, because it maintains that value is determined, not merely by desire, but by desire backed up by purchasing power, i.e., value.[38] But this is a charge which can be made with equal force against the simple demand-and-supply explanation of value determination, since it maintains that demand is a determinant of value and defines demand in terms of purchasing power. This alleged circular reasoning, however, is merely the perception on the part of the utility economists of the mutuality of relationship between exchange values. The utility theory rightly represents values as being mutually related, each value being an item in a system of interdependent values. In its fullest development it would explain how with a given set of desire (and aversion) schedules and a given distribution of accumulated wealth and of capacities for labor, saving, etc., a certain set of prices or exchange values would result. But this task has not been found feasible, even in the abstract, and the utility theorist confines himself to explaining selected and minute phases of the process of price-determination under hypothetical conditions of stability of the surrounding situation. Of no stage in his reasoning is it accurate to say that it explains value by value, though it is true—and logically irreproachable—that it makes the value of commodity w a function of the

---

than to B, but that to A the ratio between the marginal utilities of goods x and y be different from the corresponding ratio to B. If good x and good y each had for A double the marginal utility that they had for B, there would be no basis for an exchange.

[37] Cf., for example, W. H. Hamilton, in his review of Henderson's Supply and Demand, American Economic Review (March, 1923), p. 93: "His [i.e., Henderson's] admission of differences in income as affecting the amounts which purchasers are willing to pay for an article makes his 'laws,' that 'the marginal utility of a commodity to anyone diminishes with every increase in the amount he has,' applicable only to individual economy and robs it of market significance."

[38] B. M. Anderson, Social Value, chap. vi.

values of commodities x, y, and z. If this be a vicious circle, there is no merit in avoiding them.[39]

Some defects of Böhm-Bawerk's exposition of the utility theory, which were unfortunately imitated by some later writers but which many utility theorists, and especially those using the mathematical method, avoided, have given the critics some openings for well-merited criticism. Bohm-Bawerk at first did not have an adequate notion of either utility schedules or demand schedules. He built up a continuous demand schedule, which he described in subjective terms but expressed in objective terms, from a series of discontinuous, individual demand schedules, for each of which only one point was given. In his exposition, in consequence, the famous "marginal pairs" of buyers and of sellers were singled out for excessive attention, and to "the marginal buyer" was attributed the role in price-determination which, were it not more logical to attribute it alike to every unit of the demand, belonged to the marginal purchases of every purchaser. This served to obscure for Böhm-Bawerk himself for a time, and for his readers, the true character of the relationship between diminishing utility and price. On the basis of Bohm-Bawerk's exposition, many "points" can be made against the utility theory which could not be made if the exposition of other representatives of the school, such as Edgeworth, Wicksteed, or Alfred Marshall, Davenport or Fisher, Walras or Pareto, were taken as the basis for attack.[40]

· [39] Anderson first makes an unqualified charge against the Austrians of circular reasoning and then proceeds to take most of the sting out of his arraignment by the following anticlimax: "If the Austrian analysis attempt nothing more than the determination of particular prices, one at a time, on the assumption that the transactions are, in each particular case, so small as not to disturb the marginal utility of money for each buyer and seller, and on the assumption that the values and prices of all the goods owned by buyers and sellers are already determined and known, except that of the good immediately in question, it is clear that it but plays over the surface of things. If it attempt more it is involved in a circle" (*op. cit.*, p. 48). Though some mathematical economists have succeeded in relaxing somewhat the severity of these assumptions without becoming involved in circular reasoning, this is a fair enough description of what the utility theory, in the field of price-economics, has aimed to accomplish. Whether or not this is but playing on the surface depends on what is surface and what undersoil, and on how deep one must probe before one has penetrated the surface. On these matters there is room for much inconclusive and barren debate.

[40] For criticisms of the utility theory resting for their validity on the discontinuity of Bohm-Bawerk's individual demand schedules, see Anderson, *op. cit.*, pp. 29 ff.; Downey, "The Futility of Marginal Utility," *Journal of Political Economy* (April, 1910), pp. 260 ff. For criticism of Böhm-Bawerk's use of discontinuous schedules, cf. F. W. Edgeworth, "The Theory of Distribution," *Quarterly Journal of Economics* (February, 1904), pp. 189 ff. For concessions by Bohm-Bawerk to his critics, see *Kapital und Kapitalzins* (3d ed., 1912), p. 38 n.

The common criticism of the utility theory, that it is an inadequate because incomplete theory of value,[41] is really a criticism of the range of activity of the theorists who have accepted the utility theory rather than of the theory itself. The criticism comes from those who want a theory of value which will not limit itself to a static or instantaneous flashlight analysis of the value-determination process, but which will delve into the origin and growth of the wants and desires which lead to the existence of exchange values. To subdue their impatience, it might be pointed out to them that there are not, and cannot be, such things as "complete theories," and that Mill's dictum to the contrary notwithstanding, there will always continue to be some neglected phases of the value problem. When they suggest that a static theory is of no service, because the consumer becomes a different person, with a new set of values, every time he buys a cigar or a meal, they exaggerate the instability of human behavior, and they contradict their own assertions about the importance of habit and custom. When they ask for the development out of value theory of a theory of consumption they often lay down specifications which call for a theory of life.[42] But when they demand that there be added to, or substituted for, the hypotheses and the observations from crude and limited observation a body of fresh and fertile data derived from systematic and comprehensive observation of human behavior, and when they charge that utility theorists have unduly limited themselves in the range of their investigations, there is force in their remarks. There does not appear to be much promise that efforts further to refine or elaborate upon the utility theory will be productive of results commensurate with the effort involved. It may even be true that the theory has already been overrefined and overelaborated for all theoretical and practical purposes. If the flood of criticism of the utility theory results in diverting effort from its further development of the pursuit of research in fresher fields, it will have an important accomplishment to its credit. But if the utility theorists have expended too much effort on the subtleties of utility analysis, the critics have expended too much effort—and venom, also—on criticism thereof. With the need for research in new directions so urgent, and the promised harvest therefrom so rich, it is somewhat surprising that they could have

[41] Cf., especially, Thorstein Veblen, "The Limitations of Marginal Utility," in *The Place of Science in Modern Civilization* (New York, 1919), pp. 231 ff.

[42] It is to be regretted that utility theorists have often called their utility analysis a theory of consumption. It cannot be claimed for the utility theory that it does more than open a pathway to the development of such a theory, and I see no particular reason for belief that this is the most serviceable avenue of approach, even of those already available.

devoted themselves so patiently, persistently, and repetitiously to the elucidation of the allegedly palpable errors and inadequacies of the other doctrines!

There must not be denied to the utility analysis, nevertheless, some positive contributions to knowledge in the field of price-economics. It has, for the first time, afforded a satisfactory explanation of the disparity between value in use and value in exchange which so puzzled the classical economists. It provides a hypothesis, in harmony with what is known of human nature, which adequately explains the downward slope of the demand schedule and which is as yet alone in the field. It throws some light on the causes and the types of interrelationship which exist between the prices of different goods. It bridges the gap, partially at least, between the price or exchange-value theory of economics and the psychological "general theory of value" of the philosophers. Whether or not these contributions are "important" is a matter of individual definition of terms, or of individual judgment, or interest. In a subsequent article I propose to examine the significance of the utility analysis in the field of "welfare economics."

GRADATIONS OF CONSUMERS' DEMAND

Alfred Marshall

When a trader or a manufacturer buys anything to be used in production, or be sold again, his demand is based on his anticipation of the profits which he can derive from it. These profits depend at any time on speculative risks and on other causes, which will need to be considered later on. But in the long run the price which a trader or manufacturer can afford to pay for a thing depends on the prices which consumers will pay for it, or for the things made by aid of it. The ultimate regulator of all demand is therefore consumers' demand. And it is with that almost exclusively that we shall be concerned in the present Book.

Utility is taken to be correlative to Desire or Want. It has been already argued that desires cannot be measured directly, but only indirectly by the outward phenomena to which they give rise: and that in those cases with which economics is chiefly concerned the measure is found in the price which a person is willing to pay for the fulfilment or satisfaction of his desire. He may have desires and aspirations which are not consciously set for any satisfaction: but for the present we are concerned chiefly with those which do so aim; and we assume that the resultant satisfaction corresponds in general fairly well to that which was anticipated when the purchase was made.[1]

[1] It cannot be too much insisted that to measure directly, or *per se*, either desires or the satisfaction which results from their fulfilment is impossible, if not inconceivable. If we could, we should have two accounts to make up, one of desires, and the other of realized satisfactions. And the two might differ considerably. For, to say nothing of higher aspirations, some of those connected with emulation are impulsive; many result from the force of habit; some are morbid and lead only to hurt; and many are based on expectations that are never fulfilled. (See above I. II. 3, 4.) Of course many satisfactions are not common pleasures, but belong to the development of a man's higher nature, or to use a good old word, to his *beatifica-*

Source: Principles of Economics, Book III, Chapter III, Appendix notes 1 and 2. Macmillan and Co., 1930. Reprinted with permission.

There is an endless variety of wants, but there is a limit to each separate want. This familiar and fundamental tendency of human nature may be stated in the *law of satiable wants* or of *diminishing utility* thus: The *total utility* of a thing to anyone (that is, the total pleasure or other benefit it yields him) increases with every increase in his stock of it, but not as fast as his stock increases. If his stock of it increases at a uniform rate the benefit derived from it increases at a diminishing rate. In other words, the additional benefit which a person derives from a given increase of his stock of a thing, diminishes with every increase in the stock that he already has.

That part of the thing which he is only just induced to purchase may be called his *marginal purchase,* because he is on the margin of doubt whether it is worth his while to incur the outlay required to obtain it. And the utility of his marginal purchase may be called the *marginal utility* of the thing to him. Or, if instead of buying it, he makes the thing himself, then its marginal utility is the utility of that part which he thinks it only just worth his while to make. And thus the law just given may be worded:

The marginal utility of a thing to anyone diminishes with every increase in the amount of it he already has.[2]

There is however an implicit condition in this law which should be made clear. It is that we do not suppose time to be allowed for any alteration in the character or tastes of the man himself. It is therefore no exception to the law that the more good music a man hears, the stronger is his taste for it likely to become; that avarice and ambition

---

tion; and some may even partly result from self-abnegation. (See I. II. 1.) The two direct measurements then might differ. But as neither of them is possible, we fall back on the measurement which economics supplies, of the motive or moving force to action: and we make it serve, with all its faults, *both* for the desires which prompt activities and for the satisfactions that result from them. (Compare "Some remarks on Utility" by Prof. Pigou in the *Economic Journal* for March, 1903.)

[2] See Note I. in the Mathematical Appendix at the end of the Volume. This law holds a priority of position to the *law of diminishing return* from land; which however has the priority in time; since it was the first to be subjected to a rigid analysis of a semi-mathematical character. And if by anticipation we borrow some of its terms, we may say that the *return* of pleasure which a person gets from each additional *dose* of a commodity diminishes till at last a margin is reached at which it is no longer worth his while to acquire any more of it.

The term *marginal utility* (Grenz-nutz) was first used in this connection by the Austrian Wieser. It has been adopted by Prof. Wicksteed. It corresponds to the term Final used by Jevons, to whom Wieser makes his acknowledgments in the Preface (p. xxiii. of the English edition). His list of anticipators of his doctrine is headed by Gossen, 1854.

are often insatiable; or that the virtue of cleanliness and the vice of drunkenness alike grow on what they feed upon. For in such cases our observations range over some period of time; and the man is not the same at the beginning as at the end of it. If we take a man as he is, without allowing time for any change in his character, the marginal utility of a thing to him diminishes steadily with every increase in his supply of it.[3]

Now let us translate this law of diminishing utility into terms of price. Let us take an illustration from the case of a commodity such as tea, which is in constant demand and which can be purchased in small quantities. Suppose, for instance, that tea of a certain quality is to be had at 2 shillings per lb. A person might be willing to give 10 shillings for a single pound once a year rather than go without it altogether; while if he could have any amount of it for nothing he would perhaps not care to use more than 30 lbs. in the year. But as it is, he buys perhaps 10 lbs. in the year; that is to say, the difference between the satisfaction which he gets from buying 9 lbs. and 10 lbs. is enough for him to be willing to pay 2 shillings for it: while the fact that he does not buy an eleventh pound, shows that he does not think that it would be worth an extra 2 shillings to him. That is, 2 shillings a pound measures the utility to him of the tea which lies at the margin or terminus or end of his purchases; it measures the marginal utility to him. If the price which he is just willing to pay for any pound be called his *demand price*, then 2 shillings is his marginal demand price. And our law may be worded:

The larger the amount of a thing that a person has the less, other things being equal (i.e., the purchasing power of money, and the amount

---

[3] It may be noticed here, though the fact is of but little practical importance, that a small quantity of a commodity may be insufficient to meet a certain special want; and then there will be a more than proportionate increase of pleasure when the consumer gets enough of it to enable him to attain the desired end. Thus, for instance, anyone would desire less pleasure in proportion from ten pieces of wall paper than from twelve, if the latter would, and the former would not, cover the whole of the walls of his room. Or again a very short concert or a holiday may fail of its purpose of soothing and recreating: and one of double length might be of more than double total utility. This case corresponds to the fact, which we shall have to study in connection with the tendency to diminishing return, that the capital and labour already applied to any piece of land may be so inadequate for the development of its full powers, that some further expenditure on it even with the existing arts of agriculture would give a more than proportionate return; and in the fact that an improvement in the arts of agriculture may resist that tendency, we shall find an analogy to the condition just mentioned in the text as implied in the law of diminishing utility.

of money at his command being equal), will be the price which he will pay for a little more of it: or in other words his marginal demand price for it diminishes.

His demand becomes *efficient,* only when the price which he is willing to offer reaches that at which others are willing to sell.

This last sentence reminds us that we have as yet taken no account of changes in the marginal utility of money, or general purchasing power. At one and the same time, a person's material resources being unchanged, the marginal utility of money to him is a fixed quantity, so that the prices he is just willing to pay for two commodities are to one another in the same ratio as the utility of those two commodities.

A greater utility will be required to induce him to buy a thing if he is poor than if he is rich. We have seen how the clerk with £100 a year will walk to business in a heavier rain than the clerk with £300 a year.[4] But although the utility, or the benefit, that is measured in the poorer man's mind by twopence is greater than that measured by it in the richer man's mind; yet if the richer man rides a hundred times in the year and the poorer man twenty times, then the utility of the hundredth ride which the richer man is only just induced to take is measured to him by twopence; and the utility of the twentieth ride which the poorer man is only just induced to take is measured to him by twopence. For each of them the marginal utility is measured by twopence; but this marginal utility is greater in the case of the poorer man than in that of the richer.

In other words, the richer a man becomes the less is the marginal utility of money to him; every increase in his resources increases the price which he is willing to pay for any given benefit. And in the same way every diminution of his resources increases the marginal utility of money to him, and diminishes the price that he is willing to pay for any benefit.[5]

To obtain complete knowledge of demand for anything, we should have to ascertain how much of it he would be willing to purchase at each of the prices at which it is likely to be offered; and the circumstance of his demand for, say, tea can be best expressed by a list of the prices which he is willing to pay; that is, by his several demand prices for different amounts of it. (This list may be called his demand schedule.)

---

[4] See I. II. 2.
[5] See Note II. in the Mathematical Appendix.

Thus for instance we may find that he would buy

6 lbs. at 50d. per lb.	10 lbs. at 24d. per lb.
7 lbs. at 40d. per lb.	11 lbs. at 21d. per lb.
8 lbs. at 33d. per lb.	12 lbs. at 19d. per lb.
9 lbs. at 28d. per lb.	13 lbs. at 17d. per lb.

If corresponding prices were filled in for all intermediate amounts we should have an exact statement of his demand.[6] We cannot express a person's demand for a thing by the "amount he is willing to buy," or by the "intensity of his eagerness to buy a certain amount," without reference to the prices at which he would buy that amount and other amounts. We can represent it exactly only by lists of the prices at which he is willing to buy different amounts.[7]

[6] Such a demand schedule may be translated, on a plan now coming into familiar use, into a curve that may be called his *demand curve*. Let Ox and Oy be drawn the one horizontally, the other vertically. Let an inch measured along Ox represent 10 lbs. of tea, and an inch measured along Oy represent 40d.

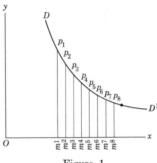

	tenths of an inch	fortieths of an inch
take	$Om_1 = 6$,	and draw $m_1p_1 = 50$
	$Om_2 = 7$,	and draw $m_2p_2 = 40$
	$Om_3 = 8$,	and draw $m_3p_3 = 33$
	$Om_4 = 9$,	and draw $m_4p_4 = 28$
	$Om_5 = 10$,	and draw $m_5p_5 = 24$
	$Om_6 = 11$,	and draw $m_6p_6 = 21$
	$Om_7 = 12$,	and draw $m_7p_7 = 19$
	$Om_8 = 13$,	and draw $m_8p_8 = 17$

Figure 1

m_1 being on Ox and m_1p_1 being drawn vertically from m_1; and so for the others. Then $p_1p_2 \ldots p_8$ are points on his demand curve for tea; or as we may say *demand points*. If we could find demand points in the same manner for every possible quantity of tea, we should get the whole continuous curve DD' as shown in the figure. This account of the demand schedule and curve is provisional; several difficulties connected with it are deferred to chapter v.

[7] Thus Mill says that we must "mean by the word demand, the quantity demanded, and remember that this is not a fixed quantity, but in general varies according to the value." (*Principles,* III. II. 4.) This account is scientific in substance; but is not clearly expressed and it has been much misunderstood. Cairnes prefers to represent "demand as the desire for commodities and services, seeking its end by an offer of general purchasing power, and supply as the desire for general purchasing power, seeking its end by an offer of specific commodities or services." He

When we say that a person's demand for anything increases, we mean that he will buy more of it than he would before at the same price, and that he will buy as much of it as before at a higher price. A general increase in his demand is an increase throughout the whole list of prices at which he is willing to purchase different amounts of it, and not merely that he is willing to buy more of it at the current prices.[8]

So far we have looked at the demand of a single individual. And in the particular case of such a thing as tea, the demand of a single person is fairly representative of the general demand of a whole market: for the demand for tea is a constant one; and, since it can be purchased in small quantities, every variation in its price is likely to affect the amount which he will buy. But even among those things which are in constant use, there are many for which the demand on the part of any single individual cannot vary continuously with every small change in price, but can move only by great leaps. For instance, a small fall in the price of hats or watches will not affect the action of every one; but it will induce a few persons, who were in doubt whether or not to get a new hat or a new watch, to decide in favour of doing so.

There are many classes of things the need for which on the part of

---

does this in order that he may be able to speak of a ratio, or equality, of demand and supply. But the quantities of two desires of the part of two different persons cannot be compared directly; their measures may be compared, but not they themselves. And in fact Cairnes is himself driven to speak of supply as "limited by the quantity of purchasing power offered for their purchase." But sellers have not a fixed quantity of commodities which they offer for sale unconditionally at whatever price they can get: buyers have not a fixed quantity of purchasing power which they are ready to spend on the specific commodities, however much they pay for them. Account must then be taken in either case of the relation between quantity and price, in order to complete Cairnes' account, and when this is done it is brought back to the lines followed by Mill. He says, indeed, that "Demand, as defined by Mill, is to be understood as measured, not, as my definition would require, by the quantity of purchasing power offered in support of the desire for commodities, but by the quantity of commodities for which such purchasing power is offered." It is true that there is a great difference between the statements, "I will buy twelve eggs," and "I will buy a shilling's worth of eggs." But there is no substantive difference between the statements, "I will buy twelve eggs at a penny each, but only six at three halfpence each," and the statement, "I will spend a shilling on eggs at a penny each, but if they cost three halfpence each I will spend ninepence on them." But while Cairnes' account when completed becomes substantially the same as Mill's, its present form is even more misleading. (See an article by the present writer on "Mill's Theory of Value" in the *Fortnightly Review* for April, 1876.)

[8] We may sometimes find it convenient to speak of this as a *raising of his demand schedule*. Geometrically it is represented by raising his demand curve, or, what comes to the same thing, moving it to the right, with perhaps some modification of its shape.

any individual is inconstant, fitful, and irregular. There can be no list of individual demand prices for wedding-cakes, or the services of an expert surgeon. But the economist has little concern with particular incidents in the lives of individuals. He studies rather "the course of action that may be expected under certain conditions from the members of an industrial group," in so far as the motives of that action are measurable by a money price; and in these broad results the variety and the fickleness of individual action are merged in the comparatively regular aggregate of the action of many.

In large markets, then—where rich and poor, old and young, men and women, persons of all varieties of tastes, temperaments and occupations are mingled together—the peculiarities in the wants of individuals will compensate one another in a comparatively regular gradation of total demand. Every fall, however slight in the price of a commodity in general use, will, other things being equal, increase the total sales of it; just as an unhealthy autumn increases the mortality of a large town, though many persons are uninjured by it. And therefore if we had the requisite knowledge, we could make a list of prices at which each amount of it could find purchasers in a given place during, say, a year.

The total demand in the place for, say, tea, is the sum of the demands of all the individuals there. Some will be richer and some poorer than the individual consumer whose demand we have just written down; some will have a greater and others a smaller liking for tea than he has. Let us suppose that there are in the place a million purchasers of tea, and that their average consumption is equal to his at each several price. Then the demand of that place is represented by the same list of prices as before, if we write a million pounds of tea instead of one pound.[9]

[9] The demand is represented by the same curve as before, only an inch measured along Ox now represents ten million pounds instead of ten pounds. And a formal definition of the demand curve for a market may be given thus: The demand curve for any commodity in a market during any given unit of time is the locus of demand points for it. That is to say, it is a curve such that if from any point P on it, a straight line PM be drawn perpendicular to Ox, PM represents the price at which purchasers will be forthcoming for an amount of the commodity represented by OM.

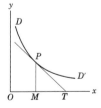

Figure 2

There is then one general *law of demand:* The greater the amount to be sold, the smaller must be the price at which it is offered in order that it may find purchasers; or, in other words, the amount demanded increases with a fall in price, and diminishes with a rise in price. There will not be any uniform relation between the fall in price and the increase of demand. A fall of one-tenth in the price may increase the sales by a twentieth or by a quarter, or it may double them. But as the numbers in the left-hand column of the demand schedule increase, those in the right-hand column will always diminish.[10]

The price will measure the marginal utility of the commodity to each purchaser individually: we cannot speak of price as measuring marginal utility in general, because the wants and circumstances of different people are different.

The demand prices in our list are those at which various quantities of a thing can be sold in a market *during a given time and under given conditions.* If the conditions vary in any respect the prices will probably require to be changed; and this has constantly to be done when the desire for anything is materially altered by a variation of custom, or by a cheapening of the supply of a rival commodity, or by the invention of a new one. For instance, the list of demand prices for tea is drawn out on the assumption that the price of coffee is known; but a failure of the coffee harvest would raise the prices for tea. The demand for gas is liable to be reduced by an improvement in electric lighting; and in the same way a fall in the price of a particular kind of tea may cause it to be substituted for an inferior but cheaper variety.[11]

Our next step will be to consider the general character of demand in

---

[10] That is, if a point moves along the curve away from Oy it will constantly approach Ox. Therefore if a straight line PT be drawn touching the curve at P and meeting Ox in T, the angle PTx is an obtuse angle. It will be found convenient to have a short way of expressing this fact; which may be done by saying that PT is *inclined negatively.* Thus the one universal rule to which the demand curve conforms is that it is *inclined negatively* throughout the whole of its length.

It will of course be understood that "the law of demand" does not apply to the demand in a campaign between groups of speculators. A group, which desires to unload a great quantity of a thing on to the market, often begins by buying some of it openly. When it has thus raised the price of the thing, it arranges to sell a great deal quietly, and through unaccustomed channels. See an article by Professor Taussig in the *Quarterly Journal of Economics* (May, 1921, p. 402).

[11] It is even conceivable, though not probable, that a simultaneous and proportionate fall in the price of all teas may diminish the demand for some particular kind of it; if it happens that those whom the increased cheapness of tea leads to substitute a superior kind for it are more numerous than those who are led to take it in the place of an inferior kind. The question where the lines of division between different commodities should be drawn must be settled by convenience of the particular discussion. For some purposes it may be best to regard Chinese and

the cases of some important commodities ready for immediate consumption. We shall thus be continuing the inquiry made in the preceding chapter as to the variety and satiability of wants; but we shall be treating it from a rather different point of view, viz. that of price-statistics.[12]

Indian teas, or even Souchong and Pekoe teas, as different commodities; and to have a separate demand schedule for each of them. While for other purposes it may be best to group together commodities as distinct as beef and mutton, or even as tea and coffee, and to have a single list to represent the demand for the two combined; but in such a case of course some convention must be made as to the number of ounces of tea which are taken as equivalent to a pound of coffee.

Again, a commodity may be simultaneously demanded for several uses (for instance there may be a "composite demand" for leather for making shoes and portmanteaus); the demand for a thing may be conditional on there being a supply of some other thing without which it would not be of much service (thus there may be a "joint demand" for raw cotton and cotton-spinners' labour). Again, the demand for a commodity on the part of dealers who buy it only with the purpose of selling it again, though governed by the demand of the ultimate consumers in the background, has some peculiarities of its own. But all such points may best be discussed at a later stage.

[12] A great change in the manner of economic thought has been brought about during the present generation by the general adoption of semimathematical language for expressing the relation between small increments of a commodity on the one hand, and on the other hand small increments in the aggregate price that will be paid for it: and by formally describing these small increments of price as measuring corresponding small increments of pleasure. The former, and by far the more important, step was taken by Cournot (*Recherches sur les Principes Mathématiques de la Théorie des Richesses*, 1838); the latter by Dupuit (*De la Mesure d'utilité des travaux public in the Annales des Ponts et Chaussées*, 1844), and by Gossen (*Entwickelung der Gesetze des menschlichen Verkehrs*, 1854). But their work was forgotten; part of it was done over again, developed and published almost simultaneously by Jevons and by Carl Menger in 1871, and by Walras a little later. Jevons almost at once arrested public attention by his brilliant lucidity and interesting style. He applied the new name final utility so ingeniously as to enable people who knew nothing of mathematical science to get clear ideas of the general relations between the small increments of two things that are gradually changing in causal connection with one another. His success was aided even by his faults. For under the honest belief that Ricardo and his followers had rendered their account of the causes that determine value hopelessly wrong by omitting to lay stress on the law of satiable wants, he led many to think he was correcting great errors; whereas he was really only adding very important explanations. He did excellent work in insisting on a fact which is none the less important, because his predecessors, and even Cournot, thought it too obvious to be explicitly mentioned, viz. that the diminution in the amount of a thing demanded in a market indicates a diminution in the intensity of the desire for it on the part of individual consumers, whose wants are becoming satiated. But he has led many of his readers into a confusion between the provinces of Hedonics and Economics, by exaggerating the applications of his favourite phrases, and speaking (*Theory*, 2nd Edn. p. 105) without qualification of the price of a thing as measuring its final utility not only to an individual, which it can do, but also to "a trading body," which it cannot

NOTES

Note I. The law of diminution of marginal utility may be expressed thus: If u be the total utility of an amount x of a commodity to a given person at a given time, then marginal utility is measured by (du/dx) δx; while du/dx measures the *marginal degree* of utility. Jevons and some other writers use "Final utility" to indicate what Jevons elsewhere calls Final degree of utility. There is room for doubt as to which mode of expression is the more convenient: no question of principle is involved in the decision. Subject to the qualifications mentioned in the text d^2u/dx^2 is always negative.

Note II. If m is the amount of money or general purchasing power at a person's disposal at any time, and μ represents its total utility to him, then $d\mu/dm$ represents the marginal degree of utility of money to him.

If p is the price which he is just willing to pay for an amount x of the commodity which gives him a total pleasure u, then

$$\frac{d\mu}{dm}\, \Delta p = \Delta u;\text{ and }\frac{d\mu}{dm}\frac{dp}{dx} = \frac{du}{dx}.$$

If p' is the price which he is just willing to pay for an amount x' of another commodity, which affords him a total pleasure u', then

$$\frac{d\mu}{dm}\cdot\frac{dp'}{dx'} = \frac{du'}{dx'};$$

and therefore

$$\frac{dp}{dx}:\frac{dp'}{dx'} = \frac{du}{dx}:\frac{du'}{dx'}.$$

(Compare Jevons' chapter on the *Theory of Exchange*, p. 151.)

Every increase in his means diminishes the marginal degree of utility of money to him; that is, $d^2\mu/dm^2$ is always negative.

Therefore, the marginal utility to him of an amount x of a commodity remaining unchanged, an increase in his means increases $(du/dx) \div (du/dm)$; i.e. it increases dp/dx, that is the rate at which he is willing to pay for further supplies of it. We may regard dp/dx as a function of m, u, and x; and then we have $d^2p/dmdx$ always positive. Of course $d^2p/dudx$ is always positive.

---

do. These points are developed later on in Appendix I. on Ricardo's Theory of Value. It should be added that Prof. Seligman has shown (*Economic Journal*, 1903, pp. 356–363) that a long-forgotten Lecture, delivered by Prof. W. F. Lloyd at Oxford in 1833, anticipated many of the central ideas of the present doctrine of utility.

An excellent bibliography of Mathematical Economics is given by Prof. Fisher as an appendix to Bacon's translation of Cournot's *Researches,* to which the reader may be referred for a more detailed account of the earlier mathematical writings on economics, as well as of those by Edgeworth, Pareto, Wicksteed, Auspitz, Lieben and others. Pantaleoni's *Pure Economics,* amid much excellent matter makes generally accessible for the first time the profoundly original and vigorous, if somewhat abstract, reasonings of Gossen.

CONSUMPTION THEORY IN TERMS OF REVEALED PREFERENCE

Paul A. Samuelson

1. INTRODUCTION

A decade ago I suggested that the economic theory of consumer's behavior can be largely built up on the notion of "revealed preference." By comparing the costs of different combinations of goods at different relative price situations, we can infer whether a given batch of goods is preferred to another batch; the individual guinea-pig, by his market behaviour, reveals his preference pattern—if there is such a consistent pattern.

Recently, Mr. Ian M. D. Little of Oxford University has made an important contribution to this field.[1] In addition to showing the changes in viewpoint that this theory may lead to, he has presented an ingenious proof that if enough judiciously selected price-quantity situations are available for two goods, we may define a locus which is the precise equivalent of the conventional indifference curve.

I should like, briefly, to present an alternative demonstration of this same result. While the proof is a direct one, it requires a little more mathematical reasoning than does his.

2. OBSERVABLE PRICE RATIOS AND A FUNDAMENTAL DIFFERENTIAL EQUATION

If we confine ourselves to the case of two commodities, x and y, we could conceptually observe for any individual a number of price-quantity situations. Since only relative prices are assumed to matter, each

---

[1] I. M. D. Little: "A Reformulation of the Theory of Consumers' Behaviour," *Oxford Economic Papers*, New Series, No. 1, January, 1949; P. A. Samuelson: *Foundations of Economic Analysis* (1947), Ch. V and VI; P. A. Samuelson: "A Note on the Pure Theory of Consumer's Behaviour; and an Addendum," *Economica* (1938), Vol. V (New Series), pp. 61–71, 353–354.

Source: Reprinted with permission from *Economica*, XV (New Series): 243–253 (November 1948).

observation consists of the triplet of numbers, $(p_x/p_y, x, y)$. By manipulating prices and income, we could cause the individual to come into equilibrium at any (x, y) point, at least within a given area. We may also make the simplifying assumption that one and only one price ratio can be associated with each combination of x and y. Theoretically, therefore, we could for any point (x, y) determine a unique p_x/p_y; or

$$\frac{p_x}{p_y} = f(x, y) \tag{1}$$

where f is an observable function, assumed to be continuous and with continuous partial derivatives.[2]

The central notion underlying the theory of revealed preference, and indeed the whole modern economic theory of index numbers, is very simple. Through any observed equilibrium point, A, draw the budget-equation straight line with arithmetical slope given by the observed price ratio. Then all combinations of goods on or within the budget line could have been bought in preference to what was actually bought. But they weren't. Hence, they are all "revealed" to be inferior to A. No other line of reasoning is needed.

As yet we have no right to speak of "indifference," and certainly no right to speak of "indifference slopes." But nobody can object to our summarising our observable information graphically by drawing a little negative "slope element" at each x and y point, with numerical gradient equal to the price ratio in question.

This is shown in Figure 1 by the numerous little arrows. These little slopes are all that we choose to draw in of the budget lines which go through each point and the directional arrows are only drawn in to guide the eye. It is a well known observation of *Gestalt* psychology that the eye tends to discern smooth contour lines from such a representation, although strictly speaking, only a finite number of little line segments are depicted, and they do not for the most part run into each other.[3] (In the present illustration the contour lines have been taken to be the familiar rectangular hyperbolae or unitary-elasticity curves and $f(x, y)$ takes the simple form $p_x/p_y = y/x$.)

---

[2] Mathematically, the above continuity assumptions are over-strict. Also, we shall make the unnecessarily strong assumption that in the region under discussion the price-quantity relations have the "simple concavity" property: $f(\partial f/\partial y)-(\partial f/\partial x) > 0$.

[3] Every student of elementary physics has dusted iron filings on a piece of paper suspended on a permanent magnet. The little filings become magnetised and orient themselves in a simple pattern. To the mind's eye these appear as "lines of force" of the magnetic field.

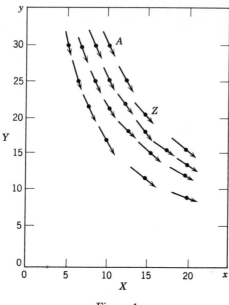

Figure 1

There is an exact mathematical counterpart of this phenomenon of *Gestalt* psychology. Let us identify a little slope, dy/dx, with each price ratio, $-p_x/p_y$. Then, from (1), we have the simplest differential equation

$$\frac{dy}{dx} = -f(x, y). \tag{2}$$

It is known mathematically that this defines a unique curve through any given point, and a (one-parameter) family of curves throughout the surrounding (x, y) plane. These solution curves (or "integral solutions" as they are often called) are such that when any one of them is substituted into the above differential equation, it will be found to satisfy that equation. Later we shall verify that these solution curves are the conventional "indifference curves" of modern economic theory. Also, and this is the novel part of the present paper, I shall show that these solution curves are in fact the limiting loci of revealed preference—or in Mr. Little's terminology they are the "behaviour curves" defined for specified initial points. This is our excuse for arbitrarily associating the differential equation system (2) with our observable pattern of prices and quantities summarised in (1).

3. THE CAUCHY-LIPSCHITZ PROCESS OF APPROXIMATION

Mathematicians are able to establish rigorously the existence of solutions to the differential equations without having to rely upon the mind's eye as a primitive "differential-analyser" or "integrator."[4] Also, mathematicians have devised rigorous methods for numerical solution of such equations to any desired (and recognisable) degree of accuracy.

It so happens that one of the simplest methods for proving the existence of, and numerically approximating, a solution is that called the "Cauchy-Lipschitz" method after the men who first made it rigorous, even though it really goes back to at least the time of Euler. In this method we approximate to our true solution curve by a connected series of straight line-segments, each line having the slope dictated by the differential equation *for the beginning point* of the straight line-segment in question. This means that our differential equation is not perfectly satisfied at all other points; but if we make our line-segments numerous and short enough, the resulting error from the true solution can be made as small as we please.

Figure 2 illustrates the Cauchy-Lipschitz approximations to the true solution passing through the point A (10, 30) and going from $x = 10$, to the vertical line $x = 15$. The top smooth curve is the true unitary-elasticity curve that we hope to approximate. The three lower broken-line curves are successive approximations, improving in accuracy as we move to higher curves.

Our crudest Cauchy-Lipschitz approximation is to use one line-segment for the whole interval. We pass a straight line through A with a slope equal to the little arrow at A, or equal to -3. This is nothing but the familiar budget line through the initial point A; it intersects the vertical line $x = 15$, at the value $y = 15$ or at the point marked Z'.[5]

(Actually, from the economic theory of index numbers and consumer's choice, we know that this first crude approximation Z': $(x, y) = (15, 15)$ clearly revealed itself to be "worse" than $(x, y) = (10, 30)$—since the former was actually chosen over the latter even though both cost the same amount. This suggests that the Cauchy-Lipschitz process will always approach the true solution curve, or "indifference curve," *from

---

[4] The usual proof found in such intermediate texts as F. R. Moulton, *Differential Equations,* Ch. XII–XIII, is that of Picard's "method of sucessive approximations." But the earlier rigorous proofs are by the Cauchy-Lipschitz method, which is very closely related to the economic theory of index numbers and revealed preference. See also, R. G. D. Allen, *Mathematical Analysis for Economists,* 1938, Ch. XVI.

[5] A Numerical Appendix gives the exact arithmetic underlying this and the following figure.

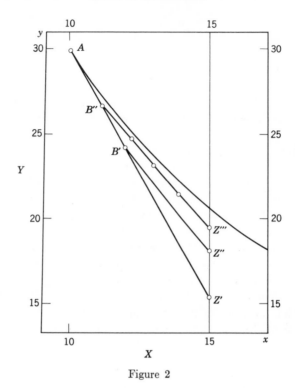

Figure 2

below. This is in fact a general truth, as we are about to see.) Can we not get a better approximation to the correct solution than this crude straight line, AZ'? Yes, if we use two line-segments instead of one. As before let us first proceed on a straight line through A with slope equal to A's little arrows. But let us travel on this line only two-fifths as far as before: to $x = 12$, rather than $x = 15$. This gives us a new point B' (12, 24), whose directional arrow is seen to have the slope of -2. Now, through B' we travel on a new straight line with this new slope; and our second, better, approximation to the true value at $x = 15$, is given by the new intersection, Z'', with the vertical line, at the level $y = 18$. (The "true" value is obviously at Z on the smooth curve where y must equal 20 if we are to be on the hyperbola with the property $xy = 10 \times 30 = 15 \times 20$; and our second approximation has only $\frac{3}{5}$ the error of our first.)

The general procedure of the Cauchy-Lipschitz process is now clear. Suppose we divide the interval between $x = 10$ and $x = 15$ into 5 equal segments; suppose we follow each straight line with slope equal to its initial arrow until we reach the end of the interval, and then begin a new straight line. Then as our numerical table shows, we get the still better approximation, $y = 19\frac{2}{7}$. In Figure 2, the broken line from A to Z''' shows our third approximation.

In the limit as we take enough sub-intervals so that the size of each line-segment becomes indefinitely small, we approach the true value of $y = 20$, and the same is true for the true value at any other x point. How do we know this? Because the pure mathematician assures us that this can be rigorously proved.

In economic terms, the individual is definitely going downhill along any one Cauchy-Lipschitz curve. For just as A was revealed to be better than Z', so also was it revealed to be better than B'. Note too that Z'' is on the budget line of B' and is hence revealed to be inferior to B', which already has been revealed to be worse than A. It follows that Z'' is worse than A.

By the same reasoning Z''' on the third approximation curve is shown to be inferior to A, although it now takes four intermediate points to make this certain. It follows as a general rule: any Cauchy-Lipschitz path always leads to a final point worse than the initial. And strictly speaking, it is only as an infinite limit that we can hope to reveal the neutral case of "indifference" along the true solution curve to the differential equation.

4. AN INDIRECT PROOF OF "LIMITING REVELATION OF INDIFFERENCE"

We have really proved only one thing so far: all points *below* the true mathematical solution passing through an initial point, A, are definitely "revealed to be worse" than A.

We have not rigorously proved that points falling on the solution contour curve are really "equal" to A. Indeed in terms of the strict algebra of "revealed preference" we have as yet no definition of what is meant by "equality" or "indifference."

Still it would be a great step forward if we could definitely prove the following: all points *above* the true mathematical solution are definitely "revealed to be better" than A.

The next following section gives a direct proof of this fact by defining a new process which is similar to the Cauchy-Lipschitz process and which definitely approximates to the true integral solution *from above*. But it may be as well to digress in this section and show that by indirect reasoning like that of Mr. Little, we may establish the proposition that all points above the solution-contour are clearly better than A.

I shall only sketch the reasoning. Suppose we take any point just vertically above the point Z and regard it as our new initial point. The mathematician assures us that a new "higher" solution-contour goes through such a point. Let us construct a Cauchy-Lipschitz process leftward, or backwards. Then by using small enough line-segments we may approach indefinitely close to *that point vertically above A which lies on the new contour line above A's contour.* A will then have to lie below the leftward-moving Cauchy-Lipschitz curve, and is thus revealed to be worse than any new initial point lying above the old contour line. Q.E.D.

We may follow Mr. Little's terminology and give the name "behaviour line" to the unique curve which lies between the points definitely shown to be better than *A*, and those definitely shown to be worse than *A*. This happens to coincide with the mathematical solution to the differential equation, and we may care to give this contour line, by courtesy, the title of an indifference curve.[6]

5. A NEW APPROXIMATION PROCESS FROM ABOVE

Let me return now to the problem of defining a new approximating process, like the conventional Cauchy-Lipschitz process, but which: (1) approaches the mathematical solution from above rather than below, and which (2) definitely reveals the economic preference of the individual at every point.

Our new process will consist of broken straight lines; and in the limit these will become numerous enough to approach a smooth curve. But the slopes of the straight line-segments will not be given by their *initial* points, as in the Cauchy-Lipschitz process. Instead, the slope will be determined by the *final* point of the sub-interval's line-segment.

After the reader ponders over this for some time and considers its geometrical significance, he may feel that he is being swindled. How can we determine the slope at the line's final point, without first determining the final point? But, how can we know the final point of the line unless its slope has already been determined? Clearly, we are at something of a circular impasse. To determine the slope, we seem already to require the slope.

The way out of this dilemma is perfectly straightforward to anyone who has grasped the mathematical solution of a simultaneous equation. The logical circle is a virtuous rather than a vicious one. By solving the implied simultaneous equation, we cut through the problem of circular

---

[6] If our preference field does not have simple concavity—and why should it?—we may observe cases where *A* is preferred to *B* at some times, and *B* to *A* at others. If this is a pattern of consistency and not of chaos, we could choose to regard *A* and *B* as "indifferent" under those circumstances. If the preference field has simple concavity, "indifference" will never explicitly reveal itself to us except as the results of an infinite limiting process.

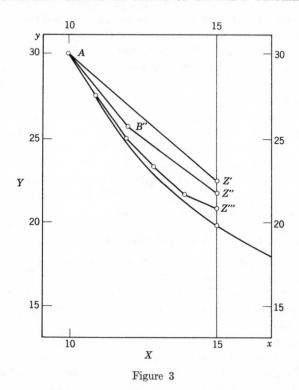

Figure 3

interdependence. And in this case we do not need an electronic computer to solve the implied equation. Our human guinea-pig, simply by following his own bent, inadvertently helps to solve our problem for us.

In Figure 3, we again begin with the initial point A. Again we wish to find the true solution for y at $x = 15$. Our first and crudest approximation will consist of one straight line. But its slope will be determined at the end of the interval and is initially unknown. Let us, therefore, through A swing a straight line through all possible angles. One and only one of these slopes will give us a line that is exactly tangent to one of the little arrows at the end of our interval. Let Z' be the point where our straight line is just tangent to an arrow lying in the vertical line. It corresponds to a y value of $22\frac{1}{2}$, which is above the true value of $y = 20$.

Economically speaking, when we rotate a straight "budget line" around an initial point A, and let the individual pick the best combination of goods in each situation, we trace out a so-called "offer curve." This curve is not drawn in on the figure, but the point Z' is the intersection of the offer curve with the vertical line. It should be obvious from our earlier reasoning that Z' and any other point on the offer curve is revealed to be better than A, since any such equal-cost point is chosen over A.

So much for our crude first approximation. Let us try dividing the interval between $x = 10$ and $x = 15$ up into two sub-intervals so that two connected straight lines may be used. If we wish the first line to end at $x = 12$, we rotate our line through A until its final slope is just equal to the indicated little arrow (or price ratio) along the vertical line $x = 12$. For the simple hyperbolae in question, where $-p_x/p_y = dy/dx = -y/x$, our straight line will be found to end at the point B'', whose (x, y) coordinates are $(12, 25\frac{4}{7})$ and whose arrow has a slope of just less than (-2).

We now begin at B'' as a new initial point and repeat the process by finding a new straight line over the interval from $x = 12$ to $x = 15$. Pivoting a line through all possible angles, we find tangency only at the point Z'', where $y = 21\frac{3}{7}$, which is a still better approximation to the true value, $y = 20$.

The interested reader may easily verify that using more sub-intervals and intermediate points will bring us indefinitely close to the true solution-contour.[7] It is clear therefore that our new process brings us to the true solution in the limit, but unlike the Cauchy-Lipschitz process, it now approaches the solution from above. And we can use the word "above" in more than a geometrical sense. Along the new process lines, the individual is revealing himself to be getting better off. For just as A is inferior to Z', it is by the same reasoning inferior to B'', which is likewise inferior to Z''; from which it follows that A is inferior to Z''.

It should be clear, therefore, that no matter how many intermediate points there are in the new process, the consumer none the less reveals himself to be travelling uphill. It follows that every point above the mathematical contour line can reveal itself to be better than A.

6. CONCLUSION

This essentially completes the present demonstration. The mathematical contour lines defined by our differential equation have been proved to be the frontier between points revealed to be inferior to A, and points revealed to be superior. The points lying literally on a (concave) frontier locus can never themselves be revealed to be better or worse than A. If we wish, then, we may speak of them as being indifferent to A.

The whole theory of consumer's behaviour can thus be based upon operationally meaningful foundations in terms of revealed preference.[8]

---

[7] He may verify that using the points $x = 10, 11, 12, 13, 14, 15$ brings us to within $\frac{2}{3}$ of $y = 20$, as shown in the second table of the Numerical Appendix.

[8] The above remarks apply without qualification to two dimensional problems where the problem of "integrability" cannot appear. In the multidimensional case there still remain some problems, awaiting a solution for more than a decade now.

NUMERICAL APPENDIX

In the Cauchy-Lipschitz process, the straight line going from (x_0, y_0) to (x_1, y_1) is defined by the explicit equation

$$y = y_0 - f(x_0, y_0)(x - x_0) = y_0 - \frac{y_0}{x_0}(x - x_0) \tag{a}$$

where $dy/dx = -f(x, y)$ is the differential equation requiring solution —in this case being $= -y/x$. The three approximations given in Figure 2 are derived numerically in the following table.

TABLE I.   CAUCHY-LIPSCHITZ APPROXIMATION

x		y	$\dfrac{dy}{dx} = -f(x, y) = -\dfrac{y}{x}$	
	First approximation			
10	initial point	30	$-\dfrac{30}{10} =$	-3
15	$30 - 3(15 - 10) =$	15		
	Second approximation			
10	initial point	30	$-\dfrac{30}{10} =$	-3
12	$30 - 3(12 - 10) =$	24	$-\dfrac{24}{12} =$	-2
15	$24 - 2(15 - 12) =$	18		
	Third approximation			
10	initial point	30	$-\dfrac{30}{10} =$	-3
11	$30 - 3(11 - 10) =$	27	$-\dfrac{27}{11} =$	$-2\dfrac{5}{11}$
12	$27 - \dfrac{27}{11}(12 - 11) = \dfrac{270}{11} =$	$24\dfrac{6}{11}$	$-\dfrac{270}{(11)(12)}$	$-2\dfrac{1}{22}$
13	$\dfrac{270}{11} - \dfrac{270}{(11)(12)}(13 - 12) = \dfrac{270}{12} = 22\dfrac{1}{2}$		$-\dfrac{270}{(12)(13)} = -1\dfrac{19}{26}$	
14	$\dfrac{270}{12} - \dfrac{270}{(12)(13)}(14 - 13) = \dfrac{270}{13} = 20\dfrac{10}{13}$		$-\dfrac{270}{(13)(14)} = -1\dfrac{44}{91}$	
15	$\dfrac{270}{13} - \dfrac{270}{(13)(14)}(15 - 14) = \dfrac{270}{14} = 19\dfrac{2}{7}$			

In the new process which approaches the true solution, $y = 300/x$, from above, the straight lines have their slopes determined by the final point of each interval, or by the implicit equation

$$y_1 = y_0 - f(x_1, y_1)(x_1 - x_0). \qquad\qquad (b)$$

In the case where $f(x, y) = y/x$, we have

$$y_1 = y_0 \frac{y_1}{x_1}(x_1 - x_0)$$

or

$$y_1 = \frac{x_1}{2x_1 - x_0} y_0.$$

Our numerical approximations are given in the following table.

TABLE 2. NEW APPROXIMATING PROCESS

x_1	$y_1 = \dfrac{x_1}{2x_1 - x_0}(y_0)$	
	First approximation	
10	initial point	30
15	$\dfrac{15}{2(15) - 10}(30)$	$= 22\dfrac{1}{3}$
	Second approximation	
10	initial point	30
12	$\dfrac{12}{2(12) - 10}(30) =$	$\dfrac{180}{7} = 25\dfrac{4}{7}$
15	$\dfrac{15}{2(15) - 12}\dfrac{180}{7} =$	$\dfrac{150}{7} = 21\dfrac{3}{7}$
	Third approximation	
10	initial point	30
11	$\dfrac{11}{2(11) - 10}(30) =$	$\dfrac{330}{12} = 27\dfrac{1}{2}$
12	$\dfrac{12}{2(12) - 11}\dfrac{330}{12} = \dfrac{12}{13}\dfrac{330}{12} =$	$\dfrac{330}{13} = 25\dfrac{5}{13}$
13	$\dfrac{13}{2(13) - 12}\dfrac{330}{13} = \dfrac{13}{14}\dfrac{330}{13} =$	$\dfrac{330}{14} = 23\dfrac{3}{7}$
14	$\dfrac{14}{2(14) - 13}\dfrac{330}{14} = \dfrac{14}{15}\dfrac{330}{14} =$	$\dfrac{330}{15} = 22$
15	$\dfrac{15}{2(15) - 14}\dfrac{330}{15} = \dfrac{15}{16}\dfrac{330}{15} =$	$\dfrac{330}{16} = 20\dfrac{5}{8}$

It may be mentioned that the third Cauchy-Lipschitz approximation satisfies the equation $270/x$ which is less than the true solution, $300/x$; and the third approximation of the new upper process satisfies the equation $330/x$, which happens to be equally in excess of the true solution.

MATHEMATICAL PSYCHICS
(The Indifference Curve)

F. Y. Edgeworth

The PROBLEM to which attention is specially directed in this introductory summary is: *How far contract is indeterminate*—an inquiry of more than theoretical importance, if it show not only that indeterminateness tends to prevent widely, but also in what direction an escape from its evils is to be sought.

DEMONSTRATIONS.[1]—The general answer is—(α) Contract without competition is indeterminate, (β) Contract with *perfect* competition is perfectly determinate, (γ) Contract with more or less perfect competition is less or more indeterminate.

(a) Let us commence with almost the simplest case of contract—two individuals, X and Y, whose interest depends on two variable quantities, which they are agreed not to vary without mutual consent. Exchange of two commodities is a particular case of this kind of contract. Let x and y be the portions interchanged, as in Professor Jevons's example.[2] Then the utility of one party, say X, may be written $\Phi_1 (a - x) + \Psi_1 (y)$; and the utility of the other party, say Y, $\Phi_2 (x) + \Psi_2 (b - y)$; where Φ and Ψ are the integrals of Professor Jevons's symbols ϕ and ψ. It is agreed that x and y shall be varied only by consent (not e.g. by violence).

More generally. Let P, the utility of X, one party, $= F(x\,y)$, and Π, the utility of Y, the other party, $= \Phi(x\,y)$. If now it is inquired at what point they will reach equilibrium, one or both refusing to move further, to what *settlement* they will consent; the answer is in general that contract by itself does not supply sufficient conditions to determine the solution; supplementary conditions as will appear being supplied by competition or ethical motives. Contract will supply only *one* condition (for the two variables), namely

$$\frac{dP}{dx}\frac{d\Pi}{dy} = \frac{dP}{dy}\frac{d\Pi}{dx}$$

[1] *Conclusions* rather, the mathematical demonstration of which is not fully exhibited.

[2] *Theory of Political Economy*, 2nd ed., p. 107.

Source: 20–29, 1881.

(corresponding to Professor Jevons's equation

$$\frac{\phi_1(a - x)}{\psi_1(y)} = \frac{\phi_2(x)}{\psi_2(b - y)}$$

Theory p. 108), which it is proposed here to investigate.

Consider $P - F(x\,y) = 0$ as a surface, P denoting the length of the ordinate drawn from any point on the plane of $x\,y$ (say the plane of the paper) to the surface. Consider $\Pi - \Phi(x\,y)$ similarly. It is required to find a point $(x\,y)$ such that, in whatever direction we take an infinitely small step, P and Π do not increase together, but that, while one increases, the other decreases. It may be shown from a variety of points of view that the locus of the required point is

$$\frac{dP}{dx}\frac{d\Pi}{dy} - \frac{dP}{dy}\frac{d\Pi}{dx} = 0;$$

which locus it is here proposed to call the *contract-curve*.

(1) Consider first in what directions X can take an indefinitely small step, say of length ρ, from any point $(x\,y)$. Since the addition to P is

$$\rho\left[\left(\frac{dP}{dx}\right)\cos\theta + \left(\frac{dP}{dy}\right)\sin\theta\right]$$

$\rho\cos\theta$ being $= dx$, and $\rho\sin\theta = dy$, it is evident that X will step only on one side of a certain line, the *line of indifference,* as it might be called; its equation being

$$(\zeta - x)\left(\frac{dP}{dx}\right) + (\eta - y)\left(\frac{dP}{dy}\right) = 0.$$

And it is to be observed, in passing, that the direction in which X will *prefer* to move, the line of force or *line of preference,* as it may be termed, is perpendicular to the line of indifference. Similar remarks apply to Π. If then we enquire in what directions X and Y will consent to move *together,* the answer is, in any direction between their respective lines of indifference, in a direction *positive* as it may be called *for both.* At what point then will they refuse to move at all? When their *lines of indifference* are coincident (and *lines of preference* not only coincident, but in opposite directions); whereof the *necessary* (but *not sufficient*) condition is

$$\left(\frac{dP}{dx}\right)\left(\frac{d\Pi}{dy}\right) - \left(\frac{dP}{dy}\right)\left(\frac{d\Pi}{dx}\right) = 0.$$

(2) The same consideration might be thus put. Let the complete variation of P be $DP = \rho[(dP/dx) \cos \theta + (dP/dy) \sin \theta]$ and similarly for Π. Then in general θ can be taken, so that $DP/D\Pi$ should be positive, say $= g^2$, and so P and Π both increase together.

$$\tan \theta = - \frac{(dP/dx) - g^2(d\Pi/dx)}{(dP/dy) - g^2(d\Pi/dy)}$$

But this solution fails when

$$\frac{(dP/dx)}{(dP/dy)} = \frac{(d\Pi/dx)}{(d\Pi/dy)}$$

In fact, in this case $DP/d\Pi$ *is the same for all directions.* If, then, that common value of $DP/D\Pi$ is *negative,* motion is impossible in any direction.

(3) Or, again, we may consider that motion is possible so long as, one party not losing, the other gains. The point of equilibrium, therefore, may be described as a *relative maximum,* the point at which e.g. Π being constant, P is a maximum. Put $P = P - c \; (\Pi - \Pi')$, where c is a constant and Π' is the supposed given value of Π. Then P is a maximum only when

$$dx\left(\frac{dP}{dx} - c\frac{d\Pi}{dx}\right) + dy\left(\frac{dP}{dy} - c\frac{d\Pi}{dy}\right) = 0;$$

whence we have as before the contract-curve.

The same result would follow if we supposed Y induced to consent to the variation, not merely by the guarantee that he should not lose, or gain infinitesimally, but by the understanding that he should gain sensibly with the gains of P. For instance, let $\Pi = k^2 P$ where k is a constant, certainly not a very practicable condition. Or, more generally, let P move subject to the condition that $DP = \theta^2 \times D\Pi$, where θ is a function of the coordinates. Then DP, *subject to this condition,* vanishes only when

$$0 = \left(\frac{dP}{dx}\right)dx + \left(\frac{dP}{dy}\right)dy + c\left\{\left(\frac{dP}{dx}\right)dx + \left(\frac{dP}{dy}\right)dy - \theta^2\right.$$
$$\left.\left[\left(\frac{d\Pi}{dx}\right)dx + \left(\frac{d\Pi}{dy}\right)dy\right]\right\}$$

where c is a constant; whence

$$\left(\frac{dP}{dx}\right)(1 + c) - c\theta^2\left(\frac{d\Pi}{dx}\right) = 0$$

and

$$\left(\frac{dP}{dx}\right)(1 + c) - c\theta^2 \left(\frac{d\Pi}{dy}\right) = 0;$$

whence as before

$$\left(\frac{dP}{dx}\right)\left(\frac{d\Pi}{dy}\right) - \left(\frac{dP}{dy}\right)\left(\frac{d\Pi}{dx}\right) = 0.$$

No doubt the one theory which has been thus differently expressed could be presented by a professed mathematician more elegantly and scientifically. What appears to the writer the most philosophical presentation may be thus indicated.

(4) Upon the hypothesis above shadowed forth,[3] human action generally, and in particular the step taken by a contractor modifying articles of contract, may be regarded as the working of a gross force *governed*, let on, and directed by a more delicate pleasure-force. From which it seems to follow upon general dynamical principles applied to this special case that equilibrium is attained when the *total pleasure-energy of the contractors is a maximum relative*,[4] or subject, to conditions; the conditions being here (i) that the pleasure-energy of X and Y considered each as a function of (certain values of) the variables x and y should be functions of the *same* values: in the metaphorical language above employed that the charioteer-pleasures should drive their teams *together* over the plane of xy; (ii) that the joint-team should never be urged in a direction contrary to the *preference*[5] of either individual; that the resultant line of force (and the momentum) of the gross, the chariot, system should be continually intermediate between the (positive directions of the) lines of the respective pleasure-forces. [We may without disadvantage make abstraction of sensible momentum, and suppose then by the condition joint-system to move towards equilibrium along a line of resultant gross force. Let it start from the origin. And let us employ an *arbitrary function* to denote the unknown *principle of compromise* between the parties; suppose the ratio of the sines of angles made by the resultant line with the respective lines of pleasure-force.] Then, by reasoning different from the preceding only in the point of view, it appears that the *total utility of the system is a relative maximum at any point on the pure contract-curve*.

It appears from (1) and (2) there is a portion of the locus (dP/dx) $(d\Pi/dy)$ — $(d\Pi/dx)$ (dP/dy) = 0, where $DP/D\Pi$ is +, *not*

[3] See pp. 13–15.
[4] See note, p. 11.
[5] See p. 22.

therefore indicating immobility, *au contraire*, the *impure* (part of the) contract-curve, as it might be called. This might be illustrated by two spheres, each having the plane of the paper as a diametral plane. The contract curve is easily seen to be the line joining the centres. Supposing that the distance between the centres is less than the less of the radii, part of the contract-curve is *impure*. If the index, as Mr. Marshall might call it, be placed anywhere in this portion it will run up to a centre. But between the centres the contract-curve is *pure;* the index placed anywhere in this portion is immovable; and if account be taken of the portions of the spheres underneath the plane of the paper, the downward ordinates representing *negative pleasures,* similar statements hold, *mutatis mutandis.*

It appears that the pure and impure parts of the contract-curve are demarcated by the points where $DP/D\Pi$ changes sign, that is (in general) where either $DP/d\sigma$ or $D\Pi/d\sigma$ ($d\sigma$ being an increment of the length of the contract-curve) either vanishes or becomes infinite. Accordingly the maxima and minima of P and Π present demarcating points; for example, the centre of each sphere, which corresponds to a maximum in reference to the upper hemisphere, a minimum in reference to the lower hemisphere. The impure contract curve is relevant to cases where the commodity of one party is a *discommodity* to the other.

But even in the pure contract-curve all points do not in the same sense indicate immobility. For, according to the consideration (3) [above, p. 162] the contract-curve may be treated as the locus where, Π being constant, P is *stationary,* either a *maximum* or *minimum.* Thus any point in our case of two intersecting spheres affords a *maximum* in relation to the upper hemisphere; but the same point (it is only an accident that it should be *the same* point—it would not be the same point if you suppose slightly distorted spheres) affords a *minimum* in relation to the lower hemisphere. This *pure, but unstable* (part of the) contract-curve is exemplified in certain cases of that[6] *unstable equilibrium of trade,* which has been pointed out by Principal Marshall and Professor Walras.

The preceding theory may easily be extended to several persons and several variables. Let $P_1 = F_1 (x\,y\,z)$ denote the utility of one of three parties, utility depending on three variables, $x\,y\,z$; and similarly $P_2 = F_2$, $P_3 = F_3$. Then the *contract-settlement,* the arrangement for the alteration of which the consent of all three parties cannot be obtained, will be (subject to reservations analogous to those analysed in the preceding

---

[6] Mr. Marshall's figure 9 but *not* his figure 8; for the delicate relation between the conceptions—instability of *Trade* (where *perfect competition* is presupposed) and instability of *contract in general*—is not one of identity.

paragraphs) *the Eliminant.*

$$\frac{dP_1}{dx} \quad \frac{dP_1}{dy} \quad \frac{dP_1}{dz}$$

$$\frac{dP_2}{dx} \quad \frac{dP_2}{dy} \quad \frac{dP_2}{dz}$$

$$\frac{dP_3}{dx} \quad \frac{dP_3}{dy} \quad \frac{dP_3}{dz}$$

In general let there be m contractors and n subjects of contract, n variables. Then by the principle (3) [above, p. 162] the state of equilibrium may be considered as such that the utility of any one contractor must be a maximum *relative to* the utilities of the other contractors being constant, or not decreasing; which may be thus mathematically expressed:

$D(l_1P_1 + l_2P_2 + \&c. + l_mP_m) = 0$, where D represents complete increment and l_1l_2 &c., are indeterminate multipliers; whence, if there be n variables $x_1x_2 \ldots x_n$, we have n equations of the form

$$l_1\frac{dP_1}{dx_1} + l_2\frac{dP}{dx_1{}^2} + \&c. + l_m\frac{dP_m}{dx_1} = 0;$$

from which, if n be not less than m, we can eliminate the ($m-1$ independent) constants l and obtain the contract-system consisting of $n - (m-1)$ equations.

The case of n being less than m may be sufficiently illustrated by a particular example. Let the abscissa x represent the single variable on which the utilities P and Π of two persons contracting depend. Then if p and π are the maximum points for the respective pleasure-curves (compare the reasoning, p. 161) it is evident that the tract of abscissa between π and p is of the nature of pure contract-curve; that the index being placed anywhere in that tract will be immovable; secus on either side beyond π and p. Similarly it may be shown that, if three individuals are in contract about two variables $x\,y$, the contract locus or region is (the space within) a curvilinear triangle in the plane $x\,y$ bounded by the *three* contract-curves presented by successively supposing each pair of individuals to be in contract with respect to x and y. And similarly for larger numbers in hyperspace.

It is not necessary for the purpose of the present study to carry the analysis further. To gather up and fix our thoughts, let us imagine a simple case—Robinson Crusoe contracting with Friday. The *articles* of contract: wages to be given by the white, labour to be given by the

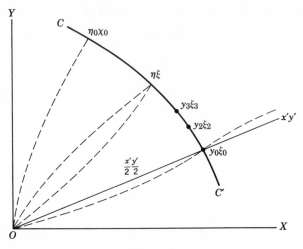

Figure 1

black. Let Robinson Crusoe $= X$. Represent y, the labour given by
Friday, by a horizontal line measured *northward* from an assumed
point, and measure x, the remuneration given by Crusoe, from the same
point along an *eastward* line (See accompanying Figure 1.). Then any
point between these lines represents a contract. It will very generally
be the interest of both parties to vary the articles of any contract taken
at random. But there is a class of contracts to the variation of which the
consent of *both* parties cannot be obtained, of *settlements*. These settlements are represented by an *indefinite number* of points, a locus, the
contract-curve CC', or rather, a certain portion of it which may be
supposed to be wholly in the space between our perpendicular lines in a
direction trending from south-east to north-west. This available portion
of the contract-curve lies between two points, say $\eta_0\chi_0$ north-west, and
$y_0\xi_0$ south-east; which are respectively the intersections with the contract-
curve of the *curves of indifference*[7] for each party drawn through the
origin. Thus the utility of the contract represented by $\eta_0\chi_0$ is for Friday
zero, or rather, the same as if there was no contract. At that point he
would as soon be off with the bargain—work by himself perhaps.

This simple case brings clearly into view the characteristic evil of
indeterminate contract, *deadlock*, undecidable opposition of interests,
ἀκριτὸς[8] ἔρις καὶ ταραχή. It is the interest of both parties that there should

---

[7] See p. 22.
[8] Demosthenes, *De Corona*.

be *some settlement,* one of the contracts represented by the contract-curve between the limits. But *which* of these contracts is arbitrary in the absence of arbitration, the interests of the two *adversâ pugnantia fronte* all along the contract-curve, Y desiring to get as far as possible south-east towards $\gamma_0\xi_0$, X north-west toward $\eta_0\chi_0$. And it further appears from the preceding analysis that in the case of any number of *articles* (for instance, Robinson Crusoe to give Friday in the way of Industrial Partnership a *fraction* of the produce as well as wages, or again, *arrangements about the mode* of work), the *contract-locus* may still be represented as a sort of line, along which the pleasure-forces of the contractors are mutually antagonistic.

MANUEL D'ECONOMIE POLITIQUE
(Ophélimité)

Vilfredo Pareto

32. For an individual, the *ophélimité* of a certain quantity of a thing, added to another known quantity (which can be equal to zero) of this thing already possessed by him, is the pleasure which this quantity affords him.

33. If this quantity is very small (infinitely small) and if the pleasure which is procured is divided by the quantity itself, we have the *OPHÉLIMITÉ ÉLÉMENTAIRE*.[1]

34. Finally, if we divide the *ophélimité élémentaire* by the price, we have the *OPHÉLIMITÉ ÉLÉMENTAIRE PONDERÉE*.[2]

35. The theory of *ophélimité* has received a new perfection. In all the reasoning used to establish it there is a weak point, which has been pointed out principally by Professor Irving Fisher.[3] We have assumed that this thing called *pleasure, value in use, economic utility, ophélimité,* was a quantity; but a demonstration has not been given. Assuming this demonstration accomplished, how would we measure this quantity? It is an error to believe that in a general fashion we could deduce the value of *ophélimité* from the law of supply and demand. We can do so only in one particular case, the unit of measure of *ophélimité* alone re-

---

[1] [Trans. note—The English term "marginal utility," being much more familiar, would perhaps be preferred by many readers. However, its use would be inappropriate in view of the earlier decision to retain *ophélimité*.]

[2] [Trans. note—Weighted marginal utility or weighted final degree of utility, the weights being the reciprocals of the prices. In symbols we would write

$$\frac{\varphi_x}{p_x}, \frac{\varphi_y}{p_y}, \frac{\varphi_z}{p_z}, \ldots$$

See Henry Schultz, "Interrelations of Demand, Price, and Income," *Journal of Political Economy*, Vol. 43, (1935), p. 437.

Thus the *ophélimité élémentaire ponderée* (weighted marginal utility) of a commodity may be defined as the increase in total utility which results from a unit increase in expenditure on the commodity. See Kenneth Boulding, *Economic Analysis*, 1st ed., (New York: Harper and Brothers, 1941), p. 644.]

[3] [Trans. note—See his *Mathematical Investigations in the Theory of Value and Prices*, (New Haven: Yale University Press, 1925), pp. 86–89; reprinted from *Transactions of the Connecticut Academy*, Vol. IX, July, 1892.]

Source: Manuel D'Economie Politique, Second Edition, 1927. Translated by Ann Stranquist Schwier; an alternative translation is forthcoming from the American Economic Association. Reprinted with permission.

maining arbitrary; this is when it is a matter of goods of a kind such that the *ophélimité* of each of them depends only on the quantity of that good, and remains independent of the quantities of other goods consumed (Appendix[4]). But in general, that is to say when the *ophélimité* of a good *A*, consumed at the same time as goods *B, C, . . .* , depends not only on the consumption of *A*, but also on the consumption of *B, C, . . .* , the *ophélimité* remains indeterminate, even after we have fixed the unit which serves as the measure (Appendix).[5]

36. Hereafter when we speak of *ophélimité*, it must always be understood that we wish simply to indicate one of the systems of indices of *ophélimité* (Par. 55).

36b. The notions of *value in use, utility, ophélimité*, indices of *ophélimité*, etc., greatly facilitate the exposition of the theory of economic equilibrium, but they are not necessary to construct this theory.

Thanks to the use of mathematics, this entire theory, as we develope it in the Appendix, rests on no more than a fact of experience, that is to say on the determination of the quantities of goods which constitute combinations indifferent for the individual[6] (Par. 52). The theory of

[4] [Trans. note—See Par. 10–12 of the Appendix.]

[5] [Trans. note—This statement represents the final conclusion of what some have called Pareto's most important contribution—his demonstration of the immeasurability of utility. See J. R. Hicks and R. G. D. Allen, "A Reconsideration of the Theory of Value," *Economica*, 1934, pp. 52–76 and 196–219. In the words of the authors, this article undertakes the task of "examining what adjustments in the statement of the marginal theory of value are made necessary by Pareto's discovery." Pareto, as it happened, had already constructed much of his theory before coming to the conclusion of the immeasurability of utility and never really carried out the reconstruction necessitated by it.

But see Oscar Lange, "The Determinateness of the Utility Function," *Review of Economic Studies*, Vol. I, (1933–34), pp. 218–225, for a demonstration that the measurability of utility can be deduced from two basic postulates both of which he finds in Pareto (IV, 32). See the footnote to that section and to III, 198 below. Ragnar Frisch has also stated that he has measured the marginal utility of money in his *New Methods of Measuring Marginal Utility*, (Beitrage zur okonomischen Theorie). Tubingen: Verlag von J. C. B. Mohr (Paul Siebeck), 1932. See Henry Schultz's review article "Frisch on the Measurement of Utility," *Journal of Political Economy*, Vol. 41, (1933), pp. 95–116. And see also Irving Fisher, "A Statistical Method for Measuring 'Marginal Utility' and Testing the Justice of a Progressive Income Tax," in *Economic Essays Contributed in Honor of John Bates Clark*, (New York: The Macmillan Company, 1927).]

[6] This cannot be understood by literary economists and metaphysicians. They will, nevertheless, want to get into it to give their opinion; and the reader who has some knowledge of mathematics can amuse himself by perusing the foolish trash which they will give out on the subject of this paragraph and of Par. 8 *et seq.* in the Appendix.

economic science thus acquires the rigor of rational mechanics; it deduces its results from experience, without bringing in any metaphysical entity.

37. As we have observed already, there can be certain constraints which prevent the modifying of phenomena to fit tastes. For example, in former times there were governments which obliged their subjects to buy a certain quantity of salt each year. It is evident, in this case, that for this matter there would be no account taken of tastes. One would not have to take account of them for any matter, if the quantity which each must buy each year would be fixed for everyone. If it were thus in practice, it would be useless to waste our time investigating the theory of tastes. But the most ordinary observation is sufficient in order to see that things do not happen that way in reality. Even when there are certain constraints, as, for example, when the State, having a monopoly of a good, fixes the price or imposes certain obstacles to production, sale, free commerce, etc., that does not absolutely prevent the individual from acting according to his tastes, within certain limits. Consequently, everyone must resolve certain problems in order to determine his consumption according to his tastes. The poor man will ask himself whether it would be better for him to buy a little sausage or a little wine; the rich man will consider whether he prefers to buy an automobile or a jewel; but everyone, more or less, solves problems of this type. Hence the necessity of considering the abstract theory which corresponds to these concrete facts.

38. We will try to explain, without making use of algebraic symbols, the results which mathematical economics reaches. We will use the symbols only in the appendix. It will be sufficient here to recall certain principles, of which the main one is, for the moment, the following. The conditions of a problem are interpreted algebraically by equations. The latter contain known quantities and unknown quantities. To determine a certain number of unknowns there must be an equal number of distinct conditions (equations), that is, of conditions such that no one of them is a consequence of the others. Moreover, they must not be contradictory. For example, if we are looking for two unknown numbers and have given for conditions (equations) that the sum of those two numbers must be equal to a given number, and the difference to another given number, the problem is completely determined, because there are two unknowns and two conditions (equations). But if, on the contrary, you were given, besides the sum of the two numbers, the sum of twice each of those numbers, the second condition would be a consequence of the first, because if 4, for example, is the sum of two unknown numbers, 8 will be the sum of twice each of those numbers. We do not have, in this case, two

distinct conditions (equations), and the problem remains indeterminate. In economic problems it is very important to know whether certain conditions completely determine the problem, or leave it indeterminate.[7]

39. *Direct effects and indirect effects of tastes.* We could make numerous hypotheses about the way in which man lets himself be guided by his tastes, and each of them would serve as a base for an abstract theory. In order to avoid exposing ourselves to a waste of time in studying useless theories, we must examine the concrete facts and inquire into what types of abstract theories fit them.

Assume an individual who buys a 3% French government bond for 99.35. Ask him why he made that transaction. It is, he will say, because he estimates that at that price it suits him to buy that bond. Having placed in balance, on the one side the expenditure of 99.35 and on the other the income of 3 francs per year, he estimates that, for him, the purchase of that annuity is worth that expenditure. If it could be purchased for 98, he would buy 6 francs of annuity instead of 3 francs. He does not raise the problem of deciding whether he would prefer to buy 3 francs at 99.35 or 6 francs at 98; that would be a useless investigation, since the setting of the price does not depend on him. He investigates, because this alone depends on him, what quantity of annuity it suits him to buy at a given price. Let us interrogate his seller. It may be that he made his decision according to exactly the same reasons. In that case, we still have the same type of contract. But towards the end of the year 1902 we would have been able to hit upon someone who would have told us: "I am selling in order to lower the price of the annuity, and thus annoy the French government." At every turn we can find someone who will tell us: "I am selling (or I am buying) to lower (or raise) the price of the annuity, in order then to turn it to account and procure for myself certain advantages." One who so operates is motivated by reasons very different from those we have previously considered: he tends to modify the price and he compares principally the positions which he reaches with different prices. We are faced with another type of contract.

40. *Types of phenomena of the effects of tastes.* The two types of phenomena that we have just indicated have a great importance for the study of political economy; let us investigate their characteristics, and

---

[7] [Trans. note. Referring to this whole section on "men's tastes" (Par. 29–38), A. R. Sweezy has this comment to make: "Pareto also [as well as Fisher] divorces subjective value from psychology, though it is difficult to see how, having effected this separation, he can maintain that his theory rests on 'facts of experience' on the subjective side." "The Interpretation of Subjective Value Theory in the Writings of the Austrian Economists," *Review of Economic Studies,* Vol. I (1933–34), pp. 176–185.]

meanwhile indicate the first type by (I) and the second by (II). We begin by considering the case where one who transforms economic goods sets for himself solely the seeking of his personal advantage; we will come later (Par. 49) to the cases where this is not so.

We will say that one who buys, or who sells, a good can be guided by two quite distinct types of considerations.

41. He can seek exclusively the satisfaction of his tastes, a certain state or condition of the market being given. He certainly contributes, but without directly seeking it, toward modifying this state, since, according to the different states of the market, he is disposed to transform a larger or smaller quantity of one good into another. He compares the successive transformations, in the same state of the market, and he seeks to find a state such that these successive transformations bring him to a point where his tastes are satisfied. We thus have type (I).

42. The individual considered can, on the other hand, seek to modify the conditions of the market in order to gain an advantage therefrom or for any other purpose whatsoever. A certain state of the market being given, exchange causes equilibrium to take place at one point; in another state, equilibrium takes place at another point. One compares these two positions and seeks that which best attains the end he has in view. After having made a choice, he busies himself in changing the conditions of the market in such a way as corresponds to that choice. We thus have type (II).

43. Evidently, though type (I) can be that of the transactions of any individual who comes on the market, type (II), on the contrary, can include only those who understand, and who can modify, the conditions of the market, which certainly is not the case for everyone.

44. Let us pursue our investigations and we will see that type (I) includes a very great number of transactions, into which enter the majority or even all the transactions which have domestic consumption for an object. When has anyone ever seen a housewife, buying chicory or coffee, concern herself with something other than the price of these objects, and say: "if I buy chicory today that may cause the price of this good to rise in the future, and I must consider the damage which the purchase that I make today will inflict on me in the future"? Who has ever abstained from ordering a suit, not in order to avoid the expenditure, but to lower, in that way, the price of suits in general? If anyone were to present himself on the market saying: "It would be agreeable to me if strawberries sold for only 30 centimes a kilogram, therefore I hold to that price," he would expose himself to ridicule. He does say, on the contrary: "at 30 centimes a kilogram I would buy 10 kilograms, at 60 centimes I would buy only 4 kilograms, at one franc I would not buy any"; and he sees whether he can thus bring himself into accord

with those who sell. This type (I) corresponds then to very numerous concrete facts, and it will not be a waste of time to build a theory on it.

45. We also find numerous examples of type (II). On the stock exchange, powerful banking companies and syndicates follow this type. Those who, thanks to powerful means, seek to monopolize some goods, evidently wish to modify the conditions of the market in order to make a profit thereby. When the French government sets the price of the tobacco it sells to the public, it operates according to type (II). All those who enjoy a monopoly, and who can draw a profit from it, behave according to this type.

46. If we look at reality, we see that type (I) occurs where there is competition among those who follow it. The persons with whom they deal may not be in competition and consequently not follow type (I). Type (I) is the more pure as competition is the more widespread and the more perfect. It is precisely because each day on the Paris Exchange there are many people who buy and sell French bonds, that it would be foolish to wish to modify the conditions of that market by buying or selling a few francs of annuity. Obviously, if all those who are selling (or who are buying) enter into an agreement, they could effectively modify these conditions to their profit; but they do not know one another, and each acts on his own account. In the midst of this confusion and this competition, each individual has nothing else to do than to occupy himself with his own affairs and seek to satisfy his own tastes, according to the different conditions which may appear on the market. All the sellers (or the buyers) of bonds clearly modify the prices, but they modify them without previous design; it is not the purpose, but the effect of their operations.

47. We observe type (II) where competition does not exist and where there is engrossment, monopoly, etc. While an individual operates in order to modify the conditions of the market to his profit, he must, if he does not want to work in vain, be sure that others will not come in to disturb his operations. And for that he must in some way rid himself of his competitors. This can happen either by the aid of the law, or because he alone possesses certain goods, or because by intrigue, trickery, by his influence or his intelligence, he removes his competitors. It may also be that he can be unconcerned about his competitors, because they have but little importance, or for any other reason.

Finally it must be noted that it often happens that a certain number of individuals join together precisely so that they can make themselves masters of the market; in this case we still have type (II), since, from certain points of view, the association can be considered as comprising only one individual.

48. We encounter an analogous, but not identical, case when a certain

number of persons or associations work together to modify certain conditions of the market, but allow complete freedom of action to the associates in regard to other conditions. Often the selling price is fixed, each member remaining free to sell as much as he can. Sometimes the quantity that each may sell is fixed, either in an absolute fashion, or in such a way that this limit cannot be exceeded without paying a certain sum to the association; it may also be stipulated that a premium will be paid to anyone who stays below the fixed quantity. As for price, it is set freely by each seller; only exceptionally are conditions of sale fixed.

For example, workers' syndicates sometimes impose uniformity of wages: one who purchases the labor of ten workmen at a certain price, cannot purchase the labor of an eleventh workman at a lower price. Moreover, the syndicates, ordinarily, also fix the price in such a way that not only is the going wage fixed, but also the conditions, and we come back to one of the preceding cases.

The law sometimes prescribes the sale at the same price of all portions of a good. It is this way in nearly all countries for railroads, which cannot charge the tenth passenger more or less than what, under identical conditions, they charge the first. A philanthropist may sell below the price in order to aid consumers or a certain class of consumers. We will see other cases when we speak of production. It is clear that they can be very numerous since they refer to the very diverse conditions that can be modified in the economic phenomenon.

49. We must examine then the diverse kinds of type (II). We must now set apart one of these kinds to which we will give the name of type (III). It is that which occurs when one wishes to organize the whole of the economic phenomenon in such a way that the maximum of well-being is procured for all those who participate. We must, however, define in a precise fashion what this well-being consists of (VI, 33, 52). Type (III) corresponds to the collectivist organization of society.

50. Note that types (I) and (II) are relative to individuals; it can then happen, and it does happen ordinarily, that when two persons contract together, one follows type (I), the other type (II); or, if a large number of persons enter into the bargaining, some follow type (I) and others type (II). It is the same for type (III), if the collectivist state allows any freedom to its members.

51. One who follows type (II) stops, according to the very definition given to this type, at a point where his tastes are not *directly* satisfied. Consequently, in comparing the condition which the individual would reach in following type (I) and that which he would reach in following type (II), we will see that the second differs from the first by certain plus or minus quantities of goods. We could then also define type (I) in

the following way: it is that in which the quantities of goods satisfy the tastes directly; and type (II) is that in which the quantities of goods are such that, the tastes being directly satisfied, there remains a positive or negative residue.

52. *Indifference lines of tastes.* Take a man who allows himself to be influenced only by his tastes and who possesses 1 kilogram of bread and 1 kilogram of wine. His tastes being given, he is disposed to have a little less bread and a little more wine, or vice versa. He consents, for example, to having only 0.9 kilogram of bread provided he have 1.2 of wine. In other words, this signifies that these two combinations, to have 1 kilogram of bread and 1 kilogram of wine or 0.9 kilogram of bread and 1.2 kilograms of wine, are equal for him; he does not prefer the second to the first, nor the first to the second; he would not know which to choose, it is *indifferent* to him to possess the one or the other of these combinations.

Starting from that combination—1 kilogram of bread and 1 kilogram of wine—we find a great number of others, between which the choice is indifferent, and we have for example

Bread	1.6	1.4	1.2	1.0	0.8	0.6
Wine	0.7	0.8	0.9	1.0	1.4	1.8

We call this series, which could be extended indefinitely, an *indifference series.*

53. The use of graphs greatly facilitates the understanding of this question:

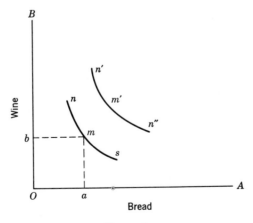

Figure 1

Draw two axes, OA, OB, perpendicular to each other; put on OA the quantities of bread, on OB the quantities of wine. [Figure 1] For example, Oa represents one of bread, Ob one of wine; the point m, where these two ordinates intersect, indicates the combination 1 kilogram of bread and 1 kilogram of wine.

54. We can represent in this manner all the preceding series, and joining all the points of that series by a continuous line, we will have the line nms which is called an *indifference line* or *indifference curve*.[8]

55. Let us give each of these combinations an index, which must satisfy the following two conditions, and which remains arbitrary in other respects: (1) Two combinations between which the choice is indifferent must have the same index; (2) of two combinations, that which is preferred to the other must have a larger index.[9, 10]

56. It follows from the above that all the combinations of one indif-

---

[8] This expression is due to Professor F. Y. Edgeworth. He assumed the existence of *utility* (*ophélimité*) and deduced the indifference curves from it. On the contrary, I consider the indifference curves as given fact, and deduce from them all that is necessary to me for the theory of equilibrium, without having recourse to *ophélimité*. [Trans. note—For a short but clear exposition of the difference between the procedures used by Edgeworth and by Pareto see Henry Schultz, "The Italian School of Mathematical Economics," *Journal of Political Economy*, Vol. 39, (1931), pp. 76–85, esp. pp. 77–80.]

[9] See IV, 32, for another condition which it is useful to add, but which it is not necessary to bring in here.

[10] [Trans. note—Here is given one of the most important postulates of the entire theory of value—namely, that an individual can tell which of two combinations has the greater utility for him, that is, he can tell whether

$$\phi_1(x_1, y_1, z_1, \ldots) \gtreqless \phi_2(x_2, y_2, z_2, \ldots)$$

and the function changes in the same direction as the utility yielded changes. The index increases as utility increases. Note that this can be *observed* in the market. The combination which is actually chosen is taken to be the one with the greatest utility for the individual considered. And on this postulate, on this fact of experience alone, the entire theory of value can be built, with no need whatsoever to "measure" utility. See Hicks and Allen, "A Reconsideration of the Theory of Value," *Economica*, (1934), pp. 52–76 and 196–219.

For a precise statement of two fundamental assumptions and their corresponding postulates involved in Pareto's theory, and their significance for the measurability of utility controversy, see Oscar Lange, "The Determinateness of the Utility Function," *Review of Economic Studies*, Vol. I, (1933–34), pp. 218–225. See also R. G. D. Allen, "A Note on the Determinateness of the Utility Function," *Review of Economic Studies*, Vol. II, (1935), pp. 155–158, for further defense of the thesis that the assumption of ordered utility is the only one needed for the theory of value.]

ference series have the same index, that is, all the points on an indifference line have the same index.

Let 1 be the index of line *nms* of Fig. 1; let *m'* (for example 1.1 of bread and 1.1 of wine) be another combination which the individual prefers to combination *m*, and give it the index 1.1. Starting from this combination *m'* we find another indifference series, that is, we describe another curve *n'm'n''*. We can continue in this fashion, considering, of course, not only combinations which are, for the individual, better than combination *m*, but also those which are worse. We will thus have several indifference series, each one having its index; in other words, we will cover the part of the plane *OAB* which we want to consider with an infinite number of indifference curves each one having its index.

57. This gives us a complete representation of the tastes of the individual in regard to bread and wine, and that is sufficient for us to determine economic equilibrium. The individual can disappear, provided he leaves us this photograph of his tastes.

It is understood, of course, that we can repeat for all goods what we have said about bread and wine.

58. The reader who uses topographical charts knows that it is customary to describe certain curves which represent the points which have, for the same curve, the same height above sea level, or above any other level whatsoever.

The curves in Fig. 1 are contour lines, if we consider the indices of *ophélimité* to represent the height above the plane *OAB*, assumed horizontal, of the points of a hill. It can be called the hill of the indices of pleasure. There are other similar ones, infinite in number, according to the arbitrary system of indices chosen.

If pleasure can be measured, if *ophélimité* exists, one of these systems of indices will be precisely that of the values of *ophélimité* (App. 3), and the corresponding hill will be the hill of pleasure or of *ophélimité*.[11]

59. An individual who possesses a certain combination of bread and wine can be represented by a point on that hill. The pleasure that this individual experiences will be represented by the height of this point above the plane *OAB*. The individual will experience a greater pleasure

---

[11] [Trans. note—The implication here is important. We start with the indifference curves which represent facts of experience, observable in the market behavior of individuals. They carry arbitrary indices, ordering but not measuring the underlying utility. And we may have an infinite number of these systems of indifference curves depending on the system of indices arbitrarily chosen. But one of these, we do not know which, would measure as well as order the utility, if utility could be subjected to an absolute scale.]

insofar as he is at a greater height; of two combinations he will always prefer that which is represented by a higher point of the hill.

60. *The paths.* Assume an individual who possesses the quantity of bread represented by *oa* and the quantity of wine represented by *ab* [Figure 2]. We say that the individual finds himself at the point on the hill which is projected at *b* on the horizontal plane *xy*, or in an elliptical fashion, that he is at *b*. Assume that at another moment the individual has *oa'* of bread and *a'b'* of wine; leaving *b* he will be at *b'*. Next if he has *oa"* of bread and *a"b"* of wine, he will have gone from *b'* to *b"*, and so on up to *o*. Assume that the points *b*, *b'*, *b"*, are very close together, and join them by a line; we will say that the individual who has had successively the quantity *oa* of bread and *ab* of wine, *oa'* of bread and *a'b'* of wine, etc., has traveled, on the hill, along a *path*, or route, or way, which is projected, on the horizontal plane *oxy*, along the line *bb'b"* . . . *c*, or, in an elliptical fashion, that he *has traveled along* the path *bc*.

61. Note that if an individual traveled along an infinite number of paths *hb*, *h'b'*, *h"b"*, . . . , and if he paused at the points *b*, *b'*, *b"*, . . . , we would have to consider him as traveling along, in reality, the path *b*, *b'*, *b"* . . . . *c*.

62. Consider a path *mn* tangent at *c* to an indifference curve *t"*; and assume that the indices of *ophélimité* increase from *t* toward *t"*, and that the path rises from *m* up to *c*, to descend then from *c* to *n*. [Figure 3] A point *a* which, starting from *m*, comes before the point *c*, and beyond which the obstacles do not permit the individual to go, will be called a TERMINAL POINT. It is encountered only in mounting from *m* toward *c*, and not in descending from *c* to *n*. Consequently, *b* would

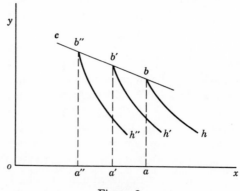

Figure 2

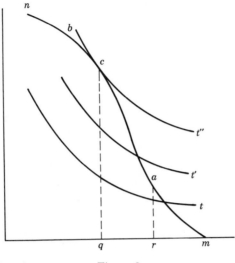

Figure 3

not be a terminal point for one who would travel along the path *mn*, but it would be for one who would travel along the path *nm*, that is, for one who, starting from *n*, would go toward *m*.

63. The terminal point and the point of tangency have a common property, namely, of being the highest point which the individual can reach in traveling along the path *mn*. The point *c* is the highest point of the entire path; the point *a* the highest point of the portion of the path *ma* which the individual is permitted to travel along.

64. It will be seen below how this way of representing the phenomena by indifference curves and paths is convenient for expounding the theories of economics.

65. *Continuous variations and discontinuous variations.* The indifference curves and the paths could be discontinuous, and they are so in reality. That is, the variations of the quantities occur in a discontinuous fashion. An individual passes from a condition in which he has 10 handkerchiefs to a condition in which he has 11, and not by intermediate conditions in which he would have, for example, 10 and 1/100 handkerchiefs, 10 and 2/100 handkerchiefs, etc.

In order to draw nearer reality, we would thus have to consider finite variations, but in that there is a technical difficulty.

Problems concerning quantities which vary by infinitely small degrees are much easier to solve than problems in which the quantities undergo finite variations. We must then, every time it is possible, replace the latter by the former; one proceeds in that way in all the physico-natural sciences. We know that in this way an error is committed; but it can be neglected either when it is small absolutely, or when it is smaller than other inevitable errors which make it useless to seek a precision which escapes us elsewhere. It is precisely so in political economy, for there we consider only average phenomena and those referring to large numbers. We speak of the individual, not in order to investigate effectively what one individual consumes or produces, but only to consider one of the elements of a collectivity, and then to total the consumption and the production of a large number of individuals.

66. When we say that an individual consumes one and one-tenth watches, it would be ridiculous to take those words literally. A tenth of a watch is an unknown object and one which is not used. But these words signify simply that, for example, one hundred individuals consume 110 watches.

When we say that equilibrium takes place when an individual consumes one and one-tenth watches, we simply mean that equilibrium takes place when 100 individuals consume—some one, others two or more watches and even none at all—in such a way that all together they consume about 110, and the average is 1.1 for each.

This manner of expression is not peculiar to political economy; it is found in a great number of sciences.

In insurance one speaks of fractions of living persons, for example twenty-seven and thirty-seven hundredths living persons. It is quite obvious that there does not exist thirty-seven hundredths of a living person!

If one did not agree to replace discontinuous variations by continuous variations, the theory of the lever could not be derived. We say that a lever having equal arms, a balance for example, is in equilibrium when it is supporting equal weights. But I might take a balance which is sensitive to a centigram, put in one of the trays a milligram more than in the other, and state that, contrary to the theory, it remains in equilibrium.

The balance in which we weigh men's tastes is such that, for certain goods, it is sensitive to the gram, for others only to the hectogram, for others to the kilogram, etc.

The only conclusion that can be drawn is that we must not demand from these balances more precision than they can give.

67. Moreover, since it is only a matter of a technical difficulty, those who have time to spare can amuse themselves by considering finite

variations; and, after stubborn and extremely long labor, they will arrive at results which, within the limit of the possible errors, do not differ from those at which we arrive easily and quickly by considering infinitesimal variations—at least in. ordinary cases. We are writing in order to investigate in an objective fashion the relations between phenomena and not to please the pedantic.

PROFESSOR SLUTSKY'S THEORY
OF CONSUMERS' CHOICE

R. G. D. Allen

In an article published in 1934,[1] Dr. J. R. Hicks and I attempted to develop a theory of consumers' choice on Paretian lines which would be, at the same time, more consistent and more complete than the theory as left by Pareto himself. Our main object was to show that the theory could be constructed without reference to any determinate or measurable concept of utility. The arbitrary element in the representation of utility was clearly pointed out by Pareto, but his theory of value was never modified to allow for it in any systematic way. In particular, we maintained that the complementary and competitive relations of goods in consumption were most inadequately described by Pareto and we advanced definitions which we considered were theoretically more satisfactory and also more serviceable from the point of view of application. In the article, much use was made of the ideas of the mathematical work of Johnson,[2] but we thought that some of the results attained, as apart from the method of approach, were entirely original. Most recently, however, our attention has been drawn to an important article by Professor Slutsky, of Charkov University, entitled *Sulla teoria del biancio del consumatore* and published in the *Giornale degli Economisti* as long ago as 1915. It is now clear that many of our results were first given explicitly by Slutsky in this article and that, though the results were not interpreted in terms of the complementary and competitive relations between goods, yet his own use of them was essentially very similar to ours. The purpose of the present article is to promote wider recognition of the value of Slutsky's work by giving a resumé of the argument of his article, omitting a great deal of the highly in-

[1] A Reconsideration of the Theory of Value, *Economica,* 1934.
[2] The Pure Theory of Utility Curves, *Economic Journal,* 1913.

Source: Reprinted with permission from *Review of Economic Studies,* III: 120–129 (February 1936).

183

volved mathematical development, and by comparing his theory with that developed independently by Hicks and myself.[3]

I

After a number of remarks on Pareto's theory of value and concept of utility, Slutsky states the basis of his own general theory by giving a definition of utility and by setting out three assumptions concerning the utility function so defined. The definition of utility is:

> The utility of a combination of goods is a quantity possessing the property of assuming greater or less values according to the degree of preference for the combination expressed by the individual considered.

If u is the utility obtained from the combination consisting of amounts x_1, x_2, . . . x_n of the various goods bought by the individual in a given period of time, then we write the utility function:

$$u = \psi(x_1, x_2, \ldots x_n)$$

Three assumptions are now made:

(1) The assumption of the continuity of the utility function and of its derivatives of the first two orders.

(2) The assumption that the utility function remains unaltered in form during the period of time considered.

(3) The assumption that the increment of utility from one combination of goods to another is not dependent on the mode of variation from the one combination to the other.

The marginal utility of the rth good is represented by the partial derivative of the utility function

$$u_r = \frac{\partial \psi}{\partial x_r}$$

and this is taken as positive since the theory of choice is here limited

---

[3] It is interesting to note the existence of a long time-lag between the publication of a highly mathematical theory, such as those of Johnson and Slutsky, and the general recognition of the main results achieved in the theory. When it is remembered, in addition, that Slutsky's article appeared in a journal of a country actively preparing for war, it cannot be considered as surprising that the work has remained completely unknown to English-speaking economists. Since the present article went to press, Professor Henry Schultz has published a long article on "Interrelations of Demand, Price and Income" (*Journal of Political Economy*, August, 1935) in which he gives the essentials of Slutsky's work. It appears that Schultz discovered Slutsky's *Giornale* article rather earlier than, but quite independently of, Hicks and myself.

to consumers who find themselves in positions where they prefer more of any good to less. The second order partial derivatives of the utility function

$$u_{rr} = \frac{\partial^2 \psi}{\partial x_r^2}; \qquad u_{rs} = \frac{\partial^2 \psi}{\partial x_r \partial x_s} = \frac{\partial^2 \psi}{\partial x_s \partial x_r}$$

then indicate the dependence of the marginal utilities on the amounts of the goods bought. There are two kinds of goods to consider, i.e. those goods for which the marginal utility decreases as more is bought ($u_{rr} < 0$) and those for which the marginal utility increases as more is bought ($u_{rr} > 0$). Goods of the first kind are called "satiable" goods and those of the second kind "nonsatiable" goods.

If i is the income of the individual in a given period, if $p_1, p_2, \ldots p_n$ are the prices of the n goods and if $x_1, x_2, \ldots x_n$ are the amounts bought, then

$$p_1 x_1 + p_2 n_2 + \cdots + p_n x_n = i \qquad (1)$$

For a stable choice, with fixed income and prices, the utility function must have a maximum value consistent with (1). The conditions for this are

$$\frac{u_1}{p_1} = \frac{u_2}{p_2} = \cdots = \frac{u_n}{p_n} = u' \qquad (2)$$

where u' is the marginal utility of money, and

$$d^2u = u_{11}dx_1^2 + u_{22}dx_2^2 + \cdots + 2u_{12}dx_1dx_2 + \cdots < 0 \qquad (3)$$

The analysis which follows makes use of a simple determinant notation. Let

$$M = \begin{vmatrix} 0 & p_1 & p_2 & \cdots & p_n \\ p_1 & u_{11} & u_{12} & \cdots & u_{1n} \\ p_2 & u_{12} & u_{22} & \cdots & u_{2n} \\ & & \cdots & & \\ p_n & u_{1n} & u_{2n} & \cdots & u_{nn} \end{vmatrix}$$

and let M_{or} denote the minor of p_r and M_{rs} the minor of u_{rs} in the determinant M (r and $s = 1, 2, \ldots n$). Finally, let R denote the minor of the element of the first row and column of M, i.e.

$$R = \begin{vmatrix} u_{11} & u_{12} & \cdots & u_{1n} \\ u_{12} & u_{22} & \cdots & u_{2n} \\ & \cdots & & \\ u_{1n} & u_{2n} & \cdots & u_{nn} \end{vmatrix}$$

These determinants take values dependent on the particular combination of amounts of the goods bought and involve the second order derivatives of the utility function. The determinants other than R also depend on the prices of the goods.

The conditions for stability of choice are given by the inequality (3) provided that the equations (2) are satisfied. A linear transformation connecting the differentials dx_1, dx_2, . . . dx_n with new differentials $d\xi_1$, $d\xi_2$, . . . $d\xi_n$ is chosen, so that d^2u takes the form:

$$d^2u = A_1 d\xi_1{}^2 + A_2 d\xi_2{}^2 + \cdot \cdot + A_n d\xi_n{}^2$$

where the co-efficients A_1, A_2, . . . A_n depend on the values of the second order partial derivatives of u at the equilibrium combination. It is shown[4] that these co-efficients are expressed as the ratios of successive principal minors of the determinant R:

$$A_1 = u_{11}; \ A_2 = \frac{\begin{vmatrix} u_{11} u_{12} \\ u_{12} u_{22} \end{vmatrix}}{u_{11}}; \ A_3 = \frac{\begin{vmatrix} u_{11} u_{12} u_{13} \\ u_{12} u_{22} u_{23} \\ u_{13} u_{23} u_{33} \end{vmatrix}}{\begin{vmatrix} u_{11} u_{12} \\ u_{12} u_{22} \end{vmatrix}}; \ \text{etc.}$$

The stability conditions are that d^2u is negative for all values of $d\xi_1$, $d\xi_2$, . . . $d\xi_n$ subject to the equations (2). These conditions are shown[5] to depend on the values of the co-efficients A_1, A_2, . . . A_{11} and on an expression Ω defined so that

$$\Omega = -\frac{M}{R}$$

The conditions can be expressed:

(1) If all the co-efficients A_1, A_2, . . . A_n are negative, the choice is called "normal" and it is always stable.

(2) If one of the co-efficients A_1, A_2, . . . A_n is positive and the others negative, the choice is called "a-normal" and it is stable only in the case where Ω is positive.

(3) If two or more of the co-efficients A_1, A_2, . . . A_n are positive, the choice is never stable.

The equilibrium conditions (1) and (2), subject to these stability conditions, determine the demands of the individual for the various

[4] Slutsky, *op. cit.*, pp. 7–8.
[5] Slutsky, *op. cit.*, pp. 4–11.

goods as functions of the income i and of the prices p_1, p_2, . . . p_n. The main problem is to investigate the variation of these demand functions as the income or the prices vary. For the variation of individual demands as functions of the income, we proceed:

The equations (2) can be written

$$u_1 = p_1 u'; \, u_2 = p_2 u'; \, \cdots ; \qquad u_n = p_n u' \tag{4}$$

Differentiating with respect to i, we obtain

$$\left.\begin{array}{l} u_{11} \dfrac{\partial x_1}{\partial i} + u_{12} \dfrac{\partial x_2}{\partial i} + \cdots + u_{1n} \dfrac{\partial x_n}{\partial i} = p_1 \dfrac{\partial u'}{\partial i} \\[2ex] u_{12} \dfrac{\partial x_1}{\partial i} + u_{22} \dfrac{\partial x_2}{\partial i} + \cdots + u_{2n} \dfrac{\partial x_n}{\partial i} = p_2 \dfrac{\partial u'}{\partial i} \\[2ex] \qquad\qquad \cdots \\[2ex] u_{1n} \dfrac{\partial x_1}{\partial i} + u_{2n} \dfrac{\partial x_2}{\partial i} + \cdots + u_{nn} \dfrac{\partial x_n}{\partial i} = p_n \dfrac{\partial u'}{\partial i} \end{array}\right\} \tag{5}$$

Differentiating the equation (1) with respect to i, we obtain

$$p_1 \frac{\partial x_1}{\partial i} + p_2 \frac{\partial x_2}{\partial i} + \cdots + p_n \frac{\partial x_n}{\partial i} = I \tag{6}$$

Solving the set of linear equations (5) and (6),

$$\frac{\partial x_r}{\partial i} = \frac{M_{or}}{M} \qquad (r = I, 2, \ldots n) \tag{7}$$

No universal results can be deduced concerning the sign of the expression $\partial x_r / \partial i$. It is only known that the expression can be positive in some cases and negative in others. A classification of the goods at any equilibrium position is thus possible; those goods of which increasing amounts are bought as income increases are called "relatively indispensable" goods and those goods of which decreasing amounts are bought as income increases are called "relatively dispensable" goods. For example, a small increase in the income of a poor family may result in a higher consumption of meat, sugar, and tea, but in a lower consumption of bread and potatoes. Meat, sugar, and tea are thus relatively indispensable, and bread and potatoes relatively dispensable in the case of such a family.

The variation of individual demands as functions of the prices is obtained in a similar way. Differentiating the equations (4) with respect to the price p_r, we obtain

$$
\left.
\begin{aligned}
u_{11}\frac{\partial x_1}{\partial p_r} + u_{12}\frac{\partial x_2}{\partial p_r} + \cdots + u_{1n}\frac{\partial x_n}{\partial p_r} &= p_1\frac{\partial u'}{\partial p_r} \\[4pt]
u_{12}\frac{\partial x_1}{\partial p_r} + u_{22}\frac{\partial x_2}{\partial p_r} + \cdots + u_{_{-}n}\frac{\partial x_n}{\partial p_r} &= p_2\frac{\partial u'}{\partial p_r} \\[2pt]
&\cdots \\[2pt]
u_{1r}\frac{\partial x_1}{\partial p_r} + u_{2r}\frac{\partial x_2}{\partial p_r} + \cdots + u_{rn}\frac{\partial x_n}{\partial p_r} &= p_r\frac{\partial u'}{\partial p_r} + u' \\[2pt]
&\cdots \\[2pt]
u_{1n}\frac{\partial x_1}{\partial p_r} + u_{2n}\frac{\partial x_2}{\partial p_r} + \cdots + u_{nn}\frac{\partial x_n}{\partial p_r} &= p_n\frac{\partial u'}{\partial p_r}
\end{aligned}
\right\} \tag{8}
$$

and, differentiating (I) similarly, we obtain

$$
p_1\frac{\partial x_1}{\partial p_r} + p_2\frac{\partial x_2}{\partial p_r} + \cdots + p_n\frac{\partial x_n}{\partial p_r} = -x_r \tag{9}
$$

Solving the set of linear equations (8) and (9) and reducing the expression of the solution, we have finally

$$
\left.
\begin{aligned}
\frac{\partial x_r}{\partial p_r} &= u'\frac{M_{rr}}{M} - x_r\frac{M_{or}}{M} \\[6pt]
\frac{\partial x_s}{\partial p_r} &= u'\frac{M_{rs}}{M} - x_r\frac{M_{os}}{M}
\end{aligned}
\right\} \quad (r \text{ and } s = 1, 2, \ldots n) \tag{10}
$$

Write

$$
k_{rr} = u'\frac{M_{rr}}{M} \quad \text{and} \quad k_{rs} = u'\frac{M_{rs}}{M}
$$

and, using the result (7), the results (10) can be written in the form

$$
\left.
\begin{aligned}
\frac{\partial x_r}{\partial p_r} &= k_{rr} - x_r\frac{\partial x_r}{\partial i} \\[6pt]
\frac{\partial x_s}{\partial p_r} &= k_{rs} - x_r\frac{\partial x_s}{\partial i}
\end{aligned}
\right\} \quad (r \text{ and } s = 1, 2, \ldots n) \tag{11}
$$

These last results have very definite economic significance. If the price of the rth good is increased by a small amount dp_r, there is an *apparent deficiency* in the individual's income equal in amount to $x_r dp_r$ since he can only purchase the same amounts of the goods as before the price change if his income is increased by this amount $x_r dp_r$. We shall call a variation dp_r in the price of the rth good accompanied by a variation in the income equal to the apparent deficiency $(x_r dp_r)$ a *compensated variation* in the price of the rth good. For such a compensated price variation, allowing for both the price change and the income change, there is a *residual variation* in the demand for the rth good equal in amount to

$$dx_r = \frac{\partial x_r}{\partial p_r} dp_r + \frac{\partial x_r}{\partial i} di = \left(\frac{\partial x_r}{\partial p_r} + x_r \frac{\partial x_r}{\partial i} \right) dp_r$$

i.e.
$$dx_r = k_{rr} dp_r$$

The residual variation in the demand for another good (the sth) is

$$dx_s = \frac{\partial x_s}{\partial p_r} dp_r + \frac{\partial x_s}{\partial i} di = \left(\frac{\partial x_s}{\partial p_r} + x_r \frac{\partial x_s}{\partial i} \right) dp_r$$

i.e.
$$dx_s = k_{rs} dp_r$$

Hence, k_{rr} and k_{rs} can be regarded as residual variations in the demands for the rth and sth goods respectively per unit compensated increase in the price of the rth good. They are called, therefore, the *residual variabilities* of x_r and x_s respectively for compensated changes in the price of the rth good.

It can now be shown[6] that, in all cases of stable choice (whether normal or a-normal), the ratio of M_{rr} to M is negative, i.e.

$$k_{rr} < 0 \qquad (r = 1, 2, \ldots n) \tag{12}$$

Further, since $M_{rs} = M_{sr}$ by the symmetry of the determinant M which follows from the third assumption concerning the utility function, we have

$$k_{rs} = k_{sr} \qquad (r \text{ and } s = 1, 2, \ldots n) \tag{13}$$

This is the "law of reversibility" of the residual variabilities.

From the results (11), together with (12) and (13), we deduce the following *laws of demand:*

I. If $\dfrac{\partial x_r}{\partial i} > 0$, then $\dfrac{\partial x_r}{\partial p_r} < 0$ necessarily,

i.e. the demand for a relatively indispensable good must decrease as

[6] Slutsky, *op. cit.*, p. 13.

the price of the good increases and must increase as the price of the good decreases.

II. If $\dfrac{\partial x_r}{\partial i} < 0$, then it is possible that $\dfrac{\partial x_r}{\partial p_r} > 0$,

i.e. the demand for a relatively dispensable good may increase as the price of the good increases and decrease as the price of the good decreases.

III. The residual variability of any good for a compensated variation in its price is necessarily negative,

i.e. the demand for any good must decrease when the price of the good increases and when, at the same time, a compensating increase equal to the apparent deficiency occurs in the income.

IV. The residual variability of one good for a compensated variation in the price of a second good is equal to the residual variability of the second good for a compensated variation in the price of the first good.

The formulae (II) belong to a category of relations not previously the object of enquiry in the social sciences. They relate quantities capable of empirical measurement and can be verified by observations of actual consumers' choices. In particular, the empirical confirmation of the law of reversibility, as expressed in the fourth of the above laws of demand, is much needed to demonstrate the truth, or at least the plausibility, of the assumption that increments of utility are not dependent on the mode of variation. It is clear, in fact, that $\partial^2 \psi / \partial x_r \partial x_s$ need not equal $\partial^2 \psi / \partial x_s \partial x_r$ if this assumption does not correspond to the real phenomena of choice, i.e. M_{rs} need not be equal to M_{sr} and the law of reversibility need not hold.

One particular case of the general theory is of special interest since it has formed the basis of most theories of marginal utility. This is the case where the marginal utility of any one good is a function of the amount of this good only, and not of the amounts of other goods. In this case, $u_{rs} = 0$ (where $r \neq s$) and the stability conditions reduce to

$$d^2u = u_{11}dx_1{}^2 + u_{22}dx_2{}^2 + \cdots + u_{nn}dx_n{}^2 < 0$$

provided that the equations (2) are satisfied. It follows that

(1) If all the partial derivatives $u_{11}, u_{22}, \ldots u_{nn}$ are negative, the choice is normal and stable in all cases.

(2) If one of the partial derivatives is positive and the others negative, the choice is a-normal and only stable if $\Omega > 0$.

(3) If two or more of the partial derivatives are positive, the choice is never stable.

The variations of the demands of the individual, as income or one of the prices varies, can now be written:

$$\frac{\partial x_r}{\partial i} = \frac{p_r}{u_{rr}\Omega}$$

$$\frac{\partial x_r}{\partial p_r} = \frac{u'(\Omega - p_r^2/u_{rr}) - p_r x_r}{u_{rr}\Omega} = u'\frac{\Omega - p_r^2/u_{rr}}{u_{rr}\Omega} - x_r\frac{\partial x_r}{\partial i}$$

and

$$\frac{\partial x_s}{\partial p_r} = -\frac{p_s(p_r u' + x_r u_{rr})}{u_{rr}u_{ss}\Omega} = -u'\frac{p_r p_s}{u_{rr}u_{ss}\Omega} - x_r\frac{\partial x_s}{\partial i}$$

where

$$\Omega = \frac{p_1^2}{u_{11}} + \frac{p_2^2}{u_{22}} + \cdots + \frac{p_n^2}{u_{nn}}$$

The following conclusions can then be drawn. If the choice is normal so that all $u_{11}, u_{22} \ldots u_{nn}$ are negative, the demand for any good increases when income increases or when the price of the good decreases. If the choice is a-normal, then one of $u_{nn}, u_{22}, \ldots u_{nn}$ is positive and the other negative, i.e. one of the goods is non-satiable and the others satiable. If the choice is also stable ($\Omega > 0$) in this case, it follows that, as income increases, the demand for the non-satiable good increases but the demands for all other goods decrease. The demand for the non-satiable good also increases as the price of the good decreases, but similar results need not hold for the other and satiable goods.

II

A comparison of Slutsky's results, as set out above, with those of Hicks and myself is now possible, but some rather general observations on the method of approach to the problem of consumers' choice can be made first.

It is to be noticed that Slutsky's statement of the basis of his theory is not entirely satisfactory. His fundamental definition should refer, not to utility, but to increments of utility if it is to be free from objection. His third assumption should then follow at once to establish the existence of a utility function, "integrating" the increments of utility into a single index of the level of utility. In any case, Slutsky's starting point is different from that of Hicks and myself. Our theory was constructed so as to be independent of the existence of an index of utility and it was only in a special case, the so-called "integrability case," that such an index was taken. This integrability case may be the most interesting and useful of all, but it remains a special case of a more general theory. Slutsky, on the other hand, assumes the special integrability case from the outset and his results are, therefore, unnecessarily limited. This is, of course, perfectly realised by Slutsky himself. His remarks on his law of reversibility, for example, provide sufficient evidence of this. The law does not hold if his third assumption does not apply and so if his utility function does not exist. His plea for statistical evidence on this point is one that we can support most strongly.

But, even when the third assumption is accepted, there still remain innumerable forms possible for the utility function. Slutsky expresses his theory in terms of one selected utility function and its partial derivatives. The arbitrariness of the utility function, however, also appears in the partial derivatives. The values of the determinant M and its various minors, which are used throughout Slutsky's analysis, are thus of no absolute significance themselves. The values vary according to the particular utility function selected from the many possible forms. It can be shown, however, that the particular determinant ratios, involved in the main formulae (7) and (10) deduced by Slutsky, are quite independent of the arbitrary element in the utility function. The results of Slutsky's analysis are thus unobjectionable in this respect; it is only the method of attaining the results that is open to objection.

It must be admitted, however, that the method of approach to a problem is of some importance. Slutsky's method, in the hands of a less sure mathematician, can lead only too easily to results which are not free from objection. It was for this reason that the theory of choice as given by Hicks and myself was developed from a position where the indeterminateness of any utility function was clearly recognised. We deliberately avoided using a particular utility function and its partial derivatives, and we replaced the concept of marginal utility by the more definite concept of a ratio of marginal utilities, i.e. by what we termed a marginal rate of substitution. From the purely methodological point of view, this seems a development preferable to that of Slutsky.

The advantage of our method of approach does not, however, lie only in the sphere of methodology. The very fact that we rejected the marginal utility concept in favour of the marginal rate of substitution concept lead to the introduction of the ideas of the elasticities of substitution and complementarity. These elasticities are defined as characteristics of the preference scale of an individual and they are of great service in the description of market phenomena. As is pointed out below, the elasticities of substitution and complementarity are proportional, at the level of market phenomena under equilibrium conditions, to Slutsky's residual variabilities. But it must be emphasized that the former are fundamental characteristics of the individual's preferences whereas the latter are not. This means that a more illuminating interpretation of results which are formally identical can be obtained in terms of substitution and complementarity than in terms of Slutsky's residual variabilities. The approach to the formulae (7) and (10) by way of marginal rates of substitution and elasticities of substitution and complementarity has, therefore, much to recommend it as compared with Slutsky's rigidly Paretian approach by way of a utility function and marginal utilities.

Passing to a more detailed comparison, we can notice first that the stability conditions are as essential to Slutsky's theory as they are to the theory of Hicks and myself. The stability conditions as stated by Slutsky in the particular case where a utility function exists are included within the last of the assumptions that Hicks and I make concerning the individual's preference scale.[7] In the more general way in which we express the stability conditions, we see that they imply the principle of increasing marginal rate of substitution.

In the problem of the variation of individual demand, Slutsky's main results, expressed by the formulae (7) and (11) above, are exactly paralleled by the results that Hicks and I obtain and express in terms of the elasticities of demand.[8] Translating the latter into Slutsky's notation, they appear:

$$\frac{\partial x_r}{\partial p_r} = - \frac{x_r}{p_r}\left(1 - \frac{x_r p_r}{i}\right)\sigma r - x_r \frac{\partial x_r}{\partial i}$$

$$\frac{\partial x_s}{\partial p_r} = - \frac{x_r x_s}{i}\sigma_{sr} - x_r \frac{\partial x_s}{\partial i}$$

where σ_r is the elasticity of substitution between the rth good and all others, and where σ_{sr} is the elasticity of complementarity of the sth good with the rth good against all others.

Each price variation of demand is compounded of two distinct and additive parts. One of the parts is written in the same way in Slutsky's formulae (11) as in our own formulae set out above. This part is due to the variation of real income consequent upon the price change considered. An increase in the price of one good causes a decrease in *real* income,

---

[7] Hicks and Allen, *op. cit.*, p. 203. This reference is to the three goods case which is effectively the general case.

[8] Hicks and Allen, *op. cit.*, p. 67, p. 71, and the formulae (13) and (16) on pp. 208–9.

i.e. an apparent deficiency in the fixed *nominal* income. The individual's demands are modified to meet this contraction of real income.

The remaining part of the price variation of demand is expressed in Slutsky's formulae (II) in a way different from that adopted by Hicks and myself. A comparison between the two expressions is interesting. Slutsky uses the notion of a change in demand due to a compensated price change, i.e. a price change accompanied by a change in income to make up the apparent deficiency, and the term under consideration appears naturally as a residual variation of demand. Since the residual variation is obtained by eliminating the effect of real income changes, it must be a substitution effect, i.e. it arises because the individual substitutes some goods for others in consumption when the relative price structure alters. This is seen by comparing our version of the direct variation $\partial x_r/\partial p_r$ with Slutsky's. Our elasticity of substitution σ_r is proportional to Slutsky's residual variability k_{rr} with its sign changed. In substitution terms, therefore, Slutsky's third law of demand simply states that the elasticity of substitution σ_r is positive and the residual demand for the rth good falls when the price rises for the reason that other goods are substituted for the good subject to the price increase.

In the same way, the elasticity of complementarity of the sth good with the rth good is proportional to Slutsky's residual variability k_{rs} with the sign changed. If this is positive, we say that the goods are complementary and the residual demand for the sth good falls when the price of the rth good rises. If it is negative, we say that the goods are competitive and the residual demand for the sth good rises with the price of the rth good. These interpretations are clear enough once the definition of complementary and competitive goods is made to depend on a substitution effect and put in a precise and quantitative form. In Slutsky's work, the complementary and competitive interpretation of the formulae remains implicit. It is at this stage of course, that the difference between the special "integrability" case assumed by Slutsky and our more general case shows itself. It is only in the special case that the complementary or competitive relation of the sth good with the rth good is the same as that of the rth good with the sth good.[9] Slutsky's law of reversibility holds only this special case and asserts the symmetry of the complementary or competitive relation between two goods.

Finally, in the particular case of "independent" goods, Slutsky's results are in agreement with those of Hicks and myself.[10] A set of independent goods can be related in a perfectly "normal" way in the

[9] Hicks and Allen, *op. cit.*, p. 72 and p. 202.
[10] Hicks and Allen, *op. cit.*, pp. 74–76 and pp. 214–7.

sense that the goods are mutually competitive and that the demand for any one good increases as income increases or as the price of the good decreases. But independent goods can also be related in a very "abnormal" way in the sense that there are strong complementary relations between them and that the demands for all goods except one decrease as income increases. Except for the explicit statement of the complementary and competitive relations, Slutsky has analysed these two possibilities with precision and elegance. In any case, there can be no difficulty about integrability or the law of reversibility when the goods are independent. But the inclusion of the "abnormal" possibility prevents the case being of much use even as a first approximation.

PART IV

The Utility Function and Risk

EXPOSITION OF A NEW THEORY
ON THE MEASUREMENT OF RISK[1]

Daniel Bernoulli

1. Ever since mathematicians first began to study the measurement of risk there has been general agreement on the following proposition: *Expected values are computed by multiplying each possible gain by the number of ways in which it can occur, and then dividing the sum of these products by the total number of possible cases where, in this theory, the consideration of cases which are all of the same probability is insisted upon.* If this rule be accepted, what remains to be done within the framework of this theory amounts to the enumeration of all alternatives, their breakdown into equi-probable cases and, finally, their insertion into corresponding classifications.

2. Proper examination of the numerous demonstrations of this proposition that have come forth indicates that they all rest upon one hypothesis: *since there is no reason to assume that of two persons encountering*

[1] Translated from Latin into English by Dr. Louise Sommer, The American University, Washington, D.C., from "Specimen Theoriae Novae de Mensura Sortis," *Commentarii Academiae Sicentiarum Imperialis Petropolitanae*, Tomus V [*Papers of the Imperial Academy of Sciences in Petersburg*, Vol. V], 1738, pp. 175–192. Professor Karl Menger, Illinois Institute of Technology has written footnotes 4, 9, 10, and 15.

Editor's Note: In view of the frequency with which Bernoulli's famous paper has been referred to in recent economic discussion, it has been thought appropriate to make it more generally available by publishing this English version. In her translation Professor Sommer has sought, in so far as possible, to retain the eighteenth century spirit of the original. The mathematical notation and much of the punctuation are reproduced without change. References to some of the recent literature concerned with Bernoulli's theory are given at the end of the article.

Translator's Note: I highly appreciate the help of Karl Menger, Professor of Mathematics, Illinois Institute of Technology, a distinguished authority on the Bernoulli problem, who has read this translation and given me expert advice. I

Source: Reprinted with permission from *Econometrica*, XXII: 23–36 (January 1954). Translated by Louise Sommer from "Specimen Theoriae Novae de Mensura Sortis," *Commentarii Academiae Scientiarum Imperialis Petropolitanae*, Tomus V, 1738.

identical risks,[2] *either should expect to have his desires more closely fulfilled, the risks anticipated by each must be deemed equal in value.* No characteristic of the persons themselves ought to be taken into consideration; only those matters should be weighed carefully that pertain to the terms of the risk. The relevant finding might then be made by the highest judges established by public authority. But really there is here no need for judgment but of deliberation, i.e., rules would be set up whereby anyone could estimate his prospects from any risky undertaking in light of one's specific financial circumstances.

3. To make this clear it is perhaps advisable to consider the following example: Somehow a very poor fellow obtains a lottery ticket that will yield with equal probability either nothing or twenty thousand ducats. Will this man evaluate his chance of winning at ten thousand ducats? Would he not be ill-advised to sell this lottery ticket for nine thousand ducats? To me it seems that the answer is in the negative. On the other hand I am inclined to believe that a rich man would be ill-advised to refuse to buy the lottery ticket for nine thousand ducats. If I am not wrong then it seems clear that all men cannot use the same rule to evaluate the gamble. The rule established in #1 must, therefore, be discarded. But anyone who considers the problem with perspicacity and interest will ascertain that the concept of *value* which we have used in this rule may be defined in a way which renders the entire procedure

---

am also grateful to Mr. William J. Baumol, Professor of Economics, Princeton University, for his valuable assistance in interpreting Bernoulli's paper in the light of modern econometrics. I wish to thank also Mr. John H. Lingenfeld, Economist, U.S. Department of Labor, for his cooperation in the English rendition of this paper. The translation is based solely upon the original Latin text.

Biographical Note: Daniel Bernoulli, a member of the famous Swiss family of distinguished mathematicians, was born in Groningen, January 29, 1700 and died in Basle, March 17, 1782. He studied mathematics and medical sciences at the University of Basle. In 1725 he accepted an invitation to the newly established academy in Petersburg, but returned to Basle in 1733 where he was appointed professor of physics and philosophy. Bernoulli was a member of the academies of Paris, Berlin, and Petersburg and the Royal Academy in London. He was the first to apply mathematical analysis to the problem of the movement of liquid bodies.

(On Bernoulli see: *Handwörterbuch der Naturwissenschaften,* second edition, 1931, pp. 800–801; "Die Basler Mathematiker Daniel Bernoulli und Leonhard Euler. Hundert Jahre nach ihrem Tode gefeiert von der Naturforschenden Gesellschaft," Basle, 1884 (Annex to part VII of the proceedings of this Society); and *Correspondance mathematique . . . ,* edited by Paul Heinrich Fuss, 1843 containing letters written by Daniel Bernoulli to Leonhard Euler, Nicolaus Fuss, and C. Goldbach.)

[2] I.e., risky propositions (gambles). [Translator]

universally acceptable without reservation. To do this the determination of the *value* of an item must not be based on its price, but rather on the *utility* it yields. The price of the item is dependent only on the thing itself and is equal for everyone; the utility, however, is dependent on the particular circumstances of the person making the estimate. Thus there is no doubt that a gain of one thousand ducats is more significant to a pauper than to a rich man though both gain the same amount.

4. The discussion has now been developed to a point where anyone may proceed with the investigation by the mere paraphrasing of one and the same principle. However, since the hypothesis is entirely new, it may nevertheless require some elucidation. I have, therefore, decided to explain by example what I have explored. Meanwhile, let us use this as a fundamental rule: *If the utility of each possible profit expectation is multiplied by the number of ways in which it can occur, and we then divide the sum of these products by the total number of possible cases, a mean utility*[3] *[moral expectation] will be obtained, and the profit which corresponds to this utility will equal the value of the risk in question.*

5. Thus it becomes evident that no valid measurement of the value of a risk can be obtained without consideration being given to its *utility*, that is to say, the utility of whatever gain accrues to the individual or, conversely, how much profit is required to yield a given utility. However it hardly seems plausible to make any precise generalizations since the utility of an item may change with circumstances. Thus, though a poor man generally obtains more utility than does a rich man from an equal gain, it is nevertheless conceivable, for example, that a rich prisoner who possesses two thousand ducats but needs two thousand ducats more to repurchase his freedom, will place a higher value on a gain of two thousand ducats than does another man who has less money than he. Though innumerable examples of this kind may be constructed, they represent exceedingly rare exceptions. We shall, therefore, do better to consider what usually happens, and in order to perceive the problem more correctly we shall assume that there is an imperceptibly small growth in the individual's wealth which proceeds continuously by infinitesimal increments. Now it is highly probable that *any increase in wealth, no matter how insignificant, will always result in an increase in utility which is inversely proportionate to the quantity of goods already possessed.* To explain this hypothesis it is necessary to define what is meant by the *quantity of goods*. By this expression I mean to connote food, clothing, all things which add to the conveniences of life, and even to luxury—anything that can contribute to the ade-

---

[3] Free translation of Bernoulli's "emolumentum medium," literally: "mean utility." [Translator]

quate satisfaction of any sort of want. There is then nobody who can be said to possess nothing at all in this sense unless he starves to death. For the great majority the most valuable portion of their possessions so defined will consist in their productive capacity, this term being taken to include even the beggar's talent: a man who is able to acquire ten ducats yearly by begging will scarcely be willing to accept a sum of fifty ducats on condition that he henceforth refrain from begging or otherwise trying to earn money. For he would have to live on this amount, and after he had spent it his existence must also come to an end. I doubt whether even those who do not possess a farthing and are burdened with financial obligations would be willing to free themselves of their debts or even to accept a still greater gift on such a condition. But if the beggar were to refuse such a contract unless immediately paid no less than one hundred ducats and the man pressed by creditors similarly demanded one thousand ducats, we might say that the former is possessed of wealth worth one hundred, and the latter of one thousand ducats, though in common parlance the former owns nothing and the latter less than nothing.

6. Having stated this definition, I return to the statement made in the previous paragraph which maintained that, in the absence of the unusual, the *utility resulting from any small increase in wealth will be inversely proportionate to the quantity of goods previously possessed.* Considering the nature of man, it seems to me that the foregoing hypothesis is apt to be valid for many people to whom this sort of comparison can be applied. Only a few do not spend their entire yearly incomes. But, if among these, one has a fortune worth a hundred thousand ducats and another a fortune worth the same number of semi-ducats and if the former receives from it a yearly income of five thousand ducats while the latter obtains the same number of semi-ducats it is quite clear that to the former a ducat has exactly the same significance as a semi-ducat to the latter, and that, therefore, the gain of one ducat will have to the former no higher value than the gain of a semi-ducat to the latter. Accordingly, if each makes a gain of one ducat the latter receives twice as much utility from it, having been enriched by two semi-ducats. This argument applies to many other cases which, therefore, need not be discussed separately. The proposition is all the more valid for the majority of men who possess no fortune apart from their working capacity which is their only source of livelihood. True, there are men to whom one ducat means more than many ducats do to others who are less rich but more generous than they. But since we shall now concern ourselves only with one individual (in different states of affluence) distinctions of this sort do not concern us. The man who is

emotionally less affected by a gain will support a loss with greater patience. Since, however, in special cases things can conceivably occur otherwise, I shall first deal with the most general case and then develop our special hypothesis in order thereby to satisfy everyone.

7. Therefore, let AB represent the quantity of goods initially possessed. Then after extending AB, a curve $BGLS$ must be constructed, whose ordinates CG, DH, EL, FM, etc., designate *utilities* corresponding to the abscissas BC, BD, BE, BF, etc., designating gains in wealth.

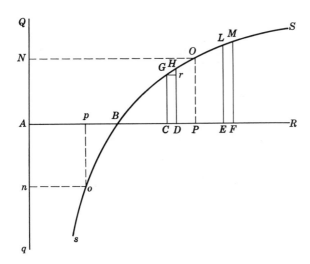

Further, let m, n, p, q, etc. be the numbers which indicate the number of ways in which gains in wealth BC, BD, BE, BF [misprinted in the original as CF], etc., can occur. Then (in accord with 4) the *moral* expectation of the risky proposition referred to is given by:

$$PO = \frac{m \cdot CG + n \cdot DH + p \cdot EL + q \cdot FM + \cdots}{m + n + p + q + \cdots}$$

Now, if we erect AQ perpendicular to AR, and on it measure off $AN = PO$, the straight line $NO - AB$ represents the gain which may properly be expected, or the value of the risky proposition in question. If we wish, further, to know how large a stake the individual should be willing to venture on this risky proposition, our curve must be extended in the opposite direction in such a way that the abscissa Bp now represents a loss and the ordinate po represents the corresponding decline in utility. Since in a fair game the disutility to be suffered by losing must be equal to the utility to be derived by winning, we must assume that

$An = AN$, or $po = PO$. Thus Bp will indicate the stake more than which persons who consider their own pecuniary status should not venture.

COROLLARY I

8. Until now scientists have usually rested their hypothesis on the assumption that all gains must be evaluated exclusively in terms of themselves, i.e., on the basis of their intrinsic qualities, and that these gains will always produce a utility directly proportionate to the gain. On this hypothesis the curve BS becomes a straight line. Now if we again have:

$$PO = \frac{m \cdot CG + n \cdot DH + p \cdot EL + q \cdot FM + \cdots}{m + n + p + q + \cdots},$$

and if, on both sides, the respective factors are introduced it follows that:

$$BP = \frac{m \cdot BC + n \cdot BD + p \cdot BE + q \cdot BF + \cdots}{m + n + p + q + \cdots},$$

which is in conformity with the usually accepted rule.

COROLLARY II

9. If AB were infinitely great, even in proportion to BF, the greatest possible gain, the arc BM may be considered very like an infinitesimally small straight line. Again in this case the usual rule [for the evaluation of risky propositions] is applicable, and may continue to be considered approximately valid in games of insignificant moment.

10. Having dealt with the problem in the most general way we turn now to the aforementioned particular hypothesis, which, indeed, deserves prior attention to all others. First of all the nature of curve sBS must be investigated under the conditions postulated in 7. Since on our hypothesis we must consider infinitesimally small gains, we shall take gains BC and BD to be nearly equal, so that their difference CD becomes infinitesimally small. If we draw Gr parallel to BR, then rH will represent the infinitesimally small gain in *utility* to a man whose fortune is AC and who obtains the small gain, CD. This *utility*, however, should be related not only to the tiny gain CD, to which it is, other things being equal, proportionate, but also to AC, the fortune previously owned to which it is inversely proportionate. We therefore set: $AC = x$, $CD = dx$, $CG = y$, $rH = dy$ and $AB = \alpha$; and if b designates some constant we obtain $dy = bdx/x$ or $y = b \log (x/\alpha)$. The curve sBS is

therefore a logarithmic curve, the subtangent[4] of which is everywhere b and whose asymptote is Qq.

11. If we now compare this result with what has been said in paragraph 7, it will appear that: $PO = b \log AP/AB$, $CG = b \log AC/AB$, $DH = b \log AD/AB$ and so on; but since we have

$$PO = \frac{m \cdot CG + n \cdot DH + p \cdot EL + q \cdot FM + \cdots}{m + n + p + q + \cdots}$$

it follows that

$$b \log \frac{AP}{AB} = \frac{\left(mb \log \dfrac{AC}{AB} + nb \log \dfrac{AD}{AB} + pb \log \dfrac{AE}{AB} + qb \log \dfrac{AF}{AB} + \cdots \right)}{(m + n + p + q + \cdots)}$$

and therefore

$$AP = AC^m \cdot AD^n \cdot AE^p \cdot AF^q \cdots)^{1/m+n+p+q+\cdots}$$

and if we subtract AB from this, the remaining magnitude, BP, will represent the value of the risky proposition in question.

12. Thus the preceding paragraph suggests the following rule: *Any gain must be added to the fortune previously possessed, then this sum must be raised to the power given by the number of possible ways in which the gain may be obtained; these terms should then be multiplied together. Then of this product a root must be extracted the degree of which is given by the number of all possible cases, and finally the value of the initial possessions must be subtracted therefrom; what then remains indicates the value of the risky proposition in question.* This principle is essential for the measurement of the value of risky propositions in various cases. I would elaborate it into a complete theory as has been done with the traditional analysis, were it not that, despite its usefulness and originality, previous obligations do not permit me to

---

[4] The tangent to the curve $y = b \log (x/a)$ at the point $(x_0, \log (x_0/a))$ is the line $y - b \log (x_0/a) = (b/x_0) (x - x_0)$. This tangent intersects the Y-axis $(x = 0$ at the point with the ordinate $b \log (x_0/a) - b$. The point of contact of the tangent with the curve has the ordinate $b \log (x_0/a)$. So also does the projection of this point on the Y-axis. The segment between the two points on the Y-axis that have been mentioned has the length b. That segment is the projection of the segment on the tangent between its intersection with the Y-axis and the point of contact. The length of this projection (which is b) is what Bernoulli here calls the "sub-tangent." Today, by the subtangent of the curve $y = f(x)$ at the point $(x_0, f(x_0))$ is meant the length of the segment on the X-axis (and not the Y-axis) between its intersection with the tangent and the projection of the point of contact. This length is $f(x_0)/f'(x_0)$. In the case of the logarithmic curve it equals $x_0 \log (x_0/a)$—Karl Menger.

undertake this task. I shall therefore, at this time, mention only the more significant points among those which have at first glance occurred to me.

13. First, it appears that in many games, even those that are absolutely fair, both of the players may expect to suffer a loss; indeed this is Nature's admonition to avoid the dice altogether. . . . This follows from the concavity of curve sBS to BR. For in making the stake, Bp, equal to the expected gain, BP, it is clear that the disutility po which results from a loss will always exceed the expected gain in utility, PO. Although this result will be quite clear to the mathematician, I shall nevertheless explain it by example, so that it will be clear to everyone. Let us assume that of two players, both possessing one hundred ducats, each puts up half this sum as a stake in a game that offers the same probabilities to both players. Under this assumption each will then have fifty ducats plus the expectation of winning yet one hundred ducats more. However, the sum of the values of these two items amounts, by the rule of 12, to only $(50^1 . 150^1)^{1/2}$ or $\sqrt{50 . 150}$, i.e., less than eighty-seven ducats, so that, though the game be played under perfectly equal conditions for both, either will suffer an expected loss of more than thirteen ducats. We must strongly emphasize this truth, although it be self evident: the imprudence of a gambler will be the greater the larger the part of his fortune which he exposes to a game of chance. For this purpose we shall modify the previous example by assuming that one of the gamblers, before putting up his fifty ducat stake possessed two hundred ducats. This gambler suffers an expected loss of $200 - \sqrt{150 . 250}$, which is not much greater than six ducats.

14. Since, therefore, everyone who bets any part of his fortune, however small, on a mathematically fair game of chance acts irrationally, it may be of interest to inquire how great an advantage the gambler must enjoy over his opponent in order to avoid any expected loss. Let us again consider a game which is as simple as possible, defined by two equiprobable outcomes one of which is favorable and the other unfavorable. Let us take a to be the gain to be won in case of a favorable outcome, and x to be the stake which is lost in the unfavorable case. If the initial quantity of goods possessed is α we have $AB = \alpha$; $BP = a$; $PO = b \log ((\alpha + a)/\alpha)$ (see 10), and since (by 7) $po = PO$ it follows by the nature of a logarithmic curve that $Bp = \alpha a/(\alpha + a)$. Since however Bp represents the stake x, we have $x = \alpha a/(\alpha + a)$ a magnitude which is always smaller than a, the expected gain. It also follows from this that a man who risks his entire fortune acts like a simpleton, however great may be the possible gain. No one will have difficulty in being persuaded of this if he has carefully examined our definitions given

above. Moreover, this result sheds light on a statement which is universally accepted in practice: it may be reasonable for some individuals to invest in a doubtful enterprise and yet be unreasonable for others to do so.

15. The procedure customarily employed by merchants in the insurance of commodities transported by sea seems to merit special attention. This may again be explained by an example. Suppose Caius,[5] a Petersburg merchant, has purchased commodities in Amsterdam which he could sell for ten thousand rubles if he had them in Petersburg. He therefore orders them to be shipped there by sea, but is in doubt whether or not to insure them. He is well aware of the fact that at this time of year of one hundred ships which sail from Amsterdam to Petersburg, five are usually lost. However, there is no insurance available below the price of eight hundred rubles a cargo, an amount which he considers outrageously high. The question is, therefore, how much wealth must Caius possess apart from the goods under consideration in order that it be sensible for him to abstain from insuring them? If x represents his fortune, then this together with the value of the expectation of the safe arrival of his goods is given by $\sqrt[100]{(x + 10000)^{95}x^5} = \sqrt[20]{(x + 10000)^{19}x}$ in case he abstains. With insurance he will have a certain fortune of $x + 9200$. Equating these two magnitudes we get: $(x + 10{,}000)^{19}x = (x + 9200)^{20}$ or, approximately, $x = 5043$. If, therefore, Caius, apart from the expectation of receiving his commodities, possesses an amount greater than 5043 rubles he will be right in not buying insurance. If, on the contrary, his wealth is less than this amount he should insure his cargo. And if the question be asked "What minimum fortune should be possessed by the man who offers to provide this insurance in order for him to be rational in doing so?" We must answer thus: let y be his fortune, then

$$\sqrt[20]{(y + 800)^{19} \cdot (y - 9200)} = y$$

or approximately, $y = 14{,}243$, a figure which is obtained from the foregoing without additional calculation. A man less wealthy than this would be foolish to provide the surety, but it makes sense for a wealthier man to do so. From this it is clear that the introduction of this sort of insurance has been so useful since it offers advantages to all persons concerned. Similarly, had Caius been able to obtain the insurance for six hundred rubles he would have been unwise to refuse it if he possessed less than 20,478 rubles, but he would have acted much too cautiously had he insured his commodities at this rate when his fortune was greater than this amount. On the other hand a man would act un-

---

[5] Caius is a Roman name, used here in the sense of our "Mr. Jones." Caius is the older form; in the later Roman period it was spelled "Gaius." [Translator]

advisedly if he were to offer to sponsor this insurance for six hundred rubles when he himself possesses less than 29,878 rubles. However, he would be well advised to do so if he possessed more than that amount. But no one, however rich, would be managing his affairs properly if he individually undertook the insurance for less than five hundred rubles.

16. Another rule which may prove useful can be derived from our theory. This is the rule that it is advisable to divide goods which are exposed to some danger into several portions rather than to risk them all together. Again I shall explain this more precisely by an example. Sempronius owns goods at home worth a total of 4000 ducats and in addition possesses 80,000 ducats worth of commodities in foreign countries from where they can only be transported by sea. However, our daily experience teaches us that of ten ships one perishes. Under these conditions I maintain that if Sempronius trusted all his 8000 ducats of goods to one ship his expectation of the commodities is worth 6751 ducats. That is

$$\sqrt[10]{12,000^9 \cdot 4000^1} - 4000.$$

If, however, he were to trust equal portions of these commodities to two ships the value of his expectation would be

$$\sqrt[100]{12,000^{81} \cdot 8000^{18} \cdot 4000} - 4000, \text{ i.e., } 7033 \text{ ducats.}$$

In this way the value of Sempronius' prospects of success will grow more favorable the smaller the proportion committed to each ship. However, his expectation will never rise in value above 7200 ducats. This counsel will be equally serviceable for those who invest their fortunes in foreign bills of exchange and other hazardous enterprises.

17. I am forced to omit many novel remarks though these would clearly not be unserviceable. And, though a person who is fairly judicious by natural instinct might have realized and spontaneously applied much of what I have here explained, hardly anyone believed it possible to define these problems with the precision we have employed in our examples. Since all our propositions harmonize perfectly with experience it would be wrong to neglect them as abstractions resting upon precarious hypotheses. This is further confirmed by the following example which inspired these thoughts, and whose history is as follows: My most honorable cousin the celebrated *Nicolas Bernoulli*, Professor utriusque iuris[6] at the University of Basle, once submitted five problems

---

[6] Faculties of law of continental European universities bestow up to the present time the title of a Doctor utriusque juris, which means Doctor of both systems of laws, the Roman and the canon law. [Translator]

to the highly distinguished[7] mathematician *Montmort*.[8] These problems are reproduced in the work *L'analyse sur les jeux de hazard de M. de Montmort*, p. 402. The last of these problems runs as follows: *Peter tosses a coin and continues to do so until it should land "heads" when it comes to the ground. He agrees to give Paul one ducat if he gets "heads" on the very first throw, two ducats if he gets it on the second, four if on the third, eight if on the fourth, and so on, so that with each additional throw the number of ducats he must pay is doubled. Suppose we seek to determine the value of Paul's expectation.* My aforementioned cousin discussed this problem in a letter to me asking for my opinion. Although the standard calculation shows[9] that the value of Paul's expectation is infinitely great, it has, he said, to be admitted that any fairly reasonable man would sell his chance, with great pleasure, for twenty ducats. The accepted method of calculation does, indeed, value Paul's prospects at infinity though no one would be willing to purchase it at a moderately high price. If however, we apply our new rule to this problem we may see the solution and thus unravel the knot. The solution of the problem by our principles is as follows.

18. The number of cases to be considered here is infinite: in one half of the cases the game will end at the first throw, in one quarter of the cases it will conclude at the second, in an eighth part of the cases with the third, in a sixteenth part with the fourth, and so on.[10] If we desig-

---

[7] Cl., i.e., Vir Clarissimus, a title of respect. [Translator]

[8] Montmort, Pierre Remond, de (1678–1719). The work referred to here is the then famous "Essai d'analyse sur les jeux de hazard," Paris, 1708. Appended to the second edition, published in 1713, is Montmort's correspondence with Jean and Nicolas Bernoulli referring to the problems of chance and probabilities. [Translator]

[9] The probability of heads turning up on the 1st throw is $\frac{1}{2}$. Since in this case Paul receives one ducat, this probability contributes $\frac{1}{2} \cdot 1 = \frac{1}{2}$ ducats to his expectation. The probability of heads turning up on the 2nd throw is $\frac{1}{4}$. Since in this case Paul receives 2 ducats, this possibility contributes $\frac{1}{4} \cdot 2 = \frac{1}{2}$ to his expectation. Similarly, for every integer n, the possibility of heads turning up on the nth throw contributes $\frac{1}{2^n} \cdot 2^{n-1} = \frac{1}{2}$ ducats to his expectation. Paul's total expectation is therefore $\frac{1}{2} + \frac{1}{2} + \cdots + \frac{1}{2} + \cdots$, and that is infinite.—Karl Menger

[10] Since the number of cases is infinite, it is impossible to speak about one half of the cases, one quarter of the cases, etc., and the letter N in Bernoulli's argument is meaningless. However, Paul's expectation on the basis of Bernoulli's hypothesis concerning evaluation can be found by the same method by which, in footnote 9, Paul's classical expectation was determined. If Paul's fortune is α ducats, then, according to Bernoulli, he attributes to a gain of 2^{n-1} ducats the value $b \log ((\alpha + 2^{n-1})/\alpha)$. If the probability of this gain is $\frac{1}{2^n}$, his expectation is $(b/2^n) \log ((\alpha + 2^{n-1})/\alpha)$. Paul's expectation resulting from the game is therefore $(b/2) \log ((\alpha + 1)/\alpha) + (b/4) \log ((\alpha + 2)/\alpha) + \cdots + (b/2^n) \log ((\alpha + 2^{n-1})/\alpha) + \cdots = b \log [(\alpha + 1)^{\frac{1}{2}} (\alpha + 2)^{\frac{1}{4}} \cdot \cdots \cdot (\alpha + 2^{n-1})^{\frac{1}{2^n}} \cdot \cdots] - b \log \alpha$. What addition D to Paul's fortune

nate the number of cases through infinity by N it is clear that there are $\frac{1}{2}N$ cases in which Paul gains one ducat, $\frac{1}{4}N$ cases in which he gains two ducats, $\frac{1}{8}N$ in which he gains fours, $\frac{1}{16}N$ in which he gains eight, and so on, ad infinitum. Let us represent Paul's fortune by α; the proposition in question will then be worth

$$\sqrt[N]{(\alpha + 1)^{N/2} \cdot (\alpha + 2)^{N/4} \cdot (\alpha + 4)^{N/8} \cdot (\alpha + 8)^{N/16} \cdots} - \alpha$$
$$= \sqrt{(\alpha + 1)} \cdot \sqrt[4]{(\alpha + 2)} \cdot \sqrt[8]{(\alpha + 4)} \cdot \sqrt[16]{(\alpha + 8)} \cdots - \alpha.$$

19. From this formula which evaluates Paul's prospective gain it follows that this value will increase with the size of Paul's fortune and will never attain an infinite value unless Paul's wealth simultaneously becomes infinite. In addition we obtain the following corollaries. If Paul owned nothing at all the value of his expectation would be

$$\sqrt[2]{1} \cdot \sqrt[4]{2} \cdot \sqrt[8]{4} \cdot \sqrt[8]{8} \cdots$$

which amounts to two ducats, precisely. If he owned ten ducats his opportunity would be worth approximately three ducats; it would be worth approximately four if his wealth were one hundred, and six if he possessed one thousand. From this we can easily see what a tremendous fortune a man must own for it to make sense for him to purchase Paul's opportunity for twenty ducats. The amount which the buyer ought to pay for this proposition differs somewhat from the amount it would be worth to him were it already in his possession. Since, however, this difference is exceedingly small if α (Paul's fortune) is great, we can take them to be equal. If we designate the purchase price by x its value can be determined by means of the equation

$$\sqrt[2]{(\alpha + 1 - x)} \cdot \sqrt[4]{(\alpha + 2 - x)} \cdot \sqrt[8]{(\alpha + 4 - x)} \cdot \sqrt[16]{(\alpha + 8 - x)} \cdots$$
$$= \alpha$$

and if α is a large number this equation will be approximately satisfied by

$$x = \sqrt[2]{\alpha + 1} \cdot \sqrt[4]{\alpha + 2} \cdot \sqrt[8]{\alpha + 4} \cdot \sqrt[16]{\alpha + 8} \cdots - \alpha.$$

After having read this paper to the Society[11] *I sent a copy to the aforementioned Mr. Nicolas Bernoulli, to obtain his opinion of my pro-*

---

has the same value for him? Clearly, $b \log ((\alpha + D)/\alpha)$ must equal the above sum. Therefore

$$D = (\alpha + 1)^{1/2}(\alpha + 2)^{1/4} \cdots \cdot (\alpha + 2^{n-1})^{1/2n} \cdots - \alpha.$$

—Karl Menger

[11] Bernoulli's paper had been submitted to the Imperial Academy of Sciences in Petersburg. [Translator]

posed solution to the difficulty he had indicated. In a letter to me written in 1732 he declared that he was in no way dissatisfied with my proposition on the evaluation of risky propositions when applied to the case of a man who is to evaluate his own prospects. However, he thinks that the case is different if a third person, somewhat in the position of a judge, is to evaluate the prospects of any participant in a game in accord with equity and justice. I myself have discussed this problem in #2. Then this distinguished scholar informed me that the celebrated mathematician, Cramer,[12] had develped a theory on the same subject several years before I produced my paper. Indeed I have found his theory so similar to mine that it seems miraculous that we independently reached such close agreement on this sort of subject. Therefore it seems worth quoting the words with which the celebrated Cramer himself first described his theory in his letter of 1728 to my cousin. His words are as follows:[13]

Perhaps I am mistaken, but I believe that I have solved the extraordinary problem which you submitted to M. de Montmort, in your letter of September 9, 1713, (problem 5, page 402). For the sake of simplicity I shall assume that A tosses a coin into the air and B commits himself to give A 1 ducat if, at the first throw, the coin falls with its cross upward; 2 if it falls thus only at the second throw, 4 if at the third throw, 8 if at the fourth throw, etc. The paradox consists in the infinite sum which calculation yields as the equivalent which A must pay to B. This seems absurd since no reasonable man would be willing to pay 20 ducats as equivalent. You ask for an explanation of the discrepancy between the mathematical calculation and the vulgar evaluation. I believe that it results from the fact that, *in their theory*, mathematicians evaluate money in proportion to its quantity while, *in practice*, people with common sense evaluate money in proportion to the utility they can obtain from it. The mathematical expectation is rendered infinite by the enormous amount which I can win if the coin does not fall with its cross upward until rather late, perhaps at the hundredth or thousandth throw. Now, as a matter of fact, if I reason as a sensible man, this sum is worth no more to me, causes me no more pleasure and influences me no more to accept the game than does a sum amounting only to ten or twenty million ducats. Let us suppose, therefore, that any amount above 10 millions, or (for the sake of simplicity) above $2^{24} = 166,777,216$ ducats be deemed by him equal in value to 2^{24} ducats or, better yet, that I can never win more than that amount, no matter how long it takes before the coin falls with its cross upward. In this case, my expectation is $\frac{1}{2} \cdot 1 + \frac{1}{4} \cdot 2 + \frac{1}{8} \cdot 4 \cdots + \frac{1}{2}^{25} \cdot 2^{24} + \frac{1}{2}^{26} \cdot 2^{24} + \frac{1}{2}^{27} \cdot 2^{24} +$

[12] Cramer, Gabriel, famous mathematician, born in Geneva, Switzerland (1704–1752). [Translator]

[13] The following passage of the original text is in French. [Translator]

$\cdots = \frac{1}{2} + \frac{1}{2} + \frac{1}{2} + \cdots$ (24 times) $\cdots + \frac{1}{2} + \frac{1}{4} + \frac{1}{8} + \cdots$
$= 12 + 1 = 13$. Thus, my moral expectation is reduced in value to
13 ducats and the equivalent to be paid for it is similarly reduced—
a result which seems much more reasonable than does rendering it
infinite.

Thus far[14] *the exposition is somewhat vague and subject to counter
argument. If it, indeed, be true that the amount 2^{25} appears to us to be
no greater than 2^{24}, no attention whatsoever should be paid to the
amount that may be won after the twenty-fourth throw, since just before making the twenty-fifth throw I am certain to end up with no less
than $2^{24} - 1$,[15] an amount that, according to this theory, may be considered equivalent to 2^{24}. Therefore it may be said correctly that my
expectation is only worth twelve ducats, not thirteen. However, in view
of the coincidence between the basic principle developed by the aforementioned author and my own, the foregoing is clearly not intended to
be taken to invalidate that principle. I refer to the proposition that
reasonable men should evaluate money in accord with the utility they
derive therefrom. I state this to avoid leading anyone to judge that
entire theory adversely. And this is exactly what Cl. C.*[16] *Cramer states,
expressing in the following manner precisely what we would ourselves
conclude. He continues thus.*[17]

The equivalent can turn out to be smaller yet if we adopt some
alternative hypothesis on the moral value of wealth. For that which
I have just assumed is not entirely valid since, while it is true that
100 millions yield more satisfaction than do 10 millions, they do
not give ten times as much. If, for example, we suppose the moral
value of goods to be directly proportionate to the square root of
their mathematical quantities, e.g., that the satisfaction provided
by 40,000,000 is double that provided by 10,000,000, my psychic
expectation becomes

$$\frac{1}{2}\sqrt{1} + \frac{1}{4}\sqrt{2} + \frac{1}{8}\sqrt{4} + \frac{1}{16}\sqrt{8} + \cdots = \frac{1}{2 - \sqrt{2}}.$$

However this magnitude is not the equivalent we seek, for this
equivalent need not be equal to my moral expectation but should
rather be of such a magnitude that the pain caused by its loss is
equal to the moral expectation of the pleasure I hope to derive
from my gain. Therefore, the equivalent must, on our hypothesis,
amount to $(1/(2 - \sqrt{2}))^2 = 1/(6 - 4\sqrt{2}) = 2.9 \ldots$, which is

[14] From here on the text is again translated from Latin. [Translator]

[15] This remark of Bernoulli's is obscure. Under the conditions of the game a gain
of $2^{24} - 1$ ducats is impossible.—Karl Menger

[16] To be translated as "the distinguished Gabriel." [Translator]

[17] Text continues in French. [Translator]

consequently less than 3, truly a trifling amount, but nevertheless, I believe, closer than is 13 to the vulgar evaluation.

REFERENCES

There exists only one other translation of Bernoulli's paper: Pringsheim, Alfred, *Die Grundlage der modernen Wertlehre: Daniel Bernoulli, Versucheiner neuen Theorie der Wertbestimmung von Glücksfällen* (Specimen Theoriao novae de Mensura Sortis). Aus dem lateinischen Übersetzt und mit Eläuterungen versehen von Alfred Pringsheim, Leipzig, Duncker und Humblot, 1896, Sammlung älterer und neuerer staats-wissenschaftlicher Schriften des In- und Auslandes hrsg. von L. Brentano und E. Leser, No. 9.

For an early discussion of the Bernoulli problem, reference is made to: Malfatti, Gianfrancosco, "Esame critico di un problema di probabilita del Signor Daniele Bernoulli, e soluzione d'un altro problema analogo al Bernoulliano," in *"Memorie di Matematica e Fisica della Societa italiana,"* Vol. I, Verona, 1782, pp. 768–824.

For more on the "St. Petersburg Paradox," including material on later discussions, see: Menger, Karl, "Das Unsicherheitsmoment in der Wertlehre. Betrachtungen im Anschluss an das sogenannte Petersburger Spiel," *Zeitschrift für Nationalökonomie,* Vol. 5, 1934.

This paper by Professor Menger, is the most extensive study on the literature of the problem, and the problem itself.

Recent interest in the Bernoulli hypothesis was aroused by its appearance in: von Neumann, John, and Oskar Morgenstern, *The Theory of Games and Economic Behavior,* second edition, Princeton: Princeton University Press, 1947, Ch. III and Appendix: "The Axiomatic Treatment of Utility."

Many contemporary references and a discussion of the utility maximization hypothesis are to be found in: Arrow, Kenneth J., "Alternative Approaches to the Theory of Choice in Risk-Taking Situations," *Econometrica,* Vol. 19, October, 1951.

More recent writings in the field include:

Alchian, A. A., "The Meaning of Utility Measurement," *American Economic Review,* Vol. XLIII, March, 1953.

Friedman, M., and Savage, L. J., "The Expected Utility-Hypothesis and the Measurability of Utility," *Journal of Political Economy,* Vol. LX, December, 1952.

Herstein, I. N., and John Milnor, "An Axiomatic Approach to Measurable Utility," *Econometrica,* Vol. 21, April, 1953.

Marschak, J., "Why 'Should' Statisticians and Businessmen Maximize 'Moral Expectation'?", *Second Berkeley Symposium on Mathematical Statistics and Probability,* 1953.

Mosteller, Frederick, and Philip Nogee, "An Experimental Measurement of Utility," *Journal of Political Economy,* lix, 5, Oct., 1951.

Samuelson, Paul A., "Probability, Utility, and the Independence Axiom," *Econometrica,* Vol. 20, Oct. 1952.

Strotz, Robert H., "Cardinal Utility," *Papers and Proceedings of the Sixty-*

Fifth Annual Meeting of the American Economic Association, American Economic Review, Vol. 43, May, 1953, and the comment by W. J. Baumol.

For dissenting views, see:

Allais, M., "Les Theories de la Psychologie du Risque de l'Ecole Americaine," *Revue d'Economie Politique,* Vol. 63, 1953.

————, "Le Comportement de l'Homme Rationnel devant le Risque: Critique des postulats et Axiomes de l'Ecole Americaine," *Econometrica,* Oct., 1953 and

Edwards, Ward, "Probability-Preferences in Gambling," *The American Journal of Psychology,* Vol. 66, July, 1953.

Textbooks dealing with Bernoulli:

Anderson, Oskar, *Einführung in die mathematische Statistik,* Wien: J. Springer, 1935.

Davis, Harold, *The Theory of Econometrics,* Bloomington, Ind.: Principia Press, 1941.

Loria, Gino, *Storia delle Matematiche, dall'alba della civiltá al secolo XIX,* Second revised ed. Milan: U. Hopli, 1950.

THE NOTION OF UTILITY

John von Neumann and Oskar Morgenstern

3.1. PREFERENCES AND UTILITIES

3.1.1. We have stated already in 2.1.1. in what way we wish to describe the fundamental concept of individual preferences by the use of a rather far-reaching notion of utility. Many economists will feel that we are assuming far too much (cf. the enumeration of the properties we postulated in 2.1.1.), and that our standpoint is a retrogression from the more cautious modern technique of "indifference curves."

Before attempting any specific discussion let us state as a general excuse that our procedure at worst is only the application of a classical preliminary device of scientific analysis: To divide the difficulties, i.e. to concentrate on one (the subject proper of the investigation in hand), and to reduce all others as far as reasonably possible, by simplifying and schematizing assumptions. We should also add that this high handed treatment of preferences and utilities is employed in the main body of our discussion, but we shall incidentally investigate to a certain extent the changes which an avoidance of the assumptions in question would cause in our theory (cf. 66., 67.).

We feel, however, that one part of our assumptions at least—that of treating utilities as numerically measurable quantities—is not quite as radical as is often assumed in the literature. We shall attempt to prove this particular point in the paragraphs which follow. It is hoped that the reader will forgive us for discussing only incidentally in a condensed form a subject of so great a conceptual importance as that of utility. It seems however that even a few remarks may be helpful, because the question of the measurability of utilities is similar in character to corresponding questions in the physical sciences.

3.1.2. Historically, utility was first conceived as quantitatively measurable, i.e., as a number. Valid objections can be and have been made

---

Source: The Theory of Games and Economic Behavior, Chapter I, Section 3, pages 15–31. Princeton University Press, Third Edition, 1953. Reprinted with permission.

against this view in its original, naive form. It is clear that every measurement—or rather every claim of measurability—must ultimately be based on some immediate sensation, which possibly cannot and certainly need not be analyzed any further.[1] In the case of utility the immediate sensation of preference—of one object or aggregate of objects as against another—provides this basis. But this permits us only to say when for one person one utility is greater than another. It is not in itself a basis for numerical comparison of utilities for one person nor of any comparison between different persons. Since there is no intuitively significant way to add two utilities for the same person, the assumption that utilities are of nonnumerical character even seems plausible. The modern method of indifference curve analysis is a mathematical procedure to describe this situation.

3.2. PRINCIPLES OF MEASUREMENT: PRELIMINARIES

3.2.1. All this is strongly reminiscent of the conditions existant at the beginning of the theory of heat: that too was based on the intuitively clear concept of one body feeling warmer than another, yet there was no immediate way to express significantly by how much, or how many times, or in what sense.

This comparison with heat also shows how little one can forecast *a priori* what the ultimate shape of such a theory will be. The above crude indications do not disclose at all what, as we now know, subsequently happened. It turned out that heat permits quantitative description not by one number but by two: the quantity of heat and temperature. The former is rather directly numerical because it turned out to be additive and also in an unexpected way connected with mechanical energy which was numerical anyhow. The latter is also numerical, but in a much more subtle way; it is not additive in any immediate sense, but a rigid numerical scale for it emerged from the study of the concordant behavior of ideal gases, and the role of absolute temperature in connection with the entropy theorem.

3.2.2. The historical development of the theory of heat indicates that one must be extremely careful in making negative assertions about any concept with the claim of finality. Even if utilities look very unnumerical today, the history of the experience in the theory of heat may repeat itself, and nobody can foretell with what ramifications and varia-

---

[1] Such as the sensations of light, heat, muscular effort, etc., in the corresponding branches of physics.

tions.[2] And it should certainly not discourage theoretical explanations of the formal possibilities of a numerical utility.

3.3. PROBABILITY AND NUMERICAL UTILITIES

3.3.1. We can go even one step beyond the above double negations—which were only cautions against premature assertions of the impossibility of a numerical utility. It can be shown that under the conditions on which the indifference curve analysis is based very little extra effort is needed to reach a numerical utility.

It has been pointed out repeatedly that a numerical utility is dependent upon the possibility of comparing differences in utilities. This may seem—and indeed is—a more far-reaching assumption than that of a mere ability to state preferences. But it will seem that the alternatives to which economic preferences must be applied are such as to obliterate this distinction.

3.3.2. Let us for the moment accept the picture of an individual whose system of preferences is all-embracing and complete, i.e. who, for any two objects or rather for any two imagined events, possesses a clear intuition of preference.

More precisely we expect him, for any two alternative events which are put before him as possibilities, to be able to tell which of the two he prefers.

It is a very natural extension of this picture to permit such an individual to compare not only events, but even combinations of events with stated probabilities.[3]

By a combination of two events we mean this: Let the two events be denoted by B and C and use, for the sake of simplicity, the probability 50%-50%. Then the "combination" is the prospect of seeing B occur with a probability of 50%. We stress that the two alternatives are mutually exclusive, so that no possibility of complementarity and the like exists. Also, that an absolute certainty of the occurrence of either B or C exists.

To restate our position. We expect the individual under consideration to possess a clear intuition whether he prefers the event A to the 50–50

[2] A good example of the wide variety of formal possibilities is given by the entirely different development of the theory of light, colors, and wave lengths. All these notions too became numerical, but in an entirely different way.

[3] Indeed this is necessary if he is engaged in economic activities which are explicitly dependent on probability. Cf. the example of agriculture in footnote 2 on p. 10 [in *The Theory of Games and Economic Behavior*].

combination of B or C, or conversely. It is clear that if he prefers A to B and also to C, then he will prefer it to the above combination as well; similarly, if he prefers B as well as C to A, then he will prefer the combination too. But if he should prefer A to, say B, but at the same time C to A, then any assertion about his preference of A against the combination contains fundamentally new information. Specifically: If he now prefers A to the 50–50 combination of B and C, this provides a plausible base for the numerical estimate that his preference of A over B is in excess of his preference of C over A.[4,5]

If this standpoint is accepted, then there is a criterion with which to compare the preference of C over A with the preference of A over B. It is well known that thereby utilities—or rather differences of utilities—become numerically measurable.

That the possibility of comparison between A, B, and C only to this extent is already sufficient for a numerical measurement of "distances" was first observed in economics by Pareto. Exactly the same argument has been made, however, by Euclid for the position of points on a line—in fact it is the very basis of his classical derivation of numerical distances.

The introduction of numerical measures can be achieved even more directly if use is made of all possible probabilities. Indeed: Consider three events, C, A, B, for which the order of the individual's preferences is the one stated. Let α be a real number between 0 and 1, such that A is exactly equally desirable with the combined event consisting of a chance of probability $1 - \alpha$ for B and the remaining chance of probability α for C. Then we suggest the use of α as a numerical estimate for the ratio of the preference of A over B to that of C over B.[6] An exact

---

[4] To give a simple example: Assume that an individual prefers the consumption of a glass of tea to that of a cup of coffee, and the cup of coffee to a glass of milk. If we now want to know whether the last preference—i.e., difference in utilities—exceeds the former, it suffices to place him in a situation where he must decide this: Does he prefer a cup of coffee to a glass the content of which will be determined by a 50%–50% chance device as tea or milk.

[5] Observe that we have only postulated an individual intuition which permits decision as to which of two "events" is preferable. But we have not directly postulated any intuitive estimate of the relative sizes of two preferences—i.e. in the subsequent terminology, of two differences of utilities.

This is important, since the former information ought to be obtainable in a reproducible way by mere "questioning."

[6] This offers a good opportunity for another illustrative example. The above technique permits a direct determination of the ratio q of the utility of possessing 1 unit of a certain good to the utility of possessing 2 units of the same good. The individual must be given the choice of obtaining 1 unit with certainty or of playing the chance to get two units with the probability α, or nothing with the

and exhaustive elaboration of these ideas requires the use of the axiomatic method. A simple treatment of this basis is indeed possible. We shall discuss it in 3.5–3.7.

3.3.3. To avoid misunderstandings let us state that the "events" which were used above as the substratum of preferences are conceived as future events so as to make all logically possible alternatives equally admissible. However, it would be an unnecessary complication, as far as our present objectives are concerned, to get entangled with the problems of the preferences between events in different periods of the future.[7] It seems, however, that such difficulties can be obviated by locating all "events" in which we are interested at one and the same, standardized, moment, preferably in the immediate future.

The above considerations are so vitally dependent upon the numerical concept of probability that a few words concerning the latter may be appropriate.

Probability has often been visualized as a subjective concept more or less in the nature of an estimation. Since we propose to use it in constructing an individual, numerical estimation of utility, the above view of probability would not serve our purpose. The simplest procedure is, therefore, to insist upon the alternative, perfectly well founded interpretation of probability as frequency in long runs. This gives directly the necessary numerical foothold.[8]

3.3.4. This procedure for a numerical measurement of the utilities of the individual depends, of course, upon the hypothesis of completeness in the system of individual preferences.[9] It is conceivable—and may even in a way be more realistic—to allow for cases where the individual is neither able to state which of two alternatives he prefers nor that they are equally desirable. In this case the treatment by indifference curves becomes impracticable too.[10]

How real this possibility is, both for individuals and for organiza-

---

probability $1 - \alpha$. If he prefers the former, then $\alpha < q$; if he prefers the latter, then $\alpha > q$; if he cannot state a preference either way, then $\alpha = q$.

[7] It is well known that this presents very interesting, but as yet extremely obscure, connections with the theory of saving and interest, etc.

[8] If one objects to the frequency interpretation of probability then the two concepts (probability and preference) can be axiomatized together. This too leads to a satisfactory numerical concept of utility which will be discussed on another occasion.

[9] We have not obtained any basis for a comparison, quantitatively or qualitatively, of the utilities of different individuals.

[10] These problems belong systematically in the mathematical theory of ordered sets. The above question in particular amounts to asking whether events, with respect to preference, form a completely or a partially ordered set. Cf. 65.3.

tions, seems to be an extremely interesting question, but it is a question of fact. It certainly deserves further study. We shall reconsider it briefly in 3.7.2.

At any rate we hope we have shown that the treatment by indifference curves implies either too much or too little: if the preferences of the individual are not all comparable, then the indifference curves do not exist.[11] If the individual's preferences are all comparable, then we can even obtain a (uniquely defined) numerical utility which renders the indifference curves superfluous.

All this becomes, of course, pointless for the entrepreneur who can calculate in terms of (monetary) costs and profits.

3.3.5. The objection could be raised that it is not necessary to go into all these intricate details concerning the measurability of utility, since evidently the common individual, whose behavior one wants to describe, does not measure his utilities exactly but rather conducts his economic activities in a sphere of considerable haziness. The same is true, of course, for much of his conduct regarding light, heat, muscular effort, etc. But in order to build a science of physics these phenomena had to be measured. And subsequently the individual has come to use the results of such measurements—directly or indirectly—even in his everyday life. The same may obtain in economics at a future date. Once a fuller understanding of economic behavior has been achieved with the aid of a theory which makes use of this instrument, the life of the individual might be materially affected. It is, therefore, not an unnecessary digression to study these problems.

3.4. PRINCIPLES OF MEASUREMENT:
DETAILED DISCUSSION

3.4.1. The reader may feel, on the basis of the foregoing, that we obtained a numerical scale of utility only by begging the principle, i.e. by really postulating the existence of such a scale. We have argued in 3.3.2. that if an individual prefers A to the 50–50 combination of B and C (while preferring C to A and A to B), this provides a plausible basis for the numerical estimate that this preference of A over B exceeds that of C over A. Are we not postulating here—or taking it for granted— that one preference may exceed another, i.e. that such statements convey a meaning? Such a view would be a complete misunderstanding of our procedure.

[11] Points on the same indifference curve must be identified and are therefore no instances of incomparability.

3.4.2. We are not postulating—or assuming—anything of the kind. We have assumed only one thing—and for this there is good empirical evidence—namely that imagined events can be combined with probabilities. And therefore the same must be assumed for the utilities attached to them,—whatever they may be. Or to put it in more mathematical language:

There frequently appear in science quantities which are *a priori* not mathematical, but attached to certain aspects of the physical world. Occasionally these quantities can be grouped together in domains within which certain natural, physically defined operations are possible. Thus the physically defined quantity of "mass" permits the operation of addition. The physico-geometrically defined quantity of "distance"[12] permits the same operations. On the other hand, the physico-geometrically defined quantity of "position" does not permit this operation,[13] but it permits the operation of forming the "center of gravity" of two positions.[14] Again other physico-geometrical concepts, usually styled "vectorial"—like velocity and acceleration—permit the operation of "addition."

3.4.3. In all these cases where such a "natural" operation is given a name which is reminiscent of a mathematical operation—like the instances of "addition" above—one must carefully avoid misunderstandings. This nomenclature is not intended as a claim that the two operations with the same name are identical—this is manifestly not the case; it only expresses the opinion that they possess similar traits, and the hope that some correspondence between them will ultimately be established. This of course—when feasible at all—is done by finding a mathematical model for the physical domain in question, within which those quantities are defined by numbers, so that in the model the mathematical operation describes the synonymous "natural" operation.

To return to our examples: "energy" and "mass" became numbers in the pertinent mathematical models, "natural" addition becoming ordinary addition. "Position" as well as the vertical quantities became triplets[15] of numbers, called coordinates or components respectively. The "natural" concept of "center of gravity" of two positions $\{x_1, x_2, x_3\}$

---

[12] Let us, for the sake of the argument, view geometry as a physical discipline—a sufficiently tenable viewpoint. By "geometry" we mean—equally for the sake of the argument—Euclidean geometry.

[13] We are thinking of a "homogeneous" Euclidean space, in which no origin or frame of reference is preferred above any other.

[14] With respect to two given masses α, β occupying those positions. It may be convenient to normalize so that the total mass is the unit, i.e. $\beta = 1 - \alpha$.

[15] We are thinking of three-dimensional Euclidean space.

and $\{x_1', x_2', x_3'\}$,[16] with the "masses" α, $1 - \alpha$ (cf. footnote 14 above), becomes

$$\{\alpha x_1 + (1 - \alpha)x_1', \ \alpha x_2 + (1 - \alpha)x_2', \ \alpha x_3 + (1 - \alpha)x_3'\}.^{[17]}$$

The "natural" operation of "addition" of vectors $\{x_1, x_2, x_3\}$ and $\{x_1', x_2', x_3'\}$ becomes $\{x_1 + x_1', x_2 + x_2', x_3 + x_3'\}$.[18]

What was said above about "natural" and mathematical operations applies equally to natural and mathematical relations. The various concepts of "greater" which occur in physics—greater energy, force, heat, velocity, etc.—are good examples.

These "natural" relations are the best base upon which to construct mathematical models and to correlate the physical domain with them.[19, 20]

3.4.4. Here a further remark must be made. Assume that a satisfactory mathematical model for a physical domain in the above sense has been found, and that the physical quantities under consideration have been correlated with numbers. In this case it is not true necessarily that the description (of the mathematical model) provides for a *unique* way of correlating the physical quantities to numbers; i.e., it may specify an entire family of such correlations—the mathematical name is mappings—any one of which can be used for the purposes of theory. Passage from one of these correlations to another amounts to a *transformation* of the numerical data describing the physical quantities. We then say that in this theory the physical quantities in question are

---

[16] We are now describing them by their three numerical coordinates.

[17] This is usually denoted by $\alpha\{x_1, x_2, x_3\} + (1-\alpha)\{x_1', x_2', x_3'\}$. Cf. (16:A:c) in 16.2.1.

[18] This is usually denoted by $\{x_1, x_2, x_3\} + \{x_1', x_2', x_3'\}$. Cf. the beginning of 16.2.1.

[19] Not the only one. Temperature is a good counter-example. The "natural" relation of "greater" would not have sufficed to establish the present day mathematical model—i.e. the absolute temperature scale. The devices actually used were different. Cf. 3.2.1.

[20] We do not want to give the misleading impression of attempting here a complete picture of the formation of mathematical models, i.e. of physical theories. It should be remembered that this is a very varied process with many unexpected phases. An important one is, e.g., the disentanglement of concepts: i.e. splitting up something which at superficial inspection seems to be one physical entity into several mathematical notions. Thus the "disentanglement" of force and energy, of quantity of heat and temperature, were decisive in their respective fields.

It is quite unforeseeable how many such differentiations still lie ahead in economic theory.

described by numbers *up* to that system of transformations. The mathematical name of such transformation systems is *groups*.[21]

Examples of such situations are numerous. Thus the geometrical concept of distance is a number, up to multiplication by (positive) constant factors.[22] The situation concerning the physical quantity of mass is the same. The physical concept of energy is a number up to any linear transformation, i.e. addition of any constant and multiplication by any (positive) constant.[23] The concept of position is defined up to an inhomogeneous orthogonal linear transformation.[24, 25] The vectorial concepts are defined up to homogeneous transformations of the same kind.[26, 27]

3.4.5. It is even conceivable that a physical quantity is a number up to any monotone transformation. This is the case for quantities for which only a "natural" relation "greater" exists—and nothing else. E.g. this was the case for temperature as long as only the concept of "warmer" was known;[5] it applies to the Mohs' scale of hardness of minerals; it applies to the notion of utility when this is based on the conventional idea of preference. In these cases one may be tempted to take the view that the quantity in question is not numerical at all, considering how arbitrary the description by numbers is. It seems to be preferable, however, to refrain from such qualitative statements and to state instead objectively up to what system of transformations the numerical description is determined. The case when the system consists of all monotone transformations is, of course, a rather extreme one; various graduations at the other end of the scale are the transformation systems mentioned above: inhomogeneous or homogeneous orthogonal

---

[21] We shall encounter groups in another context in 28.1.1, where references to the literature are also found.

[22] I.e. there is nothing in Euclidean geometry to fix a unit of distance.

[23] I.e. there is nothing in mechanics to fix a zero or a unit of energy. Cf. with footnote 2 above. Distance has a natural zero—the distance of any point from itself.

[24] I.e. $\{x_1, x_2, x_3\}$ are to be replaced by $\{x_1{}^*, x_2{}^*, x_3{}^*\}$ where

$$x_1{}^* = a_{11}x_1 + a_{12}x_2 + a_{13}x_3 + b_1,$$
$$x_2{}^* = a_{21}x_1 + a_{22}x_2 + a_{23}x_3 + b_2,$$
$$x_3{}^* = a_{31}x_1 + a_{32}x_2 + a_{33}x_3 + b_3,$$

the a_{ij}, b_i being constants, and the matrix (a_{ij}) what is known as orthogonal.

[25] I.e. there is nothing in geometry to fix either origin or the frame of reference when vectors are concerned.

[26] I.e. the $b_i = 0$ in footnote 24. Sometimes a wider concept of matrices is permissible—all those with determinants $\neq 0$. We need not discuss these matters here.

[27] But no quantitatively reproducible method of thermometry.

linear transformations in space, linear transformations in space, linear transformations of one numerical variable, multiplication of that variable by a constant.[28] *In fine*, the case even occurs where no transformations at all need be tolerated.[29]

3.4.6. Given a physical quantity, the system of transformations up to which it is described by numbers may vary in time, i.e. with the stage of development of the subject. Thus temperature was originally a number only up to any monotone transformation.[30] With the development of thermometry—particularly of the concordant ideal gas thermometry—the transformations were restricted to the linear ones, i.e. only the absolute zero and the absolute unit were missing. Subsequent developments of thermodynamics even fixed the absolute zero so that the transformation system in thermodynamics consists only of the multiplication by constants. Examples could be multiplied but there seems to be no need to go into this subject further.

For utility the situation seems to be of a similar nature. One may take the attitude that the only "natural" datum in this domain is the relation "greater," i.e. the concept of preference. In this case utilities are numerical up to a monotone transformation. This is, indeed, the generally accepted standpoint in economic literature, best expressed in the technique of indifference curves.

To narrow the system of transformations it would be necessary to discover further "natural" operations or relations in the domain of utility. Thus it was pointed out by Pareto[31] that an equality relation for utility differences would suffice; in our terminology it would reduce the transformation system to the linear transformations.[32] However, since it does not seem that this relation is really a "natural" one—i.e. one which can be interpreted by reproducible observations—the suggestion does not achieve the purpose.

[28] One could also imagine intermediate cases of greater transformation systems than these but not containing all monotone transformations. Various forms of the theory of relativity give rather technical examples of this.

[29] In the usual language this would hold for physical quantities where an absolute zero as well as an absolute unit can be defined. This is, e.g., the case for the absolute value (not the vector!) of velocity in such physical theories as those in which light velocity plays a normative role: Maxwellian electrodynamics, special relativity.

[30] As long as only the concept of "warmer"—i.e., a "natural" relation "greater"— was known. We discussed this *in extenso* previously.

[31] V. *Pareto,* Manuel d'Economie Politique, Paris, 1907, p. 264.

[32] This is exactly what Euclid did for position on a line. The utility concept of "preference" corresponds to the relation of "lying to the right of" there, and the (desired) relation of the equality of utility differences to the geometrical congruence of intervals.

3.5. CONCEPTUAL STRUCTURE OF THE AXIOMATIC TREATMENT OF NUMERICAL UTILITIES

3.5.1. The failure of one particular device need not exclude the possibility of achieving the same end by another device. Our contention is that the domain of utility contains a "natural" operation which narrows the system of transformations to precisely the same extent as the other device would have done. This is the combination of two utilities with two given alternative probabilities α, $1 - \alpha$, $(0 < \alpha < 1)$ as described in 3.3.2. The process is so similar to the formation of centers of gravity mentioned in 3.4.3. that it may be advantageous to use the same terminology. Thus we have for utilities u, v the "natural" *relation* $u > v$ (read: u is preferable to v), and the "natural" *operation* $\alpha u + (1 - \alpha)v$, $(0 < \alpha < 1)$, (read: center of gravity of u, v with the respective weights α, $1 - \alpha$; or: combination of u, v with the alternative probabilities α, $1 - \alpha$). If the existence—and reproducible observability—of these concepts is conceded, then our way is clear: We must find a correspondence between utilities and numbers which carries the relation $u > v$ and the operation $\alpha u + (1 - \alpha)v$ for utilities into the synonymous concepts for numbers.

Denote the correspondence by

$$u \to p = V(u),$$

u being the utility and $V(u)$ the number which the correspondence attaches to it. Our requirements are then:

$$u > v \qquad \text{implies} \qquad V(u) > V(v), \qquad (3{:}1{:}\text{a})$$

$$V[\alpha u + (1 - \alpha)v] = \alpha V(u) + (1 - \alpha)V(v).^{33} \qquad (3{:}1{:}\text{b})$$

If two such correspondences

$$u \to \rho = V(u), \qquad (3{:}2{:}\text{a})$$

$$u \to \rho' = V'(u), \qquad (3{:}2{:}\text{b})$$

should exist, then they set up a correspondence between numbers

$$\rho \leftrightarrows \rho', \qquad (3{:}3)$$

for which we may also write

$$\rho' = \phi(\rho). \qquad (3{:}4)$$

---

[33] Observe that in each case the left-hand side has the "natural" concepts for utilities, and the right-hand side the conventional ones for numbers.

Since (3:2:a), (3:2:b) fulfill (3:1:a), (3:1:b), the correspondence (3:3), i.e. the function $\phi(\rho)$ in (3:4) must leave the relation $\rho > \sigma$[34] and the operation $\alpha\rho + (1 - \alpha)\sigma$ unaffected. (Cf footnote 33.) I.e.

$$\rho > \sigma \quad \text{implies} \quad \phi(\rho) > \phi(\sigma), \quad\quad\quad (3:5:a)$$

$$\phi[\alpha\rho + (1 - \alpha)\sigma] = \alpha\phi(\rho) + (1 - \alpha)\phi(\sigma). \quad\quad\quad (3:5:b)$$

Hence $\phi(\rho)$ must be a linear function, i.e.

$$\rho' = \phi(\rho) \equiv \omega_0\rho + \omega_1, \quad\quad\quad (3:6)$$

where ω_0, ω_1 are fixed numbers (constants) with $\omega_0 > 0$.

So we see: If such a numerical valuation of utilities[35] exists at all, then it is determined up to a linear transformation.[36, 37] I.e. then utility is a number up to a linear transformation.

In order that a numerical valuation in the above sense should exist it is necessary to postulate certain properties of the relation $u > v$ and the operation $\alpha u + (1 - \alpha)v$ for utilities. The selection of these postulates or axioms and their subsequent analysis leads to problems of a certain mathematical interest. In what follows we give a general outline of the situation for the orientation of the reader; a complete discussion is found in the Appendix.

3.5.2. A choice of axioms is not a purely objective task. It is usually expected to achieve some definite aim—some specific theorem or theorems are to be derivable from the axioms—and to this extent the problem is exact and objective. But beyond this there are always other important desiderata of a less exact nature: The axioms should not be too numerous, their system is to be as simple and transparent as possible, and each axiom should have an immediate intuitive meaning by which its appropriateness may be judged directly.[38] In a situation like

---

[34] Now these are applied to numbers ρ, σ!

[35] I.e. a correspondence (3:2:a) which fulfills (3:1:a), (3:1:b).

[36] I.e. one of the form (3:6).

[37] Remember the physical examples of the same situation given in 3.4.4. (Our present discussion is somewhat more detailed.) We do not undertake to fix an absolute zero and an absolute unit of utility.

[38] The first and the last principle may represent—at least to a certain extent—opposite influences: If we reduce the number of axioms by merging them as far as technically possible, we may lose the possibility of distinguishing the various intuitive backgrounds. Thus we could have expressed the group (3:B) in 3.6.1. by a smaller number of axioms, but this would have obscured the subsequent analysis of 3.6.2.

To strike a proper balance is a matter of practical—and to some extent even esthetic—judgment.

ours this last requirement is particularly vital, in spite of its vagueness: we want to make an intuitive concept amenable to mathematical treatment and to see as clearly as possible what hypotheses this requires.

The objective part of our problem is clear: the postulates must imply the existence of a correspondence (3:2:a) with the properties (3:1:a), (3:1:b) as described in 3.5.1. The further heuristic, and even esthetic desiderata, indicated above, do not determine a unique way of finding this axiomatic treatment. In what follows we shall formulate a set of axioms which seems to be essentially satisfactory.

3.6. THE AXIOMS AND THEIR INTERPRETATION

3.6.1. Our axioms are these:

We consider a system U of entities[39] $u, v, w, \ldots$ In U a *relation* is given, $u > v$, and for any number α, $(0 < \alpha < 1)$, an operation

$$\alpha u + (1 - \alpha)v = w.$$

These concepts satisfy the following axioms:

(3:A)   u > v *is a complete ordering of* U.[40]

This means: Write $u < v$ when $v > u$. Then:

For any two u, v one and only one of three following relations holds:

$$u = v, \qquad u > v, \qquad u < v. \qquad\qquad (3\text{:}A\text{:}a)$$

$$u > v, v > w \text{ implies } u > w.[41] \qquad\qquad (3\text{:}A\text{:}b)$$

(3:B)   *Ordering and combining.*[42]

$$u < v \text{ implies that } u < \alpha u + (1 - \alpha)v. \qquad\qquad (3\text{:}B\text{:}a)$$

$$u > v \text{ implies that } u > \alpha u + (1 - \alpha)v. \qquad\qquad (3\text{:}B\text{:}b)$$

$u < w < v$ implies the existence of an α with

$$\alpha u + (1 - \alpha)v < w. \qquad\qquad (3\text{:}B\text{:}c)$$

---

[39] This is, of course, meant to be the system of (abstract) utilities, to be characterized by our axioms. Concerning the general nature of the axiomatic method, cf. the remarks and references in the last part of 10.1.1.

[40] For a more systematic mathematical discussion of this notion, cf. 65.3.1. The equivalent concept of the completeness of the system of preferences was previously considered at the beginning of 3.3.2. and of 3.4.6.

[41] These conditions (3:A:a), (3:A:b) correspond to (65:A:a), (65:A:b) in 65.3.1.

[42] Remember that the α, β, γ occurring here are always $> 0, < 1$.

$u > w > v$ implies the existence of an α with

$$\alpha u + (1 - \alpha)v > w. \qquad (3\!:\!B\!:\!d)$$

(3:C)   *Algebra of combining.*

$$\alpha u + (1 - \alpha)v = (1 - \alpha)v + \alpha u. \qquad (3\!:\!C\!:\!a)$$

$$\alpha[\beta u + (1 - \beta)v] + (1 - \alpha)v = \gamma u + (1 - \gamma)v \qquad (3\!:\!C\!:\!b)$$

where $\gamma = \alpha\beta$.

One can show that these axioms imply the existence of a correspondence (3:2:a) with the properties (3:1:a), (3:1:b) as described in 3.5.1. Hence the conclusions of 3.5.1 hold good: The system U—i.e. in our present interpretation, the system of (abstract) utilities—is one of numbers up to a linear transformation.

The construction of (3:2:a) [with (3:1:a), (3:1:b) by means of the axioms (3:A)–(3:C)] is a purely mathematical task which is somewhat lengthy, although it runs along conventional lines and presents no particular difficulties. (Cf. Appendix.)

It seems equally unnecessary to carry out the usual logistic discussion of these axioms[43] on this occasion.

We shall however say a few more words about the intuitive meaning —i.e. the justification—of each one of our axioms (3:A)–(3:C).

3.6.2. The analysis of our postulates follows:

(3:A:a*)   This is the statement of the completeness of the system of individual preferences. It is customary to assume this when discussing utilities or preferences, e.g. in the "indifference curve analysis method." These questions were already considered in 3.3.4. and 3.4.6.

(3:A:b*)   This is the "transitivity" of preference, a plausible and generally accepted property.

(3:B:a*)   We state here: If v is preferable to u, then even a chance $1 - \alpha$ of v—alternatively to u—is preferable. This is legitimate since any kind of complementarity (or the opposite) has been excluded, cf. the beginning of 3.3.2.

(3:B:b*)   This is the dual of (3:B:a*), with "less preferable" in place of "preferable."

(3:B:c*)   We state here: If w is preferable to u, and an even more preferable v is also given, then the combination of u with a chance $1 - \alpha$ of v will not affect w's preferability to it if this chance is small

---

[43] A similar situation is dealt with more exhaustively in 10.; those axioms describe a subject which is more vital for our main objective. The logistic discussion is indicated there in 10.2. Some of the general remarks of 10.3. apply to the present case also.

enough. I.e.: However desirable v may be in itself, one can make its influence as real as desired by giving it a sufficiently small chance. This is a plausible "continuity" assumption.

(3:B:d*) This is the dual of (3:B:c*), with "less preferable" in place of "preferable."

(3:C:a*) This is the statement that it is irrelevant in which order the constituents u, v of a combination are named. It is legitimate, particularly since the constituents are alternative events, cf. (3:B:a*) above.

(3:C:b*) This is the statement that it is irrelevant whether a combination of two constituents is obtained in two successive steps— first the probabilities α, $1 - \alpha$, the the probabilities β, $1 - \beta$; or in one operation—the probabilities γ, $1 - \gamma$ where $\gamma = \alpha\beta$.[44] The same things can be said for this as for (3:C:a*) above. It may be, however, that this postulate has a deeper significance, to which one allusion is made in 3.7.1. below.

3.7. GENERAL REMARKS CONCERNING THE AXIOMS

3.7.1. At this point it may be well to stop and to reconsider the situation. Have we not shown too much? We can derive from the postulates (3:A)–(3:C) the numerical character of utility in the sense of (3:2:a) and (3:1:a), (3:1:b) in 3.5.1.; and (3:1:b) states that the numerical values of utility combine (with probabilities) like mathematical expectation! And yet the concept of mathematical expectation has been often questioned, and its legitimateness is certainly dependent upon some hypothesis concerning the nature of an "expectation."[45] Have we not then begged the hypotheses which bring in the mathematical expectation?

More specifically: May there not exist in an individual a (positive or negative) utility of the mere act of "taking a chance," of gambling, which the use of the mathematical expectation obliterates?

How did our axioms (3:A)–(3:C) get around this possibility?

As far as we can see, our postulates (3:A)–(3:C) do not attempt to avoid it. Even that one which gets closest to excluding a "utility of

---

[44] This is of course the correct arithmetic of accounting for two successive admixtures of v with u.

[45] Cf. *Karl Menger:* Das Unsicherheitsmoment in der Wertlehre, Zeitschrift für Nationalökonomie, vol. 5, (1934) pp. 459 ff. and *Gerhard Tintner:* A contribution to the non-static Theory of Choice, Quarterly Journal of Economics, vol. LVI, (1942) pp. 274 ff.

gambling" (3:C:b) (cf. its discussion in 3.6.2), seems to be plausible and legitimate—unless a much more refined system of psychology is used than the one now available for the purposes of economics. The fact that a numerical utility—with a formula amounting to the use of mathematical expectations—can be built upon (3:A)–(3:C), seems to indicate this: We have practically defined numerical utility as being that thing for which the calculus of mathematical expectations is legitimate.[46] Since (3:A)–(3:C) secure that the necessary construction can be carried out, concepts like a "specific utility of gambling" cannot be formulated free of contradiction on this level.[47]

3.7.2. As we have stated, the last time in 3.6.1., our axioms are based on the relation $u > v$ and on the operation $\alpha u + (1 - \alpha)v$ for utilities. It seems noteworthy that the latter may be regarded as more immediately given than the former: one can hardly doubt that anybody who could imagine two alternative situations with the respective utilities u, v could not also conceive the prospect of having both with the given respective probabilities α, $1 - \alpha$. On the other hand one may question the postulate of axiom (3:A:a) for $u > v$, i.e. the completeness of this ordering.

Let us consider this point for a moment. We have conceded that one may doubt whether a person can always decide which of two alternatives—with the utilities u, v—he prefers.[48] But, whatever the merits of this doubt are, this possibility—i.e. the completeness of the system of (individual) preferences—must be assumed even for the purposes of the "indifference curve method" [cf. our remarks on (3:A:a) in 3.6.2.]. But if this property of $u > v$[49] is assumed, then our use of the much less questionable $\alpha u + (1 - \alpha)v$[50] yields the numerical utilities too![51]

---

[46] Thus Daniel Bernoulli's well known suggestion to "solve" the "St. Petersburg Paradox" by the use of the so-called "moral expectation" (instead of the mathematical expectation) means defining the utility numerically as the logarithm of one's monetary possessions.

[47] This may seem to be a paradoxical assertion. But anybody who has seriously tried to axiomatic that elusive concept, will probably concur with it.

[48] Or that he can assert that they are precisely equally desirable.

[49] I.e. the completeness postulate (3:A:a).

[50] I.e. the postulates (3:B), (3:C) together with the obvious postulate (3:A:b).

[51] At this point the reader may recall the familiar argument according to which the unnumerical ("indifference curve") treatment of utilities is preferable to any numerical one, because it is simpler and based on fewer hypotheses. This objection might be legitimate if the numerical treatment were based on Pareto's equality relation for utility differences (cf. the end of 3.4.6). This relation is, indeed, a stronger and more complicated hypothesis, added to the original ones concerning the general comparability of utilities (completeness of preferences).

However, we used the operation $\alpha u + (1 - \alpha)v$ instead, and we hope that the

If the general comparability assumption is not made,[52] a mathematical theory—based on $\alpha u + (1 - \alpha) v$ together with what remains of $u > v$—is still possible.[53] It leads to what may be described as a many-dimensional vector concept of utility. This is a more complicated and less satisfactory set-up, but we do not propose to treat it systematically at this time.

3.7.3. This brief exposition does not claim to exhaust the subject, but we hope to have conveyed the essential points. To avoid misunderstanding, the following further remarks may be useful.

(1) We re-emphasize that we are considering only utilities experienced by one person. These considerations do not imply anything concerning the comparisons of the utilities belonging to different individuals.

(2) It cannot be denied that the analysis of the methods which make use of mathematical expectation (cf. footnote 1 on p. 28. for the literature) is far from concluded at present. Our remarks in 3.7.1. lie in this direction, but much more should be said in this respect. There are many interesting questions involved, which however lie beyond the scope of this work. For our purpose it suffices to observe that the validity of the simple and plausible axioms (3:A)–(3:C) in 3.6.1. for the relation $u > v$ and the operation $\alpha u + (1 - \alpha) v$ makes the utilities numbers up to a linear transformation in the sense discussed in these sections.

3.8. THE ROLE OF THE CONCEPT OF MARGINAL UTILITY

3.8.1. The preceding analysis made it clear that we feel free to make use of a numerical conception of utility. On the other hand, subsequent discussions will show that we cannot avoid the assumption that all subjects of the economy under consideration are completely informed about the physical characteristics of the situation in which they operate and are able to perform all statistical, mathematical, etc., operations which this knowledge makes possible. The nature and importance of

---

reader will agree with us that it represents an even safer assumption than that of the completeness of preferences.

We think therefore that our procedure, as distinguished from Pareto's, is not open to the objections based on the necessity of artificial assumptions and a loss of simplicity.

[52] This amounts to weakening (3:A:a) to an (3:A:a') by replacing in it "one and only one" by "at most one." The conditions (3:A:a'), (3:A:b) then correspond to (65:B:a), (65:B:b).

[53] In this case some modifications in the groups of postulates (3:B), (3:C) are also necessary.

this assumption has been given extensive attention in the literature and the subject is probably very far from being exhausted. We propose not to enter upon it. The question is too vast and too difficult and we believe that it is best to "divide difficulties." I.e. we wish to avoid this complication which, while interesting in its own right, should be considered separately from our present problem.

Actually we think that our investigations—although they assume "complete information" without any further discussion—do make a contribution to the study of this subject. It will be seen that many economic and social phenomena which are usually ascribed to the individual's state of "incomplete information" make their appearance in our theory and can be satisfactorily interpreted with its help. Since our theory assumes "complete information," we conclude from this will be found in the concepts of "discrimination" in 33.1., of "incomplete exploitation" in 38.3., and of the "transfer" or "tribute" in 46.11., 46.12.

On the basis of the above we would even venture to question the importance usually ascribed to incomplete information in its conventional sense[54] in economic and social theory. It will appear that some phenomena which would *prima facie* have to be attributed to this factor, have nothing to do with it.[55]

3.8.2. Let us now consider an isolated individual with definite physical characteristics and with definite quantities of goods at his disposal. In view of what was said above, he is in a position to determine the maximum utility which can be obtained in this situation. Since the maximum is a well-defined quantity, the same is true for the increase which occurs when a unit of any definite good is added to the stock of all goods in the possession of the individual. This is, of course, the classical notion of the marginal unity of a unit of the commodity in question.[56]

These quantities are clearly of decisive importance in the "Robinson Crusoe" economy. The above marginal utility obviously corresponds to the maximum effort which he will be willing to make—if he behaves according to the customary criteria of rationality—in order to obtain a further unit of that commodity.

---

[54] We shall see that the rules of the games considered may explicitly prescribe that certain participants should not possess certain pieces of information. Cf. 6.3., 6.4. [Games in which this does not happen are referred to in 14.8. and in (15:B) of 15.3.2., and are called games with "perfect information."] We shall recognize and utilize this kind of "incomplete information" (according to the above, rather to be called "imperfect information"). But we reject all other types, vaguely defined by the use of concepts like complication, intelligence, etc.

[55] Our theory attributes these phenomena to the possibility of multiple "stable standards of behavior" cf. 4.6. and the end of 4.7.

[56] More precisely: the so-called "indirectly dependent expected utility."

It is not clear at all, however, what significance it has in determining the behavior of a participant in a social exchange economy. We saw that the principles of rational behavior in this case still await formulation, and that they are certainly not expressed by a maximum requirement of the Crusoe type. Thus it must be uncertain whether marginal utility has any meaning at all in this case.[57]

Positive statements on this subject will be possible only after we have succeeded in developing a theory of rational behavior in a social exchange economy, that is, as was stated before, with the help of the theory of "games of strategy." It will be seen that marginal utility does, indeed, play an important role in this case too, but in a more subtle way then is usually assumed.

[57] All this is understood within the domain of our several simplifying assumptions. If they are relaxed, then various further difficulties ensue.

THE UTILITY ANALYSIS OF CHOICES INVOLVING RISK[1]

Milton Friedman and Leonard J. Savage

1. THE PROBLEM AND ITS BACKGROUND

The purpose of this paper is to suggest that an important class of reactions of individuals to risk can be rationalized by a rather simple extension of orthodox utility analysis.

Individuals frequently must, or can, choose among alternatives that differ, among other things, in the degree of risk to which the individual will be subject. The clearest examples are provided by insurance and gambling. An individual who buys fire insurance on a house he owns is accepting the certain loss of a small sum (the insurance premium) in preference to the combination of a small chance of a much larger loss (the value of the house) and a large chance of no loss. That is, he is choosing certainty in preference to uncertainty. An individual who buys a lottery ticket is subjecting himself to a large chance of losing a small amount (the price of the lottery ticket) plus a small chance of winning a large amount (a prize) in preference to avoiding both risks. He is choosing uncertainty in preference to certainty.

This choice among different degrees of risk so prominent in insurance and gambling, is clearly present and important in a much broader range of economic choices. Occupations differ greatly in the variability of the income they promise: in some, for example, civil service employment, the prospective income is rather clearly defined and is almost certain to be within rather narrow limits; in others, for example, salaried employment as an accountant, there is somewhat more variability yet almost no chance of either an extremely high or an extremely low income; in still others, for example, motion-picture acting, there is extreme variability, with a small chance of an extremely high income and a larger

---

[1] The fundamental ideas of this paper were worked out jointly by the two authors. The paper was written primarily by the senior author.

Source: Reprinted with permission from The Journal of Political Economy, LVI: 279–304 (August 1948).

chance of an extremely low income. Securities vary similarly, from government bonds and industrial "blue chips" to "blue-sky" common stocks; and so do business enterprises or lines of business activity. Whether or not they realize it and whether or not they take explicit account of the varying degree of risk involved, individuals choosing among occupations, securities, or lines of business activity are making choices analogous to those that they make when they decide whether to buy insurance or to gamble. Is there any consistency among the choices of this kind that individuals make? Do they neglect the element of risk? Or does it play a central role? If so, what is that role?

These problems have, of course, been considered by economic theorists, particularly in their discussions of earnings in different occupations and of profits in different lines of business.[2] Their treatment of these problems has, however, never been integrated with their explanation of choices among riskless alternatives. Choices among riskless alternatives are explained in terms of maximization of utility: individuals are supposed to choose as they would if they attributed some common quantitative characteristic—designated utility—to various goods and then selected the combination of goods that yielded the largest total amount of this common characteristic. Choices among alternatives involving different degrees of risk, for example, among different occupations, are explained in utterly different terms—by ignorance of the odds or by the fact that "young men of an adventurous disposition are more attracted by the prospects of a great success than they are deterred by the fear of failure," by "the overweening conceit which the greater part of men have of their own abilities," by "their absurd presumption in their own good fortune," or by some similar *deus ex machina*.[3]

The rejection of utility maximization as an explanation of choices among different degrees of risk was a direct consequence of the belief in diminishing marginal utility. If the marginal utility of money diminishes, an individual seeking to maximize utility will never participate in a "fair" game of chance, for example, a game in which he has an equal chance of winning or losing a dollar. The gain in utility from winning a dollar will be less than the loss in utility from losing a dollar, so that the expected utility from participation in the game is negative. Diminishing marginal utility plus maximization of expected utility would thus imply that individuals would always have to be paid to

[2] E.g., see Adam Smith, *The Wealth of Nations,* Book I, Ch. x (Modern Library reprint of Cannan ed.), pp. 106–11; Alfred Marshall, *Principles of Economics* (8th ed.; London: Macmillan & Co., Ltd., 1920), pp. 398–400, 554–55, 613.

[3] Marshall, *op. cit.,* p. 554 (first quotation); Smith, *op. cit.,* p. 107 (last two quotations).

induce them to bear risk.[4] But this implication is clearly contradicted by actual behavior. People not only engage in fair games of chance, they engage freely and often eagerly in such unfair games as lotteries. Not only do risky occupations and risky investments not always yield a higher average return than relatively safe occupations or investments, they frequently yield a much lower average return.

Marshall resolved this contradiction by rejecting utility maximization as an explanation of choices involving risk. He need not have done so, since he did not need diminishing marginal utility—or, indeed, any quantitative concept of utility—for the analysis of riskless choices. The shift from the kind of utility analysis employed by Marshall to the indifference-curve analysis of F. Y. Edgeworth, Irving Fisher, and Vilfredo Pareto revealed that to rationalize riskless choices, it is sufficient to suppose that individuals can rank baskets of goods by total utility. It is unnecessary to suppose that they can compare differences between utilities. But diminishing, or increasing, marginal utility implies a comparison of differences between utilities and hence is an entirely gratuitous assumption in interpreting riskless choices.

The idea that choices among alternatives involving risk can be explained by the maximization of expected utility is ancient, dating back at least to D. Bernoulli's celebrated analysis of the St. Petersburg paradox.[5] It has been repeatedly referred to since then but almost in-

---

[4] See Marshall, *op. cit.*, p. 135 n.; Mathematical Appendix, n. ix (p. 843). "Gambling involves an economic loss, even when conducted on perfectly fair and even terms. . . . A theoretically fair insurance against risks is always an economic gain" (p. 135). "The argument that fair gambling is an economic blunder . . . requires no further assumption than that, firstly the pleasures of gambling may be neglected; and, secondly $\phi''(x)$ is negative for all values of x, where $\phi(x)$ is the pleasure derived from wealth equal to x. . . . It is true that this loss of probable happiness need not be greater than the pleasure derived from the excitement of gambling, and we are then thrown back upon the induction that pleasures of gambling are in Bentham's phrase 'impure'; since experience shows that they are likely to engender a restless, feverish character, unsuited for steady work as well as for the higher and more solid pleasures of life" (p. 843).

[5] See Daniel Bernoulli, *Versuch einer neuen Theorie der Wertbestimmung von Glücksfällen* (Leipzig, 1896), translated by A. Pringsheim from "Specimen theoriae novae de mensura sortis," *Commentarii academiae scientiarum imperialis Petropolitanae*, Vol. V, for the years 1730 and 1731, published in 1738.

In an interesting note appended to his paper Bernoulli points out that Cramer [presumably Gabriel Cramer (1704–52)], a famous mathematician of the time, had anticipated some of his own views by a few years. The passages that he quotes from a letter in French by Cramer contain what, to us, is the truly essential point in Bernoulli's paper, namely, the idea of using the mathematical expectation of utility (the "moral expectation") instead of the mathematical expectation of income to compare alternatives involving risk. Cramer has not in general been

variably rejected as the correct explanation—commonly because the prevailing belief in diminishing marginal utility made it appear that the existence of gambling could not be so explained. Even since the wide-spread recognition that the assumption of diminishing marginal utility is unnecessary to explain riskless choices, writers have continued to reject maximization of expected utility as "unrealistic."[6] This rejection of maximization of expected utility has been challenged by John von Neumann and Oskar Morgenstern in their recent book, *Theory of Games and Economic Behavior*.[7] They argue that "under the conditions on which the indifference curve analysis is based very little extra effort is needed to reach a numerical utility," the expected value of which is maximized in choosing among alternatives involving risk.[8] The present paper is based on their treatment but has been made self-contained by the paraphrasing of essential parts of their argument.

If an individual shows by his market behavior that he prefers A to B and B to C, it is traditional to rationalize this behavior by supposing that he attaches more utility to A than to B and more utility to B than to C. All utility functions that give the same ranking to possible alternatives will provide equally good rationalizations of such choices, and it will make no difference which particular one is used. If, in addition,

---

attributed this much credit, apparently because the essential point in Bernoulli's paper has been taken to be the suggestion that the logarithm of income is an appropriate utility function.

[6] "It has been the assumption in the classical literature on this subject that the individual in question will always try to maximize the mathematical expectation of his gain or utility. . . . This may appear plausible, but it is certainly not an assumption which must hold true in all cases. It has been pointed out that the individual may also be interested in, and influenced by, the range or the standard deviation of the different possible utilities derived or some other measure of dispersion. It appears pretty evident from the behavior of people in lotteries or foot-ball pools that they are not a little influenced by the skewness of the probability distribution" [Gerhard Tintner, "A Contribution to the Non-Static Theory of Choice," *Quarterly Journal of Economics*, Vol. LVI (February, 1942), p. 278].

"It would be definitely unrealistic . . . to confine ourselves to the mathematical expectation only, which is the usual but not justifiable practice of the traditional calculus of 'moral probabilities'" [J. Marschak, "Money and the Theory of Assets," *Econometrica*, Vol. VI (1938), p. 320].

Tintner's inference, apparently also shared by Marschak, that the facts he cites are necessarily inconsistent with maximization of expected utility is erroneous (see Secs. III and IV below). He is led to consider a formally more general solution because of his failure to appreciate the real generality of the kinds of behavior explicable by the maximization of expected utility.

[7] Princeton University Press, 1st ed., 1944; 2d ed., 1947; pp. 15–31 (both eds.), pp. 617–32 (2d ed. only); succeeding references are to 2d ed.

[8] *Ibid.*, p. 17.

the individual should show by his market behavior that he prefers a 50–50 chance of A or C to the certainty of B, it seems natural to rationalize this behavior by supposing that the *difference* between the utilities he attaches to A and B is greater than the *difference* between the utilities he attaches to B and C, so that the *expected* utility of the preferred combination is greater than the utility of B. The class of utility functions, if there be any, that can provide the same ranking of alternatives that involve risk is much more restricted than the class that can provide the same ranking of alternatives that are certain. It consists of utility functions that differ only in origin and unit of measure (i.e., the utility functions in the class are linear functions of one another).[9] Thus, in effect, the ordinal properties of utility functions can be used to rationalize riskless choices, the numerical properties to rationalize choices involving risk.

It does not, of course, follow that there will exist a utility function that will rationalize in this way the reactions of individuals to risk. It may be that individuals behave inconsistently—sometimes choosing a 50–50 chance of A or C instead of B and sometimes the reverse; or sometimes choosing A instead of B, B instead of C, and C instead of A—or that in some other way their behavior is different from what it would be if they were seeking rationally to maximize expected utility in accordance with a given utility function. Or it may be that some types of reactions to risk can be rationalized in this way while others cannot. Whether a numerical utility function will in fact serve to rationalize any particular class of reactions to risk is an empirical question to be tested; there is no obvious contradiction such as was once thought to exist.

This paper attempts to provide a crude empirical test by bringing together a few broad observations about the behavior of individuals in choosing among alternatives involving risk (Sec. II) and investigating whether these observations are consistent with the hypothesis revived by von Neumann and Morgenstern (Secs. III and IV). It turns out that these empirical observations are entirely consistent with the hypothesis if a rather special shape is given to the total utility curve of money (Sec. IV). This special shape, which can be given a tolerably satisfactory interpretation (Sec. V), not only brings under the aegis of rational utility maximization much behavior that is ordinarily explained in other terms but also has implications about observable behavior not used in deriving it (Sec. VI). Further empirical work should make it possible to determine whether or not these implications conform to reality.

[9] *Ibid.*, pp. 15–31, esp. p. 25.

It is a testimony to the strength of the belief in diminishing marginal utility that it has taken so long for the possibility of interpreting gambling and similar phenomena as a contradiction of universal diminishing marginal utility, rather than of utility maximization, to be recognized. The initial mistake must have been at least partly a product of a strong introspective belief in diminishing marginal utility: a dollar must mean less to a rich man than to a poor man; see how much more a man will spend when he is rich than when he is poor to avoid any given amount of pain or discomfort.[10] Some of the comments that have been published by competent economists on the utility analysis of von Neumann and Morgenstern are even more remarkable testimony to the hold that diminishing marginal utility has on economists. Vickrey remarks:

> There is abundant evidence that individual decisions in situations involving risk are not always made in ways that are compatible with the assumption that the decisions are made rationally with a view to maximizing the mathematical expectation of a utility function. The purchase of tickets in lotteries, sweepstakes, and 'numbers' pools would imply, on such a basis, that the marginal utility of money is an increasing rather than a decreasing function of income. Such a conclusion is obviously unacceptable as a guide to social policy.[11]

Kaysen remarks,

> Unfortunately, these postulates (underlying the von Neumann and Morgenstern discussion of utility measurement) involve an assumption about economic behavior which is contrary to experience. . . . That this assumption is contradicted by experience can easily be shown by hundreds of examples (including) the participation of individuals in lotteries in which their mathematical expectation of gain (utility) is negative.[12]

[10] This elemental argument seems so clearly to justify diminishing marginal utility that it may be desirable even now to state explicitly how this phenomenon can be rationalized equally well on the assumption of increasing marginal utility of money. It is only necessary to suppose that the avoidance of pain and the other goods that can be bought with money are related goods and that, while the marginal utility of money increases as the amount of money increases, the marginal utility of avoiding pain increases even faster.

[11] William Vickrey, "Measuring Marginal Utility by Reactions to Risk," *Econometrica*, Vol. XIII (1945), pp. 319–33. The quotation is from pp. 327 and 328. "The purchase of tickets in lotteries, sweepstakes, and 'numbers' pools" does not imply that marginal utility of money increases with income everywhere (See Sec. IV below). Moreover, it is entirely unnecessary to identify the quantity that individuals are to be interpreted as maximizing with a quantity that should be given special importance in public policy.

[12] C. Kaysen, "A Revolution in Economic Theory?" *Review of Economic Studies,* Vol. XIV, No. 35 (1946–47), pp. 1–15; quotation is from p. 13.

II. OBSERVABLE BEHAVIOR TO BE RATIONALIZED

The economic phenomena to which the hypothesis revived by von Neumann and Morgenstern is relevant can be divided into, first, the phenomena ordinarily regarded as gambling and insurance; second, other economic phenomena involving risk. The latter are clearly the more important, and the ultimate significance of the hypothesis will depend primarily on the contribution it makes to an understanding of them. At the same time, the influence of risk is revealed most markedly in gambling and insurance, so that these phenomena have a significance for testing and elaborating the hypothesis out of proportion to their importance in actual economic behavior.

At the outset it should be confessed that we have conducted no extensive empirical investigation of either class of phenomena. For the present, we are content to use what is already available in the literature, or obvious from casual observation, to provide a first test of the hypothesis and to impose significant substantive restrictions on it.

The major economic decisions of an individual in which risk plays an important role concern the employment of the resources he controls: what occupation to follow, what entrepreneurial activity to engage in, how to invest (nonhuman) capital. Alternative possible uses of resources can be classified into three broad groups according to the degree of risk involved: (a) those involving little or no risk about the money return to be received—occupations like schoolteaching, other civil service employment, clerical work; business undertakings of a standard, predictable type like many public utilities; securities like government bonds, high-grade industrial bonds; some real property, particularly owner-occupied housing; (b) those involving a moderate degree of risk but unlikely to lead to either extreme gains or extreme losses—occupations like dentistry, accountancy, some kinds of managerial work; business undertakings of fairly standard kinds in which, however, there is sufficient competition to make the outcome fairly uncertain; securities like lower-grade bonds, preferred stocks, higher-grade common stocks; (c) those involving much risk, with some possibility of extremely large gains and some of extremely large losses—occupations involving physical risks, like piloting aircraft, automobile racing, or professions like medicine and law; business undertakings in untried fields; securities like highly speculative stocks; some types of real property.

The most significant generalization in the literature about choices among these three uses of resources is that, other things the same, uses a or c tend in general to be preferred to use b; that is, people must in general be paid a premium to induce them to undertake moderate risks instead of subjecting themselves to either small or large risks. Thus Marshall says:

> There are many people of a sober steady-going temper, who like to know what is before them, and who would far rather have an appointment which offered a certain income of say £400 a year than one which was not unlikely to yield £600, but had an equal chance of affording only £200. Uncertainty, therefore, which does not appeal to great ambitions and lofty aspirations, has special attractions for very few; while it acts as a deterrent to many of those who are making their choice of a career. And as a rule the certainty of moderate success attracts more than an expectation of an uncertain success that has an equal actuarial value.
>
> But on the other hand, if an occupation offers a few extremely high prizes, its attractiveness is increased out of all proportion to their aggregate value.[13]

Adam Smith comments similarly about occupational choices and, in addition, says of entrepreneurial undertakings:

> The ordinary rate of profits always rises more or less with the risk. It does not, however, seem to rise in proportion to it, or so as to compensate it completely. . . . The presumptuous hope of success seems to act here as upon all other occasions, and to entice so many adventurers into those hazardous trades, that their competition reduces the profit below what is sufficient to compensate the risk.[14]

Edwin Cannan, in discussing the rate of return on investments, concludes that "the probability is that the classes of investments which on the average return most to the investor are neither the very safest of all nor the very riskiest, but the intermediate classes which do not appeal either to timidity or to the gambling instinct."[15]

This asserted preference for extremely safe or extremely risky investments over investments with an intermediate degree of risk has its direct counterpart in the willingness of persons to buy insurance and also to buy lottery tickets or engage in other forms of gambling involving a small chance of a large gain. The extensive market for highly speculative stocks—the kind of stocks that "blue-sky" laws are intended to control—is a border-line case that could equally well be designated as investment or gambling.

---

[13] *Op. cit.*, pp. 554–55.

[14] *Op. cit.*, p. 111.

[15] Article on "Profit," in *Dictionary of Political Economy*, ed. R. H. Inglis Palgrave (new edition, ed. Henry Higgs; London, 1926); see also the summary of the views of different writers on risk-taking in F. H. Knight, *Risk, Uncertainty, and Profit* (New York, 1921; reprint London School of Economics and Political Science, 1933), pp. 362–67.

The empirical evidence for the willingness of persons of all income classes to buy insurance is extensive.[16] Since insurance companies have

[16] E.g., see U.S. Bureau of Labor Statistics, *Bulletin 648: Family Expenditures in Selected Cities, 1935–36;* Vol. I: *Family Expenditures for Housing, 1935–36;* Vol. VI: *Family Expenditures for Transportation, 1935–36;* and Vol. VIII: *Changes in Assets and Liabilities, 1935–36.*

Table 6 of the Tabular Summary of Vol. I gives the percentage of home-owning families reporting the payment of premiums for insurance on the house. These percentages are given separately for each income class in each of a number of cities or groups of cities. Since premiums are often paid less frequently than once a year, the percentages given definitely understate the percentage of families carrying insurance. Yet the bulk of the percentages are well over 40.

Table 5 of the Tabular Summary of Vol. VI gives the percentage of families (again by income classes and cities or groups of cities) reporting expenditures for automobile insurance. These figures show a very rapid increase in the percentage of automobile operators that had insurance (this figure is derived by dividing the percentage of families reporting automobile insurance by the percentage of families operating cars) as income increases. In the bottom income classes, where operation of a car is infrequent, only a minority of those who operate cars carry insurance. In the upper income classes, where most families operate cars, the majority of operators carry insurance. A convenient summary of these percentages for selected income classes in six large cities, given in text Table 10 (p. 26), has 42 entries. These vary from 4% to 98%, and 23 are over 50%.

Table 3 of the Tabular Summary of Vol. VIII gives the percentage of families in each income class in various cities or groups of cities reporting the payment of life, endowment, or annuity insurance premiums. The percentages are uniformly high. For example, for New York City the percentage of white families reporting the payment of insurance premiums is 75% or higher for every income class listed and varies from 75% in the income class $500–$749 to over 95% in the upper-income classes; the percentage of Negro families purchasing insurance was 38% for the $1000–$1249 class but 60% or higher for every other class. This story is repeated for city after city, the bulk of the entries in the table for the percentage of families purchasing insurance begin above 80%.

These figures cannot be regarded as direct estimates of the percentage of families willing to pay something—that is, to accept a smaller actuarial value—in order to escape risk, the technical meaning of the purchase of insurance that is relevant for our purpose. (1) The purchase of automobile and housing insurance may not be a matter of choice. Most owned homes have mortgages (see Vol. I, p. 361, Table L) and the mortgage may require that insurance be carried. The relevant figure for mortgaged homes would be the fraction of owners carrying a larger amount of insurance than is required by the mortgage. Similarly, finance companies generally require that insurance be carried on automobiles purchased on the instalment plan and not fully paid for, and the purchase of automobile insurance is compulsory in some states. (2) For automobile property damage and liability insurance (but not collision insurance) the risks to the operator and to the insurance company may not be the same, particularly to persons in the lower-income classes. The loss to the uninsured operator is limited by his wealth and borrowing power, and the maximum amount that he can lose may be well below the face value of the policy that he would purchase. The excess of the premium over the costs of operation that are covered by their premium receipts, the purchaser is obviously paying a larger premium than the average compensation he can expect to receive for the losses against which he carries insurance. That is, he is paying something to escape risk.

The empirical evidence for the willingness of individuals to purchase lottery tickets, or engage in similar forms of gambling, is also extensive. Many governments find, and more governments have found, lotteries an effective means of raising revenue.[17] Though illegal, the "numbers"

---

expected loss is thus greater for him than for a person with more wealth or borrowing power. The rise in the percentage of persons carrying automobile insurance as income rises may therefore reflect not an increased willingness to carry insurance but a reduction in the effective price that must be paid for insurance. (3) This tendency may be reversed for the relatively high-income classes for both automobile and housing insurance by the operation of the income tax. Uninsured losses are in many instances deductible from income before computation of income tax under the United States federal income tax, while insurance premiums are not. This tends to make the net expected loss less for the individual than for the insurance company. This effect is almost certainly negligible for the figures cited above, both because they do not effectively cover very high incomes and because the federal income tax was relatively low in 1935–36. (4) Life insurance at times comes closer to gambling (the choice of an uncertain alternative in preference to a certain alternative with a higher expected value) than to the payment of a premium to escape risk. For example, special life insurance policies purchased to cover a single railroad or airplane trip are probably more nearly comparable to a lottery ticket than a means of achieving certainty. (5) Even aside from these qualifications, actual purchase of insurance would give at best a lower limit to the number willing to buy insurance, since there will always be some who will regard the price asked as too high.

These qualifications offset one another to some extent. It seems highly unlikely that their net effect could be sufficient to reverse the conclusion suggested by the evidence cited that a large fraction of people in all income classes are willing to buy insurance.

[17] France, Spain, and Mexico, to name but three examples, currently conduct lotteries for revenue. Russia attaches a lottery feature to bonds sold to the public. Great Britain conducted lotteries from 1694 to 1826. In the United States lotteries were used extensively before the Revolution and for some time thereafter, both directly by state governments and under state charters granted to further specific projects deemed to have a state interest. For the history of lotteries in Great Britain see C. L'Estrange Ewen, *Lotteries and Sweepstakes* (London, 1932); in New York State, A. F. Ross, "History of Lotteries in New York," *Magazine of History*, Vol. V (New York, 1907). There seem to be no direct estimates of the fraction of the people who purchase tickets in state or other legal lotteries, and it is clear that such figures would be difficult to get from data obtained in connection with running the lotteries. The receipts from legal lotteries, and casual impressions of observers, suggest that a substantial fraction of the relevant units (families or, alternatively, individual income recipients) purchase tickets.

game and similar forms of gambling are reported to flourish in the United States,[18] particularly among the lower-income classes.

It seems highly unlikely that there is a sharp dichotomy between the individuals who purchase insurance and those who gamble. It seems much more likely that many do both or, at any rate, would be willing to. We can cite no direct evidence for this aserted fact, though indirect evidence and casual observation give us considerable confidence that it is correct. Its validity is suggested by the extensiveness of both gambling and the purchase of insurance. It is also suggested by some of the available evidence on how people invest their funds. The widespread legislation against "bucket shops" suggests that relatively poor people must have been willing to buy extremely speculative stocks of a "blue-sky" variety. Yet the bulk of the property income of the lower-income classes consists of interest and rents and relatively little of dividends, whereas the reverse is true for the upper-income classes.[19] Rents and interest are types of receipts that tend to be derived from investments with relatively little risk, and so correspond to the purchase of insurance, whereas investment in speculative stocks corresponds to the purchase of lottery tickets.

Offhand it appears inconsistent for the same person both to buy insurance and to gamble: he is willing to pay a premium, in the one case, to avoid risk, in the other, to bear risk. And indeed it would be inconsistent for a person to be willing to pay something (no matter how little) in excess of actuarial value to avoid every possible risk and also something in excess of actuarial value to assume every possible risk. One must distinguish among different kinds of insurance and different kinds of gambling, since a willingness to pay something for only some kinds of insurance would not necessarily be inconsistent with a willingness to engage in only some kinds of gambling. Unfortunately, very little empirical evidence is readily available on the kinds of insurance that people are willing to buy and the kinds of gambling that they are willing to engage in. About the only clear indication is that people are willing

---

[18] Evidence from wagering on horse races, where this has been legalized, is too ambiguous to be of much value. Since most legal wagering is at the track, gambling is available only to those who go to watch the races and is combined with participation in the mechanics of the game of chance.

[19] *Delaware Income Statistics,* Vol. I (Bureau of Economic and Business Research, University of Delaware, 1941), Table 1; *Minnesota Incomes,* 1938–39, Vol. II (Minnesota Resources Commission, 1942), Table 27; F. A. Hanna, J. A. Pechman, S. M. Lerner, *Analysis of Wisconsin Income* ["Studies in Income and Wealth," Vol. IX (National Bureau of Economic Research, 1948)], Part II, Table 1.

to enter into gambles that offer a small chance of a large gain—as in lotteries and "blue-sky" securities.

Lotteries seem to be an extremely fruitful, and much neglected, source of information about reactions of individuals to risk. They present risk in relatively pure form, with little admixture of other factors; they have been conducted in many countries and for many centuries, so that a great deal of evidence is available about them; there has been extensive experimentation with the terms and conditions that would make them attractive, and much competition in conducting them, so that any regularities they may show would have to be interpreted as reflecting corresponding regularities in human behavior.[20] It is, of course, not certain that inferences from lotteries would carry over to other choices involving risk. There would, however, seem to be some presumption that they would do so, though of course the validity of this presumption would have to be tested.[21]

The one general feature of lotteries that is worth noting in this preliminary survey, in addition to the general willingness of people to participate in them, is the structure of prizes that seems to have developed. Lotteries rarely have just a single prize equal to the total sum to be paid out as prizes. Instead, they tend to have several or many prizes. The largest prize is ordinarily not very much larger than the next largest, and often there is not one largest prize but several of the same size.[22] This tendency is so general that one would expect it to reflect some consistent feature of individual reactions, and any hypothesis designed to explain reactions to uncertainty should explain it.

III. THE FORMAL HYPOTHESIS

The hypothesis that is proposed for rationalizing the behavior just summarized can be stated compactly as follows: In choosing among

[20] Aside from their value in providing information about reactions to risk, data from lotteries may be of broader interest in providing evidence about the stability of tastes and preferences over time and their similarity in different parts of the world. Here is a "commodity" which has remained unchanged over centuries, which is the same all over the globe, and which has been dealt in widely for the entire period and over much of the globe. It is hard to conceive of any other commodity for which this is true.

[21] See Smith, *op. cit.*, p. 108, for a precedent.

[22] See Ewen, *op. cit., passim,* but esp. descriptions of state lotteries in Ch. VII, pp. 199–244; see also the large numbers of bills advertising lotteries in John Ashton, *A History of English Lotteries* (London: Leadenhall Press, 1893).

alternatives open to it, whether or not these alternatives involve risk, a consumer unit (generally a family, sometimes an individual) behaves as if (a) it had a consistent set of preferences; (b) these preferences could be completely described by a function attaching a numerical value—to be designated "utility"—to alternatives each of which is regarded as certain; (c) its objective were to make its expected utility as large as possible. It is the contribution of von Neumann and Morgenstern to have shown that an alternative statement of the same hypothesis is: An individual chooses in accordance with a system of preferences which has the following properties:

(1) The system is complete and consistent; that is, an individual can tell which of two objects he prefers or whether he is indifferent between them, and if he does not prefer C to B and does not prefer B to A, then he does not prefer C to A.[23] (In this context, the word "object" includes combinations of objects with stated probabilities; for example, if A and B are objects, a 40–60 chance of A or B is also an object.)

(2) Any object which is a combination of other objects with stated probabilities is never preferred to every one of these other objects, nor is every one of them ever preferred to the combination.

(3) If the object A is preferred to the object B and B to the object C, there will be some probability combination of A and C such that the individual is indifferent between it and B.[24]

This form of statement is designed to show that there is little difference between the plausibility of this hypothesis and the usual indifference-curve explanation of riskless choices.

These statements of the hypothesis conceal by their very compactness

[23] The transitivity of the relation of indifference assumed in this postulate is, of course, an idealization. It is clearly possible that the difference between successive pairs of alternatives in a series might be imperceptible to an individual, yet the first of the series definitely preferable to the last. This idealization, which is but a special case of the idealization involved in the geometric concept of a dimensionless point, seems to us unobjectionable. However, the use of this idealization in indifference-curve analysis is the major criticism offered by W. E. Armstrong in an attack on indifference-curve analysis in his article "The Determinateness of the Utility Function," *Economic Journal,* Vol. XLIX (September, 1939), pp. 453–67. In a more recent article ["Uncertainty and the Utility Function," *Economic Journal,* Vol. LVIII (March, 1948), pp. 1–10] Armstrong repeats this criticism and adds to it the criticism that choices involving risk cannot be rationalized by the ordinal properties of utility functions.

[24] For a rigorous presentation of the second statement and a rigorous proof that the statements are equivalent see von Neumann and Morgenstern, *op. cit.,* pp. 26–27, 617–32.

most of its implications. It will pay us, therefore, to elaborate them. It simplifies matters, and involves no loss in generality, to regard the alternatives open to the consumer unit as capable of being expressed entirely in terms of money or money income. Actual alternatives are not, of course, capable of being so expressed: the same money income may be valued very differently according to the terms under which it is to be received, the nonpecuniary advantages or disadvantages associated with it, and so on. We can abstract from these factors, which play no role in the present problem, by supposing either that they are the same for different incomes compared or that they can be converted into equivalent sums of money income.[25] This permits us to consider total utility a function of money income alone.

Let I represent the income of a consumer unit per unit time, and $U(I)$ the utility attached to that income if it is regarded as certain. Measure I along the horizontal axis of a graph and U along the vertical. In general, $U(I)$ will not be defined for all values of I, since there will be a lower limit to the income a consumer unit can receive, namely, a negative income equal (in absolute value) to the maximum amount that the consumer unit can lose per unit time for the period to which the utility curve refers.

Alternatives open to the consumer unit that involve no risk consist of possible incomes, say I', I'', ... The hypothesis then implies simply that the consumer unit will choose the income to which it attaches the most utility. Other things the same, we know from even casual observation that the consumer unit will in general choose the largest income: put differently, we consider it pathological for an individual literally to throw money away, yet this means of choosing a smaller income is always available. It follows that the hypothesis can rationalize riskless choices of the limited kind considered here if, and only if, the utility of money income is larger, the higher the income. Consideration of riskless choices imposes no further requirements on the utility function.

Alternatives involving risk consist of probability distributions of possible incomes. Fortunately, it will suffice for our purpose to consider

[25] The other factors abstracted from must not, of course, include any that cannot in fact be held constant while money income varies. For example, a higher income is desired because it enables a consumer unit to purchase a wider variety of commodities. The consumption pattern of the consumer unit must not therefore be supposed to be the same at different incomes. As another example, a higher income may mean that a consumer unit must pay a higher price for a particular commodity (e.g., medical service). Such variation in price should not be impounded in *ceteris paribus*, though price changes not necessarily associated with changes in the consumer unit's income should be.

only a particularly simple kind of alternative involving risk, namely (A) a chance $a(0 < a < 1)$ of an income I_1, and a chance $(1 - a)$ of an income I_2, where for simplicity I_2 is supposed always greater than I_1. This simplification is possible because, as we shall see later, the original hypothesis implies that choices of consumer units among more complicated alternatives can be predicted from complete knowledge of their preferences among alternatives like A and a riskless alternative (B) consisting of a certain income I_0.

Since "other things" are supposed the same for alternatives A and B, the utility of the two alternatives may be taken to be functions solely of the incomes and probabilities involved and not also of attendant circumstances. The utility of alternative B is $U(I_0)$. The expected utility of A is given by

$$\bar{U}(A) = aU(I_1) + (1 - a)U(I_2)$$

According to the hypothesis, a consumer unit will choose A if $\bar{U} > U(I_0)$, will choose B if $\bar{U} < U(I_0)$, and will be indifferent between A and B if $\bar{U} = U(I_0)$.

Let $\bar{I}(A)$ be the actuarial value of A, i.e., $\bar{I}(A) = aI_1 + (1 - a)I_2$. If I_0 is equal to $\bar{I}$, the "gamble" or "insurance" is said t be "fair" since the consumer unit gets the same actuarial value whichever alternative it chooses. If, under these circumstances, the consumer unit chooses A, it shows a preference for this risk. This is to be interpreted as meaning that $\bar{U} > U(\bar{I})$ and indeed $\bar{U} - U(\bar{I})$ may be taken to measure the utility it attaches to this particular risk.[26] If the consumer unit chooses B, it shows a preference for certainty. This is to be interpreted as meaning that $\bar{U} < U(\bar{I})$. Indifference between A and B is to be interpreted as meaning that $\bar{U} = U(\bar{I})$.

Let I^* be the certain income that has the same utility as A, that is, $U(I^*) = \bar{U}$.[27] Call I^* the income equivalent to A. The requirement,

---

[26] This interpretation of $\bar{U} - U(\bar{I})$ as the utility attached to a particular risk is directly relevant to a point to which von Neumann and Morgenstern and commentators on their work have given a good deal of attention, namely, whether there may "not exist in an individual a (positive or negative) utility of the mere act of 'taking a chance,' of gambling, which the use of the mathematical expectation obliterates" (von Neumann and Morgenstern, *op. cit.*, p. 28). In our view the hypothesis is better interpreted as a rather special explanation why gambling has utility or disutility to a consumer unit, and as providing a particular measure of the utility or disutility, than as a denial that gambling has utility (see *ibid.*, pp. 28, 629–32).

[27] Since U has been assumed strictly monotonic to rationalize riskless choices, there will be only one income, if any, that has the same utility as A. There will be one if U is continuous which, for simplicity, we assume to be the case throughout this paper.

derived from consideration of riskless choices, that utility increase with income means that

$$\bar{U} \gtreqless U(\bar{I})$$

implies

$$I^* \gtreqless \bar{I}$$

If I^* is greater than $\bar{I}$, the consumer unit prefers this particular risk to a certain income of the same actuarial value and would be willing to pay a maximum of $I^* - \bar{I}$ for the privilege of "gambling." If I^* is less than $\bar{I}$, the consumer unit prefers certainty and is willing to pay a maximum of $\bar{I} - I^*$ for "insurance" against this risk.

These concepts are illustrated for a consumer unit who is willing to pay for insurance $(\bar{I} > I^*)$ in Figure 1a, and for a consumer unit who is willing to pay for the privilege of gambling $(\bar{I} < I^*)$ in Figure 1b. In both figures, money income is measured along the horizontal axis, and utility along the vertical. On the horizontal axis, designate I_1 and I_2, $\bar{I}$, the actuarial value of I_1 and I_2, is then represented by a point that divides the interval I_1 to I_2 in the proportion

$$\frac{1-a}{a} \quad \left(\text{i.e.,} \frac{\bar{I}-I_1}{I_2-\bar{I}} = \frac{1-a}{a}\right)$$

Draw the utility curve (CDE in both figures). Connect the points $[I_1, U(I_1)]$, $[I_2, U(I_2)]$ by a straight line (CFE). The vertical distance of this line from the horizontal axis at $\bar{I}$ is then equal to $\bar{U}$. [Since $\bar{I}$ divides the distance between I_1 and I_2 in the proportion $(1-a)/a$, F divides the vertical distance between C and E in the same proportion, so the

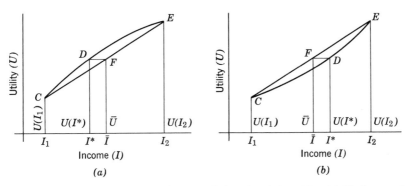

Figure 1. Illustration of utility analysis of choices involving risk: (a) Preference for certainty; (b) Preference for risk.

vertical distance from F to the horizontal axis is the expected value of $U(I_1)$ and $U(I_2)$]. Draw a horizontal line through F and find the income corresponding to its intersection with the utility curve (point D). This is the income the utility of which is the same as the expected utility of A, hence by definition is I^*.

In Figure 1a, the utility curve is so drawn as to make I^* less than $\bar{I}$. If the consumer unit is offered a choice between A and a certain income I_0 greater than I^*, it will choose the certain income. If this certain income I_0 were less than $\bar{I}$, the consumer unit would be paying $\bar{I} - I_0$ for certainty—in ordinary parlance it would be "buying insurance"; if the certain income were greater than $\bar{I}$, it would be being paid $I_0 - \bar{I}$ for accepting certainty, even though it is willing to pay for certainty—we might say that it is "selling a gamble" rather than "buying insurance." If the consumer unit were offered a choice between A and a certain income I_0 less than I^*, it would choose A because, while it is willing to pay a price for certainty, it is being asked to pay more than the maximum amount $(\bar{I} - I^*)$ that it is willing to pay. The price of insurance has become so high that it has, as it were, been converted into a seller rather than a buyer of insurance.

In Figure 1b, the utility curve is so drawn as to make I^* greater than $\bar{I}$. If the consumer unit is offered a choice between A and a certain income I_0 less than I^*, it will choose A. If this certain income I_0 were greater than $\bar{I}$, the consumer unit would be paying $I_0 - \bar{I}$ for this risk—in ordinary parlance, it would be choosing to gamble or, one might say, "to buy a gamble"; if the certain income were less than $\bar{I}$, it would be being paid $\bar{I} - I_0$ for accepting this risk even though it is willing to pay for the risk—we might say that it is "selling insurance" rather than "buying a gamble." If the consumer unit is offered a choice between A and a certain income I_0 greater than I^*, it will choose the certain income because, while it is willing to pay something for a gamble, it is not willing to pay more than $I^* - \bar{I}$. The price of the gamble has become so high that it is converted into a seller, rather than a buyer, of gambles.

It is clear that the graphical condition for a consumer unit to be willing to pay something for certainty is that the utility function be above its chord at $\bar{I}$. This is simply a direct translation of the condition that $U(\bar{I}) > \bar{U}$. Similarly, a consumer unit will be willing to pay something for a risk if the utility function is below its chord at $\bar{I}$. The relationship between these formalized "insurance" and "gambling" situations and what are ordinarily called insurance and gambling is fairly straightforward. A consumer unit contemplating buying insurance is to be regarded as having a current income of I_2 and as being subject to a chance of losing a sum equal to $I_2 - I_1$, so that if this loss should occur its income would be reduced to I_1. It can insure against this loss by paying a premium equal to $I_2 - I_0$. The premium, in general, will be larger than $I_2 - \bar{I}$, the "loading" being equal to $\bar{I} - I_0$. Purchase of insurance therefore means accepting the certainty of an income equal to I_0 instead of a pair of alternative incomes having a higher expected value. Similarly, a consumer unit deciding whether to gamble (e.g., to purchase a lottery ticket) can be interpreted as having a current income equal to I_0. It can have a chance $(1 - a)$ of a gain equal to $I_2 - I_0$ by subjecting itself to a chance a of losing a sum equal to $I_0 - I_1$. If it gambles, the actuarial value of its income is $\bar{I}$, which in general is less than I_0. $I_0 - \bar{I}$ is the premium it is paying for the chance to gamble (the "take" of the house, or the "banker's cut").

It should be emphasized that this analysis is all an elaboration of a particular hypothesis about the way consumer units choose among alternatives involving risk. This hypothesis describes the reactions of consumer units in terms of a utility function, unique except for origin and unit of measure, which gives the utility assigned to certain incomes and which has so far been taken for granted. Yet for choices among certain incomes only a trivial characteristic of this function is relevant, namely, that it rises with income. The remaining characteristics of the function are relevant only to choices among alternatives involving risk and can therefore be inferred only from observation of such choices. The precise manner in which these characteristics are implicit in the consumer unit's preferences among alternatives involving risk can be indicated most easily by describing a conceptual experiment for determining the utility function.

Select any two incomes, say $500 and $1000. Assign any arbitrary utilities to these incomes, say 0 utiles and 1 utile, respectively. This corresponds to an arbitrary choice of origin and unit of measure. Select any intermediate income, say $600. Offer the consumer unit the choice between (A) a chance a of $500 and $(1 - a)$ of $1000 or (B) a certainty of $600, varying a until the consumer unit is indifferent between the two (i.e., until $I^* = \$600$). Suppose this indifference value of a is $\frac{2}{5}$. If the hypothesis is correct, it follows that

$$U(600) = \tfrac{2}{5}U(500) + \tfrac{3}{5}U(1000) = \tfrac{2}{5} \cdot 0 + \tfrac{3}{5} \cdot 1 = \tfrac{3}{5} = .60$$

In this way the utility attached to every income between $500 and $1000 can be determined. To get the utility attached to any income outside the interval $500 to $1000, say $10,000, offer the consumer unit a choice between (A) a chance a of $500 and $(1 - a)$ of $10,000 or (B) a certainty of $1000, varying a until the consumer unit is indifferent between the two (i.e., until $I^* = \$1000$). Suppose this indifference value of a is $\frac{4}{5}$. If the hypothesis is correct, it follows that

$$\tfrac{4}{5}U(500) + \tfrac{1}{5}U(10{,}000) = U(1000)$$

or

$$\tfrac{4}{5} \cdot 0 + \tfrac{1}{5}U(10{,}000) = 1$$

or

$$U(10{,}000) = 5$$

In principle, the possibility of carrying out this experiment, and the reproducibility of the results, would provide a test of the hypothesis. For example, the consistency of behavior assumed by the hypothesis would be contradicted if a repetition of the experiment using two initial incomes other than \$500 and \$1000 yielded a utility function differing in more than origin and unit of measure from the one initially obtained.

Given a utility function obtained in this way, it is possible, if the hypothesis is correct, to compute the utility attached to (that is, the expected utility of) any set or sets of possible incomes and associated probabilities and thereby to predict which of a number of such sets will be chosen. This is the precise meaning of the statement made toward the beginning of this section that, if the hypothesis were correct, complete knowledge of the preferences of consumer units among alternatives like A and B would make it possible to predict their reactions to any other choices involving risk.

The choices a consumer unit makes that involve risk are typically far more complicated than the simple choice between A and B that we have used to elaborate the hypothesis. There are two chief sources of complication: Any particular alternative typically offers an indefinitely large number of possible incomes, and "other things" are generally not the same.

The multiplicity of possible incomes is very general: losses insured against ordinarily have more than one possible value; lotteries ordinarily have more than one prize; the possible income from a particular occupation, investment, or business enterprise may be equal to any of an indefinitely large number of values. A hypothesis that the essence of choices among the degrees of risk involved in such complex alternatives is contained in such simple choices as the choice between A and B is by no means tautological.

The hypothesis does not, of course, pretend to say anything about how consumer choices will be affected by differences in things other than degree of risk. The significance for our purposes of such differences is rather that they greatly increase the difficulty of getting evidence about reactions to differences in risk alone. Much casual experience, particularly experience bearing on what is ordinarily regarded as gambling, is likely to be misinterpreted, and erroneously regarded as contradictory to the hypothesis, if this difficulty is not explicitly recognized. In much so-called gambling the individual chooses not only to bear risk but also to participate in the mechanics of a game of chance; he buys, that is, a gamble, in our technical sense, and entertainment. We can conceive of separating these two commodities: he could buy entertainment alone by paying admission to participate in a game using valueless chips; he could buy the gamble alone by having an agent play the game of chance for him according to detailed instructions.[28] Further, insurance and gambles are often purchased in almost pure form. This is notably true of insurance. It is true also of gambling by the purchase of lottery tickets when the purchaser is not a spectator to the drawing of the winners (e.g., Irish sweepstakes tickets bought in this country or the "numbers" game), and of much stock-market speculation.

An example of behavior that would definitely contradict the assertion, contained in the hypothesis, that the same utility function can be used to explain choices that do and do not involve risk would be willingness by an individual to pay more for a gamble than the maximum amount he could win. In order to explain riskless choices it is necessary to suppose that utility increases with income. It follows that the average utility of two incomes can never exceed the utility of the larger income and hence that an individual will never be willing to pay, for example, a dollar for a chance of winning, at most, 99 cents.

More subtle observation would be required to contradict the assertion that the reactions of persons to complicated gambles can be inferred from their reactions to simple gambles. For example, suppose an individual refuses an opportunity to toss a coin for a dollar and also to toss a coin for two dollars but then accepts an opportunity to toss two coins in succession, the first to determine whether the second toss is to be for one dollar or for two dollars. This behavior would definitely contradict the hypothesis. On the hypothesis, the utility of the third gamble is an average of the utility of the first two. His refusal of the first two indicates that each of them has a lower utility than the alternative of not gambling; hence, if the hypothesis were correct, the third should have a lower utility than the same alternative, and he should refuse it.

---

[28] It does not, of course, follow that the price an individual is willing to pay for the joint commodity is simply the sum of the prices he is willing to pay for them separately. Indeed, it may well be the possible existence of such a difference that people have in mind when they speak of a "specific utility of gambling."

IV. RESTRICTIONS ON UTILITY FUNCTION REQUIRED
TO RATIONALIZE OBSERVABLE BEHAVIOR

The one restriction imposed on the utility function in the preceding section is that total utility increase with the size of money income. This restriction was imposed to rationalize the first of the facts listed below. We are now ready to see whether the behavior described in Section II can be rationalized by the hypothesis, and, if so, what additional restrictions this behavior imposes on the utility function. To simplify the task, we shall take as a summary of the essential features of the behavior described in Section II the following five statements, alleged to be facts: (1) consumer units prefer larger to smaller certain incomes; (2) low-income consumer units buy, or are willing to buy, insurance; (3) low-income consumer units buy, or are willing to buy, lottery tickets; (4) many low-income consumer units buy, or are willing to buy, both insurance and lottery tickets; (5) lotteries typically have more than one prize.

These particular statements are selected not because they are the most important in and of themselves but because they are convenient to handle and the restrictions imposed to rationalize them turn out to be sufficient to rationalize all the behavior described in Section II.

It is obvious from Figure 1 and our discussion of it that if the utility function were everywhere convex from above (for utility functions with a continuous derivative, if the marginal utility of money does not increase for any income), the consumer unit, on our hypothesis, would be willing to enter into any fair insurance plan but would be unwilling to pay anything in excess of the actuarial value for any gamble. If the utility function were everywhere concave from above (for functions with a continuous derivative, if the marginal utility of money does not diminish for any income), the consumer unit would be willing to enter into any fair gamble but would be unwilling to pay anything in excess of the actuarial value for insurance against any risk.

It follows that our hypothesis can rationalize statement 2, the purchase of insurance by low-income consumer units, only if the utility functions of the corresponding units are not everywhere concave from above; that it can rationalize statement 3, the purchase of lottery tickets by low-income consumer units, only if the utility functions of the corresponding units are not everywhere convex from above; and that it can rationalize statement 4, the purchase of both insurance and lottery tickets by low-income consumer units, only if the utility functions of the corresponding units are neither everywhere concave from above nor everywhere convex from above.

The simplest utility function (with a continuous derivative) that can rationalize all three statements simultaneously is one that has a segment convex from above followed by a segment concave from above and no other segments.[29] The convex segment must precede the concave segment because of the kind of insurance and of gambling the low-income consumer units are said to engage in: a chord from the existing income to a lower income must be below the utility function to rationalize the purchase of insurance against the risk of loss; a chord from the immediate neighborhood of the existing income to a higher income must be above the utility function at the existing income to rationalize the purchase for a small sum of a small chance of a large gain.[30]

Figure 2 illustrates a utility function satisfying these requirements. Let this utility function be for a low-income consumer unit whose current income is in the initial convex segment, say at the point designated I^*. If some risk should arise of incurring a loss, the consumer unit would clearly (on our hypothesis) be willing to insure against the loss (if it did not have to pay too much "loading") since a chord from the utility curve at I^* to the utility curve at the lower income that would be the consequence of the actual occurrence of the loss would everywhere be below the utility function. The consumer unit would not be willing to engage in

[29] A kink or a jump in the utility function could rationalize either the gambling or the insurance. For example, the utility function could be composed of two convex or two concave segments joined in a kink. There is no essential loss in generality in neglecting such cases, as we shall do from here on, since one can always think of rounding the kind ever so slightly.

[30] If there are more than two segments and a continuous derivative, a convex segment necessarily precedes a concave segment.

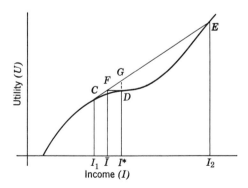

Figure 2. Illustration of utility function consistent with willingness of a low-income consumer unit both to purchase insurance and to gamble.

small gambling. But suppose it is offered a fair gamble of the kind represented by a lottery involving a small chance of winning a relatively large sum equal to $I_2 - I^*$ and a large chance of losing a relatively small sum equal to $I^* - I_1$. The consumer unit would clearly prefer the gamble, since the expected utility (I^*G) is greater than the utility of I^*. Indeed it would be willing to pay any premium up to $I^* - \bar{I}$ for the privilege of gambling; that is, even if the expected value of the gamble were almost as low as $\bar{I}$, it would accept the gamble in preference to a certainty of receiving I^*. The utility curve in Figure 2 is therefore clearly consistent with statements 2, 3, and 4.

These statements refer solely to the behavior of relatively low-income consumer units. It is tempting to seek to restrict further the shape of the utility function, and to test the restrictions so far imposed, by appealing to casual observation of the behavior of relatively high-income consumer units.[31] It does not seem desirable to do so, however, for two major reasons: (1) it is far more difficult to accumulate reliable information about the behavior of relatively high-income consumer units than about the behavior of the more numerous low-income units: (2) perhaps even more important, the progressive income tax so affects the terms under which the relatively high-income consumer units purchase insurance or gamble as to make evidence on their behavior hard to interpret for our purposes.[32] Therefore, instead of using observations about the

---

[31] For example, a high-income consumer unit that had a utility function like that in Fig. 2 and a current income of I_2 would be willing to participate in a wide variety of gambling, including the purchase of lottery tickets; it would be unwilling to insure against losses that had a small expected value (i.e., involved payment of a small premium) though it might be willing to insure against losses that had a large expected value. Consequently, unwillingness of relatively high-income consumer units to purchase lottery tickets, or willingness to purchase low-premium insurance, would contradict the utility function of Fig. 2 and require the imposition of further restrictions.

[32] The effect of the income tax, already referred to in footnote 16 above, depends greatly on the specific provisions of the tax law and of the insurance or gambling plan. For example, if an uninsured loss is deductible in computing taxable income (as is loss of an owned home by fire under the federal income tax) while the premium for insuring against the loss is not (as a fire insurance premium on an owned home is not), the expected value of the loss is less to the consumer unit than to the firm selling insurance. A premium equal to the actuarial value of the loss to the insurance company then exceeds the actuarial value of the loss to the consumer unit. That is, the government in effect pays part of the loss but none of the premium. On the other hand, if the premium is deductible (as a health insurance premium may be), while an uninsured loss is not (as the excess of medical bills over $2500 for a family is not), the net premium to the consumer unit is less than the premium received by the insurance company. Similarly, gambling gains in excess of gambling losses are taxable under the federal income tax, while

behavior of relatively high-income consumer units, we shall seek to learn more about the upper end of the curve by using statement 5, the tendency for lotteries to have more than one prize.

In order to determine the implications of this statement for the utility function, we must investigate briefly the economics of lotteries. Consider an entrepreneur conducting a lottery and seeking to maximize his income from it. For simplicity, suppose that he conduct the lottery by deciding in advance the number of tickets to offer and then auctioning them off at the highest price he can get.[33] Aside from advertising and the like, the variables at his disposal are the terms of the lottery: the number of tickets to sell, the total amount to offer as prizes (which together, of course, determine the actuarial value of a ticket), and the structure of prizes to offer. For any given values of the first two, the optimum structure of prizes is clearly that which maximizes the price he can get per ticket or, what is the same thing, the excess of the price of a ticket over its actuarial value—the "loading" per ticket.

In the discussion of Figure 2, it was noted that $I^* - \bar{I}$ was the maximum amount in excess of the actuarial value that the corresponding consumer unit would pay for a gamble involving a chance $(1 - a)$ of winning $I_2 - I^*$ and a chance a of losing $I^* - I_1$. This gamble is equivalent to a lottery offering a chance $(1 - a)$ of a prize $I_2 - I_1$ in return for the purchase of a ticket at a price of $I^* - I_1$, the chance of winning the prize being such that $\bar{I} - I_1$ is the actuarial worth of a ticket [i.e., is equal to $(1 - a) \times (I_2 - I_1)$]. If the consumer unit won the prize, its net winnings would be $I_2 - I^*$, since it would have to subtract the cost of the ticket from the gross prize. The problem of the entrepreneur, then, is to choose the structure of prizes that will maximize $I^* - \bar{I}$ for a given

---

gambling losses in excess of gambling gains are not deductible. The special treatment of capital gains and losses under the existing United States federal income tax adds still further complications.

Even if both the premium and the uninsured loss are deductible, or a gain taxable and the corresponding loss deductible, the income tax may change the terms because of the progressive rates. The tax saving from a large loss may be a smaller fraction of the loss than the tax payable on the gain is of the gain.

These comments clearly apply not only to insurance and gambling proper but also to other economic decisions involving risk—the purchase of securities, choice of occupation or business, etc. The neglect of these considerations has frequently led to the erroneous belief that a progressive income tax does not affect the allocation of resources and is in this way fundamentally different from excise taxes.

[33] This was, in fact, the way in which the British government conducted many of its official lotteries. It frequently auctioned off the tickets to lottery dealers, who served as the means of distributing the tickets to the public (see Ewen, *op. cit.*, pp. 234–40).

actuarial value of a ticket, that is, for a given value of $\bar{I} - I_1$. Changes
in the structure of prizes involve changes in $I_2 - I_1$. If there is a single
prize, $I_2 - I_1$ is equal to the total amount to be distributed [$(1 - a)$ is
equal to the reciprocal of the number of tickets]. If there are two equal
prizes, $I_2 - I_1$ is cut in half [$(1 - a)$ is then equal to twice the reciprocal
of the number of tickets]. Suppose Figure 2 referred to this latter situation
in which there were two equal prizes, I^* on the diagram designating both
the current income of the consumer unit and the income equivalent
to the lottery. If the price and actuarial worth of the ticket were kept
unchanged, but a single prize was substituted for the two prizes [and
$(1 - a)$ correspondingly reduced], the gamble would clearly become more
attractive to the consumer unit. I_2 would move to the right, the chord
connecting $U(I_1)$ and $U(I_2)$ would rotate upward, $\bar{U}$ would increase, and
the consumer unit would be paying less than the maximum amount it
was willing to pay. The price of the ticket could accordingly be increased;
that is, I_2, $\bar{I}$, and I_1 could be moved to the left until the I^* for the new
gamble were equal to the consumer unit's current income (the I^* for
the old gamble). The optimum structure of prizes clearly consists therefore of a single prize, since this makes $I_2 - I_1$ as large as possible.

Statement 5, that lotteries typically have more than one prize, is
therefore inconsistent with the utility function of Figure 2. This additional
fact can be rationalized by terminating the utility curve with a suitable
convex segment. This yields a utility curve like that drawn in Figure 3.
With such a utility curve, $I^* - \bar{I}$ would be a maximum at the point at
which a chord from $U(I_1)$ was tangent to the utility curve, and a larger
prize would yield a smaller value of $I^* - \bar{I}$.[34]

A utility curve like that drawn in Figure 3 is the simplest one consistent with the five statements listed at the outset of this section.

It seems well to digress at this point to consider two questions that,

---

[34] An additional convex segment guarantees that there will always exist current
incomes of the consumer unit for which (a) attractive gambles exist and (b) the
optimum prize for attractive gambles has a maximum. It does not guarantee that
b will be true for every income for which attractive gambles exist. The condition
on the current income that attractive gambles exist is that the tangent to the
utility curve at the current income be below the utility curve for some income (this
argument, like many in later technical footnotes, holds not only for the utility function of Fig. 3 but for any differentiable utility function). A single prize will be
the optimum, no matter what the amount distributed in prizes or the fixed actuarial worth of the prize if, and only if, every chord from the utility curve at the
current income to the utility of a higher income is everywhere above the utility
curve. A particular, and somewhat interesting, class of utility functions for which
b will be true for every income for which a is true is the class for which utility
approaches a finite limit as income increases.

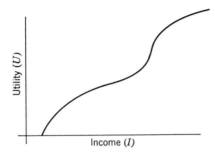

Figure 3. Illustration of typical shape of utility curve.

while not strictly relevant to our main theme, are likely to occur to many readers: first, is not the hypothesis patently unrealistic; second, can any plausible interpretation be given to the rather peculiar utility function of Figure 3?

THE DESCRIPTIVE "REALISM" OF THE HYPOTHESIS

An objection to the hypothesis just presented that is likely to be raised by many, if not most, readers is that it conflicts with the way human beings actually behave and choose. Is it not patently unrealistic to suppose that individuals consult a wiggly utility curve before gambling or buying insurance, that they know the odds involved in the gambles or insurance plans open to them, that they can compute the expected utility of a gamble or insurance plan, and that they base their decision on the size of the expected utility?

While entirely natural and understandable, this objection is not strictly relevant. The hypothesis does not assert that individuals explicitly or consciously calculate and compare expected utilities. Indeed, it is not at all clear what such an assertion would mean or how it could be tested. The hypothesis asserts rather that, in making a particular class of decisions, individuals behave *as if* they calculated and compared expected utility and *as if* they knew the odds. The validity of this assertion does not depend on whether individuals know the precise odds, much less on whether they say that they calculate and compare expected utilities or think that they do, or whether it appears to others that they do, or whether psychologists can uncover any evidence that they do, but solely on whether it yields sufficiently accurate predictions about the class of decisions with which the hypothesis deals. Stated differently, the test by results is the only possible method of determining whether the *as if* statement is or is not a sufficiently good approximation to reality for the purpose at hand.

A simple example may help to clarify the point at issue. Consider the problem of predicting, before each shot, the direction of travel of a billiard ball hit by an expert billiard player. It would be possible to construct one or more mathematical formulas that would give the directions of travel that would score points and, among these, would indicate the one (or more) that would leave the balls in the best positions. The formulas might, of course, be extremely complicated, since they would necessarily take account of the location of the balls in relation to one another and to the cushions and of the complicated phenomena introduced by "english." Nonetheless, it seems not at all unreasonable that excellent predictions would be yielded by the hypothesis that the billiard player made his shots *as if* he knew the formulas, could estimate accurately by eye the angles, etc., describing the location of the balls, could make lightning calculations from the formulas, and could then make the ball travel in the direction indicated by the formulas. It would in no way disprove or contradict the hypothesis, or weaken our confidence in it, if it should turn out that the billiard player had never studied any branch of mathematics and was utterly incapable of making the necessary calculations: unless he was capable in some way of reaching approximately the same result as that obtained from the formulas, he would not in fact be likely to be an expert billiard player.

The same considerations are relevant to our utility hypothesis. Whatever the psychological mechanism whereby individuals make choices, these choices appear to display some consistency, which can apparently be described by our utility hypothesis. This hypothesis enables predictions to be made about phenomena on which there is not yet reliable evidence. The hypothesis cannot be declared invalid for a particular class of behavior until a prediction about that class proves false. No other test of its validity is decisive.

A POSSIBLE INTERPRETATION OF THE UTILITY FUNCTION

A possible interpretation of the utility function of Figure 3 is to regard the two convex segments as corresponding to qualitatively different socio-economic levels, and the concave segment to the transition between the two levels. On this interpretation, increases in income that raise the relative position of the consumer unit in its own class but do not shift the unit out of its class yield diminishing marginal utility, while increases that shift it into a new class, that give it a new social and economic status, yield increasing marginal utility. An unskilled worker may prefer the certainty of an income about the same as that of the majority of unskilled workers to an actuarially fair gamble that at best would make him one of the most prosperous unskilled workers and at worst one of the least prosperous. Yet he may jump at an actuarially fair gamble that offers a small chance of lifting him out of the class of unskilled workers and into the "middle" or "upper" class, even though it is far more likely than the preceding gamble to make him one of the least prosperous unskilled workers. Men will and do take great risks to distinguish themselves, even when they know what the risks are. May not the concave segment of the utility curve of Figure 3 translate the economic counterpart of this phenomenon appropriately?

A number of additions to the hypothesis are suggested by this interpretation. In the first place, may there not be more than two qualitatively distinguishable socioeconomic classes? If so, might not each be reflected by a convex segment in the utility function? At the moment, there seems to be no observed behavior that requires the introduction of additional convex segments, so it seems undesirable and unnecessary to complicate the hypothesis further. It may well be, however, that it will be necessary to add such segments to account for behavior revealed by further empirical evidence. In the second place, if different segments of the curve correspond to different socioeconomic classes, should not the dividing points between the segments occur at roughly the same income for different consumer units in the same community? If they did, the fruitfulness of the hypothesis would be greatly extended. Not only could the general shape of the utility function be supposed typical; so also could the actual income separating the various segments. The initial convex segment could be described as applicable to "relatively low-income consumer units" and the terminal convex segment as applicable to "relatively high-income consumer units"; and the groups so designated could be identified by the actual income or wealth of different consumer units.

Interpreting the different segments of the curve as corresponding to different socioeconomic classes would, of course, still permit wide variation among consumer units in the exact shape and height of the curve. In addition, it would not be necessary to suppose anything more than rough similarity in the location of the incomes separating the various segments. Different socioeconomic classes are not sharply demarcated from one another; each merges into the next by imperceptible gradations (which, of course, accounts for the income range encompassed by the concave segment); and the generally accepted dividing line between classes will vary from time to time, place to place, and consumer unit to consumer unit. Finally, it is not necessary that every consumer unit have a utility curve like that in Figure 3. Some may be inveterate gamblers; others, inveterately cautious. It is enough that many consumer units have such a utility curve.

VI. FURTHER IMPLICATIONS OF THE HYPOTHESIS

To return to our main theme, we have two tasks yet to perform: first, to show that the utility function of Figure 3 is consistent with those features of the behavior described in Section II not used in deriving it; second, to suggest additional implications of the hypothesis capable of providing a test of it.

The chief generalization of Section II not so far used is that people must in general be paid a premium to induce them to bear moderate risks instead of either small of large risks. Is this generalization consistent with the utility function of Figure 3?

It clearly is for a consumer unit whose income places it in the initial convex segment. Such a relatively low-income consumer unit will be willing to pay something more than the actuarial value for insurance against any kind of risk that may arise; it will be averse to small fair gambles; it may be averse to all fair gambles; if not, it will be attracted by fair gambles that offer a small chance of a large gain; the attractiveness of such gambles, with a given possible loss and actuarial value, will initially increase as the size of the possible gain increases and will eventually decrease.[35] Such consumer units therefore prefer either certainty

---

[35] The willingness of a consumer unit in the initial convex segment to pay something more than the actuarial value for insurance against any kind of risk follows from the fact that a chord connecting the utility of its current income with the utility of any lower income to which it might be reduced by the risk in question will everywhere be below the utility curve. The expected utility is therefore less than the utility of the expected income.

To analyze the reaction of such a consumer unit to different gambles, consider the limiting case in which the gamble is fair, i.e., $\bar{I} = I_0$. $\bar{I}$ then is both the expected income of the consumer unit if it takes the gamble and its actual income if it does not (i.e., its current income). The possible gains (and associated probabilities) that will be attractive to the unit for a given value of I_1 (i.e., a given possible loss) can be determined by drawing a straight line through $U(I_1)$ and $U(\bar{I})$. All values of $I_2 > \bar{I}$ for which $U(I_2)$ is greater than the ordinate of the extended straight line will be attractive; no others will be.

Since $\bar{I}$ is assumed to be in the first convex segment, there will always exist some values of $I_2 > \bar{I}$ for which $U(I_2)$ is less than the ordinate of the extended straight line. This is the basis for the statement that the consumer unit will be averse to small gambles.

Consider the line that touches the curve at only two points and is nowhere below the utility curve. Call the income at the first of the points at which it touches the curve, which may be the lowest possible income, I', and the income at the second

or a risk that offers a small chance of a large gain to a risk that offers the possibility of moderate gains or losses. They will therefore have to be paid a premium to induce them to undertake such moderate risks.

The generalization is clearly false for a consumer unit whose income places it in the concave segment. Such an "intermediate-income" consumer unit will be attracted by every small fair gamble; it may be attracted by every fair gamble; it may be averse to all fair insurance; if not, it will be attracted by insurance against relatively large losses.[36] Such consumer units will therefore be willing to pay a premium in order to assume moderate risks.

The generalization is partly true, partly false, for a consumer unit whose income places it in the terminal convex segment. Such a relatively high-income consumer unit will be willing to insure against any small possible loss and may be attracted to every fair insurance plan; the only insurance plans it may be averse to are plans involving rather large losses; it may be averse to all fair gambles; if not, it will be attracted by gambles that involve a reasonably sure, though fairly small, gain, with a small possibility of a sizable loss; it will be averse to gambles of the lottery variety.[37] These consumer units therefore prefer certainty to moderate risks; in this respect they conform to the generalization. However, they may prefer moderate risks to extreme risks, though these

---

point, I''. The consumer unit will be averse to all gambles if its income ($I_0 = \bar{I}$) is equal to or less than I'. This follows from the fact that a tangent to the curve at $\bar{I}$ will then be steeper than the "double tangent" and will intersect the latter prior to I'; a chord from $\bar{I}$ to a lower income will be even steeper. This is the basis for the statement that the consumer unit may be averse to all gambles.

If the income is above I', there will always be some attractive gambles. These will offer a small chance of a large gain. The statement about the changing attractiveness of the gamble as the size of the possible gain changes follows from the analysis in Sec. IV of the conditions under which it would be advantageous to have a single prize in a lottery.

[36] Consider the tangent to the utility curve at the income the consumer unit would have if it did not take the gamble ($\bar{I} - I_0$). If this income is in the concave section, the tangent will be below the utility curve at least for an interval of incomes surrounding $\bar{I}$. A chord connecting any two points of the utility curve on opposite sides of $\bar{I}$ and within this interval will always be above the utility curve at $\bar{I}$ (i.e., the expected utility will be above the utility of the expected income), so these gambles will be attractive. The tangent may lie below the utility curve for all incomes. In this case, every fair gamble will be attractive. The unit will be averse to insuring against a loss, whatever the chance of its occurring, if a chord from the current income to the lower income to which it would be reduced by the loss is everywhere above the utility curve. This will surely be true for small losses and may be true for all possible losses.

[37] These statements follow directly from considerations like those in the two preceding footnotes.

adjectives hardly suffice to characterize the rather complex pattern of risk preferences implied for high-income consumer units by a utility curve like that of Figure 3. Nonetheless, in this respect the implied behavior of the high-income consumer units is either neutral or contrary to the generalization.

Our hypothesis does not therefore lead inevitably to a rate of return higher to uses of resources involving moderate risk than to uses involving little or much risk. It leads to a rate of return higher for uses involving moderate risk than for uses involving little risk only if consumer units in the two convex segments outweigh in importance, for the resource use in question, consumer units in the concave segment.[38] Similarly, it leads to a rate of return higher for uses involving moderate risk than for uses involving much risk only if consumer units in the initial convex segment outweigh in importance consumer units in both the concave and the terminal convex segments—though this may be a more stringent condition than is necessary in view of the uncertainty about the exact role of consumer units in the terminal convex segment.

This relative distribution of consumer units among the various segments could be considered an additional restriction that would have to be imposed to rationalize the alleged higher rate of return to moderately risky uses of resources. It is not clear, however, that it need be so considered, since there are two independent lines of reasoning that, taken together, establish something of a presumption that relatively few consumer units are in the concave segment.

One line of reasoning is based on the interpretation of the utility function suggested in Section V above. If the concave segment is a border line between two qualitatively different social classes, one would expect relatively few consumer units to be between the two classes.

The other line of reasoning is based on the implications of the hypothesis for the relative stability of the economic status of consumer units in the different segments. Units in the intermediate segment are tempted by every small gamble and at least some large ones. If opportunities are available, they will be continually subjecting themselves to risk. In consequence, they are likely to move out of the segment; upwards, if they are lucky; downwards, if they are not. Consumer units in the two convex segments, on the other hand, are less likely to move into the intermediate segment. The gambles that units in the initial segment accept will rarely pay off and, when they do, are likely to shift them

---

[38] This statement is deliberately vague. The actual relative rates of return will depend not only on the conditions of demand for risks of different kinds but also on the conditions of supply, and both would have to be taken into account in a comprehensive statement.

all the way into the terminal convex segment. The gambles that units in the terminal segment accept will rarely involve losses and, when they do, may shift them all the way into the lower segment. Under these conditions, maintenance of a stable distribution of the population among the three segments would require that the two convex segments contain many more individuals than the concave segment. These considerations, while persuasive, are not, of course, conclusive. Opportunities to assume risks may not exist. More important, the status of consumer units is determined not alone by the outcome of risks deliberately assumed but also by random events over which they cannot choose and have no control; and it is conceivable that these random events might be distributed in such a way that their main effect was to multiply the number in the concave segment.

The absolute number of persons in the various segments will count most for choices among the uses of human resources; wealth will count most for choices among uses of nonhuman resources.[39] In consequence, one might expect that the premium for bearing moderate risks instead of large risks would be greater for occupations than for investments. Indeed, for investments, the differential might in some cases be reversed, since the relatively high-income consumer units (those in the terminal segment) count for more in wealth than in numbers and they may prefer moderate to extreme risks.

In judging the implications of our hypothesis for the market as a whole, we have found it necessary to consider separately its implications for different income groups. These offer additional possibilities of empirical test. Perhaps the most fruitful source of data would be the investment policies of different income groups.

It was noted in Section II that, although many persons with low incomes are apparently willing to buy extremely speculative stocks, the low-income group receives the bulk of its property income in the form of interest and rents. These observations are clearly consistent with our hypothesis. Relatively high-income groups might be expected, on our hypothesis, to prefer bonds and relatively safe stocks. They might be expected to avoid the more speculative common stocks but to be attracted to higher-grade preferred stocks, which pay a higher nominal rate of return than high-grade bonds to compensate for a small risk of capital loss. Intermediate income groups might be expected to hold

---

[39] This distinction requires qualification because of the need for capital to enter some types of occupations and the consequent existence of "noncompeting groups"; see Milton Friedman and Simon Kuznets, *Income from Independent Professional Practice* (New York: National Bureau of Economic Research, 1945), Ch. III, Sec. 3; Ch. IV, Sec. 2.

relatively large shares of their assets in moderately speculative common stocks and to furnish a disproportionate fraction of entrepreneurs.

Of course, any empirical study along these lines will have to take into account, as noted above, the effect of the progressive income tax in modifying the terms of investment. The current United States federal income tax has conflicting effects: the progressive rates discourage risky investments; the favored treatment of capital gains encourages them. In addition, such a study will have to consider the risk of investments as a group, rather than of individual investments, since the rich may be in a position to "average" risks.

Another implication referred to above that may be susceptible of empirical test, and the last one we shall cite, is the implied difference in the stability of the relative income status of various economic groups. The unattractiveness of small risks to both high- and low-income consumer units would tend to give them a relatively stable status. By contrast, suppose the utility curve had no terminal convex segment but was like the curve of Figure 2. Low-income consumer units would still have a relatively stable status: their willingness to take gambles at long odds would pay off too seldom to shift many from one class to another. High-income consumer units would not. They would then take almost any gamble, and those who had high incomes today almost certainly would not have high incomes tomorrow. The average period from "shirt sleeves to shirt sleeves" would be far shorter than "three generations."[40] Unlike the other two groups, the middle-income class might be expected to display considerable instability of relative income status.[41]

VII. CONCLUSION

A plausible generalization of the available empirical evidence on the behavior of consumer units in choosing among alternatives open to them is provided by the hypothesis that a consumer unit (generally a family,

---

[40] We did not use the absence of such instability to derive the upper convex segment because of the difficulty of allowing for the effect of the income tax.

[41] The existing data on stability of relative income status are too meager to contradict or to confirm this implication. In their study of professional incomes Friedman and Kuznets found that relative income status was about equally stable in all income levels. However, this study is hardly relevant, since it was for homogeneous occupational groups that would tend to fall in a single one of the classes considered here. Mendershausen's analysis along similar lines for family incomes in 1929 and 1933 is inconclusive. See Friedman and Kuznets, op. cit., chap. VII; Horst Mendershausen, Changes in Income Distribution during the Great Depression (New York: National Bureau of Economic Research, 1946), chap. III.

sometimes an individual) behaves as if

(1) It had a consistent set of preferences;

(2) These preferences could be completely described by attaching a numerical value—to be designated "utility"—to alternatives each of which is regarded as certain;

(3) The consumer unit chose among alternatives not involving risk that one which has the largest utility;

(4) It chose among alternatives involving risk that one for which the expected utility (as contrasted with the utility of the expected income) is largest;

(5) The function describing the utility of money income had in general the following properties:

(a) Utility rises with income, i.e., marginal utility of money income everywhere positive;

(b) It is convex from above below some income, concave between that income and some larger income, and convex for all higher incomes, i.e., diminishing marginal utility of money income for incomes below some income, increasing marginal utility of money income for incomes between that income and some larger income, and diminishing marginal utility of money income for all higher incomes;

(6) Most consumer units tend to have incomes that place them in the segments of the utility function for which marginal utility of money income diminishes.

Points 1, 2, 3, and 5a of this hypothesis are implicit in the orthodox theory of choice; point 4 is an ancient idea recently revived and given new content by von Neumann and Morgenstern; and points 5b and 6 are the consequence of the attempt in this paper to use this idea to rationalize existing knowledge about the choices people make among alternatives involving risk.

Point 5b is inferred from the following phenomena: (a) low-income consumer units buy, or are willing to buy, insurance; (b) low-income consumer units buy, or are willing to buy, lottery tickets; (c) many consumer units buy, or are willing to buy, both insurance and lottery tickets; (d) lotteries typically have more than one prize. These statements are taken as a summary of the essential features of observed behavior not because they are the most important features in and of themselves but because they are convenient to handle and the restrictions imposed to rationalize them turn out to be sufficient to rationalize all the behavior described in Section II of this paper.

A possible interpretation of the various segments of the utility curve specified in 5b is that the segments of diminishing marginal utility correspond to socioeconomic classes, the segment of increasing marginal utility to a transitional stage between a lower and a higher socioeconomic class. On this interpretation the boundaries of the segments should be roughly similar for different people in the same community; and this is one of several independent lines of reasoning leading to point 6.

This hypothesis has implications for behavior, in addition to those used in deriving it, that are capable of being contradicted by observable data. In particular, the fundamental supposition that a single utility curve can generalize both riskless choices and choices involving risk would be contradicted if (a) individuals were observed to choose the larger of two certain incomes offered to them but (b) individuals were willing to pay more than the largest possible gain for the privilege of bearing risk. The supposition that individuals seek to maximize expected utility would be contradicted if individuals' reactions to complicated gambles could not be inferred from their reactions to simple ones. The particular shape of the utility curve specified in 5b would be contradicted by any of a large number of observations, for example, (a) general willingness of individuals, whatever their income, who buy insurance against small risks to enter into small fair gambles under circumstances under which they are not also buying "entertainment," (b) the converse of a, namely an unwillingness to engage in small fair gambles by individuals who are not willing to buy fair insurance against small risks, (c) a higher average rate of return to uses of resources involving little risk than to uses involving a moderate amount of risk when other things are the same, (d) a concentration of investment portfolios of relatively low-income groups on speculative (but not highly speculative) investments or of relatively high-income groups on either moderately or highly speculative investments, (e) great instability in the relative income status of high-income groups or of low-income groups as a consequence of a propensity to engage in speculative activities.

CLASSIC AND CURRENT NOTIONS OF "MEASURABLE UTILITY"

D. Ellsburg

I

It is ten years since von Neumann and Morgenstern, in their famous aside to the economic profession, announced they had succeeded in synthesizing "measurable utility." That feat split their audience along old party lines. It appeared that a mathematician had performed some elegant sleight-of-hand and produced, instead of a rabbit, a dead horse.

The most common reaction was dismay. To "literary" economists who had freshly amputated their intuitive feelings of cardinal utility at the bidding of some *other* mathematicians, it seemed wanton of von Neumann and Morgenstern so soon to sprinkle salt in their wounds with the statement:[1] "It can be shown that under the conditions on which the indifference curve analysis is based very little extra effort is needed to reach a numerical utility." To others, who had said all along that surgery was unnecessary, the verdict was no surprise but still welcome, coming as it did from an unexpected (non-Cambridge) source. But before long both these groups had joined in expressing doubts that von Neumann and Morgenstern had succeeded in doing what (these readers believed) they had set out to do. The spokesman for the "cardinalists," interpreting their cause as his own, was forced to conclude that they "seem to me to have done as much harm as good to the cause to which they have lent their distinguished aid."[2]

However, it is now clear that the impression that von Neumann and Morgenstern were leading a reactionary movement was erroneous. Their cause, if it can be so dignified, is a new one, not that to which Professor Robertson alluded. The operations that define their concepts are essentially new, and their results are neither intended nor suited to fill the main functions of the older, more familiar brands of "cardinal utility." It is unfortunate that old terms have been retained, for their associations arouse both hopes and antagonisms that have no real roots in the new context.

Source: Reprinted with permission from *Economic Journal,* LXIV: 528–556 (September 1954).

Footnotes for this article are on pp. 292–296.

In the latest writings the theory has been formulated unambiguously, so that the subject presents little difficulty to one approaching it now for the first time. This article is directed, instead, at readers who came early to the controversy, and who followed the theory in its various stages closely enough to become thoroughly confused.

By concentrating their discussion on the general concept of "measurability," von Neumann and Morgenstern unfortunately obscured the unique features of their particular construction. Later expositions have tended to follow them in this,[3] or to stress the empirical content of the von Neumann-Morgenstern results.[4] Very little attention has been given to the major source of misunderstandings: ambiguity concerning the differences in derivation and application between the new notion of "measurable utility" and the concept of the same name implied in the writings, say, of Marshall and Jevons. This article will attempt to distinguish clearly between the two concepts, chiefly by examining the different operations by which they are defined and tested.[5]

This procedure may provide some valuable exercise in the use of the operational approach, which in economic literature has been honored chiefly in footnotes. This approach regards the basic definition of a technical concept in scientific usage as: "What is measured by" a particular set of operations. Two different sets of operations are presumed to measure two different "things," although under certain conditions (discussed later) it is justifiable to treat the two concepts as identical. A scientific proposition is operationally meaningful if definite conceivable results of given operations are defined which would *refute* the statement; if it does not *restrict* the class of results which are to be expected, it cannot be useful for scientific purposes. The meaningfulness of concepts and propositions is a necessary, though not a sufficient, condition for their scientific usefulness.[6] This point of view will prove useful in the concluding section in clarifying the *difference* in meaning of two concepts bearing the same name.

The next section will describe the similarities between the old and new approaches to a "cardinal utility" and will present, in advance, some of the conclusions to be drawn as to their points of contrast. The next two parts examine the operational bases of the two theories, and the final section will analyse in detail the peculiarities of the von Neumann-Morgenstern construction.

II

Suppose that a man who prefers A to B, B to C and A to C must choose between having B for certain or having a "lottery ticket" offering A with probability p or C with probability $1 - p$.[7] Without asking him outright, is it possible to predict his choice? If so, what sort of data are necessary?

Economists of the school of Jevons, Menger, Walras and Marshall, on the one hand, and on the other those following von Neumann and Morgenstern would answer "Yes" to the first question. But their predictions would be based on quite different types of data.

For von Neumann and Morgenstern, it would be necessary to observe the man's behavior in other risk-situations, involving different outcomes or the same outcomes with different probabilities. The older economists, of whom we will take Marshall as typical, would ask no knowledge of his other risk-behavior. They assumed it possible, by observation or interrogation, to discover a man's intensities of liking for sure outcomes; on the basis of this knowledge alone, they were ready either to predict or to prescribe his choice between prospects.

This divergence is concealed by the fact that both schools would summarise the results of their investigations in the same symbolic shorthand, arriving at expressions that are formally identical. Under both procedures the results of experiment would be expressed by assigning a triplet of numbers, U_a, U_b and U_c to the three outcomes, with the property: $U_a > U_b > U_c$. This triplet is a utility index for the three outcomes, since their order of magnitude reflects the order of preference. Next, both Marshall and von Neumann-Morgenstern would form the expression:

$$1 \cdot U_b \gtreqless p \cdot U_a + (1 - p)U_c \qquad (1)$$

where p and $1 - p$ are the respective probabilities of A and C. Each side of this relationship is a sum of the utility numbers corresponding to the outcomes of a given prospect multiplied by their respective probability numbers. Since the probabilities sum to unity, the result is a weighted arithmetic mean of the utilities, variously known as the mathematical expectation of utility, the expected utility, the moral expectation, moral expectancy, actuarial value of utility and the first moment of the utility-probability distribution.[8]

In each case the prediction (or advice) would have the man choose the prospect with the highest mathematical expectation of utility. Or, if the two sides of the relationship (1) were equal, we should be indifferent between the two prospects. A man whose behavior conformed to this rule could be said to be "maximizing the mathematical expectation of utility."

With this much similarity between the two approaches, it is natural that they should commonly be confused. Yet the most misleading point of similarity remains: the fact that in both cases "utility" is said to be "measurable." The necessity of this assumption is seen more clearly if the left-hand side of expression (1) is rewritten $p \cdot U_b + (1 - p)U_b$ and terms collected to form the relationship:

$$p(U_a - U_b) - (1 - p)(U_b - U_c) \gtreqless 0 \qquad (2)$$

This is merely relationship (1) in a different form. The rule would now have the man accept the prospective offering A or C if the left-hand side of (2) were positive, reject it if the left-hand side were negative, or be indifferent between it and the sure outcome B if the left-hand side were equal to zero. The important point here is that relationship (2) shows clearly that the rules rely on comparing *differences* in utility.

If only preferences were known, the triplet of utility numbers could be replaced by another with the same ordinal relationships. In general, such a monotonic transformation would not preserve equality, or give inequalities, among differences between utility numbers. The rule of maximising expected utility would lead to prediction or advice which would depend on the particular index used, and if preferences were the only guide, the choice of index would be arbitrary. The rule would be meaningless, therefore useless.

In order for the rule to give definite results, it would be necessary to find some "natural"[9] operation that would give meaning to differences in utility numbers, hence to the numerical operations implied by the rule. The new index, summarising the results of the additional operation as well as preferences, would belong to a more restricted set of indices than the set of all ordinal utility indices. Any two indices in which corresponding differences as well as absolute utilities satisfied the same inequalities would be related by a linear, and not merely any monotonic, transformation.[10] It is, then, necessary to find some aspect of behavior that can be described only by a set of numbers determined up to a linear transformation: a set, moreover, which is one of those expressing preferences. So much is necessary in order for the rule of maximising expected utility to be meaningful. Its usefulness, if any, must depend on the particular aspect of behavior which serves this purpose, if one can be found.

To say that both the Marshallian and the von Neumann-Morgenstern theories require a "measurable utility" is precisely to say that they require a utility index determined up to a linear transformation. At this point the similarity ends. In general, the order of magnitude of the differences between corresponding numbers would be different for the two indices; therefore, predictions based on the rule of maximising moral expectation would differ for the two approaches. Moreover, it might be possible to find a measurable index by one method and not the other. Even if both should "exist," they would be in general monotonic, and not linear, transformations of each other.

III

Such theorists as Jevons, Menger, Walras and Marshall conceived of the crucial natural operation in the measurement of utility as taking place within the mind of a subject; it was a process of weighing introspectively the amounts of "satisfaction" associated with different outcomes.

Such an operation appeared more of an objective basis for theory to them than it would to modern economists. In their view, in the realm of reasonable men one man's introspection was as good as another's, and the theorist's own internal calculations were likely to correspond roughly to those of his subject; to this extent the results of the subject's operation were "observable." However, if challenged to produce less-subjective evidence, it would undoubtedly have occurred to Jevons that the most natural way to obtain the results of the man's introspective measurements would be to ask for them.

The first rough outline of the subject's pattern of "satisfaction" would emerge from an "indifference-map" experiment, in which he is asked to rank the events, A, B and C in order of preference. If he can compare the events and if his preferences are transitive ("consistent"), e.g., if he prefers A to B, B to C and A to C, the results of this experiment are summarised by any triplet of numbers satisfying: $U_a > U_b > U_c$. This triplet is a "non-measurable" utility index, determined up to a monotonic transformation.

In what we will call a "Jevonsian"[11] experiment the man would next be asked to rank his preferences of A to B and his preference of B to C. If he finds that he can state, for example, that his preference of A to B exceeds his preference of B to C, we could summarise this information by any triplet of numbers satisfying the two inequalities: (a) $U_a > U_b > U_c$, and (b) $U_a - U_b > U_b - U_c$.

Finally, if A and B were sums of money, we could ask the man to vary the sum of money represented by B until he could tell us that he found his preference of A to B' equal to his preference of B' to C. If he finds such a B', then the results of this last operation would be expressed by any triplet of numbers satisfying the relationships: (a) $U_a > U_b > U_c$, and (b) $U_a - U_b = U_b - U_c$. Any two triplets obeying these relationships must be related by a linear transformation; they represent utility indices differing only by scale and origin.

The Jevonsian index for the individual, if one can be found, is thus "measurable"; which in this case means nothing more or less than that the subject was able to give consistent answers to these particular questions. It might be objected that in fact subjects will be unable to answer the questions, or will answer them inconsistently. This is an empirical matter. If the events were the possession of (a) one million dollars, (b) two dollars, and (c) one dollar, it seems likely that most people would answer the question (and, moreover, would state specifically that their preference of A to B exceeded their preference of B to C).[12] For such people, the notion of a cardinal utility index would not be "meaningless"; if it had no other meaning, it might at least imply that their answers to this sort of question could be predicted. Inconsistency is to be expected, particularly with respect to utility differences that are almost equal. But inconsistency also appears (in lesser degree) in the "indifference-map" experiment; in each case the most important information gained concerns choices which the subject finds easy to make.[13]

The more damaging attack has been on the usefulness of the method, though here again the case is not conclusive. If the only "consistency" discovered were consistency of answers with other answers, the results would be trivial. But Marshall and his predecessors regarded such answers as revealing the subject's internal measurements of satisfaction.[14] Since they believed the man based his decisions to act on the results of this introspective operation, they hoped to use the results of a Jevonsian experiment to predict his decision.

As the ordinalists have demonstrated, decisions in the marketplace under conditions of certainty can be predicted on the basis of the "indifference-map" experiment alone. But this is not true of behavior under uncertainty or risk. With a Jevonsian utility index, on the other hand, it is possible to frame meaningful hypotheses placing definite restrictions on observable behavior in risk-situations.

The particular rule which Marshall and Jevons proposed (rather more for normative purposes than descriptive) was that the "rational" man would maximise the mathematical expectation of utility. In terms of the expression (1) cited earlier:

$$U_b - p \cdot U_a + (1 - p)U_c \qquad (1)$$

the rational man should (would) choose the prospect if the right-hand side were greater, the sure outcome B if the left-hand side were greater. If U_b, the utility that can be had for certain if the prospect is rejected, is regarded as the opportunity cost of the prospect, then the expression (2):

$$p(U_a - U_b) - (1 - p)(U_b - U_c) \gtreqless 0 \qquad (2)$$

represents the mathematical expectation of *gain* (measured in utility) associated with the prospect. The first term is the amount of utility that the man stands to win by accepting the gamble (in excess of the utility cost of the gamble) multiplied by the probability of winning, and the second term is the amount of utility he stands to lose multiplied by the probability of losing. The man should take any gambles whose expectation of gain is positive, reject all whose expectation of gain is negative, be indifferent to those whose expectation of gain is zero.

One point about this procedure must be emphasised, for it is in sharp contrast to that of von Neumann and Morgenstern. The utility index, and its measurability, on which the Marshallian predictions were based was not derived from any risk-behavior. The rule of maximising expected utility on the basis of a Jevonsian index led to prediction, or prescription, of a man's choice among prospects without any previous observation of his behavior in the face of risk.

Actually, in the main field of consumer behavior characterised by risk-gambling-Marshall was not sanguine about the usefulness of the rule as a descriptive hypothesis. He took it as a universal empirical law that answers in the Jevonsian experiment would reveal diminishing marginal utility. In other words, if A, B and C are three sums of money such that $A > B > C$, and if $A - B = B - C$, then he assumed that corresponding utility numbers would satisfy the inequality: $U_a - U_b < U_b - U_c$. A "fair" gamble is defined as one in which the mathematical expectation of *money* gain is zero, expressed by:

$$p(A - B) - (1 - p)(B - C) = 0 \tag{3}$$

where p is the probability of winning A, $1 - p$ the probability of winning C and B is the cost of the gamble (in the above case, p must equal $\frac{1}{2}$). But, granted decreasing marginal utility, the corresponding expectation of *utility* gain is negative, so the rational man would never accept a fair gamble, or, *a fortiori*, an unfair gamble.

As Marshall was well aware, people did accept fair and even unfair gambles; but this behavior disputed their rationality, not (the curvature of) their utility index. The latter was established once and for all by tests that did not involve risk. Because of the existence of "pleasures of gambling"[15] (which Marshall measured by the acceptance of unfair bets), Marshall would have rejected the observation of risk-behavior as an alternative operation for measuring people's intensities of liking for outcomes.

The particular Marshallian rule governing risk-behavior is not implied by his concept of utility or by the methods of measuring it. An early form of the rule is stated by Jevons:[16]

> If the probability is only one in ten that I shall have a certain day of pleasure, I ought to anticipate the pleasure with one-tenth of the force which would belong to it if certain. In selecting a course of action which depends on uncertain events, as, in fact, does every-

thing in life, I should multiply the quantity of feeling attaching to every future event by the fraction denoting its probability.

The reliance of this approach on measurability (of "quantity of feeling") is obvious; but it is equally obvious that the measurability of "pleasure," and even the general principle that likings for prospects should be based on likings for outcomes and their probabilities, does not imply this particular rule of decision-making. On the basis of a given Jevonsian index, Marshall or Jevons could just have easily proposed that the rational man base his preference on the mode, the median, the range, variance or other properties of the distribution of properties of the distribution of utilities. These rules would have been just as meaningful, and possibly more useful (especially if they took into account measures of "risk" as well as "central tendency"). In fact, it was the feeling that the emphasis on mathematical expectation was arbitrary and unrealistic which led to the decline of the concept even before doubts arose that a measurable utility could be discovered to make it meaningful.

IV

What von Neumann and Morgenstern asserted, in their famous digression,[17] was the possibility that the notion of maximising the mathematical expectation of utility might (a) be made meaningful, and (b) describe a wider range of risk-behavior than in its old usage, *if "utility" were measured (defined) in a special way.* Since they were concerned only with risk-behavior, the operation they proposed was the observation of choices in risk-situations. If a person's preferences among *prospects*— described merely in ordinal terms—should satisfy certain, apparently weak, axiomatic restrictions, then von Neumann has proved that it would be possible to find a set of numbers which could express these preferences in a particularly convenient way.

This set of numbers would be a utility index, because it would be one among all the sets of numbers (related by monotonic transformations) expressing the person's preferences (*not* "intensities of preference" or "quantities of feeling") among sure outcomes. The novelty would be that this same set of numbers, applying explicitly only to sure outcomes, could also summarise the person's preferences among prospects. In a complete description of the individual's entire preference-structure, it would be unnecessary to list prospects separately or to record explicitly his preferences among prospects; these preferences would be known, through observation, but they could be expressed implicitly by the numbers attached to sure outcomes.

Clearly, the class of indices which could express with such economy preferences both among sure outcomes and among prospects must be smaller than the Class of all ordinal utility indices in most of which it would be necessary to list prospects individually. In fact, it turns out that all indices with this property, if any exist, will be related by linear transformations. Yet the index is not "measurable" in the sense that it is correlated with any significant economic quantity such as quantity of feeling or satisfaction, or intensity, such as intensity of liking or preference. It is derived from *choices*, and describes only *preferences*. It would be "cardinal" ("measurable") only to the extent that the numerical operation of forming mathematical expectations on the basis of these numbers would be related to observable behavior, so as to be empirically meaningful.

Von Neumann and Morgenstern might simply have proposed the empirical hypothesis that an index of the desired sort could be found for certain individuals. However, this proposition, which we will call the Hypothesis on Moral Expectations, has little inherent plausibility. The major feat of von Neumann and Morgenstern is to show that the Hypothesis on Moral Expectations is *logically equivalent* to the hypothesis that the behavior of given individuals satisfies certain axiomatic restrictions. Since these axioms appear, at first glance, highly "reasonable," the second hypothesis seems far more intuitively appealing than the equivalent Hypothesis on Moral Expectations. It is thus more likely to be accepted on the basis of casual observation and introspection, although the two hypotheses would both be contradicted by exactly the same observations.

Most expositions follow von Neumann and Morgenstern in focusing all attention on the second hypothesis, i.e., on the empirical relevance of the axioms. Once this is accepted, the Hypothesis on Moral Expectations "goes along free" in the form of the Theorem on Moral Expectations, which states conditionally that *if* an individual's behavior conforms to the axioms, a von Neumann-Morgenstern index can be computed for him (this proposition rests on logic rather than observation, and it has been established by several different proofs). Empirical test of the proposition is thus displaced to the axioms which imply it. The logical relationship of the axioms to the Hypothesis is usually left obscure, for the demonstration is too difficult for most readers.[18] Therefore the reader must generally take it on faith that behavior violating a particular axiom conflicts with the possibility of finding a von Neumann-Morgenstern index. Instead, we will follow the straighter, though less persuasive, route of describing how the Hypothesis on Moral Expectations would be tested directly.

We can state the Hypothesis in the following form. For a given individual (it is asserted that) a set of numbers *exists* (i.e., can be found) with the two properties: (1) it is one of the sets expressing the individual's actual preferences among sure outcomes (i.e., it is one of his ordinal utility indices); (2) numbers are assigned to sure outcomes in such a way that, if "moral expectations" of *prospects* were computed on the basis of these numbers, one prospect would have a higher moral expectation than another if, and only if, the person actually preferred the former to the latter, and two prospects would have the same moral expectation if and only if the person were indifferent between them.

If, from the set of all utility indices (related by monotonic transformations) one index can be found such that "moral expectations" computed on the basis of this particular set of "utilities" arrange prospects according to an individual's actual preferences among them, then any other index related to the first by a linear (not merely by any monotonic) transformation will also have this property. Thus, if one such index exists, an infinite set will exist: though still a tiny subset of all indices expressing ordinal preferences among outcomes. The Theorem on Moral Expectations states that such a set does exist, if and when the axioms apply. The Hypothesis states that the index actually does exist for given persons.

Having found such an index, we could submit it to a monotonic increasing transformation—e.g., we could take the square or the log of each number—and the resulting set of numbers would be a perfectly valid utility index of outcomes. But it would not serve any more as a utility index of prospects as well; it would no longer be true that moral expectancies would correspond to the individual's actual preferences among prospects.

Our approach will consist of trying to find an index (hypothetically) with the two properties specified, noting in the process the type of behavior which would make this impossible. The "operational content" of the theory should be most obvious from this point of view, since it is intimately related to the body of behavior "ruled out" by the Hypothesis. The greater the amount and importance of this behavior, the more powerful does the Hypothesis appear, though the less immediately plausible.

The basic operation in deriving a von Neumann-Morgenstern utility index is the observation of an individual's behavior in the very simplest situation involving risk: a choice between a sure outcome and a prospect involving two possible outcomes with given probabilities. The essential restriction the Hypothesis puts on behavior is that, by observing a person's choices in situations of this simple type, it must be possible to predict his choices among sets of prospects each offering a multitude of prizes with complex odds (some of the prizes possibly being other prospects). In the discussion below, the notation $(A, p; B)$ signifies a prospect offering outcome A with probability p or B with probability $1 - p$.

To fix the origin and unit of the utility index we seek, we assign arbitrary numbers to two outcomes (order of magnitude in order of preference); this guarantees that the index, if we can find one, will be unique. For example, let us assign to the money sums \$1000 and \$0 the utility numbers 10 and 0: i.e., $U_{1000} = 10$, $U_0 = 0$. Now we consider a third sum, say \$500, which the individual ranks between the first two; the problem is to find a utility number U_{500} that satisfies the Hypothesis on Moral Expectations, consistent with his preferences and with the two numbers already assigned arbitrarily. The crucial datum in the procedure is the probability $\dot{p}$ at which the person is indifferent between having \$500 with certainty or a prospect (\$1000, $\dot{p}$; \$0).[19] Suppose that this $\dot{p}$ is $\frac{8}{10}$; i.e., he tells us, or we observe, that he is indifferent between \$500 and (\$1000, $\frac{8}{10}$; \$10). The Hypothesis on Moral Expectations then implies that it is possible to find a number U_{500} with the two properties:

$$0 < U_{500} < 10 \text{ (since he prefers \$1000 to \$500 and \$500 to \$0)} \quad (4.1)$$

$$1 \cdot U_{500} = \tfrac{8}{10} \cdot 10 + \tfrac{2}{10} \cdot 0 \quad (4.2)$$

Obviously, such a number *can* be found: $U_{500} = 8$. So the Hypothesis has passed the first test.

Even in this first application, the Hypothesis was not tautologous. It was conceivable that the individual would prefer the certainty of \$500 to any prospect (\$1000, p; \$0) for *any* p whatever: perhaps from extreme conservative principles or moral scruples against gambling. The Hypothesis would then imply that it was possible to find a number U_{500} satisfying both the following two relationships:

$$0 < U_{500} < 10 \quad (5.1)$$

and

$$U_{500} > p \cdot 10 + (1 - p) \cdot 0 \qquad \text{for all } p, 0 < p < 1. \quad (5.2)$$

But no such number exists; for any given U_{500} satisfying (5.1), there would exist a p, such that (5.2) would not hold. Therefore the Hypothesis would be contradicted.

Similarly, the Hypothesis would be contradicted if the individual should prefer any prospect (\$1000, p; \$0) to the certainty of \$500; say, from an obsession with gambling.

It might seem that such behavior might well occur, thus rejecting the Hypothesis on the basis of one observation. But proponents of the Hypothesis could point out that it is unusual to have such "absolute" likes or dislikes: to feel so strongly either for or against gambling as to ignore entirely the relative stakes and odds.[20] They might suggest that such behavior, though it may exist, is statistically unimportant, so that it is reasonable to hypothesise that there will be *some* $\dot{p}$ at which the subject will be indifferent. A man with a marked taste for security might pick $\dot{p} = 9999/10,000$; a born gambler might indicate $\dot{p} = 1/1000$. In either case it would be possible to find a number U_{500} consistent with these preferences.

Thus, the Hypothesis puts very weak limitations in this initial application to the man's preferences among risky alternatives. The drastic test is to investigate whether or not his other choices will be "consistent" with this first choice. Let us return to our original result, $U_{500} = 8$. On the basis of our single observation (fixing $\dot{p}$ at $\frac{8}{10}$) we must be able to predict the individual's choice among any set of prospects involving the three outcomes, \$1000, \$500 or \$0, with any probabilities. Given any set of prospects, we simply compute the moral expectations of each on the basis of the utility numbers (two of which, in this case, were fixed arbitrarily and the third derived from a single observed choice), and pick the prospect with the highest moral expectancy. No rationale for this procedure has been given here. It is not suggested that the individual makes his choice by a similar calculation. We are merely examining the implications of the hypothesis that it is possible to describe his behavior "as though" he did.

Thus, we compute the moral expectation of the prospect (\$1000, $\frac{1}{2}$; \$0) as: $\frac{1}{2} \cdot 10 + \frac{1}{2} \cdot 0 = 5$. If, when confronted with the choice between this prospect and the certainty of \$500 ($U_{500} = 8$), our subject does not definitely prefer the latter, then it is not true that moral expectations on the basis of our utility numbers arrange prospects according to the individual's actual preference; our triplet does not have properties of a von Neumann-Morgenstern index. More than that, if this triplet is not one of these whose existence is implied by the Moral Expectations Hypothesis, *then no such triplet can be found*, and the hypothesis is thereby invalidated. For, once two numbers had been arbitrarily chosen, and the third one was uniquely determined by our initial observation;[21] any other value for U_{500} would be inconsistent (in terms of our hypothesis with that particular choice).

If, on the contrary, no serious[22] inconsistency appears, we can proceed to find utility numbers for other sums of money. If we observed that the subject was indifferent between \$200 and (\$500, $\frac{1}{4}$; \$0), we would define $U_{200} = 2$. Our set of utility numbers corresponding to \$0, \$200, \$500 and \$1000 is now 0, 2, 8, 10. If these are the unique set implied by the Hypothesis, then the individual should be indifferent between a 50–50 chance of \$0, \$200 or \$500, since: $\frac{1}{2} \cdot 0 + \frac{1}{2} \cdot 10 = \frac{1}{2} \cdot 2 + \frac{1}{2} \cdot 8$. If, in fact, he prefers one to another, then the existence theorem is contradicted; the axioms on which it may be based do not apply to this individual.

More complicated tests can be devised. One of the "prizes" in a prospect might be another prospect, say, a "lottery ticket" offering a $\frac{4}{5}$ chance of $1000 and a $\frac{1}{5}$ chance of $0; if the other prize is $200, the two prizes being offered at equal odds, this would appear in our notation: [$200, $\frac{1}{2}$; ($1000, $\frac{4}{5}$; $0)]. This "complex" prospect might be compared to the "simple" prospect: ($500, $\frac{5}{8}$; $0). The person "should" be indifferent between them, since:

$$\tfrac{1}{2} \cdot 2 + \tfrac{1}{2}(\tfrac{4}{5} \cdot 10 + \tfrac{1}{5} \cdot 0) = \tfrac{5}{8} \cdot 8 + \tfrac{3}{8} \cdot 0$$

A new test would be to confront the subject with a choice between the above complex prospect and the simple prospect with three prizes: ($1000, $\frac{2}{5}$; $200, $\frac{1}{2}$; $0, $\frac{1}{10}$). Suppose that U_{200} is yet to be computed, and that the individual is found to prefer the complex "lottery ticket" to the above simple one. Then the Hypothesis would imply that a number U_{200} can be found satisfying both:

$$0 < U_{200} < 10, \tag{6.1}$$

and

$$\tfrac{2}{5} \cdot 10 + \tfrac{1}{10} \cdot 0 + \tfrac{1}{2} \cdot U_{200} < \tfrac{1}{2}(\tfrac{4}{5} \cdot 10 + \tfrac{1}{5} \cdot 0 + \tfrac{1}{2} \cdot U_{200}) \tag{6.2}$$

Since (6.2) implies $U_{200} < U_{200}$, it is clearly impossible to find a number with the desired properties.

Von Neumann and Morgenstern's controversial Axiom 3:C:b^{23} rules out this type of behavior by assuming that a person will be indifferent between two prospects which are derivable from each other according to the rules of probabilities. By application of these rules, any complex prospect offering other prospects as prizes may be reduced to a simple prospect, and the axioms require the individual to be indifferent between this derived prospect and the original one. This implies that the individual is indifferent to the number of steps taken to determine the outcome. On the contrary, a sensible person might easily prefer a lottery which held several intermediate drawings to determine who was still "in" for the final drawing; in other words, he might be willing to pay for the possibility of winning intermediate drawings and "staying in," even though the chances of winning the pot were not improved thereby. A longer time-period of suspense would usually also be involved, but it need not be. The crucial factor is "pleasure of winning," which may be aroused by intermediate wins even if one subsequently fails to receive the prize. Many, perhaps most, slot-machine players know the odds are very unfavorable, and are not really motivated by hopes of winning the jackpot. They feel that they have had their money's worth if it takes them a long while to lose a modest sum, mean-while enjoying a number of intermediate wins—which go back into the machine to pay for the pleasure of the next win. Von Neumann and Morgenstern single out axiom $3:C:b$, which excludes this type of behavior, as the "really critical" axiom[24]—"that one which gets closest to excluding a 'utility of gambling'."[25]

The final major test of the Hypothesis would be to give the subject a choice between two such prospects as ($500, p; $1000) and ($200, p; $1000), where p is the same in each and where $500 is preferred to $200. For any p he must prefer the first to the second. If, for example, he was indifferent between them at some $p = P$, the Hypothesis would imply that there was a U_{500} such that:

$$2 < U_{500} < 10, \tag{7.1}$$

and

$$p \cdot U_{500} + (1 - P)10 = P \cdot 2 + (1 - P)10. \tag{7.2}$$

Together these imply that $U_{500} > 2$ and $U_{500} = 2$, which can be true of no number (we are assuming in this example that U_{500} has not already been determined by some other experiment).

It is the "Strong Independence Axiom" ruling out this sort of preference which Samuelson has emphasised, presenting it as the "crucial" axiom.[26] It seems rather hard to justify this emphasis, since the axioms seems indubitably the most plausible of the lot. After all, all of the axioms are necessary to the final result, and this particular one is almost impregnable (even people who did not follow it in practice would probably admit, on reflection, that they should) whereas others (such as $3:C:b$) are contradicted by much everyday experience. One might almost suspect Samuelson, who counts himself a "fellow traveller"[27] of the von Neumann-Morgenstern theory, of using the axiom (his invention) as a mantrap, luring critics past the really vulnerable points to waste their strength on the Independence Assumption."[28]

In all this it has been emphasised that the Hypothesis on Moral Expectations sets a double condition for an acceptable index, the first part being that it must be one of the individual's ordinal utility index. Some critics seem to have overlooked this; for example, I. M. D. Little:[29]

> Suppose that . . . we have given C, A, B, the utility numbers $10\frac{4}{5}$, 10, 9, because the consumer was 'indifferent' between (A certain) and (C with probability $\frac{5}{9}$ or B with probability $\frac{4}{9}$). It follows that . . . if the consumer is given the choice between B and A, A must be taken. In fact B might well be taken.

If, as the last sentence suggests, the consumer preferred B to A (and C to both), we would start the experiment with this information. If we should then observe that he was indifferent between A and $(C, \frac{5}{9}, B)$, then we would not be able to assign any utility number at all to A, for it would be impossible to find one satisfying the two conditions: $U_a < U_b < U_c$ and $U_c = \frac{4}{9} \cdot B + \frac{5}{9}C$. This behavior contradicts the Hypothesis, but the conflict would show up in the impossibility of finding a von Neumann-Morgenstern index, not in the index, once having been "certified," turning out to be inconsistent with ordinal preferences. This is a small point, but criticism which may be quite pertinent loses force if framed in a way that suggests the critic has not understood the conditions of the experiment.

Another type of criticism that goes wide of the mark uses examples involving only "utils," with no mention of the sums they represent or the particular observations on which they were based. Baumol, for example, cites two lottery tickets with prizes expressed in utils (i.e., utility units, rather than money).[30] He computes their moral expectations, but asks, "yet who is to say" that it is "pathological" for the subject to prefer the one with the lower expectation. To this a defender can retort: (a) Baumol gives no indication that the utility numbers were correctly derived; (b) it would not, of course, be "pathological" in any case; but (c) if it happened that the utility numbers were actually derived, for example, from the person's previous choice between the very two prospects cited, then it would be "inconsistency" of a sort usually defined as non-rational for him to switch his choice on this occasion. The crux of the matter is that it is impossible to decide on intuitive grounds whether it is "plausible" to choose the prospect with the higher moral expectation if only utils are cited and if the person's past choices are not known, since an appraisal of "plausibility" must be based on the money sums involved and on the person's pattern of behavior in risk-situations.

We have described above the main types of behavior that conflict with the Hypothesis on Moral Expectations. It is possible to give long lists of factors in risk-situations which would lead to these types of behavior.[31] Among those which have not been mentioned earlier are: feelings of skill, or, in general, the feeling that the "real" odds are more favorable than the stated odds (e.g., belief in personal luck, or in "winning streaks"); inability to compute compound probabilities, and thus to derive simple prospects from complex ones; influence of the other elements in the risk-situation besides the money prizes and the probabilities—e.g., the atmosphere of the gaming-room. The Theorem could possibly be framed so as to allow for these considerations, but in any practical application they would undoubtedly have some effect.

Whether or not these factors would lead to *serious* inconsistency is open to question; it seems very likely that they would in the field of gambling, but Samuelson suggests that they may be less important in business and statistical problems.[32]

The only laboratory test of the Hypothesis has been performed by Professor Frederick Mosteller, who derived utility curves for a group of subjects on the basis of their choice among simple gambles, and used these data to predict their choices among other and more complicated gambles.[33] The experiment side-stepped pitfalls which could not be avoided in practical application by abstracting from the major sources of inconsistent behavior: (a) all probabilities were known; (b) all calculations were performed for the subjects and their misconceptions eliminated;[34] (c) only small sums were used; (d) no social influences or any "other factors" were present; (e) behavior was observed only in one special risk-context (and that an artificial one). The fact that Mosteller found only mild consistency despite these "ideal" conditions might be interpreted as distinctly unfavorable to the hypothesis (though, considered in themselves, the results were inconclusive).

V

In deriving a "Jevonsian" utility index, we would begin as in the preceding section by assigning two arbitrary values; since, like the von Neumann-Morgenstern index, it is determined up to a linear transformation (if it can be found at all). As before, we might assign the utility numbers 10 and 0 to the outcomes $1000 and $0. To find U_{500} instead of confronting the individual with a choice between prospects, we would ask him to rank his preference of $1000 to $500 and his preference of $500 to $0. Suppose he should tell us that the two preferences were equal; we would then assign the utility number $U_{500} = 5$. But on the basis of the von Neumann-Morgenstern experiment (let us assume that the same individual was the subject) we assigned the number $U_{500} = 8$. Is there not a conflict here?

To anyone who has skimmed the literature in this field it will not be obvious that the two sets of results are independent, hence do not conflict, for certain passages, particularly in *The Theory of Games*, gives quite the opposite impression. A close examination of the texts can, in fact, settle the question definitely. Instead of referring immediately to the literature, however, it is rewarding to examine a more general type of analysis, which might have made the issues intelligible to economists from the beginning.

Bridgman states the central proposition of the operational approach thus:[35]

> We must demand that the set of operations equivalent to any concept be a unique set, for otherwise there are possibilities of ambiguity in practical applications which we cannot admit . . . .

*If we have more than one set of operations we have more than
one concept,* and strictly there should be a separate name to correspond to each different set of operations.

The word "should" above should be interpreted as meaning that it is
useful, in terms of certain specific purposes, to adopt the proposed
point of view (this applies as well to the word "should" in this sentence). Because of incautious phrasing in his early writing, it has often
been thought that Bridgman regarded his own definitions and classifications as logical imperatives. Actually (as he has since made explicit), it
is not necessary to insist on his approach dogmatically or exclusively;
without making any unique claims, it is easy to show the value of his
point of view (which admittedly is not the most natural) in helping to
avoid certain types of confusion.

Of course, in everyday usage we very commonly use the same term to
cover different operations, on the grounds that they measure the "same
thing." If we take the strict operational point of view that a "thing" is
"what is measured by a particular operation," we need not ban the
practice of treating two different operations as measuring the "same
thing," but we must insist that it be justified by a direct argument. In
an important passage, Bridgman indicates the nature of an adequate
justification:[36]

> If we deal with phenomena outside the domain in which we originally
> defined our concepts, we may find physical hindrances to performing
> the operations of the original definition, so that the original op-
> erations have to be replaced by others. These new operations, are,
> of course, to be chosen so that they give, within experimental error,
> the same numerical results in the domain in which the two sets of
> operations may be both applied; but we must recognize in prin-
> ciple that in changing the operations we have really changed the
> concept . . . . The practical justification for retaining the same
> name is that within our present experimental limits a numerical
> difference between the results of the two sorts of operations has not
> been detected.

It would hardly be possible to find a passage more pertinent to a
comparison of the economic theories discussed here. It may be helpful to
give some economic illustrations; several examples of pairs of operations
which differ but are usually treated as equivalent exist within the
boundaries of our discussion.

(1) In the indifference map experiment the operations (a) of inter-
rogating the individual as to his preferences, or (b) observing his actual
choices (Samuelson's "revealed preference"), are usually regarded as
alternative.

(2) In the "Jevonsian" experiment two operations are usually thought to be involved: (a) inquiring of the subject how he ranks his preferences; (b) the subject's own subjective process of "weighing" satisfactions. The first is said to measure differences in satisfaction on the assumption that it approximates the results of the second. The basis of this assumption is that in the area where they can both be applied—the area of our own introspection—they give identical results (to the extent that we *can* balance satisfactions and that we tell the truth).

(3) In the von Neumann-Morgenstern experiment we used the operation (a) of asking the subject to name a p at which he would be indifferent; but we also suggested the possibility (b) of observing his choices when confronted with various pairs of prospects many times. Mosteller used the latter operation in his empirical tests.

In each case, the alternative operations are regarded as roughly identical. Actually, most economists who have had practical experience in applied theory are well aware that the results of interrogation and of observing actual behavior are almost never identical. Moreover, minor differences in the operations (such as the wording of questions) do "make a difference."[37] When a pair of operations is accepted as measuring the "same thing" it is because the divergence between the results is not regarded as significant. But as the range of application of each operation is widened over time, divergences appear in the area of overlap, and as pecision increases, small differences become significant. Too often, theorists are unprepared for these phenomena and are thrown into confusion at the emergence of ambiguity and paradox.[38] One who accepts the propositions of the operational approach, on the other hand, not only expects these problems to arise but also knows where to watch for them. This (and nothing more pretentious) is the chief virtue which is claimed for the approach.

The relevance of the above discussion to the present problem can now be stated. Probably many readers of *The Theory of Games* and some later articles have received the impression that the third pair of operations above was being proposed as "measuring the same thing" as the second pair. In other words, many have interpreted the von Neumann-Morgenstern experiment as a more precise or practical, though indirect, approach to the results of the Jevonsian experiment: i.e., basically, to the results of the subjective calculation of satisfactions. But if the operational point of view were more common as a habit of thought, readers would have placed the burden of proof on the (supposed) exponents of such an equivalence challenging them to exhibit evidence. In fact, as they would have discovered, there are no such exponents. And the evidence does not exist, for in general the two operations do not produce even approximately the same results.

Let us recall the results of our hypothetical von Neumann-Morgenstern experiment: $U_0 = 0$, $U_{200} = 2$, $U_{500} = 8$, $U_{1000} = 10$. If the von Neumann-Morgenstern index for this individual were plotted as a function of money incomes, interpolating a smooth curve, the graph would be concave upward between \$0 and \$500; in this range it would show "increasing marginal utility." This shape would reflect merely the fact that in this range of money outcomes the individual accepted "unfair" bets and that his choices among prospects showed consistency of a certain type.

In contrast to this, Marshall and Jevons predicted almost unconditionally one general feature of a "utility" curve derived from an experiment of the Jevonsian type; it would be concave downwards throughout its whole length, exhibiting non-increasing marginal utility at all points. Among those economists who believe that a Jevonsian experiment can have consistent results at all, few have ever disputed this opinion.

If Marshall's prediction does hold, then the numbers inferred from the two experiments will certainly conflict for any person who is observed to accept a gamble at odds which are not distinctly favorable, let alone odds that are actually unfair. If such a person has a von Neumann-Morgenstern index it will have a range of increasing marginal utility, which is assumed to be contradictory to the Jevonsian index. Marshall himself pointed out that there were such people, even among those otherwise "rational."

Thus we can state: the von Neumann-Morgenstern and Jevons-Marshall operations do *not* measure the "same thing." The former do not simply tend to measure the Marshallian "utilities" with greater precision, i.e., to a higher number of significant figures. In general, the ranking of first differences in "utility" as a function of money will be different, depending on which "utility" is being measured; if the functions are continuous, the second derivatives will not in general have the same sign.

To those who accepted the apparent inference that the gambling operation allowed an "estimate" of the results of a Jevonsian experiment, a moments's thought should have suggested the question: Why is an estimate necessary? If risk-behavior reveals something about differences in satisfaction, presumably it is because those differences in satisfaction are the decisive factor in decision-making. But in that case we might as well ask about satisfactions directly.[39]

This discussion has not established yet that von Neumann and

Morgenstern do not themselves regard their operation, mistakenly, as measuring differences in satisfaction. The evidence for this is their repeated rejection of the notion that an individual reaches decisions in risk-situations by calculating differences in utilities, their brand or any other (such as Jevonsian utilities). But much confusion probably stems from the fact that they are prone to write in large, clear type about comparing differences in preferences and to discard such notions in fine print at the bottom of the page. Thus, they formulate their "continuity" axiom (which rules out the "absolute" rejection of lottery tickets or the "absolute" love of gambling discussed earlier) as follows:[40]

> No matter how much the utility of v exceeds . . . the utility of u, and no matter how little the utility of w exceeds . . . the utility of u, if v is admixed to u with a sufficiently small numerical probability, the difference that this admixture makes from u will be less than the difference of w from u.

This leaves a strong impression, to put it mildly, that the notions of quantity of utility and differences in quantities are an integral part of the argument . . . unless the reader follows a footnote on the next page:[41]

> The reader will also note that we are talking of entities like 'the excess of v over u,' or 'the excess of u over v' or (to combine the two former) the 'discrepancy of u and v' (u, v, being utilities) merely to facilitate the verbal discussion—they are not part of our rigorous, axiomatic system.

One other passage in the "literary" discussion is probably the greatest single source of misunderstanding; it concerns a situation in which an individual is offered a choice between a sure outcome, A, and a 50–50 chance of B or C, where C is preferred to A and A to B:[42]

> Any assertion about his preference of A against the combination contains fundamentally new information. Specially: If he now prefers A to the 50–50 combination of B and C, this provides a plausible base for the numerical estimate that his preference of A over B is in excess of his preference of C over A.

This passage seems clearly to imply that the von Neumann-Morgenstern operation aims at the same "entities" (i.e., utility differences) as the Jevonsian experiment, being merely more indirect. But again, the crucial withdrawal is in the footnote:[43]

> Observe that we have only postulated an individual intuition which permits decision as to which of the two events is preferable. But we have not directly postulated any intuitive estimate of the relative sizes of two preferences—i.e., in the subsequent terminology, of two differences of utilities.

The equivocal word here is "estimate." This implies that the procedure tries to approximate the results of an introspective operation. Actually, in the von Neumann-Morgenstern experiment described above utility differences were not "estimated" but computed exactly. They were related precisely to certain risk-choices; no other evidence, intuitive or otherwise, was allowed to influence the results.

The authors themselves point out the ambiguity:

> Are we not postulating here—or taking it for granted—that one preference may exceed another, i.e., that such statements convey a meaning? Such a view would be a complete misunderstanding of our procedure."[44]

Their procedure is actually to use the risk-chocies to *define* the utility differences—to make this notion meaningful in a new way—not to "estimate" them. Very likely it was the above passage which led Professor D. H. Robertson to imagine that von Neumann and Morgenstern had proposed a method for estimating relative differences in desirability. It is easy to spot this inference in his critical account of their theory:[45]

> Thus in the case of a man who does not know how to choose—i.e., who chooses by the toss of a mental coin—between the certainty of B and an even chance of A or C, these authors offer 1 as a measure of the ratio of AB to BC. . . . But it is clear that this would only be *true* for a particular type of man, namely, one who is content to be governed entirely by mathematical expectations. . . . [My italics.]

In the case of the behavior described, von Neumann and Morgenstern would *define* the ratio of utility differences as 1; and in a matter of definition there can be no question of truth and falsity. Those standards could be applied only to a *hypothesis* that the scale defined by von Neumann and Morgenstern bore some empirical relation to some other data, not involving risk: for example, the hypothesis that it approximated the results of a Jevonsian measurement. It is clear from the context of Robertson's remarks that he believed, like most readers, such a hypothesis was implied. It has been the argument of this paper that this belief is mistaken.

In the same passage Robertson adopts essentially the Marshallian position:[46] ". . . we can make no sense of his actions in the face of uncertainty without supposing that he can form some estimate of the relative difference in desirability between pairs of situations." Whatever the plausibility of this argument, it has no relevance to the von Neumann-Morgenstern theory. Where Marshall postulated a type of "consistency" between men's risk-choices and their feelings of relative differences in desirability of the outcomes, von Neumann and Morgenstern hypothesise simply a consistency between risk-choices and other risk-choices. By coincidence, it happens that the particular form of "consistency" prescribed by Marshall (he might well have chosen some other rule than the maximisation of "expected utility") would imply von Neumann-Morgenstern "consistency"; though not vice versa. A man who had a Jevonsian index *and* who obeyed Marshall's dictum would have a von Neumann-Morgenstern index; but the existence of the latter index implies neither of the first two conditions (and the existence of the former index implies neither of the last two conditions). Thus the von Neumann-Morgenstern axioms cover all those who are "rational" in the Marshallian sense; in addition, they may apply to others who would be "irrational" in Marshall's terms, e.g., bettors who accepted unfair bets:[47] and still others for who no Jevonsian index can be defined.

Von Neumann and Morgenstern describe their procedure thus: "We have practically defined numerical utility as being that thing for which a calculus of mathematical expectations legitimate."[48] The word "practically" is unnecessary; from an operational point of view, they *have* so defined it. Does such a "thing" exist? Friedman and Savage have emphasised the use of the axioms, which put definite restrictions on behavior, as a basis for testable and fairly powerful predictions concerning risk-choices.[49] *Should* it exist? Marschak has proposed that the axioms be regarded as defining "rational" behavior in risk-situations; according to this view, which no other writer has supported, the axioms are of interest for normative purposes, even if no one actually does conform to them.[50]

Von Neumann and Morgenstern cited only the descriptive aspect of the theory. They were not particularly interested in predicting or prescribing people's preferences among prospects, but merely in describing them in terms of mathematical expectation: a necessity in their own theory of games, a convenience in any context. This original view of the subject, by far the least pretentious, is probably the most appropriate. The emphasis by Friedman and Savage on the meaningfulness of the hypothesis obscures the fact that many other hypotheses are just as meaningful, perhaps more useful, and even more convenient for predictive purposes (though not for description). For example, hypotheses in terms of parameters of the *money* distribution, such as mathematical expectation and variance, might produce fully as good predictions as those based on a derived von Neumann-Morgenstern index, and they would certainly be easier to test. As for the normative aspect, there seems very little reason to advise a man who is extremely reckless (or excessively conservative) in some of his risk-choices that he should be consistently reckless (or conservative) in his remaining risk-choices. Nor does it seem that a person who behaves approximately in accordance with a von Neumann-Morgenstern index would be in any sense better off if he behaved *more* in accordance with it. If these conclusions are accepted (and von Neumann and Morgenstern would probably accept them), then one must answer the question, "What does it matter whether such a 'thing' exists?" very conservatively.

At any rate, it should be clear that Baumol's impression that "Neumann and Morgenstern consider the utility index obtained by them as the *only* true one"[51] is quite mistaken. So far as behavior under certainty is concerned, only the ordinal features of the index are relevant. The only numerical operation permitted is that of forming mathematical expectations, which is related to risk-behavior; it makes no sense, for example, to *add* von Neumann-Morgenstern utilities. The cardinal features of the index—relative differences between utility numbers—are used only to predict or describe risk-behavior, and, moreover, are derived solely from risk-behavior. Therefore the results of a von Neumann-Morgenstern experiment cannot be "checked" against the results of any experiment not involving risk-choices. This applies to simple introspection, to the Jevonsian experiment, and also to other attempts to base a cardinal utility on consumer behavior.[52] These latter have been rather thoroughly discredited by Samuelson and others because of their use of special unrealistic assumptions. But the existence or non-existence of a von Neumann-Morgenstern index and the existence of "measurable" indices based on these other operations are entirely independent matters. Each method might, out of the whole set of ordinal utility indices, select a different subset of indices reflecting some type of data in addition to preferences; if the indices inside each subset were related by linear transformations, each method would result in a "measurable" utility index. These indices might have entirely different shapes, but so long as they did not entirely overlap in application, there would be no need to single out any one of them as being the "true" utility index. Certainly von Neumann and Morgenstern make no such claims for their construction; they cite only its convenience in formalising risk-behavior. There is no reason to believe that a "measurable utility" derived by some other method could do this;[53] on the other hand, the von Neumann-Morgenstern index could not do the main jobs for which other constructions are intended. It would be of no aid whatsoever in formalising consumer behavior under certainty (the goal of the Fisher-Frisch constructions: see Bishop, *op. cit.*), nor would it seem to be of any relevance in welfare evaluations (whereas a Jevonsian index might be).[54] If it is true, as Professor Robertson has complained, that von Neumann and Morgenstern have actually done harm to "the cause of creating acceptance for a measurable utility with these last two objectives,[55] this is but a measure of the general misinterpretation of their results: a confusion for which they cannot evade all responsibility.

FOOTNOTES

[1] Von Neumann and Morgenstern, *The Theory of Games* (Princeton, 1944), p. 17.

[2] Professor D. H. Robertson, *Utility and all That* (London, 1952), p. 28.

[3] This is the only shortcoming of the otherwise excellent article by Alchian, "The Meaning of Utility Measurement," *American Economic Review*, March 1953, p. 26. The present paper may serve as a complement to Alchian's.

[4] Friedman and Savage, "The Utility Analysis of Choices Involving Risk," *Journal of Political Economy*, August 1948, p. 279. Mosteller and Nogee, "An Experimental Measurement of Utility," *Journal of Political Economy*, October 1951, p. 371. I have also benefited from reading as yet unpublished papers by Professors Bishop, Marschak and Allais.

[5] This paper was originally written as the first chapter in a thesis, entitled "Theories of Rational Choice Under Uncertainty: The Contributions of von Neumann and Morgenstern," submitted for undergraduate honors at Harvard University, April 1952. The thesis was written under the valuable guidance of Professor John Chipman. I am also greatly indebted to Professors Paul Samuelson, Robert Bishop, Oskar Morgenstern and Frederick Mosteller for the opportunity to discuss problems and to read unpublished writings on the subject, and to Mr. Nicholas Kaldor for his comments.

[6] These concepts and the general point of view were first formulated explicitly by Percy W. Bridgman, in *The Logic of Modern Physics* (New York, 1927), who declared them to be implicit in the thinking of modern physicists. The terms, and the emphasis on restrictiveness and refutability of propositions, have become familiar to economists largely through Samuelson's *Foundations of Economic Analysis* (Cambridge, 1948), but the other main propositions are less well known.

[7] A "lottery ticket" of this sort, offering a set of alternative outcomes with stated probabilities summing to unity, will hereafter be known as a *prospect*. If one outcome is offered with unit probability, i.e., with no uncertainty, it will be known as a *sure outcome*.

[8] Of these, "mathematical expectation of utility" and its shorter form, moral expectation," will be used below. Both must be carefully distinguished from the "mathematical expectation of *money*," which is a weighted sum of the money outcomes, rather than of their utility numbers.

[9] Von Neumann and Morgenstern use this term to signify an operation other than numerical or logical manipulation of a mathematical model. A mathematical model is useful if the results of a "natural" operation can be correlated with numbers in such a way that numerical operations can symbolise and substitute for the "natural" operation.

[10] For an excellent exposition of the concepts of linear and monotonic transformations, the reader is referred to the article by Alchian, *op. cit.* Briefly two indices are related by a linear transformation if for every point x on one index, the corresponding point y on the other index satisfies a relationship of the form: $y =$

$ax + b$, where a and b are constants. The two indices differ only with respect to scale and origin.

If the difference between two numbers in one index is greater than, less than or equal to the difference between two other numbers, the corresponding differences in the other index will have the same ordinal relationship.

[11] This name is suggested by J. C. Weldon, who points out that it implies no more than that Jevons assumed that preferences could be directly compared. "A Note on Measures of Utility," *Canadian Journal of Economics and Political Science,* May 1950, p. 230.

[12] At least, they would probably do so if asked point-blank and not given time for doubts as to whether the question "meant" anything (induced, perhaps, by the writings of Samuelson). This could be made part of the conditions of the experiment.

[13] The above discussion follows Weldon, *op. cit.*

[14] Such information might by itself be of interest in welfare economics; it might, though it need not, influence the evaulations on which a social-welfare function must be based.

[15] Unfair gambling could be "rationalised" if introspective tests revealed that the happiness derived from gambling outweighed the "expected loss of satisfaction" implied by the odds. However, Marshall wished to retain the normative connotation of "rationality" at the expense of predictive value. In his view, the pleasures of gambling "are likely to engender a restless, feverish character, unsuited for steady work. . . ." (*Principles of Economics* (London, 1925). Mathematical Appendix, Note IX, p. 843.) Granted that marginal utility was decreasing and that pleasures of gambling could be ignored because "impure," then unfair gambling was unequivocally irrational, an "economic blunder."

[16] W. Stanley Jevons, *The Theory of Political Economy* (London, 1911), p. 36.

[17] The theory which follows occupies only a few pages in the introduction to their book, and plays no role in the theory of games. The latter theory requires a commodity which is not only measurable but intercomparable and freely transferable, so pay-offs are expressed in money, not in von Neumann-Morgenstern "utility."

[18] Von Neumann and Morgenstern did not present a proof deriving the Theorem from the axioms until the second edition of *The Theory of Games* (1947); they describe it, with terrific understatement, as "rather lengthy and maybe somewhat tiring for the mathematically untrained reader" (p. 617). A different, slightly easier proof, is given by Marschak in "Rational Behaviour, Uncertain Prospects, and Measurable Utility," *Econometrica,* April 1950. A genuinely simple proof has finally been presented by Samuelson, in "Utility, Preference, and Probability," abstract of paper given before the conference of *Les Fondements et Applications de la Theories du Risque en Econometric,* 1952.

[19] The axioms require that he be indifferent at one and only one p. Tests have already shown that this perfect consistency is never encountered, but "indifference" might be defined stochastically (e.g., if an individual rejected a prospect with given odds as often as he accepted it, he might be said to be "indifferent" to it).

[20] As John Chipman has put it, this is the "every man has his price" axiom.

[21] Since indices satisfying the Hypothesis are determined "up to two arbitrary constants," the specification of two values determines the index uniquely.

[22] In a real experiment we would have to decide in statistical terms what to regard as a "reasonable" approximation to consistency with the Theorem.

[23] Von Neumann and Morgenstern, *op. cit.,* p. 26.

[24] *Ibid.,* p. 632.

[25] *Ibid.,* p. 28.

[26] Samuelson, "Utility, Preference, and Probability," *op. cit.* Also, "Probability, Utility, and the Independence Axiom," *Econometrica,* October 1952, p. 672.

[27] Samuelson, "Probability, Utility, and the Independence Axiom," *op. cit.,* p. 677.

[28] Dr. Alan S. Manne's article, "The Strong Independence Assumption—Gasoline Blends and Probability Mixtures," *Econometrica,* October 1952, p. 665, gives an interesting example of a physical situation in which superposition does not apply, which may be more relevant to linear programming than to the present subject. Although it raises a doubt, I do not think his criticism is really damaging in this context. The argument in the same issue by H. Wold, "Ordinal Preferences or Cardinal Utility?" is definitely invalid.

[29] I. M. D. Little, A *Critique of Welfare Economics* (Oxford, 1950), p. 30.

[30] William Baumol, "The Neumann-Morgenstern Utility Index—An Ordinalist View" *Journal of Political Economy,* February 1951, p. 65.

[31] Maurice Allais, in "Notes theoriques sur l'Incertitude de l'Avenir et la Risque" (as yet unpublished), and Professor Robert Bishop, in a paper that has not been published as yet, outline these considerations in detail.

[32] Samuelson, "Probability, Utility, and the Independence Axiom," *op. cit.,* p. 677.

[33] Frederick Mosteller and Philip Nogee, "An Experimental Measurement of Utility," *Journal of Political Economy,* October 1951, p. 399.

[34] In the first two sessions subjects were not instructed on computing odds, and calculations were not performed for them. Behavior in these sessions was quite different from behavior in the rest of the experiment. Although these interesting results were not discussed in the article cited, Mosteller informed me that a definite finding of the experiment was that all the subjects behaved very differently before and after they had received lectures on dealing with probabilities. Moreover, their behavior showed a trend factor throughout the experiments as they grew increasingly familiar with the various gambles.

Even if the final conclusions had been much more favorable than they were, these observations would have dictated great caution in extrapolating them to situations outside the laboratory.

[35] Percy W. Bridgman, *The Logic of Modern Physics* (New York, 1927). The first sentence is on p. 6, the second on p. 10 (my italics).

Although such notions as the meaningfulness and restrictiveness of hypotheses have been made familiar to many economists by followers of Bridgman, the above proposition and the following ones, which are the very heart of the operational approach, are not widely known among economists.

[36] Percy W. Bridgman, *The Logic of Modern Physics* (New York, 1927); the first two sentences are on p. 23; the third, on p. 16 (in the latter sentence, Bridgman refers to the measurement of length by ordinary and by Einstein's operations).

[37] The operational approach may be useful in reminding us that differently worded questionnaires measure, in general, "different things."

[38] Such confusion was prevalent in physics prior to the revolutionary theories of Einstein and Planck. The operational approach was proposed as a means of avoiding such a state of mind in the future.

[39] It is perhaps conceivable, though unlikely, that his feelings of satisfaction might be difficult for an individual directly, being only semi-conscious, though influencing his behavior. But if it were true that his risk-behavior was a reliable and convenient guide to his feelings of differences in satisfaction this would ensure that the Jevonsian experiment *could* always be performed. For even if the subject were an economist, say, who detested introspection, he could note tacitly his reactions to hypothetical lottery tickets (or even, if conscientious, plot his behavior at bingo games and horse races) before replying to questions about differences in satisfaction.

On the other hand, to say that the Jevonsian experiment cannot lead to consistent results is to say that any consistency revealed by the von Neumann-Morgenstern experiment is not closely related to satisfaction.

[40] Von Neumann and Morgenstern, *op. cit.,* p. 630. Since the content of this passage is not under discussion, the reader is advised to pass his eyes over it rather swiftly.

[41] *Ibid.,* p. 631 n. This is not the only time in their book that the authors introduce notions in a "literary" discussion of their theorems that they simultaneously disown, informing the reader that it all comes out in the axioms. Of course, the very inclusion of a verbal discussion is a concession to non-mathematicians; but one can do only so much in the name of "heuristic devices." It is not a recommendation of the empirical relevance of axioms to say that they can be made plausible in literary translation only by identifying them with notions (such as subjective utility differences) which are actually irrelevant.

[42] *Op. cit.,* p. 18.

[43] *Ibid.,* p. 18 n.

[44] *Ibid.,* p. 20.

[45] D. H. Robertson, *Utility and all That* (London, 1952), p. 28.

[46] *Ibid.,* p. 28.

[47] The theory, since it allows for this sort of behavior, cannot be said to rule out all forms of "pleasure in gambling." But proponents have rather overplayed this point. Although acceptance of unfair bets does not contradict the theory, there is ample behavior which does, including some other forms of "pleasure in gambling."

[48] *Op. cit.,* p. 28.

[49] Friedman and Savage, *op. cit.*

[50] Marschak, *op. cit.,* p. 139; also, "Why 'Should' Statisticians and Businessmen Maximise 'Moral Expectation'?" *Proceedings of the Second Berkeley Symposium on Mathematical Statistics and Probability* (Los Angeles, 1951), p. 493.

[51] Baumol, "The Neumann-Morgenstern Utility Index—an Ordinalist View," *Journal of Political Economy,* February 1951, p. 61.

[52] See Robert Bishop, "Consumer's Surplus and Cardinal Utility," *Quarterly Journal of Economics,* May 1943. For criticism of these approaches see Samuelson, *Foundations of Economic Analysis,* pp. 174-9.

[53] Thus, Alchian is mistaken in asserting that "measurability 'up to a linear transform' both *implies* and is implied by the possibility of predicting choices among uncertain prospects, the universal situation" ["The Meaning of Utility Measurement," p. 49 (my italics)]. Actually, it is easy to conceive a "measurable" utility index which is neither derived from nor used to predict risk-behavior.

[54] After I had reached these conclusions, I had the great benefit of conversation with Professor Oskar Morgenstern, who was kind enough to read and discuss with me an earlier version of this paper. Professor Morgenstern confirmed what were then speculations on the implications of the theory; he particularly confirmed that he and von Neumann had envisioned only limited application, to risk-behavior alone.

[55] Robertson, *op. cit.,* p. 28.

PART V

Utility and Welfare Economics

THE UTILITY CONCEPT IN VALUE THEORY AND ITS CRITICS, II. THE UTILITY CONCEPT IN WELFARE ECONOMICS

Jacob Viner

THE LEGITIMACY OF WELFARE ECONOMICS

In the recent literature on economic methodology, of which an outstanding characteristic has been the demonstration on a priori grounds of the lack of validity of the a priori method, protests recur, resting also on a priori grounds, against the conduct of economic analysis in welfare terms. One basis for such protests is that welfare is an ethical concept, involving the making of ethical evaluations, and that such evaluations are repugnant to the inherent nature of uncorrupted scientific analysis. There does not seem to be any essential conflict between this dogma of the laboratory and the use of the utility concept, not only in price-economics, but even in analysis intended to provide a basis for the making of welfare judgments.

Let us assume for the present that welfare consists of a flow of utility and that utility means satisfaction. Economists can accept satisfaction as a quantity, without committing themselves to any position with respect to its ethical quality. If they be welfare economists, they can consider the bearing of economic institutions and processes on "maximum satisfaction," but if they refrain from taking any position with respect to the goodness or the evil of these satisfaction consequences they will have succeeded in keeping their analysis free from ethical taint. Economics suffers, however, from the fact that it shares its terminology with other disciplines and with the language of common sense. The term "utility" suggests a particular school of ethics, while "welfare" is hard to distinguish from the *summum bonum* of most humanist schools of ethical doctrine. But economics can conceivably employ these

Source: Reprinted with permission from *The Journal of Political Economy,* XXXIII: 638–659 (December 1925).

concepts without giving them ethical meaning within the proper limits of its own range of inquiry. If economics wishes to make its findings helpful in the making of ethical appraisals, which is surely not an illegitimate aim, it may well apply itself to the study of the consequences, for whatever is the ethical *bonum,* of economic structure and process. By the selection of the data which he investigates the economist may suggest by implication what in his judgment is the proper basis for ethical judgment, but provided he does not defend his selection on ethical grounds it is at least not obvious that he has offended the scientific properties.

That utility and welfare have been used in economics as ethical concepts may be conceded, but it does not follow that their use necessarily involves ethical judgment. When Knight cites the use of utility by economists in the justification of progressive taxation as illustrating the ethical nature of the concept,[1] he merely points out that it has been used for ethical purposes. It is not the acceptance of utility as an economic *datum,* but the acceptance of maximum satisfaction as the *summum bonum,* or as an important element therein, which serves some economists as the justification for progressive taxation. If there are utility theorists who hold with Knight that "men who know what they do want—and who have not sapped their vitality by unnatural living or too much of a certain kind of thinking—[do not] want their wants satisfied"[2] they might come to the same conclusion as other utility theorists with respect to the contribution of progressive taxation to maximum satisfaction of wants, but would use this conclusion as the basis for an ethical condemnation of progressive taxation. Whatever ethical implications the conclusions of the economist with respect to utilities may carry with them, these implications are for the ethicist or for the economist only in other than his professional capacity to act upon.

In any case, most welfare economists carefully disclaim any intention of pronouncing final ethical judgments.[3] For most of them, it is true, there is no difference in kind between the economic welfare with which they attempt to deal and total or general welfare, but merely the limitation in the range of welfare problems considered and in the comprehensiveness of their analysis thereof which professional division of labor

---

[1] F. H. Knight, *American Economic Review Supplement* (March, 1921), p. 145.

[2] *Ibid.,* "Ethics and the Economic Interpretation," *Quarterly Journal of Economics* (May, 1922), p. 470.

[3] Fetter, however, asserts that it is necessary for welfare economists to distinguish between the "good" and the "bad" in acts of individual choice ("Value and the Larger Economics. II," *Journal of Political Economy* [December, 1923], p. 792).

enforces upon them.[4] They are always ready to admit, however, the possibility of serious conflict between the economic and the non-economic utilities. They ordinarily go no farther toward ethical judgment than to claim the existence of a strong presumption that an increase in economic satisfactions or in economic welfare will contribute to total welfare.[5] If their welfare economics is in any degree an encroachment upon the field of ethics it is so as a casuistry in a partial and tentative ethics which admittedly does not take into account all the elements necessary for final ethical judgment.

UTILITY AS A WELFARE CONCEPT

The welfare economist, if he is of the utility school, generally defines and measures welfare in subjective terms of utility. But there pervades the utility economics a threefold ambiguity in the use of the term "utility," whose persistence is facilitated by the lingering traces of psychological hedonism in its analysis and by the lack of clearly defined dividing lines in its organization between price problems and welfare problems. Utility is sometimes used to signify satisfaction, pleasure, happiness, or whatever the stuff of welfare is thought to be;[6] at other times to signify the capacity of goods to contribute to welfare, or to yield satisfactions.[7] In recent years there has been a tendency to confine its meaning to "capacity to satisfy desire" or "desiredness," and then to abandon it, because of its ambiguity, for the latter term.[8] The time seems to be approaching when there will be a utility economics which carefully avoids employing the term which originally gave it its name!

Among welfare economists of the utility school it has been the general tendency to take satisfaction (in some cases, pleasure) as the unit of welfare. If the function of welfare economics is to contribute data which will serve the social philosopher or the statesman in the making

---

[4] Cf. A. C. Pigou, *The Economics of Welfare* (London, 1924), pp. 10 ff.

[5] Cf., for example, Henry Sidgwick, *Principles of Political Economy* (London, 1883), pp. 518 ff.; A. C. Pigou, *op. cit.*, p. 20.

[6] Cf. Alfred Marshall, *Principles of Economics*, 6th ed., p. 93: "The total utility of a thing to anyone [that is, the total pleasure or other benefit it yields him]. . . . ."

[7] Cf. F. A. Fetter, *Economic Principles* (New York, 1915), pp. 25, 509.

[8] Cf. A. C. Pigou, *op. cit.*, p. 23. For this meaning of the word "utility," "capacity to excite or induce desire" would be preferable, as less ambiguous, than "capacity to satisfy desire."

of ultimate welfare judgments, this tendency leads, perhaps, to a hedonistic ethics. It is not necessarily entangled, however, in a hedonistic psychology, since if it avoids using price as a measure of satisfaction it need not commit itself to the existence of any close relationship between desire and satisfaction. The day seems definitely to have passed, however, when the philosophically-minded and the psychologically-sophisticated would give their support to an ethics written in terms of a pleasure element alone, or of any other single element. To say nothing of transcendentalists engaged in the pursuit of absolute values which derive their sanctions from other sources than current human desires and satisfactions, there are many who would place greater stress on the importance of the process of desire-fulfilment itself than on the gratifications or other states of consciousness which result from such fulfilment. Some emphasize the absence of unfulfilled desires, therefore, as more conducive to welfare than a great flow of satisfactions which still leaves their recipient discontented. The economist, whether naively or as a *modus operandi* while awaiting the solution by other disciplines of their own problems, has given scant attention to these difficulties.[9] Directly

[9] Exception must be made for F. H. Knight, who has probed these problems to their epistemological depths with a zeal, and with a capacity, for the subtleties of metaphysical inquiry each of which is surely unsurpassed among contemporary economists. His writings cannot be disregarded by anyone who wishes to cope seriously with the problem of the nature of the fundamental concepts of economics as a welfare discipline. At first inclined to limit economic inquiry to investigation of data external to man and of human behavior in its strictly objective manifestations, he later found this position untenable, and has reached the conclusion that economics, like even the physical sciences, though in greater degree, must deal with the metaphysical entities which lie behind the objective regularities which can be observed in the external world. He now not only concedes the legitimacy of economic investigation in terms of desire or of satisfaction, but he characterizes this as an intermediate or tentative stage preparing the way for an inquiry into the origin of the judgments upon which man builds a hierarchy of good-and-bad, higher-and-lower values, by which he subjects desires to an evaluation more fundamental than the merely quantitative standard of more-or-less satisfaction, or pleasure. I am disposed to accept his reasoning up to a certain point. Whether or no there is a hierarchy of absolute values which overlays the evaluation in terms of more-or-less satisfaction, we must for pragmatic reasons proceed as if for our purposes quantity of satisfaction were an adequate basis for welfare judgments. Knight would set us a task with which few of us are adequately equipped to grapple. We still have so far to go before we will have attained adequate control of the technique of the satisfaction-calculus that it seems unwise to attempt an even more difficult and more elusive type of subjective mensuration.

The progressive development of Knight's thinking on these and allied problems can be traced in the following of his writings: *Risk, Uncertainty, and Profit* (Boston, 1921), chap. iii; "Ethics and the Economic Interpretation," *Quarterly Journal of Economics,* May, 1922; "The Ethics of Competition," ibid., August, 1923; "Rela-

or indirectly influenced by the utilitarian tradition which has been so powerful and persistent in economics, he has seemed content to make his analyses in satisfaction terms, without evidencing much fear that a new revelation in philosophy or psychology, or old knowledge newly applied, would expose a lack of relevance of his analyses or his conclusions to human welfare. He is quite possibly wrong, but in the absence of clearer light he can but hope that there is a sufficient element of truth in his premises to give enough validity to his conclusions to justify —in a utilitarian sense—the effort expended in reaching them.

OBJECTIVE INDICIA OF WELFARE

Whatever may be the content of welfare, it is a matter of general agreement that it is subjective, internal, rather than objective, external, to man. But the difficulty, if not the complete impossibility, of measuring subjective quantities directly (and the doubt on the part of some whether qualitative differences between desires or between satisfactions do not so completely overlay quantitative differences as to make futile, even for the purposes of abstract speculation, the idea of a subjective calculus of welfare) has led to attempts to find objective indicia of welfare. Most notable has been the attempt to use price or exchange-value as the measure, or as an element in the measure, of welfare. Perhaps the chief contribution of the utility school to welfare economics has been the negative one of demonstrating the inadequacy at their best of such measures of welfare, because in many respects they conceal or are inapplicable to the very problems for whose solution they are intended to serve as instruments.

The inadequacies of price as a measure of welfare may be illustrated in connection with the problem of tracing the changes in welfare from one period in time to another for a given community.

1. If money income be proposed as a measure of the trend of welfare, there is the obvious objection that the monetary unit, from the point of view of the thing it specifically measures, objective exchange-value, is a yardstick which varies arbitrarily in its own length from time to time. If allowance is made, by reference to a perfect index number, for the year-to-year fluctuations in the exchange-value of the monetary unit,

tions between Economics and Ethics," *American Economic Review Supplement,* March, 1922; "Economic Psychology and the Value Problem," *Quarterly Journal of Economics,* May, 1925; "Fact and Metaphysics in Economic Psychology," *American Economic Review,* June, 1925.

there is left virtually "real" or objective income, the flow of goods and services, as the measure of welfare. This is still inadequate, if for no other reasons than those adduced below.

2. The summation of miscellaneous goods and services must necessarily be accomplished in terms of relative price. Granting that a satisfactory method is devised to make provision for the constant shifting in relative values, prices measure the relative marginal significance for purchasers of the different goods, and welfare is a matter of total utilities (or total satisfactions), not marginal ones. This can readily be demonstrated by reference to the paradox of value that exchange value diminishes as total utility approaches its maximum.

3. Even if an objective measure were devised which would make allowance in terms of a common objective denominator for shifts in the relative total significance of different goods, this would still leave unsolved the problem presented by absolute changes throughout the range of goods in their total significance for the individuals comprising the community. If all prices remained the same, and every person's real income were doubled, an objective measure would indicate a doubling of welfare. But the diminishing-utility principle would establish a presumption that a doubling of objective income would less than double welfare.[10] Moreover, more goods may be needed if new evils are to be warded off[11] while maintaining the same flow of positive satisfactions. Or changes may occur in the total attitude of individuals to material income, a trend toward the simple life, or a greater appreciation of leisure, or, through the progress of education and physical well-being, an increase in the zest with which the material goods of life are enjoyed. A measure of welfare in terms of objective income will not reflect such changes in the slightest degree.

4. Changes in the relative distribution of income as between different classes will bring about changes in the amount of welfare, even though the aggregate real income of the community remains the same.[12] This is

---

[10] Thus Ricardo, lacking full possession of this principle, stated that if a man gets two sacks of corn where formerly he had gotten only one, "he gets, indeed, double the quantity of riches—double the quantity of utility—double the quantity of what Adam Smith calls value in use" (*Principles of Political Economy,* chap. xx, p. 265, in Gonner's edition).

[11] E.g., transportation costs resulting from greater distances between places of employment and available residential sites; medical expenses, because of greater prevalence of disease.

[12] Cf. Henry Sidgwick, *Principles of Political Economy,* p. 76: "If wealth were measured by its utility, 'amount of wealth' would partly be determined by the manner in which the wealth is distributed; and we could not say how much wealth there was in a country till we knew how it was shared among its inhabitants."

so generally accepted a corollary of the law of diminishing utility that further elaboration is unnecessary here.

5. Real income as a measure of welfare breaks down completely in the case of the transfer of commodities from the "free goods" class to the "economic goods" class in consequence of greater scarcity of the commodities in question, and is in the same degree ill-adapted to indicate changes in welfare resulting from such increases in the available amounts of commodities as take them out of the class of "economic goods" and put them into the class of "free goods." An adequate welfare calculus must take into consideration the importance for welfare of free goods, and no calculus in terms of price can do this.

6. Real income as a measure of welfare is ill-adapted to deal with public goods, an increasingly important element in welfare. Estimates of the trend of real income either ignore the services rendered gratuitously to individuals by the government or, measuring them through the inclusion in the community income of the amounts paid as taxes, include them at their money costs, which may grossly exaggerate or grossly underestimate their welfare significance as compared to commodities measured in terms of their market values.

7. A calculus of welfare in terms of real income would reflect only the flow of welfare on the consumption side, and would leave out of the picture the satisfactions and the disutilities accruing from the process of production itself. An increase in real income resulting from an increase in the length of the working day may mean a decrease, rather than an increase, in human welfare. A constant flow of real income, if accompanied by a progressive diminution in the fatigues and pains of production and by an increase in the amount of satisfaction derived from the productive effort itself, as distinguished from its material products, will be consistent with a steady upward trend in welfare.

8. Even if price, or real income measured in terms of price, could be used as a measure of subjective quantities, what it would reflect would be the extent of desire for goods, and not the amount of satisfaction derived from their acquisition and consumption. A measure of desire can serve the purpose of a measure of satisfaction only if the two are quantitatively closely related, and there is abundant ground for scepticism in this regard.[13] If welfare is a quantity of satisfaction, price, therefore, would not be an acceptable measure even if it did measure desire accurately.

The important contribution of the utility theory to welfare economics seems, up to the present, to have consisted in just such demonstrations

[13] See *infra*.

of the inadequacy of price, and of all objective measures formulated in terms of price, as measures of welfare, and in exposition of the qualifications which must accordingly be made in conclusions with respect to welfare based on a price-calculus thereof.[14] The utility theorists, however, have often concentrated their attention on the single factor of inequality in the distribution of wealth, to the neglect of the other factors which militate against the acceptance of price as an adequate measure of welfare. In several notable instances economists who have formally accepted the utility analysis but were not well disposed toward a calculus in subjective terms have found irksome its questioning of the validity of objective measurement of welfare, and by minimizing, on one pretext or another, the degree of conflict between analysis in utility terms and analysis in objective terms, or by selecting for consideration only those problems in which the conflict is least sharp, or perhaps least apparent, have succeeded in reverting to measurement of welfare in terms of price, while retaining the language and the superficial appearance of subjective measurement.

The chief offender in this respect was Alfred Marshall. He disposed very neatly of inequality in the distribution of income as an objection to the measurement of welfare in price terms. "On the whole, however," says Marshall, "it happens that by far the greater number of the events with which economics deals affect in about equal proportions all the different classes of society; so that if the money measures of the happiness caused by two events are equal, there is not in general any very great difference between the amounts of the happiness in the two cases."[15] This has been justly characterized as a "cavalier dismissal of the effect of 'differences of wealth' and 'differences in sensibility.' "[16]

Granted that there are some problems in connection with which the

---

[14] For early analyses in utility terms of the inadequacy of price as a measure of welfare, see especially F. Y. Edgeworth, *Mathematical Physics* (London, 1881), *passim;* Henry Sidgwick, *Principles of Political Economy* (London, 1883), chap. iii; Philip Wicksteed, *Alphabet of Economic Science* (London, 1888), pp. 75 ff., 80 ff. Reference should be made also to two recent articles by F. Y. Edgeworth in which, with characteristic penetration and finesse of technique, he discusses the problem of objective indicia of welfare ("The Plurality of Index Numbers," *Economic Journal,* September, 1925, and "The Element of Probability in Index Numbers," *Journal of the Royal Statistical Society,* July, 1925).

[15] *Principles of Economics,* 6th ed., p. 131. For the same argument, in very much the same language, see Z. C. Dickinson, "The Relations of Recent Psychological Developments to Economic Theory," *Quarterly Journal of Economics* (May, 1919), p. 407.

[16] C. E. Persons, "Marginal Utility and Marginal Disutility as Ultimate Standards of Value," *Quarterly Journal of Economics* (August, 1913), p. 548.

existence of inequality in incomes may be safely disregarded, it is nevertheless difficult to overestimate the extent to which the problem of inequality pervades and underlies the important problems to which economics has traditionally applied itself. It is necessary only to mention taxation, government expenditures, poor relief, immigration, land policy, and, above all, the problem of inequality itself to make clear that a calculus of welfare which abstracts from inequalities in the distribution of wealth and income is a *Hamlet* with Hamlet omitted from the cast.

The problems raised for welfare economics by the possibility of disparity between desire and satisfaction have been quite generally evaded by utility theorists in very much the same manner as Marshall evaded the problem of inequality. As has already been pointed out, utility theorists as a rule take welfare to mean satisfaction. Now price, if it measures any subjective quantity, measures desire, and is a measure of satisfaction only to the degree in which desire is an accurate reflection of satisfaction. But if there exists a welfare economics it is as an unsystematic and very much incidental appendage to price analysis, very imperfectly differentiated in technique and in objectives. A welfare economist who accepts satisfaction as the content of welfare cannot, therefore, accept price as a measure of welfare unless he accepts desire as an accurate, or at least approximate, measure of satisfaction; but rejection of price as the measure of welfare involves an arduous reconstruction and reorganization of his thinking and of his economic "system." If appeal could be made to the hedonistic psychology, there would be no problem. Desire could be taken as a fairly accurate reflection of the satisfaction which would result from its fulfilment, and whatever was acceptable as a measure of desire would therefore be acceptable also as a measure of satisfaction. But the modern utility theorist disavows faith in the hedonistic psychology and in the complete rationality of human behavior. He nevertheless finds ingenious ways of proceeding with the discussion of desire quantities as if they were satisfaction quantities, while maintaining the appearance of logical consistency.

Pigou, for instance, concedes that the possibility of disparity between desire and satisfaction "obviously has great theoretical importance," but denies that it has great practical importance because "it is fair to suppose that most commodities, especially those of wide consumption that are required, as articles of food and clothing are, for direct personal use, will be wanted as a means to satisfaction and will, consequently, be desired with intensities proportioned to the satisfactions they are expected to yield."[17] This need be conceded only if expectations are

[17] *Economics of Welfare*, p. 24. Cf. also, to much the same effect, Vilfredo Pareto, *Manuel D'Économie Politique*, Paris, 1909: "Quant à la substitution de la

never grossly mistaken, if the desires for "food and clothing" *are* simply desires for instruments for the satisfaction of primary physical needs whose serviceability for the purpose in view can be accurately judged by the ordinary purchaser,[18] and if desires, even if originating in a careful calculation of the satisfaction-potentialities of commodities, may not persist after a change in circumstances has deprived them of their rational basis[19]—a rather formidable series of qualifications. And Marshall, after citing impulse, habit, morbidity, self-abnegation, mistaken expectations, and other possible causes of disparity between desire and satisfaction, concludes that as direct measurement of neither desire nor satisfaction is possible, it is necessary to fall back on price and make it serve, "with all its faults, both for the desires which prompt activities and for the satisfactions which result from them."[20] So also Dickinson cites, with apparent approval, Böhm-Bawerk's justification of the assumption of general harmony between desire and satisfaction on the ground that the causes of disparity "are usually such as cannot be reduced to any general principles, and the undue emphasis of them simply leads to agnosticism."[21]

To assume the lack of disparity between desire and satisfaction is arbitrarily and unwisely to limit the scope of welfare economics. The effects of ignorance on the part of the buyers of the degree of suitability of commodities offered for sale for their intended purposes, the practice of fraud, cunning, misrepresentation on the part of sellers—in fact, the whole problem of unfair methods in trade in so far as the unfairness is to the buyers—these are current evils which would not exist if the as-

---

sensation de la consommation possible à la sensation de la consommation effective, si on considère des actions qui se répètent, et c'est ce que fait l'économie politique, ces deux sensations, en somme, se trouvent dans un rapport constant et tel que, sans erreur grave, la première peut remplacer la seconde."

[18] Cf. F. H. Knight, "Ethics and the Economic Interpretation," *Quarterly Journal of Economics* (May, 1922), pp. 463 ff. for an interpretation of desires for food, shelter, and clothing as desires for a whole set of cultural values rather than desires for mere nourishment, protection from the elements, etc.

[19] Even as pronounced a hedonist as J. S. Mill saw the necessity of this qualification. Cf. his *System of Logic*, 8th ed., Bk. VI, chap. ii, p. 4: "As we proceed in the formation of habits and become accustomed to will a particular act or a particular course of conduct because it is pleasurable, we at last continue to will it without any reference to its being pleasurable. Although, from some change in us or in our circumstances, we have ceased to find any pleasure in the action, or perhaps to anticipate any pleasure as the consequence of it, we still continue to desire the action, and consequently to do it. In this manner it is that habits of hurtful excess continue to be practiced although they have ceased to be pleasurable."

[20] *Principles of Economics*, p. 92, note.

[21] Z. C. Dickinson, *op. cit.*, p. 401.

sumptions of Pigou and of Marshall were in accordance with the facts. There is a range of problems here, not to be dismissed without investigation as unimportant, and, without effort to find uniformities, as unsusceptible to scientific generalization. Is it not probable, for instance, that the modern development of aggressive salesmanship is tending to increase the disparity between desire and satisfaction, and that commodities pushed by intensive methods of selling are overdesired in comparison to the satisfactions they will yield, and play a disproportionate part in the ordinary consumer's budget as compared to the few commodities which are still permitted to make their own appeal? Is it not possible that there is a common underestimate of the contribution which governmental services make to individual welfare, resulting from the favorable advertising which private enterprise provides for its own products—and to the unfavorable advertising which it often spreads with respect to the products of government activity?

In one respect, however, the utility school has made systematic allowance for the disparity between desire and satisfaction, namely, where a substantial interval of time elapses between the experience of the desire and its satisfaction. With the exception of Pantaleoni, who, to preserve inviolate the purity of his hedonic economics, here maintains an elegant consistency,[22] the utility school uniformly recognizes a definite bias in favor of present satisfactions as against satisfactions distant in time. They make this bias, in conjunction with the actuarial allowances for the uncertain duration of life, the risk of changes in wants, and the chances of augmented income in the future, an integral part of their interest theory, as explaining the preference for present over future consumption.[23] The same procedure, if extended to other phases of disparity between desire and satisfaction, would quite conceivably afford a basis for equally serviceable generalizations.

Though we should conclude, in spite of the tendency even of utility theorists to revert to price as a measure of welfare, that price is not an adequate measure, it might be argued that we should, nevertheless, abandon the fruitless search for a practical subjective measure and resort to some objective measure other than price. Such, for instance, seems to be the position of Wesley Mitchell: "In becoming consciously a science of human behavior, economics will lay less stress upon wealth

---

[22] *Pure Economics* (London, 1898), pp. 86 ff. Cf. also Wieser, *Natural Value* (London, 1893), pp. 16 ff.

[23] Pigou also makes some important applications of it to welfare problems, as establishing presumptions in favor of government measures for the conservation of exhaustible resources and against taxation which tends to fall heavily on capital (*op. cit.*, pp. 24 ff.).

and more stress upon welfare. . . . At present welfare thus conceived is rather vague, but it is capable of being made objective and definite in reference to such matters as food, clothing, shelter, sanitation, education, fatigue, leisure."[24] True enough, if taken one at a time, and for one individual at a time, and at a particular moment of time, which, for most practical purposes, means not true at all. What if more or better shelter involves more fatigue? Or what if more food for Jones involves less food for Smith? Or what if more food for Jones now involves less food for Jones next year? An objective criterion of welfare cannot handle problems involving such conflicts of interest without equating them in terms of price. If this is done we are back to wealth as the measure of welfare. And the important and difficult problems of welfare are important and difficult precisely because they arise out of just such conflicts of interest.

WELFARE AS A LONG-RUN CONCEPT

A common shortcoming of the welfare economics of the utility school, and one, moreover, from which their classical predecessors were in large part free,[25] is their typically short-run approach to the problems of economic welfare. It is especially true of the Austrian school that they have restricted their discussion of the realization of utilities from the consumption of transitory goods to the immediately realizable utilities, to the neglect of the consequences for future welfare resulting from such consumption. This preoccupation with the immediate effects of consumption could not be explained away by reference to the assumption of an omniscient economic man, competent adequately to take into account the entire flow of utilities, immediate and prospective, positive and negative, which would result from a given act of consumption, for, as has been shown, even the economic man was not presumed to give adequate weight to future utilities. The explanation probably is to be found in the adequacy for price-economics of a utility concept which expresses only immediate desires, and in the fear of the ethical entanglements which would apparently result from any departure from immediate intensity of desire as an all-sufficient test from the economic point of view of the comparative worth of goods.

The utility concept, however, if given so narrow an interpretation,

---

[24] "The Prospects of Economics" in *The Trend of Economics* (R. G. Tugwell, editor), New York, 1924, p. 31.

[25] Cf., for example, the classical treatment of the effects of high standards of consumption on future population and wages.

cannot adequately serve the needs of a welfare calculus. Consider, for example, this explanation of the meaning of utility from a widely-used text:

> Anything that is capable of satisfying a human want is a good, and possesses utility. We need here to guard against a misunderstanding which the word "utility" might suggest. Utility is the power to satisfy wants, not the power to confer benefits. Cigars are as "useful" in the economic sense as bread or books, for all three satisfy wants. Economic wants may be serious, frivolous, or even positively pernicious, but the objects of these wants all alike possess utility in the economic sense.[26]

If the immediate satisfaction to an individual from the consumption of a given quantity of whiskey and a given quantity of ennobling literature be the same, but if the consumption of whiskey would result in future pains and frustrations for its consumer, whereas the acquisition and study of the good literature would contribute to a happy old age, the economist must, for welfare-calculus purposes, attribute greater utility or greater importance to the books than to the whiskey.[27]

INDIVIDUALISTIC VS. GROUP MEASUREMENT OF UTILITY

Most utility theorists may also justly be charged with failure to distinguish between an individualistic and a group concept of welfare, and to make adequate use of the latter. The "individualistic" concept of welfare may be taken to be that which bases its measurements of welfare solely in terms of the additions to, or the subtractions from, the welfare of the particular individuals, taken one at a time, who are directly affected by the institution or activity under investigation at the moment. A group concept of welfare, on the other hand, would endeavor to take into account the totality of influence, favorable or unfavorable, of such institution or activity on all who are affected thereby, directly

[26] R. T. Ely, *Outlines of Economics* (1920), p. 105. Compare with Marshall's definition: "The total utility of a thing to anyone (that is, the total pleasure *or other benefit* it yields him) . . . ." (*Principles*, p. 93. Italics mine.)

[27] Fetter distinguishes between welfare "in an immediate or narrow sense," as an important factor in the determination of exchange values, and welfare "in a broader and truer sense . . . the abiding condition of well-being" as the important quantity with which welfare economics must concern itself [*Economic Principles* (1915), p. 509]. So also McGoun's distinction between "higher" and "lower" desires ultimately rests on comparisons of the satisfactions derived *in the long run* from their realization [A. F. McGoun, "Higher and Lower Desires," *Quarterly Journal of Economics* (February, 1923), pp. 291 ff.].

or indirectly. It would thus take into account in connection with any particular price-transaction not merely those utilities which influence the determination of that price, but also those utilities, or disutilities, which accrue therefrom to persons who played no direct part in the transaction.

The laissez faire philosophy, with its fundamental assumption of an essential harmony between individual and group interests, covered up the need for a distinction between individual and group welfare, and was itself reinforced by the failure to test actual institutions in terms of such a distinction. But just as there have been few economists who were unqualified exponents of the laissez faire philosophy, so also there have been few economists who have concerned themselves with welfare problems as such without at times applying the group standard in their welfare appraisals. With but rare exceptions, however, welfare economists of the utility school confined their use of the group standard to problems which affected groups of persons *en masse* and could not possibly be handled in terms of solitary individuals. The entire range of economic activities which were wholly or mainly under the governance of the price system and of the principle of free contract, such as buying and selling, hiring and firing, saving and spending, assumption and avoidance of risk, they appraised solely in terms of an individualistic analysis. They took it for granted that every freely contracted purchase-and-sale transaction brought gain to each of the two active participants, not only disregarding, as we have seen, the effects of ignorance and fraud on the part of one or the other of these participants, but overlooking the possibility that economic transactions may have vital bearing on the welfare of persons not directly concerned therewith, and failing to perceive that mere disparity in bargaining power might lead to exploitation of one party to a "free" contract by the other, even though both were honest, equally intelligent, and equally well-informed.[28]

Nevertheless, even when the utility theorists used an individualistic test of welfare, there was throughout their discussion the implication,

---

[28] Recognition of the importance of disparity in bargaining power as affecting the terms of the wage contract, and consequently the expediency of adherence to a policy of strict laissez faire, is lacking in even so late a work as W. S. Jevons, *The State in Relation to Labor*, London, 1887. See p. 42: "Laissez faire policy might still be maintained [i.e., wisely and justly] if everybody understood his interests." But even during the period of undisputed sway of the classical economics among the learned there was a current tendency in the business and political world even to exaggerate the extent to which superiority of financial resources could determine the outcome of commercial competition, to the disregard of community interests and of genuine advantages in productive efficiency (cf. my *Dumping: A Problem in International Trade*, p. 46).

either clearly expressed or readily to be inferred, that it was the welfare of the group which was important, and the welfare of individuals as comprising in their aggregate the group. And in dealing with matters of governmental policy, and especially in their support of specific departures from the laissez faire policy and in their treatment of the problems of government finance, they wholly abandoned the individualistic standard. These problems could not be handled at all in terms of the welfare of individuals taken singly, either because it was too obvious to be overlooked that an activity which would bring profit to some might injure others, or because these problems concerned benefits of an intangible and indivisible sort, accruing to the community as a whole and not imputable in measurable proportions to particular individuals. They here used a group standard of welfare, though there is little evidence in their writings that they were conscious of their change in standards as they proceeded from the discussion of problems of free contract to the treatment of the relationship between government and its citizens.[29]

UTILITY ANALYSIS AS CAPITALISTIC APOLOGETICS

In its early stages of development the utility analysis was made use of to explode the Marxian surplus-value theory. It was, consequently, charged by the Socialists with being merely a retreat by orthodox economics to a new line of defense made necessary by the successful Marxian attack on the classical argument for laissez faire.[30] In recent years it has again been attacked, and by learned economists who are themselves fully equipped with the traditions and the technique of the orthodox doctrines, as by its nature necessarily leading to a capitalistic apologetics. The grounds upon which this modern attack is based can be adequately indicated by citations from two of the foremost critics. "Political economy," writes J. M. Clark, "does not defend the existing system, but it selects for explanation the elements of cooperation in it, which are the elements that everybody approves of. The Austrian theory . . . is relevant to these good elements in the existing system, and it is not *positively and constructively* relevant to any other side of the

[29] Cf., however, F. von Wieser, *Natural Value* (London, 1893), pp. 228–42, for a discussion of the differences in standards actually operative as between the realm of free contract and the sphere of government activity, and for further elaboration of these differences, his "Theorie der gesellschaftlichen Wirtschaft," in *Grundriss der Sozialökonomik* (2d ed., Tubengen, 1924), Vol. I, Part II, pp. 292–302.

[30] Cf. H. M. Hyndman, *The Economics of Socialism* (London, 1896), chap. vii.

case."[31] "The study of utility seems to be oriented by the question: To what is value equal? rather than by the broader question: How does value function in relation to human wants?"[32] "When theory has studied the meaning of value in terms of utility, its very attitude and inquiry have presupposed an equilibrium between utilities, and thus have been oriented by a static point of view and static assumptions. The emancipated counterpart of this equilibrium inquiry is a study of the entire process of economic guidance, in which the utility theory appears as an interpretation of one phase only of guidance by one agency only, viz., the static or the hedonistic phase of guidance which falls within the requirements of a theory of equilibrium."[33] "That economic theorist," says Hamilton, "is indeed an expert at logomachy who can use a nomenclature of 'utility,' 'disutility,' and 'productivity' and yet hedge the words about in such a way that he escapes the implication of making the system of prices as a whole represent such a use of limited resources in satisfying wants as to insure to society the greatest surplus of utility over disutility."[34]

Clark is obviously making a tacit assumption that utility analysis has been strictly confined within the limits of price economics, and he attributes to the utility school as a whole and as a logically inevitable outcome of its mode of analysis a restricted scope of inquiry and a type of conclusion therefrom which fairly characterizes only some of its exponents. Hamilton's assertion that only by word-juggling can utility analysis avoid leading to a defense of the status quo puts the cart before the horse, for it is only by word-juggling that utility theorists have avoided facing the serious questioning of the status quo which the utility analysis logically leads to. The utility analysis yields different products to different men. Most of its exponents may probably be rightly classed as conservative in their outlook on economic problems, and some of them have unquestionably used the utility theory to support their faith in the goodness of things as they are. Others of its exponents have been radicals, and have found the utility analysis a serviceable weapon in

[32] "Economic Theory in an Era of Social Readjustment," *American Economic Review Supplement* (March, 1919), p. 284. Italics his.

[32] "Economic Theory in an Era of Social Readjustment," *American Ecoonmic Review Supplement* (March, 1919), p. 289. This contrasts with Knight's complaint that utility tends to become an ethical concept, and to take us "from the realm of fact to that of what ought to be" ("Normal Price in Value and Distribution," *Quarterly Journal of Economics,* November, 1917, p. 67).

[33] "Economics and Modern Psychology," *Journal of Political Economy* (January, 1918), p. 3. Cf. Wieser, "Value in the Economy of the State," *Natural Value,* Bk. V.

[34] W. H. Hamilton, "The Place of Value Theory in Economics," *Journal of Political Economy* (April, 1918), p. 392.

their assaults upon private property and the capitalistic organization of society.[35] It is altogether questionable that the utility school as a group has been more ardent in its defense of things as they are than its classical predecessors, and it seems apparent that utility analysis, if applied in the field of welfare economics, makes defense of laissez faire and eulogy of the capitalistic system more, rather than less, difficult than it would be to an economics written wholly in pecuniary terms.

I have already argued that much of what passes for utility theory is really objective price-theory presented in the purloined terminology of subjective analysis, and that it was by reversion in fact to price-calculus, while maintaining the semblance of subjective calculus, that many utility theorists managed to avoid dealing with the less pleasing aspects of private property and the unrestrained operation of the profit motive. But in spite of the generally conservative tendencies of the utility economists and the selective discrimination with which they chose the problems to be subjected to the utility analysis,[36] the utility theory seems on the whole to have shaken, rather than strengthened, their belief in the virtues of the existing economic organization.[37] It was not wholly without basis that J. S. Nicholson, in 1894, in his presidential address before the economics section of the British Association for the Advancement of Science, warned his audience that the new-fangled diminishing utility and maximum satisfaction doctrines were leading economists to socialism and away from the rock-ribbed individualism of the classical economics.[38] The utility theory is a mode of analysis, not a set of conclusions, and what conclusions will be reached by it will depend on the character and the fullness of the data to which it is applied and the skill and honesty with which it is used.[39] It would be trite, were it not for the extent to which the principle *Maledicti sunt qui ante nos nostra dixerunt* seems to pervade certain phases of recent American economic theorizing, to suggest the possibility that some, at least, of the

[35] Cf. especially Adolphe Landry's *L'Utilité Sociale de la Propriété Individuelle,* Paris, 1901, where a vigorous attack on private property by means of price analysis is intensified in the second half of the book by the application of the utility analysis.

[36] Rather than, as Clark puts it, the selective character of the technique itself.

[37] Compare, for example, Edgeworth's *Mathematical Psychics,* or the concluding chapter of Wieser's *Natural Value,* or in this country, Fetter's or Davenport's writings, with the typical surviving expositions of pre-utility economics.

[38] *Report of Sixty-third Meeting* (London, 1894), pp. 843 ff.

[39] Cf. W. C. Mitchell, "Wieser's Theory of Social Economics," *Political Science Quarterly* (March, 1917), p. 111: "[The utility theory] has been . . . adopted as a substitute for Marxism by one set of socialists and decried as a covert defense of the established order by another set."

older utility theorists applied the analysis honestly, and that intellectual curiosity occasionally got the best of social bias with the others.

PRACTICABILITY OF A SUBJECTIVE CALCULUS

The advocate of a subjective calculus of welfare encounters the objection that it is not possible to measure subjective quantities, whether they be desires, satisfactions, pleasures, or pains, except through their objective manifestations in price offers or other types of behavior. I believe the answer lies in the fact that we all do repeatedly measure desires and satisfactions as such, our own and those of other persons, and that much of our family relations, our contacts with our friends and neighbors, and the relations of government with its citizens are actually guided, whether well or ill, by such calculations. Such calculations of subjective quantities may never be exact, and may often be grossly inaccurate, but they can, and often must, be made in the absence of means to more precise measurement. Moreover, no one asks that economics abandon the pecuniary calculus and substitute therefor a purely subjective one. For many purposes the pecuniary calculus serves all needs. In any case, it is an institutional fact, an important force in human behavior and in the guidance of economic activity, and must be fully reckoned with by the economist. But for many purposes the pecuniary calculus is a grossly imperfect instrument whose results require modification by calculations of subjective quantities before they can serve as an acceptable guide to action or to understanding.

The subjective type of measurement cannot, at least not as yet, yield absolute quantities as its product. The most it can attain is the discovery of more-or-less relationships, and even that with a very small degree of reliability. But there is a wide range of human activity in which only imperfect instruments are available with which to guide conduct toward perfection. Those who insist that welfare economics confine itself to measurement in terms of prices, because prices are data for statistical investigation, whereas the subjective conditions reflected by prices are not, have succumbed to an all-too-prevalent methodological fanaticism which prefers the accurate but superficial to the approximate but fundamental, and which makes adaptability to its special technique of investigation, rather than importance, the standard for the selection of problems and the delimitation of the scope of inquiry. Statistics is a tool, not an end. The imperfect measurement of variations in welfare may serve as a better guide to action than the perfect measurement of something which has something to do with welfare.

THE FOUNDATIONS OF
ECONOMIC ANALYSIS

(WELFARE ECONOMICS)

Paul A. Samuelson

Beginning as it did in the writings of philosophers, theologians, pamphleteers, special pleaders, and reformers, economics has always been concerned with problems of public policy and welfare. And at least from the time of the physiocrats and Adam Smith there has never been absent from the main body of economic literature the feeling that in some sense perfect competition represented an optimal situation. Of course, over time the exact form of this doctrine has undergone modification (not always in any one direction), and there is considerable diversity in the attempted proofs (in the amazingly few places where rigorous proof was attempted).

Although this doctrine is often thought to be conservative or reactionary in its implication and to reflect the "kept" status of the economist, it is important to emphasize that it was "radical" in the eighteenth century, and there is some evidence from events of the last decades (e.g., the T.N.E.C. and economists' role and views with respect to Anti-Trust) that it has become a thorn in the side of what are usually thought of as conservative interests. Furthermore, some Socialist writers, who in their youth became interested in analytical economics, find in this doctrine a possible device for expediting planning in a socialized state.

Early uncritical allegiance to this doctrine arose in part from the understandable eighteenth-century tendency to find teleological significance in the workings of what is after all an equilibrium system which is not devoid of aesthetic content regarded simply as a mechanism.[1] But it would be unfair to the older economists to believe that

---

[1] It would be out of place here to discuss the relationship of this doctrine to that of "natural rights"; to that of competition as an immutable law with which man cannot interfere even if he should wish to; to the inverted doctrine of natural

---

Source: Chapter VIII, pages 203–253, Harvard University Press, 1953. Reprinted with permission.

their case ended with a simple argument from design, even if such a charge can be sustained with respect to certain Epigoni.

This can best be seen in the writings on International Trade where the issue of the tariff brings out most clearly the welfare and policy beliefs of economists, even down to the present day. For free trade is but one dramatic exemplification of pure competition, and in this field formal attempts at proof were made, or we can at least in many cases piece together the implicit beliefs of the author.

1. Perhaps the most common reason for believing competition to be optimal stemmed from the recognition that no party could be hurt by exchange as compared to his position before trade, since he could always refuse to trade. *Thus, trade is better than no trade; exchange is mutually beneficial; one party does not gain what the other loses.* If we examine the argument carefully, we find that it does not really imply that pure competition is optimal, even though properly interpreted it can provide a case against *prohibitive tariffs*.

2. A second more sophisticated argument, which includes the first and more, rests upon the fact that the equilibrium position reached in pure competition represents an optimum for each individual, consistent with his original endowment of commodities and the market situation with which he is confronted. But every individual may be making the best of a situation without implying that that best is very good or is optimal; although each individual in pure competition takes price as given, for the market it is a variable, and it is quite possible that conditions other than pure competition might lead to better results in terms of any of the usual ethical notions. But, leaving aside all ethical notions, is it not equally clear that under (say) monopoly, both buyer and seller are doing the best that they can for themselves under existing market situations? The only distinguishing feature of pure competition, as compared to any other mode of behavior, is that the market conditions facing each individual are taken (by him) to be "straight lines" involving trade at unchanging price ratios. And it is precisely the question of the sense in which this is optimal which is left unanswered.

It does not appear that Walras ever reached beyond this second stage

---

selection whereby the results of competition were judged to be best by means of a circular definition of the "fittest" as those who survive; to the Malthusian view that hardship and competition are necessary to bring out the "best" in a man; to the view that competition was good enough for our predecessors and therefore good enough for us; and other arguments designed to preserve the *status quo*.

of the argument.[2] His cardinal failing consists not so much in the fact that he jumps from incomplete premises to sweeping conclusions, but in the fact that he is satisfied with this very limited kind of an optimum, which by a play on words he seems to confuse with the more usual and important senses in which perfect competition is conceived to be optimal.[3]

3. Still a third stage of reasoning attempts to show, *not* that *each* individual is made best off by competition since this is impossible unless each can take all, but that in some sense the sum total of satisfactions is maximized, that perfect competition effects an ideal compromise of mutual benefit, or in its most nebulous form that free trade (perfect competition) maximizes world (all individuals') *income.* Of course, this involves the notion of adding the utilities of different individuals, of somehow being able to compare and weight the utilities of different individuals. Although the marginal utility economists, with the exception of Jevons who made an interesting slip in connection with the concept of the utility of the "trading body," knew that it was not necessary to make interpersonal comparisons of utility in describing exchange under pure competition, they nevertheless did not have the modern reticence about making such assumptions.

Launhardt seems to have been the only economist who attempted to give rigorous proof of this theorem. As Wicksell has pointed out in the section just cited, his argument is mathematically and logically false. Yet he must be given credit for having made an attempt at rigor, and we can learn more from his unambiguous failure than from many pages of fuzzy literary effusion.

To many modern economists the difficulty with this third line of reasoning lies in the fact that it assumes that the utilities of different individuals can be compared, in fact added together. This they would regard

[2] Compare the very penetrating remarks of Wicksell on this point. K. Wicksell, *Lectures on Political Economy* (English translation, New York: Macmillan, 1934), I, 72–83.

[3] If interpreted literally, he would seem to imply that each and every person is made better off by perfect competition, a conclusion which, as Wicksell observes, goes farther than the free traders themselves, "for the latter have not denied that a restriction of free competition might be most advantageous to a small privileged minority." *Ibid.,* p. 76.

Actually there is one qualification in Walras' argument which makes it not so much wrong as trivial. He maintains that perfect competition creates a maximum of satisfaction, *consistent with trading at uniform prices.* Waiving the trivial objection that under nondiscriminating monopoly trading is also done at uniform prices, I find this confusing. Except for positions of multiple equilibria which we may provisionally ignore, the equilibrium position under competition is uniquely determined. Instead of being the *optimum* condition under these conditions, it is the only one possible. Thus, it is the worst position as well as the best.

as "unscientific." But to the preceding generation of economists, inter-individual comparisons of utility were made almost without question; to a man like Edgeworth, steeped as he was in the Utilitarian tradition, individual utility—nay social utility—was as real as his morning jam. And with Marshall the apostrophe in consumers' surplus was always after the *s*.

Both Marshall and Wicksell objected to what they considered to be a prevalent notion that perfect competition leads to the maximum of satisfaction. Both enter as a minor objection the fact that there may be multiple positions of equilibrium; actually this is largely irrelevant since each stable equilibrium might be a relative maximum as compared to points in its immediate neighborhood (*im kleinen*) even if it were not the *maximum maximorum*. But their major objection consists in the fact that with existing distributions of wealth and ability, the processes of imputation under competition will give rise to great inequalities in the personal distribution of income so that unless individuals are very different in their natures the marginal utilities of income will not be equal for each individual. Both recognize that in these circumstances any interference (à la Robin Hood) with perfect competition which transfers income from rich to poor would be beneficial.

4. It might be thought that at this stage Marshall and Wicksell would enunciate a fourth proposition, that exchange under perfect competition is optimal provided the distribution of income is optimal. In the case of Wicksell the proof which he gives (*Lectures*, p. 80) to show why perfect competition is *not* optimal when the distribution of income is inappropriate paves the way for a proof as to why perfect competition is optimal when the distribution of income is appropriate.[4] Wicksell also realizes that when the distribution of income is not optimal, the creation of a condition of imperfect competition may improve the situation, but that this is not the best way of improving the situation, since perfect competition is a necessary condition to "maximize production." I return to this point a little later in this historical review.

Although inappropriateness in distribution is thought by Marshall to

---

[4] Actually his proof seems to suffer from one minor drawback. In effect, his evaluation of the change in utility resulting from a change in price from the competitive level assumes that in the noncompetitive situation all individuals are still on their offer curves. Strictly speaking, this is not possible. It would perhaps be correct to say that his proof (with slight modifications) shows that transfer of goods or income from one individual to another could not improve the competitive conditions. There is also an unfortunate minor slip in expression, perhaps in translation, in the statement that "free competition would secure a maximum satisfaction *to all* parties to the exchange." (Ibid, p. 81, my italics.) Actually, it is the sum of all and not the utility *of each* that is maximized.

render the competitive position suspect, he was of the belief that many decisions involve alternatives which affect all classes more or less equally. He has been criticized for this too facile assumption, but it is nevertheless true that many modern economists, and this includes some purists, by use of the principle of sufficient reason (or is it insufficient reason?) argue in such terms for or against a price change of a commodity which is not presumed to relate more to the poor than to the rich.

However, aside from problems raised by the inappropriateness of the distribution of income, Marshall had important objections to the equilibrium position realized under perfect competition. These objections resulted from his analysis of consumers' surplus, an analysis which was regarded as almost the most significant contribution of his *Principles*. By a comparison of geometrical areas he arrived at the conclusion that increasing cost industries would be pushed to too great a margin under competition, and that the output of decreasing cost industries would be too small under competition. From the modern standpoint it is clear that these conclusions are true in only a very limited sense. And if Marshall did arrive at conclusions which are not completely wrong, it is nevertheless clear that he arrived at them for the wrong reasons.

It is not easy in a few paragraphs to delineate the various faults in the Marshallian reasoning. In the first place, his exposition in Book V, chapter xiii, is extremely sketchy, and, in the second place, it is impossible to avoid the somewhat extraneous difficulties arising from the admittedly unsatisfactory treatment of decreasing cost by Marshall. However, the latter is simply the most dramatic exemplification of the paradox that Marshall, with whom the doctrines of partial equilibrium and industry analysis are inseparably associated, nowhere presents a complete or satisfactory theory of the industry in its relationship to the firms which make it up. If anyone doubts this, he need only compare the treatment of these problems by Pigou, Marshall's shining pupil, in his 1912 *Wealth and Welfare* with his treatment in the late editions of the *Economics of Welfare* or with that of Viner in the *Zeitschrift* article cited in chapter iii.

Another inadequacy, but one that can be easily remedied, lies in the fact that Marshall neglects producers' surplus instead of treating this symmetrically with consumers' surplus, so that it is possible by the reasoning of page 468, footnote 2, to arrive at the curious conclusion that industries of increasing costs should in many cases be contracted even if there are no decreasing cost industries to expand.

There seems to be no point in discussing the Marshallian reasoning at greater length except to note that Pigou nowhere makes essential use of the concept of consumers' surplus in his welfare analysis. He originally enunciated essentially the Marshallian conditions with respect to increasing and decreasing cost industries, but as a result of the criticisms of Allyn Young, Knight, and Robertson he seriously modified these conclusions.[5] In its final form his doctrine holds that the equilibrium of a closed economy under competition is correct except where there are technological external economies or diseconomies. Under these conditions, since each individual's actions have effects on others which he does not take into account in making his decision, there is a *prima facie* case for intervention. But this holds only for technological factors (smoke nuisance, etc.); changes in factor prices resulting from the expansion of demand by firms in an industry represent transfers which are irrelevant for determination of ideal output. (In all fairness it should be admitted that the correct use of consumers' surplus and producers' surplus might have helped to avoid error in this regard.)

There would be no reason to rake over these old ashes were it not for the fact that Professor Hicks has recently lent the weight of his authority to the view that the doctrine of consumers' surplus has a claim to importance in the welfare field.[6] As I have indicated in chapter vii, careful perusal of his argument simply confirms my belief that the economist—mathematical, literary, beginner, expert—had best dispense with consumers' surplus. It is a tool which can be used only by one who can get along without its use, and not by all such. As Hicks admits, it is not useful in the exposition of the conditions of "equilibrium" or "optimum." And even in the case of a Crusoe economy where the problems raised by many individuals can be sidestepped, it is usually only devised to give the loss in utility resulting from a deviation from the optimum in the amount of one good.

In this connection its principal conclusion states that the (second order) change in utility resulting from a deviation in the amount of one commodity, other commodities continuing to be optimally adjusted, depends upon the amount of the discrepancy in that good times the discrepancy in the equilibrium condition. This conclusion is no more plausibly derived from consumers' surplus than from simple intuition. And if one probes deeper, one finds in any case that the theorem is incorrect

[5] F. H. Knight, "Fallacies in the Interpretation of Social Cost," *Quarterly Journal of Economics* (1923). Reprinted in *The Ethics of Competition* (New York: Harper, 1935), pp. 215–236. Allyn Young, "Pigou's Wealth and Welfare," *Quarterly Journal of Economics*, XXVII (1913), 672–686. D. H. Robertson, "Those Empty Boxes," *Economic Journal*, XXXIV (1924), 16–31.

[6] J. R. Hicks, "The Rehabilitation of Consumers' Surplus," *Review of Economic Studies*, VIII (1941), 108–116.

even to the order of infinitesimals (second) at which the argument is pitched.

Thus in the most favorable case to consumers' surplus where one commodity, x_{n+1}, has literally constant marginal utility so that

$$U = L(x_1, x_2, \cdots, x_n) + mx_{n+1},\qquad(1)$$

and where the goods can be converted into each other at constant technological rates as indicated by the relation

$$\sum_1^{n+1} b_i x_i = c,\qquad(2)$$

for this conclusion to be correct it would be necessary that the change in utility resulting from a small change in the amount of x_1 be

$$\delta^2 U = 0 + \tfrac{1}{2} L_{11} \delta x_1{}^2.\qquad(3)$$

Actually, by a simple extension of the reasoning in chapter iii, it is given by

$$\delta^2 U = 0 + \tfrac{1}{2} \sum_1^n \sum_1^n L_{ij} \delta x_i \delta x_j.\qquad(4)$$

If we proceed to higher orders of infinitesimals, the case is worse, and the same can be said if we drop the unrealistic assumption about the utility of the numeraire, and if the original position is not one of equilibrium.

Even if consumers' surplus did give a cardinal measure of the change in utility from a given change, it is hard to see what use this could serve. Only in the contemplation of alternative movements which begin or end in the same point could this cardinal measure have any significance, and then only because it is an indicator of ordinal preference. Such situations are comparatively rare as far as questions of social policy are concerned, being in the nature of the somewhat academic question as to whether the introduction of a little monopoly evil into one industry, all others being competitive before and after the change, is better or worse than introduction of some monopoly in another.

In connection with monopolistic competition the frequent occurrence of decreasing cost and indivisible initial costs inevitably raises problems of an "all or none" character. Waiving the difficulties arising from many individuals, we see that correct decisions necessitate reference to ordinal indifference curves and to nothing else. Certain difficulties connected with the determination of the optimal amount of differentiation of product were properly posed by Chamberlin, Cassels, and Kahn without the use of consumers' surplus.[7]

We may conclude from this lengthy digression that after making due allowances for external economies and for certain omissions in their expositions, the founders of neo-classical economics believed that perfect competition led to an optimum in "exchange and production" provided that the distribution of income was appropriate. But they did not believe that incomes imputed by the competitive process as of a given historical distribution of ownership of factors of production and personal abilities was in any sense the best one, and not subject to modification by appropriate mechanisms.

5. Before analyzing the problems encountered under the headings of optimum "production" and optimum "exchange," I should like to note briefly the existence of economists who attempted to establish the stronger position that incomes imputed under competition were actually right and best. Thus at an earlier date, Bastiat, whose powers of analysis were hardly of the highest order even in his way, hoped to show that beneficient competition would lead to ". . . an amount of utility and enjoyment, always greater, and more and more equally distributed. . . ."[8]

Confronted with the undeniable fact of considerable inequality of income and possessing the latent Western European prejudice against inequality, writers had either to refer to a future day when competition would achieve better results, or attribute existing inequalities to the admittedly large institutional deviations from competition, or to look for inequalities among individuals' characteristics (including property ownership) to justify differences in income.

To anyone with knowledge of the world the perverse relationship between exertion and income made necessary a revision of the classical real cost doctrine in its simplest form, although the promotion by Senior of abstinence to the rank of a full-bodied real cost helped to bolster that doctrine. But ultimately refuge was found in the undeniable fact of differences in personal "ability" and the related doctrine of noncompeting groups. This raised many questions as to the extent to which the relevant abilities were or were not "acquired characteristics" and the degree of correspondence between the distribution of abilities and

---

[7] E. H. Chamberlin, *The Theory of Monopolistic Competition* (3rd ed.; Cambridge: Harvard University Press, 1938), p. 94. J. M. Cassels, "Excess Capacity and Monopolistic Competition," *Quarterly Journal of Economics*, LI (1937), 426–443. R. F. Kahn, "Some Notes on Ideal Output," *Economic Journal*, XLV (1935), 1–35.

[8] F. Bastiat, *Harmonies of Political Economy* (2nd ed.; Edinburgh, 1880), p. 301.

income. That much of this discussion was meaningless and from most points of view irrelevant does not detract from its significance from the standpoint of the history of ideas.

Among analytical economists J. B. Clark[9] is best known for his belief that not only will factors of production have imputed to them their marginal productivity under competition, but that this is a "natural law" which is "morally justifiable" since this is their "actual," "specific" product. Indeed Clark himself considered that the principal way that his independently discovered marginal productivity doctrine represented an improvement upon von Thünen lay in his demonstration of its ethical fairness as compared to the latter's belief that the doctrine involved exploitation. That Clark, who clearly states the distinction between personal and functional income, should have thought that he had proved the ethical fairness of income determination under competition is simply a reflection of the fact that where emotional beliefs in right and wrong enter into analysis, it is usually not to the advantage of the latter. As we shall see, even if all income resulted from personal services, Clark's proposition is not consistent with widely held ethical views; and if it is accepted as a definition rather than a theorem, it will be found to be consistent with *no* unambiguous ethical evaluation of different individuals' welfare. Nevertheless, it has considerable appeal, especially in a frontier society, where each individual could be thought of as working by himself under conditions where "his" product could be identified. Analytically, it is almost precisely in these terms that Clark first perceived his doctrine, going with painful slowness from the (broad) "zone of indifference" to the concept of the internal margin.

6. While Wicksell and Marshall held that competition would be optimal if the distribution of income were appropriate, it was left for Pareto[10] to take the stronger position that competition produces a *maximum d'utilité collective* regardless of the distribution of income, and indeed even if the utilities of different individuals were not considered to be comparable. *An optimum position in this sense was defined by the requirement that there should not exist any possible variation or movement which would make everybody better off.*

His discussion is not easy to follow, and it has not received attention from economists commensurate with the importance which he attached to it. Yet it forms the basis of many modern notions, and it led directly to the important contribution of Barone. Pareto also seems to have been one of the first to discuss criteria of planning under collectivism.

[9] J. B. Clark, *The Distribution of Wealth*, (New York, 1899).
[10] V. Pareto, *Manuel D'Economie Politique* (1909), chap. vi; also the Mathematical Appendix, par. 89, *passim*.

Pareto's exposition is complicated by the fact that he works with differentials or first order (infinitesimal) variations. This was a very common practice with mathematicians and physicists of the nineteenth century, and because of its formal heuristic conveniences is still often used today. And under proper qualifications this practice can be given a rigorous, unambiguous basis. Nevertheless, where delicate problems of interpretation are involved it often obscures more than it reveals, especially if the problem arises as to whether any given differential expression is an "exact" differential.

Pareto is unwilling to add the utility or *ophelimité* of different individuals together, either *in toto*, i.e. $(U^1 + U^2 \cdots)$, or for small variations $(\delta U^1 + \delta U^2 + \cdots)$. For that would involve a comparison of different individuals' utility, and in addition it would depend upon the particular cardinal index of *ophelimité* selected for each. But he was interested in comparing the summed variation in the utility of each, after these expressions have been divided by the marginal utility of any one good, a, selected as numeraire. For if we examine the dimensionality of the expression

$$\frac{1}{U_a{}^1}\, \delta U^1 + \frac{1}{U_a{}^2}\, \delta U^2 + \cdots , \tag{5}$$

where as usual subscripts represent partial differentiation, but where the superscript is taken to indicate different individuals, we shall see that this has the dimensionality of the good, a, and nothing else.

Pareto attempts to show that if the orginal position is one of equilibrium under perfect competition, then no possible variations, consistent with the fundamental scarcity of goods and given technology, can make the above expression positive. If it could, he says, it would be possible to arrange things so that each term in the expression could be made positive, and then everyone would be better off. But the expression *cannot* be made positive. Actually, regarded as a differential expression (of the first order), the above expression can be shown to be zero, in consequence of the fact that each commodity is sold at minimum unit cost (proportionality of marginal products, etc.,[11] and in consequence of the tangency of each individual's indifference curves to mutual price exchange loci. If recourse is had to differentials of higher order, the secondary maximum-minimum conditions of firms and individuals will guarantee that the expression (5) will be negative for all finite deviations from the competitive position, or so Pareto attempted to show.

Although Pareto's treatment is somewhat sketchy and in need of ex-

[11] *Ibid.*, p. 646.

pansion, part of which Barone later provided, the main outlines are reasonably clear. But in connection with the fundamentals of interpretation of the significance of his maximum, there do arise certain problems. First, can the differential expression of (5) be regarded as the exact differential of some expression? Actually, Pareto later gives a name to this expression, calling it δU; but is there an expression U (social utility?) of which this is an exact differential? Pareto does not tell us, but presumably he would answer, no, if he were on guard when the question was asked. As we shall see, Barone does work with an expression whose differential corresponds to (5), but he clearly recognizes that it is a construction, not involving the dimension of utility, but rather that of the numeraire good.

But the most important objection to Pareto's exposition is his lack of emphasis upon the fact that an optimum point, in his sense, is not a unique point.[12] If transfers of income from one individual to another are arbitrarily imposed, there will be a new optimum point, and there is absolutely no way of deciding whether the new point is better or worse than the old. His optimum points constitute a manifold infinity of values. This locus can be obtained under regimes quite different from perfect competition (e.g., by multilateral monopoly). Within Pareto's system it is impossible to decide, by his differential criterion or otherwise, which of two points on what may be called the "generalized contract locus" are better, or even that a given movement off the contract locus and hence to a non-optimal point is good or bad. Actually in terms of the wider reference schemes of ordinary economic thought, such a movement may be deemed eminently desirable. But Pareto shows that however desirable such a move may be, there exists still a better move, which for the same (ordinal) amount of harm to those who "should" be harmed, will yield more benefit for the worthy ones who are to be benefited. This is an important contribution.

7. In a masterly article, written in 1908 in Italian, but not translated into English until 1935,[13] Barone developed further and in greater detail the Paretian conditions of optimum, especially as they relate to the planning of production under collectivism. By avoiding all mention of utility and indeed without introducing even the notion of indifference curves, Barone was able to break new ground along lines which have in

---

[12] In his earlier *Cours* discussion, II, 90 ff., he explicitly assumes the distribution of income to be *"convenable,"* but in his later *Manuel* treatment the dependence of the optimum point on the initial distribution of income, and hence its lack of uniqueness, is not brought to the foreground.

[13] Reprinted as an Appendix in F. A. Hayek, ed., *Collectivist Economic Planning* (London: Routledge, 1935), pp. 245–290.

recent years become associated with the economic theory of index numbers.

Unlike most of the writers discussed above, Barone is unsatisfied with the statement that free competition maximizes product, or sums of product, which can then be distributed in any given fashion. Heterogeneous products cannot be added. Furthermore, leisure may be preferred to the maximization of output. It is significant that those writers who do not explicitly introduce the equations of general equilibrium should gloss over the definition of "product" which is allegedly maximized. Thus, Wicksell[14] confines his demonstration to a case where the same product can be provided by different sources, and only in this case shows that various marginal conditions are optimal. The same is true of the very excellent treatment by Knight, in which the movement of goods over alternative roads is analyzed for optimum conditions.[15]

It is remarkable that Professor Pigou, who reaches substantially correct conclusions, never squarely meets the problem of the definition of social product. His index number discussion represents an important contribution in its own right, but it is offered at best as an approximate criterion or indicator of changes in individual and social welfare. He would not seriously suggest that the thing to be maximized is the money value of output deflated by an ideal index of prices. Nor will the more exact limits of index number theory such as are discussed in chapter vi avail.

Barone proposes to add different products after they have been weighted by their respective prices; it is usually taken to be convenient to express these prices as ratios to the numeraire good, a. For Barone, productive services can be treated simply as algebraically negative goods and services. Thus, decisions between more or less work can be included in his welfare system. Then if the sum total of each good consumed by all individuals together is written as

$$A = a^1 + a^2 + \cdots$$
$$B = b^1 + b^2 + \cdots \tag{6}$$
$$\text{etc.,}$$

and recalling that

$$\delta U^i = U_a{}^i \delta_a{}^i + U_b{}^i \delta b^i + \cdots, \tag{7}$$

we can write Pareto's equation (5) above in the equivalent form

$$1(\delta a^1 + \delta a^2 + \cdots) + \rho_b(\delta b^1 + \delta b^2 + \cdots) + \cdots$$
$$= \delta A + \rho_b \delta B + \cdots \tag{8}$$

[14] Wicksell, op. cit., p. 140, passim.
[15] Knight, op. cit., p. 219.

In passing from (4) to (8), use is made of the fact that the ratios of marginal utilities of two goods for each individual are equal to their price ratios. Barone himself does not use this terminology, but no doubt he would have to if the connection with Pareto were to be shown.

The expression in (8) can be regarded as the variation in the following expression when prices are regarded as constants:

$$\Phi = A + \rho_b B + \cdots . \tag{9}$$

If productive services were known to be constant so that they could be neglected, (9) would equal (except for dynamic factors involving capital which we can ignore) money value of national product. If all productive factors are included, it will represent the net difference between value of consumers' goods and the return to productive services. Under many assumptions this quantity must be zero under the full conditions of perfect competition.

Barone shows that perfect competition maximizes this expression, prices being taken as fixed parameters, i.e., any variation from a condition of price equal to minimum cost must make $\delta\Phi$ as given in (8) negative. Thus, if we are at conditions other than perfect competition, with (8) not equal to zero for all possible variations, it will be possible to specify a movement which will make $\delta\Phi$ positive. But we can think of $\delta\Phi$ as being made up of the sum of a similar expression referring to each individual

$$\delta\Phi = \delta_\varphi{}^1 + \delta_\varphi{}^2 + \cdots = (\delta a^1 + \rho_b \delta b^1 + \cdots) \\ + (\delta a^2 + \rho_b \delta b^2 + \cdots) + \cdots . \tag{10}$$

If for any movement, the total $\delta\Phi$ is positive, it is not necessary that each and every one of the individual's δ_φ be positive; but it is necessary that those which are positive should outweight those which are negative. Thus, those who are hurt could be compensated by those who are helped, and there would still be a net gain left to be parceled out among the individuals.

This is essentially the gist of the Barone argument. The one point which will occur to the critical reader is the fact that arbitrary prices are assumed in evaluating the expression to be maximized. Which prices are to be used? Barone employs the prices which prevailed before a contemplated break with the conditions of competition are made, and this suffices if one merely wishes to demonstrate that not all individuals can be improved by any departure from competition.[16]

[16] Actually, Barone discusses varying prices in a passage which seems obscure to me. *Op. cit.*, p. 255.

Unlike Pareto, Barone satisfies himself with deriving optimal *production* conditions without going into the fact that under competition no additional individual exchanges of fixed amounts of goods would be mutually profitable. No doubt this oversight resulted from his wish to avoid the use of indifference curves and utility, but even without these constructions, by the use of the index number notions which he pioneered, the enlarged conditions of exchange could have been included. It is a tribute to this work that a third of a century after it was written there is no better statement of the problem in the English language to which the attention of students may be turned.

8. The next writer who deserves our attention is A. P. Lerner, who comparatively recently developed, presumably independently, the Paretian conditions which show that the marginal equivalences realized by perfect competition lead to an optimum of production and exchange in the special senses discussed above.[17] Actually, in the field of production his statement of the problem is slightly different from that of Pareto and Barone. They showed that a movement to conditions of perfect competition in the field of production and cost could make everyone better off because they could be given more of every good. But they still worked with individuals. Even in a collectivized state where the existence of the individual is not assumed, the Lerner formulation of the sense in which output is optimal would still hold: *the marginal equivalences of competition are such as to give a maximum of any one product for given specified amounts of all others.* This is almost identical with the Pareto-Barone production propositions, but not quite.

Professor Hotelling, also presumably independently, developed in two articles[18] conditions closely related to the Pareto production and exchange conditions of optimum. In particular, he has insisted upon the fact that marginal rather than average costs provide the appropriate basis for pricing, and he developed the dramatic applications of this to the problem of railroad rates and decreasing cost public utilities in general. On the analytic side each thing which he sets out to prove he does prove with great elegance and generality, but his fundamental primitive assumptions are only implicitly related to each other and to the equations of general equilibrium. Moreover, his welfare work really

---

[17] A. P. Lerner, "The Concept of Monopoly and the Measure of Monopoly Power," *Review of Economics Studies,* I (1934), 157–175. "Economic Theory and Socialist Economy," *Review of Economic Studies,* II (1934), 51–61.

[18] H. Hotelling, "The General Welfare in Relation to Problems of Taxation and of Railway and Utility Rates," *Econometrica,* VI (1938), 242–269, "Edgeworth's Taxation Paradox and the Nature of Demand and Supply Functions," *Journal of Political Economy,* XL (1932), 577–616.

falls into two distinct headings; on the one hand, that of the first article cited and much of the second article, and on the other hand, that of the second section of his second article referring to the "fundamental theorem" (especially pp. 248–256). Roughly these two diverse contributions of Hotelling fall respectively under the headings of optimal *production* and optimal *exchange* conditions; or, on the analytic side, to the difference between firms with unlimited budgets and the consumer with limited budget, to each of which fields Professor Hotelling has contributed much in the way of demand analysis. This dualism explains why so discerning a reader as Professor Frisch should have been puzzled by the Hotelling proof.[19]

9. The last writer to be mentioned is Professor A. Bergson.[20] He is the first who understands the contributions of all previous contributors, and who is able to form a synthesis of them. In addition, he is the first to develop explicitly the notion of an ordinal social welfare function in terms of which all the various schools of thought can be interpreted, and in terms of which they for the first time assume significance. In view of his own very generous acknowledgments of the work of others, even where he himself had independently rediscovered many basic theorems in an improved form, it is regrettable that his contribution has received so little notice. No doubt this stems in part from the mathematical character of his exposition, and to the fact that he uses the rather difficult notation of differentials throughout. The analysis that follows is simply an enlargement and development of his important work.[21]

[19] Space cannot permit a detailed examination of the exact steps in the Hotelling reasoning, this being particularly unnecessary since it is clear that his conclusions are impeccable. In the original specification of his system Professor Hotelling essentially generalizes the Dupuit-Marshall partial equilibrium set-up to many interrelated industries. However, unless we confine ourselves to the production problem alone, this will not lead to the equations of general equilibrium. These require the addition of the special demand functions of consumers for goods and their supply functions of productive services. In the mixed consumer-firm system the integrability conditions which give meaning to Hotelling's line integral, dead loss, and price potential (equal to the Barone Φ function) are not satisfied. Nor when it came to interpretation would it matter for the validity of the Pareto-Barone-Lerner conditions if they were. While Hotelling gives separate consideration to consumers when discussing excises, the two treatments are never adequately integrated.

[20] A. Bergson, "A Reformulation of Certain Aspects of Welfare Economics," *Quarterly Journal of Economics*, LII (1938), 310–334.

[21] In recent years Kaldor and Hicks have given an exposition of certain aspects of welfare economics. N. Kaldor, "Welfare Propositions in Economics," *Economic Journal*, XLIX (1939), 549–552. J. R. Hicks, "Foundations of Welfare Economics," *Economic Journal*, XLIX (1939), 696–712. Mention should also be made of an

THE SOCIAL WELFARE FUNCTION

It is fashionable for the modern economist to insist that ethical value judgments have no place in scientific analysis. Professor Robbins in particular has insisted upon this point,[22] and today it is customary to make a distinction between the pure analysis of Robbins *qua* economist and his propaganda, condemnations, and policy recommendations *qua* citizen. In practice, if pushed to extremes, this somewhat schizophrenic rule becomes difficult to adhere to, and it leads to rather tedious circumlocutions. But in essence Robbins is undoubtedly correct. Wishful thinking is a powerful deterrent of good analysis and description, and ethical conclusions cannot be derived in the same way that scientific hypotheses are inferred or verified.

But it is not valid to conclude from this that there is no room in economics for what goes under the name of "welfare economics." It is a legitimate exercise of economic analysis to examine the consequences of various value judgments, whether or not they are shared by the theorist, just as the study of comparative ethics is itself a science like any other branch of anthropology. If it is appropriate for the economist to analyze the way Robinson Crusoe directs production so as to maximize his (curious) preferences, the economist does not thereby commit himself to those tastes or inquire concerning the manner in which they were or ought to have been formed. No more does the astronomer, who enunciates the principle that the paths of planets are such as to minimize certain integrals, care whether or not these should be minimized; neither

---

important article which indicates the modification in the Pigouvian analysis necessitated by the considerations of monopolistic competition. R. F. Kahn, "Some Notes on Ideal Output," *Economic Journal*, XLV (1935), 1–35. A convenient compact summary of welfare economics is provided by O. Lange, "The Foundations of Welfare Economics," *Econometrica*, X (1942), 215–228. An advance in the discussion is represented by T. Scitovsky, "A Note on Welfare Propositions in Economics," *Review of Economic Studies*, IX (1941), 77–88. Because discussions of Free Trade illuminate the beliefs of economists upon these matters, and because this subject provides a convenient illustration, it would be desirable to review its literature. However, reference can only be made here to the survey in J. Viner, *Studies in the Theory of International Trade* (New York: Harper, 1937); to T. Scitovsky, "A Reconsideration of the Theory of Tariffs," *Review of Economic Studies*, IX (1942), 89–110; P. A. Samuelson, "Welfare Economics and International Trade," *American Economic Review*, XXVIII (1938), 261–266; "The Gains from International Trade," *Canadian Journal of Economics and Political Science*, V (1939), 195–205.

[22] L. Robbins, *An Essay on the Nature and Significance of Economic Science* (London, 1932).

for all we know do the stars care. Our above historical review should show that there is meaty and weighty content to the field of welfare economics, without invoking new methods in economic thought. In saying this, I do not mean to imply that the field of welfare economics has scientific content because a number of its theorems do *not* require inter-personal comparisons of utility; this after all is a mere detail. That part which *does* involve inter-personal comparisons of utility also has real content and interest for the scientific analyst, even though the scientist does not consider it any part of his task to deduce or verify (except on the anthropological level) the value judgments whose implications he grinds out. In the same way, the mathematical theory of probability accepts as a primitive undefined assumption whose validity is not its concern the initial specification of "equally likely" events, the measure of various "classes" or the "collective," and it then proceeds to grind out the mathematical implications of these and subsidiary hypotheses. It is only fair to point out, however, that the theorems enunciated under the heading of welfare economics are not meaningful propositions or hypotheses in the technical sense. For they represent the deductive implications of assumptions which are not themselves meaningful refutable hypotheses about reality.

Without inquiring into its origins, we take as a starting point for our discussion a function of all the economic magnitudes of a system which is supposed to characterize some ethical belief—that of a benevolent despot, or a complete egotist, or "all men of good will," a misanthrope, the state, race, or group mind, God, etc. Any possible opinion is admissible, including my own, although it is best in the first instance, in view of human frailty where one's own beliefs are involved, to omit the latter. We only require that the belief be such as to admit of an unequivocal answer as to whether one configuration of the economic system is "better" or "worse" than any other or "indifferent," and that these relationships are transitive; i.e., A better than B, B better than C, implies A better than C, etc. The function need only be ordinally defined, and it may or may not be convenient to work with (any) one cardinal index or indicator. There is no need to assume any particular curvature of the loci (in hyper-space) of indifference of this function. Utilizing one out of an infinity of possible indicators or cardinal indices, we may write this function in the form

$$W = W(z_1, z_2, \ldots), \tag{11}$$

where the z's represent all possible variables, many of them non-economic in character.

Between these z's there will be a number of "technological" relations limiting our freedom to vary the z's independently. Just what the content of these technological relations will be depends upon the level of abstraction at which the specifier of the value judgments wishes to work. If he is an out and out Utopian he may wish to ignore various institutional relations regardless of their empirical importance; indeed, he may go all out and repeal the laws of conservation of energy and widen greatly the technological productivities of the system. On the other hand, he may wish to take as fixed and immutable all social and economic institutions except those relating to the Central Bank. (Indeed those of fatalistic temperament may regard the restraints to be so numerous as to leave no problem of choice.) In other words, the auxiliary constraints imposed upon the variables are not themselves the proper subject matter of welfare economics but must be taken as givens.

Subject to these constraints, which may be written in the most general way as

$$g^i(z_1, z_2, \ . \ . \ .) = 0 \tag{12}$$

there will presumably be an upper bound to W (even though no unique value of the z's need correspond to this maximum level). If certain assumptions of regularity are made, it would be possible to indicate formal conditions for the maximum, involving Lagrangean multipliers, matrices, rank, and quadratic forms definite under constraint, etc. However, there is no particular point in developing this formalism.

The subject could end with these banalities were it not for the fact that numerous individuals find it of interest to specialize the form of W, the nature of the variables, z, and the nature of the constraints.

1. For one thing, prices are not usually included in the welfare function itself, except very indirectly through the effects of different prices and wages upon the quantities of consumption, work, etc.

2. Also certain of the variables can be thought of as referring to a particular individual or family; e.g., one of the z's may be the amount of tea consumed by John Jones, or the amount of unskilled labor which he provides.

3. It is often further assumed that the quantities of a given commodity consumed by one individual are of the same type as those consumed by another; technically, this means that certain of the variables enter in the technical side-conditions in sums, which relate the total amount produced of a commodity to input, regardless of the ultimate distribution of that output. Whatever may be said about the admissibility of this, the matter is still worse when a similar assumption is made concerning the homogeneity of the various services provided by different

individuals. However, even if in the most rigorous sense each individual's talents are unique, society rarely has the time or patience to learn to appreciate the flavor of each man, and, in the absence of perfect "screening" of different individuals, it does treat them as if they were perfectly substitutable; thus for our purposes they may be assumed to be so in many cases. This does not mean that we work with a single grade of labor; on the contrary, the number of grades may be very large and the classification minute, but it is assumed that there are many individuals in each grade, actually or potentially.

4. Not infrequently it is assumed that a given grade of productive service may be used indifferently in a number of uses. Technically this means that certain of the z's enter into the welfare function only as certain sums. As Bergson has pointed out, this involves implicit value judgments, so that Robbins when he discusses the problem of allocating resources as between alternative uses so as to maximize (in some sense) output or personal utility is not able even on the Robinson Crusoe level to avoid these notions; or rather, if resources are not assumed indifferent between at least two uses, few interesting marginal conditions can be deduced.

5. A more extreme assumption, which stems from the individualist philosophy of modern Western Civilization, states that individuals' preferences are to "count." If any movement leaves an individual on the same indifference curve, then the social welfare function is unchanged, and similarly for an increase or decrease. Actually, an examination of the principles of jurisprudence, the folkways and mores, shows that in its extreme form this assumption is rarely seriously proposed. Even "sane" adults are not permitted to eat and drink what they think best, individuals cannot sell themselves in order to consume more in the present, milk ration tickets cannot be exchanged for beer at the will of the owner, etc.

But economists in the orthodox tradition have tended to consider the above cases as exceptions.[23] However, in recent years many economists,

---

[23] Consider, however, the following interesting quotation from Edwin Cannan who was very much in the classical tradition: "We shall never decide whether to put a penny on beer or to further steepen the super-tax on incomes by considering how much the loss of a penny pinches the beer-drinker and the duke: we shall, and we do, decide it by making some rough estimate of the aggregate advantage in the long run of the two methods to society at large. For example, if we find that cheaper beer means better food for underfed children while less super-tax means more training of horses to run fast for a short distance with a very light burden, we incline to the super-tax: but if we find cheaper beer means more beer for drunkards and less super-tax means more houses for the people to inhabit in comfort and health, we incline to the beer tax." From an *Economic Journal* review of

Frank Knight being a notable example, have insisted upon the degree to which individual tastes and wants are socially conditioned by advertising and custom so that they can hardly be said to belong to him in any ultimate sense. All this is recognized in the witticism of the soap box speaker who said to the recalcitrant listener, "When the revolution comes, you will eat strawberries and cream, and like it!" Attention should also be called to the fact that even the classical economist does not literally have the individual in mind, so much as the family; of course, some hardy souls will pursue the will-o'-the-wisp of sovereignty within the family so as to reduce even these collective indifference curves to an individualistic basis.

6. One does not have to be a John Donne then to find fault with the above assumption, especially if we consider the closely related assumption that an individual's preference depends only upon the things which *he* consumes and not upon what others consume. As Veblen characteristically pointed out, much of the motivation for consumption is related to the fact that others do or do not have the same thing. Conspicuous expenditure, "keeping up with the Joneses," snob appeal, maintenance of face, are important in any realistic appraisal of consumption habits; and if we turn to the field of power analysis, it is not only on the national scale that "satisfactions" are relative and dog-in-the-manger tactics are rational.

If this sixth assumption is not made, many of the conclusions of welfare economics will remain valid, but they will require modifications to allow for certain "external" consumption economies not dissimilar analytically to the external technological economies and diseconomies of the Marshall-Pigou type.

7. All of the above assumptions are more or less tacitly accepted by extremely divergent schools of thought. The next assumption involves a more controversial value judgment, but one which has been characteristic of much of modern thought of the last century, and which is especially typical of the beliefs of the classical and neo-classical economists. *It is that the welfare function is completely (or very nearly) symmetrical with respect to the consumption of all individuals.*

Taken in connection with previous assumptions, in its strict form it is not consistent with the patent fact of considerable differences in individuals' overt preference patterns. Thus, in addition to involving a very significant value judgment, it also involves a very definite assumption of fact. This was not appreciated by economists, who tended to believe in the desirability of an equality of income, leaving it to the in-

---

Sir Josiah Stamp's *Fundamental Principles of Taxation in the Light of Modern Developments,* reprinted in *An Economist's Protest* (London, 1927), p. 279.

dividual to determine the exact form of his consumption. However, it is easy to show that the rule of equality of income (measured in dollars, numeraire, abstract purchasing power) applied to individuals of different tastes, but made to hold in all circumstances, is actually inconsistent with any determinate, definite W function. Equality becomes a fetish or shibboleth, albeit a useful one, in that the means becomes the end, and the letter of the law takes precedence over the spirit.

For the decision of equal incomes as optimal in one situation implies a certain relative well-being as between vegetarians and nonvegetarians; at different relative prices between vegetables and nonvegetables an equal distribution of income can no longer be optimal. Actually this does not render invalid the reasoning based upon this seventh premise since the adherents of this view implicitly held that individuals were very much alike, and if given equality of treatment would develop the same want patterns. Moreover, they could in all logic take the milder position that a great deal less inequality than existed in real life would be desirable even if one did not believe in complete equality.[24]

In a similar way, the belief that the individual should rightfully receive his imputed productivities is not consistent with a W function having properties (1) through (6). A change in the technological situation will alter individuals' fortunes so that the final result cannot be optimal if the initial situation was deemed so. Perhaps the bourgeois penchant for laissez-faire is the only case on record where a substantial number of individuals have made idols of partial derivatives, i.e., imputed marginal productivities.

One could similarly multiply expressions and beliefs which are part of everyday parlance, which upon examination turn out to be inconsistent and meaningless. The slogan, "the greatest good for the greatest number," was shown by Edgeworth to be one such; and we might add the dictum, "each to count for one and only one." As Professor Knight has ceaselessly insisted, Western Man is a hodgepodge of beliefs stemming from diverse and inconsistent sources. Fortunately his life is sufficiently compartmentalized so that he can assume his various roles with a tolerable amount of ambiguity in each; and only the most introspective worry about this enough to become disorganized.

8. A final essentially unnecessary assumption, which was especially characteristic of the last generation of economists, was *the definition of*

---

[24] It is not the purport of the above lines that the use of a welfare function leads to a belief in inequality as compared to equality. It merely shows that equality of money income where there is diversity of tastes involves the equality of nothing important. It is in lesser degree like the Anatole France aphorism concerning the equality of the law in its treatment of rich and poor. Before Bergson's treatment one could have sensed, but not analyzed, this subtlety.

the welfare function, which was to be maximized, as the sum of cardinal utilities experienced by each individual. Before the time of Bergson this was not uncommonly met even in the advanced literature, and vestiges can be found today. It stemmed from the main Utilitarian stream of economic thought, when utility was used interchangeably in a behavioristic, in a psychological, in a physiological, in an ethical sense.

It was not uncommon for older writers to ponder over the question as to whether utility was being maximized or whether pain was being minimized; whether by and large man was operating "in the red" below absolute zero, but making the best of a bad lot. The answer depended upon the author's theology and endocrine glands at the moment. Paley, Sidgwick, and others could seriously ask whether it was better to have a tremendous population, each contributing a little to a vast amount of Social Utility, or whether it was better to have less Social Utility, provided its average amount per head was maximized.

In the field of Public Finance the assumption of additive individual utilities plus the law of diminishing utility were used to justify the imposition of progressive taxes. In its most sweeping form this doctrine set up minimum aggregate sacrifice or maximum total utility as appropriate goals of action. This goal can be obtained only if the marginal utility of income (after taxes) is equal for all individuals; or if individuals are essentially alike, only with equal incomes for all.[25] On the other hand, the criterion that a given sum of taxes should be raised so as to lead to *equal sacrifice* for all is a much more conservative doctrine; following it we can only be sure that taxes should increase with income, but not necessarily in proportion with income.[26]

[25] F. Y. Edgeworth, "The Pure Theory of Taxation," *Economic Journal*, VII (1897), 550–571.

[26] The condition of equality of sacrifice is satisfied at each level of income if

$$U(X) - U(X - t) = \text{constant for all } X.$$

Differentiating this so as to determine the explicit change in t with respect to X,

$$\frac{dt}{dX} = \frac{U'(X - t) - U'(X)}{U'(X - t)}.$$

Because of diminishing marginal utility this is positive. But if we wish to have progressive taxation, the elasticity of *income after taxes* against income before taxes must be less than one. But

$$\frac{X}{X - t} \frac{d(X - t)}{dX} = \frac{XU'(X)}{(X - t)U'(X - t)},$$

which is less than one if, and only if, the elasticity of the marginal utility curve is less than unity. Thus, for Bernoulli's law of utility, equality of sacrifice would imply proportional rather than progressive taxation.

Today such arguments are not very fashionable since it is as easy to assume one's conclusions with respect to appropriate policy as to assume the premises of these arguments. Not only is the former more direct, but it is more honest. Nevertheless, some of the considerations which enter into the above arguments are latent in much of modern discussion and thought. In the distribution of war burden the moderately well-to-do tend to point to their rather large sacrifices and to call upon the lower classes to share in these and make new ones. The relatively poorer farmers and laborers concentrate upon how much the rich have left after they have made substantial sacrifices, and how little they themselves have in any case, not in comparison with what they had before the war, but compared to what they consider fair. Whether war times are the appropriate times to redress ancient wrongs or not, it is too much to expect that the bargaining advantages which the war brings will not be used for this purpose.

In connection with this eighth assumption it was implicitly assumed that real income could be treated as a homogeneous quantity to be distributed among individuals. This could be literally true only in a one-commodity world, or in a world where all relative prices were fixed constants. Actually prices will vary depending how money income is distributed. Strictly speaking, therefore, the real judgments embodied in the welfare function must be judgments concerning a multitude of diverse goods. This would be quite a problem even for a man with definite opinions and great preoccupation with value judgments. If, however, he takes refuge in assumption (5) that individual preferences are to count, the individual can be left to decide for himself how he will spend his money at given prices. Our ethical observer need only decide then what his preferences are as between the given levels of satisfaction of different individuals.

It might be thought that our ethical observer, even if the individuals themselves had no unique cardinal indexes of utility, would have to find cardinal indicators. But this would be quite incorrect. Of course, if utilities are to be added, one would have to catch hold of them first, but there is no need to add utilities.[27] The cardinal utilities enter into the W

---

[27] Even if one wished to add utilities, it would seem silly from any ethical viewpoint to have one's opinions as to correct taxation influenced by how consumers spend their income on goods. Yet that is what the recent attempts to measure marginal utility must imply if they have any pretensions to relevance for policy. R. Frisch, *New Methods of Measuring Marginal Utility* (Tübingen, 1932). I. Fisher, "A Statistical Method for Measuring 'Marginal Utility' and Testing the Justice of a Progressive Income Tax," in *Economic Essays Contributed in Honor of John Bates Clark* (New York, 1927).

function as independent variables if assumption (5) is made. But the W function is itself only ordinally determinable so that there are an infinity of equally good indicators of it which can be used. Thus, if one of these is written as

$$W = F(U^1,\ U^2,\ \ldots),\qquad\qquad (13)$$

and if we were to change from one set of cardinal indexes of individual utility to another set $(V^1,\ V^2,\ \ldots)$, we should simply change the form of the function F so as to leave all social decisions invariant. Thus, let us move from one configuration of goods going to the different individuals to another configuration which leaves W unchanged or which is socially indifferent. Then no redefinition of the U's or of F can change this fact: the social indifference loci are independent of cardinal numbering. And in this terminology the significance of assumption (5) that individual tastes shall count is contained in the requirement that the social indifference slopes between two goods *going to the same individual* are exactly the same as the individuals' indifference ratios. Assumption (6) adds that these curves are unaffected by changes in the goods going to other individuals.

MATHEMATICAL ANALYSIS

The assumptions discussed above can be given mathematical formulation. Thus, assumptions (2) and (3) imply that the important variables of our system can be regarded as a number of commodities and productive services $(X_1,\ X_2,\ \ldots,\ X_n,\ V_1,\ V_2,\ \ldots,\ V_m)$. These totals can be distributed among s individuals of the system; the amounts going to each can be written with a superscript which identifies the individual and a subscript identifying the commodity or service. (While productive services could be written as negative commodities, I have chosen to conform to the more common procedure encountered in the literature.)

$$
\begin{aligned}
X_i &= \sum_{k=1}^{s} x_i{}^k, \qquad (i = 1,\ \ldots,\ n)\\[2mm]
V_j &= \sum_{k=1}^{s} v_j{}^k. \qquad (j = 1,\ \ldots,\ m)
\end{aligned}
\qquad (14)
$$

The social welfare function involves only the amounts going to each individual, not prices or totals. Therefore, equation (11) is specialized to

$$W = W(x_1^1, \ldots, x_n^1; \ldots; x_1^s, \ldots, x_n^s;$$
$$v_1^1, \ldots, v_m^1; \ldots; v_1^s, \ldots, v_m^s). \quad (15)$$

This exhausts the implications of the first four assumptions.

Assumptions (5) and (6) further specialize (11) so that the welfare function can be written as

$$W = W[U^1(x_1^1, \ldots, x_n^1; v_1^1, \ldots, v_m^1), \ldots,$$
$$U^s(x_1^s, \ldots, x_n^s; v_1^s, \ldots, v_m^s)], \quad (16)$$

where the cardinal forms of the U's and the W are arbitrary. Assumption (7) is meaningless unless the respective U's can be made identical; but if this can be done, W must then be a symmetric function of the U's. Assumption (8) requires that there exist a cardinal W and cardinal U's such that W is a summation of the U's. On the anthropological level this involves (aside from its arbitrariness) definite restrictions on the social rates of indifference between the commodities and services of the same and different individuals. These are similar to the empirical restrictions of independent individual utility as discussed in chapter vii.

In the previous section it was noted that the "technical" restraints must be assumed with the same arbitrariness as the welfare function itself. However, since the formulation of general equilibrium by Walras, it has been customary to take as given by the engineer the fundamental relationships between inputs and outputs and that production itself takes place in firms or industries which are distinct from the individuals, having no value in and of themselves. Under modern industrial conditions this is not unrealistic. But even here many interesting alternatives can arise. What one calls economics, economic engineering, engineering, etc., is to a considerable degree a matter of choice. One can assume that all production decisions involving relative marginal productivities are the concern of the engineer, or economic engineer, and that the economist can take as already derived a transformation relationship between the X's and V's of the form

$$T(X_1, X_2, \ldots, X_n; V_1, V_2, \ldots, V_m) = 0. \quad (17)$$

This implicit relation is interpreted to give the maximum amount of any one output as of given amounts of all inputs and all other outputs, or the minimum amount of any one input as of given amounts of all outputs and all other inputs.

But if one starts from more primitive technological assumptions, such as the production functions of each commodity, the transformation locus is a derived theorem and not an axiom. Behind it lie many interesting optimal production conditions involving marginal productivities and other magnitudes usually thought of as economic rather than engineering.

PRODUCTION CONDITIONS

In a synthesis of welfare economics we can derive first a set of production conditions which require for their validity the weakest of all ethical assumptions: *simply that more of any one output, other commodities or services being constant, is desirable; similarly, less input for the same outputs is desirable.*

Under the simplest technological conditions we can take as given the production function relating each output to the inputs devoted to it.

$$X_i = X^i(v_{1i}, v_{2i}, \ldots, v_{mi}), \qquad (i = 1, \ldots, n) \tag{18}$$

where the first subscript indicates the kind of productive factor and the second subscript the commodity to which it is applied. Of course, the total applied to all commodities is given by

$$V_j = v_{j1} + v_{j2} + \cdots + v_{jn}. \qquad (j = 1, \ldots, m) \tag{19}$$

Ordinarily it is assumed that the production function possesses partial derivatives (marginal productivities), but the above formulation includes the case of so-called fixed proportions or fixed coefficients where the production function has contour lines with corners.

Equations (18) and (19) represent $(n + m)$ relations. If we specify arbitrarily all but one output (service), we can maximize (minimize) the remaining one. This is an extremum problem in which there are auxiliary constraints. The first order partial derivative conditions can be expressed directly as proportionalities and rank properties of the matrix of first partial derivatives of our functions. But it is illuminating to express these directly by means of the artifice of Lagrangean undetermined multipliers. To do this we set up the function

$$\Phi = \pi_1 X_1 + \pi_2 X_2 + \cdots + \pi_n X_n + \lambda_1 V_1 + \lambda_2 V_2 + \cdots + \lambda_m V_m \tag{20}$$

and *pretend* to maximize it treating all the variables *as if* they were independent, and treating the π's and λ's as (undetermined) constants. If the correct secondary extremum conditions are written out in full, it will be seen that they are quite different from those that would have to hold if the Φ function were really to be maximized. *Only by accident* would these secondary conditions coincide; only by accident would Φ not be at a minimum or would it be at an extremum rather than simply at a stationary value.

This may seem to be an esoteric and recondite point of little practical significance. It is the primary contention of the present work that *everything* interesting is contained in the inequalities associated with an extremum position, rather than in the equalities. This is no less true of the field of welfare economics. From a deeper point of view *market prices, regarded as parameters by perfect competitors, are nothing more nor less than Lagrangean multipliers*. The Langrangean expression Φ corresponds to Barone's Φ function or to Hotelling's price potential and can be regarded as the value of output or national product, expressed in terms of money or any numeraire, and generalized by the subtraction of factor costs.

If the *game* of competition leads to optimal conditions, it does so partly by accident. For it is precisely under the conditions favorable to the maintenance of atomistic competition (briefly absence of decreasing costs) that the secondary conditions of the correct maximum problem agree with those guaranteeing the maximization of the money value of output as of fixed prices. Where there are substantial technological increasing returns, competition as an empirical phenomenon breaks down. It is in such conditions that collectivism is likely to be considered seriously as a social policy. If then a socialist regime should insist upon mechanically playing the game of competition with prices regarded as parameters à la Lange,[28] its managers would rush away from the minimization of Φ, even though this *minimization* may be precisely what is required under decreasing cost if welfare is to be *maximized*.

The moral is not that prices should cease to be related to marginal cost, or that planning under socialism is impossible. It is simply that the decentralized operators in a planned society should refrain from a literal aping of atomistic, passive, parametric price behavior. Instead of pretending that demand curves are infinitely elastic when they are not, the correct shape of the curve is to be taken into account. This does not mean that the decentralized operators should take account of their influence on price as a monopolist would.[29]

After the elimination of Lagrangean multipliers, the first order maxi-

---

[28] O. Lange, article in *On the Economic Theory of Socialism*, B. E. Lippincott, ed. (Minneapolis: University of Minnesota Press, 1938), pp. 55–142.

[29] When we come to the full statement of welfare conditions, it will be seen that unusual difficulties do arise in the decreasing cost case in determining whether a given maximum position represents a *maximum maximorum* or whether the number of differentiated products should be reduced.

mum conditions take the form

$$\frac{\partial X_i/\partial v_{1i}}{\partial X_k/\partial v_{1k}} = \cdots = \frac{\partial X_i/\partial v_{mi}}{\partial X_k/\partial v_{mk}} = \frac{T_{x_k}}{T_{x_i}}, \qquad (i, k = 1, \ldots, n) \quad (21)$$

or the equivalent form

$$\frac{\partial X_1/\partial v_{j1}}{\partial X_1/\partial v_{r1}} = \cdots = \frac{\partial X_n/\partial v_{jn}}{\partial X_n/\partial v_{rn}} = \frac{T_{v_j}}{T_{v_r}}. \qquad (j, r = 1, \ldots, m) \quad (22)$$

In words this takes the form: *productive factors are correctly allocated if the marginal productivity of a given factor in one line is to the marginal productivity of the same factor in a second line as the marginal productivity of any other factor in the first line is to its marginal productivity in the second line. The value of the common factor of proportionality can be shown to be equal to the marginal cost of the first good in terms of the (displaced amount of the) second good.*[30]

Geometrically these conditions can be easily derived in the two good, two factor case by means of a Jevons-Edgeworth-Bowley-Lerner diagram consisting of a box whose respective sides are equal to the available total amounts of the two factors. Any point within the box, if oriented with respect to the lower left-hand corner, can be thought of as representing the amounts of the two factors used in the production of the first good, and the iso-product contour lines can be sketched in. The same point when referred to the upper right-hand corner represents the allocation to the second good, whose contour lines can also be superimposed on the same diagram.

If we specify the amount of one of the goods and restrict movements to one of these contour lines, the optimum position is reached only when we have touched the highest output line of the other good, or at a point of tangency of the opposing iso-product lines. The geometrical diagram indicates the correct secondary conditions which are quite different from conventional diminishing returns. The locus of all such points of tangency, which can appropriately be called a "generalized contract" curve, represents the infinity of optimum positions. If along this locus we read off the amounts of the respective products, and plot one of these magnitudes against the other, the resulting locus is the substitution, transformation, or opportunity cost curve, T. The slope of this curve at any

[30] By introducing as variables inputs and outputs of different dates optimal behavior over time can be included in the above information. However, when this is done, it will be seen that contrary to the belief of most economists since the time of Böhm-Bawerk, no single real interest rate is implied for a capitalist or socialist state. Equality would be a necessity only in the highly unusual case where relative prices of all goods remain the same over time.

point represents the marginal cost of one of the goods in terms of the other, or the ratio of marginal costs expressed in terms of some third magnitude.[31]

The substitution curve is drawn up as of given amounts of the factors of production and will shift with any changes in the latter. For a given transformation curve to be of any relevance, the factors of production must be regarded as being indifferent as between different uses.[32]

If constant returns to scale and only one factor (perhaps equal to a composite dose) are assumed, we have the classical case of a straight line transformation curve. If the first of these assumptions is made, but there is more than one factor of production, unless the goods should just happen to use the factors in the same proportion, the transformation curve will be concave to the origin because of the law of diminishing returns to varying proportions. The curve can also assume this shape for other reasons relating to returns to scale. In the decreasing cost case, however this arises, the curve will be convex to the origin.

In all of these cases let the firms or planners really take prices as given and attempt to maximize value of output or Φ. In the constant returns case there will be complete specialization on one of the goods (the one with comparative advantage) or complete indifference at the critical price ratio equal to the cost transformation ratio. If both goods are consumed, and if the economy is a closed one, the latter critical price ratio is sure to be the only relevant one.

In the increasing cost case at given price ratios the firm will come into equilibrium at the levels of output which make prices proportional to marginal (transformation or factor) costs. However, in the decreasing cost case the planners in a socialist state attempting to maximize at fixed prices would concentrate on one or the other of the two commodities. But this would be optimal only in an open economy which would really trade with the outside world (in unlimited amounts) at the

---

[31] For the geometrical picture see W. F. Stolper and P. A. Samuelson, "Protection and Real Wages," *Review of Economic Studies,* IX (1941), 58–74.

[32] It is only when the last two unnecessary and unrealistic assumptions are made that the so-called opportunity cost doctrine is even formally valid. Even under these conditions the usual formulation is rather a mumbo jumbo of high sounding gibberish, which does not state the conditions of equilibrium in a very direct way. All this is further complicated by the fact that most enunciations of the opportunity cost doctrine are purely verbal: leisure is treated as a displaced good! Inevitably, therefore, when the opportunity cost doctrine is carefully stated and qualified, it degenerates into the full conditions of general equilibrium in which factor supply and preference equations must be introduced if only as inequalities. This is not to imply that one must accept the dubious psychological language and interpretations of classical real cost theorists.

given price ratio. In a closed planned state it might be desirable to produce something of both, to have price ratios equal to marginal cost ratios even if that meant a minimization of Φ. If we regard the passive approach of the decentralized planners as an equilibrium process, it is clear that the correct optimum, being a minimum and not a maximum, would not be an equilibrium point at all. Or if the planners acted like Balaam's ass, it could be regarded as a highly unstable equilibrium point from which they would rush at the slightest disturbance.

Thus it is only accidentally—the first two cases—that competition is optimal. For it is in those cases that the Lagrangean expression (20) is at a maximum when we are at the correct maximum of (18). In these accidental cases, if we like, we may think of our production decisions as being independent of preferences, in the sense that they are *uniformly* best with respect to the most extreme weightings of the commodities. Under increasing returns we may even never settle on society's best transformation curve.

Actually our production conditions might have been introduced in more complex form than as single, isolated production functions of the form (18). It is to a certain extent arbitrary as to how much preliminary maximizing behavior we consider as being done by the engineer and how much by the economist. Under competitive conditions the relevance of prices to the decision is taken as the dividing line; but for welfare purposes we may dispense with prices completely. However, it would seem somewhat awkward then to term the problem one of engineering; still some economists might prefer to begin with the transformation function, T.

If we examine production possibilities more closely, it will be apparent that in many cases it will not be possible to end up with a single transformation function, T. Thus suppose that commodities divide up into two or more groups such that no productive factor is used in more than one group. Then there will be at least as many independent transformation curves as there are groups. Of course, formally these can be combined into a single implicit equation, e.g., by equating their summed squares to zero, but this is trivial. No indeterminacy arises, however, from the multiplicity of transformation curves; we have fewer choices to make and therefore fewer marginal conditions.

PURE EXCHANGE CONDITIONS

The production conditions of the previous section were derivable on the basis of rather mild assumptions by virtue of the fact that more of all goods, however they are to be divided, would seem better than less. These conditions are still only *necessary*. They are not *sufficient*, since decisions must still be made as to how to divide up given available goods, and as to which of the available amounts of production will actually be used.

Even if the last of these two decisions is made, there remains the problem of dividing up a given total of all commodities and services among individuals. Once there has been specified a clearly defined W function, the final optimum point can be easily determined. But at this point after assuming, if only implicitly, the first six serious assumptions, the modern welfare economist becomes timid and hesitates to make assumption (7) or indeed any other specific welfare function. He has been conditioned against making ethical assumptions. If possible, therefore, he would like to develop further optimum conditions which are within broad limits independent of the form of the W specified. In fact, as has been known since the time of Pareto at least, it is possible to gratify this wish and to specify still another set of *necessary*, but not *sufficient*, conditions which must prevail as between individuals.

Here the simple assumption is made that W is undefined, or unspecified, except to the extent that it is a monotonic increasing function of the individual U's. We are not able to plot in the (U^1, U^2) plane a locus of points along which W is constant. We know only that a movement in the northeast direction of the plane increases W and is good, a movement in the southwest direction decreases W and is bad; a movement into either of the other two quadrants taken around a given point is indeterminate.

In words, the simple assumption is made that only if all individuals are made better (worse) off can we definitely state that a given movement is good (bad). Otherwise we must reserve judgment. Mathematically it is clear that for the levels of utility of all but one individual being arbitrarily specified, it is a necessary condition of equilibrium that the utility of the remaining individual be at a maximum, subject to the condition that there be fixed totals of all goods. For

$$\sum_{j=1}^{s} x_i^j = \bar{X}_i, \ \sum_{j=1}^{s} v_r^j = \bar{V}_r, \tag{23}$$

$$U^i(x_1^j, \ldots, x_n^j, v_1^j, \ldots, v_m^j) = \bar{U}^i \qquad (j \neq k)$$

we must maximize

$$U^k = U^k(x_1^k, \ldots, x_n^k, v_1^k, \ldots, v_m^k). \tag{24}$$

By using Lagrangean multipliers or by direct methods, it can be easily shown that in equilibrium the ratio between marginal utilities of two goods consumed by one individual must be the same as the ratio of marginal utilities of the same to any other individual who consumes the same goods. If one or more of the goods is absent from the consumption of an individual, certain inequalities can be introduced to generalize the above conditions. We may write the first order conditions of equilibrium in the form

$$\frac{U_i^1}{U_j^1} = \frac{U_i^2}{U_j^2} = \cdots = \frac{U_i^s}{U_j^s} \tag{25}$$

It will be noted that only ratios of marginal utilities for the same individuals are ever involved.[33] Thus, there is no need for numerical utility even for a single individual and no need to compare the utilities of different individuals.

Graphically the equilibrium may be represented by the same box-type diagram as was mentioned in the last section. The dimensions of the box represent the fixed totals of the commodities in existence. Any interior point oriented with respect to the lower left-hand corner represents the amount of consumption of the first individual, and the contour lines are now to be interpreted as indifference curves. Referred to the upper right-hand corner, a point represents the second individual's consumption, and his contour lines may be superimposed on the other. Specifying the utility of the second individual, we maximize that of the first by moving along the given indifference line of the second individual until we reach (at a point of tangency) the highest indifference curve of the first. Because the original specification of the second man's utility was arbitrary, the final equilibrium is also arbitrary and not unique. The locus of all such arbitrary points is, of course, the familiar Edgeworthian contract curve and represents the set of points satisfying necessary exchange conditions.

After the discussion of the previous section it will not be necessary to reiterate at length the contention that the equality of the various ratios can be expressed without Lagrangean multipliers and without price ratios; moreover, in by no means impossible cases, even playing the game of competition would lead away from rather than toward the correct optimal position. As before, this is because the secondary conditions for a constrained maximum are not the same as the secondary conditions necessary literally to bring the Lagrangean expression to an extremum.

---

[33] Equilibrium conditions regarding the factors of production need not be indicated separately if it is remembered that they may be treated as negative commodities.

It will be noted that from any point off the contract curve there exists a movement toward it which would be beneficial to both individuals. This is not the same thing as to say, with Edgeworth, that exchange will in fact necessarily cease somewhere on the contract curve; for in many types of bilateral monopoly a final equilibrium may be reached off the contract curve. Nor is it the same as to say that points on the contract curve are better than points off the contract curve. Later I shall discuss the correct formulation of the significance of this condition.

But first it is well to write down the full first order conditions of equilibrium which must hold if we are to have an optimum of both production and exchange, that is, if we combine with the conditions of this section the conditions of the last section. *Then (1) we must have a common marginal rate of indifference between any two goods for every individual; this common indifference ratio must, moreover, be equal to the ratio at which one of these goods can be transformed into the other in a production sense, the transformation to come about as the result of transferring any resource from one good's production to the other's. (2) We must have for all individuals a common ratio of indifference between supplying more of any factor of production and enjoying more consumption of a given good; this common ratio must be equal to the rate at which supplying more of that factor results in greater production of the good in question.*

Mathematically, as Lange has shown,

$$\frac{U_{x_i}^{1}}{U_{x_j}^{1}} = \cdots = \frac{U_{x_i}^{s}}{U_{x_j}^{s}} = \frac{T_{X_i}}{T_{X_j}}, \qquad (i, j = 1, \ldots, n) \qquad (26)$$

$$\frac{U_{v_k}^{1}}{U_{x_i}^{1}} = \cdots = \frac{U_{v_k}^{s}}{U_{x_i}^{s}} = \frac{\partial X_i}{\partial v_{ki}} = \frac{T_{V_k}}{T_{V_i}} \qquad \begin{matrix} (i = 1, \ldots, n) \\ (k = 1, \ldots, m) \end{matrix}$$

These conditions may be rewritten in a variety of ways but only being (at the first order level) necessary conditions rather than sufficient conditions, they are necessarily less in number than the number of the unknowns of the system. This is after taking account of the fact that the total of factors used in every use and the total of commodities consumed must equal the sums of these magnitudes over all individuals, i.e., even after taking into account equations (14). We are still short $(s - 1)$ equations. These can only be supplied on the basis of definite assumptions concerning how different individuals enter into the W function. This will be discussed in detail in the next section.

Returning to the combined production and exchange conditions of equations (26), I should like to point out various alternative formulations of them. First, it is easy to derive from them the conditions that the ratios of indifference between any two factors must be uniform for all individuals, and equal to the relative marginal productivities of the two factors in any line of production.

Second, it is sometimes convenient to interpret the first of these equilibrium conditions as specifying the equality of price and marginal utility ratios to the *ratios* of marginal cost. There is occasionally some uncertainty in the literature as to whether prices should *equal* marginal costs or just bear the same percentage discrepancy in every line. The distinction is especially important if decreasing costs are very prevalent, for then it is impossible for capitalistic monopolies or socialist bureaus to recover their full costs of production if they charge only prices equal to marginal costs. Recourse must be had to direct taxation to cover the difference or to the imputed revenues accruing to state-owned factors of production, revenue which in a world of constant returns to scale would be available for distribution to the citizens of the state.

So long as only price ratios are used it is not necessary to state the units in which costs are measured, dollars, labor, fertilizer, or opportunity-substitution costs. In the usual exposition partial equilibrium conditions are implicitly assumed, and costs, wages, and prices are expressed in terms of dollars. In these conditions must prices be equal to marginal costs, or just proportional? The answer is *equality* if we take into account the conditions relating to factors of production such as are embodied in the second part of equations (26). If all factors of production were indifferent between different uses and completely fixed in amount (the pure Austrian case), then we could dispense with these conditions, and proportionality of prices and marginal cost would be sufficient. But if we drop these highly special assumptions, for which there is not in any case empirical or theoretical warrant, then if all prices were proportional to (say double) marginal costs, we should not have an optimum situation. By working a little more or less everybody could be made better off since in the described situation the preferred terms at which they exchange leisure and goods are not equal to the true productivity terms at which they can be transformed into each other.

I need not remind the reader that first order conditions are really of secondary importance as compared to the full inequalities implied by an optimum position. Also it should not be necessary to show in detail that the above conditions hold only if every factor of production is actually used in every line of production, and if something is produced of every good, and if all production and indifference functions have continuous partial derivatives. If any of these conditions fail, the number of equalities may be diminished, but in every case the correct general inequalities will prevent there being any essential ambiguities in the characterization of the optimum position. A closely related problem arises when there are multiple positions of equilibrium. With strongly convex indifference fields and strongly concave cost functions such cannot occur. But there is no reason why human nature should display the simple, regular properties which the observer-economist finds convenient. And it is the essence of the decreasing cost, increasing returns, lumpiness, indivisibility phenomena that improper curvature on the cost side should enter the picture.

Especially where differentiation of product arises as a result of monopolistic competition or as its cause, there arises the problem as to whether or not a commodity should be produced at all. If it is produced, the marginal cost conditions of (26) should be realized, but there may be a better maximum where none is produced. Here the extremum position is of the corner type, and the conventional equalities must be replaced by inequalities. This involves decision making at a distance; we cannot feel our way to the optimum, step by step, but must boldly experiment with diverse combinations. Where such "all or none" phenomena are concerned, things often get worse before they get better, and so decisions *im kleinen* will not suffice. Even aside from the difficulties of the paragraph after next, we cannot decide that a thing should be produced if a perfectly discriminating monopolist or government bureau could recover its total cost by some sort of a take-it-or-leave-it offer. In these cases involving finite decisions we must ask consumers (or Robinson Crusoe) whether a given abundance of fewer commodities is preferred to an alternative scarcity of a greater range of commodities.[34] At this point there will inevitably arise questions concerning the rationality of individual choice, questions which had been summarily suppressed by a cavalier acceptance of the validity of assumptions five and six set out in the third section back. But these questions, whatever their importance, cannot be settled by deductive analysis.

The equality of price to marginal cost creates confusions in the minds of many concerning the question as to whether or not costs which are fixed in the short run are not variable in the long run and hence should be covered by price. They ask whether price should not exceed short run marginal cost since the latter excludes elements of long range variable costs. There are two confusions revealed by this question. First, marginal cost is sometimes treated as a part of total unit costs, which it is not. Marginal cost is the difference between costs in two situations and cannot be identified in general with given components of cost, labor, mate-

[34] In certain special cases consumer's surplus may be employed to describe finite inequalities. But these cases are rare, and in any case we are rather better off if we use direct methods.

rials, etc. Symptomatic of this confusion is the statement that competition tends to drive price down to prime or variable costs so that full costs are not recovered. Of course, pure competition (which is not really implied in the previous sentence) involves price equal to marginal cost, which may far exceed full unit costs depending upon the scale of output and the level of price. Not only did Alfred Marshall speak loosely on this matter, but so great a contribution as J. M. Clark's *Economics of Overhead Costs* errs, at least in exposition, in its diagnosis of the role of overhead costs in the breakdown of competitive theory. An examination of the character of agriculture, the last stronghold of pure competition, would show a high level of overhead costs with no tendency toward the breakdown of competition. Aside from non-imitable differentiation of product the principal cause of disintegration of competition is decreasing long run unit costs of each firm at levels representing large fractions of total demand for the product; this would be true even if all goods could be produced to order.

Marginal cost is not part of cost which must be met, and the equality of price and marginal cost has nothing to do with a recovery of full costs, determination of fair return on investments, correct imputation of factor shares, etc. Its purpose is to secure correct factor allocation, and avoid anomalous product allocation. This is accented if one considers a wavy cost curve or a cost curve showing a corner at the point of capacity (long run or short run). At the latter point marginal cost is undefined, or, if you prefer, it is anywhere from a finite amount to infinity. There is no clue as to proper price determination, but this is of no consequence so long as production does actually take place at the capacity point. Similarly, as demand fluctuates for a commodity whose cost curve shows waves because of lumpiness, etc., the correct price charged will vary greatly; rather than let a train set out with a single empty seat, the price should fall to zero. It is no argument against this statement that such pricing may not recover full costs, or that passengers will tend to wait until trains are least crowded. What could be more desirable socially than the evening out of traffic? Does not a railroad company which gives out passes to its own employees often follow the sound principle that they may ride as they please so long as they add nothing to costs? Incidentally, it will be seen from this discussion that where small changes in demand create great changes in social cost, posted, administered, relatively stable prices are not optimal devices.

The second and less important confusion involved in the statement that price should exceed short run marginal cost stems from the fallacious belief that long run marginal cost "inclusive of changes in long run variable factors" is greater than short run marginal cost. Actually, we know from the Wong-Viner-Harrod envelope theorem that they are equal for instantaneous rates of change if production is taking place at the anticipated level. For an actual, finite, forward movement from this point, short run marginal cost "exclusive of the fixed factors" is of course *greater* not smaller than marginal cost when all factors are varied optimally. Whether or not output is at the anticipated level, price equal to short run marginal cost is necessary in order that the existing plant be used optimally; the relationship between price and long run marginal cost is relevant to a decision as to whether to change the size of plant, when that decision arises. If one dropped the first order statement of optimum conditions and replaced them by the general inequalities which must be satisfied, it would be obvious that the optimum position must satisfy a different maximum condition (inequality) for every alternative which can be contemplated. Thus, it must not pay to make a small step forward or backward, a middling step, a sizable step, a huge step, to shut down completely or open a new line, etc., etc. Each of these implies a relationship between price or revenue and entirely different measures of marginal or differential cost.[35]

INTERPERSONAL OPTIMAL CONDITIONS

In the last two sections an attempt was made to derive as general conditions as possible with a minimum of controversial assumptions. Nevertheless, we have seen that it is not possible to deduce a unique equilibrium unless we have more to build upon. This is only as it should be, for intuition assures us that it is not possible to deduce a unique equilibrium unless we have more to build upon. This is only as it should be, for intuition assures us that there cannot be an optimum position which is independent of the exact form of the W function. Even if all of the necessary conditions of production and exchange are satisfied, we are short as many equations as there are individuals in excess of unity. In a Robinson Crusoe world where there is but one individual (*pace* Friday!) there are no individuals in excess of unity and the equilibrium in unique. But as soon as we have more than one individual, our previous conditions simply assure us that we are on the "generalized

---

[35] Once this fact is mastered, the whole question of "allocation of perfectly joint costs" is seen to be a false and irrelevant problem for either a firm or society. It derives its present day empirical importance from the intrusion, not necessarily irrationally, of "full cost" considerations into price formation, and to problems of government regulation, e.g., T.V.A., Tariff Commissions, etc.

contract locus" from which there are no possible movements which are advantageous to each and every individual.

An infinity of such positions exists ranging from a situation in which all of the advantage is enjoyed by one individual, through some sort of compromise position, to one in which another individual has all the advantage. Without a well-defined W function, i.e., without assumptions concerning interpersonal comparisons of utility, it is impossible to decide which of these points is best. In terms of a given set of ethical notions which define a *Welfare* function the best point on the generalized contract locus can be determined, and only then.

All of this may be formulated mathematically as follows. The optimal conditions of production and exchange as given in equations (26) which summarize the argument of the previous two sections permit us to reduce the level of indeterminacy of the system to an implicit equation between the levels of well-being of the different individuals in the system. This may be written as

$$P(U^1, U^2, \ldots, U^s) = 0. \tag{27}$$

This says that we may specify at will the levels of well-being of all but one of the individuals, and the last one's well-being is uniquely determined. The essential shape of this *Possibility function* depends of course upon the technological and other assumed restraints of the system as well as upon the tastes of the different individuals. Notationally, the same implicit function can be written in many different ways, but the locus in question is invariant under these purely terminological changes. One should note, however, that since the exact numerical form of each U is arbitrary, no importance attaches to the curvature properties of this locus.

If we have a given definite welfare function, then we are to maximize

$$W = W(U^1, \ldots, U^s) \tag{28}$$

subject to the above constraint. The first order condition of equilibrium takes the form

$$\frac{W_i}{W_j} = \frac{P_i}{P_j}. \qquad (i, j = 1, \ldots, s) \tag{29}$$

These conditions, like the correct secondary conditions which need not be written explicitly, are independent of purely notational ambiguities involved in the welfare function, the possibility function, and the selection of particular cardinal indices of individual utility.

Equations (29) give us the missing $(s - 1)$ conditions of equilibrium, and our equilibrium is seen to be finally determinate. It is not at all necessary to take the expositional path followed above. Thus, Professor Pigou, who does not hesitate from the very beginning to make inter-individual comparisons of utility, moves directly via a maximization of (11) subject to (12) to the same equilibrium which Pareto-Barone-Lerner reach after they have admitted into their systems interpersonal comparisons of utility. And as will be discussed at greater length below, they end up with no optimum and no final definite conclusions if they are unwilling to permit others to introduce such ethical considerations.

The real significance of their analysis lies in the fact that they provide a relatively easy opening for the introduction of ethical notions. For it follows from their analysis that all of the action necessary to achieve a given ethical *desideratum* may take the form of *lump-sum taxes* or *bounties*. These may be given in the form of abstract purchasing power or in kind, it being necessary, however, that the latter should be freely exchangeable against other goods. Thus, instead of having to decide how much to allocate of each and every good to each individual, the ethical authority need only decide on the allocation of final incomes between individuals.

Working directly from a well-defined (ordinal) welfare function, we require that W be maximized subject to the physical constraints of the system. We may express the final conditions in many different forms, with or without Lagrangean multipliers. One such compact method which avoids as far as possible duplicating the exact form (but not the substance) of the conditions of the previous section is given as follows:

$$
\begin{aligned}
\frac{\partial W}{\partial x_i^1} = \cdots &= \frac{\partial W}{\partial x_i^s} = \frac{\partial W}{\partial X_i}, \quad (i = 1, \ldots, n) \\
&\qquad\qquad\qquad\qquad (j = 1, \ldots, m) \\
\frac{\partial W}{\partial v_j^1} = \cdots &= \frac{\partial W}{\partial v_j^s} = \frac{\partial W}{\partial V_j} = \frac{\partial W}{\partial X_1}\frac{\partial X_1}{\partial v_{j1}} = \cdots = \frac{\partial W}{\partial X_n}\frac{\partial X_n}{\partial v_{jn}}.
\end{aligned}
\tag{30}
$$

Not only are these equations very similar to the famous Note XIV which summarizes much of what is best in Marshall's *Principles*, but they are cast almost exactly in the form followed by Professor Pigou in his *Economics of Welfare*. In words, two conditions are implied: *first, the marginal social utility (disutility) of the same good (service) must be equal for each individual; second, each factor of production must be divided among different possible uses so that its indirect, derived marginal social utility must be the same in every use and equal to its marginal social disutility.*

We may leave to the reader the task of showing the necessary modifications if the supply of a factor is inelastic, if a factor of production is not indifferent between different uses, if there is joint production, if there are external technological economies or diseconomies (so that the production function of a good contains in it factors of production devoted to other uses), etc. By dividing the above equations through by any single partial derivative, they may be thrown into a form which is independent of the particular cardinal representation of W.

While the Lerner production conditions are contained in the above set of equations, the exchange conditions are not. However, if we make the individualistic assumptions five and six above so that the welfare function takes on the special form given in equation (13), then in virtue of the identities

$$\frac{\partial W}{\partial x_i^r} = \frac{\partial W}{\partial U^r} \frac{\partial U^r}{\partial x_i^r} \tag{31}$$

the exchange conditions of the previous section are also included in these equations. Thus, the production and exchange conditions which constitute the "new welfare economics" are included in the old, but are themselves incomplete.

If we substitute the last identities in the fundamental equations (30), they can easily be thrown into the production and exchange conditions given in (26) plus the new interpersonal element guaranteeing us that the distribution of incomes and lump-sum allowances is optimal. This takes the mathematical form of equality of marginal social utility of income (expressed in terms of any good) for all individuals.

$$\frac{\partial W}{\partial x_i^1} = \frac{\partial W}{\partial x_i^2} = \cdots = \frac{\partial W}{\partial x_i^s} \tag{32}$$

The statement that any "individualistic" ethical optimum can be effected by lump-sum taxes is a theorem, not an axiom. For its proof we require only that the individual indifference curves be such that they can be swung into final equilibrium by operating upon their incomes, letting them trade mechanically at fixed prices. The vast importance of this theorem for social policy in a planned or free enterprise economy is deserving of the greatest emphasis. Yet its greatest significance is in the realm of administration and tactics. From the standpoint of the logic of welfare analysis it is not fundamental. In fact it is not universally true.

First, the indifference curves of one or more individuals may have curvature properties such that the individual who believes or pretends to believe that prices are parameters beyond his control will rush away from rather than toward the correct optimum position. The remarks in the section above dealing with production which discuss the analogy between prices and Lagrangean multipliers and secondary conditions may be referred to here.

Second, and of more practical importance, the optimum position may be reached by means of discriminating all or none offers, sliding scales, etc., rather than by trading at uniform prices. The important thing is the realization of appropriate marginal conditions rather than what happens to the intra-marginal units. (Compare on this point the discussion above of recovery of full cost as a goal of pricing.) In a regime such as this, lump-sum allowances may not suffice to realize the optimum point.

Third, it is not really easy to devise in practice a tax or subsidy which is of a purely lump-sum character. A tax upon income affects marginal decisions with respect to effort and risk-taking. This is obvious. Less conspicuous is the fact that the usual ethical notions compel us to set our allowances according to a man's "circumstances," which are partially the result of his own actions and decision. Analytically, the problem resembles that of determining fair piece rates or of setting a fair "handicap" for golfers of different ability. We wish to equalize opportunity for all contestants, but we do not want them to hold back from playing their best because of a fear of losing their favorable handicap. Ideally, the social managers would have to know the potentialities of every individual; and to remedy the distortions of imperfect lump-sum taxes, they would have to set a system of quotas and penalties based upon potentialities rather than upon performance.

Thus, we might decide that everyone should have at least a minimum income, that Society will make up the deficiency between what the less fortunate can earn and this minimum. Once this is realized by those who fall below the minimum, there is no longer an incentive for them to work at the margin, at least in pecuniary material terms. This is clearly bad social policy, not because I have a vulgar prejudice in favor of work and against leisure. On the contrary, the increases in real income in the years ahead probably will be spent in considerable degree on leisure. It is wrong because it forces the rest of society to give up leisure. Its fault lies in the fact that the individual's allowance is not a lump-sum one. It varies inversely with his effort, and thus penalizes effort. It would be tolerable only if a small percentage of the population were below the minimum, or if we could rely upon new motivations in the Utopia of the future. I, myself, put considerable stock in the possibility of changing conventional patterns of motivation. However, this will not provide comfort to those who wish to utilize a parametric pricing system with algebraic lump-sum allowances, since these same considerations undermine the "individualistic" assumptions upon which their analysis is based.[36]

Fourth, because decisions need only be made concerning incomes, the problem of formulating political slogans and beliefs which will command wide approbation is simplified. However desirable this may be from a political point of view, it must never be forgotten that from a consistent ethical point of view decisions should be made concerning the welfare function itself. Beliefs concerning the distribution of income are derivative rather than fundamental. Except in the admittedly unrealistic case where all tastes are identical, setting up such beliefs as goals is equivalent to accepting a "shibboleth" and to embracing an ambiguous, undefinable welfare function. Among other things such a procedure involves making a shibboleth of the existing distribution of relative technological scarcities of goods. (Of course, whether this is a bad practice is not in itself part of the content of welfare economics, which does not presume to deduce appropriate beliefs. However, welfare economics can legitimately point out the implications of different ethical propositions.)

NEW VERSUS OLD WELFARE ECONOMICS

While in a real sense there is only one all-inclusive welfare economics, which reaches its most complete formulation in the writings of Bergson, it is possible to distinguish between the New Welfare Economics, which involves roughly the contents of the sections on production and exchange and which makes no assumptions concerning interpersonal comparability of utility, and the Old Welfare Economics which starts out with such assumptions. Roughly it is the distinction between Pareto and Pigou. From our above discussion it will be clear that the former is included in the latter, but not vice versa.

Strictly speaking there is no opposition between the two points of view. However, it is not uncommon for expositors of the "new" set of doctrines to imagine that their results have significance even if one is unwilling to make any ethical assumptions. In fact this belief is almost a necessity for anyone who has taken seriously Robbins' dicta concerning the in-

---

[36] The clash between equity and incentive is not unimportant for the present stage of modern capitalism. To an important first approximation the adverse effects of high marginal rates of taxation stem not from the level of the rates, provided they are less than 100 per cent, but from the "curvature" of the tax formula whereby gains increase tax liability more than equivalent losses reduce tax liability. But the essence of "progression" in taxation and in income redistribution is curvature. The only solution lies in pooling risks, and in drafting tax legislation so as to produce a maximum of averaging over time. If this does not suffice, equity may still be worth considerable unavoidable costs.

admissibility of welfare economics in the body of economic theory. Once it is apprehended that the latter notion is a delusion, the need to believe in the significance of the production and exchange conditions divorced from the interpersonal conditions will disappear. Nevertheless, it may be desirable to appraise their significance taken by themselves.

I pass over as being obvious from our discussion of the first six assumptions about the W function that it is not literally true that the new welfare economics is devoid of *any* ethical assumptions. Admittedly, however, its assumptions are more general and less controversial, and it is for this reason that it gives incomplete necessary conditions, whose full significance emerges only after one has made interpersonal assumptions. To refuse to take the last step renders the first two steps nugatory; like pouring out a glass of water and then refusing to drink. To say that the first two conditions should be realized, but that the third is meaningless, is like saying that it does not matter whether or not a man has hair, so long as it is curly!

A limited significance remains for the new welfare economics if we hold that a welfare function is definable but undefined, and if we look for conditions which hold true uniformly for all possible definitions. It cannot tell us which of *any* two situations is better, but it can occasionally rule out one given situation as being worse than another in the sense that everyone is worse off. It cannot tell us when society really has a choice between two given situations. Most important of all it cannot tell us that a movement about which it can give a determinate answer is better than a movement about which it cannot give an answer. If we are at a point not on the Possibility Function, it assures us that there exists a still better point. But it cannot assert that a given point on the Possibility Function is better than all, or many, points not on the Possibility locus.

Concretely, the new welfare economics is supposed to be able to throw light on such questions as to whether the Corn Laws should have been repealed. This act would help many individuals, but hurt landowners. It is usually assumed, although not necessarily quite rigorously, that free trade can be expected to lead to a new "situation" in which those who are benefited can afford to bribe those who are hurt. It is thought that this constitutes a "case" for free trade. Actually, this leads to no positive guide to action. For the new welfare economics cannot state definitely: "The Corn Laws should be repealed, and the landowners should be compensated." Occasionally such a statement is implicit in a writer's formulation, but it is clear that this involves an unwarranted assumption as to the adequacy of the *status quo,* an assumption which the new welfare economics holds to be neither right nor wrong, but meaningless.

On the other hand, the new welfare economics cannot make the definite statement: "The Corn Laws should be repealed, and the owners should *not* be compensated." It can only assert in a negative way: " 'Twere better that the Corn Laws be repealed, and compensation be paid, *if necessary*." It gives no real guide to action. Nor does our experience with man as a social animal suggest that one can safely predict, as a factual matter, that "educated and intelligent men of goodwill" in point of fact tend to move to the generalized contract locus. As an empirical statement of fact we cannot agree with the assertion of Edgeworth that bilateral monopolists must end up somewhere on the contract curve. They may end up elsewhere, because one or both is unwilling to discuss the possibility of making a mutually favorable movement for fear that the discussion may imperil the existing tolerable *status quo*.

Scitovsky[37] has attempted to remedy certain deficiencies in the usual statement of the new welfare economists by developing a double test of the desirability of two situations, in which the distribution of income of the new situation is treated symmetrically with that of the old situation. While his is an improvement on certain earlier statements, it is so primarily in a negative way, to the extent that it delimits the scope of the new welfare economics. His own positive formulation is also a " 'twere better" statement, and not a positive guide to action. Such statements are not without value, but they are not at all substitutes for the policy dictates which stemmed from the old welfare economics.

Within the limited scope of the " 'twere better" statements there is an ambiguity which Scitovsky alone seems to have sensed. The term "situation" can mean a number of different things. It can refer to an actual position reached by every individual prior to the repeal of a tariff, and to the new situation which would actually be attained by each individual after new action is taken, i.e., repeal with varying or no amounts of compensation. Or it can mean the totality of all possible positions available with the Corn Laws unrepealed, and the totality of all possible positions with the Corn Laws repealed. The latter is the more significant sense, and can be given significance in terms of the Possibility Function developed above. Thus, a perfectly legitimate " 'twere better" statement can be made as follows: "Technological change can make everybody better off in the sense that it will shift the Possibility Function outwards."[38] We cannot deduce from this the dictum: "Tech-

---

[37] T. Scitovsky, "A Note on Welfare Propositions in Economics," and "A Reconsideration of the Theory of Tariffs," *Review of Economic Studies*, IX (1941–42), 77–88 and 89–110.

[38] In effect Scitovsky recognizes the case where the Possibility Function is given a twist rather than everywhere being shifted outward.

nological change is a good thing," since the introduction of technological change will in fact mean a vector movement from the old positions of every individual to their new positions which can hardly bode good to all.

At this point the new welfare economist will fall back on the vague statement that "probably technological change will result in good on balance." Not only is this argument on its probability side based upon ignorance rather than knowledge, but it is meaningless as well unless the admissibility of a W function is admitted.

In closing I should like to point out that the point of view which I have been calling the new welfare economics is really only a caricature. On the whole, Pareto, Barone, Hotelling, and Lerner sidestepped interpersonal judgments rather than denied them. Bergson synthesizes the various aspects, as does Lange. Whether Kaldor and Hicks are open to the criticism along the lines which Stigler has recently advanced,[39] the reader must decide.

CONCLUSION

In the present chapter I have attempted to give a brief but fairly complete survey of the whole field of welfare economics. It would be possible to develop the subject further in many respects and to consider a number of related problems. However, limitations of space preclude this, and I shall content myself with two final remarks.

First, what is the best procedure if for some reason a number of the optimum conditions are not realized? What shall we do about the remaining ones which are in our power? Shall we argue that "two wrongs do not make a right" and attempt to satisfy those we can? Or is it possible that failure of a number of the conditions necessitates modifying the rest? Clearly the latter alternative is the correct one. A given divergence in a subset of the optimum conditions necessitates alterations in the remaining ones. Thus, in a world where almost all industries are producing at marginal social cost less than price (either because of monopoly or external economies) it would not be desirable for the rest

---

[39] N. Kaldor, "Welfare Propositions in Economics," *Economic Journal* XLIX (1939), 549–552; J. R. Hicks, "Foundations of Welfare Economics," *Economic Journal*, XLIX (1939), 696–712; G. J. Stigler, "The New Welfare Economics," *American Economic Review*, XXXIII (1943), 355–359; P. A. Samuelson, "Further Commentary on Welfare Economics," *American Economic Review*, XXXIII (1943), 604–607. See also P. A. Samuelson, "Welfare Economics and International Trade," *American Economic Review*, XXVIII (1938), 261–266.

to produce up to the point where marginal cost equals price. Neither would it be quite correct to seek the same percentage or absolute divergence from the optimum conditions in each case; although in this particular example, if the elasticity of the supplies of the factors of production were zero, the proportionality of prices to marginal cost would be as good as the exact equality. Still another example to show that failure of some conditions necessitates alteration of the rest is provided by the possibility of increasing welfare by deliberately selling below marginal costs to groups with a high marginal (social) utility of income. Given a faulty distribution of income, this can improve the situation, although it would be still better to have the full optimal conditions realized.

The last point consists of the warning that the introduction of dynamic conditions into our analysis necessitates a considerable change in the statement of optimal conditions.[40] The difference is not one of principle, but it is nevertheless important. Judged purely on statical grounds, monopolies or a patent system may appear as unmitigated evils, and certainly inferior to atomistic competition and free trade. But in a dynamical world these judgments may have to be reversed; viz. the infant industry argument for protection, the stimulus to large scale research which only a monopolist can afford, the (alleged) necessity to hold out incentives to inventors, etc. Indeed the measure of support which capitalism commands is most importantly related to precisely these factors of development.

In admitting the superiority of monopoly to atomistic competition in certain respects, we do not imply that it is the best possible organization of an industry. There necessarily exists a still better third alternative, which may or may not be less Utopian than the restoration and maintenance of atomistic competition.

[40] Arguments which allege that individuals, under capitalism or socialism, decide what goods they shall consume, but are not capable of making a correct decision with respect to saving seem to suggest that there is a qualitative difference introduced by dynamics. I refer to the argument that wealthy men are necessary in order to provide for saving and capital formation, and that in a socialist state the government should decide what the appropriate amounts of capital formation should be. If one specifies a W function satisfying the first six assumptions and includes in it as separate variables future goods and services, both of these views are wrong whether there is capitalism or socialism. However, especially where problems of the present and future are concerned, modern philosophers balk at the assumption that what people think is best for them really is. Naturally, when the individualistic assumption six is dropped, our conditions are altered. But the same would be true if we denied this assumption in a statical world.

ON THE DENOTATION OF THE IDEAL

William J. Baumol

I

We come now to an essential question on which we have touched several times before—precisely what meaning are we prepared to impute to the term "ideal" which we are taking as the central norm in our discussion? We have defined an ideal situation as one where no change in the behaviour of the individuals in question can increase the efficiency with which they pursue whatever goals they happen to have chosen for themselves. The question need involve no ethical implications. The aims of the group are meant to be taken without question for purposes of a pedestrian inquiry into the efficiency with which the behaviour of the members of that group is engineered to promote them.[1]

The difficulty, in formulating a general criterion, arises, as indicated above, from the ambiguity involved in the concept of the aims of the group, for there may well be conflicting or unrelated aims on the part of the various members. Only if we can develop some criterion as to the relative value or importance of the opinions of these individuals, i.e. only with the development of a criterion for the interpersonal comparison of utility, does the problem seem to admit of a ready solution.[2]

II

Mr. Kaldor[3] has proposed a device similar to that which we have been using and which it was hoped would resolve this difficulty in many cases. Roughly, under the terms of Mr. Kaldor's suggestion, any potential change should be subjected to the following test. All persons who would suffer deleterious effects as a result of the innovation would be asked how much (in money terms) they should consider the minimum amount necessary to compensate them for the inconvenience to which the innovation put them. Similarly, all persons who would benefit from the innovation would be asked to estimate how much money they are willing to give up rather than forgo the benefits to be obtained. The innovation

Source: Welfare Economics and the Theory of the State, Chapter X, pages 161–172. London School of Economics, Harvard University Press, 2nd edition, 1965. Reprinted with permission.

is judged socially desirable so long as the latter sum is greater than the former.

The essence of Mr. Kaldor's innovation is found in the assertion that the community can be considered to be indifferent to an innovation (its real income can be considered unchanged) ". . . if *supposing* that those who are worse off were exactly compensated for their loss at the expense of those who are better off, this redistribution of incomes would leave the real incomes of everyone the same as before."[4] Observe that the condition does not require that the compensation actually be made.

In the words of Dr. Hicks: "A 'permitted reorganization' must . . . be taken . . . to mean a reorganization which will *allow* of compensation being paid, and which will yet show a net advantage. The position is not optimum so long as such reorganization is possible."[5]

Now it is true, as Hicks suggests, and as already mentioned above, that where a "permitted reorganization" is possible the community could, so to speak, do better for itself. The absence of such a possibility is clearly necessary in order that the situation be in some sense optimum, if we approve of a change which harms no one and is desired by some. But caution is here required in applying Mr. Kaldor's principle, for while it contains a necessary condition it is by no means sufficient foundation for an economic optimum. Thus I believe it is quite possible to conceive of "permitted reorganizations" which (it can be argued on utilitarian but non-economic grounds) leave the community as a whole in a worse state than before. And I maintain, moreover, that only by assuming some criterion for the interpersonal comparison of utility can we always distinguish the sheep from the goats, the desirable from the undesirable "permitted reorganizations."

The applicability of Mr. Kaldor's device is, I believe, weakened by one crucial characteristic, namely, that it does not require that persons injured by some economic phenomenon must *actually be compensated* in full by those who have gained from it. It is true that if, upon the establishment of any such innovation, not only were a survey made of the money value of gains and losses but compensation was actually paid, then we would be justified in concluding from this transaction that no persons had lost and at least some persons had gained.[6] In fact, we would be returning to Pareto's criterion: "Consider any situation whatsoever, and suppose there is a very small departure from it, consistent with the circumstances of the case. If, as a result, the well-being of everybody in the group is augmented, it is evident that the new position is preferable to everyone in the group, and vice versa, it is undesirable if the well-being of everyone is diminished. The well-being of some may, moreover, remain constant without affecting our conclusions. . . . It is these considerations which lead us to define a situation to be one of maximum ophelimity if it is such that it is impossible to depart from it slightly in such a manner that all the ophelimity enjoyed by the individuals concerned increases or remains constant."[7]

But what if the compensation suggested (but not required) by Mr. Kaldor's criterion is not in fact made? Are we justified in assuming because the money measure of a gain to one set of individuals is greater than the money measure of the loss to a *different* set of individuals, that society as a whole has indeed benefited? To take a crude illustration, let us assume that all the persons who gain from an innovation are very rich, whereas all the losers are in a highly impoverished state. Is it then reasonable to assume that the subjective value of money does not vary from one group to another? Certainly the fact that the richer group has gained (in money terms) slightly more than the poorer group has lost, is meagre evidence that there has indeed been a balancing between satisfactions and dis-satisfactions. Indeed, it seems very plausible that the same amount of money might well represent a much greater loss to the poorer group than the corresponding gain to the richer.[8]

It turns out then that Mr. Kaldor's criterion has not eliminated the problem of interpersonal comparison of utility. It has only subjected utility to the measuring rod of money, a measuring rod which bends and stretches, and ultimately falls to pieces in our hands. It is my belief that we are not entitled to say merely because one part of the group is able profitably to compensate its other members for any inconvenience caused to the latter that the change in question necessarily involves a gain to the group.[9]

Professor Scitovsky has shown[10] that because of Mr. Kaldor's resort to this flexible yardstick, his criterion may give inconsistent results when the gain from an innovation is compared to the loss from the elimination of that same innovation. Thus both the innovation and its elimination may turn out to be "permitted reorganizations." This results from the possibility that the distribution of "wealth" may be so different in these two cases that in either case those who gain from the change will be more than able to compensate those who lose by it. These arguments are meant to apply even to the restricted alternative criterion proposed by Scitovsky whereby no conclusions would be drawn in those cases where the original criterion led to this type of inconsistency. For it is my contention that a rubber yardstick is not necessarily trustworthy even in those cases where its elasticity is insufficient to permit the conclusion that one distance is simultaneously greater and smaller than another.[11]

The difficulty stems from the fact that we have not discovered what may not be discoverable—an "objective" criterion for an optimum distribution of income, and in any problem in the field of welfare economics we are therefore forced to take the distribution of income as a datum. As soon as a redistribution of income is involved in some innovation with some people having more and some less than before, the economist is prevented from passing judgment upon the desirability (to those affected) of that innovation.

The entire argument of this section can be brought out more clearly with the aid of Professor Samuelson's utility possibility curve.[12] Considering an economy composed of two individuals, let us indicate in Fig. 12 the state of welfare or utility of one individual, X, along the x axis, and that of the other, Y, along the vertical axis. It is not necessary for our purpose to be able to measure utility or welfare, for we insist merely that the index whereby we measure utility increases when the individual in question feels himself better off, decreases when he feels his welfare diminished, and otherwise remains unchanged. Thus we are interested in an ordinal rather than a cardinal measure of utility, and any index having the required characteristics will do equally well, i.e. we have, as Samuelson put it, "rubber axes."

Suppose now that in a given situation the possible combinations of the welfare of X and Y, obtainable by modification of the system of distribution and nothing else, is shown by line AA'. This line is drawn in such a way that if the welfare position of X is given by OX, then XT is the best that can be done for Y under the circumstances. From the stipulation that it is the distribution of welfare which is affected by a movement along AA', we may expect that AA' will be downward sloping, i.e. that an increase in the welfare of X will involve a deterioration in Y's position.[13]

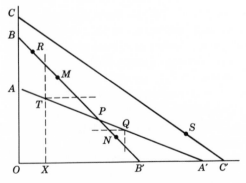

Figure 12

Suppose now that some change occurs, such as the removal of a tariff, and that as a result our utility possibility curve shifts from AA' to BB' where the two lines intersect at P. Is the change in question desirable? Clearly, if the initial situation were represented by point T, and the new situation by point M, both X and Y would now be better off. On the other hand, if the initial situation were represented by point Q on AA' while the new situation was that indicated by N, both parties would have preferred the initial circumstances. The change is thus not unambiguously desirable or undesirable.

We may now distinguish four criteria that have been suggested:

(a) *Pareto's criterion:* To apply this we must know the initial point and the point after the change. Then the change is an improvement if it involves a movement from a point like T to a point like M, so that both parties benefit. Similarly, the change is socially undesirable if it involves a movement from a point like Q to a point like N. In all other cases we cannot judge.

(b) *Bergson's criterion:* To apply this we must have an exhaustive social evaluation which indicates how society regards all the possible distributions of welfare to the individuals concerned, indicated by the various points on the map. Interpersonal comparison of worth is generally involved in this, and it is the social value judgment *par excellence.* The description of the evaluation decided upon is called the social welfare function,[14] and may be represented by drawing indifference curves all over the diagram. The change in question is an improvement if and only if it involves a movement to a higher indifference curve. Note that this criterion is more complete than Pareto's, and like it, requires that we know the actual points representing the situations before and after the change. Pareto's criterion, however, goes as far as is possible without passing judgment on what constitutes a desirable distribution.

(c) *Kaldor's criterion:* If the initial situation is given by T, then the change is taken to be an improvement if there exists on the new utility possibility curve *any* point such as M which leaves both X and Y better off than before. For if there exists any such point it is always *possible* to make the change in a way which leaves both parties better off, i.e. by moving from T to M. Mr. Kaldor suggests that the possibility of a movement from T to M proves that a change from T to any point on BB' is an improvement, even a change to point N, which involves a loss to Y. The argument of this section has been that the Kaldor criterion tacitly assumes all points on any utility possibility curve to be equally desirable, i.e. that the utility possibility curves are taken to be the indifference curves of the social welfare function. For then, if there exists any point such as M on BB' which is superior to point T by Pareto's criterion then any point on BB' must be superior to T.[15]

We come finally to

(d) *Scitovsky's double criterion:* If the changeover in question involves a movement from a point like T to a point like N, then by Kaldor's criterion the change from AA' to BB' is an improvement since there is a point M on BB' superior to T. But the change back from BB' to AA' is also an improvement, since there is a point Q on AA' which is superior to N. Thus by Kaldor's criterion both the change and its elimination represent improvements. To eliminate the difficulty Scitovsky proposes to call the change an improvement only if the change from the first point is an improvement on Kaldor's criterion, and if, at the same time, the change back is undesirable on Kaldor's criterion. Thus if the change is from T to, say, R it is an improvement on Scitovsky's criterion, since the movement from T to any point on BB' is an improvement on Kaldor's criterion, as before, but the movement from R to AA' is undesirable, since there are no points on AA' which leave both X and Y better off than they are at R. On the other hand, on the Scitovsky double criterion we can pass no judgment on a movement from T to N. If my argument about the tacit assumption behind the Kaldor criterion is correct the difficulty is not yet taken care of, for if all points on AA' are taken to be equally desirable, and all points on BB' are equally desirable, we cannot, as we do, have point M on BB' superior to point T on AA', and at the same time point Q on AA' superior to point N on BB'. Thus, where the utility possibility curves intersect, there is an implicit contradiction in the use of Mr. Kaldor's criterion; this because the curves are used as indifference curves, and such a difficulty arises any time indifference curves intersect.[16]

The contradiction can of course be eliminated by confining the use of the criterion to changes which involve non-intersecting utility possibility curves, e.g. a change which moves the curve from AA' to CC'. But this still avoids the basic difficulty. Thus point S on CC' represents an improvement in the position of X, and a deterioration in the position of Y as compared to the situation represented by point R. We can then only clearly choose between S and R if we are prepared to take a stand on how we believe welfare should be distributed, i.e. only with the use of Bergson's criterion.[17]

Little has recently formulated another criterion:[18] a change is an improvement if and only if (a) its elimination is not improvement in terms of Kaldor's criterion and (b) the resulting redistribution of welfare is judged desirable. In other words, the losers must not be able profitably to bribe the gainers to oppose the change and the ethical predilections of the examiner must be satisfied by the change in distribution resulting. In terms of Fig. 12 the change from Q to M will be an improvement on Little's criterion if the movement along possibility curve AA' from Q to T is judged desirable. For a movement along a possibility curve is what Little means by a redistribution of welfare, and at M the distribution of welfare may be judged roughly similar to that at T. Moreover, M is above AA' so that there is no point on AA' better than M for both persons. Thus losers can never bribe gainers back to AA', i.e. to Q.[19] This criterion may be considered a useful special form of the Bergson criterion, for as Little points out,[20] the construction of a complete social welfare function or any appreciable segment of one is generally quite inconceivable in practice. On the other hand, judgment of the desirability of a change in distribution seems to be a question begging device which makes the rest of the procedure somewhat pointless.

III

Which of these criteria can we accept then? We have seen that Mr. Kaldor has indeed provided us with a necessary criterion for the ideal in that the possibility of a "permitted reorganization," i.e. one which allows of compensation to be paid and yet shows a net advantage, means that the group could indeed do better for itself by making the change in question complete with compensations if there is no other way. We may then say that the ideal is a member of that set of situations from which no "permitted reorganization" is possible.

That still leaves us the unhappy task of segregation within this set, for it is by no means certain that all the members of the set in question are ideal. Here no satisfactory answer has been developed. The best that can be done is to say that the problem is a political one and that it can be solved only by some sort of collective decision by the group. This answer obviously leaves much to be desired, but I can see no alternative.

With this rather feeble result, how are we to interpret our entire analysis, dependent as it is on the concept of the ideal? There are two alternatives possible. The one which involves the strictest interpretation of our results can be developed on the assumption that the political decisions in question have somehow been made. These being taken for granted it follows that there is some sort of unambiguous definition of the ideal, and the rest follows without difficulty. However, a more restricted interpretation is also possible. If in the discussion we take a departure from the ideal to mean a change which could be eliminated by instituting a "permitted reorganization," and by interpreting a change to the ideal to mean the institution of a "permitted reorganization" *with* compensation, then the argument employed requires no modification.

This latter form of the argument may well be preferred on the ground that its procedure is less questionable, but it requires considerable care in interpreting the results, for the ideal does not then mean exactly what we would like it to mean.

In terms of the analysis at the end of the last section, I have just suggested that we must adopt either Pareto's or Bergson's criterion. The reason I feel the other criteria we have considered are unsatisfactory I have already gone into at length. For most of our arguments we have employed and shall employ no more than Pareto's criterion.

Now it is clear that Pareto's criterion cannot in all cases give us unambiguous results, and if, indeed, as Professor Samuelson has suggested,[21] we should require perfection in our recommendations, this criterion can never give us any results. Thus if we draw a utility possibility map in Fig. 13 and consider the point R which lies below the utility possibility curve BB', it is clear that on Pareto's criterion any point lying on the segment CC' of BB' within the quadrant given by NRM (RN and RM being parallel to the Y and X axes respectively) is superior to point R, since any point on CC' leaves both parties better off than they were at R. But we have no assurance that there are no other points on BB' which are superior to every point on CC'. Indeed there may even be points below BB' which are superior to every point on CC'. Thus, suppose that Y is a notorious war criminal, and we are unwilling to give him very much at X's expense. Then point H, which leaves X better off than he would be anywhere on CC', may be considered preferable, even though Y is here in a worse position than he is anywhere on CC'. It follows that on Pareto's criterion alone we can never find the "best" point possible, and as a result Professor Samuelson seems to feel that we can do nothing with the criterion by way of recommendation.

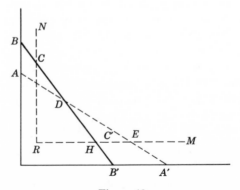

Figure 13

It is my opinion, however, that such extreme perfectionism is unnecessary. Surely, in the absence of further information, unless we specifically desire to do someone dirt, we are permitted to say concerning the situation shown in the figure that if we are at R then we are fools if we do not move to some point on CC' unless we soon expect more information. Of course, if there is another utility possibility curve such as AA' which lies above and to the right of some parts of BB' in the quadrant MRN, where we might for example attain AA' by modifying a tariff, then we must recommend a move to somewhere on CDE, or more generally to a point on the envelope of all the utility possibility curves lying in MRN. This is the approach we have employed in our discussion. We have defined a situation as not ideal if, like R, it lies below some utility possibility curve, and we argue that rationality then requires that there be a changeover from R to some point on the envelope of the utility possibility curves lying in MRN, this in the absence of better information.

NOTES

[1] Professor Knight has cast doubts on the legitimacy of this entire procedure by advocating a more dynamic approach to the problem of ends (goals). He suggests that goals may be modified in the process of seeking their attainment, that the nature of the modification is not independent of the means chosen for their pursuit, and indeed, that means are themselves ends in many cases. No doubt these contentions are quite valid, yet a government or an individual must take some ends as given at every moment of time or else be doomed either to pointless activity or complete inaction. No doubt the ends taken as given must at all times be under revision, but no more than this can be conceded without giving up all activity in hopeless confusion. For otherwise, if every course taken by anyone involved no distinct set of ends for him at a moment taken as initial, he could never decide which course to pursue, there being no frame of reference. Even with this concession a great deal of strength is lost to the argument, for while rational decision remains possible, *ex post* evaluation of the rationality of past activity becomes impossible—a person cannot, in general, judge whether an alternative course would have made him happier than the one he actually did take, since he is in effect a different person from the one he would have been had he adopted the alternative procedure.

Since, however, *ex ante* evaluation remains valid under the assumption of a given set of ends at any moment, and since it is this which is relevant to decision and policy, our analysis can proceed on the basis of this contention.

[2] Cf. Lionel Robbins, *The Nature and Significance of Economic Science,* Chapter VI.

See also Kenneth Arrow's illuminating discussion of the entire problem of an acceptable reconciliation of choices in his *Social choice and Individual Values.*

[3] Nicholas Kaldor, "Welfare Propositions in Economics," *Economic Journal,* September 1939, pp. 549–52. For earlier versions see Barone, "The Ministry of Produc-

tion in the Collectivist State," in *Collectivist Economic Planning,* F. A. Hayek, editor, pp. 255–6; and Jacob Viner, *Studies in the Theory of International Trade,* pp. 532–4, where the argument is stated and applied in detail, but the pitfalls of the Hicks-Kaldor version are neatly avoided by scrupulous interpretation of the welfare implications.

[4] Kaldor, "A Note on Tariffs and the Terms of Trade," *Economica,* November 1940, p. 378 (my italics).

[5] J. R. Hicks, "The Foundations of Welfare Economics," *Economic Journal,* December 1939, p. 706 (my italics).

[6] Professor Viner argues that even this may be conceding too much, because people may judge incorrectly as to the amount of compensation required to leave them indifferent. Also a reorganization may have impaired their relative standing in the community, even though their absolute share has increased, and it may be the former which is the more important. This criticism can be avoided in a circular manner by assuming that compensation demands take account of all psychological damage, including the ill effects of loss of standing.

[7] Vilfredo Pareto, *Manuel d'Economie Politique,* 2nd edition, pp. 617–18. Cf., however, Wicksell's objections, *Lectures on Political Economy,* Volume I, pp. 83.

[8] ". . . a pound's worth of satisfaction to an ordinary poor man is a much greater thing than a pound's worth of satisfaction to an ordinary rich man. . . ." Marshall, *Principles of Economics,* eighth edition, p. 130.

[9] But see Kaldor's reply, *Review of Economic Studies,* 1946–7, also Arrow's elucidation of my position, *op. cit.,* pp. 38–40.

[10] "A Note on Welfare Propositions in Economics," *Review of Economic Studies,* November 1941, pp. 77–88.

[11] Scitovsky does, however, briefly consider the point now being argued. He states: ". . . it might be argued that the abolition of the Corn Laws should not have been advocated by economists in their capacity of pure economists without advocating at the same time the full compensation of landowners out of taxes levied on those favoured by the cheapening of corn. Yet, in a sense, and regarded from a long-run point of view, such propositions are not independent of value judgments between alternative income distributions either. For, going out of their way to preserve the existing distribution of income, they imply a preference for the *status quo*" (*op. cit.,* p. 79). Cf., on the other hand, M. Reder, *Studies in the Theory of Welfare Economics,* Chapter VIII, I; and I. M. D. Little, "The Foundations of Welfare Economics," *Oxford Economic Papers,* 1949, p. 233.

But of course it is not my argument that the *status quo* should be preserved, or that the economist *should* in fact always recommend full compensation. But I do claim that *qua* positivist he can only differentiate between an improvement and a deterioration in general welfare when compensation is in fact made. In order to be able to distinguish an improvement in the general case, and indeed, to decide what should be done about compensation, he must resort tacitly or explicitly to his political postulates, which include among them a criterion for interpersonal comparison of worth. It is in fact my contention that the criterion under discussion is the one which exhibits a predilection for the distributive *status quo,* in that it is weighted by the "compensating power" of the individuals involved. Note that I do not argue against Little's view (*op. cit.,* pp. 243–4) that interpersonal comparison of utility involves no value judgments. Yet in welfare economics I think we require somewhat more than comparison of *utility*. We need to decide whether we weigh the brahmin's and the untouchable's utility equally once having compared them, and this certainly does require a value judgment.

[12] Cf. *Foundations of Economic Analysis,* Chapter VIII, especially p. 243 *et seq.;* also the same author's "Evaluation of Real National Income," *Oxford Economic Papers,* January 1950.

[13] Where there are external economies of consumption, it is conceivable that the utility possibility curve will slope upwards for part of its range, e.g. if Y gets so much joy out of a gift to X that they both benefit by a transfer of goods from Y to X. Mr. Graaff has also shown that where we draw the utility possibility curve subject to the condition that all other members of the economy are kept indifferent to the transfers involved, then an upward-sloping utility possibility curve may in some queer cases result from the existence of external *diseconomies* of consumption. See J. de V. Gaaaff, "On Optimum Tariff Structures," *Review of Economic Studies,* 1949–50, p. 49, footnote 2.

[14] Cf. A. Bergson, "A Reformulation of Certain Aspects of Welfare Economics," *Quarterly Journal of Economics,* February 1938. Most writers seem to be content to specialize the social welfare function to

$$W = W[U_1(x_{11}, \ . \ . \ . \ ,x_{1n}), \ . \ . \ . \ ,U_s(X_{s1} \ . \ . \ . \ ,x_{sn})];$$

where there are s individuals and n goods and services in the system, and where xij is the quantity of the jth good going to the ith person, and Ui is one of the ith person's preference functions whose cardinal form, like that of W, is arbitrary; cf., for example, Paul A. Samuelson, *Foundations of Economic Analysis,* pp. 221–30. (But see Gerhard Tintner, "A Note on Welfare Economics," *Econometrica,* 1946, for a formulation which avoids the strictures of this note.)

It is, of course, one of my main contentions here that this involves an over-simplification, and that by neglecting the fact that in practice

$$Ui = Ui(x_{11}, \ . \ . \ . \ ,x_{1n},x_{21}, \ . \ . \ . \ ,x_{2n}, \ . \ . \ . \ ,x_{i1}, \ . \ . \ . \ ,x_{in}, \ . \ . \ . \ ,x_{sn})$$

(external economies of consumption), we permit some of the most interesting problems of welfare economics to slip through our fingers.

As a consequence of this neglect Samuelson accepts, though guardedly, the argument widely proposed among economists that it might be socially beneficial to permit free sale of ration coupons by those not desiring to use them (*op. cit.,* p. 171), this on the ground that both parties to such a voluntary exchange must benefit by it if they are to be induced to engage in it at all. But this view neglects the possibility (which I believe to be very real) that less affluent persons would suffer considerable annoyance at the prospect of the wealthy being thus able to augment their rations in times of shortage, and that while they might sell their rations once such a free market were established, they could still prefer to prevent such supplementation of the consumption of the rich altogether. Is it not for a similar reason that the purchase of replacements by affluent conscripts is no longer permitted? I suggest that anyone who thinks this argument is far fetched consider the probable reaction to such a proposal. In addition there is the danger that some persons might be led by such a scheme to neglect their health, and this (especially in a world where military preparation is valued highly) may have marked external diseconomies. (Note I am *not* arguing that the individual is not the best judge of the amount of effort to be devoted to health insofar as it affects only him.) A similar objection may apply to Reder's view that rationing of incomes is superior to rationing of individual commodities. ("Welfare Economics and Rationing," *Quarterly Journal of Economics,* November 1942.) For the consumption of some goods by a minority may have external diseconomies (e.g. cheese- and meat-lovers may still bid away all protein foods with a resultant deterioration in the health of others which itself has external diseconomies). Also limitation of some consumption having direct external diseconomies (alcohols?) may be desired. This may also make some excise taxes preferable to income taxes. Cf. also W. C. Haraldson, "Welfare Economics and Rationing," *Quarterly Journal of Economics,* November 1943.

[15] The illustrative argument which compared the compensating ability of a rich and a poor man and indicated that the same change might, by Mr. Kaldor's criterion, be desirable or undesirable, depending on whether the person who gained from the change was the rich or the poor man, can be translated into our diagram by assuming that the axes are measured in some sort of true (cardinal) utility units. In this case the utilitarian bias in which a unit of utility of one man is worth as much as that of another would result in straight-line downward-sloping indifference curves, representing our social welfare function, making a 45-degree angle with either axis. This would mean that the loss of one utility unit by X must be offset by the gain of exactly one utility unit by Y in order that the change may leave society indifferent. Now the diminishing marginal utility of income would mean that the utility possibility curve is concave to the origin, since constant gains in utility to X by means of money transfers from Y must mean ever greater losses in utility to Y. When conceived this way it follows that the utility possibility curve and the indifference curve of the social welfare functions cannot possibly be the same. The argument is meant to indicate that Mr. Kaldor's implicit use of the utility possibility curve as an indifference curve does not seem to be in line with some often accepted value judgments on interpersonal comparisons.

[16] Indeed I believe this is the reason we have the possibility of intersection of the community indifference curves (which are constructed on Kaldor's criterion), cf. Chapter 3, Section II above.

[17] This is essentially my objection to a fifth criterion proposed by Samuelson in his lectures at the London School of Economics in the autumn of 1948, whereby a change is an improvement if and only if the new utility possibility curve nowhere intersects the old curve and lies above it at all points, as in the change from AA' to CC'. This criterion has recently been discussed in print in Samuelson's "Evaluation of Real National Income," *Oxford Economic Papers,* January 1950, pp. 10–11. Some objections are mentioned on p. 11.

[18] I. M. D. Little, *A Critique of Welfare Economics,* Appendix and Chapters VI and VII.

[19] Thus Little's criterion permits us to judge between points like Q and M, but not between points like T and N. The reverse holds for the Kaldor criterion. However, Little argues that (say) rather than move from T to N the community might better redistribute income and move to Q. This may neglect political feasibility.

[20] I. M. D. Little, *op. cit.,* Chapter VII.

[21] Cf. P. A. Samuelson, "Welfare Economics and International Trade," *American Economic Review,* 1938; also *Foundations,* pp. 249–52.

MANUEL D'ECONOMIE POLITIQUE
(Ophélimité)

Vilfredo Pareto

32. Property of equilibrium. Equilibrium, according to the conditions in which it is obtained, possesses certain properties which it is important to know.

33. We will begin by defining a term which it is profitable to use in order to avoid length. We will say that the members of a collectivity enjoy, in a certain position, the *maximum of ophélimité,* when it is impossible to find a means of moving away a very little from that position, in such a way that the *ophélimité* which each of the individuals of that collectivity enjoys increases or decreases. That is to say, any small displacement departing from that position has necessarily for an effect to increase the *ophélimité* which certain individuals enjoy, and to decrease that which others enjoy: to be agreeable to some, disagreeable to others.

34. Equilibrium of exchange. We have the following theorem:

For phenomena of type (I), when equilibrium takes place at a point where the indifference curves of the contracting parties are tangent, the members of the collectivity under consideration enjoy the maximum of ophélimité.

Let us note that we can arrive at this position of equilibrium either by a rectilinear path, that is to say, with prices constant, or by any path whatsoever.

35. A rigorous demonstration of this theorem can be given with the aid of mathematics (Appendix); we will content ourselves here with giving a rough sketch.

Let us begin by considering exchange between two individuals [Figure 50]. For the first one, the axes are ox and oy, and for the second $\omega\alpha$ and $\omega\beta$; and let us lay them out in a way that the paths travelled by the two individuals meld into a single line on figure 16 (III, 116). The in-

Source: Manuel D'Economie Politique, Second Edition, 1927. Translated by Ann Stranquist Schwier; an alternative translation is forthcoming by the American Economic Association. Reprinted with permission.

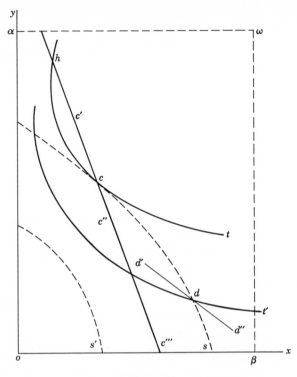

Figure 50

difference lines are t, t', t'', . . . , for the first individual, and s, s', s'', . . . , for the second. For the first one the hill of pleasure ascends from o toward ω, and for the second, on the contrary, it ascends from ω toward o.

For phenomena of type (I), it is known that the point of equilibrium must be found at a point of tangency of the indifference curves of the two individuals. Let c be one of these points. If we move away from it following the route cc', we ascend the hill of pleasure of the first individual, descend that of the second; and inversely if we follow the route cc''. It is not then possible to move away from c helping, or harming, both individuals at one time; but necessarily, if it is agreeable to the one, it is disagreeable to the other.

It is not the same for points, such as d, where two indifference curves intersect. If we follow the route dd', we increase the pleasure of both individuals; if we follow the line dd'', we decrease it for both.

36. For phenomena of type (I) equilibrium takes place at a point

such as c; for phenomena of type (II), equilibrium takes place at a point such as d; hence the difference between these two types of phenomena, in regard to the maximum of *ophélimité*.

37. Returning to fig. 50,[1] we see intuitively that, by extending the path cc' towards h, we always descend the hill of pleasure of the second individual, whereas, on the contrary, we indeed begin by climbing the hill of pleasure of the first individual, but then we descend, when we are beyond the point where $cc'h$ is tangent to an indifference line. Consequently, if we move away from the position of equilibrium a finite distance along a straight line, the *ophélimités* which the two individuals enjoy can vary in such a way that the one increases while the other decreases, or they both decrease together; but they cannot increase together. That is true, however, only for goods the *ophélimités* of which are independent, or in the cases where these goods have a dependence of the first type (IV, 42).

Mathematics alone (Appendix) allows the giving of a rigorous proof, not only in this case, but also in the general case of several goods and several individuals.

38. If we could perform on human society experiments such as the chemist performs in his laboratory, the preceding theorem would permit us to resolve the following problem:

A given collectivity is considered; the indices of ophélimité of its members are unknown; it is known that with the exchange of certain quantities there is equilibrium; we ask whether it is obtained in the same conditions in which it would be obtained by free competition?

We must perform an experiment in order to see whether, the manner in which exchangers are made remaining the same, we can add (note well: add and not substitute) other exchanges, made at constant prices, which please all the individuals. If so, equilibrium does not take place as when free competition exists, if not, it takes place in these conditions.

39. *Equilibrium of production.* We must distinguish here several cases:

(1) *Selling prices constant.* (α) Coefficients of production variable with the total quantity, that is to say goods whose cost of production varies with the quantity. (β) Coefficients of production constant with the quantity, that is to say goods whose cost of production is constant.

(2) *Selling prices variable.*

40. 1 (α). This case is given us by fig. 46 (Par. 4). The points of equilibrium c, c' are not those which give the maximum of *ophélimité* in

---

[1] [Trans. note—The French text reads fig. 49 but clearly means fig. 50.]

the transformation (Appendix). Consequently, there can be a point which is not on the line of complete transformations and such that the transforming enterprise has a profit there, while the consumers are better off than at c, c'. This case, in reality, is occasionally realized with trusts.

41. 1 (β). This is the case of fig. 44 (Par. 1). The point of equilibrium c gives the maximum of *ophélimité* for the transformations (Appendix).

42. 2. The variable prices can be such that they produce a phenomenon analogous to that of case 1 (α).

But if we can arrange these prices to obtain the maximum of *ophélimité* in the transformations, we can in this way reach the point e, fig. 51, which gives this maximum (Appendix).

43. If we follow the path amu of complete transformations, we certainly arrive there; the same also if we follow a path avu, which coincides with that line only in the part veu; or finally a path $all'e$ tangent at e to the line of complete transformations and to the indifference line t.

In reality, this last path is very difficult to follow, because one must guess precisely where point e is found; the first two paths, on the contrary, can be followed without knowing precisely where point e is.

44. It is probable that the greatest part of production is of the type in which the cost of production varies with the quantity produced; we can, consequently, assert that the system of constant prices, which is generally used in our society, does not procure the maximum of *ophélimité;* and if we take into account the great number of products

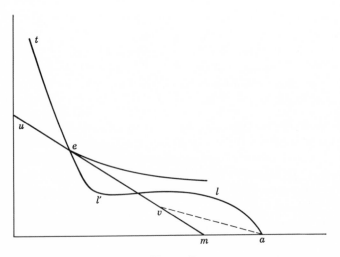

Figure 51

to which this conclusion applies, it appears that the loss of *ophélimité* must be very great.

45. It is because of this that, even in our social organization, producers have an advantage in practicing variable prices; and, as they cannot do it directly, they endeavour to do it indirectly by expedients which can only very crudely approach the solution which would give the maximum of *ophélimité*.

Generally, variable prices are practiced by distinguishing the consumers by categories; and this expedient is better than nothing, but it is indeed far from the solution which would make prices vary for all consumers.

46. The very grave error which judges economic facts according to moral standards leads many people, in a more or less conscious fashion, to think that the profit of the producer can be only the loss of the consumer and vice versa. Consequently, if the producer gains nothing, if he is on the line of complete transformations, it is imagined that the consumer cannot suffer any loss.

Without insisting on the fact that, as we have already seen (Par. 10), the line of complete transformations may be obtained with an excess cost of production, it is well not to forget the very frequent case indicated in Par. 39.1 (α).

47. Assume, for example, that a country consumes 100 of a good X and that this good is produced by home factories at a cost of 5 per unit. The total cost is 500; and if the total selling price is also 500, the home producers make no profit.

It happens now that they produce 200, which lowers the cost of production to 3. They sell 120 within the country at a price of 3.50, and 80 abroad at a price of 2.50. In total they receive 620 for a good which costs them 600, and consequently they make a profit. The domestic consumers moan because they pay more for the good than that which is sold to foreigners; but, at bottom, they pay less for it than they paid before, and consequently they have an advantage, and not a loss.

It may be, but it is not certain, that a similar phenomenon takes place occasionally in Germany, where the producers sell to foreigners at a lower price than that which they obtain within the country; for in this way they can increase the quantity produced and reduce the cost of production.

48. The phenomena which we have just studied suggest, in an abstract way and without taking into account the practical difficulties, a considerable argument in favor of collectivist production. Much better than the production partially subject to competition, partially to monopolies, which we actually have, it could make use of variable prices which

would permit the following of the line of complete transformations, and consequently reach point *e* of fig. 46 (Par. 4), whereas actually we must stop at point *c'*, or even at point *c*. The advantage which society would have could be so great that it would compensate for the inevitable losses of a production of this type. But in order to do so the collectivist production would have to have for its only purpose an endeavour to obtain the maximum of *ophélimité* in production, and not to procure the profits of monopoly for the workers, or to pursue humanitarian ideals.[2] As the old economists had clearly seen, the research of greatest advantage for society is a problem of production.

Even cooperative societies could bring us on to the line of complete transformations, but that does not happen because they allow themselves to deviate from their purpose through their ethical, philanthropic, humanitarian views. One cannot pursue two hares at once.

If we consider the phenomenon from the point of view of the economic theories exclusively, it is a very poor way of organizing the private enterprise of railroads which exacts from the societies which exploit them, as has been done in Italy, a fixed deduction on the gross product (or even on the net product) for the profit of the state, because in that way, instead of impelling them to approach the line of complete transformations, they are detracted from it.

49. Free competition determines the coefficients of production in a way to assure the maximum of *ophélimité* (Appendix). It tends to render equal the net revenues of the capital goods which can be produced by means of saving; in effect, saving is evidently transformed into the capital goods which yield the most revenue, until the abundance of these capital goods makes the net revenue from them fall to the common level. This equality of net revenues is equally a condition for obtaining the maximum of *ophélimité* from the use of these capital goods. Even in this case, rigorous proof can be given only with mathematics;[3] we can here only indicate somewhat the course of the phenomenon.

50. In regard to the revenue of capital goods, we can remark that if savings obtain a greater income in one certain use than in another, that signifies that the first use is more "productive" than the second. Consequently there is an advantage for "society" in decreasing the second use of savings in order to increase the first,[4] and we also arrive at the equality of the net revenues in the two cases. But this reasoning is cer-

---

[2] Among the socialists, G. Sorel has the great merit of having understood that the problem which collectivism must solve is principally a problem of production.

[3] Cours, Par. 724.

[4] [Trans. note—The French text reverses the words "first" and "second" in this sentence.]

tainly not very precise, not at all rigorous, and consequently, by itself alone, it could indeed prove nothing.

51. A little better, but a very little, is the reasoning which, without making use of mathematics, brings in the coefficients of production.

Enterprises determine them in a way to have the minimum cost; but competition drives them onto the line of complete transformations; consequently, it is their customers, buyers and sellers, who definitely derive an advantage from the work accomplished by the enterprises.

The fault of this type of proofs does not rest only in that they lack precision, but also, and principally, in that they do not give a clear idea of the conditions necessary in order that the theorems be true.

52. *Equilibrium in the collectivist society.* We must now speak of phenomena of type (III), to which we have, up to now, simply alluded (III, 49).

In order to give them a concrete form, and by an abstraction analogous to that of the *homo oeconomicus,* let us consider a collectivist society, which has for an end to procure to its members the maximum[5] of *ophélimité.*

53. The problem divides into two others which are completely different and which cannot be solved by the same criteria: (1) We have a problem of distribution: how ought the goods which the society possesses or produces be divided among the members? (III, 12, 16). We must bring in ethical considerations, social considerations of a different type, comparisons of *ophélimité* between different individuals, etc. We do not have to occupy ourselves with that here. We will therefore assume this problem solved. (2) We have a problem of production: how to produce the economic goods in such a way that, on distributing them then according to the rules obtained by the solution of the first problem, the members of the society obtain the maximum of *ophélimité?*

54. After all that we have said, the solution of this problem is easy.[6]

Prices, the net interest on capital goods can disappear, if however that is possible, as real entities; but they will remain as accounting entities; without them the *minister of production* would move along

---

[5] [Trans. note—The French text reads "minimum" which is obviously an error.]

[6] [Trans. note—The classic work on this subject is, of course, Barone's famous article "Il Ministro della produzione nello stato collectivista," in the *Giornale degli economisti,* 1908, and available in English in *Collectivist Economic Planning,* F. A. von Hayek, ed., (London: George Routledge and Sons, Ltd., 1935). Schumpeter points out that the essential idea of Barone's argument—namely, that the "logical core" of the economic process, the theory of production, is essentially independent of its "institutional garb," the social organization—is clearly indicated by Pareto here. "Vilfredo Pareto," *Quarterly Journal of Economics,* Vol. LXIII, (1949), pp. 147–173.]

blindly and would not know how to organize production. It is clearly understood that if the state is the owner of all capital goods, all the net interest goes to it.

55. In order to obtain the maximum of *ophélimité*, the collectivist state must render the different net interests equal and determine the coefficients of production in the same way that free competition determines them. Moreover, after having made the distribution according to the rules of the first problem, it must permit a new distribution which the members of the collectivity can operate among themselves, or that the socialist state can make, but which, in any case, must take place as if it were operated by free competition.

56. The difference between the phenomena of type (I) and those of type (III) resides, then, principally in the division of incomes. In the phenomena of type (I), this division operates according to all the historical and economic contingencies within which the society has evolved; in the phenomena of type (III); it is the result of certain ethico-social principles.

APPENDIX

89. (γ) *Maximum of ophélimité*. It is convenient first of all to define this term exactly. There are, as we have seen (VI, 53), two problems to resolve to procure the maximum of well being for a collectivity. Certain rules of distribution being adopted, we can investigate which position gives, always following these rules, the greatest well-being possible to the individuals of a collectivity.

Consider any position whatsoever, and assume that we move away from it by a very small quantity, compatibly with the interconnections. If in doing that we increase the well-being of all the individuals of the collectivity, it is evident that the new position is more advantageous to each one of them; and vice versa, it is less so if we decrease the well-being of all the individuals. The well-being of certain ones among them can, moreover, remain constant, without these conclusions changing. But if, on the contrary, this small movements increases the well-being of certain individuals and decreases that of the others, we can no longer assume that it is advantageous to the entire collectivity to effect that movement.

These are the considerations which lead to defining as the position of maximum *ophélimité* that from which it is impossible to move away by a very small amount, in such a way that all the *ophélimités* which the individuals enjoy, except those which remain constant, each receive an increase or a decrease (VI, 33).

Let us indicate by δ any variations whatsoever, as for example when we pass from one path to another (Par. 22); and by Φ_1, Φ_2, . . . , the total *ophélmités* for each individual. Consider the expression

$$\frac{1}{\varphi_{1a}} \delta\Phi_1 + \frac{1}{\varphi_{2a}} \delta\Phi_2 + \frac{1}{\varphi_{3a}} \delta\Phi_3 + \cdots \qquad (112)$$

If we exclude the case where the $\delta\Phi_1$, $\delta\Phi_2$, . . . , are zero, it is seen that, the quantities φ_{1a}, φ_{2a}, . . . , being essentially positive, this expression (112) can become zero only if a portion of the $\delta\Phi$ is positive, and another portion is negative; a portion can, however, still be zero. Consequently, if we set up

$$0 = \frac{1}{\varphi_{1a}} \delta\Phi_{1a} + \frac{1}{\varphi_{2a}} \delta\Phi_{2a} + \frac{1}{\varphi_{3a}} \delta\Phi_{3a} + \cdots , \qquad (113)$$

we exclude the case where all the variations are positive, or negative. Equation (113) characterizes, then, according to our definition, the maximum of *ophélimité* for the collectivity under consideration. The variations which are found in this equation must all be those which are compatible with the interconnections of the system.

It is convenient to choose the definition of the maximum of *ophélimité* for a collectivity in such a way that it coincides with that which is valid for a single individual, when the collectivity is reduced to that single individual. This is effectively what occurs for the definition which we have just given (Par. 116).

A NOTE ON TARIFFS AND THE TERMS OF TRADE

Nicholas Kaldor

1. In the foregoing paper Dr. Benham raises the question whether the advantage accruing to a country through improvement in the terms of trade, consequent upon the imposition of a tariff, could compensate for the disadvantage arising on account of a smaller volume of trade.

It can be demonstrated that the introduction of a system of import duties will always improve the position of the country imposing it, provided that the rate of duty is below a certain critical level, and provided also that the introduction of the tariff does not lead to retaliation, in the form of the imposition of higher duties, by other countries.[1] It can also be shown that there is a particular rate of duty which makes the net advantage accruing from the tariff a maximum.[2]

2. Our demonstration is based on the Edgeworth barter diagram, and since the two parties in question here are two nations, and not two individuals, it employs the concept of "community indifference curves," of which it is necessary to say a few words. A "community indifference curve" is the locus of points representing a constant real income for the community as a whole. In so far as individuals' tastes differ or their money-incomes differ, or the distribution of incomes varies, positions representing a constant real income for the community as a whole do

---

[1] We shall ignore here the possible disadvantages due to increased unemployment in the export trades.

[2] The argument which follows is of course not new. Cf. Bickerdike, "The Theory of Incipient Taxes," *Economic Journal*, December, 1906, and Edgeworth, *Collected Papers*, Vol. ii, pp. 340 ff. But the modern indifference curve technique permits a simple demonstration of it which it may be worth while to reproduce; and it also shows that the proposition is quite independent of any assumption as to a measurable utility function (with which at one time it was erroneously thought to be associated).

Source: Reprinted with permission from *Economica*, VII (New Series): 377–380 (November 1940).

not imply an unchanged real income for each individual taken separately. Some individuals will be worse off (as between two such positions) and others better off. But the real income can nevertheless be regarded as constant for the community as a whole, if, supposing that those who are worse off were exactly compensated for their loss at the expense of those who are better off, this redistribution of incomes would leave the real income of everyone the same as before. In other words in order that two situations, A and B, should represent constant total real income, it is necessary to suppose that, if all those who are better off in B than in A were taxed to the extent necessary to make them indifferent as between A and B, and those who are worse off in B than in A were subsidised by an amount which would make them indifferent as between A and B, the total amount of taxes to be imposed would be equal to the total amount of subsidies to be paid.[3,4]

3. Let us now suppose that there are two countries, France and England, and two commodities, wine and coal. In the diagram we measure the amount of coal bought by France (and sold by England) along Ox and the amount of wine bought by England (and sold by France) along Oy. The indifference curve I_{F_0} which passes through O then represents the level of real income of the French community in the absence of coal purchases from England, and the indifference curve I_{E_0} (passing through O) the real income of the English community deprived of French wine. OE and OF represent the two offer curves: the English demand curve for wine (and supply curve of coal) and the French demand curve for coal (and supply curve of wine). In the absence of import duties and transport

[3] For a further discussion of this concept, cf. my note "Welfare Propositions of Economics and Interpersonal Comparisons of Utility," *Economic Journal*, September, 1939, and Hicks, "The Foundations of Welfare Economics," *Economic Journal*, December, 1939.

[4] The derivation of the community indifference curve is as follows: Let us assume two commodities, a and b. Take an arbitrary point, P_1 on the line R_1. Since along R_1 the ratio a/b is constant, it is clear that all points on R_1 to the right of P_1 represent real incomes higher than P_1, and all points on the left, lower real incomes. It follows, therefore, that there cannot be two points along R_1 which represent the *same* total real income. This must be equally true of any other line R_2 (representing a different

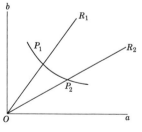

ratio a/b). Hence there can be only one point (P_2) along R_2 where the real income is the same as at P_1. Finding these points for each of the radiuses R_3 . . . etc., and connecting up the corresponding points P_3 . . . etc., we obtain the community indifference curve representing the real income at P_1. The shape of this curve should be similar to the shape of an ordinary indifference curve.

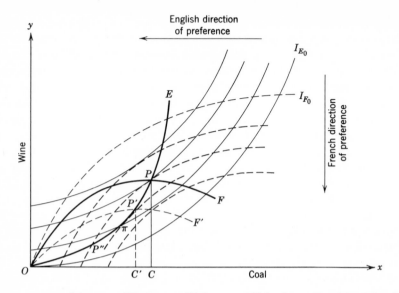

costs, competitive equilibrium will be established at P with PC wine exchanged against OC coal, the French terms of trade being OC/PC. If we now suppose that France imposes an import duty on coal, the French demand curve will be shifted (to OF'), in such a way that the difference in the height at any point between the old demand curve and the new represents the revenue of the French State (import duty x amount bought) in terms of wine. The resulting new equilibrium is at P', with $P'C'$ wine being exchanged against OC' coal. It is clear that the new position secures a higher real income for France so long as P' is to the right of P''—the point on the English demand curve which passes through the *same* French indifference curve as at P. The optimal rate of import duty is the one which secures equilibrium at π—this being the point on the English demand curve which is tangential to one of France's indifference curves (i.e., which therefore places France in the best position compatible with the English demand for wine). With the same reasoning it can also be shown that a subsidy on exports, by shifting the offer curve in the opposite direction, necessarily places the country in a worse position than before.

4. π is in fact the optimum monopoly position, and the corresponding price the optimum monopoly price—i.e., the price which would result in the absence of a tariff, if the French wine trade were in the hands of a monopolist who decided to exploit his monopoly power to the full. Our analysis shows, therefore, that the introduction of import duties can reproduce exactly the same effects as the introduction of monopoly. The

extent to which it is possible to exploit the foreigner in this way depends on the country's monopoly power; i.e., the elasticity of foreign demand for its products, and the extent to which the foreign power desires, or is able, to retaliate. (Retaliation will improve the position of the exploited country, but it might leave both countries worse off than they were originally.) Provided that the elasticity of foreign demand is less than infinite there is always *some* rate of duty which it is advantageous to introduce in the absence of retaliation; and if the elasticity of the country's own demand for foreign products is markedly higher than the elasticity of foreign demand for its own products—an unusual case— this policy may be advantageous even if the "optimum degree of retaliation" of foreign countries is allowed for.

A NOTE ON WELFARE PROPOSITIONS IN ECONOMICS

Tibor de Scitovszky

Modern economic theory draws a sharp distinction between positive economics, which explains the working of the economic system, and welfare economics, which prescribes policy. In the domain of welfare economics the impossibility of interpersonal utility comparisons has for a long time been believed to impose strict limitations on the economist, which kept this branch of economic theory in the background. Recently, however, there has been a reawakening of interest in welfare problems, following assertions that these limitations are less restrictive than they were hitherto supposed to be.[1] The present note attempts to analyse the problem in detail.

I

The aim of welfare economics is to test the efficiency of economic institutions in making use of the productive resources of a community. For analytical and historical reasons it is useful to distinguish between welfare propositions based on the assumption of a fixed quantity of employed resources and those that regard that quantity as a variable. The former are concerned with the allocating efficiency of the system;[2]

[1] Cf. N. Kaldor: "Welfare Propositions of Economics and Interpersonal Comparisons of Utility," *Economic Journal*, vol. 49 (1939), p. 549; J. R. Hicks: "Foundations of Welfare Economics," *Economic Journal*, vol. 49 (1939), p. 696. See also N. Kaldor "A Note on Tariffs and the Terms of Trade," *Economica* (N. S.), vol. 7 (1940), p. 377; and J. R. Hicks: "The Rehabilitation of Consumers' Surplus," *Review of Economic Studies*, vol. 8 (1941), p. 108. The present note is a criticism of the principle enunciated in Mr. Kaldor's first-quoted article and underlying the argument of the others. It is not presented in polemic form, in order to enable the reader not acquainted with the articles here quoted to follow its argument.

[2] This expression was suggested to me by Mr. George Jaszi to whom I am also indebted for reading the manuscript and making valuable suggestions.

Source: Reprinted with permission from *Review of Economic Studies,* IX:77–88 (November 1941).

i.e. with its ability of best allocating a given quantity of utilised resources among their various uses in consumption and production. They can be conceived of as criteria for judging institutions and policy in a closed community whose potential resources are fixed and can be trusted to be fully employed, either because of the automatism of the system or because of the existence of a governmental policy aiming at full employment.

The latter, which may be called welfare propositions in the wider sense, are in addition to the above problems concerned also with the total quantity of resources available to an open group and the degree of utilisation of those resources. They are therefore relevant, first of all, to problems of international trade from the point of view of a single country; and secondly, to the general problem of employment.

II

All the welfare propositions of the classical economists—viz., perfect competition, free trade, and direct taxation—belong in the first category; a fact which has not always been realised. They are all based on the principle that given the total quantity of utilised resources, they will be best distributed among different uses if their rates of substitution are everywhere and for every person equal; for only in such a situation will each person's satisfaction be carried to that maximum beyond which it cannot be increased without diminishing someone else's. Perfect competition, free trade, and direct taxation are one (probably the simplest) among the many ways of achieving this aim.

By limiting our universe of discourse to two commodities and two persons, we can illustrate this principle on a simple diagram. Let us draw the indifference maps of the two individuals superposed on each other, one of them reversed, with the axes parallel and in such a position that their intersection gives the quantities of the two goods jointly possessed by the two people. Every point of the rectangle enclosed by the axes corresponds to a given distribution of the two goods between the two persons, and the two indifference curves going through that point show their respective welfare positions. At some points, indifference curves do not cut but are tangential one to another. At these points the rate of substitution of the two goods is equal for the two persons, and they represent optimum situations, because once such a point has been reached no redistribution of the two goods can increase the welfare of either person without diminishing that of the other. The locus of all optimum points gives the contract curve.

We judge the allocating efficiency of economic institutions by the criterion whether or not they enable people so to redistribute goods and services among themselves (irrespective of their initial position) as to arrive on the contract curve. That perfect competition or, from the point of view of the universe, free trade are efficient in the above sense can be proved by showing that all pairs of offer (reciprocal demand) curves drawn from any point within the rectangle intersect on the contract curve. Similarly, excise taxes and, from the point of view of the universe, import and export duties are inefficient, because they can be represented as distortions of offer curves that make them intersect outside the contract curve. The arguments based on this diagram can be generalized for any number of persons and commodities.[3] It implies only one limitation: the quantities of goods available to the community as a whole must be fixed; for they determine the points of intersection of the axes and the position of the contract cruve. This shows that the propositions illustrated by the diagram are allocative welfare propositions; and it also appears to limit their applicability to the problem of the exchange of goods whose quantities coming onto the market are given. It can be proved, however, that our arguments are equally valid when instead of these quantities those of the factors utilised in their production are considered to be fixed. For the formal proof of the geometrical arguments and their generalisations the reader is referred to the original sources and to textbooks dealing with the subject.[4]

III

We have seen above that allocative welfare propositions are based on the criterion of economic efficiency. They state that of alternative situations, brought about by different institutions or courses of policy, one is superior to the other in the sense that it would make everybody better off for every distribution of welfare, *if* that were the same in the two situations. This is different from saying that one situation is actually better than the other from everybody's point of view, because a change in institutions or policy almost always redistributes welfare sufficiently not to have a uniform effect on everybody but to favour some people and prejudice others. It follows from this that economic welfare propositions cannot as a rule be made independently of interpersonal comparisons of utility.

---

[3] This also holds good for all arguments based on other diagrams in this note.

[4] Cf. F. Y. Edgeworth: *Mathematical Psychics*, London, 1881, and "The Pure Theory of International Trade," *Economic Journal*, vol. 4 (1894); Alfred Marshall: *The Pure Theory of Foreign Trade* (1879), London School reprint, 1930; and his *Principles of Economics*, Bk. V, Chap. II. Note on Barter and Mathematical Note XII; A. P. Lerner: "The Symmetry between Export and Import Taxes," *Economica* (N.S.), vol. 3 (1936); J. R. Hicks: *Value and Capital*, Oxford, 1939, etc. For the best analysis of the nature of this kind of diagram see A. L. Bowley: *The Mathematical Groundwork of Economics*, Oxford, 1924.

It would hardly be satisfactory, however, to confine the economist's value judgments to cases where one situation is superior to the other from the point of view of everybody affected. It is doubtful if in practice any choice comes within this category; besides, there would not be much point in soliciting the economist's expert opinion when everybody is unanimous, except in order to enlighten people as to their true interest.

Favouring an improvement in the organization of production and exchange *only* when it is accompanied by a corrective redistribution of income fully compensating those prejudiced by it might seem to be a way out of the difficulty, because such a change would make some people better off without making anyone worse off. For instance, it might be argued that the abolition of the Corn Laws should not have been advocated by economists in their capacity of pure economists without advocating at the same time the full compensation of landowners out of taxes levied on those favoured by the cheapening of corn. Yet, in a sense, and regarded from a long-run point of view, such propositions are not independent of value judgments between alternative income distributions either. For, going out of their way to preserve the existing distribution of income, they imply a preference for the *status quo*.

There seem to be two solutions of the problem. First of all, in addition to admitting his inability to compare different people's satisfaction, the economist may postulate that such comparisons are impossible, and that therefore there is nothing to choose between one distribution of income and another. He may then make value judgments on the sole criterion of efficiency without bothering about concomitant shifts in the distribution of income, since he considers one income distribution as good as any other.[5] In this case, however, he cannot claim that his value judgments are independent of interpersonal utility comparisons, because they depend on the assumption of their impossibility.

Secondly, the economists may put forward his welfare propositions with due emphasis on their limitations, as being based on the sole criterion of efficiency. He may then point out the nature of eventual redistributions of income likely to accompany a given change, and stress the necessity of basing economic policy on considerations both of

---

[5] This, I think, was the attitude of the classical economists; at least of those who did not, like Bastiat, impute ethical values to the distribution of income under perfect competition. It seems to be the correct interpretation of that fairly representative statement of Cairnes': ". . . standards of abstract justice . . . are inefficacious as means of solving the actual problems of . . . distribution. . . . If our present system of industry (perfect competition) is to be justified, it must . . . find its justification . . . in the fact that it secures for the mass of mankind a greater amount of material and moral well-being, and provides more effectively for its progress in civilization than any other plan."

economic efficiency and of social justice.[6] Such an attitude, which I think is the only correct one, may diminish the force of the economist's welfare propositions but does not make them less useful. The above considerations qualify also the welfare propositions to be discussed below.

IV

When we come to the problem of welfare propositions in the wider sense, we can no longer illustrate a change in economic institutions or policy on a single diagram. For such a change will no longer mean a mere redistribution of income and alteration of the rules of production and exchange; but may also involve a change both in the total quantity of resources available to the community, and in their degree of utilisation. The former may be due to the imposition of a duty on international trade, which from the point of view of an individual country alters the quantities of imports and retained exports available for home consumption; while the latter may be caused by this or any other change, if it affects the propensity to save or the inducement to invest and thereby changes employment. Analytically there is no difference between the two cases. In both, the quantities of resources available for consumption are changed, hence the relative position of the indifference maps is altered; whence it follows that welfare propositions in the wider sense must involve the comparison of two diagrams. Since these are constructed from the identical two indifference maps and differ only in the latter's relative position to each other, such comparisons are not the hopeless task they might seem at first sight. For we can represent some (not all) welfare positions on both diagrams; and it is possible to represent on one diagram the welfare positions corresponding to all those points of the other diagram's contract curve that are inferior to its "own" contract curve. This follows from the fact that our diagrams admit the representation of all welfare situations that are inferior (worse from the point of view of at least one of the two persons) to their contract curve, while welfare positions superior to the contract curve cannot be represented on them.

Our welfare propositions may necessitate the comparison of points on the contract curves of the two diagrams or of points suboptimal to them, or of a point on one contract curve with a point suboptimal to the other contract curve. The first case is that where the system's allocating efficiency is at an optimum both before and after the given change; the second, where it is suboptimal both before and after the change; the

---

[6] Or, of course, he may also renounce his claim to purity and base his own recommendations on both criteria.

third, where the change affects allocating efficiency. Taking an example from the theory of international trade, the first case may be illustrated by the imposition of an import duty by a country in which taxation is direct and domestic markets are perfectly competitive;[7] the second case can be represented by a duty imposed in a monopolistic world; and the third by a duty which favours the formation of monopolies or is linked with an excise tax on the home production of import substitutes.

V

Let us draw two diagrams (Fig. 1), both consisting of the superposed indifference maps of individuals A and B, but with the difference that in the second, B's map has been shifted by $O_B O_B'$; so that the joint possessions of A and B have increased by $x_0 x_1$ of X and $y_0 y_1$ of Y compared with what they were in the first. This shift will bring into a position of tangency indifference curves that in the first diagram have neither touched nor intersected, and will thus make the second diagram's contract curve superior to that of the first diagram throughout its range. This follows from that fundamental postulate of economic theory that indifference curves can never have a positive slope, and it will be the case whenever the shift in the relative position of the indifference maps represents an increase in the quantity of at least one of the two commodities without a diminution in that of the other. From the fact that the second diagram's contract curve is superior to that of the first, it follows that the latter can be represented on the second diagram by tracing the locus of the points of intersection of all the indifference curves that in the first diagram are tangential to each other. This will give us a curve on each side of the second diagram's contract curve, and the area between them represents welfare positions that are superior to the first diagram's contract curve. Hence, a change that brings the welfare of our groups from a point of the first diagram's contract curve onto a point of the second diagram's contract curve (or at least within the area between the broken lines), can be said to be desirable with the same generality and significance with which perfect competition or direct taxation are said to be desirable on the ground of their allocating efficiency. In other words, while it need not actually improve everybody's

---

[7] A tariff on foreign trade is not incompatible with the tariff imposing country's domestic trade and production being of optimum allocating efficiency. The reader must not let himself be confused by the fact that similar diagrams have been used for illustrating the waste caused by tariffs from the point of view of the universe as a whole. We are here solely concerned with the effects of a tariff on the welfare of a single country, consequently the indifference maps that constitute our diagrams belong to inhabitants of the same country.

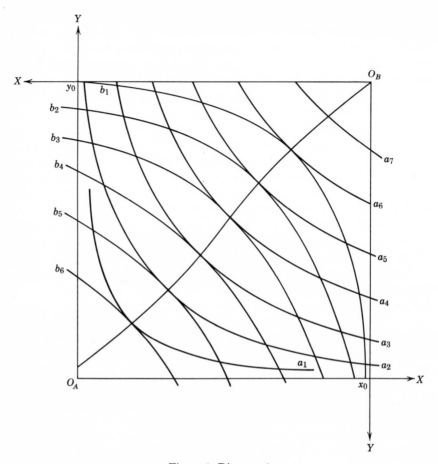

Figure 1. Diagram 1.

position, it would do so for every possible distribution of welfare if the change were to leave that distribution unaffected.

The above argument is an explicit formulation of the statement that getting more of some (or all) commodities at no cost of foregoing others is a good thing. This may be considered as overpedantic, since that statement seems to be obvious; on the other hand, it is subject to the same limitations that qualify allocative welfare propositions (cf. section 3 above); and besides, it is not even always true. Increased plenty is a good thing only if it is not linked with a redistribution of welfare, too retrogressive from the point of view of social justice; and if it does not lead to a serious deterioration of the allocating efficiency of the economic system. For the former there exists no objective criterion, but there is a simple test for the latter. To test whether a diminution in allocating efficiency has not obviated the advantages of increased plenty, we must see if after the change, it is possible fully to compensate people prejudiced by it out of funds levied on those favoured by the change, without thereby completely eliminating the latter's gain. From the geometrical argument above it follows that if this test is fulfilled for one initial income distribution, it will be fulfilled for all possible initial income distributions, and *vice versa*. Our test is completely general also in the sense that it is applicable whether or not the initial situation is of optimum allocating efficiency. (I.e. whether or not it lies on the contract curve.)

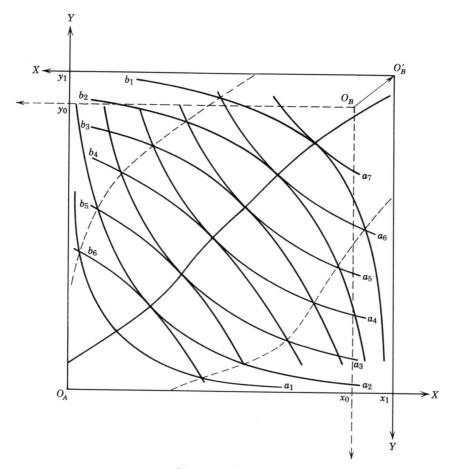

Figure 1. Diagram 2.

VI

The kind of change contemplated above, where the quantity of some or all goods is increased without a diminution in others, is likely to occur as a result of increased employment, capital accumulation, technical progress, better utilization of strategic advantages in international trade (by putting a duty on the export of goods for which foreign demand is inelastic), and the like. Another kind of change, especially important in international trade, is that where the quantity of some resources is increased and that of others diminished.[8] In Fig. 2 this is represented by a parallel displacement of one of the two indifference maps in the negative direction; so that the quantity of X is diminished by $x_0 x_1$ and that of Y increased by $y_0 y_1$. Nothing general can be said about the relationship of the shape of the indifference maps. It is possible that the change will result in superior welfare positions throughout the whole range of the contract curve, in the same way as was depicted in Fig. 1. This is especially likely to happen when the increase is large and the diminution small. When on the other hand, the diminution is large and the increase small, the change may result in inferior positions throughout the contract curve; a situation which can be visualised by thinking of diagram 2 (Fig. 1) as showing the initial, and diagram 1 the new, position. Between these two extremes lies the more general case in which some sectors of the new contract curve are superior to the old one, while others are inferior to it. Its simplest example is illustrated in Fig. 2, where P_0 is a common point of the two contract curves, to the left of which the new contract curve, $\pi\pi$, represents welfare positions superior to the corresponding welfare positions of the old contract curve, PP; while to the right of P_0, the old contract curve is superior to the new one. In each diagram the broken lines show the welfare positions corresponding to the other diagram's contract curve wherever that is inferior to the diagram's own contract curve.

The economic meaning of this is that the identical change in the composition of the national income would improve general welfare for some hypothetical welfare distributions and worsen it for others. Imagine members of a community divided into two groups according to their preference for goods Y and X respectively.[9] Then assume a change that increases the quantity of Y and diminishes that of X, but leaves the

---

[8] This is the effect of important and export duties whenever the foreigners' reciprocal demand for exports is not inelastic and employment is given.

[9] The term "preference" is used in a loose sense. It denotes the whole shape of indifference surfaces and not only their slope at the relevant point, which in equilibrium conditions is the same for everybody.

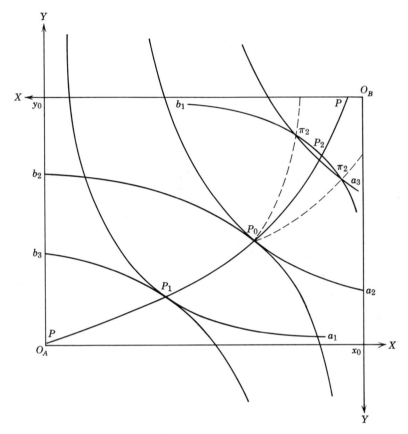

Figure 2. Diagram 1.

distribution of money income between our two groups unaffected. From the point of view of individuals, the change will appear as a shift in relative prices; which, given the distribution of income, will be likely to make those with a special preference for Y better off, and those with a liking for X worse off, than they were before. Assume next that the members of our first group are rich and those of the second poor. Then the gain of the first group expressed in money (or in terms of any single commodity) will be greater than the money equivalent of the loss suffered by the second group. Therefore, if we so redistributed income as to restore approximately the initial distribution of welfare, there would be a net gain, making members of both groups better off than they were before. Conversely, if the people favoured by the changes were poor, and those prejudiced by it were rich, the money equivalent of the former's

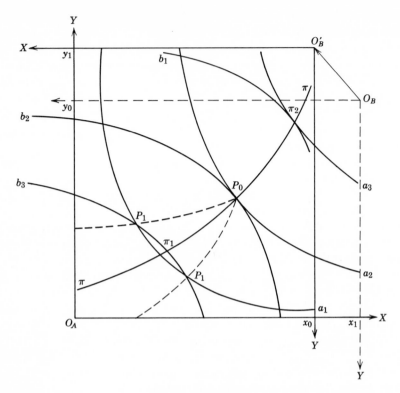

Figure 2. Diagram 2.

gain would be insufficient fully to compensate the latter's loss, so that a redistribution of income tending to restore the initial distribution of welfare would result in a net loss of satisfaction for everybody.

What significance are we to attach to this case? To refrain altogether, as the classical economists did, from making welfare propositions relating to it, seems unduly restrictive. It is true that as we have seen such a change would improve general welfare for some welfare distributions and worsen it for others; on the other hand, we are not interested in all possible welfare distributions. There are only two distributions of welfare that really matter. Those actually obtaining immediately before and after the change contemplated.[10] It seems therefore sufficient to concentrate on these and to investigate how the change would affect general

[10] The reader's attention is called to the fact that in reality the distribution of income is not *given* as we have assumed in the argument above. As a rule, the change will affect the distribution of welfare not only by shifting relative prices but also by boosting some industries and depressing others, and thereby redistributing money income.

welfare if it were to leave the distribution of welfare unaffected and if that were both before and after it, first what it actually is before, secondly what it actually is after, the change. Whenever these two comparisons yield identical results, we can make welfare propositions of almost the same generality and significance as the allocative welfare propositions of the classical economists; especially since the identical results for the two welfare distributions imply a strong presumption in favour of the same result holding for all intermediate welfare distributions as well.

We propose, therefore, to make welfare propositions on the following principle. We must first see whether it is possible in the new situation so to redistribute income as to make everybody better off than he was in the initial situation; secondly, we must see whether starting from the initial situation it is not possible by a mere redistribution of income to reach a position superior to the new situation, again from everybody's point of view. If the first is possible and the second impossible, we shall say that the new situation is better than the old was. If the first is impossible but the second possible, we shall say that the new situation is worse; whereas if both are possible or both are impossible, we shall refrain from making a welfare proposition.[11]

We can illustrate this procedure in Fig. 2 for the special case when allocating efficiency is at its optimum both before and after the change. Each situation can then be represented by a point on its respective contract curve and compared with the corresponding point on the other contract curve. If both points lie to the left of P_0 on their respective contract curves, the change will increase general welfare, because starting from the new situation on the second diagram's contract curve it is always possible to travel along that curve by redistributing income and arrive at a point which is superior to the initial situation from everybody's point of view; whereas starting from the initial situation on the first diagram's contract curve, it is impossible by travelling along that curve to reach a position superior to the new situation. If on the other hand, both points lie to the right of the common point P_0, the change can be said to diminish general welfare on the same reasoning; while if one point lies to the left and the other to the right, we can make no welfare propositions relative to our group.

VII

Our two criteria for making welfare propositions bear a close resemblance to Paasche's and Laspeyre's formulae in the theory of cost of

[11] It need hardly be recalled that in the situation discussed in section 5—that is, when the quantities of goods and services all change in the same direction—this last case can never occur, and we can always make welfare propositions.

living index numbers. There, just as here, the difficulty lies in comparing averages whose weighting is different;[12] and the solution is sought in comparing the two real situations not one with another, but each with a hypothetical situation, which resembles it in weighting but is otherwise identical with the other real situation. In the theory of index numbers, budgets of different dates or places are compared each with the cost of the identical bundle of commodities at the prices of the other date or place; and these two comparisons, expressed as ratios (Paasche's and Laspeyre's formulae), are the limits within which the true difference in the cost of living must lie.[13] In welfare problems, of course, we can aim neither at a "true" answer nor at its quantitative expression without measuring satisfaction and comparing different people's. But our two criteria are exactly analogous to Paasche's and Laspeyre's formulae. For we compare the first welfare situation with what general welfare would be if the satisfaction, yielded by the physical income of the second situation were distributed as it was in the first; and contrast the second situation with the welfare that the first situation's physical income would yield to each person if it were so distributed as to make the distribution of welfare similar to that of the second situation.[14]

VIII

Mr. Kaldor and Professor Hicks have asserted that it is *always* possible to tell whether a given change improves general welfare, even if not all people gain by it and some lose. The test suggested by them: to see whether it is possible after the change fully to compensate the losers at a cost to those favoured that falls short of their total gain, is fundamentally identical with the first of our two criteria. The objection to using this criterion by itself is that it is asymmetrical, because it attributes undue importance to the particular distribution of welfare obtaining before the contemplated change. If the government had a special attachment to the *status quo* before the change and would actually undertake to reproduce that welfare distribution by differential taxation after the change, then Mr. Kaldor's test would be sufficient. For then, the economist could regard that particular welfare distribution as the

---

[12] Because the general welfare can be conceived of as average welfare.

[13] Cf. Henry Schultz: "A Misunderstanding in Index Number Theory," *Econometrica*, vol. 7 (1939), p. 1; and A. A. Konus: "The Problem of the True Index of the Cost of Living," *Econometrica*, vol. 7 (1939), p. 10.

[14] We say that the distribution of welfare is similar in two situations if every member of the community prefers the same situation. A more exact definition would be unnecessary for our purposes; besides, it is also impossible, since welfare cannot be measured.

only relevant one and would be entitled to use it as his sole standard of reference. But in the absence of such a governmental policy there can be no justification in attaching greater importance to the welfare distribution as it was before than as it is after the change.

To illustrate the pitfalls of this one-sided criterion, imagine a change, say the imposition of a duty on imports, that brings the welfare of A and B from P_1 (Fig. 2) on the contract curve of diagram 1 onto π_2 on the contract curve of diagram 2. According to Mr. Kaldor's test this change is desirable, because by redistributing income we could travel from π_2 along the $\pi\pi$ curve to π_1, which is superior to P_1. But once the tariff has been imposed and situation π_2 established, it will be free trade and the resulting (original) situation P_1 that will appear preferable *by the same test*, because starting from P_1, income could be so redistributed (travelling along the PP curve in the first diagram this time) as to reach P_2, which is superior to π_2. So the two situations can be shown each to be preferable to the other by the identical criterion: an absurd result, which can only be avoided by using our double criterion.

A REFORMULATION OF
CERTAIN ASPECTS OF
WELFARE ECONOMICS

Abram Bergson

The object of this paper is to state in a precise form the value judgments required for the derivation of the conditions of maximum economic welfare which have been advanced in the studies of the Cambridge economists,[1] Pareto and Barone, and Mr. Lerner.[2] Such a formulation, I hope, will clarify certain aspects of the contribution of these writers, and at the same time provide a basis for a more precise understanding of the principles of welfare.

I shall develop my analysis under a set of assumptions which in certain respects differ from those introduced in the welfare studies. It will

[1] I use this caption to designate those economists whose names are directly attached to the Cambridge School—Marshall, Professor Pigou, Mr. Kahn—as well as others, such as Edgeworth, whose welfare analysis is in all essentials the same as that of the Cambridge group. But in the course of my discussion I shall refer mainly to the studies of the first group of economists. This will ease my task considerably, and, I believe, will involve no loss of generality.

[2] The studies referred to are Alfred Marshall, *Principles of Economics* (all references to the third—London, 1895—edition); A. C. Pigou, *Economics of Welfare* (all references to the fourth—London, 1932—edition); R. F. Kahn, "Notes on Ideal Output," *Economic Journal,* March 1935; Vilfredo Pareto, *Cours d'Economie Politique* (all references to the Lausanne—1897—edition); Enrico Barone, "The Ministry of Production in a Socialist State," (translated from the Italian article of the same title in *Giornale degli Economisti,* 1908; the translation appearing in F. A. von Hayek, ed., *Collectivist Economic Planning,* London, 1935); and A. P. Lerner, "The Concept of Monopoly and the Measurement of Monopoly Power," *Review of Economic Studies,* June 1934, and A. P. Lerner, "Economic Theory and Socialist Economy," *Review of Economic Studies,* October 1934.

Source: Originally published in the *Quarterly Journal of Economics,* February 1938, with grateful acknowledgement to Mr. Paul Samuelson "for suggestions on many points." With the kind permission of the Belknap Press of the Harvard University Press, use is made here of a slightly edited version appearing in Abram Bergson, *Essays in Normative Economics,* Cambridge, Mass., 1966.

be assumed throughout the discussion that the amounts of all the factors of production, other than labor, are fixed and, for convenience, non-depreciating. While a variable capital supply is included in some of the welfare studies, this is not a well-developed part of the analysis, and for present purposes it will be desirable to confine to the simpler case the discussion of the evaluations required.[3] I shall assume, also, that the variables involved in the analysis—the amounts of the various commodities consumed and services performed—are infinitesimally divisible. This assumption will be interpreted more strictly than is usually done; otherwise it is the postulate of the welfare writers, and its introduction here will involve no significant departure from their analyses. Finally, I shall assume that there are only two kinds of consumers' goods, two kinds of labor, and two factors of production other than labor in the community, and that each commodity is produced, with labor and the other factors, in a single production unit. This assumption is introduced only to simplify the notation employed. The discussion will apply, with no modification, to the many-commodity, many-factor, and many-production unit case.[4]

THE MAXIMUM CONDITIONS IN GENERAL

Among the elements affecting the welfare of the community during any given period of time are the amounts of each of the factors of production, other than labor, employed in the different production units, the amounts of the various commodities consumed, the amounts of the different kinds of work done, and the production unit for which this work is performed by each individual in the community during that period of time. If we use A and B to denote the two kinds of labor; C and D to denote the two factors of production other than labor; and X and Y to denote the two consumers' goods; we may express this relationship in the form

$$W = W(x_1, y_1, a_1^x, b_1^x, a_1^y, b_1^y, \ldots ,$$
$$x_n, y_n, a_n^x, b_n^x, a_n^y, b_n^y, C^x, D^x, C^y, D^y, r, s, t, \ldots). \quad (1)$$

[3] On a simple model, similar to that of Barone, the analysis may be extended to the case of a variable capital supply.

[4] The assumption that each commodity is produced in one production unit, it is true, excludes an element of "external economies" from the analysis. But in the present essay I am interested only in the maximum conditions for the community's welfare, and not in the departures from the maximum under a given institutional set-up. To the extent that in the many-production unit case there are external economies, these will require no modification in the maximum conditions I shall present, for these conditions relate only to marginal *social* value productivities.

Here C^x and D^x are the amounts of the nonlabor factors of production C and D employed in the production unit producing the consumers' good X; C^y and D^y are the amounts of these factors employed in the production unit producing the consumers' good Y; x_i and y_i are the amounts of X and Y consumed by the ith individual; and a_i^x, b_i^x, a_i^y, and b_i^y are the amounts of each kind of work performed by him for each production unit during the given period of time.[5] The symbols r, s, t, . . . , denote elements other than the amounts of commodities, the amounts of work of each type, and the amounts of the nonlabor factors in each of the production units, affecting the welfare of the community.

Some of the elements r, s, t, . . . , may affect welfare, not only directly, but indirectly through their effect on (say) the amounts of X and Y produced with any given amount of resources—for example, the effects of a change in the weather. On the other hand, it is conceivable that variations in the amounts of commodities, the amounts of work of each type, and the amounts of nonlabor factors in each of the production units also will have a direct and indirect effect on welfare; as, for instance, a sufficient diminution of x_i and y_i may be accompanied by an overturn of the government. But for relatively small changes in these variables, other elements in welfare, I believe, will not be significantly affected. To the extent that this is so, a partial analysis is feasible.

I shall designate the function,

$$E = E(x_1, y_1, a_1^x, b_1^x, a_1^y, b_1^y, \ldots ,$$
$$x_n, y_n, a_n^x, b_n^x, a_n^y, b_n^y, C^x, D^x, C^y, D^y), \quad (2)$$

which is obtained by taking r, s, t, . . . , in (1) as given, the Economic Welfare Function.[6]

Let us write the amounts of X and Y produced respectively by the X and Y production units as functions,

$$X = X(A^x, B^x, C^x, D^x); \qquad Y = Y(A^y, B^y, C^y, D^y), \quad (3)$$

where A^x and B^x are the amounts of the two kinds of labor and C^x and D^x are the amounts of the other two factors of production employed in the X production unit; and A^y, B^y, C^y, D^y are defined similarly for the Y production unit.

If we assume that E varies continuously with x_1, y_1, . . . , we may write as a general condition for a position of maximum economic wel-

---

[5] I am assuming that an individual's labor time may be divided among the different types of work in any desired proportions.

[6] It should be emphasized that in (2) other factors affecting welfare are taken as given. I do *not* assume that economic welfare is an independent element which may be added to other welfare to get total welfare.

fare that, subject to the limitations of the given technique of production and the given amounts of resources,

$$dE = 0. \tag{4}$$

Equation (4) requires that in the neighborhood of the maximum position any small adjustment will leave the welfare of the community unchanged. By use of (3) and (4) it is possible immediately to state in general terms the conditions for a maximum welfare.[7]

One group of maximum conditions relates to the consumption and supply of services by each individual in the community. They require that the marginal economic welfare of each commodity and the marginal economic diswelfare of each type of work be the same with respect to each individual in the community.[8] If we denote the marginal economic welfare of commodity X with respect to the ith individual, $\partial E/\partial x_i$, and of Y, $\partial E/\partial y_i$, the first group of these conditions requires that, for all i, and for some p, q, and ω,

$$\frac{\partial E}{\partial x_i} = \omega p \tag{5}$$

and

$$\frac{\partial E}{\partial y_i} = \omega q \tag{6}$$

Similarly, if we denote the marginal economic diswelfare of the various types of work with respect to the ith individual $\partial E/\partial a_i{}^x$, $\partial E/\partial b_i{}^x$, $\partial E/\partial a_i{}^y$, $\partial E/\partial b_i{}^y$, the second group of these conditions requires that, for all i and for some g^x, h^x, g^y, h^y, and for the ω already chosen,

$$-\frac{\partial E}{\partial a_i{}^x} = \omega g^x, \tag{7}$$

$$-\frac{\partial E}{\partial a_i{}^y} = \omega g^y, \tag{8}$$

---

[7] The conditions I shall develop in this section are a group of necessary conditions for a maximum. They are also the conditions for any critical point, and are sufficient in number to determine the location of such a point (or points) if there is one. Below, pp. 23 ff. I consider the problem of determining whether a given critical point is a maximum or not.

[8] This rather awkward terminology is adopted instead of, say, the phrase "marginal economic welfare *of* the ith individual" in order to include the possibility that an increment of X or Y given to the ith individual will affect the welfare of others.

$$-\frac{\partial E}{\partial b_i{}^x} = \omega h^x, \tag{9}$$

$$-\frac{\partial E}{\partial b_i{}^y} = \omega h^y. \tag{10}$$

The minus signs and the multiplicative factor ω are inserted in these equations for convenience.

The remaining maximum conditions relate to production. They require that the economic welfare of the consumers' goods produced by a marginal increment of each type of work should equal the negative of the diswelfare of that increment of work, and that the increment of economic welfare due to the shift of a marginal unit of factors C and D from one production unit to another should equal the negative of the diswelfare caused by this adjustment. Using the notation $\partial X/\partial A^x$ for the marginal productivity of A^x, and a similar notation for the other marginal productivities, we may write these conditions in the form,

$$p\,\frac{\partial X}{\partial A^x} = g^x, \tag{11}$$

$$q\,\frac{\partial Y}{\partial A^y} = g^y, \tag{12}$$

$$p\,\frac{\partial X}{\partial B^x} = h^x, \tag{13}$$

$$q\,\frac{\partial Y}{\partial B^y} = h^y, \tag{14}$$

and,

$$\omega\left(p\,\frac{\partial X}{\partial C^x} - q\,\frac{\partial Y}{\partial C^y}\right) = -\left(\frac{\partial E}{\partial C^x} - \frac{\partial E}{\partial C^y}\right), \tag{15}$$

$$\omega\left(p\,\frac{\partial X}{\partial D^x} - q\,\frac{\partial Y}{\partial D^y}\right) = -\left(\frac{\partial E}{\partial D^x} - \frac{\partial E}{\partial D^y}\right) \tag{16}$$

In equations (11) through (14), ω, which was present in all terms, has been divided out.[9] The derivatives on the right-hand sides of (15) and (16) indicate the effect on welfare of an adjustment in C or D for which all other elements—x^i, y^i, etc.—in welfare are constant. Such an effect would arise, for example, through a positive or negative evaluation of

[9] Strictly speaking, this procedure assumes a value proposition, which we shall introduce later, to the effect that ω is unequal to zero.

the relative amounts and kinds of "factory smoke" emitted in the two production units for varying amounts of one or the other factors employed in each unit.

It will be convenient to designate p the *price* of X; q the *price* of Y; and g^x, g^y, h^x, h^y, the *wage* respectively of the types of work A^x, A^y, B^x, B^y. Equations (5) and (6) thus require that the marginal economic welfare per "dollar's worth" of each commodity, $\partial E/\partial x_i \cdot 1/p$ and $\partial E/\partial y_i \cdot 1/q$, be the same for each commodity and for all individuals in the community. Similarly, equations (7) through (10) require that the marginal economic diswelfare per "dollar's worth" of each kind of work be the same with respect to each kind of work and each individual in the community; equations (11) through (14) require that the wages of each type of labor should equal the marginal value productivity of that type of labor,[10] and with an analogous interpretation, equations (15) and (16) require that the marginal value productivity equal the cost due to a shift in C or D from one use to another.

MAXIMUM CONDITIONS IN DIFFERENT ANALYSES

The maximum conditions just presented are the general conditions for a position of maximum economic welfare for any Economic Welfare Function. The maximum conditions presented in the welfare studies relate to a particular family of welfare functions. Their derivation thus requires the introduction of restrictions on the shape of the Economic Welfare Function presented here. Three groups of value propositions suffice for this purpose.

I shall designate the various maximum conditions derived by the names of those writers, or groups of writers, who have been especially responsible for their elucidation. For reasons which will appear I have altered somewhat the content of the conditions, and there are differences in the analyses of the various writers which must also be noted. The latter differences will be pointed out in this section and in the one following.

The Lerner Conditions. The First Group of Value Propositions: *a shift in a unit of any factor of production, other than labor, from one production unit to another would leave economic welfare unchanged, provided the amounts of all the other elements in welfare were constant.*

The First Group of Value Propositions enables us to state certain of the maximum conditions in terms of the production functions alone.

[10] In the present essay it will be understood that all value productivities are *social* value productivities. Compare n.4 above.

From these evaluations the right-hand side of (15) and of (16) must equal zero. To refer again to the example mentioned above, the net effect on the community's welfare of the "factory smoke" arising from a shift of the nonlabor factors from one use to another is taken as zero. The two equations thus may be written,

$$p \frac{\partial X}{\partial C^x} = q \frac{\partial Y}{\partial C^y}, \tag{17}$$

$$p \frac{\partial X}{\partial D^x} = q \frac{\partial Y}{\partial D^y}, \tag{18}$$

and they now impose the condition that the marginal value productivity of factors other than labor be the same in every use.

Equations (17) and (18) still contain the variables p and q, which involve derivatives of the Economic Welfare Function. If we combine (17) and (18), however, we have two equations,

$$\frac{q}{p} = \frac{\partial X/\partial C^x}{\partial Y/\partial C^y} = \frac{\partial X/\partial D^x}{\partial Y/\partial D^y}, \tag{19}$$

the second of which involves only the derivatives of the production functions. It requires that in the maximum position the ratio of the marginal productivity of a factor in one use to its marginal productivity in any other use be the same for all factors of production, other than labor. The first equation of (19) requires that all these ratios equal the price ratio.

The significance of (19) for the determination of maximum welfare may be expressed in the following manner: whatever the relative evaluations of commodity X and commodity Y, that is, in Barone's terminology, whatever their ratio of equivalence, (19) requires that in the maximum position, given that one factor C is so distributed that a small shift from one production unit to another would alter the amounts of X and Y in such a manner as to leave welfare unchanged—that is, given that C is so distributed that $(\partial X/\partial C^x)/(\partial Y/\partial C^y)$ equals the ratio of equivalence of the two commodities, then the other factors in order to be so distributed must have a ratio of marginal productivities equal to $(\partial X/\partial C^x)/(\partial Y/\partial C^y)$.

The condition (19) can also be interpreted in another manner, which, however, does not bring out as directly the significance of the condition for a position of maximum *welfare*. The equality of the marginal productivity ratios implies that there is no possible further adjustment for which the amount of one commodity will be increased without that of another being reduced. A shift in one factor from X to Y can at best be just compensated by a shift of another from Y to X, if (19) is satisfied.[11]

The Pareto-Barone-Cambridge Conditions. The Fundamental Value Propositions of Individual Preference: *if the amounts of the various commodities and types of work were constant for all individuals in the community except any ith individual, and if the ith individual consumed the various commodities and performed the various types of work in combinations which were indifferent to him, economic welfare would be constant.*

The First Group of Value Propositions, which were set forth previously, imply that under the assumption that the amounts of the factors of production other than labor are constant, the Economic Welfare Function may be written as

$$E = E(x_1, y_1, a_1{}^x, b_1{}^x, a_1{}^y, b_1{}^y, \ldots, x_n, y_n, a_n{}^x, b_n{}^x, a_n{}^y, b_n{}^y). \quad (20)$$

For from these propositions a shift in C or D from one production unit to another would have no effect on welfare, if all the other elements were constant. The Fundamental Value Propositions require that E be some function of the form,

$$E = E[(S^1(x_1, y_1, a_1{}^x, b_1{}^x, a_1{}^y, b_1{}^y), \ldots,$$
$$S^n(x_n, y_n, a_n{}^x, b_n{}^x, a_n{}^y, b_n{}^y)], \quad (21)$$

where the function

$$S^i = S^i(x_i, y_i, a_i{}^x, b_i{}^x, a_i{}^y, b_i{}^y) \quad (22)$$

expresses the loci of combinations of commodities consumed and work performed which are indifferent to the ith individual.

The Fundamental Value Propositions enable us to restate all the consumption and labor supply conditions in terms of the individual indifference functions, S^i. The conditions must be expressed, however, rela-

---

[11] Mr. Lerner, as far as I am aware, is the only economist to present (17) and (18) in the form of (19), his interpretation being the second of the two alternatives I have voted. In the studies of Pareto, Barone, and Marshall the conditions (17) and (18) are presented with the price ratios already equated to the individual marginal rates of substitution (see below). In the studies of Professor Pigou and Mr. Kahn the procedure is the same as that of Pareto, Barone, and Marshall except that Pigou and Kahn include in their analysis the possibility of departures from (17) and (18) due to aspects such as "factory smoke."

Mr. Lerner advances the conditions (19) for all factors of production, labor as well as nonlabor (*Review of Economic Studies,* October 1934, p. 57). On the face of the matter this formulation is inconsistent with Mr. Lerner's own advocacy of the supremacy of individual tastes in the sphere of consumption, and I have therefore taken the liberty to modify his conditions accordingly. The other economists also do not allow in their analysis for individual preferences as between employment in different units, as distinct from different kinds of labor.

tively to some one of them, say, (5). Thus consider the equation

$$\frac{\partial E/\partial x_i}{\partial E/\partial y_i} = \frac{p}{q}, \tag{23}$$

obtained from (5) and (6) by division. Using the Fundamental Value Propositions,

$$\frac{\partial E/\partial x_i}{\partial E/\partial y_i} = \frac{(\partial E/\partial S^i)(\partial S^i/\partial x_i)}{(\partial E/\partial S^i)(\partial S^i/\partial y_i)} = \frac{\partial S^i/\partial x_i}{\partial S^i/\partial y_i}. \tag{24}$$

The last ratio in (24) represents the slope of the indifference locus of the ith individual, or in the Hicks and Allen terminology, the marginal rate of substitution of commodity Y for commodity X.[12] Thus (23) requires that the marginal rate of substitution of the two commodities be the same for all individuals. By successively combining (5) with equations (7) through (10), a similar result is obtained with respect to the other elements of welfare.

All the production conditions may now be stated in terms of the indifference functions and the production functions. For equations (11) through (14), the statement that the wage of each type of work should equal its marginal value productivity may be interpreted to mean that the marginal product of a given type of work employed in producing a given commodity should equal the marginal rate of substitution of that commodity for that type of work. In the same manner, conditions (19) not only require that the ratios of marginal productivities of the various factors other than labor be equal, but that these ratios should equal the marginal rate of substitution of the two commodities.

The Fundamental Value Propositions thus require that, whatever the ratios of equivalence between the various commodities and types of work, given that the types of work performed and commodities consumed by one individual are so fixed that for any small adjustment among them economic welfare is unchanged—that is, given that the marginal rates of substitution and marginal productivities for this individual equal the respective ratios of equivalence—then for all other individuals to be similarly situated, their marginal rates of substitution must be the same as those of this individual. Under our implicit assumption of homogeneous factors, the respective marginal productivities, of course, must in any case be equal for all individuals.

Again, the Fundamental Value Propositions may be interpreted also

---

[12] See J. R. Hicks and R. G. D. Allen, "A Reconsideration of the Theory of Value," *Economica*, February 1934.

to mean that in the maximum position it is impossible to improve the situation of any one individual without rendering another worse off.[13]

The Cambridge Conditions. Let us designate

$$m_i = px_i + gy_i - g^x a_i{}^x - h^x b_i{}^x - g^y a_i{}^y - h^y b_i{}^y, \qquad (25)$$

the Share of the ith individual. In (25), p, q, etc., are taken proportional to the respective marginal rates of substitution of individuals. Thus m^i is defined, aside from a proportionality factor. The sum of m^i for the community as a whole is equal to the difference between the total wages and the total value of consumers' goods in the community.

The Propositions of Equal Shares: *If the Shares of any ith and kth individuals were equal, and if the prices and wage rates were fixed, the transfer of a small amount of the Share of i to k would leave welfare unchanged.*

The Propositions of Equal Shares enable us to state in terms of the distribution of Shares the remaining condition (5) to which we related consumption and labor supply conditions in order to reformulate them in terms of individual indifference functions (above, p. 11). According to the Propositions of Equal Shares, if the Shares of i and k are equal, then for the given price-wage situation,

$$dE = \frac{\partial E}{\partial m_i} dm_i + \frac{\partial E}{\partial m_k} dm_k = 0, \qquad (26)$$

for $dm_i = -dm_k$. Equation (26) is equivalent to the condition imposed by (5) that the marginal economic welfare per "dollar's worth" of X is

---

[13] The Pareto-Barone-Cambridge Conditions are developed by Marshall in the *Principles* (pp. 413–415, 526–527; Appendix XIV), but the derivation of the production conditions is based upon the very simple illustrative assumption of a producer-consumer expending his capital and labor in such a manner as to maximize his utility. Under more general assumptions the conditions are developed, without the utility calculus used by Marshall, by Pareto (*Cours,* I, pp. 20 ff, II, pp. 90 ff) and Barone; ("Ministry of Production"), and with the utility calculus, by Professor Pigou (*Economic Journal,* March 1935). All of these writers either develop the consumption conditions independently of their formulation of the production conditions (Marshall, Pareto) or assume the consumption conditions *ab initio* (Barone, Pigou, Kahn); and, as we shall indicate, the interpretations vary. Mr. Lerner in his study in the *Review of Economic Studies,* June 1934, presents all the conditions together, and interprets them most lucidly in the second of the two senses I have pointed out.

As I have noted elsewhere (n. 11), none of these writers includes in his analysis individual preferences between production units. Also, Professor Pigou and Mr. Kahn include the possibility of departures from (19), and perhaps from (11), (12), (13), 14), for the direct effects on welfare of shifts of the factors of production from one use to another.

the same for i and k.[14] Thus, if the Shares of all individuals are equal, the condition (5) is satisfied.[15]

The three groups of value propositions are not only sufficient for the derivation of the maximum conditions presented in the welfare studies; they are necessary for this procedure. For it is possible, and I shall leave

[14] The proof is as follows:

$$\frac{\partial E}{\partial m_i} = \frac{\partial E}{\partial x_i}\frac{\partial x_i}{\partial m_i} + \frac{\partial E}{\partial y_i}\frac{\partial y_i}{\partial m_i} + \frac{\partial E}{\partial a_i^x}\frac{\partial a_i^x}{\partial m_i} + \frac{\partial E}{\partial b_i^x}\frac{\partial b_i^x}{\partial m_i} + \frac{\partial E}{\partial a_i^y}\frac{\partial a_i^y}{\partial m_i} + \frac{\partial E}{\partial b_i^y}\frac{\partial b_i^y}{\partial m_i}.$$

By (25),

$$1 = p\frac{\partial x_i}{\partial m_i} + q\frac{\partial y_i}{\partial m_i} - g^x\frac{\partial a_i^x}{\partial m_i} - h^x\frac{\partial b_i^x}{\partial m_i} - g^y\frac{\partial a_i^y}{\partial m_i} - h^y\frac{\partial b_i^y}{\partial m_i}.$$

Using this equation, (23), and other similar equations,

$$\frac{\partial E}{\partial m_i} = \frac{\partial E}{\partial x_i} \cdot \frac{1}{p}.$$

[15] Among the welfare studies the Cambridge Conditions are the distinctive characteristic of the writings of the members of the Cambridge School. They are advanced in the works of all the Cambridge economists, and in none of the other welfare studies we have considered. But certain qualifications must be noted.

The Cambridge economists require an equal distribution of incomes, $(px_i + qy_i)$, rather than of Shares, as the condition for equality of the marginal economic welfare per "dollar" for all individuals (with qualifications which we shall vote directly, cf. Kahn, *Economic Journal*, March 1935, p. 1–2; Pigou, *Economics of Welfare*, pp. 82 ff; Marshall, *Principles*, p. 795). If it is assumed that the amounts of the various types of labor performed by each individual in the community are given, this condition is of course the same as ours. But otherwise for a requirement of equal incomes there is unlikely to be any position which satisfies all the conditions for a maximum. For it would be necessary that in the neighborhood of the maximum position the marginal productivity and marginal diswelfare of each type of work be zero.

The condition of equal incomes is not necessarily inconsistent with the other postulates. There might be some indifference functions and production functions such that all the maximum conditions are satisfied. But it may be noted here, in general, as a minimum requirement, that the various conditions must be consistent with each other. Compare Lange, *Review of Economic Studies*, October 1936, pp. 64–65, and Lerner, *Review of Economic Studies*, October 1936, p. 73.

For convenience I have presented the Cambridge Conditions in a rather simple form. In a more elaborate exposition of the conditions advanced by the Cambridge economists I should have to introduce—and on *a priori* grounds I believe it desirable to introduce—modifications in the distribution of Shares for changes in the price-wage situation which might affect different individuals differently—some moving to a more preferable position, and others to a less preferable one—and for other special differences between individuals. See the reference to the distribution of *wealth* in Marshall, pp. 527, 595, and to the distribution of the *Dividend* in Pigou, p. 89; but also see the reference to the distribution of *money incomes,* in Kahn, pp. 1–2.

the development of the argument to the reader, to deduce from the maximum conditions presented the restriction imposed upon the Economic Welfare Function by the value judgments introduced.

But it should be noted that the particular value judgments I have stated are not necessary to the welfare analysis. They are essential only for the establishment of a particular group of maximum conditions.[16] If the production functions and individual indifference functions are known, they provide sufficient information concerning the Economic Welfare Function for the determination of the maximum position, if it exists. In general, any set of value propositions which is sufficient for the evaluation of all alternatives may be introduced, and for each of these sets of propositions there corresponds a maximum position. The number of sets is infinite, and in any particular case the selection of one of them must be determined by its compatibility with the values prevailing in the community the welfare of which is being studied. For only if the welfare principles are based upon prevailing values can they be relevant to the activity of the community in question. But the determination of prevailing values for a given community, while I regard it as both a proper and necessary task for the economist, and of the same general character as the investigation of the indifference functions for individuals, is a project which I shall not undertake here. For the present I do not attempt more than the presentation of the values current in economic literature in a form for which empirical investigation is feasible.[17]

DIFFERENT ANALYSES FURTHER CONSIDERED

The formulation I have used to derive the maximum conditions of economic welfare differs in several respects from that of the welfare

---

[16] See footnote 7.

[17] This conception of the basis for the welfare principles should meet Lionel Robbins' requirement that the economist take the values of the community as data. But insofar as I urge that the economist also *study* these data it represents perhaps a more positive attitude than might be inferred as desirable from his essays. See *The Nature and Significance of Economics* (London, 1932), particularly chap. vi. Whether the approach will prove a fruitful one remains to be seen.

It may be noted that though Professor Robbins is averse to the study of indifference curves (pp. 96 ff), his own analysis requires an assumption that a movement of labor from one use to another is indifferent to the laborer and that a shift of other factors of production is indifferent to the community. Without these assumptions, for which I can see no *a priori* justification, his whole discussion of alternative *indifferent* uses, and his references to the most adequate satisfaction of demand from a given amount of means are without basis.

studies. It will be desirable to review briefly the relevant points of the various expositions, and the departures of the present essay from them. I shall continue to use the set of assumptions stated on page 4.

In the Cambridge analysis,[18] the welfare of the community, stated symbolically,[19] is an aggregate of the form,[20]

$$E = \Sigma U^i(x_i, y_i, a_i^x, b_i^y, a_i^y, b_i^y). \tag{27}$$

In this expression U^i is some function of the indifference function, S^i, and measures the satisfactions derived by the ith individual from x_i, y_i, a_i^x, b_i^x, a_i^y, b_i^y. If individual temperaments are about the same—that is, if individuals are capable of equal satisfactions—the marginal utilities or derivatives of the utility functions of different individuals, it is assumed, will be equal for an equal distribution of Shares.[21]

It is possible to derive all the maximum conditions, in specific terms, from the equation

$$\Sigma dU^i = 0. \tag{28}$$

The technique used by the Cambridge economists is less direct and varies in certain respects. For our present purposes these procedural differences are of little special interest, but it will facilitate our discussion of the analysis of Pareto and Barone if we append the following notes.

Marshall develops the Pareto-Barone-Cambridge consumption and labor supply conditions separately from the rest of his analysis.[22] These conditions are that for some price-wage situation, p, q, g^x, h^x, g^y, h^y, and for all i,

$$w^i = \frac{U_1^i}{p} = \frac{U_2^i}{q} = \frac{-U_3^i}{g^x} = \frac{-U_4^i}{h^x} = \frac{-U_5^i}{g^y} = \frac{-U_6^i}{h^y}. \tag{29}$$

[18] The passages in the Cambridge studies which are particularly informative as to the Cambridge concept of welfare are Marshall, pp. 80 ff, 200 ff, 527, 804; Pigou, pp. 10–11, 87, 97; Kahn, pp. 1, 2, 19; and also F. Y. Edgeworth, *Papers Relating to Political Economy*, II (London, 1925), p. 102 (from the *Economic Journal*, 1897).

[19] Aside from Marshall's appendices, the exposition of Marshall, Professor Pigou, and Mr. Kahn is nonmathematical, but the few relationships we discuss here may be presented most conveniently in a mathematical form. This will also facilitate comparison with the studies of Pareto and Barone.

[20] In the analyses of Professor Pigou and Mr. Kahn some modification of (27) would be introduced to take care of the direct effects (as in the case of "factory smoke") on aggregate welfare of shifts of factors of production from one use to another.

[21] With the qualifications of n. 15 above.

[22] See the references in n. 13 above.

In (29), w^i is the marginal utility of money to the ith individual and $U_1{}^i$, $U_2{}^i$, $U_3{}^i$, etc., are the marginal utilities of the various commodities and disutilities of the various types of work. In Marshall's exposition it is shown that, for any given amounts of X, Y, A^x, B^x, A^y, B^y, if the conditions (29) are not satisfied some U^i can be increased without any other being decreased. Thus for (28) to hold, (29) must be satisfied. Professor Pigou and Mr. Kahn do not develop the conditions (29), but assume them *ab initio* in their analysis.

If the conditions (29) are satisfied, (28) may be written in the form

$$\Sigma w^i \Delta_i = 0, \tag{30}$$

where

$$\Delta_i = p \, dx_i + q \, dy_i - g^x \, da_i{}^x - h^x \, db_i{}^x - g^y \, da_i{}^y - h^y \, db_i{}^y. \tag{31}$$

The remaining conditions again may be derived from (30). However, in Mr. Kahn's reformulation of Professor Pigou's analysis,[23] it is assumed also that the Shares are distributed equally, and the remaining conditions are developed from the requirement that

$$\Sigma \Delta_i = 0. \tag{32}$$

The summation in (32), with certain qualifications, is Professor Pigou's index of the National Dividend.[24] The procedures of Professor Pigou and Marshall differ from this, but the variations need not be elaborated here.[25]

Pareto and Barone also assume initially that conditions (29) are satisfied, but Pareto, like Marshall, shows in an early section of his work that, otherwise, it is possible to increase the *ophélimité* of some individuals without that of any others being decreased.[26] To develop the remaining conditions, aside from the Cambridge Conditions, Pareto expressedly avoids the use of (28) on the ground that "nous ne pouvons ni comparer ni sommer celles-ci [dU^1, dU^2, etc.], car nous ignorons le rapport des unités en lesquelles elles sont exprimées."[27] Instead Pareto proceeds directly to (32) and deduces the maximum conditions for pro-

---

[23] *Economic Journal,* March 1935.

[24] Professor Pigou's index does not include cost elements; it relates to large adjustments—whence the problem of backward and forward comparisons; and it is expressed as a percentage of the total value product at the initial position. See *Economics of Welfare,* chap. vi.

[25] But see pp. 419–422, below.

[26] *Cours,* I, pp. 20 ff.

[27] *Ibid.,* II, p. 93.

duction from it. In this, evidently for the same reason, Barone follows.[28]
Neither Pareto nor Barone introduces the Cambridge Conditions into
his analysis. Pareto merely assumes that the shares are distributed
"suivant la régle qu'il plaira d'adopter," or in a "maniére convenable,"[29]
and Barone that they are distributed according to some "ethical
criteria."[30]

The basis for developing production conditions directly from (32), for
Pareto, is that this equation will assure that if the quantities of products
"étaient convenablement distribuées, il en resulterait un maximum
d'ophélimite pour chaque individu dont se compose la société."[31]

Barone adopts the requirement that the sum be zero because, in his
words,

> this means that every other series of equivalents different from
> that which accords with this definition would make that sum nega-
> tive. That is to say, either it causes a decline in the welfare of all,
> or if some decline while others are raised, the gain of the latter is
> less than the loss of the former (so that even taking all their gain
> from those who gained in the change, reducing them to their former
> position, to give it completely to those who lost, the latter would
> always remain in a worse position than their preceding one without
> the situation of others being improved).[32]

Mr. Lerner, in the first of his two studies on welfare, advances as a
criterion for maximum position the condition that it should be impossible
in this position to increase the welfare of one individual without decreasing that of another. From this criterion he develops graphically
various maximum conditions. Like Pareto and Barone, he does not introduce the Cambridge Conditions into his analysis but, as he indicates,
ignores the problem of distribution.[33] In his later paper Mr. Lerner
presents our first group of maximum conditions, on the basis of the
criterion for a maximum that it should be impossible to increase the
production of one commodity without decreasing that of another.[34]

In my opinion the utility calculus introduced by the Cambridge
economists is not a useful tool for welfare economics. The approach does
not provide an alternative to the introduction of value judgments. First
of all, the comparison of the utilities of different individuals must involve an evaluation of the relative economic positions of these individ-

---

[28] See Barone, p. 246.
[29] *Cours,* II, pp. 91, 93, 94.
[30] Barone, p. 265.
[31] *Cours,* II, pp. 93, 94.
[32] Barone, p. 271.
[33] *Review of Economic Studies,* June 1934.
[34] *Review of Economic Studies,* October 1934.

uals. No extension of the methods of measuring utilities will dispense with the necessity for the introduction of value propositions to give these utilities a common dimension. Secondly, the evaluation of the different commodities cannot be avoided, even though this evaluation may consist only in a decision to accept the evaluations of the individual members of the community. And, finally, whether the direct effects on aggregate utility of a shift of factors of production from one use to another are given a zero value, as in Marshall's analysis, or a significant one, as in the analyses of Professor Pigou and Mr. Kahn,[35] alternatives are involved, and accordingly value judgments must be introduced.

While the utility calculus does not dispense with value judgments, the manner in which these value judgments are introduced is a misleading one. Statements as to the aggregative character of total welfare, or as to the equality of marginal utilities when there is an equal distribution of Shares, provided temperaments are about the same, do have the ring of *factual* propositions, and are likely to obscure the evaluations implied. The note by Mr. Kahn, in reference to his own formulation of the maximum conditions for economic welfare, that "many will share Mr. Dobb's suspicion 'that to strive after such a maximum is very much like looking in a dark room for a black hat which may be entirely subjective after all' "[36] is not one to reassure the reader as to the nature of the welfare principles derived in this manner. To the extent that the utility calculus does conceal the role of value judgments in the derivation of welfare principles, the criticism directed against the Cambridge procedure by Professor Robbins and others[37] is not without justification.

The approach, it must also be noted, requires a group of value propositions additional to those I have presented. So far as the Cambridge economists require that the economic welfare of the community be an *aggregate* of individual welfares, value judgments must be introduced to the effect that each individual contributes independently to the total welfare. These value propositions, which imply the complete measurability of the Economic Welfare Function aside from an arbitrary origin and a scalar constant, are not necessary for the derivation of the maximum conditions, and accordingly are not essential to the analysis.[38]

---

[35] See p. 407, and n. 20 above.

[36] *Economic Journal,* March 1935, p. 2n.

[37] Robbins, *The Nature and Significance of Economic Science;* C. Sutton, "The relation between Economic Theory and Economic Policy," *Economic Journal,* March 1937.

[38] Lange's discussion of utility determinateness (O. Lange, "On the Determinateness of the Utility Function," *Review of Economic Studies,* June 1934) errs insofar as it implies that welfare economics requires the summation of the independently measurable utilities of individuals, that is, his second utility postulate.

The derivation of conditions of maximum economic welfare without the summation of individual utilities, by Pareto, Barone, and Mr. Lerner, is a stride forward from the Cambridge formulation. Pareto's exposition of the basis for the procedure is somewhat ambiguous. Properly stated, the argument for developing production conditions directly from (32) is the same as that used in developing consumption conditions. The increment Δ_i in (31) indicates the preference direction of the ith individual.[39] If Δ_i is positive, the ith individual moves to a preferable position. The condition that $\Sigma\Delta_i$ be equal to zero does not assure that the *ophélimité* of each individual be a maximum, but that it be impossible to improve the position of one individual without making that of another worse. This, disregarding the misleading comparison of losses and gains, is the interpretation of Barone, and it is also the condition for a maximum used by Mr. Lerner.

But in avoiding the addition of utilities, Pareto, Barone, and Mr. Lerner also exclude the Cambridge Conditions from their analyses. None of the writers indicates his reasons for the exclusion, and I believe it has not proved an advantageous one. The first two groups of value propositions are introduced in the studies of Pareto and Barone by the use of, and in the argument as to the use of (32) as a basis for deriving maximum conditions, and in the analysis of Mr. Lerner by the criteria adopted for a maximum. In this respect the formulations differ little from that of the Cambridge economists. With the accompanying statements by Pareto and Barone that *the distribution of Shares* is decided on the basis of some "ethical criteria" or "rule," or with the complete exclusion of the problem by Mr. Lerner, this approach is not more conducive to an apprehension of the value content of the first two groups of maximum conditions. In the case of Mr. Lerner's study a misinterpretation does in fact appear. For in his analysis the first group of maximum conditions are advanced as objective in a sense which clearly implies that they require no value judgments for their derivation.[40]

Further, it must be emphasized, though the point is surely an obvious one, that unless the Cambridge Conditions, or a modified form of these conditions, is introduced there is no reason in general why it is more preferable to have the other conditions satisfied than otherwise. Placing $\Sigma\Delta_i$ equal to zero does not assure that there are no other positions for which welfare is greater, but only that there are no other positions for which the welfare of one individual is greater without that of another being less. In general, if conditions regarding distribution are not satis-

---

[39] R. G. D. Allen, "The Foundation of a Mathematical Theory of Exchange," *Economica*, May 1932.

[40] *Review of Economic Studies,* October 1934, p. 57.

fied, it is just as likely as not that any position for which $\Sigma\Delta_i$ does not equal zero will be *more* desirable than any position for which it does equal zero.

In the Pareto-Barone analysis, though not in that of Mr. Lerner, there is reason to believe that, in a general form, maximum conditions regarding distribution are assumed to be satisfied. While the distribution of Shares is not specified, it is consistent with some "ethical criteria," or "rule." Whatever the rule is, it should follow that in the maximum position the marginal economic welfare "per dollar" with respect to all individuals is the same. Otherwise, in the light of that rule, some other distribution would be preferable. If this interpretation is correct, the special exposition used by Pareto and Barone to support their derivation of maximum conditions is inappropriate. In (32) it is true that each dollar does not express the same amount of utility in the Cambridge sense, since the value propositions of independence are not introduced. But each dollar does express the same amount of welfare. The argument used to place (32) equal to zero is thus not the Pareto-Barone one, but that if it were unequal to zero, a further adjustment increasing the summation would be possible, and this would directly increase welfare, *regardless* of whether the position of some individuals were improved and that of others worsened by the change.[41]

EVALUATION OF A CHANGE IN WELFARE

I have noted elsewhere that the conditions for a maximum welfare which are presented on pages 403–413 are the conditions for any critical point. They are sufficient to inform us whether or not we are at the top or bottom of a hill, or at the top with respect to one variable, and the bottom with respect to another. The requirement for a *maximum* position is that it be possible to reach the position from any neighboring point by a series of positive adjustments. For the determination of such a position, it is necessary to know the sign $(+, -, 0)$ of any increment of welfare.

In the welfare studies the sign of dE is specified only for limited groups of adjustments. It will be of interest to note these conditions, and the value judgments required, though I shall not review again the formulations of the various writers.

(i) If we assume that all the conditions for a critical point are satisfied, except those relating to the distribution of the factors of produc-

---

[41] This argument is more fully developed in the section following.

tion between different uses, one additional group of value judgments gives us sufficient information concerning the shape of the Economic Welfare Function to determine the sign of an increment of welfare. These value propositions are: *if all individuals except any ith individual moves to a position which is preferable to him, economic welfare increases.* If we denote a more preferable position by a positive movement of S^i, these value propositions require that

$$\frac{\partial E}{\partial S^i} > 0, \tag{33}$$

for any i. Let us write from (21)

$$dE = \sum \frac{\partial E}{\partial x_i} dx_i + \frac{\partial E}{\partial y_i} dy_i + \frac{\partial E}{\partial a_i^x} da_i^x + \frac{\partial E}{\partial b_i^x} db_i^x$$

$$+ \frac{\partial E}{\partial a_i^y} da_i^y + \frac{\partial E}{\partial b_i^y} db_i^y. \tag{34}$$

Using equations (5) through (10), and the notation of (31),

$$dE = \omega \Sigma \Delta_i. \tag{35}$$

By (33) and the equations (5) through (10), ω must have the same sign as the price-wage rates in Δ_i. We shall take this sign as positive. Thus if the Shares are distributed equally, and if the prices and wage rates are proportionate to the marginal rates of substitution of the different kinds of commodities and types of work, economic welfare has the sign of Professor Pigou's index of the National Dividend. It will be increased by any adjustment which results in the movement of factors of production to a position of higher marginal value productivity.

(ii) If the assumption that the Cambridge Conditions are satisfied is relaxed, (35) may be written in the form

$$dE = \Sigma \omega^i \Delta_i \tag{36}$$

where ω^i is the marginal economic welfare per dollar with respect to the ith individual. Using the evaluation in (33) it follows that, for any adjustment for which no Δ_i decreases and some Δ_i increases, economic welfare will increase.

(iii) Continuing to use the assumptions of (ii), let us write

$$\lambda_{ik} = \frac{\omega^i}{\omega^k}, \tag{37}$$

and

$$dE = \omega^k \Sigma \lambda_{ik} \Delta_i. \tag{38}$$

Let us introduce the value propositions: *for a given price-wage situation, and any i and k, if the Share of i is greater than that of k, a decrease in the Share of k would have to be accompanied by a larger increase in the Share of i, for economic welfare to remain unchanged.* Since it can be shown that if the Share of the ith individual increases by dm_i a concomitant decrease, $-\lambda_{ik}dm_i$, in the share of the kth will leave economic welfare unchanged,[42] these value propositions require that λ_{ik} be less than unity. It follows that, for any given adjustment, if $\Sigma\Delta_i$ is positive, and if Δ_i does not vary with λ_{ik}, or if it decreases with λ_{ik}, economic welfare will increase. In other words, if the change in the National Dividend is not counteracted by a change in its distribution, the welfare of the community will be increased, even if some Δ_i increase and others decrease.

The adjustments in (i) are those considered by Mr. Kahn; in (ii) by Pareto, Barone, and Mr. Lerner; and in (iii) by Marshall and Professor Pigou. As Professor Pigou has pointed out,[43] the sign of an increment of welfare for some adjustments is left undetermined in his analysis. To determine the sign of dE for all adjustments, all the λ's would have to be evaluated, and a similar group of value judgments for the case where prices and wages are not proportional to the marginal rates of substitution would have to be introduced. On *a priori* grounds there is no reason why more information should not be obtained, since the comparison involved in evaluating the λ's is the same as that required for the Value Propositions of Equal Shares. For some additional and fairly rough evaluations, the range of adjustments included can be extended considerably, though an element of uncertainty is involved. Two such approximations, perhaps, are of sufficient interest to note, though they are not introduced in the welfare studies.

(iv) The assumptions of (ii) are retained. Let us suppose that with respect to some individual, say the kth,

$$\Sigma\lambda_{ik} = N, \qquad (39)$$

the sum being taken for all i. Thus ω^k is the average ω. If we write

$$\alpha_i = \lambda_{ik} - 1; \qquad \beta_i = \Delta_i - \frac{\Sigma\Delta_i}{N}; \qquad (40)$$

[42] This relationship follows immediately from the equations:

$$dE = \frac{\partial E}{\partial m_i} dm_i + \frac{\partial E}{\partial m_k} dm_k = \omega^i dm_i + \omega^k dm_k.$$

[43] *Economics of Welfare*, p. 645.

then

$$dE = \omega^k(\Sigma\alpha_i\beta_i + \Sigma\Delta_i). \qquad (41)$$

The first term in the brackets may be regarded as an index of the distribution of the National Dividend. It follows immediately from (41) that: (a) if Δ_i is positively correlated with λ_{ik}, dE will be positive for an increase in the Dividend and conversely; (b) if the coefficient of variation of the ω's is less than one hundred per cent, that is, if the standard deviation of λ_{ik} is less than unity, and if the coefficient of variation of Δ_i is also less than one hundred per cent, dE will have the sign of the index of the Dividend *regardless* of changes in its distribution.[44]

To determine precisely whether the conditions enumerated are satisfied would, of course, require a complete evaluation of the λ's. But the following rough evaluations would be sufficient to assure the likelihood of the results. For (a), it must be possible to say that "on the average" the change in distribution does not affect the "poor" more than the "rich," or vice versa. For (b) it is necessary to conceive of an individual or group of individuals who are, on the whole, in an average position from the point of view of welfare, and to determine whether, for a given position, ω^i "on the average" is likely to be somewhat less than twice the marginal economic welfare per "dollar" for the average individuals, that is, less than twice ω^k. (This should be stated in terms of the average shift in Shares for which welfare remains unchanged.) If it is determined that such a position is occupied, it would be likely that if tastes did not vary greatly—that is, if the relative variation of Δ_i were not very large —dE would increase for an increase in the Dividend. Since, however, the relative variation of Δ_i would ordinarily become excessively large as $\Sigma\Delta_i$ approached zero, it would be highly uncertain, for adjustments close to the maximum, whether or not an unfavorable change in distribution would obliterate the change in the Dividend.

[44] From (41),

$$dE = \omega^k(Nr_{\lambda\Delta}\sigma_\lambda\sigma_\Delta + \Sigma\Delta)$$
$$= \omega^k(Nr_{\lambda\Delta}\sigma_\lambda\sigma_\Delta/\Sigma\Delta + 1)\Sigma\Delta$$

The proposition (a) follows immediately, and (b) is based on the fact that $r_{\lambda\Delta}$ must be less than unity.

The last two methods of social choice, dictatorship and convention,
ve in their formal structure a certain definiteness absent from voting
the market mechanism. In ideal dictatorship there is but one will in-
lved in choice, in an ideal society ruled by convention there is but the
vine will or perhaps, by assumption, a common will of all individuals
ncerning social decision, so in either case no conflict of individual wills
involved.[2] The methods of voting and the market, on the other hand,
e methods of amalgamating the tastes of many individuals in the mak-
g of social choices. The methods of dictatorship and convention are,
· can be, rational in the sense that any individual can be rational in
s choices. Can such consistency be attributed to collective modes of
oice, where the wills of many people are involved?

It should be emphasized here that the present study is concerned only
ith the formal aspects of the above question. That is, we ask if it is
rmally possible to construct a procedure for passing from a set of
nown individual tastes to a pattern of social decision-making, the pro-
edure in question being required to satisfy certain natural conditions.
n illustration of the problem is the following well-known "paradox of
oting." Suppose there is a community consisting of three voters, and
nis community must choose among three alternative modes of social
ction (e.g., disarmament, cold war, or hot war). It is expected that
hoices of this type have to be made repeatedly, but sometimes not all of
he three alternatives will be available. In analogy with the usual utility
nalysis of the individual consumer under conditions of constant wants
nd variable price-income situations, rational behavior on the part of

---

ode, the interpretation will pass into the hands of a single individual or a small
roup alone deemed qualified.

The classification of methods of social choice given here corresponds to Professor
Knight's distinction among custom, authority, and consensus, except that I have
ubdivided consensus into the two categories of voting and the market (F. H.
Knight, "Human Nature and World Democracy," in *Freedom and Reform*, New
York: Harper and Bros., 1947, pp. 308–310).

[2] It is assumed, of course, that the dictator, like the usual economic man, can
always make a decision when confronted with a range of alternatives and that he
will make the same decision each time he is faced with the same range of alternatives. The ability to make consistent decisions is one of the symptoms of an integrated personality. When we pass to social decision methods involving many individuals (voting or the market), the problem of arriving at consistent decisions
might analogously be referred to as that of the existence of an integrated society.
Whether or not this psychiatric analogy is useful remains to be seen. The formal
existence of methods of aggregating individual choices, the problem posed in this
study, is certainly a necessary condition for an integrated society in the above
sense; but whether the existence of such methods is sufficient or even forms an
important part of the sufficient condition for integration is dubious.

SOCIAL CHOICE AN
INDIVIDUAL VALUE

Kenneth J. Arrow

I. INTRODUCTION

1. THE TYPES OF SOCIAL CHOICE

In a capitalist democracy there are essentially two n
social choices can be made: voting, typically used to
decisions, and the market mechanism, typically used to i
decisions. In the emerging democracies with mixed ec
Great Britain, France, and Scandinavia, the same two i
social choices prevail, though more scope is given to the
ing and decisions based directly or indirectly on it and le
the price mechanism. Elsewhere in the world, and even i
units within the democracies, social decisions are some
single individuals or small groups and sometimes (more i
in this modern world) by a widely encompassing set of t
for making the social choice in any given situation, e.g., a

[1] The last two methods of making social choices are in a sense e
developments of conflicting tendencies in a democracy. The rule c
vidual is the extreme of administrative discretion, the rule of a
extreme of rule by law. But in dynamic situations the rule of a s
by insensible steps to dictatorship. The code needs interpretatio
change, and, no matter how explicit the code may have been in i
determining how society shall act in different circumstances, its n
ambiguous with the passage of time. It might conceivably happen
interpretation passes to society as a whole, acting through some de
—"vox populi, vox dei." Or it can happen that interpretation pass
of the people individually and not collectively; in this case, as soc
of opinion arise, the religious code loses all its force as a guide i
See, for example, the ultimate consequences in the field of econom
Protestant insistence on the right of each individual to interpret th
(R. H. Tawney, *Religion and the Rise of Capitalism*, London: J
pp. 97–100). But more likely, in view of the authoritarian characte

Source: Chapters I–III, pages 1–33. John Wiley and Sons, Second
Reprinted with permission.

the community would mean that the community orders the three alternatives according to its collective preferences once for all, and then chooses in any given case that alternative among those actually available which stands highest on this list. A natural way of arriving at the collective preference scale would be to say that one alternative is preferred to another if a majority of the community prefer the first alternative to the second, i.e., would choose the first over the second if those were the only two alternatives. Let A, B, and C be the three alternatives, and 1, 2, and 3 the three individuals. Suppose individual 1 prefers A to B to C (and therefore A to C), individual 2 prefers B to C and C to A (and therefore B to A), and individual 3 prefers C to A and A to B (and therefore C to B). Then a majority prefer A to B, and a majority prefer B to C. We may therefore say that the community prefers A to B and B to C. If the community is to be regarded as behaving rationally, we are forced to say that A is preferred to C. But in fact a majority of the community prefer C to A.[3] So the method just outlined for passing from individual to collective tastes fails to satisfy the condition of rationality, as we ordinarily understand it. Can we find other methods of aggregating individual tastes which imply rational behavior on the part of the community and which will be satisfactory in other ways?[4]

If we continue the traditional identification of rationality with maximization of some sort (to be discussed at greater length below) then the problem of achieving a social maximum derived from individual desires is precisely the problem which has been central to the field of welfare economics. There is no need to review the history of this subject in detail.[5] There has been controversy as to whether or not the economist

[3] It may be added that the method of decision sketched above is essentially that used in deliberative bodies, where a whole range of alternatives usually comes up for decision in the form of successive pair-wise comparisons. The phenomenon described in the text can be seen in a pure form in the disposition of the proposals before recent Congresses for federal aid to state education, the three alternatives being no federal aid, federal aid to public schools only, federal aid to both public and parochial schools. The "paradox of voting" seems to have been first pointed out by E. J. Nanson (*Transactions and Proceedings of the Royal Society of Victoria*, Vol. 19, 1882, pp. 197–240). I am indebted for this reference to C. P. Wright, University of New Brunswick.

[4] The problem of collective rationality has been discussed by Knight, but chiefly in terms of the socio-psychological prerequisites. See "The Planful Act: The Possibilities and Limitations of Collective Rationality," in *Freedom and Reform, op. cit.*, pp. 335–369, especially pp. 346–365.

[5] Good sketches will be found in P. A. Samuelson's *Foundations of Economic Analysis*, Cambridge, Massachusetts: Harvard University Press, 1947, Chapter VIII; and A. Bergson (Burk), "A Reformulation of Certain Aspects of Welfare Economics," *Quarterly Journal of Economics*, Vol. 52, February, 1938, pp. 310–334. A summary of recent developments will be found in the article, "Socialist Economics,"

qua economist could make statements saying that one social state is better than another. If we admit meaning to interpersonal comparisons of utility, then presumably we could order social states according to the sum of the utilities of individuals under each, and this is the solution of Jeremy Bentham, accepted by Edgeworth and Marshall.[6] Even in this case we have a choice of different mathematical forms of the social utility function in terms of individual utilities; thus, the social utility might be the sum of the individual utilities or their product or the product of their logarithms or the sum of their products taken two at a time. So, as Professor Bergson has pointed out, there are value judgments implicit even at this level.[7] The case is clearly much worse if we deny the possibility of making interpersonal comparisons of utility. It was on the latter grounds that Professor Robbins so strongly attacked the concept that economists could make any policy recommendations,[8] at least without losing their status as economists and passing over into the realm of ethics. On the other hand, Mr. Kaldor and, following him, Professor Hicks have argued that there is a meaningful sense in which we can say that one state is better than another from an economic point of view,[9] even without assuming the reality of interpersonal comparison of utilities. The particular mechanism by which they propose to accomplish the comparison of different social states, the compensation principle, will be examined in more detail in Chapter IV.

---

by A. Bergson, in *A Survey of Contemporary Economics,* H. S. Ellis, ed., Philadelphia: The Blakiston Co., 1948, Chapter XII. In addition to the above, restatements of the present state of the field will be found in O. Lange, "The Foundations of Welfare Economics," *Econometrica,* Vol. 10, July–October, 1942, pp. 215–228; and M. W. Reder, *Studies in the Theory of Welfare Economics,* New York: Columbia University Press, 1947, Chapters I–V.

   [6] F. Y. Edgeworth, *Mathematical Psychics,* London: C. Kegan Paul and Co., 1881, pp. 56–82, especially p. 57; "The Pure Theory of Taxation," in *Papers Relating to Political Economy,* London: Macmillan and Co., 1925, Vol. II, pp. 63–125, especially pp. 100–122. The interpretation of social utility as the sum of individual utilities is implicit in Marshall's use of the doctrine of consumers' surplus, though other assumptions are also involved. (A. Marshall, *Principles of Economics,* New York: The Macmillan Co., eighth edition, 1949, pp. 130–134, 467–476.)

   [7] Bergson, "A Reformulation . . . ," *op. cit., passim.* See also Samuelson, *op. cit.,* pp. 219–252.

   [8] L. Robbins, *An Essay on the Nature and Significance of Economic Science,* second edition, London: Macmillan and Co., 1935, Chapter VI; "Interpersonal Comparisons of Utility: A Comment," *Economic Journal,* Vol. 43, December, 1938, pp. 635–641.

   [9] N. Kaldor, "Welfare Propositions of Economics and Interpersonal Comparisons of Utility," *Economic Journal,* Vol. 49, September, 1939, pp. 549–552; J. R. Hicks, "The Foundations of Welfare Economics," *Economic Journal,* Vol. 49, December, 1939, pp. 696–700, 711–712.

The controversy involves a certain confusion between two levels of argument. There can be no doubt that, even if interpersonal comparison is assumed, a value judgment is implied in any given way of making social choices based on individual utilities; so much Bergson has shown clearly. But, given these basic value judgments as to the mode of aggregating individual desires, the economist should investigate those mechanisms for social choice which satisfy the value judgments and should check their consequences to see if still other value judgments might be violated. In particular, he should ask the question whether or not the value judgments are consistent with each other, i.e., do there exist any mechanisms of social choice which will in fact satisfy the value judgments made? For example, in the voting paradox discussed above, if the method of majority choice is regarded as itself a value judgment, then we are forced to the conclusion that the value judgment in question, applied to the particular situation indicated, is self-contradictory.

In the matter of consistency, the question of interpersonal comparison of utilities becomes important. Bergson considers it possible to establish an ordering of social states which is based on indifference maps of individuals, and Samuelson has agreed.[10] On the other hand, Professor Lange, in his discussion of the social welfare function, has assumed the interpersonal measurability of utility,[11] and elsewhere he has insisted on the absolute necessity of measurable utility for normative social judgments.[12] Professor Lerner similarly has assumed the meaningfulness of an interpersonal comparison of intensities of utility in his recent work on welfare economics.[13]

In the following discussion of the consistency of various value judgments as to the mode of social choice, the distinction between voting and the market mechanism will be disregarded, both being regarded as special cases of the more general category of collective social choice. The analogy between economic choice and political choice has been pointed out a number of times. For example, Professor Zassenhaus considered the structure of a planned economy by considering the free market replaced by influence conceived generally as a means of distributing the

---

[10] See the discussion of the Fundamental Value Propositions of Individual Preference in Bergson, "A Reformulation . . . ," op. cit., pp. 318–320; Samuelson, op. cit., p. 228.

[11] Lange, op. cit., pp. 219–224, especially top of p. 222; but there are contradictory statements on p. 223 and at the top of p. 224.

[12] O. Lange, "The Determinateness of the Utility Function," Review of Economic Studies, Vol. 1, June, 1934, pp. 224–225.

[13] A. P. Lerner, Economics of Control, New York: The Macmillian Co., 1944, Chapter III.

social product.[14] He argued that, under conditions analogous to free competition, the market for exchanging influence for goods would come to equilibrium in a manner analogous to that of the ordinary market, political influence taking the place of initial distribution of goods. His model, however, is expressed only in very general terms, and it is not easy to see how it would operate in a socialist democracy, for example.

Dr. Howard Bowen has considered voting as the demand for collective consumption.[15] In his treatment he regards distribution of income and costs as given, and other simplifying assumptions are made. Close analogies are found with the ordinary market demand curve.

Knight has also stressed the analogy between voting and the market in that both involve collective choice among a limited range of alternatives.[16] He has also stressed certain differences, particularly that there is likely to be a greater tendency toward inequality under voting than under the market; these differences are, however, largely of a socio-psychological type rather than of the formal type which alone is relevant here.

More recently, there has been a series of papers by Professor Duncan Black, dealing with various aspects of the theory of political choice under certain special assumptions and emphasizing the close similarity between the problems of market and electoral choice.[17] His work will be dealt with in greater detail in Chapter VII, Section 2. There is also a literature on the technical problems of election. The chief relevant point here is that virtually every particular scheme proposed for election from single-member constituencies has been shown to have certain arbitrary features. The problem of choosing by election one among a number of candidates for a single position, such as the Presidency of the United States or membership in a legislative body when each district returns only a single member, is clearly of the same character as choosing one out of

[14] H. Zassenhaus, "Über die okonomische Theorie der Planwirtschaft," *Zeitschrift für Nationalokonomie,* Vol. 5, 1934, pp. 502–532.

[15] H. R. Bowen, "The Interpretation of Voting in the Allocation of Economic Resources," *Quarterly Journal of Economics,* Vol. 58, November, 1943, pp. 27–48.

[16] F. H. Knight, "Economic Theory and Nationalism," in *The Ethics of Competition and Other Essays,* New York: Harper and Bros., 1931, pp. 294–305.

[17] D. Black, "On the Rationale of Group Decision-Making," *Journal of Political Economy,* Vol. 56, February, 1948, pp. 23–34; "The Decisions of a Committee Using a Special Majority," *Econometrica,* Vol. 16, July, 1948, pp. 245–261; "The Elasticity of Committee Decisions with an Altering Size of Majority," *ibid.,* pp. 262–270; and "Un approccio alla teoria delle decisioni di comitato," *Giornale degli economistie e annali di economica,* Vol. 7, Nuova Serie, 1948, pp. 262–284. For the analogy between voting and the market, see especially "The Elasticity of Committee Decisions . . . ," pp. 262, 270; and "Un approccio . . . ," pp. 262–269.

a number of alternative social policies; indeed, selection among candidates is presumably a device for achieving selection among policies.

2. SOME LIMITATIONS OF THE ANALYSIS

It has been stated above that the present study confines itself to the formal aspects of collective social choice. The aspects not discussed may be conveniently described as the game aspects, especially since that term has acquired a double meaning. In the first place, no consideration is given to the enjoyment of the decision process as a form of play. There is no need to stress the obvious importance of the desire to play and win the game as such in both economic behavior and political.[18] That such considerations are real and should be considered in determining the mechanics of social choice is not to be doubted; but this is beyond the scope of the present study.

The other meaning of the term "game" is that which has been brought to the attention of economists by Professors von Neumann and Morgenstern.[19] The point here, broadly speaking, is that, once a machinery for making social choices from individual tastes is established, individuals will find it profitable, from a rational point of view, to misrepresent their tastes by their actions, either because such misrepresentation is somehow directly profitable[20] or, more usually, because some other individual will be made so much better off by the first individual's misrepresentation that he could compensate the first individual in such a way that both are better off than if everyone really acted in direct accordance with his tastes. Thus, in an electoral system based on plurality voting, it is notorious that an individual who really favors a minor party candidate will frequently vote for the less undesirable of the major party candidates rather than "throw away his vote." Even in a case where it is possible to construct a procedure showing how to aggregate individual tastes into a consistent social preference pattern, there still remains the problem of devising rules of the game so that individuals will actually express their true tastes even when they are acting rationally. This problem is allied to the problem of constructing games of fair division, in which the rules are to be such that each individual, by playing rationally, will succeed in getting a preassigned fair share; in the case of

---

[18] Knight has constantly emphasized the importance of play motives in human life; see, for example, the reference in fn. 16. The importance of emulative motives has nowhere been so forcefully stressed as by T. Veblen (*The Theory of the Leisure Class,* New York: The Macmillan Co., 1899).

[19] J. von Neumann and O. Morgenstern, *Theory of Games and Economic Behavior,* second edition, Princeton: Princeton University Press, 1947.

[20] A similar point is made by Bowen, *op. cit.,* pp. 45, 48.

two people and equal division, the game is the very familiar one in which one player divides the total stock of goods into two parts, and the second player chooses which part he likes.[21]

In addition to ignoring game aspects of the problem of social choice, we will also assume in the present study that individual values are taken as data and are not capable of being altered by the nature of the decision process itself. This, of course, is the standard view in economic theory (though the unreality of this assumption has been asserted by such writers as Veblen, Professor J. M. Clark, and Knight[22]) and also in the classical liberal creed.[23] If individual values can themselves be affected by the method of social choice, it becomes much more difficult to learn what is meant by one method's being preferable to another.

Finally, it is assumed that all individuals in the society are rational. The precise meaning of this assumption will be enlarged on in the next chapter.

II. THE NATURE OF PREFERENCE AND CHOICE

1. MEASURABILITY AND INTERPERSONAL COMPARABILITY OF UTILITY

The viewpoint will be taken here that interpersonal comparison of utilities has no meaning and, in fact, that there is no meaning relevant to welfare comparisons in the measurability of individual utility. The controversy is well-known and hardly need be recited here. During the entire controversy, the proponents of measurable utility have been unable to produce any proposition of economic behavior which could be explained by their hypothesis and not by those of the indifference-curve

---

[21] See H. Steinhaus, "The Problem of Fair Division" (abstract), *Econometrica*, Vol. 16, January, 1948, pp. 101–104.

[22] Veblen, *The Theory of the Leisure Class, op. cit.*, and "Why is Economics Not an Evolutionary Science?" in *The Place of Science in Modern Civilisation and Other Essays*, New York: B. W. Huebsch, 1919, pp. 73–74; J. M. Clark, "Economics and Modern Psychology," in *Preface to Social Economics*, New York: Farrar and Rinehart, 1936, pp. 92–160, and "Realism and Relevance in the Theory of Demand," *Journal of Political Economy*, Vol. 54, August, 1946, pp. 347–351; F. H. Knight, "Ethics and the Economic Interpretation," in *The Ethics of Competition and Other Essays, op. cit.*, pp. 19–40, *passim*.

[23] "*Liberalism takes the individual as given*, and views the social problem as one of right relations between given individuals." (Italics in the original.) F. H. Knight, "Ethics and Economic Reform," in *Freedom and Reform, op. cit.*, p. 69.

theorists.[1] Indeed, the only meaning the concepts of utility can be said to have is their indications of actual behavior, and, if any course of behavior can be explained by a given utility function, it has been amply demonstrated that such a course of behavior can be equally well explained by any other utility function which is a strictly increasing function of the first. If we cannot have measurable utility, in this sense, we cannot have interpersonal comparability of utilities *a fortiori*.

Recently, the issue of measurable utility has been reopened by the results of Professors von Neumann and Morgenstern.[2] These results have been widely misunderstood. They consider a preference pattern not only among certain alternatives but also among alternative probability distributions. Making certain plausible assumptions as to the relations among preferences for related probability distributions, they find that there is a utility indicator (unique up to a linear transformation) which has the property that the value of the utility function for any probability distribution of certain alternatives is the mathematical expectation of the utility. Put otherwise, there is one way (unique up to a linear transformation) of assigning utilities to probability distributions such that behavior is described by saying that the individual seeks to maximize his expected utility.

This theorem does not, as far as I can see, give any special ethical significance to the particular utility scale found. For instead of using the utility scale found by von Neumann and Morgenstern, we could use the square of that scale; then behavior is described by saying that the individual seeks to maximize the expected value of the square root of his utility. This is not to deny the usefulness of the von Neumann-Morgenstern theorem; what it does say is that among the many different ways of assigning a utility indicator to the preferences among alternative probability distributions, there is one method (more precisely, a whole set of methods which are linear transforms of each other) which has

---

[1] Classical demand theory leaves ambiguous the relation between the indifference map of a household and the indifference maps of the individual members thereof. It is the former which is relevant for the behavior of the market. The passage from individual to household maps is a special case of the passage from individual to social orderings; if the present thesis is accepted, household indifference maps can, indeed, only arise from the presence of common standards of value of some sort. But these are, as will be seen, empirically determinable by examination of the individual indifference maps and are not based on some type of intrinsic comparison of intensities of feeling. In what follows we shall ignore the distinction between individual and household indifference maps; this action may be regarded as meaning either that the intra-household aggregation is somehow solved or that that problem is being considered simultaneously with the general problem.

[2] *Op. cit.*, pp. 15–31, 617–632. See also W. S. Vickrey, "Measuring Marginal Utility by Reactions to Risk," *Econometrica*, Vol. 13, October, 1945, pp. 319–333.

the property of stating the laws of rational behavior in a particularly convenient way. This is a very useful matter from the point of view of developing the descriptive economic theory of behavior in the presence of random events, but it has nothing to do with welfare considerations, particularly if we are interested primarily in making a social choice among alternative policies in which no random elements enter. To say otherwise would be to assert that the distribution of the social income is to be governed by the tastes of individuals for gambling.

The problem of measuring utility has frequently been compared with the problem of measuring temperature. This comparison is very apt. Operationally, the temperature of a body is the volume of a unit mass of a perfect gas placed in contact with it (provided the mass of the gas is small compared with the mass of the body). Why, it might be asked, was not the logarithm of the volume or perhaps the cube root of the volume of the gas used instead? The reason is simply that the general gas equation assumes a particularly simple form when temperature is defined in the way indicated. But there is no deeper significance. Does it make any sense to say that an increase of temperature from 0° to 1° is just as intense as an increase of temperature from 100° to 101°? No more can it be said that there is any meaning in comparing marginal utilities at different levels of well-being.

Even if, for some reason, we should admit the measurability of utility for an individual, there still remains the question of aggregating the individual utilities. At best, it is contended that, for an individual, his utility function is uniquely determined up to a linear transformation; we must still choose one out of the infinite family of indicators to represent the individual, and the values of the aggregate (say a sum) are dependent on how the choice is made for each individual. In general, there seems to be no method intrinsic to utility measurement which will make the choice compatible.[3] It requires a definite value judgment not derivable from individual sensations to make the utilities of different

---

[3] It must be granted, though, that, if it is assumed to begin with that all preference scales for individuals are the same (all individuals have the same tastes), then we could choose the utility function the same for all. However, if we take seriously the idea of interpersonal comparison of utilities, we must allow for the possibility that, of two individuals with the same indifference map, one is twice as sensitive as the other, and so the proper utility function for one should be just double that for another. It would be interesting, indeed, to see an operational significance attached to this concept of differing sensitivity.

Von Neumann and Morgenstern (*op. cit.*, pp. 608–616) have considered a case where two individuals have differing powers of discernment, but they have not represented this case by assuming different utilities for the same bundle of goods. Instead, they assume both utility scales can take on only discrete values, though one can take on more such values than the other.

individuals dimensionally compatible and still a further value judgment to aggregate them according to any particular mathematical formula. If we look away from the mathematical aspects of the matter, it seems to make no sense to add the utility of one individual, a psychic magnitude in his mind, with the utility of another individual. Even Bentham had his doubts on this point.[4]

We will therefore assume throughout this book that the behavior of an individual in making choices is describable by means of a preference scale without any cardinal significance, either individual or interpersonal.

2. A NOTATION FOR PREFERENCES AND CHOICE

In this study it is found convenient to represent preference by a notation not customarily employed in economics, though familiar in mathematics and particularly in symbolic logic. We assume that there is a basic set of alternatives which could conceivably be presented to the chooser. In the theory of consumer's choice, each alternative would be a complete decision on all inputs and outputs; in welfare economics, each alternative would be a distribution of commodities and labor requirements. In general, an alternative is a vector; however, in the theory of elections, the alternatives are candidates. These alternatives are mutually exclusive; they are denoted by the small letters x, y, z, ... On any given occasion, the chooser has available to him a subset S of all possible alternatives, and he is required to choose one out of this set. The set S is a generalization of the well-known opportunity curve; thus, in the theory of consumer's choice under perfect competition it would be the budget plane. It is assumed further that the choice is made in this way: Before knowing the set S, the chooser considers in turn all possible pairs of alternatives, say x and y, and for each such pair he makes one and only one of three decisions: x is preferred to y, x is indifferent to y, or y is preferred to x. The decisions made for different pairs are assumed to be consistent with each other, so, for example, if x is preferred to y and y to z, then x is preferred to z; similarly, if x is indifferent to y and y to z, then x is indifferent to z. Having this ordering of all possible alternatives, the chooser is now confronted with a particular opportunity set S. If there is one alternative in S which is preferred to all others in S, the chooser selects that one alternative. Suppose, however, there is a subset of alternatives in S such that the alternatives in the

<hr>

[4] " 'Tis in vain to talk of adding quantities which after the addition will continue distinct as they were before, one man's happiness will never be another man's happiness: a gain to one man is no gain to another: you might as well pretend to add 20 apples to 20 pears. . . ." (Quoted by W. C. Mitchell in "Bentham's Felicific Calculus," in *The Backward Art of Spending Money and Other Essays*, New York: McGraw-Hill Book Co., 1937, p. 184.)

subset are each preferred to every alternative not in the subset, while the alternatives in the subset are indifferent to each other. This case would be one in which the highest indifference curve that has a point in common with a given opportunity curve has at least two points in common with it. In this case, the best thing to say is that the choice made in S is the whole subset; the first case discussed is one in which the subset in question, the choice, contains a single element.

Since we have not restricted the type of sets allowed, a third possibility presents itself; there may be no alternative in S which is preferred or indifferent to all others. That is, for every alternative in S, there is another which is preferred to it. For example, suppose that an individual prefers more money to less and that the alternatives in S include every integral number of dollars. Or, if we wish to require that S is in some sense bounded, consider the sequence of alternatives $\frac{1}{2}$, $\frac{2}{3}$, $\frac{3}{4}$, . . . , $1 - (1/n)$, . . . dollars. There cannot really be said to be any rational choice in this case. However, this mathematical point will not play any part in the present work.

Preference and indifference are relations between alternatives. Instead of working with two relations, it will be slightly more convenient to use a single relation, "preferred or indifferent." The statement "x is preferred or indifferent to y" will be symbolized by $x\,R\,y$. The letter R, by itself, will be the name of the relation and will stand for a knowledge of all pairs such that $x\,R\,y$. From our previous discussion, we have that, for any pair of alternatives x and y, either x is preferred to y or y to x, or the two are indifferent. That is, we have assumed that any two alternatives are comparable.[5] But this assumption may be written symbolically, as

AXIOM I: *For all x and y, either $x\,R\,y$ or $y\,R\,x$,*

A relation R which satisfies Axiom I will be said to be connected. Note that Axiom I is presumed to hold when $x = y$, as well as when x is distinct from y, for we ordinarily say that x is indifferent to itself for any x, and this implies $x\,R\,x$.[6] Note also that the word "or" in the statement of

---

[5] The assumption of comparability of all alternatives is the heart of the integrability controversy in the theory of consumer's choice. See V. Pareto, *Manuel d'économie politique,* deuxième édition, Paris: M. Giard, 192, pp. 546–569. For some of the paradoxical consequences, of nonintegrability (which is equivalent to noncomparability of alternatives not infinitesimally close together), see N. Georgescu-Roegen, "The Pure Theory of Consumer's Behavior," *Quarterly Journal of Economics,* Vol. 50, August, 1936, pp. 545–569. Professor Ville has derived the integrability condition, and therewith the comparability of all alternatives, from some plausible hypotheses on the nature of demand functions (J. Ville, "Sur les conditions d'existence d'une ophélimité totale et d'un indice du niveau des prix," *Annales de l'Universite de Lyon,* Section A, Vol. 3, No. 9, 1946, pp. 32–39).

Axiom I does not exclude the possibility of both $x R y$ and $y R x$. That word merely asserts that at least one of the two events must occur; both may.

The property mentioned above of consistency in the preferences between different pairs of alternatives may be stated more precisely, as follows: If x is preferred or indifferent to y and y is preferred or indifferent to z, then x must be either preferred or indifferent to z. In symbols,

AXIOM II: *For all $x, y,$ and $z, x R y$ and $y R z$ imply $x R z$*

A relation satisfying Axiom II is said to be transitive.[7] A relation satisfying both Axioms I and II is termed a weak ordering or sometimes simply an ordering. It is clear that a relation having these two properties taken together does create a ranking of the various alternatives. The adjective "weak" refers to the fact that the ordering does not exclude indifference, i.e., Axioms I and II do not exclude the possibility that for some distinct x and y, both $x R y$ and $y R x$. A strong ordering, on the other hand, is a ranking in which no ties are possible.[8] A weak ordering is a generalization of the concept "greater than or equal to" applied to real numbers; a strong ordering generalizes the concept "greater than" applied to the same realm.[9]

It might be felt that the two axioms in question do not completely characterize the concept of a preference pattern. For example, we ordinarily feel that not only the relation R but also the relations of (strict) preference and of indifference are transitive. We shall show that, by defining preference and indifference suitably in terms of R, it will follow that all the usually desired properties of preference patterns obtain.

DEFINITION 1: *$x P y$ is defined to mean not $y R x$.* The statement "*$x P y$*" is read "*x is preferred to y.*"

DEFINITION 2: *$x I y$ means $x R y$ and $y R x$.* The statement "*$x I y$*" is read "*x is indifferent to y.*"

---

[6] Strictly speaking, a relation is said to be connected if Axiom I holds for $x \neq y$. A relation R is said to be reflexive if, for all x, $x R x$. (See A. Tarski, *Introduction to Logic*, New York: Oxford University Press, 1941, pp. 93–94.) Thus a relation satisfying Axiom I is both connected and reflexive. However, for convenience, we will use the slightly inaccurate terminology in the text, that is, we will use the word "connected" for the longer expression "connected and reflexive."

[7] Tarski, *ibid.*, p. 94.

[8] Frequently, indeed, the term "ordering relation" is reserved for strong orderings (Tarski, *ibid.*, pp. 96–96). However, in the present book the unmodified term "ordering" or "ordering relation" will be reserved for weak orderings.

[9] A formal characterization of strong ordering relations will be given later, in discussing the recent work of Professor Duncan Black on the theory of elections; see Chapter VII, Section 2.

It is clear that P and I, so defined, correspond to the ordinary notions of preference and indifference, respectively.

LEMMA 1: (a) *For all x, $x R x$.*

(b) *If $x P y$, then $x R y$.*

(c) *If $x P y$ and $y P z$, then $x P z$.*

(d) *If $x I y$ and $y I z$, then $x I z$.*

(e) *For all x and y, either $x R y$ or $y P x$.*

(f) *If $x P y$ and $y R z$, then $x P z$.*

All these statements are intuitively self-evident from the interpretations placed on the symbols. However, it may be as well to give sketches of the proofs, both to show that Axioms I and II really imply all that we wish to imply about the nature of orderings of alternatives and to illustrate the type of reasoning to be used subsequently.

PROOF: (a) In Axiom I, let $y = x$; then for all x, either $x R x$ or $x R x$, which is to say, $x R x$.

(b) Directly from Definition 1 and Axiom I.

(c) From $x P y$ and $y P z$, we can, by (b), deduce $x R y$. Suppose $z R x$. Then, from $z R x$ and $x R y$, we could deduce $z R y$ by Axiom II. However, from $y P z$, we have, by Definition 1, not $z R y$. Hence the supposition $z R x$ leads to a contradiction, so that we may assert not $z R x$, or $x P z$, by Definition 1.

(d) From $x I y$ and $y I z$, we can, by Definition 2, deduce $x R y$ and $y R z$. From Axiom II, then, $x R z$. Also from $x I y$ and $y I z$, by Definition 2, we have $z R y$ and $y R x$, which imply $z R x$, by Axiom II. Since both $x R z$ and $z R x$, $x I z$ by Definition 2.

(e) Directly from Definition 1.

(f) Suppose $z R x$. From $z R x$ and $y R z$ follows $y R x$, by Axiom II. But, by Definition 1, $x P y$ implies not $y R x$. Hence the supposition $z R x$, leads to a contradiction. Therefore, not $z R x$, or $x P z$.

For clarity, we will avoid the use of the terms "preference scale" or "preference pattern" when referring to R, since we wish to avoid confusion with the concept of preference proper, denoted by P. We will refer to R as an "ordering relation" or "weak ordering relation," or, more simply, as an "ordering" or "weak ordering." The term "preference relation" will refer to the relation P.

In terms of the relation R, we may now define the concept of choice, recalling that in general we must regard the choice from a given set of alternatives as itself a set. If S is the set of alternatives available, which we will term the *environment*,[10] let $C(S)$ be the alternative or alternatives chosen out of S. $C(S)$ is, of course, a subset of S. Each element of

[10] This term is J. Marschak's.

$C(S)$ is to be preferred to all elements of S not in $C(S)$ and indifferent to all elements of $C(S)$; and, therefore, if x belongs to $C(S)$, $x R y$ for all y in S. On the other hand, if in fact, $x R y$ for all y in S and if x belongs to S, then, by Definition 1, there is no element z in S such that $z P x$. Hence, we may define $C(S)$ formally as follows:

DEFINITION 3: $C(S)$ *is the set of all alternatives x in S such that, for every y in S, $x R y$.*

$C(S)$, it is to be noted, describes a functional relationship in that it assigns a chance to each possible environment. We may call it the choice function; it is a straightforward generalization of the demand function as it appears in the theory of consumer's choice under perfect competition, the sets S there being budget planes.

Let $[x,y]$ be the set composed of the two alternatives x and y. Suppose $x P y$. Then $x R y$, by Lemma 1(b), and $x R x$, by Lemma 1(a), so that x belongs to $C([x,y])$; but, again by Definition 1, since $x P y$, not $y R x$, so that y does not belong to $C([x,y])$, i.e., $C([x,y])$ contains the single element x.

Conversely, suppose $C([x,y])$ contains the single element x. Since y does not belong to $C([x,y])$, not $y R x$; by Definition 1, $x P y$.

LEMMA 2: *A necessary and sufficient condition that $x P y$ is that x be the sole element of $C([x,y])$.*

In case neither $x P y$ nor $y P x$, we have, clearly, $x I y$, and this is equivalent to saying the $C([x,y])$ contains both x and y. If, then, we know $C([x,y])$ for all two-element sets, we have completely defined the relations P and I and therefore the relation R; but, by Definition 3, knowing the relation R completely determines the choice function $C(S)$ for all sets of alternatives. Hence, one of the consequences of the assumptions of rational choice is that the choice in any environment can be determined by a knowledge of the choices in two-element environments.[11]

---

[11] Instead of starting, as here, with a weak ordering relation R satisfying certain axioms and then obtaining a choice function, it is possible to impose certain axioms directly on the choice function. It is not hard, in fact, to construct a set of plausible axioms concerning the choice function from which it is possible to deduce that there exists a weak ordering relation which could have generated the choice function, so that the two approaches are logically equivalent. Starting with the choice function instead of the ordering relation is analogous to the approach of Cournot, who started with demand functions having postulated properties instead of deriving those properties from a consideration of indifference maps or utility functions. (A. Cournot, *Mathematical Principles of the Theory of Wealth*, English translation, New York: The Macmillan Co., 1897, pp. 49–50). The assumptions made by Cournot about the demand function were not very restrictive. More

The representation of the choice mechanism by ordering relations, as suggested above, has certain advantages for the present analysis over the more conventional representations in terms of indifference maps or utility functions. In regard to indifference maps, there is first the obvious advantage of being able to consider alternatives which are represented by vectors with more than two components. Second, the usefulness of an indifference map usually rests to a large measure on the assumption that the chooser desires more of each component of the alternative to less, all other components remaining the same; this assumption serves to orient the chart.[12] Since the present study is concerned with the choice of a social state, each alternative has many components which may be desirable under certain circumstances and undesirable under others. Third, the use of an indifference map involves assumptions of continuity which are unnecessarily restrictive for the present purpose, especially since, in order to handle such problems as indivisibilities, which have been productive of so much controversy in the field of welfare economics, it is necesary to assume that some of the components of the social state are discrete variables.

As for utility functions, there is first of all the formal difficulty that, if insufficient continuity assumptions are made about the ordering, there may exist no way of assigning real numbers to the various alternatives in such a way as to satisfy the usual requirements of a utility function. In any case, we would simply be replacing the expression $x \, R \, y$ by the expression $U(x) \geq U(y)$, and the structure of all proofs would be unchanged, while the elegance of the whole exposition would be marred by the introduction of the superfluous function $U(x)$, whose significance lies entirely in its ordinal properties. If we are concerned with ordinal properties, it seems better to represent these directly.[13]

---

sophisticated treatment of demand from this point of view is to be found in the work of Ville, *op. cit.*, and Samuelson, *op. cit.*, pp. 11–117. Both treatments concern only the case of consumer's choice under perfectly competitive conditions, but suitable generalization to imperfectly competitive environments does not seem impossible.

[12] This brief statement is not accurate when the existence of a point of saturation is assumed. However, the chart is then at least oriented uniformly within each of several large segments, and the interesting economic problems presumably occur in the region where the assumption made in the text holds.

[13] Similarly, in the field of production economics, it seems more natural to express the transformation restrictions by saying that the input-output vector lies in a certain point set than to introduce a transformation function and then subject the operations of the firm to the conditions $T = 0$. In this case, the irrelevance of the functional representation is even clearer since, if $F(t) = 0$ if and only if $t = 0$, then $F(T)$ can be used as the transformation function just as well as T.

3. THE ORDERING OF SOCIAL STATES

In the present study the objects of choice are social states. The most precise definition of a social state would be a complete description of the amount of each type of commodity in the hands of each individual, the amount of labor to be supplied by each individual, the amount of each productive resource invested in each type of productive activity, and the amounts of various types of collective activity, such as municipal services, diplomacy and its continuation by other means, and the erection of statues to famous men. It is assumed that each individual in the community has a definite ordering of all conceivable social states, in terms of their desirability to him. It is not assumed here that an individual's attitude toward different social states is determined exclusively by the commodity bundles which accrue to his lot under each. It is simply assumed that the individual orders all social states by whatever standards he deems relevant. A member of Veblen's leisure class might order the states solely on the criterion of his relative income standing in each; a believer in the equality of man might order them in accordance with some measure of income equality. Indeed, since, as mentioned above, some of the components of the social state, considered as a vector, are collective activities, purely individualistic assumptions are useless in analyzing such problems as the division of the national income between public and private expenditure. The present notation permits perfect generality in this respect. Needless to say, this generality is not without its price. More information would be available for analysis if the generality were restricted by a prior knowledge of the nature of individual orderings of social states. This problem will be touched on again.

In general, there will, then, be a difference between the ordering of social states according to the direct consumption of the individual and the ordering when the individual adds his general standards of equity (or perhaps his standards of pecuniary emulation).[14] We may refer to the former ordering as reflecting his values. The distinction between the two is by no means clear-cut. An individual with esthetic feelings certainly derives pleasure from his neighbor's having a well-tended lawn. Under the system of a free market, such feelings play no direct part in social choice; yet psychologically they differ only slightly from the pleasure in one's own lawn. Intuitively, of course, we feel that not all the possible preferences which an individual might have ought to count;

[14] This distinction has been stressed to the author by M. Friedman, The University of Chicago.

his preferences for matters which are "none of his business" should be irrelevant. Without challenging this view, I should like to emphasize that the decision as to which preferences are relevant and which are not is itself a value judgment and cannot be settled on an a priori basis. From a formal point of view, one cannot distinguish between an individual's dislike for having his grounds ruined by factory smoke and his extreme distaste for the existence of heathenism in Central Africa. There are probably not a few individuals in this country who would regard the former feeling as irrelevant for social policy and the latter as relevant, though the majority would probably reverse the judgment. I merely wish to emphasize here that we must look at the entire system of values, including values about values, in seeking for a truly general theory of social welfare.

It is the ordering according to values which takes into account all the desires of the individual, including the highly important socializing desires, and which is primarily relevant for the achievement of a social maximum. The market mechanism, however, takes into account only the ordering according to tastes. This distinction is the analogue, on the side of consumption, of the divergence between social and private costs in production developed by Professor Pigou.[15]

As for notation, we will let R_i be the ordering relation for alternative social states from the standpoint of individual i. Sometimes, when several different ordering relations are being considered for the same individual, the symbols will be distinguished by adding a superscript. Corresponding to the ordering relation R_i, we have the (strict) preference relation P_i and the indifference relation I_i. If the symbol for the ordering has a prime or second attached (thus, $R_i{}'$, $R_i{}''$), then the corresponding symbols for preference and indifference will have the prime or second attached, respectively.

Similarly, society as a whole will be considered provisionally to have a social ordering relation for alternative social states, which will be designated by R, sometimes with a prime or second. Social preference and indifference will be denoted by P and I, respectively, primes or seconds being attached when they are attached to the relation R.

Throughout this analysis it will be assumed that individuals are rational, by which is meant that the ordering relations R_i satisfy Axioms I and II. The problem will be to construct an ordering relation for society

---

[15] A. C. Pigou, *The Economics of Welfare,* London: Macmillan and Co., 1920, Part II, Chapter VI. For the analogy, see Samuelson, *op. cit.,* p. 224; Reder, *op. cit.,* pp. 64–67; G. Tintner, "A Note on Welfare Economics," *Econometrica,* Vol. 14, January, 1946, pp. 69–78.

as a whole that will also reflect rational choice-making so that R may also be assumed to satisfy Axioms I and II.

4. A DIGRESSION ON RATIONALITY AND CHOICE

The concept of rationality used thoughout this study is at the heart of modern economic analysis, and it cannot be denied that it has great intuitive appeal; but closer analysis reveals difficulties. These may be illustrated by consideration of the modern developments in the theory of games used, in particular, the theory of zero-sum two-person games.[16]

As noted in Chapter II, Section 2, one of the consequences of the assumption of rationality is that the choice to be made from any set of alternatives can be determined by the choices made between pairs of alternatives. Suppose, however, that the situation is such that the chooser is never confronted with choices between pairs of alternatives; instead, the environment may always involve many alternatives. Indeed, that is precisely the situation in the theory of consumer's choice under perfect competition; the actual environment is always a whole line or plane. But, under certain plausible conditions, we can say that the choices made from the actual environments can be explained as though they were derived from choices between pairs of alternatives; and, at least conceptually, it makes sense to imagine the choices actually being made from pairs of alternatives.

Superficially, the theory of rational behavior in the zero-sum two-person game seems to fall into the same pattern. We could imagine each of the players considering all his possible strategies in turn, ordering them on the basis of the minimum profit (or maximum loss) that he could expect under each, and then choosing his best strategy by going as

---

[16] The theory of games involving more than two persons or games in which the sum of the payments to the various players is not independent of the methods of play is still in a dubious state despite the mathematically beautiful development in von Neumann and Morgenstern, *op. cit.*, Chapters V–XII. For example, the highly developed mechanism of compensations needed for their theory of rational behavior in such games appears to have little counterpart in the real world, as was pointed out by Professor Bain in another connection (J. S. Bain, "Output Quotas in Imperfect Cartels," *Quarterly Journal of Economics,* Vol. 62, August, 1948, pp. 617–622). On the other hand, there can be little doubt that the theory of rational play of a zero-sum two-person game has been completely solved, at least under certain restrictive assumptions as to the risk-neutrality of the players and as to the completeness of their information concerning the rules of the game. (See J. von Neumann, "Zur Theorie der Gesellschaftsspiele," *Mathematische Annalen,* Vol. 100, August, 1928, pp. 295–320; von Neumann and Morgenstern, *op. cit.*, Chapters III–IV.) Hence the theory of behavior in zero-sum two-person games affords some sort of check on the concepts of rationality derived to a large extent by analogy with the static theory of the firm under perfect competition.

high up on the resulting scale as he can. But the only reason why we regard this solution as truly rational is that, if both players follow it, neither one will have any incentive to change his strategy even if he finds out the opponent's. This is the essence of the famous min-max or saddle-point theorem. The validity of this theorem, however, arises from the fact that every time we admit a set of pure strategies into the player's environment, we also admit all mixtures of them, i.e., all probability distributions over such a set of pure strategies. Hence, the environment (set of admissible strategies), if it contains more than one strategy, automatically contains an infinite number. Nor can we even conceptually imagine the choice between two strategies; for, if this limitation were real, a saddle-point would exist only in special cases, and the ordering of strategies by minimum profit would not lead to a solution having the stability properties described above.

Thus, the model of rational choice as built up from pair-wise comparisons does not seem to suit well the case of rational behavior in the described game situation. It seems that the essential point is, and this is of general bearing, that, if conceptually we imagine a choice being made between two alternatives, we cannot exclude any probability distribution over those two choices as a possible alternative. The precise shape of a formulation of rationality which takes the last point into account or the consequences of such a reformulation on the theory of choice in general or the theory of social choice in particular cannot be foreseen; but it is at least a possibility, to which attention should be drawn, that the paradox to be discussed below might be resolved by such a broader concept of rationality.

Many writers have felt that the assumption of rationality, in the sense of a one-dimensional ordering of all possible alternatives, is absolutely necessary for economic theorizing; for example, Professor Rothschild remarks, "Unless economic units act in conformity with some rational pattern no general theory about what would follow from certain premises would be possible."[17] There seems to be no logical necessity for this viewpoint; we could just as well build up our economic theory on other assumptions as to the structure of choice functions if the facts

---

[17] K. W. Rothschild, "The Meaning of Rationality: A Note on Professor Lange's Article," *Review of Economic Studies,* Vol. 14, No. 1, 1946–47, p. 50. Rothschild also attributes this view to Professor Lange, but there seems to be a misinterpretation. Lange regards the assumption of rationality (which he identifies with ordering) as a highly convenient postulate, if true, but not necessary. (O. Lange, "The Scope and Method of Economics," *ibid.,* Vol. 13, No. 1, 1945–46, p. 30).

seemed to call for it.[18] The work of the institutionalist school may be regarded in part as such an attempt, though no systematic treatment has emerged.

The concept of choice functions not built up from orderings seems to correspond to Rothschild's "real irrationality"; however, such choice functions need not be the product of impulsive behavior but may conceivably arise from full reflection, as in the theory of games discussed above.

III. THE SOCIAL WELFARE FUNCTION

1. FORMAL STATEMENT OF THE PROBLEM OF SOCIAL CHOICE

I will largely restate Professor Bergson's formulation of the problem of making welfare judgments[1] in the terminology here adopted. The various arguments of his social welfare function are the components of what I have here termed the social state, so that essentially he is describing the process of assigning a numerical social utility to each social state, the aim of society then being described by saying that it seeks to maximize the social utility or social welfare subject to whatever technological or resource constraints are relevant or, put otherwise, that it chooses the social state yielding the highest possible social welfare within the environment. As with any type of behavior described by maximization, the measurability of social welfare need not be assumed; all that matters is the existence of a social ordering satisfying Axioms I and II. As before, all that is needed to define such an ordering is to know the relative ranking of each pair of alternatives.

The relative ranking of a fixed pair of alternative social states will vary, in general, with changes in the values of at least some individuals; to assume that the ranking does not change with any changes in individual values is to assume, with traditional social philosophy of the Platonic realist variety, that there exists an objective social good defined independently of individual desires. This social good, it was frequently held, could best be apprehended by the methods of philosophic inquiry.

---

[18] Like Lange, the present author regards economics as an attempt to discover uniformities in a certain part of reality and not as the drawing of logical consequences from a certain set of assumptions regardless of their relevance to actuality. Simplified theory-building is an absolute necessity for empirical analysis; but it is a means not an end.

[1] Bergson, "A Reformulation . . . ," *op. cit., passim.*

Such a philosophy could be and was used to justify government by the elite, secular or religious, although we shall see below that the connection is not a necessary one.

To the nominalist temperament of the modern period, the assumption of the existence of the social ideal in some Platonic realm of being was meaningless. The utilitarian philosophy of Jeremy Bentham and his followers sought instead to ground the social good on the good of individuals. The hedonist psychology associated with utilitarian philosophy was further used to imply that each individual's good was identical with his desires. Hence, the social good was in some sense to be a composite of the desires of individuals. A viewpoint of this type serves as a justification of both political democracy and laissez-faire economics or at least an economic system involving free choice of goods by consumers and of occupations by workers.

The hedonist psychology finds its expression here in the assumption that individuals' behavior is expressed by individual ordering relations R_i. Utilitarian philosophy is expressed by saying that for each pair of social states the choice depends on the ordering relations of all individuals, i.e., depends on $R_1, \ldots, R_n$, where n is the number of individuals in the community. Put otherwise, the whole social ordering relation R is to be determined by the individual ordering relations for social states, $R_1, \ldots, R_n$. We do not exclude here the possibility that some or all of the choices between pairs of social states made by society might be independent of the preferences of certain particular individuals, just as a function of several variables might be independent of some of them.

DEFINITION 4: *By a social welfare function will be meant a process rule which, for each set of individual orderings $R_1, \ldots, R_n$ for alternative social states (one ordering for each individual), states a corresponding social ordering of alternative social states, R.*

As a matter of notation, we will let R be the social ordering corresponding to the set of individual orderings $R_1, \ldots, R_n$, the correspondence being that established by a given social welfare function; if primes or seconds are added to the symbols for the individual orderings, primes or seconds will be added to the symbol for the corresponding social ordering.

There is some difference between the concept of social welfare function used here and that employed by Bergson. The individual orderings which enter as arguments into the social welfare function as defined here refer to the values of individuals rather than to their tastes. Bergson supposes individual values to be such as to yield a social value judgment leading to a particular rule for determining the allocation of productive resources and the distribution of leisure and final products in accordance with individual tastes. In effect, the social welfare function described here is a method of choosing which social welfare function of the Bergson type will be applicable, though, of course, I do not exclude the possibility that the social choice actually arrived at will not be consistent with the particular value judgments formulated by Bergson. But in the formal aspect the difference between the two definitions of social welfare function is not too important. In Bergson's treatment, the tastes of individuals (each for his own consumption) are represented by utility functions, i.e., essentially by ordering relations; hence the Bergson social welfare function is also a rule for assigning to each set of individual orderings a social ordering of social states. Furthermore, as already indicated, no sharp line can be drawn between tastes and values.

A special type of social welfare function would be one which assigns the same social ordering for every set of individual orderings. In this case, of course, social choices are completely independent of individual tastes, and we are back in the Platonic case.

If we do not wish to require any prior knowledge of the tastes of individuals before specifying our social welfare function, that function will have to be defined for every logically possible set of individual orderings. Such a social welfare function would be universal in the sense that it would be applicable to any community. This ideal seems to be implicit in Benthamite social ethics and in its latter-day descendant, welfare economics.

However, we need not ask ourselves if such a universal social welfare function can be defined. Let an *admissible* set of individual ordering relations be a set for which the social welfare function defines a corresponding social ordering, i.e., a relation satisfying Axioms I and II. A universal social welfare function would be one for which every set of individual orderings was admissible. However, we may feel on some sort of a priori grounds that certain types of individual orderings need not be admissible. For example, it has frequently been assumed or implied in welfare economics that each individual values different social states solely according to his consumption under them. If this be the case, we should only require that our social welfare function be defined for those sets of individual orderings which are of the type described; only such should be admissible.

We will, however, suppose that our a priori knowledge about the occurrence of individual orderings is incomplete, to the extent that there are at least three among all the alternatives under consideration for which the ordering by any given individual is completely unknown in advance. That is, every logically possible set of individual orderings of a certain set S of three alternatives can be obtained from some admissible set of individual orderings of all alternatives. More formally, we have

CONDITION 1: *Among all the alternatives there is a set of S of three alternatives such that, for any set of individual orderings $T_1, \ldots, T_n$ of the alternatives in S, there is an admissible set of individual orderings $R_1, \ldots, R_n$ of all the alternatives such that, for each individual i, $x R_i y$ if and only if $x T_i y$ for x and y in S.*

Condition 1, it should be emphasized, is a restriction on the form of the social welfare function since, by definition of an admissible set of individual orderings, we are requiring that, for some sufficiently wide range of sets of individual orderings, the social welfare function give rise to a true social ordering.

We also wish to impose several other apparently reasonable conditions on the social welfare function.

2. POSITIVE ASSOCIATION OF SOCIAL AND INDIVIDUAL VALUES

Since we are trying to describe social welfare and not some sort of illfare, we must assume that the social welfare function is such that the social ordering responds positively to alterations in individual values, or at least not negatively. Hence, if one alternative social state rises or remains still in the ordering of every individual without any other change in those orderings, we expect that it rises, or at least does not fall, in the social ordering.

This condition can be reformulated as follows: Suppose, in the initial position, that individual values are given by a set of individual orderings $R_1, \ldots, R_n$, and suppose that the corresponding social ordering R is such that $x P y$, where x and y are two given alternatives and P is the preference relation corresponding to R, i.e., defined in terms of R in accordance with Definition 1. Suppose values subsequently change in such a way that for each individual the only change in relative rankings, if any, is that x is higher in the scale than before. If we call the new individual orderings (those expressing the new set of values) $R_1', \ldots, R_n'$ and the social ordering corresponding to them R', then we would certainly expect that $x P' y$, where P' is the preference relation corresponding to R'. This is a natural requirement since no individual ranks x lower than he formerly did; if society formerly ranked x above y, we should certainly expect that it still does.

We have still to express formally the condition that x be not lower on each individual's scale while all other comparisons remain unchanged. The last part of the condition can be expressed by saying that, among pairs of alternatives neither of which is x, the relation R_i' will obtain for those pairs for which the relation R_i holds and only such; in symbols, for all $x' \neq x$ and $y' \neq x$, $x' R_i' y'$ if and only if $x' R_i y'$. The condition that x be not lower on the R_i' scale than x was on the R_i scale means that x is preferred on the R_i' scale to any alternative to which it was preferred on the old (R_i) scale and also that x is preferred or indifferent to any alternative to which it was formerly indifferent. The two conditions of the last sentence, taken together, are equivalent to the following two conditions: (1) x is preferred on the new scale to any alternative to which it was formerly preferred; (2) x is preferred or indifferent on the new scale to any alternative to which it was formerly preferred or indifferent. In symbols, for all y', $x R_i y'$ implies $x R_i' y'$, and $x P_i y'$ implies $x P_i' y'$. We can now state the second condition which our social welfare function must satisfy.

CONDITION 2: *Let $R_1, \ldots, R_n$ and $R_1', \ldots, R_n'$ be two sets of individual ordering relations, R and R' the corresponding social orderings, and P and P' the corresponding social preference relations. Suppose that for each i the two individual ordering relations are connected in the following ways: for x' and y' distinct from a given alternative x, $x' R_i' y'$ if and only if $x' R_i y'$; for all y', $x R_i y'$ implies $x R_i' y'$; for all y', $x P_i y'$ implies $x P_i' y'$. Then, if $x P y$, $x P' y$.*

3. THE INDEPENDENCE OF IRRELEVANT ALTERNATIVES

If we consider $C(S)$, the choice function derived from the social ordering R, to be the choice which society would actually make if confronted with a set of alternatives S, then, just as for a single individual, the choice made from any fixed environment S should be independent of the very existence of alternatives outside of S. For example, suppose that an election system has been devised whereby each individual lists all the candidates in order of his preference and then, by a preassigned procedure, the winning candidate is derived from these lists. (All actual election procedures are of this type, although in most the entire list is not required for the choice.) Suppose that an election is held, with a certain number of candidates in the field, each individual filing his list of preferences, and then one of the candidates dies. Surely the social choice should be made by taking each of the individual's preference lists, blotting out completely the dead candidate's name, and considering only the orderings of the remaining names in going through the procedure of determining the winner. That is, the choice to be made among the set S of surviving candidates should be independent of the preferences of individuals for candidates not in S. To assume otherwise would be to make the result of the election dependent on the obviously accidental circumstance of whether a candidate died before or after the date of polling. Therefore, we may require of our social welfare function that the choice made by society from a given environment depend only on the orderings of individuals among the alternatives in that environment. Alternatively stated, if we consider two sets of individual orderings such that, for each individual, his ordering of those particular alternatives in a given environment is the same each time, then we require that the choice made by society from that environment be the same when individual values are given by the first set of orderings as they are when given by the second.

CONDITION 3: *Let $R_1, \ldots, R_n$ and $R_1', \ldots, R_n'$ be two sets of individual orderings and let $C(S)$ and $C'(S)$ be the corresponding social choice functions. If, for all individuals i and all x and y in a given environment S, $x\, R_1\, y$ if and only if $x\, R_i'\, y$, then $C(S)$ and $C'(S)$ are the same (independence of irrelevant alternatives).*

The reasonableness of this condition can be seen by consideration of the possible results in a method of choice which does not satisfy Condition 3, the rank-order method of voting frequently used in clubs.[2] With a finite number of candidates, let each individual rank all the candidates, i.e., designate his first-choice candidate, second-choice candidate, etc. Let preassigned weights be given to the first, second, etc., choices, the higher weight to the higher choice, and then let the candidate with the highest weighted sum of votes be elected. In particular, suppose that there are three voters and four candidates, $x, y, z,$ and w. Let the weights for the first, second, third, and fourth choices be 4, 3, 2, and 1, respectively. Suppose that individuals 1 and 2 rank the candidates in the order $x, y, z,$ and w, while individual 3 ranks them in the order $z, w, x,$ and y. Under the given electoral system, x is chosen. Then, certainly, if y is deleted from the ranks of the candidates, the system applied to the remaining candidates should yield the same results, especially since, in this case y is inferior to x according to the tastes of every individual; but, if y is in fact deleted, the indicated electoral system would yield a tie between x and z.

A similar problem arises in ranking teams in a contest which is essentially individual, e.g., a foot race in which there are several runners from each college, and where it is desired to rank the institutions on the basis of rankings of the individual runners. This problem has been studied by Professor E. V. Huntington,[3] who showed by means of an

---

[2] This example was suggested by a discussion with G. E. Forsythe, National Bureau of Standards.

[3] E. V. Huntington, "A Paradox in the Scoring of Competing Teams," *Science,* Vol. 88, September 23, 1938, pp. 287–288. I am indebted for this reference to J. Marschak.

example that the usual method of team scoring in those circumstances, a method analogous to the rank-order method of voting, was inconsistent with a condition analogous to Condition 3, which Huntington termed the postulate of relevancy.

The condition of the independence of irrelevant alternatives implies that in a generalized sense all methods of social choice are of the type of voting. If S is the set $[x,y]$ consisting of the two alternatives x and y, Condition 3 tells us that the choice between x and y is determined solely by the preferences of the members of the community as between x and y. That is, if we know which members of the community prefer x to y, which are indifferent, and which prefer y to x, then we know what choice the community makes. Knowing the social choices made in pairwise comparisons in turn determines the entire social ordering and therewith the social choice function $C(S)$ for all possible environments. Condition 2 guarantees that voting for a certain alternative has the usual effect of making surer that that alternative will be adopted.

Condition 1 says, in effect, that, as the environment varies and individual orderings remain fixed, the different choices made shall bear a certain type of consistent relation to each other. Conditions 2 and 3, on the other hand, suppose a fixed environment and say that, for certain particular types of variation in individual values, the various choices made have a certain type of consistency.

4. THE CONDITION OF CITIZENS' SOVEREIGNTY

We certainly wish to assume that the individuals in our society are free to choose, by varying their values, among the alternatives available. That is, we do not wish our social welfare function to be such as to prevent us, by its very definition, from expressing a preference for some given alternative over another.

DEFINITION 5: *A social welfare function will be said to be imposed if, for some pair of distinct alternatives x and y, $x R y$ for any set of individual orderings $R_1, \ldots, R_n$, where R is the social ordering corresponding to $R_1, \ldots, R_n$.*

In other words, when the social welfare function is imposed, there is some pair of alternatives x and y such that the community can never express a preference for y over x no matter what the tastes of all individuals are, even if all individuals prefer y to x; some preferences are taboo. (Note that, by Definition 1, asserting that $x R y$ holds for all sets of individual orderings is equivalent to asserting that $y P x$ never holds.)

At the beginning of this study, allusion was made to the type of social choice in which decisions are made in accordance with a customary code. It is arguable whether or not Definition 5 catches the essence of the intuitive idea of conventional choice. In the true case of customary restraints on social choice, presumably the restraints are not felt as such but really are part of the tastes of the individuals. The problems here involve psychological subtleties; can we speak, in the given situation, of true desires of the individual members of the society which are in conflict with the custom of the group?

If the answer to the last question is yes, then Definition 5 is indeed a correct formalization of the concept of conventionality. But we need not give a definite answer, and that is especially fortunate since an examination of the question would take us very far afield indeed. For certainly we wish to impose on our social welfare function the condition that it not be imposed in the sense of Definition 5; we certainly wish all choices to be possible if unanimously desired by the group. If Definition 5 is not a model of customary choice, it is at least a model of external control, such as obtains in a colony or an occupied country.

CONDITION 4: *The social welfare function is not to be imposed.*

Condition 4 is stronger than need be for the present argument. Some decisions as between given pairs of alternatives may be assumed to be imposed. All that is required really is that there be a set S of three alternatives such that the choice between any pair is not constrained in advance by the social welfare function. This set S must also have the properties indicated in Condition 1.

If the answer to the question asked earlier is that there is no sense in speaking of a conflict of wills between the individual and the sacred code, then we have a situation in which it is known in advance that the individual orderings of social alternatives conform to certain restrictions, i.e., that certain of the choices made by individuals are preassigned. In that case, we might desire that the social welfare function be defined only for sets of individual orderings compatible with the known socio-ethical norms of the community; this requirement may involve a weakening of Condition 1. This point will be discussed at greater length in Chapter VII.

It should also be noted that Condition 4 excludes the Platonic case discussed in Section 1 of this chapter. It expresses fully the idea that all social choices are determined by individual desires. In conjunction with Condition 2 (which insures that the determination is in the direction of agreeing with individual desires), Condition 4 expresses the same idea as Bergson's Fundamental Value Propositions of Individual Preference, which state that, between two alternatives between which all individuals but one are indifferent, the community will prefer one over the other or be indifferent between the two according as the one individual prefers one over the other or is indifferent between the two.[4] Conditions 2 and 4 togther correspond to the usual concept of consumer's sovereignty; since we are here referring to values rather than tastes, we might refer to them as expressing the idea of citizens' sovereignty.

5. THE CONDITION OF NONDICTATORSHIP

A second form of social choice not of a collective character is the choice by dictatorship. In its pure form, it means that social choices are to be based solely on the preferences of one man. That is, whenever the dictator prefers x to y, so does society. If the dictator is indifferent between x and y, presumably he will then leave the choice up to some or all of the other members of society.

DEFINITION 6: *A social welfare function is said to be dictatorial if there exists an individual i such that, for all x and y, $x P_i y$ implies $x P y$ regardless of the orderings R_i, . . . , R_n of all individuals other than i, where P is the social preference relation corresponding to R_1, . . . , R_n.*

Since we are interested in the construction of collective methods of social choice, we wish to exclude dictatorial social welfare functions.

CONDITION 5: *The social welfare function is not to be dictatorial (non-dictatorship).*

Again, it cannot be claimed that Definition 6 is a true model of actual dictatorship. There is normally an element of consent by the members of the community or at least a good many of them. This may be expressed formally by saying that the desires of those individuals include a liking for having social decisions made by a dictator[5] or at least a liking for the particular social decisions which they expect of individuals will be discussed in Chapter VII at somewhat greater length. However, in any case, Condition 5 is certainly a reasonable one to impose on the form of the social welfare function.

We have now imposed five apparently reasonable conditions on the construction of a social welfare function. These conditions are, of course, value judgments and could be called into question; taken together they

---

[4] Bergson, "A Reformulation . . . ," *op. cit.*, pp. 318–320. The Fundamental Value Propositions of Individual Preference are not, strictly speaking, implied by Conditions 2 and 4 (in conjunction with Conditions 1 and 3), though something very similar to them is so implied; see Consequence 3 in Chapter V, Section 3. A slightly stronger form of Condition 2 than that stated here would suffice to yield the desired implication.

[5] See E. Fromm, *Escape from Freedom,* New York: Rinehart and Co., 1941, 305 pp.

express the doctrines of citizens' sovereignty and rationality in a very general form, with the citizens being allowed to have a wide range of values. The question raised is that of constructing a social ordering of all conceivable alternative social states from any given set of individual orderings of those social states, the method of construction being in accordance with the value judgments of citizens' sovereignty and rationality as expressed in Conditions 1–5.

6. THE SUMMATION OF UTILITIES

It may be instructive to consider that proposed social welfare function which has the longest history, the Bentham-Edgeworth sum of individual utilities. As it stands, this form seems to be excluded by the entire nature of the present approach, since, in Chapter II, Section 1, we agreed to reject the idea of cardinal utility, and especially of interpersonally comparable utility. However, presumably the sum of utilities could be reformulated in a way which depends only on the individual orderings and not on the utility indicators. This seems to be implied by Bergson's discussion of this social welfare function;[6] though he presents a number of cogent arguments against the sum-of-utilities form, he does not find that it contradicts the Fundamental Value Propositions of Individual Preference (see Section 4 above), which he would have to if he did not consider that form to be determined by the individual orderings. The only way that I can see of making the sum of utilities depend only on the indifference loci is the following: Since to each individual ordering there corresponds an infinite number of utility indicators, set up an arbitrary rule which assigns to each indifference map one of its utility indicators; then the sum of the particular utility indicators chosen by the rule is a function of the individual orderings and can be used to establish a social ordering.

Obviously, this formation of the sum of utilities will lead to different decisions in a given situation with different choices of the rule. For any rule, Condition 1 is satisfied. However, Conditions 2 and 3 essentially prescribe that, for a given environment, the choice made shall vary in a particular way with certain variations in the orderings of individuals. This being so, it is clear that for the sum of utilities to satisfy Conditions 2 and 3, it would be necessary for the rule to be stringently limited; in fact, the general theorem, established in Chapter V, guarantees that the only rules which would make the sum of utilities satisfy Conditions 2 and 3, if any, lead it to violate either Condition 4 or Condition 5. In-

---

[6] Bergson, "A Reformulation . . . ," *op. cit.*, pp. 324, 327–328.

deed, according to Theorem 3 in Chapter VI, Section 3, the same would be true even if it were assumed that the utility of each individual depended solely on his own consumption. I have not been able to construct a special proof of this fact for the sum of utilities which is essentially different from the proof of the general theorem.

It may be of interest, however, to consider a particular rule for assigning utility indicators to individual orderings.[7] Assume that the individual orderings for probability distributions over alternatives obey the axioms of von Neumann and Morgenstern;[8] then there is a method of assigning utilities to the alternatives, unique up to a linear transformation, which has the property that the probability distributions over alternatives are ordered by the expected value of utility. Assume that for each individual there is always one alternative which is preferred or indifferent to all other conceivable alternatives and one to which all other alternatives are preferred or indifferent. Then, for each individual, the utility indicator can be defined uniquely among the previously defined class, which is unique up to a linear transformation, by assigning the utility 1 to the best conceivable alternative and 0 to the worst conceivable alternative. This assignment of values is designed to make individual utilities interpersonally comparable.

It is not hard to see that the suggested assignment of utilities is extremely unsatisfactory. Suppose there are altogether three alternatives and three individuals. Let two of the individuals have the utility 1 for alternatives x, .9 for y, and 0 for z; and let the third individual have the utility 1 for y, .5 for x, and 0 for z. According to the above criterion, y is preferred to x. Clearly, z is a very undesirable alternative since each individual regards it as worst. If z were blotted out of existence, it should not make any difference to the final outcome; yet, under the proposed rule for assigning utilities to alternatives, doing so would cause the first two individuals to have utility 1 for x and 0 for y, while the third individual has utility 0 for x and 1 for y, so that the ordering by sum of utilities would cause x to be preferred to y.

A simple modification of the above argument shows that the proposed rule does not lead to a sum-of-utilities social welfare function consistent with Condition 3. Instead of blotting z out of existence, let the individual orderings change in such a way that the first two individuals find z indifferent to x and the third now finds z indifferent to y, while the relative positions of x and y are unchanged in all individual orderings. Then the assignment of utilities to x and y becomes the same as it became in

[7] This particular rule was suggested by A. Kaplan.
[8] See fn. 1, Chapter II.

the case of blotting out z entirely, so that again the choice between x and y is altered, contrary to Condition 3.

The above result appears to depend on the particular method of choosing the units of utility. But this is not true, although the paradox is not so obvious in other cases. The point is, in general, that the choice of two particular alternatives to produce given utilities (say 0 and 1) is an arbitrary act, and this arbitrariness is ultimately reflected in the failure of the implied social welfare function to satisfy one of the conditions laid down.